THE CAMBRIDGE
ANCIENT HISTORY

VOLUME V

THE CAMBRIDGE ANCIENT HISTORY

SECOND EDITION

VOLUME V

The Fifth Century B.C.

Edited by

D. M. LEWIS F.B.A.

Professor of Ancient History in the University of Oxford

JOHN BOARDMAN F.B.A.

Lincoln Professor of Classical Archaeology and Art in the University of Oxford

J. K. DAVIES F.B.A.

Rathbone Professor of Ancient History and Classical Archaeology in the University of Liverpool

M. OSTWALD

*William R. Kenan, Jr, Professor of Classics, Swarthmore College
and Professor of Classical Studies, University of Pennsylvania*

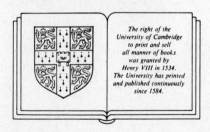

The right of the
University of Cambridge
to print and sell
all manner of books
was granted by
Henry VIII in 1534.
The University has printed
and published continuously
since 1584.

CAMBRIDGE UNIVERSITY PRESS

CAMBRIDGE

NEW YORK   PORT CHESTER

MELBOURNE   SYDNEY

Published by the Press Syndicate of the University of Cambridge
The Pitt Building, Trumpington Street, Cambridge CB2 1RP
40 West 20th Street, New York, NY 10011-4211, USA
10 Stamford Road, Oakleigh, Victoria 3166, Australia

First published 1992

Printed and bound in Great Britain by
Woolnough Bookbinding Ltd, Irthlingborough, Northamptonshire

A catalogue record for this book is available from the British Library

Library of Congress card no. 75-85719

ISBN 0 521 23347 X hardback

SE

CONTENTS

MAPS

TEXT-FIGURES

PREFACE

This volume is unlike any which has preceded it. Earlier volumes have covered the whole of the Mediterranean and Near East. We hardly stray beyond Greece, deferring developments elsewhere to Volume VI. We are thus stressing that this is a period when, for the first and last time before the Romans, great political and military power on the one hand and cultural importance on the other, including the presence of historians to describe that power, are located in the same place. By contrast, Persia and the empires which preceded it were powerful but not articulate; the Jews were articulate but not powerful. This gives the volume a coherence which its predecessors and immediate successors lack.

Some of the coherence arises from the nature of our sources, which make an Athenian standpoint hard to avoid. That point was noticed by Sallust in the first century B.C.:

As I reckon it, the actions of the Athenians were indeed vast and magnificent, but rather less substantial than report makes them. But because writers of genius grew up there, Athenian deeds are renowned as the greatest throughout the world. The talent of those who did them is judged by the powers of praise of these outstanding literary geniuses. (*Bell. Cat.* 8.2–4)

In this volume we shift Sallust's emphasis, and regard the efflorescence of literature (and art) as itself a major historical phenomenon to be examined and explained. Much of the cultural achievement survives, for us to assess by our own criteria. Fluctuations in the reputation of individuals and of styles will continue, but they are not likely to diminish the position of the fifth century, particularly at Athens, as the first Classic age of European civilization, important not only for its own achievements, but for the power of those achievements to influence later generations and take new forms in their hands. Even if the events of the period had no intrinsic interest, they would still be precious for our understanding of the cultural heritage.

The events themselves certainly do have great intrinsic interest. The transformation of the Delian League, created to continue the Greek fight against Persia, into an empire run in the interests of Athens, is a textbook case in the history of imperialism. The development of Athenian democracy, the beginnings of which we saw in the last volume, into an experiment in direct government by a largish citizen body, produced political concepts and political thinking which have remained of permanent importance. That the volume ends with the collapse of both the empire and the democracy raises perennial questions about the reconciliation of political justice and political efficiency. These themes are visible in many of our sources, but were most notably transmitted and interpreted by Thucydides, one of the most gifted historians of any age: it should be added that perhaps his most remarkable achievement was to transmute even military narrative into a commentary on the human condition.

On the international plane, events were shaped by the break, at first gradual, which split the victorious Greek allies of 480–79. There were always those, at both Athens and Sparta, whose ideal was continued collaboration; but events were too strong for them, and our concept of the century is shaped by the polarity between the Spartan alliance, land-based, with a fairly narrow and specialized governing group at its centre, and the Athenian empire, largely maritime and with a democracy at its centre. Various later generations have found contemporary resonances which have encouraged them to perpetuate the concept of this polarity. The different nature of the power-bases certainly did much to shape the course of the eventual struggle of the Peloponnesian War.

Some of the factors which made the cultural achievement possible are clear. First, success in the Persian Wars was itself a heroic achievement, which provided new epic themes and the impulse to celebrate them. Secondly, as Athens became more important politically, it became more likely to attract individuals who might find it a more stimulating environment than their own cities. This was a cumulative process and must have developed existing talent. Thirdly, the economic gains of empire (not simply the tribute paid by the allies, important though that was) made projects possible for the Athenians which had hitherto been peculiar to kings and tyrants. Why the Athenian citizen-body itself commanded a gene-pool of such potentiality is beyond us.

Though Athens dominates our sources for this volume, it is nevertheless called 'The Fifth Century' instead of the 'Athens' of the first edition. But we have tried not to draw too sharp a line between Archaic and Classical Greece; and there is a sense in which the last decade of our period, with a weakened Athens and a renascent Persia, looks forward to the shape of the fourth century. The more general title reflects the fact that the story of the fifth century is not just an Athenian story. Even at the cultural level, the temple of Zeus at Olympia had emerged, some years earlier than the Parthenon, from a separate and different set of social and political circumstances. The great sanctuaries continued to follow their own individual lines of development, and their festivals created forms of literature not found at Athens. Developments in the many minor Greek states were influenced by emulation of their larger neighbours. Models of comfort and society elsewhere stimulated urban development in more backward areas. Smaller communities saw the advantages of combining into bigger ones, for example, Olynthus in 432 and Rhodes in 408. Exiles and migrants from long-established states took their ideas of the good life to foundations like Thurii and Amphipolis or areas like Macedon where urbanism did not exist.

This presupposed the polis as the Greek way of life. There were other forms of political development, but they are harder to trace during our period. Gelon's creation of an extended Syracuse collapsed. Successive kings of Macedon struggled to preserve and centralize their kingdom; they too used urbanization as one of their principal tools. The Athenians, who had exploited ties of racial relationship with their allies when they created the Delian League, nevertheless did not use them to break down citizenship barriers between one polis and another. Athenian citizenship became more, not less, restricted during our period. Pericles boasted of the advantages of equal opportunity for citizens at home, but neither he nor the Athenian people saw merit in extending it further. Cleon may have been right to say that democracy could not rule an empire. This volume closes in uncertainty as to whether the Spartan oligarchy would be more successful.

The framework of this volume is different from that of the first edition. We have been more explicit on questions of historical method. We have tried to achieve closer integration of Athenian external and internal history. Separate chapters on drama, philosophy, historiography and art have been replaced by an attempt to show the cultural achievements in their historical, social and religious contexts. The bibliographies in such intensely cultivated fields can make no real attempt at completeness and mostly represent work directly referred to by our contributors; we have slightly amplified the form of reference to them used in previous volumes. We continue our practice of including a map reference after a name in the index, instead of compiling a separate index of names for each map.

The volume has been long in preparation, and scrutiny of our attempts to keep it up to date may well reveal unavoidable inconsistencies. Of our contributors, Professor A. Andrewes, who gave sage counsel in the planning stage and thereafter, and Professor R. E. Wycherley have not lived to see the completed volume; these are personal losses as well as losses to scholarship.

We are grateful to Simon Hornblower for help in the closing stages of

preparation, and for the patience, skill and care with which we have been
tended by the staff of the Cambridge University Press, in particular by
Pauline Hire. Professor Rhodes wishes to thank Dr O. P. T. K.
Dickinson, and, for financial assistance, the University of Durham. Text
illustrations, when not derived from a stated source, have been prepared
by Marion Cox. Fuller illustration will appear in the Plates Volume
which is intended to accompany both Volume v and the forthcoming
Volume vi. The maps have been drawn by Euromap Ltd; the index was
compiled by Barbara Hird.

D. M. L.

J. B.

J. K. D.

M. O.

NOTE ON FOOTNOTE REFERENCES

Works cited in the various sections of the Bibliography are referred to in
footnotes by author and date, followed by the appropriate section letter, the
number assigned to the work in that section, the volume number, page
references etc. Thus Pritchett 1965 (A 100) 1 5 is a reference to p. 5 of vol. 1 of
W. K. Pritchett's *Studies in Ancient Greek Topography* – no. 100 of Bibliography A:
General.

CHAPTER 1

SOURCES, CHRONOLOGY, METHOD

D. M. LEWIS

As far as source material is concerned, the period covered by this volume falls, for the writer of political history, into three sections, which present sharply contrasting problems of method.[1] For the period from 435 to 411 B.C. Thucydides provides a firm framework. For the period from 478 to 435, he gives us some relatively full narrative on special points and a sketchy narrative from 477 to 440; the only connected narrative of any size is that by Diodorus Siculus. For 411 to 404 we have two connected narratives, by Xenophon and Diodorus.

Thucydides,[2] son of Olorus of the deme Halimous, born perhaps about 460, was related in some way to Cimon and to Thucydides son of Melesias.[3] Like Cimon, he had Thracian connexions, as is indicated by his father's name (cf. Hdt. VI.39.3) and his own statement (IV.105.1) that he had possessions in the gold mines east of the river Strymon which gave him great influence with the mainlanders of that area. Of his early life we know nothing, but can readily infer his total immersion in the intellectual excitement which the sophists were bringing to Athens.[4] His military career begins and ends for us with his tenure of the generalship in 424/3 (p. 427 below). After his failure at Amphipolis he was in exile from Athens for twenty years (V.26.5), and this gave him the opportunity to watch events, not less from the Peloponnesian side; he says nothing of his ability to watch Athens. His intention of writing a history of the Peloponnesian War had in some sense been formed from its beginning in 431 (I.1.1). How long he lived after 404, we have no means of telling.[5]

Our manuscripts call his book *Historiai*; there is no reason to think that this, 'Investigations', would have been his title for what he probably thought of as his *xyngraphe* or *xyngramma*, 'Composition'. They divide it into eight books (a division into thirteen books was also current in antiquity). Of these, Book I is introductory and carries the story down to

---

[1] For most of the topics covered in this chapter, see also Gomme, *HCT* Introduction.

[2] On Thucydides in general see Luschnat 1971 (C 68), Dover 1973 (C 27), Hornblower 1987 (C 52). [3] Cavaignac 1929 (D 13); Wade-Gery 1958 (A 121) 246–7; Davies 1971 (L 27) 233–6.

[4] Finley 1942 (C 30) 36–73, and see pp. 359–62 below; cf. e.g. Macleod 1983 (A 82) 54–6, 125–31.

[5] It has been argued by Pouilloux and Salviat 1983 (C 79) that he was still writing Book VIII after 396; I do not accept their evidence (see also Cartledge 1984 (F 15) and p. 44 n. 36).

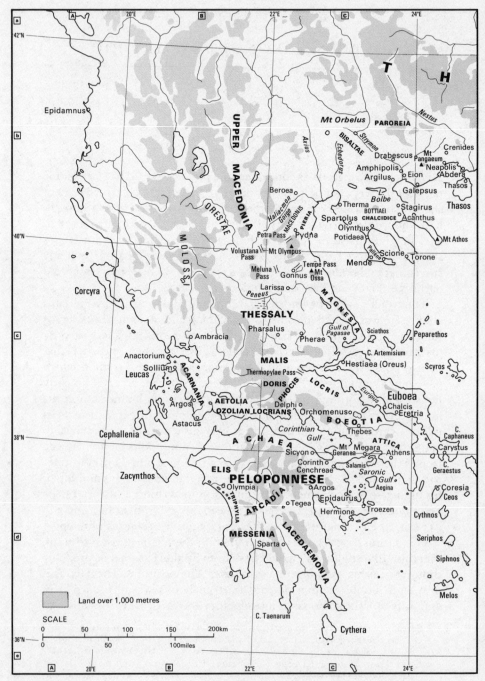

1 Greece and Western Asia Minor

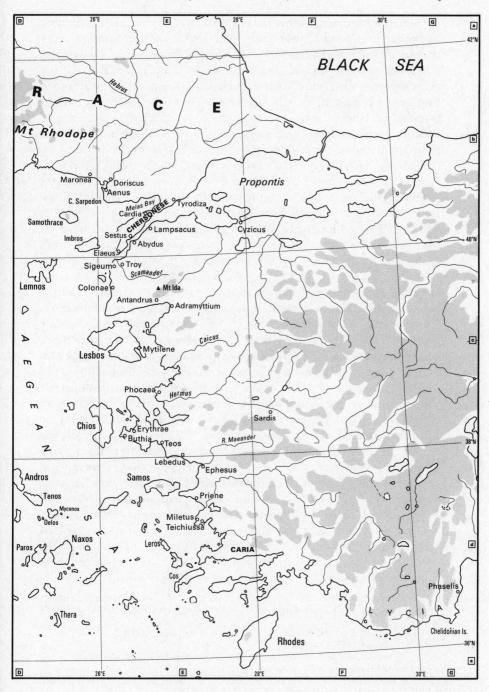

BLACK SEA

T H R A C E

Mt Rhodope

Hebrus

Maronea
Doriscus
Aenus
C. Sarpedon
Melas Bay
Cardia
CHERSONESE
Tyrodiza
Propontis
Sestus
Lampsacus
Cyzicus
Abydus
Elaeus
Sigeum
Troy
Scamander
Colonae
▲ Mt Ida
Antandrus
Adramyttium
Caicus
Mytilene
Lesbos
Phocaea
Hermus
Sardis
Chios
Erythrae
Buthia
Teos
R. Maeander
Lebedus
Ephesus
Samos
Priene
Miletus
Teichiussa
Leros
CARIA
Cos
Phaselis
L Y C I A
Chelidohian Is.
Rhodes

Samothrace
Imbros
Lemnos

A E G E A N   S E A

Andros
Tenos
Myconos
Delos
Paros
Naxos
Thera

the period immediately before the outbreak of war in 431. The remaining books are organized by war-years, each divided into a summer and a winter. This distinguishes the work sharply from that of Herodotus, which has no open chronological scheme, less sharply from that of other contemporary writers (he has at least Hellanicus in mind), who arranged by other types of year, by Athenian archons or by the year of the current priestess of Hera at Argos (v.19.2, cf. II.2.1). Such arrangements he thought imprecise (v.19.3, cf. 1.97.2); how great a degree of precision is to be attributed to the beginning and end of his seasons is disputed.

There is general agreement that Book VIII, which breaks off in mid-sentence in late summer 411, represents a fairly early stage of composition; parallel narratives, sometimes hardly more than extended notes, stand side by side without close correlation, and there are no speeches worked up into direct speech; there is no reason to think that what we have was written at all long after the events described.[6] Book V, from chapter 27 to its end, also has no speeches, apart from the Melian Dialogue (v.85–113; see pp. 445–6), but, apart from this, what has appeared incompleteness may be in some part due to the nature of the subject matter.[7] For the rest of the work arguments tend to be subjective. There are passages, notably II.65.12, VI.15.3–4, which were certainly written in or after 404, but there is no means of telling how much continuous attention Thucydides gave to his manuscript or whether his criteria of incompleteness would have been the same as ours.[8]

The introductory chapters of Book I, intended in form to demonstrate the greatness of the Peloponnesian War, give by the way a history of early Greece, and carry an ever-growing weight of observation on historical method. There are limitations, we are told (1.21), on the amount of truth which can be asserted about the past; 1.22 passes to the limitations of his work on the war. Speeches were hard to remember in detail both by him and by his informants, and there will be some subjectivity (ὡς δ' ἂν ἐδόκουν ἐμοὶ ἕκαστοι περὶ τῶν αἰεὶ παρόντων τὰ δέοντα μάλιστ' εἰπεῖν, 'as I thought the several individuals or groups would have said what they had to say about the situation'); that point is at least clear, whatever the nuances of the qualifications;[9] correspondingly the speeches in the work are normally introduced and concluded with indefinite pronouns (e.g. οἱ μὲν Κερκυραῖοι ἔλεξαν τοιάδε (1.31.4) . . .

---

[6] For all this see Andrewes, HCT v, including pp. 4, 369–75, for arguments about the date of writing, ignored by Pouilloux and Salviat (above, n. 5). But see Connor 1984 (C 22) 217–21 (hardly tenable).

[7] Andrewes, HCT IV 63, Connor 1984 (C 22) 44–7, but see Andrewes, HCT v 375–9.

[8] See Andrewes, HCT v 363, 400–5.

[9] For discussions of what Thucydides is saying here and his actual practice in speech-writing (not necessarily the same thing), see: Gomme 1937 (A 49) 156–9 and HCT I 146–8; Andrewes 1962 (C 5) 64–71; de Ste Croix 1972 (G36) 7–16; Stadter, ed. 1973 (C 95); Andrewes, HCT v 393–9; Macleod 1983 (A 82) 52–3, 68–70; Hornblower 1987 (C 52) 45–72.

τοιαῦτα μὲν οἱ Κερκυραῖοι εἶπον (1.36.4)), by contrast with the definite pronouns which introduce and conclude documents (e.g. IV.117.3, 119.3; V.17.2, 20.1). The subjectivity allowed for speeches is explicitly renounced for facts:

as for the events of what was done in the war, I did not think it right to write them on the basis of eyewitness reports or my own opinion [οὐδ' ὡς ἐμοὶ ἐδόκει responding to ὡς δ' ἂν ἐδόκουν ἐμοὶ above], but by checking every detail as carefully as possible, both where I was present and when I heard from others. Investigation was laborious, because those present at each event did not say the same things about the same event, but were influenced by their partisanship or memory.

Only very occasionally does Thucydides underline uncertainty about facts, but for the battle of Mantinea in 418, where he has occasion to report a difficulty about finding out the truth (v.68.2), the indefinite pronoun of uncertainty recurs (v.79.1 καὶ ἡ μὲν μάχη τοιαύτη καὶ ὅτι ἐγγύτατα τούτων ἐγένετο, 'and the battle happened *in such a way*, as near as possible to this').

Thucydides' high competence and devotion to truth are not to be doubted, and we can place much greater reliance on what he gives us for the years 435–411 than on our materials for most other periods of ancient history.[10] The difficulty here lies in our dependence on what he gives us. This is a great deal, but he has assimilated his source material and concealed his workings. On the other hand, there has inevitably been selectivity, and we should not expect to be told everything that happened. Sometimes there is warning, as, for example, when all the Athenian invasions of the Megarid from 431 to 424 are disposed of in advance (II.31.3), not to be recalled until they are again relevant (IV.66.1, slightly discrepant). Sometimes there is not, and we are left to wonder, for example, whether there were indeed only three tribute-collecting expeditions during the Archidamian War (II.69.1, III.19, IV.50.1), or whether it is not rather the case that these were regular annual events (cf. Arist. *Ath.Pol.* 24.3) which Thucydides only reports when something of interest occurred. These possibilities on the plane of simple military operations turn into certainties when we contemplate the more political developments which he chose to describe in general terms or to indicate by a brief statement about hostility between individuals (e.g. IV.27.5, VI.15.2) when it seemed relevant. Nothing is said of the personal stories about Pericles' political difficulties in the years before the war, even though they were already current in the fifth century. The ostracism of Hyperbolus (below, p. 442), which must have started as a major political event, is not reported in its place. That Thucydides does not report an

---

[10] For a recent investigation of why we feel this, see Connor 1985 (C 23).

event is not a reason for believing that it did not happen, and, if our interests take us that way, we have a duty to try to fill the gaps. But when he does report an event, it is only at our peril that we try to reinterpret it and it will seldom be good method to do so.

These considerations are valid to an even greater degree for the period 479–435. The formal narrative of this period (1.89–118) is set in the framework of the decision of the Spartan Assembly in 432 that the Athenians had broken the Thirty Years' Peace of 446. This decision is to some extent (see p. 371) motivated by Spartan fear of the growing power of the Athenians, since they saw that most of Hellas was already subject to them (1.88). 'This is how the Athenians came to power' (1.89.1), and we are plunged into a fairly detailed narrative of events of 478 and 477 in a style perhaps nearer to story-telling than that in which the war itself is described. When the story reaches 477 and the establishment of the Delian League, we get a more extended second introduction, which begins by saying that his motive for telling the story of the 'Fifty Years' (known to modern scholarship as the *Pentekontaetia*) was to fill a gap left by all his predecessors except Hellanicus, and adds, almost as an afterthought, that the story also demonstrates the growth of Athenian power (1.97.2). There follows a fairly breathless survey of events down to the end of the Samian revolt, notably short, after a reflective passage at 1.99 and a brief comment at 1.103.4, of material to direct the reader's mind in any particular direction, until a resumptive passage at 1.118.1–2 brings us back to the main narrative. This section on the Fifty Years is supplemented by a separate account of the careers of Pausanias and Themistocles (1.128–38), an account very close in style to 1.89–96, which may reasonably be thought to be more vulnerable than normal Thucydidean narrative to suspicions about the nature and value of the underlying evidence.[11]

The reference to Hellanicus' work could point to a date of composition after 406, since Hellanicus covered events of that year (*FGrH* 323a F 25–6), but need not date more than the sentence in which it appears. Further speculation is inseparably bound up with more general worries about the extent of Thucydides' changes of mind and plan.[12] My own conviction is that there was a relatively late change of plan and that material originally written for other purposes has been incompletely integrated into the work as we have it,[13] but the methodological principle has to remain unaltered. Even those who suspect that we are dealing with work by Thucydides which is incomplete and insufficiently scrutinized depart at their peril from what we actually have.

[11] Rhodes 1970 (C 82); Westlake 1977 (C 108).
[12] See Andrewes, *HCT* v 384–444, and below, p. 372.
[13] But see Walker 1957 (C 106); Connor 1984 (C 22) 42–7.

The work of Diodorus of Agyrium in Sicily (frequently Diodorus Siculus), who was writing in the third quarter of the first century B.C., is a very different matter.[14] He covers the events of this volume, in Books XI.38–fin., XII–XIII of his *Bibliotheke*. Despite some modern scepticism,[15] the position established by nineteenth-century scholarship[16] still stands, that his basic method was to summarize one previous author at a time, and that for the fifth century that author was Ephorus.[17] Ephorus wrote *kata genos*, one subject at a time, and it is not clear how much chronology he gave and how he organized it. As the work comes through in Diodorus, it has been chopped up into 'years' which equate Roman consular-years and Athenian archon-years; in reality, these were never coterminous. The operation was conducted with little care or skill, and the appearance of any event in Diodorus' main narrative under a particular year is not to be regarded as evidence for its dating.[18] There are items at the end, more rarely at the beginning of years, which are derived from a chronological handbook and are more likely to be reliable. But the danger of trusting Diodorus' competence can be seen most clearly from the fact that he has read his chronological handbook as dating the reign of Archidamus from 476 to 434 (XI. 48.2, XII.35.4), but still reports his activity in the early years of the Archidamian War.

Through Diodorus and from other evidence, we can form some judgement of Ephorus of Cyme in Asia Minor, writing a universal history in the third quarter of the fourth century.[19] It is clear that he relied substantially on good earlier sources for our period, successively Herodotus, Thucydides and the author of the *Hellenica Oxyrhynchia* (see below). Sometimes he added from other sources, sometimes he simply reworked the material for his own purposes. These puposes are not easy to see through Diodorus' perhaps selective treatment of him, and we are, for example, left uncertain whether he attempted a general account of the political events and cultural achievement of the Periclean age. But there is no reason to attribute to him a preference for truth over what was stylistically appropriate and congenial to his own outlook. Sound method will not construe a sentence of Diodorus closely to provide strict evidence, and one should not be too hasty to assume information independent of Thucydides if there is nothing else un-Thucydidean in the context.

---

[14] On Diodorus in general, see Schwartz 1903 (C 88), Griffith 1968 (C 38) 204–5, 237, J. Hornblower 1981 (C 51) 18–39.

[15] E.g. Laqueur 1958 (C 65); Drews 1962 (C 28); Casevitz 1972 (C 15) xiii–xv.

[16] Volquardsen 1868 (C 103); Holzapfel 1879 (C 49).

[17] For some qualifications about the history of the West, see *CAH* VI², ch.5.

[18] Modern scholars, nevertheless, particularly for the fourth century, often act on an undeclared principle that Diodorus is right except when he is demonstrably wrong.

[19] On Ephorus in general see Schwartz 1907 (C 89), *FGrH* IIC 22–35, Barber 1935 (C 9).

One continuator of Thucydides has already been mentioned, the author of the *Hellenica Oxyrhynchia*. This work is represented for us by three groups of papyrus fragments, two small, covering various events in 409–407, one large, covering events of 396 and 395.[20] The groups cohere in style, in intelligence, and in their obvious relationship to Diodorus. We are dealing with a continuator of Thucydides, presumably starting with the year 411 (with some back-references), writing towards the middle of the fourth century; the terminal date of the work cannot be established. The only author's name which we possess which can be plausibly attached to it is that of the Athenian Cratippus, but even that attribution is not without difficulty.[21] The importance of the fragments lies not only in their direct contributions, but also in the assurance which they offer that a sober historian lies somewhere behind Diodorus. Much recent work on the late fifth and early fourth centuries has been based on a growing preference for Diodorus over Xenophon.[22]

Xenophon's *Hellenica* is the only continuation of Thucydides which survives complete. As we have it, it begins a few weeks after the end of Thucydides' account in 411 and runs down to 362. It is virtually impossible to establish at what stages in Xenophon's life, mostly spent in exile from Athens in the Peloponnese and ending around 350, any given section was written; differences in attitude and style appear to separate, for example, the account of the Peloponnesian War to its end (II.2.23 or II.3.9) from the account of the Thirty at Athens.[23] At times more vivid in detail than Thucydides, the work has had few whole-hearted admirers in recent years, although its faults perhaps arise more from deficiencies of information and intellectual grip than from pro-Spartan bias;[24] Xenophon can criticize Sparta and Spartans. The first two books have come down to us with a spurious and inconsistent chronological framework;[25] Xenophon's own attempts at chronological accuracy are sporadic and inefficient.

Theopompus of Chios (*c.* 380–*c.* 315), a more intelligent, but less

[20] The only complete edition is McKechnie and Kern 1988 (c 69). The large London group and the small Florence group are edited by Bartoletti 1959 (c 10), with a commentary by Bruce 1967 (c 14). For the Cairo fragments see Koenen 1976 (c 62).

[21] The best discussion of authorship (based on the London fragments only) is by Bloch 1940 (c 11). For our direct information about Cratippus, see *FGrH* 64. He surely covered the right material and had an interest in Thucydides. The difficulty about the attribution is that Dionysius of Halicarnassus, though claiming knowledge of Cratippus (*de Thuc.* 16), says that no one after Thucydides wrote by summers and winters (*ibid.* 9 fin.); our author seems to have done this (IX.1).

[22] For the fifth century, see Andrewes 1974 (D 2) and 1982 (G 6), Littman 1968 (G 25), Ehrhardt 1970 (G 13). For the beginnings of a reaction see Tuplin 1986 (C 101).

[23] On Xenophon in general, see Breitenbach 1967 (c 13), Anderson 1974 (c 3). Delebecque 1957 (c 25) provides an over-confident attempt to analyse and date the composition of the *Hellenica*. See also Hatzfeld 1930 (c 46), Maclaren 1934 (c 70).

[24] Breitenbach 1950 (c 12); Sordi 1950–1 (c 93); Cawkwell 1979 (c 16) 15–46; Montgomery 1965 (c 73).   [25] Raubitschek 1973 (c 80) attempts vainly to defend it; see Lotze 1974 (c 67).

amiable figure, wrote two relevant works.[26] The *Hellenica*, a continuation of Thucydides from 411 to 394, is thought to be a relatively youthful work; few fragments survive. We know rather more about two books of his *Philippica*, which covered much of importance for the fifth century, Book x, on the Athenian Demagogues, and Book xxv, on Athenian Lies.[27] The second and probably the first were largely polemic in character, and Theopompus clearly took pleasure in saying what might be unusual and unpopular. But he combined learning with an acute appreciation of some types of political reality, and it is regrettable that those authors who have transmitted his fragments had a marked penchant for the sensational. As far as the nature of his narrative in the *Hellenica* is concerned, there is important testimony by Porphyry of Tyre (A.D. 234–*c*. 302), an excellent judge, that it was heavily dependent on Xenophon, but changed for the worse (*FGrH* 115 F 21).

So far we have been dealing with historians,[28] but this is not an appropriate designation for the remaining major source for the fifth century, Plutarch of Chaeronea (A.D. *c*. 50–*c*. 120).[29] Mistakes can be made if he is taken to be writing history rather than ethical studies of character, for which facts serve as illustrations, but he can allow interest in his story to run away with him. We would be substantially worse off without the one Spartan (*Lysander*) and six Athenian (*Themistocles, Aristides, Cimon, Pericles, Nicias, Alcibiades*) lives which cover the fifth century, since an enormous body of reading lies behind them; the older fashion for believing that it was not his own reading is in disrepute.[30] The *Nicias* indeed is relatively slight, adding not much more than a few comic fragments to a reworking of Thucydides' account, but the rest draw on a large body of material, even to judge by the authors cited by name. These range from intelligent fifth-century sources (Ion of Chios, Critias), through scandal-mongers of the fifth (Stesimbrotus of Thasos) and the late fourth (Idomeneus) centuries, to the fourth-century philosophers, and significant detail is sought from all of them. It is normally harder to determine the source of narrative passages, when the source has not survived. My own inclination is to attach importance to

[26] The fragments are collected in *FGrH* 115. On Theopompus in general, see Von Fritz 1941 (C 33), Connor 1967 (C 20), Lane Fox 1986 (C 64).   [27] A full treatment in Connor 1968 (C 21).

[28] Of those not so far mentioned, Aristodemus (not later than second century A.D.; *FGrH* 104; also *P. Oxy.* XXVII 2469) adds nothing to our knowledge of the Ephorean tradition. The work of Pompeius Trogus (first century B.C.) is potentially more interesting, but the Latin epitome by Justin through which we mainly know it is so incompetently executed as to make certainties hard to find.

[29] For Plutarch's historical methods, see Gomme, *HCT* I 54–84, Stadter 1965 (C 94), Pelling 1980 (C 78). Russell 1963 (C 86) is a particularly valuable study of his dealings with a source we still possess.

[30] The classical attempt to establish intermediate sources is Meyer 1899 (A 87) 1–87, but see Theander 1951 (C 99), Hamilton 1969 (C 41) xliii–xlvi, Frost 1980 (C 36) 40–50.

demonstrable use of Theopompus in the *Pericles*[31] and to the large
number of places in the *Alcibiades* and the *Lysander* where the narrative is
visibly closer to that of Xenophon than to that of Diodorus, without
being quite the same. On Porphyry's showing, these may well depend on
Theopompus, despite Plutarch's suspicions about his attitudes (*Lys.*
30.2).

Plutarch took his material where he found it and as he could use it, and
his judgement about the nature and aims of his sources is not impeccable.
In the *Pericles* (4.6–6.1), for example, he uses Plato for Pericles' education
without noticing the marked irony of the original. On a larger scale, he
has to struggle with the disagreement of his sources about Pericles. He
solves the trouble that Theopompus thought him a demagogue and
Thucydides thought him a great statesman by positing a great change
after the ostracism of Thucydides son of Melesias (16.3). He is less happy
with the difficulty that, whereas Thucydides thought him a great
statesman, everyone else said that he had precipitated an unnecessary and
damaging war for personal reasons, and eventually leaves it unresolved.
Neither he nor Ephorus before him had the ability to evaluate justly the
evidence of Old Comedy and pamphleteers. We should not ourselves be
too confident that we fully understand fragments torn from their
context.

For the last quarter of the fifth century, the contemporary evidence of
comedy and oratory begins to be of value.[32] The evaluation of comic
evidence is a complex matter, but it is frequently possible to distinguish
between a joke or a piece of abuse and the fact which makes the joke or
abuse meaningful; Ar. *Knights* 465–9 is not evidence for Cleon's
treachery, but it is evidence for negotiations with Argos (see p. 387
below). Similar situations arise in using oratory. One may sometimes
have to distinguish between a public fact, which must correspond to
something within the jury's knowledge, and the assertion of a private
fact, which need not.[33] In general, one should always try to envisage the
lost argument of an opponent.

One last literary category remains, that of the *Atthides*, the chronicles
devoted to Athenian history.[34] Closely related to these is the *Athenian
Constitution* of Aristotle.[35] The earliest *Atthis*, composed by Hellanicus

[31] Wade-Gery 1958 (A 121) 233–9.

[32] Standing by itself is the Pseudo-Xenophontine *Athenaion Politeia*, sometimes known as 'the
Old Oligarch', a short pamphlet, of which the aims and date are disputed. On its aims see, e.g.,
Gomme 1962 (A 51) 38–69, Lewis 1969 (c 66).

[33] Take, e.g., Lys. xx. That Polystratus was elected to office by his fellow-tribesmen (2) is a public
fact; that he wrote down nine thousand names (13) is not, but the second statement is normally given
more credit than the first. See Andrewes, *HCT* v 204–6 and p. 475 below.

[34] On the *Atthides* in general, see Jacoby 1949 (c 57) and *FGrH* III B with commentary.

[35] On all matters connected with this work, see Rhodes 1981 (c 83), who does not believe in
Aristotelian authorship. There is no doubt that it was written between 335 and 322 and was
attributed to Aristotle in antiquity. The present volume will be found to vary in its practice as to
how its author is referred to.

of Lesbos, contained, as we have seen, events of the year 406, though its composition may have started earlier. A number of successors followed, notably Androtion, probably a main source for Aristotle and composing in the 340s,[36] and the third-century Philochorus.[37] Their main importance for us is chronological, since they arranged events by Athenian archons. Not only direct quotations, but dates given in this form by scholiasts are likely to go back to them. The temptation is to believe that a date given by an *Atthis* must be sound, at any rate for the fifth century, but occasionally one may wonder how such a date could have been fixed, even by Hellanicus. The *Athenian Constitution*, well preserved, but not without confusion and bias, not only presents special problems, better discussed in relation to particular episodes, but sometimes makes one wonder whether a well-preserved *Atthis* would enjoy the confidence which the fragments currently command.

Much depends on the evidence which we think Hellanicus could have found and whether he used it. Here we are dependent on our evidence from inscriptions on stone. These suggest that some archival material existed well before the end of the century, not necessarily that it was well ordered and usable.[38] Decrees of the people on stone only occasionally bear archon-dates before 421.[39] Building accounts, expense accounts and records of tribute-payment[40] are datable rather earlier, so that we are in a position to say that tribute-payment was recorded at Athens from spring 453 (*IG* I[3] 259) and that the first year of payments for the Parthenon was 447/6 (*IG* I[3] 436). No one doubts that the amount on public record substantially increased after the reforms of Ephialtes (see below, p. 70), but towards the beginning of our period it is not easy to see how some dates could be known for certain. And what applies to dates might apply still more to the historical circumstances of a fact or decision, even if the fact or decision was itself dated. Herodotus and Thucydides reflect much oral tradition, and there was of course much more to be acquired, but, when we consider the farrago of confused nonsense which Andocides (III.3–9) could parade to an Athenian jury in 391 as fifth-century history, we will not be disposed to place much confidence in oral tradition about Athens' external history.[41]

Thucydides' disapproval (V.20.2) of archon-dating systems rested on the ground that to talk about the beginning, middle or end of an archonship was not precise, though it must be admitted that we do not necessarily get much further with placing events in his summers and

[36] *FGrH* 324. See also Harding 1977 (C 44).   [37] *FGrH* 328.
[38] On public archives in the fifth century, see Boegehold 1972 (D 8).
[39] Mattingly 1961 (E 45) 124, and 1963 (E 47) 272 n. 73, thinks that virtually none do.
[40] Strictly speaking, payments of tribute were not recorded on stone. What we possess (edited in *ATL*; see also *IG* I[3] 259–90) are records of the one-sixtieth (a mina in every talent) which went to Athena.
[41] But W. E. Thompson 1967 (C 100) thinks that Andocides was dependent on Hellanicus. On oral tradition see now Thomas 1989 (A 114).

winters.[42] We could add that events separated by one archonship, though describable as 'in the third year' (τρίτῳ ἔτει, with inclusive count), might be anything from 14 to 34 months apart. Nevertheless, archon-dates have the advantage for us that we do possess a continuous list of Athenian archons which we can relate to Julian years from 480 to 292 B.C.[43] and that there is therefore a chronological system in use in the fifth century which we can relate to our own.[44]

Athenian archon-years were lunar years starting with a mid-summer new moon. As lunar years, they needed the frequent intercalation of a thirteenth month to bring them and their festivals into line with the sun; they therefore varied in length, having 354 or 355, 383 or 384 days. For a long period in the fifth century, ending in 407 or 406, the Council of Five Hundred operated on a solar year, normally of 366 days, not coterminous with the archon-year; such years, designated by the name of the first of the ten secretaries of the year, were occasionally used for dating purposes (*IG* I³ 46.19–20, 364, etc.). We may assume that the dating of the Atthidographers was intended to conform to a real Attic year. It is most unlikely that Diodorus understood what he was doing enough to intend anything of the kind, even for events relating to Athens; other late historians, notably Arrian and Josephus, also used the sequence of Attic years for general chronology. Even in Attic contexts, things might sometimes go wrong; for example, Alcibiades' return to Athens in 407 (see p. 487 below) cannot have been in the archonship of Antigenes (407/6) (Schol. Ar. *Frogs* 1422).

A fixed point for the start of our period is provided by Herodotus' confidence (VIII.51.1) that Athens was captured in the archonship of Calliades (480/79). This gives us 480 as the year of Salamis,[45] 479 for Plataea and Mycale, and we can be reasonably confident that Pausanias' campaign to Cyprus and Byzantium (Thuc. I. 94–5; see p. 35 below) belongs to 478. There is equally no doubt that the Peloponnesian War started in 431; this is confirmed not only by Thucydides' archon-date (II.2.1), but by the eclipse of the sun (27 July) which he places in the same summer. The interval which he asserts (II.2.1) had elapsed since the Thirty Years' Peace seems to place that in winter 446/5.[46]

For the years from 478 to 446 we are much worse placed. As we have seen, we have contemporary evidence for dating the start of the tribute record at Athens to spring 453 and of work on the Parthenon to the Attic year 447/6, but neither of these events is recorded by Thucydides, so that

---

[42] For discussion of the beginnings and ends of Thucydidean seasons, see van der Waerden and Pritchett 1961 (B 17), Meritt 1964 (G 29), Gomme, *HCT* III 699–715, Andrewes, *HCT* IV 18–21.

[43] The framework for this is provided by Diodorus and Dionysius of Halicarnassus' *Dinarchus*.

[44] How closely we can get to Julian dates by month and day is another matter; see below, n. 52.

[45] Correspondingly the eclipse of Hdt. IX.10.3 is that of 2 October 480.

[46] He will have been thinking more precisely at II.2.1 than at II.21.1, where he carelessly transposes the fourteen years into a different context.

we cannot relate them to his account. No relevant eclipse appears in the
tradition, and the only useful event datable outside the Athenian system
is the death of Xerxes, recently firmly dated to August 465;[47] Diodorus,
who places it under 465/4 (XI.69), got it right.

Despite Thucydides' complaint (1.97.2) that Hellanicus' treatment of
the period was short and chronologically imprecise, his own dates, as he
has left them, are insufficient for a complete chronology of the events
which he describes, and events which he does not mention present even
greater difficulties.[48] He frequently simply links events with temporal
adverbs. Often he does speak in terms of years, but interpretation of the
word 'year' has varied. Given his general attitude, conscious use of
archon-years can be ruled out, but it sometimes makes a difference if one
takes a year to be analogous to the use in the main body of the work, a
twelve-month period covering a summer and a winter, or if one takes it
to be a campaigning season. A slight variation on the campaigning-
season concept would be to think of the period from one winter public
funeral to another. That possibility is particularly relevant to us, since we
possess a funeral monument of the Erechtheid tribe with the names of
those who fell 'in Cyprus, Phoenicia and in Egypt, at Halieis, Aegina and
Megara, in the same year' (τοῦ αὐτοῦ ἐνιαυτοῦ; M–L 33). This should be
the first year of the Egyptian expedition, 460 or 459 (see below, p. 501).
More trouble arises over doubts as to whether events are recounted in a
rigid order[49] or with forward and backward references; at least one
resumptive passage seems to break the order at 1.109.

A vital clue comes from elsewhere in Thucydides' work. In IV.102.2–3
it is asserted that the first attempt to settle the site of Amphipolis was
made by Aristagoras of Miletus (cf. CAH IV². 485–6), that the Athenians
came thirty-two years later and met with disaster at Drabescus (cf.
1.100.3 and p. 46 below), but came again in the 27th year under Hagnon
and finally founded Amphipolis (see p. 145 below). In what terms these
time-intervals came to Thucydides we cannot know. Fortunately, we
have a date for Hagnon's foundation, 437/6, twice transmitted, once
apparently from an *Atthis* (Schol. Aeschin. 11.31), once from Diodorus'
chronological source (XII.32[50]). The disaster at Drabescus consequently
belongs about 465/4,[51] with uncertainty about the correlation between
the archon-year for Amphipolis and whatever form of year Thucydides

[47] A Babylonian eclipse text has 'Xerxes' son killed him' against a date equivalent to somewhere
between 4 and 8 August (Stolper 1988 (B 15) 196–7). The accession of Artaxerxes was known in
southern Egypt by 4 January 464 (Cowley 1923 (A 21) no. 6); the year is referred to as the 21st year of
Xerxes and the accession year of Artaxerxes.
[48] The most useful comprehensive treatments are those by Gomme, HCT 1 389–413, ATL III
158–80, Hammond 1955 (B 5); see also Deane 1972 (B 4), Bayer and Heideking 1975 (B 2), Badian
1988 (B 1).   [49] As held by ATL III 162.
[50] Note that the main narrative event given to the year cannot belong to it.
[51] The date of 453/2 given by Schol. Aeschin. 11.31 cannot be right, despite Badian 1988 (B 1).

is using, and this should also give us an approximate date for the
neighbouring events, the revolt of Thasos (p. 44 below) and the
beginning of the Helot Revolt (pp. 108–9 below).

The periods before and after 465/4 each contain one major problem.
Thucydides has been universally followed in his belief (shared with
another fifth-century author, Charon of Lampsacus) that, when Themistocles fled to Asia, Artaxerxes was already on the throne; fourth-century
and later authors brought him to the court of his old enemy Xerxes.
Accepting this presents problems if Thucydides' casual allusion to the
siege of Naxos coinciding with Themistocles' flight (1.137.2) is taken
seriously. Thucydides' statement (1.103.1) that the Helot Revolt ended in
its tenth year is in hopeless conflict with any belief in the rigidity of his
chronological order. These and smaller problems are dealt with in the
narrative chapters or in the Chronological Notes at the end of the book;
it will be seen that we frequently run short of events to fill the period. We
are still far from having agreed solutions on major matters. Scholars may
legitimately disagree by up to five or six years about the date of the battle
of the Eurymedon or the end of the Helot Revolt, and for the death of
Pausanias the margin is even wider.

When Thucydides' main narrative starts, the problems change character and arguments may concern weeks rather than years. There are
events in the Peloponnesian War for which very close dates in the Julian
calendar can be plausibly argued on the basis of the inter-relationship
between the two Athenian calendars and on epigraphic evidence,[52] but
the historical consequences are seldom substantial. Problems do multiply after the end of Thucydides because of the nature of the sources. It
may be hoped that we do now know whether Alcibiades came back to
Athens in 408 or 407 (below, pp. 503–5), but it takes a complex argument
to get the answer. This volume may sometimes be found surprisingly
sceptical or critical of Thucydides, but chronology is only one index of
the difference between having his guidance and losing it.

---

[52] Meritt's successive tables of Julian equivalences for the late fifth century (1928 (C 146) 84–122;
1932 (C 147) 174–9; 1961 (C 149) 202–19; 1971 and 1978 (G 30)) have been criticized by Pritchett (e.g.
1957 (C 157) 293–300), on the ground that we cannot control the amount of irregular intercalation
the Athenians may have indulged in, but see Dover, HCT IV 264–70.

CHAPTER 2

GREECE AFTER THE PERSIAN WARS

J. K. DAVIES

Throughout Books VII–IX Herodotus refers to those who resisted the Persian invasion as 'the Greeks'.[1] His shorthand is understandable, but over-simplifies: 'those who, being Greeks, submitted to the Persians without compulsion' (Hdt. VII.132.2) were no marginal group, not to speak of those Greeks who stood aloof, or had pressing business elsewhere, or were already willing or unwilling Persian vassals.[2] Yet his phraseology is important: copied by Thucydides in his survey of the development of 'what is now called Hellas' (1.2.1), and even by the otherwise chauvinistic writers of Athenian funeral speeches,[3] it reflects both the language of war-time diplomacy (Hdt. VII.130.3, 132.2, 148.1) and the poetry of the post-war decades, especially Aeschylus' *Persae* and the epigrams of Simonides. Plainly, to Greeks of the time 'the Greeks' were an entity, and 'Greece' much more than a geographical expression. To attempt to define the nature of that entity is therefore not just a task of historical analysis. It is also, at least in part, a matter of reconstructing a collective consciousness, and the two tasks are separate but not independent.

To identify the Greek world as a cultural system is at first sight fairly easy. One can define it first and foremost by *language*. For all the divergences of phonology and vocabulary among and within the four major dialect groupings (Attic/Ionic, Arcado-Cypriot, Aeolic, and Doric/North-west Greek), the dialects were mutually intelligible: the main perceived gulf was not between dialects but between Greek and all other languages. The pan-Greek use of Doric and of Homeric Ionic as literary dialects plainly attuned ears well enough, and Aristophanes evidently saw little point in jokes of mutual incomprehension when depicting Athenians' conversations with Megarians, Thebans, and Spartans (*Ach.* 729ff and 860ff, *Lys.* 980ff and 1070ff). His evidence therefore counts, even though his concern was with dramatic colour rather than with philology and though comparison with epigraphic evidence has revealed some false forms.[4] Again, without mutual compre-

[1] *ATL* III 97 n. 12: Brunt 1953–4 (A 10) 145f. Hdt. VII.145.1 is exceptional.
[2] Gillis 1979 (A 46) 59–71.   [3] Strasburger 1958 (C 98) 23f.   [4] Elliott 1914 (J 35) 207ff.

hension, institutions such as the Panhellenic Games, oracles, Amphictyonies, inter-city diplomacy, or the campaigns of a multi-city alliance
would have been impractical, not to speak of cross-border or maritime
trading: the particularisms of the writing systems for numerals, of month
names, or of calendars in general, though tiresome, were not insuperable
handicaps.[5]

In contrast, the boundary between Greeks and others had long since
crystallized in the word *barbaros*.[6] Significantly, its first known use refers
to language, that of the 'barbarian-voiced Carians' (Καρῶν βαρβαρο-
φώνων, Hom. *Il.* II. 267). Significantly too, it was this word, the very
formation of which betrays a primarily linguistic perception of the
boundary, which came to prevail, rather than the wholly obscure loan-
word *karban/karbanos* used on occasion by Aeschylus (*Suppl.* 118, 914;
Ag. 1061). *Barbaros* retained its linguistic connotation throughout the
fifth century and beyond, but as early as Heraclitus it was also carrying an
extended semantic load: 'eyes and ears are bad witnesses for men, since
they have barbarian souls' (D–K 22 B 107). Heraclitus' point, purely
epistemological, was that by itself the evidence of the senses lacked *logos*
(rational cohesion), but the implication was that those who lacked
certain essential qualities were thereby 'barbarian': those who were
(linguistically) unintelligible were well on their way to being seen as
unintelligent (thus, rightly, Diller 1962 (A 24) 40), and by the early fifth
century the attribution of cultural superiority to Greeks by Greeks was
coming to provide a second, highly subjective definition of Greek
cultural unity. Aeschylus and Herodotus document it in various ways,
which reflect as much the need to explain Greek success in the Persian
Wars as the ethnographic interests and compilations of the previous
generation. True, Herodotus in his *philobarbaros* mood was quite capable
of contrasting the anthropomorphic simple-mindedness of Greek theology unfavourably with the greater sophistication of the barbarians (sc.
Persians).[7] Likewise, ethnographic juxtapositions could yield comparisons which were neutral, or explicitly dodged value judgements (as in
Herodotus' report of Darius' experiment confronting Greek and Indian
funeral customs, III.38), or even made Greeks come off worst (Hdt.
I.133.2, 153.1–2, IV.79.3). However, the bias of judgement is represented
rather by the claims of superior Greek '*arete*, the product of wisdom and
strict law' which Demaratus advances in his conversation with Xerxes
(Hdt. VII.101–4, esp. 102.1 and 104.4). Examples to the same effect were
the failure of Danaus' herald and daughters respectively to respect Greek

[5] Dow 1952 (A 28); Samuel 1972 (B 11) 57–138.
[6] Jüthner 1923 (A 70); Bacon 1961 (J 2); Schwabl 1962 (A 110); Backhaus 1976 (J 1).
[7] Hdt. 1.60.3 with the unemended text vindicated by Burkert 1963 (J 13) 97–8 and Lloyd-Jones
1971 (J 70) 180 n. 45.

gods and the sanctuary their altars offered (Aesch. *Suppl.*893ff), and to understand that a king was not necessarily a despot (*ibid.* 365–75), or the portrait in both Aeschylus and Herodotus of Xerxes' blasphemous failure to understand or respect the divine ordering of the world. Small wonder that for Anacharsis 'the Greeks were all occupied in the pursuit of every kind of knowledge, except the Lacedaemonians: who, however, alone knew how to converse sensibly' (Hdt. IV.77.1). No doubt such claims were the idle invention of the Greeks themselves (Hdt. IV.77.2), but they reveal well enough the profile which, complacently but with some justice, they thought they presented to the barbarian world.

Certain shared norms, inherent in shared customs and common values as expressed in a common language, provided a third facet of Greek cultural unity. *Hybris* (offensive behaviour damaging the honour of another), *ate* (blind guilty rashness and its destructive consequences), *timē* (honour), *dike* (justice), *arete* (virtue, excellence), *charis* (grace, obligation, favour), and other complex or loaded words denoted values and expectations which would willy-nilly be shared by all Greek speakers and which did to some degree constitute a single interlocking system of thought and belief. Together with institutions such as blood-guilt, recognition of suppliants, monogamous marriage, chattel slavery, patrilinear and patrilocal descent, and inheritance without right of primogeniture, they could be thought of as the '*nomoi* (laws/customs) of the Greeks'.[8] Granted, the phrase should not be pushed too hard. The divergences among Greek states in legal practice, principle and authority were too great to allow the Greeks to be a 'people of the Law' in the way the Jews became. *Nomos* could denote alike the customs of human society in general, those of non-Greek societies, or those of a particular Greek polity.[9] Nevertheless, the contrast between Greek freedom under law and the arbitrariness of a monarch, thought to be characteristic of non-Greek societies, was plainly felt and expressed.

Lastly, and in some formal sense, cult and ritual helped to define Greek cultural unity. Not transparently so, for in many ways Greek religion was not *sui generis*. The components of Greek ritual – prayer/benefit/gratitude, altar/shrine/temple/*temenos*, offerings/procession/festival/contest, purification/oracle/mysteries, polytheism more or less ordered – were not peculiarly Greek, nor was the Greek mixture of them unique (Egyptian religion was a closely analogous system, to name no other). Nor could Greek be clearly distinguished from non-Greek gods. The origin of many was outlandish or opaque enough, while Pindar himself provides evidence in just our period not only of the rapprochement between Greek and non-Greek deity which identified, e.g., Zeus

---

[8] E.g. Hdt. VI.86β2; Thuc. 1.41. Other references in Ostwald 1969 (D 64) 33–7.
[9] Finley 1966 (A 37); Ostwald 1969 (D 64) 20–56.

with the Egyptian oracle-god Ammon, but also of Greek receptivity for foreign gods such as the Great Mother.[10] Nevertheless, what matters in a polytheistic system is not the individual gods so much as the interlocking structure, and that was specific to Greek culture. It was admittedly a loose-knit structure, reflecting the interplay in the Dark and Archaic periods between local multi-functional deities on the one hand and on the other the greater theological tidiness diffused through the panhellenic shrines and the literary tradition,[11] but precisely for that reason it managed to accommodate the attachments of deities to specific Greek localities within a framework which defined the relationship of the major deities to each other. This framework, inevitably genealogical with gods so anthropomorphic as the Greek, not only unified into a divine family the powers of the natural and psychological worlds which the gods were imputed to command, but also (and thereby) integrated with the divine order all the social groups and activities which the gods collectively or individually could be invoked to protect. Here above all the Greekness of the system was to be found. Just as the family of Olympian Gods had a uniquely Greek locus, or as the cult titles applied to each deity in its various capacities – Zeus Horkios (of the oath), Athene Ergane (of craftsmanship), Hermes Enagonios (of the contest), and so on – were nearly all transparently Greek, so too the deities and institutions to which they gave cohesion and protection – lineage, village, 'tribe', polis, occupational group, age-group, or hazard-group such as seafarers or women in labour – came to define each other, and to define Greek space, symbolically. 'In this way the sacrificial community is a model of Greek society' (Burkert 1985 (κ 16) 255). That such definitions could exclude non-Greeks from this or that festival or sanctuary (Hdt. v.22) is a measure of the system's success in creating Greek consciousness; that they could also exclude certain sorts of Greek[12] reminds us that other boundaries could also be important.

II

If we now think of the Greek world of the 470s not as a cultural system but as an economic system, its unity is much less perspicuous, for there are intractable problems involved in relating description to theory in the domain of Greek economic history. Detailed discussion of them is reserved to a later chapter focused on Athens (chapter 8g), since the shifts in behaviour which have provoked much of the recent debate took place

---

[10] Classen 1959 (κ 18) (Ammon); Bowra 1964 (J 9) 50f; Nilsson 1967 (κ 69) 747f.
[11] Vernant 1974 (A 118) 103ff = Vernant 1980 (A 119) 92ff; Burkert 1977 (κ 13) 331–43; Sourvinou-Inwood 1978 (κ 86).
[12] Hdt. 1.143.3–144.1, v.72.3; DGE 773; Alty 1982 (A 1) 13.

there and are best attested there. In the present context, the complexities emerge best if we distinguish at least three levels or modes or sectors of economic activity. The first and fundamental one consisted of the exploitation of an incalculable number of privately owned farms or estates, large or small, unitary or fragmented, worked by the owner and his family, by the owner with slave help, by a bailiff and slaves, by share-croppers, tenants, or serfs, in each case with or without temporary hired help from labourers of 'free' status. These estates produced in very varying proportions both the Mediterranean staples – cereals (wheat or barley), olive-oil and wine – and their essential complements such as fruit and vegetables, and cheese, meat and wool from sheep, goats, cattle and pigs.

At this primary level the Greek world showed much uniformity but little interaction. Its uniformity derived in part from its ecological and climatic limits, in that Greeks had not penetrated as agricultural settlers either beyond the northern limit of olive cultivation or beyond dry-farming zones into areas of very low rainfall which required large-scale irrigation. In part it derived from the overwhelming primacy of the widely distributed private beneficial ownership of land. Though there were free landless men, and owners of broad acres, social and military pressures had so far worked effectively against the polarization of society between such extremes and in favour of the largely autarkic peasant, each working his own *kleros* (inherited lot)[13] and entitled to status within the community, or obliged to provide services to it, in proportion to the size of that *kleros*. True, some land was owned by deities, by cult-groups, or collectively, and was rented out to individual tenants,[14] but such assignments never made Greek deities and temples into the preponder-ant landholders and economic powers which they became in Egypt, the East Mediterranean seaboard, or Babylonia. On the contrary the patchy evidence we have for Attica suggests that gods, cult-groups and collectives owned at most 10 per cent of the land in the Classical period, and probably rather less.[15]

Such uniformity and lack of interaction may also have derived in part from *autarkeia* (self-sufficiency) as a cultural ideal and as an economic strategy. As a strategy it still persists in present-day Greece, as revealed by the practices of having a little of everything and of deliberately so

[13] Gschnitzer 1981 (L 63) 37. The importance of serfdom in Thessaly and Laconia derogates somewhat from this picture, but not totally even there (Cartledge 1979 (F 14) 160–95, esp. 165–70; Hodkinson 1986 (F 31) 386ff).

[14] E.g. Rheneia, half of which was owned by Apollo after the 520s (Kent 1948 (L 88)), or the *orgas* on the border between Attica and the Megarid (*LSCG* no. 32).

[15] Lewis 1973 (L 94) 198–9; Andreyev 1974 (L 1); Walbank 1983 (C 174); Osborne 1988 (L 109). The allotment to Athena of one-tenth of the land of Lesbos in 427 (Thuc. III.50.2) could formally be a tithe of war-spoils, but may still be a corroborative hint.

planning the planting of wheat as to ensure a surplus over consumption in an average year.[16] Similarly the fragmentation of the landholdings of one householder, whether in a village or more widely over a landscape or even over an entire polis-territory, clear in Classical Athens (see chapter 8g below), may indeed have been an inconvenient consequence of dowry-giving, of division of the *kleros* among siblings, or of land division following collective clearance in the Archaic period, but may also have been a deliberate strategy adopted to spread risks and crops among a variety of soils and micro-environments.[17] Certainly the fifth-century Gortyn code encouraged division of the *kleros* among siblings (*Cod. Gort.* iv.37–48 and v.28–54), as did fourth-century theory and practice.[18] So too, though the requirements incumbent upon each Spartiate to contribute specified minimum amounts of barley, wine, cheese, figs and money to his *syssition* (communal mess) monthly[19] tell us nothing about the layout or partition of his *kleros*, they confirm the existence, at least in Spartan political society, of a prejudice against agricultural specialization. It is a moot point how far such prejudices made *autarkeia* a cultural ideal. It was a very ambivalent ideal, for though its main formulations in fourth-century political theory are couched in terms of the self-sufficiency of the city,[20] earlier literary portrayals were as much concerned with the self-sufficiency of the individual *oikos* or agronomic unit,[21] while the individual or psychological dimension of self-sufficiency which was later to figure so prominently in Cynicism is itself prefigured in the later fifth century by Democritus, Hippias of Elis and Antisthenes.[22]

That this cultural ideal had economic effects, in the form of resistance to and distrust towards markets, exchanges, profit-making, selling and so forth, can scarcely be doubted, though the texts which illustrate that resistance are nearly all of the fourth century (Hdt. ii.166–7 excepted). All the same, however much we may wish to ascribe a leading role to the autarkic *oikos* in the Classical Greek economy, the pressures on it and on the domestic mode of production to yield a surplus were considerable. Some were dictated by prudence or social pressure, such as the need to insure against a crop failure next year, to provide a daughter's dowry, or

[16] Forbes 1982 (L 44) 356–76.

[17] Forbes 1982 (L 44) 324–55 with earlier references and comparative material.

[18] Pl. *Leg.* v, 745d; Arist. *Pol.* ii, 1263a21ff; *SIG* 141.16–17, with Salviat and Vatin 1974 (L 124) 260.

[19] The quantities are variously reported by Dicaearchus F 74 Wehrli and Plut. *Lyc.* 12; Cartledge 1979 (F 14) 170.

[20] Main texts: Pl. *Leg.* iv, 704a ff; Arist. *Pol.* i, 1252b27ff, iii, 1275b20, iv, 1291a10, vii, 1326b1ff; Austin and Vidal-Naquet 1977 (L 4) 41f, 162–8, 203f.

[21] Hes. *Op.* 342–367; Finley 1962 (A 36) ch. 3.

[22] Respectively D–K 68 B 246; D–K 86 A 1 and B 12; F 80 Caizzi. For Cynic *autarkeia* see Rich 1956 (J 88); Paquet 1975 (J 83).

to contribute to collective feasts or acts of mutual support via the complex relationship of gift and counter-gift expressed in the word *eranos*.[23] Others, such as the obligations to provide tithes of produce to a deity (cf. M–L 73) or to bespeak man-days for military or political duties, were the product of the political systems in which all Greek house-holders and landowners were caught up. Yet others were the products of the search for power and social prestige, such as ostentatious generosity to the poor,[24] conspicuous consumption at funerals of the kind that Solon had had to legislate against (Plut. *Solon* 21.6), or duly lavish performance of the quasi-obligatory public services (*leitourgiai*) for festival or military purposes which were becoming an increasingly important component of the public economy in the early fifth century in Athens and elsewhere (see p. 29 below). Others, lastly, emerged from the limitations of self-sufficiency. Since few *oikoi* could produce salt or fish on their own, let alone pottery, cut stone, spices, metal weaponry or jewellery, acquisition and exchange of some sort was essential.

Such processes bring us to economic activity at a second level. By the early fifth century it had of course been an established part of life in Greek lands and elsewhere for centuries if not millennia. It had been one of the preconditions of the colonizing movement, and it continued to provide an impetus for war: Miltiades' expedition against Paros in 489, intended simultaneously to satisfy a private quarrel, punish Paros for medizing, and enrich the participants (Hdt. VI.132–3), shows how the nexus of action subsisted. Yet neither this activity, nor the contacts and conflicts which it engendered, need have much eroded autarky, in practice or in theory, or have gone far to create a unified 'Greek economy' or even an 'economy' as such in the sense of an autonomous area of activity, obeying its own behavioural norms and inter-relating with cultural or political systems as a partner of equal status. On the contrary, acquisition at this level can very properly be regarded as embedded in Greek cultures and politics and as largely taking such institutional and value-buttressed forms as were consistent with the *oikos* framework. The principal forms were gift-exchange between chiefs and *aristoi* of the kind illustrated repeatedly in the *Odyssey*; barter, whether the silent sea-shore variety of the kind ascribed to the Carthaginians in West Africa by Herodotus[25] or the more sociable but socially edgy variety engaged in by Homeric *prekteres* (*Od.* VIII.162); seizure (συλή) and piracy;[26] or straightforward war. Such activity did not have to involve specifically developed places (markets), specific media of exchange

[23] Jameson 1983 (L 81) (famine); Gernet 1968 (A 45) (*eranos*).
[24] Notably Cimon's in just this period (Davies 1971 (L 27) 311).
[25] IV.196, with Whittaker 1974 (A 124) 68.
[26] Ormerod 1924 (A 94); Bravo 1980 (L 14). For a comparable list relating to the early medieval period, Grierson 1959 (L 62).

(coinage), specific callings (merchants), or specific value-structures (profit-making). Nor did it entail action by any polity; indeed the colonizing activity of polities, being directed towards moving mouths towards food and other resources rather than the reverse, worked more towards re-establishing autarky than eroding it (though *emporia*, as will be seen, are a different matter). Equally such a pattern of acquisition must have begun by being, and must long have remained, marginal. It might be carried on in marginal time, like Hesiod's seafaring (*Op.* 663ff and 678ff). It might be conducted by those marginal to agrarian society because young or landless.[27] Or it might involve the acquisition of commodities such as jewellery, precious metals, spices, or fine textiles, which met the needs of status and display but hardly rated as basic commodities of survival as did corn, or metals for weaponry.

Whether it remained marginal after the Persian Wars is the crucial problem. There are three usable criteria: (*a*) the extent to which the actual volume of goods exchanged or acquired grew, (*b*) the extent to which trade emancipated itself from gift-exchange, etc., and (*c*) the extent to which the demands of exchange stimulated institutional innovation elsewhere, even in the behaviour of polities.[28]

The first criterion is non-controversial but of limited value. Some flows, such as those of metal ores, marble for statuary and architecture, or Attic painted pottery, had plainly grown considerably in the late Archaic period. Yet the two latter commodities at least may have been minor in bulk and value even at their zenith,[29] while other commodities such as slaves, timber, livestock, and most agrarian products will have left no direct trace whatever and therefore cannot begin to be measured. Evidence from the frequency of shipwrecks, of the kind which has proved diagnostic for later Mediterranean history, is as yet neither large enough nor sufficiently precise in date to signal trends unambiguously. The second criterion has aroused more debate, with claims that the flows mentioned above, and others, can be accommodated within a framework of commission and patronage. Not all such claims are equally persuasive, for the 'trademarks' on Corinthian and Attic painted pottery suggest detachment as much from patronage as from domestic production, while

27 Humphreys 1978 (A 66) 165f.
28 There is little point in adducing a fourth criterion, that of identifying men active in maritime trading, sometimes for high profit. The standard pre-400 examples, such as Colaeus of Samos (Hdt. IV.152.1), Sostratus of Aegina (Hdt. IV.152.3 with Johnston 1972 (L 83) and Johnston 1979 (L 85) 44, 49, 189 with 240 nn. 1–2), and possibly the Anaxagores of the Berezan letter (Bravo 1977 (L 13) = Bravo 1980 (L 14) 879–85), yield meagre and anecdotal results and are far from proving a structural change in activity. In general, Reed 1980 (L 119) ch. 4 and (in sharp contrast of approach) Roebuck, *CAH* IV² 446–60.
29 Webster 1972 (I 177) 42–62, 270–300; Webster 1973 (L 140) 127–45; Starr 1977 (A 113) 64ff; Snodgrass 1980 (A 112) 126–9; Snodgrass 1983 (L 129) 18–25; Cartledge 1983 (L 21) 13f.

we know too little of archaic and early classical blacksmithing for its social position to emerge clearly.[30]

The third criterion is the most revealing, for by the early fifth century there was in place a network of institutions and practices which both reflected a degree of existing (though patchy and marginal) emancipation of exchange from 'political' contexts in favour of integration across Greek political and social frontiers, and was to permit a much greater degree of such emancipation in subsequent decades. Some such practices were of long standing, such as the pattern of behaviour which since Homer had been denoted by the words *emporos* and *emporia*.[31] Even older, in fact if not in name, was the *emporion* such as Ischia or Naucratis. At first this comprised a port of trade outside the Greek culture area, settled or frequented by Greeks, but lying within the orbit of an established power which was able to limit and to define Greek penetration. It differed from a colony in having no formal act of foundation by a specific polis, in having no agricultural *chora*, and in involving little or no subordination of the indigenous population.

However, most of the other constituents of the network were sixth-century innovations. Prime among them, because requiring decisions and investment of labour not by private persons but by states or rulers, were the early stages of harbour constructions and short cuts,[32] for even if they were undertaken for military or cultic reasons they were available for other purposes. So, too, the *emporion* proposed by the Phocaeans *c.* 540 for the Oinoussai islands (Hdt. 1.165.1) would presumably have involved harbour installations, while mercantile purposes cannot have been wholly absent from the planning of Piraeus from 493/2 onwards,[33] though Thucydides' language emphasizes its military aspect (1.93) and though the *horoi* (boundary markers) delimiting the *emporion* there (*IG* I^3 1101) appear to be as late as *c.* 450. Another innovation taking shape in this period was the use of coinage. Though few would now claim that its adoption throughout most of Greece in the course of the sixth century had anything intrinsically to do with exchange among individuals, rather than fiscal payments to the state and distributions or payments by the state for services to it, none the less the hoard evidence does suggest that by the late sixth century certain coinages at least, especially those of Athens, Macedonia and Thrace, were being used to facilitate long-

[30] Burford 1972 (L 18) *passim*; Johnston 1974 (L 84); Johnston 1979 (L 85) 48–53. *Contra* Humphreys 1978 (A 66) 169 and Cartledge 1983 (L 21) 13f.

[31] Knorringa 1926 (L 89); Bravo 1974 (C 122); Bravo 1977 (L 13); Starr 1977 (A 113) 55ff; Mele 1979 (L 100); Vélissaropoulos 1980 (L 137); Reed 1980 (L 119).

[32] Surveys in Blackman 1982 (L 7) and Parry 1987 (L 112).

[33] For the mercantile aspect, Boersma 1970 (I 23) 37f, 46–50, with Judeich 1931 (I 85) 430–56; Gomme, *HCT* I 261–70; Martin 1951 (I 105) 105–10; Panagos 1968 (L 111); Garland 1987 (L 51).

distance exchange.[34] Be it said, however, that further innovation was
required in order to supplement capital concentration via *oikos-* or
patronage-relationships by more formalized, impersonal, interest-bearing loan arrangements, for only such arrangements could exploit the
growing pool of large-value coinage fully enough to create something
like a real money market. One of the two innovations which these
pressures and opportunities produced, viz. the bottomry loan, was
probably a creation of the generation after the Persian Wars, though it is
not attested till 421 (though evidently familiar enough by then) and only
for Athens in the fifth century.[35] It is certainly not chance that the other
financial innovation of the mid-fifth century, which stemmed from the
gradual though still weak monetization of Greek economies, viz. the
bank (τράπεζα, 'table'), probably developed in the same period, being
first attested, albeit by dubious evidence, in Corinth in the 460s.
However, its function seems to have been primarily that of facilitating
the exchange of coin of one currency or weight standard for that of
another, and only secondarily that of accumulating and lending out
capital sums deposited.[36]

However, a further sub-group of linked innovations, certainly under
way in the immediate post-war period in some localities, was to have far
more radical consequences. These innovations comprised the start of
small-value coinages, of small-scale retail trading, of the gradual shift of
the locus of such exchange away from the periphery towards the centre
of the civic space of a polity, and of the consequent enlargement and
redefinition of the function of the Agora. Each of these processes was
patchy, long-drawn-out, and the product of different concatenations of
circumstances. Small-value coinage, for example, took decades to move
down from the threshold represented in early Ionian issues by the
relatively common but still high-value 1/96 fractions of the electrum
stater even to that represented in later Archaic Ionia and the *Wappenmün-
zen* period of Attica by silver ¼-obols,[37] let alone further down still. The
first experiments with base-metal coinages (iron and bronze, cast or
minted) at Olbia and in south Italy and Sicily do not much pre-date 450,
though interestingly the suggestion that Athens should follow suit was
being made before 443.[38] Yet the smaller-scale trading which such

[34] Most recent summary by Kraay, *CAH* iv², ch. 7d, building on Cook 1958 (c 183); Kraay 1964
(c 188); Price and Waggoner 1975 (c 196); Kraay 1976 (c 190) 318–28; Kraay 1977 (c 191); Grierson
1977 (c 185).
[35] *P. Oxy.* 2741 = Eupolis F 192.96–8 K–A, with de Ste Croix 1974 (L 122) 44 and n. 13; Harvey
1976 (L 66); Reed 1980 (L 119) 54ff with 110 n. 54 (dismissing earlier alleged evidence).
[36] [Them.] *Ep.* vi and vii, with Bogaert 1966 (L 10) 135–44 and Bogaert 1968 (L 11) 94f, 305–7.
The word χρυσαμοιβός in Aesch. *Ag.* 437 proves – unsurprisingly – the concept formulated before
458.   [37] Kraay 1964 (c 188) 87f; Kraay 1976 (c 190) 318 n. 2.
[38] Price 1968 (c 195) 94, on the assumption that Dionysius (*PA* 4084), to whom Callimachus (F
430 *ap.* Ath. xv.669D) attributed the suggestion, did not return from Thurii.

coinage assisted was clearly in being well before then. Immediate proof comes not so much from Cyrus' reported rude remarks, at a dramatic date in the 540s, about Greeks who cheat on oath while buying and selling in the Agora (Hdt. 1.153.1–2), for that *mot* presumably stems from the later contrast between him as father (*pater*) and Darios as petty retailer (*kapelos*, Hdt. III.89.3); but rather from Hipponax' use of the verb *kapeleuein* (F79.19 Degani). Yet Cyrus' *mot* is historically important, for he is made to locate those deplorable activities 'in the middle of the city' (ἐν μέσῃ τῇ πόλει). Such a locus was new. The archaic Greek Agora as an open space had had political, legal, cultic, theatrical and athletic-competitive functions,[39] but the place for such exchange as took place outside the framework of social relationships seems to have lain on a frontier or in a no-mans'-land, whether physical, such as a seashore (cf. later *emporia* and towns called Agora (cf. Hdt. VIII.58.2)), or political, such as the 'frontier Agora' from which murderers were excluded by Draco's law.[40] That such exchange should enter the Agora proper – and in fact should end by extruding much other public activity from it, and by permanently altering the uses of words such as ἀγοράζω or ἀγορά itself – was a long-drawn-out process, not reflected in literary texts till Herodotus,[41] but one weighty enough in its eventual impact to yield two separate functionally distinct *agorai* at Athens, Piraeus and elsewhere.[42]

A final group of innovations returns us to the seaways, the ships and the seafarers. First, the late sixth and early fifth centuries saw knowledge about far-away places rise from the level of prodigies and fabulous tales to that of increasingly sober and practical descriptive treatment. Granted, some parts of this process were known to Greeks only at second hand, such as the account by a Carthaginian, the elder Hanno, of his circumnavigation of Africa *c*. 600 B.C. (Hdt. IV.42), or not at all, such as the younger Hanno's report of his colonizing expedition down the West African coast to Senegal if not to Mt Cameroun.[43] However, knowledge of the *Description of the Earth* by the Milesian Hecataeus should have been well diffused by the 470s, and will have been supplemented by other more autobiographical travel descriptions, such

[39] McDonald 1943 (I 100) ch. 4; Martin 1951 (I 105) 149ff; Wycherley 1962 (I 184) 50ff; Martin 1974 (I 107) 30–47, 266–75; Kolb 1981 (I 92) 1–19.

[40] *IG* I³ 104.27–8, with Davies, *CAH* IV² 369 n. 7; Martin 1951 (I 105) 284ff. Add now Peacock 1982 (A 97) 156f for comparative material.

[41] Martin 1951 (I 105) 279ff; *Epig. Hom.* XIV.5 is undatable. *Cod. Gort.* VII.10–11 already uses *agora* to denote the slave-market.

[42] Thessaly: Arist. *Pol.* VII, 1331a30ff. with Newman *ad loc.* and Xen. *Cyr.* 1.2.3–5 (ἐλευθεραὶ ἀγοραί). Athens: Apollodorus *FGrH* 244 F 113, with Oikonomides 1962 (I 118), Wycherley 1966 (I 186) (sceptical); Travlos 1971 (I 171) 1; Kolb 1981 (I 92) 20–2. Piraeus: Garland 1987 (L 51) 141f, 152f. Distinct commodity markets in fourth-century Athens: Stroud 1974 (C 167) 180; Sparkes 1975 (I 156) 132.

[43] Text *GGM* I 1–14 (Eng. tr. in Carpenter 1966 (A 15) 82–5); Cary and Warmington 1963 (A 18) 63ff; Momigliano 1975 (A 89) 137 (probably 500–450); full discussion in Huss 1985 (A 68) 75–83.

as Skylax' account of his voyage from the Indies to Suez, and possibly also by Euthymenes of Massilia's earlier account of the African coast or by whatever lay behind the western Mediterranean portion of Avienus' *Ora maritima*.[44] Secondly, shipbuilding had shown a radical change in the generation before 480, with a real and major divergence between warship and merchantman. The two had long been distinguished as much by the presence or absence of a beak as by shape, so that Herodotus' report that the Phocaeans used to make their western Mediterranean voyages in pentekonters, not in round ships (II.163.1–2), is less odd than it appears, given the likely dangers from Etruscan or Carthaginian warships or pirates. That that expedient was unsatisfactory is suggested by the invention of the 'samaina', 'which has a beak turned up like a pig's snout, but is rounder and belly-shaped, so that it can both carry cargo and sail swiftly. It was so called because it appeared first in Samos, on the initiative of Polykrates the tyrant' (Plut.*Per.* 26.4). The idea presumably was to have it both ways, by increasing cargo space without sacrificing offensive capability, but that the risk–benefit balance was tipping even further towards larger capacity and smaller crew is clear from the development by the 520s of the merchant ship propelled entirely by sail.[45] It is no accident that such a ship type would have best suited the lengthy round trips from the Aegean to the Black Sea and back, which were to become (if they were not already) a prime component of Classical Greek seaborne trade and for which the essential staging posts were mostly in place by then.[46] Teus plainly was not the only place to be permanently dependent on imported grain by *c.* 470 (M–L 30A). Such trips are evidence of that profound revolution in the logistics of antiquity which comprised moving a staple food supply to its consumers at an acceptable social price instead of moving them to it through colonization. As later in Rome and Constantinople, so now in the Aegean and probably at Carthage too, the political consequences of that revolution were to overwhelm household autarky, to involve the state in the process, and hence to help both to define the shape and to broaden the scope of the public economy. Slowly, jerkily, and via a process responding to need but mostly flowing outside the political framework, the single loosely inter-related economic system, which the Greek world and some of its non-Greek neighbours had long been for

[44] Euthymenes: *FHG* IV 409, with Hdt. II.22, if it is not a forger's version of the younger Hanno. Avienus: Hind 1972 (L 67); Boardman 1980 (A 6) 224.

[45] First secure attestation on the Attic black-figure cup, London BM B 436; reproduction and/or discussion in Casson 1959 (A 19) 86–7 and pl. 7; Morrison and Williams 1968 (A 91) 109 Arch. 85 and pl. 19; Casson 1971 (A 20) figs. 81–2; de Ste Croix 1972 (G 36) 393–6; Humphreys 1978 (A 66) 168f, 171; Snodgrass 1983 (L 129) 16f.

[46] Hdt. VII.147.2, with Noonan 1973 (L 104); Davies 1978 (A 23) 58; Bravo 1983 (L 15). Scepticism in Garnsey 1985 (L 53) and Garnsey 1988 (L 54) 107–19.

certain marginal purposes, was being expanded to take in an even greater proportion of flows, transactions and commodities.

III

Developments of a rather different kind were affecting the public, intellectual, and social life of the 470s and were exposing the strains and contradictions inherent in the very institution which had shaped Greek political life for so long, the republican polis. They affected alike its form, its inner dynamics, and its external relationships, and interacted so closely with the economic shifts just described as to erode the presuppositions of value and function which had underpinned it since the eighth century.

To diagnose crisis, at a moment when the Persian Wars had just been fought in defence of and in terms of the polis and when their outcome had to all appearance vindicated it as a system of government, may seem as paradoxical as it is unconventional. Indeed, at first sight it is the consolidation of the polis-form of polity in the 470s which strikes the eye rather than its erosion. For one thing, tyranny, monarchy and *dynasteiai* (narrow oligarchies) were on the retreat. Even before the Persian Wars many had succumbed to that pressure for wider participation in decision making, and thereby for greater equality between ruler and ruled, which had come to be labelled *isonomia*.[47] In the post-war period the fact that many such regimes, such as those in Thessaly or Thebes,[48] had been pro-Persian helped to quicken the rout, especially in the vulnerable areas of Asia Minor and Propontis, where the Athenians had a compounded interest in eliminating them.[49] However, the same process was under way from purely internal impulses in Cyrene, where the Battiad monarchy was overthrown by a democracy sometime after 460,[50] in Sicily, where by the late 460s the Deinomenid regime had been dismantled and the republican status quo restored (Diod. XI.76.4–6) (see chapter 7), and even in Epirus if Thucydides' note on the Chaones and Thesproti as kingless in 430 (II.80.5) has significance. In the Greek-speaking area indeed, only Sparta, Molossia, Macedonia and Cyprus had monarchies deep-rooted enough to survive the egalitarian winds of the fifth century.

Fashionable instead were the various processes loosely called synoecism.[51] The use of the term in Greek sources is unhelpfully elastic,

---

[47] Ostwald 1969 (D 64).   [48] Forrest, *CAH* III³. 3, 291–9.

[49] See the survey in Berve 1967 (A 5) I 186–9.

[50] Schol. Pind. *Pyth.* IV *inscr.* b, and Arist. fr. 611.7, with Chamoux 1953 (F 17) 202–10; Mitchell 1966 (F 51) 108–13; Hornblower 1983 (A 65) 58–62.

[51] Kuhn 1878 (F 40), still valuable; Kahrstedt 1932 (F 38); Moggi 1976 (F 53); Hornblower 1982 (A 64) 78.

ranging for this period alone from (i) joint foundation of colonies through (ii) the forcible transfer of population, (iii) imposed amalgamation, (iv) the creation of an urban centre, and (v) the creation of a political central place, to (vi) annexation.[52] To such uses, moreover, one may add not only examples which are inferred rather than directly attested,[53] but also (with reservations) federal structures such as the Arcadian League. The boundaries of the phenomenon are therefore not closely definable. None the less the early fifth century does appear to have experienced a clear shift of mood towards amalgamating political units or towards unifying areas which had hitherto been little more than ethnic or geographical expressions and had no one political central place. Gelon's creation of a Greater Syracuse in the 480s exemplifies the former, while the synoecisms of Elis, Mantineia and Tegea in the 470s may exemplify the latter to varying degrees.[54]

To the extension of polis-style government and the extension of participation in its processes may be added the extension of its role and responsibilities. This took various forms. It is clear, for example, in the area of cult, where the late Archaic period had seen religion and the state redefine themselves and their function in ways which subtly but significantly favoured the state.[55] So, too, the state's power to coerce recalcitrant members was slowly advancing. At the social level, though the drastic and unparalleled inculcation of social values and skills, which was encapsulated in the Spartan *agoge*, had not yet become the social paradigm elsewhere in Greece that it was to become by the 420s,[56] Athens at least may already have been developing more formal means of control over public order and pirate action; the first employment of a corps of Scythian archers as a police force may belong in this period,[57] while the capacity to prosecute was being extended, via a process impossible to date or to trace in detail, to a wider range of persons and to a wider range of offences.[58] At the political level the prosecutions of Miltiades in 493 and 489, the Athenian ostracisms of the 480s, the imitation of ostracism elsewhere,[59] or the various legal or quasi-legal actions successfully mounted against no fewer than three Spartan kings

---

[52] Respectively (i) Thuc. I.24.2, VI.2.6 etc., with Moggi 1975 (F 52); (ii) Hdt. VII.156; (iii) Str. VIII.3.20, with Moggi 1976 (F 53) 166 no. 26; (iv) Thuc. I.10.2; (v) *LSS* 10. col. ii, with Parke 1977 (K 71) 31 and Hornblower 1982 (A 64) 79 n. 9; (vi) Paus. VIII.27.1, with Moggi 1976 (F 53) 127 no. 22.

[53] E.g. Olbia and Berezan (Graham 1978 (F 27) 106), or the Mesara plain in Crete (Kirsten 1956 (A 73) 110).

[54] Thus orthodoxy (e.g. Moggi 1976 (F 53) 131ff nos. 23–5), but there is room for doubt (below, p. 103). [55] Davies, *CAH* IV² 368–88.

[56] Ollier 1933 (F 55) 42–54, 119–38; Tigerstadt 1965 (F 68); Rawson 1969 (A 104) 12ff; Hodkinson 1983 (F 30) 245 ff, with earlier references.

[57] Andoc. III.5 and Aeschin. II.173, with Plassart 1913 (D 68) and Vos 1963 (I 173).

[58] Mainly by the *graphe* procedure, but also by *apagoge* and *endeixis*: Hansen 1976 (D 30A) 115.

[59] Schol. Ar. *Knights* 855; Diod. XI.86.5–87.6.

within fifteen years, all suggest that public opinion was willing to create and to use formal procedures (rather than acquiescence or assassination) against errant politicians in a way barely conceivable fifty years previously.

At the fiscal level, too, increased pressure must be assumed, for even though *misthos* (pay) for public office lay nearly a generation in the future, even at Athens, new needs were outstripping older modes of public finance. There had of course long been tithes, fines and confiscations, while the linkage between socio-economic ranking and the responsibility to contribute, militarily or otherwise, to the needs of the state, which was encapsulated in the barely translatable word *telos* (property/obligation group),[60] re-emerged with the four Solonian property-classes (*Ath.Pol.* 7.3), and survived to provide the background to oligarchic notions of distributive justice. So, too, communities had long assigned a *temenos* (precinct) to a god or an official on the understanding that its produce or revenues would defray the expenses of cult or office. Yet the often morally dubious fiscal improvisations attributed to sixth-century tyrants in [Aristotle]'s *Oeconomica* II and elsewhere were already symptoms of strain, and one military innovation in particular – the trireme – must have generated further and greater pressures. By our period its impact on Greek public finance was being felt all over the Aegean, and if Herodotus' terminology can be trusted it had yielded by the early fifth century a uniform solution in the form of the trierarchy. Attested at Samos in 494 (Hdt. VI.14.2) and at Aegina, Naxos and elsewhere (Hdt. VII.181.1, VIII.46.3, VIII.90.4) as well as Athens in 480, this fiscal expedient reflected the new relationship imposed by the necessity for the state to meet the capital cost of the hulls.[61] Part magistracy, part an extended *telos*-type obligation, part aristocratic euergetism, it cleverly accommodated the new fiscal interests of the state within the archaic value-framework of *timē* (prestige) and *charis* (obligation).[62] Much the same is true for the other form of *leitourgia* or public service, viz. that concerned with the provision of spectacles and contests during religious festivals, which appeared in its fully developed form first in Athens with the *choregia* in 502/1 and speedily proliferated there, though unlike the trierarchy it seems to have been slow to spread elsewhere.[63]

To some such pressures, then, some Greek communities could and did respond from the early fifth century on by extending and adapting

---

[60] Van Effenterre 1979 (L 135) 27ff is now the point of departure; add (on its likely Mycenaean ancestry in /tereta/ or /tereja/) Baumbach 1968 (C 115) 237ff and Gschnitzer 1981 (L 63) 19ff.

[61] A vestige of the older system of privately built hulls at Hdt. VIII.17.

[62] Veyne 1976 (A 120) 186–200; Davies 1981 (D 18) 92–105.

[63] Capps 1943 (C 125); Davies 1967 (D 17). The word *choregos* at Hdt. V.83.3 (Aegina) and Arist. *Pol.* VIII, 1341a33 (Sparta) probably has its intrinsic meaning 'chorus-leader', as in Alcman's *Partheneion* (line 44 Page).

the polis and its governmental mechanisms. Yet – and herein lies the basic paradox – the more the polis increased and consolidated its role in Greek society, the more it encountered contradictions which could not be resolved within that polis framework. The main contradiction was military. Thessaly, for example, was to see in the fifth century a hitherto effective mechanism for unifying military resources on land eroded by separatist pressure from the growing individual poleis.[64] Maritime polities faced the opposite pressure. Thucydides is explicit that the costs of triremes and trierarchies bore heavily on the Athenian allies and induced many of them (he implies in the 460s) to commute ship contributions to the payment of tribute (1.99). Thucydides sees this within a context of their capacity or incapacity to revolt, but it has wider implications; the logic of contemporary naval technology was dividing Greek states into two classes, those who could and those who could not keep up with the costs.

The effect was compounded by international pressures. In the West, where polis-particularism had shallower roots than in Old Greece and where self-identification as 'Ionian' or as 'Dorian' provided an alternative exploitable focus, Carthaginian encroachment provided reason – or excuse – first for tightly interlocking dynastic connexions and later for so enlarging the polis, by forcible amalgamations and transfers of population, that Greater Syracuse by 480 was no longer a polis but a territorial state. Likewise the dwarf states of Old Greece had been dragged willy-nilly back into the concert of eastern Mediterranean powers by half a century of Persian invasions. As in 546 and 499, so too in 491 and 481 resistance had entailed cooperation and alliance, for no one polis by itself could survive militarily in such an environment, while the successive decisions taken by the Aegean seaboard states at Samos in 479, Byzantium in 478 and Delos in 477 had indicated that here too, as in the Peloponnese, military activity would take place for the foreseeable future within the framework of a regional hegemony. The contradiction was fundamental. The polis as a military unit on its own was dead, while the polis as an administrative and cultural unit was not.

That by itself would have been enough to constitute a fifth-century crisis, but other contradictions and tensions in post-war Greek society made it worse. For example, the more the polis extended its range of activity, and opened its polity or even its magistracies to all citizens, the more anomalous became the position of those whose activities put them without the city framework. Seers (*manteis*) and their more disreputable confrères, the *chresmologoi* and shamans, were a case in point, as shown by the way the Spartans had to break all their own rules in order to

[64] Hornblower 1983 (A 65) 79–83; Kraay 1976 (C 190) 115–17.

accommodate the talents of Teisamenos of Elis.[65] So were poets and artists such as Bacchylides or Polygnotus or Alcamenes, who moved from commission to commission. So too were the many Aegean islanders who rowed more and more Athenian ships as commutation gathered pace – mercenaries in all but name.[66] So, too, were the sea-traders (*emporoi* and *naukleroi*), whose economic role might well come to be central to the existence of the very cities which had no control over them and within which they had no intrinsic legal standing.[67]

A second, closely allied, contradiction was that presented by chattel slavery in the household, in craftwork, in mining and in agriculture. The problem here was not so much that presented by the conceptual conflict between slave as instrument and slave as human being, which Aristotle later found so intractable (*Pol.* 1253b23ff), nor even the conflict between slavery as an efficient (because mobile and controllable) means of concentrating a labour force for productive or display purposes and slavery as intrinsically inefficient, because goodwill and cooperation could not be extracted from a structurally alienated workforce.[68] Rather, the problem arose from the presence, within a polis and its *chora*, of a growing (it seems) number of deracinés of alien speech and culture, whose labour was necessary (or highly desirable) but whose presence was potentially dangerous, whose immediate ambitions for freedom and wealth challenged the very roots of a descent-group-defined agrarian society, and whose life-style, if 'living apart' from their masters as money-making investments for the latter, might differ so little from that of poor citizens as to present status contradictions of their own.

A third tension, visible in the literature and thought of the 470s, is that between, on the one hand, paradigms of the world couched in terms of myth and, on the other, systematic non-theistic descriptions of the world and of man's predicament based either on observation or on the primacy of reasoned argument as the way to truth. It was precisely because the Hesiodic tradition, best represented in this decade by Pindar, was challenged equally strongly from two basically incompatible directions, that Greek intellectual life, not (so far as one can see) hitherto greatly fractured or discordant or at loggerheads with political life *as such* (which is not to say that poets might not be fiercely partisan or denunciatory), now began to show increasing alienation from the traditional framework of Greek political, social and cultural life. Already in the previous generation Xenophanes had been caustically questioning the point of

---

[65] Hdt. IX.33–6, with Kett 1966 (K 50); Nilsson 1967 (K 69) 618–20; Burkert 1977 (K 13) 20.
[66] On whom Roy 1967 (A 107) 322.
[67] de Ste Croix 1972 (G 36) 264–7, 393–6; Van Effenterre 1979 (L 136); Reed 1981 (L 119) *passim*.
[68] Thus Vernant 1974 (A 118) 29.

athletic victories and other aristocratic values. Heraclitus in his idiosyn-
cratic way had more recently followed suit, while the Pythagoreans in
south Italy were making their Freemason-style groups the main focus of
social life, and more and more intellectuals were moving away from their
own cities to where the action was.[69]

A fourth source of tension is identified – or caricatured – after the
event by the Old Oligarch: 'the demos has put down the athletes at
Athens and the practitioners of *mousike*' ([Xen.] *Ath.Pol.* 1.13). Prepos-
terous at first sight in the century of Sophocles, his allegation is echoed
and expanded, at least for music proper, by Plato (*Laws* III,700–1) and
has some truth. The Archaic period had seen the emergence, and
differentiation from a continuing peasant society, of an upper-class
cultural and behavioural norm. It was multiply characterized: by affected
ostentation in dress; by social contacts and intermarriage across political
frontiers; by ritualized conflict and competition at the Panhellenic
Games and elsewhere; by institutions of restricted membership such as
the *palaistra* or the *symposion* with their accompanying etiquette and
social prestige; by being both the locus and the focus of predominant art
forms such as dithyrambic, lyric, or elegiac poetry, the *kouros* statue, or
elegant table-ware in silver or fine pottery; by pederasty; by the specific
vogue-words *kalos kagathos* (perhaps 'gentleman') and *asteios* (urban,
witty); and by the gravitation of those involved and of their activities
away from the *chora* of the gauche unaccomplished country bumpkin
with his sheepskin cloak towards the nucleated polis with its 'polite'
atmosphere.[70] This high urbane sub-culture of Archaic Greece was now
subject to erosion – or rather was so attractive as to generate pressure to
extend it down the social scale. The sudden emergence of formal schools
in the 490s, even in such remote places as Astypalaea, is one symptom of
pressure.[71] Another is the break-up of the formal frontal *kouros*-pose in
sculpture from *c.* 480 onwards in favour of the sort of representation of
action or of heroic archetype which had already long come to predominate in the much cheaper and therefore less aristocratic bronze or
terracotta statuettes. A third is the amalgamation of upper-class lyric
with the significantly out-of-town bucolic Dionysiac ritual of the *komos*
and the *tragos*, in order to produce the upstart, hybrid (if not bastard),
vulgarly spectacular art forms of comedy and tragedy which appealed to
a mass audience newly culturally enfranchised and which put other
poetic art forms in the shade.

[69] Xenophanes D–K B 2; Heraclitus D–K B 15. See Ostwald, ch.8*h* below.
[70] Various aspects of this general picture in Gschnitzer 1981 (L 63) 60ff, 126ff; Roebuck, *CAH*
III².3, 438–41; Lloyd 1983 (A 79); Bowie 1986 (J 5).
[71] Paus. VI.9.6, with other references in Marrou 1956 (A 84) 369 n. 7; Immerwahr 1964 (I 79);
Harvey 1966 (L 65) 629–35; Giroux 1980 (L 59).

To these areas of difficulty we can add others, such as the tension in state after state between an existing polity based on subordination – whether by serfdom, helotization, or the control of non-participant outlying communities by a dominant centre – and an ideal polity based, like most colonies, on equality and likeness (ἐπὶ ἴσῃ καὶ ὁμοίᾳ). The picture which emerges is of a post-war Greece in the grip of what was at best uncomfortable transition in many fields of social activity at once, if not of acute crisis. That is not a conventional view of the early fifth century, but the case stands.

CHAPTER 3

THE DELIAN LEAGUE TO 449 B.C.

P. J. RHODES

I. THE FOUNDATION OF THE LEAGUE

It is unlikely that the Greeks who fought against the Persians at Plataea in 479 entered into any commitment relevant to this chapter. There may well be authentic material behind the various texts of an oath said to have been sworn before the battle (Tod, *GHI* 204, 21–51; Lycurg. *Leoc.* 80–1; Diod. XI.29.2–3: Theopomp. *FGrH* 115 F 153 rejected it as an Athenian fabrication), but the clause requiring temples destroyed by the Persians to be left in ruins does not appear in the inscribed version and is hard to accept.[1] After the battle the Plataeans were promised freedom from attack on condition that they cared for the graves of the fallen (Thuc. II.72, III.58.4), but the Greek festival of freedom appears to be a Hellenistic institution, and Plutarch's combination with this of a Greek force to wage war against the barbarian is unlikely to represent a decision taken after Plataea (Diod. XI.29.1; Plut. *Arist.* 21.1–2).[2]

However, if we may believe Herodotus, the question of carrying the war back to Persian territory and liberating Greeks under Persian rule was raised in 480–479. Thoughts of the future attributed to Themistocles (VIII.108.4, 109.5) may be suspect, but there is no need to doubt the envoys appealing for the liberation of Ionia early in 479 (VIII.132), or the futher appeal from Samos later in the year (IX.90). After the battle of Mycale, we are told, the Greeks considered abandoning Ionia and giving the Ionians new homes in Greece: the proposal was supported by the Peloponnesians, but successfully resisted by the Athenians, who claimed a special relationship with the Ionians; after which Samos, Chios, Lesbos and 'the other islanders who were campaigning along with the Greeks'

This chapter, written at short notice in 1985/6, gives an argued narrative based on the review of problems by Rhodes 1985 (E 68). Major works for the whole of this chapter are Meritt *et al.* 1939–53 (E 55), Meiggs 1972 (E 53). These will be cited as *ATL* and Meiggs respectively.

[1] The clause is accepted by Dinsmoor 1941 (I 59) 158 n. 322; Raubitschek 1965 (C 163) 516–18; Meiggs 504–7; and (though he finds several examples of its breach) Boersma 1970 (I 23) 50–1, etc. It is rejected by Siewert 1972 (F 65) 102–8. Cf. *CAH* IV² 604.

[2] There are attempts to defend part of this by Larsen 1933 (F 42) 262–4, Raubitschek 1960 (A 102) and 1965 (C 163), Meiggs 507–8. For the arguments against, see *ATL* III 101–4; Brunt 1953–4 (A 10) 153–6; Frost 1961 (C 35); Etienne and Piérart 1975 (C 131).

(but not, it appears, any mainlanders) were admitted to the Greek alliance (IX.106).

Herodotus has conditioned us to thinking of the Persian Wars as ending in 479, but the Greeks could not be certain at that point that the Persians would not attack again, and it should cause no surprise that in 478 the Spartan-led Greek alliance continued the war – on a smaller scale, because there was no longer an immediate threat to Greece. Pausanias, who had commanded on land in 479, took command of the fleet; and it may have been in the same year that Leotychidas, commander of the fleet in 479, took a land expedition to punish medizers in Thessaly (Hdt. VI.71).[3] Pausanias first sailed out of the Aegean and overran most of Cyprus (to which the Persian fleet had perhaps withdrawn), then made for the Bosporus and drove the Persians out of Byzantium (Thuc. 1.94): this was anti-Persian action, not pro-Ionian. But, though he had laughed at Persian grandeur after Plataea (Hdt. IX.82), power now went to his head, and his arrogance and severity offended the allies. Thucydides is convinced that he was also guilty of medism; but when recalled to Sparta he was acquitted on that charge; he was not in Byzantium long enough to send and receive the letters which Thucydides quotes, and there is no reason why after his victories over the Persians he should at this point have begun to collude with them (Thuc. 1.95, 128.4–130).[4]

Reports reached Sparta, and Pausanias was recalled; by the time Dorcis had arrived as his successor, the leadership had been taken over by the Athenians. Not only Sparta but the other Peloponnesians, and Aegina, which could hardly be expected to submit to Athenian leadership,[5] remained outside the new League. Athens had supported the Ionians at the beginning (but only at the beginning) of their revolt against Persia in 498;[6] she had opposed the Peloponnesians' proposal to transport the Ionians to Greece; and at the end of 479 she had led a campaign against Sestos after the Peloponnesian contingents had returned home (Hdt. IX.114–21, cf. Thuc. 1.89.2). She had by far the largest navy of any Greek state. There is thus nothing surprising in Athenian leadership for the kind of war that could be expected.

According to Thucydides, the allies took the initiative and pressed the leadership on Athens (1.95.1–2, cf. 75.2), but other texts ascribe the initiative to Athens (Hdt. VIII.3.2; *Ath. Pol.* 23.4). It may not have been clear who had first made the suggestion, but there must have been willingness on both sides. The Ionian Revolt, with no strong leader, had ended in disaster, while in mainland Greece Sparta had built up in the

---

[3] Cf. pp. 97, 499, where a slightly later date is considered.

[4] See especially Lippold 1965 (F 46); Fornara 1966 (F 23) 263–5; Lang 1967/8 (F 41); Rhodes 1970 (C 82) 387—90; Blamire 1970 (F 6) 296–8; Lazenby 1975 (F 44) 235–8.

[5] Cf. *CAH* IV² 339–40, 365–7.   [6] Cf. *CAH* IV² 482–3.

Peloponnesian League a strong alliance which had not noticeably diminished its members' freedom, and the larger union under Spartan leadership of nearly all the southern Greeks had succeeded in repelling the Persian invasion. The prospect of a strong leader must have been attractive to the eastern Greeks, and after the Ionian Revolt the chief danger to be feared from Athens must have seemed not that she would wield too much power over her allies but that she would not persevere in what was their cause more than hers: the permanent nature of the alliance (below) may have been seen as binding Athens rather than the allies. So in 478/7 (*Ath. Pol.* 23.5; Diod. XI.47[7] narrates it under 477/6) a new alliance was formed.

For the organization of the League we are largely dependent on two tantalizing chapters of Thucydides (1.96–7). The objective, clearly, was in some sense to continue the war against Persia. Thucydides writes that 'the pretext [*proschema*, in contrast with the aims which Athens came to pursue[8]] was to obtain revenge for what they had suffered by ravaging the King's land' (1.96.1). Technically what was formed was a full offensive and defensive alliance, intended to last until lumps of metal rose from the bottom of the sea (*Ath. Pol.* 23.5), and although Thucydides does not mention the freedom of the Greeks here he does so elsewhere (III.10.3, VI.76.3–4): we have seen that the idea was mooted in 479, and we need not doubt that that was part of the reason for the formation of a permanent alliance against the Persians.[9]

How large the League is likely to have been at its foundation depends partly on how much enthusiasm for war against Persia can be postulated among the states of the Aegean, partly on how we interpret the word 'Ionian' in Hdt. IX.104, Thuc. 1.89.2, 95.1, and *Ath. Pol.* 23.4–5. Some have wanted to take 'Ionian' strictly, as referring to the eastern states which belonged to the Ionian strand of the Greek people and shared in the *Panionion*, but the founder members must have included at any rate the Aeolian states of Lesbos (Hdt. IX.106) and Dorian Byzantium. Persia's settlement after the Ionian Revolt had been mild (Hdt. VI.42–3), and it seems not to have been so strongly thought up to the time of the Persian Wars as it came to be afterwards that Greeks and barbarians were fundamentally different; but the eastern Greeks had not submitted to Persia enthusiastically (cf. Hdt. 1.141, 152–3), and we may assume that as long as the chances of success seemed good many will have welcomed a

[7] On Diodorus' dates see p. 7.
[8] Cf. Rawlings 1977 (E 66). French 1979 (E 29) denies the contrast, but it should be accepted. Athens may not have had ulterior motives from the beginning, but she soon found ways of using the League to her own advantage, and by the third quarter of the century was openly treating the League as an Athenian empire.
[9] Sealey 1966 (E 82) limits the original objective of the League to raiding for booty, but see Jackson 1969 (E 37), Meiggs 462–4. The theme of retaliation is stressed by Raaflaub 1979 (E 65).

continuing war against Persia. The League should have attracted a fair number of members from the outset.[10]

There was to be a treasury on Delos, and meetings of the allies were to be held there (Thuc. 1.96.2); hence the modern name for the alliance, the Delian League. Delos with its sanctuary of Apollo was important to the Ionians in the strict sense of that term (Thuc. III.104). Originally the dominant influence there had been that of Naxos; an Athenian interest had been shown by the sixth-century tyrant Pisistratus, who had 'purified' Delos by removing graves from the area of the sanctuary (Hdt. 1.64.2; Thuc. III.104.1).[11] The use of the term 'Ionians' with reference to a League whose members included eastern Greeks of all strands is thus not just an accident of our sources: at its foundation the League was represented as an Ionian league (which may have helped to justify Athens' leadership and make it acceptable to Sparta), and eastern Greeks of other kinds were assimilated to the Ionians.

Some allies were to provide ships, others were to make payments in cash (*phoros*, usually translated 'tribute'). According to Thucydides the Athenians decided which members should contribute in which way and provided the financial officials (*hellenotamiai*, Greek treasurers), and the total tribute was originally assessed at 460 talents, presumably per annum (1.96). Athens provided the commanders of League expeditions, and it should not surprise us that she also provided the League treasurers:[12] if the alliance was to be effective, the leader needed to be able to exercise her leadership, and to do so over all the allies, those which paid tribute as well as those which sent their own ships. (The members were partners in a full alliance, and it should not be supposed that a tribute-payer could discharge its full obligation by making its annual payment: the leader could require soldiers from all the allies, and was to do so in Greece in the 450s.[13]) The first assessment of contributions is elsewhere attributed to the Athenian Aristides (*Ath. Pol.* 23.5; Plut. *Arist.* 24, cf. Thuc. v.18.5), and deciding the form of individual contributions will no doubt have formed part of that exercise. It has sometimes been thought that for the cities to which it applied Aristides took over the assessment made by Artaphernes at the end of the Ionian Revolt, but this implication should not be read into Hdt. vi.42, and it appears that Artaphernes considered agricultural land only but the Athenians took into account other forms of wealth.[14]

[10] See, for a small League at the beginning, Walker, *CAH* v¹ 42–4; Highby 1936 (E 35) 39–57; Sealey 1966 (E 82) 243–4; cf. (for a strict interpretation of 'Ionians') Hammond 1967 (E 33) 43–7 (= A 54, 315–21). A large League is preferred by Gomme, *HCT* I 289–95, cf. 257, 271–2; *ATL* III 194–224; Meiggs 50–8. [11] Cf. *CAH* III².3, 403.

[12] But Woodhead 1959 (E 95) suggested that at first the treasurers were appointed by the League.
[13] Cf. p. 114.
[14] Cf. Murray 1966 (A 93). Evans 1976 (A 35) argues that Aristides did use Artaphernes' land survey as his basis.

The scale of the first assessment is notoriously problematic. Thucydides gives a total of 460 talents, in language suggesting that that was the amount contributed by payers of tribute; yet the evidence of the tribute quota-lists indicates that in the late 450s, when the League had more members, and more tribute-paying members, the total assessment was only c. 500 talents. Similarly, Thuc. II.13.3 states that the total tribute in 431 was 600 talents, but the quota-lists for the late 430s point to an assessment of c. 430 talents.[15] Various solutions have been attempted.[16] The one assessment list which we know in detail, that of 425, is an extremely optimistic list,[17] and it may be that Thucydides' 460 talents is derived from an optimistic list covering not only the states which did join the League at the beginning but all which Athens hoped would join. This list will have covered both tribute-payers and (perhaps at the rate of one ship for 1 talent) ship-providers: only a large state could afford the manpower to contribute several ships for a campaigning season every year, and it has been estimated that more than half of the likely members of the League could not regularly provide even one trireme, and only 15 per cent could regularly provide more than two.[18] Even if Thucydides' figure is artificially high, the first assessment is problematic in another way too. We do not know how large were the forces with which the League campaigned, or for how long a season (Plut. Per. 11.4 refers to sixty ships sent out for eight months, but we do not know of which period, if any, this is true), but if Athens, though not assessed for tribute, made a substantial contribution from her own resources, it is hard to think that large sums would need to be spent from the tribute – and a papyrus fragment may tell us that 5,000 talents had accumulated in the League's treasury by the middle of the century.[19] Later a proportion of the tribute was given as an offering to Athena in Athens, and at first we may assume that a proportion was given to Apollo on Delos: work on a new temple there was begun in the second quarter of the fifth century, and was abandoned about the middle of the century, when the League's treasury had been removed to Athens.[20]

Thucydides says that the allies 'at first were autonomous and deliberated in common councils' (1.97.1); he goes on to mention cases in which

[15] For the figures calculated from the tribute quota-lists see Meiggs 62–3 with 63 n. 1, 527; it is arguable that the figure for the late 450s, which assumes that all members except Lesbos, Chios and Samos had become tribute-payers, is slightly too low. Thucydides' figures recur in Plut. Arist. 24.4, but Diod. XI.47.1, XII.40.2, has different figures.
[16] See Walker, CAH v¹ 44–6; Gomme, HCT I 273–9; ATL III 236–43; Chambers 1958 (E 15); Eddy 1968 (E 18); Meiggs 58–67; French 1972 (E 28); Unz 1985 (E 86).
[17] IG I³ 71; see pp. 420–1.
[18] Ruschenbusch 1983 (E 73–74). Eddy 1968 (E 18) suggested that 1 talent was reckoned as equivalent to one ship; various questions concerning contributions of ships are discussed by Blackman 1969 (E 10).   [19] Cf. pp. 126 n. 26.
[20] See Courby 1931 (I 54) 1–106, summarized by Bruneau and Ducat 1965 (I 32) 84–5 no. 13.

Athens infringed the autonomy of the allies, and the councils reappear only in a speech in which the Mytilenaeans say that at first Athens 'led on a basis of equality', and refer to the many votes (*polypsephia*) of the allies and to the allies' being 'equal in votes' (*isopsephoi*) to Athens (III.10.4–5, 11.4). Probably there was a single council, in which Athens had one vote along with every other member;[21] and probably by the middle of the century the council had ceased to meet.[22] Originally, we must assume, Athens and the allies sent their forces and their representatives on the council to Delos each spring, and the plan of campaign for the year was decided then. Athens, as the leader providing the commander and the largest number of ships, had a virtual veto, as she could hardly be made to undertake a campaign which she did not want; but it would be difficult for her to campaign with reluctant allies, and an ally with strong objections might refuse to serve in a campaign of which she disapproved, as Corinth had deserted Sparta *c.* 506 (Hdt. v.75).[23] In 459 the decision to fight in Egypt seems to have been taken neither in the member cities nor at the regular council but by the commanders of the forces which had gone to Cyprus (p.52). Probably it was not thought necessary at the outset to stipulate that the members were to be autonomous: the word αὐτόνομος is first attested in 441 (Soph. *Ant.* 821, already metaphorical), and it has been suggested that it was coined with reference to the kind of freedom which the members of the League found to be increasingly at risk and became anxious to retain.[24]

The Second Athenian League, founded in 378 to resist Spartan imperialism, was in many respects differently organized.[25] It was based on a purely defensive alliance. There was a council of allies in permanent session in Athens, with its own presidential apparatus, which performed a probouleutic function in parallel with the Athenian *boule*, while the Athenian Assembly had the last word (but presumably could not commit the allies against their will). Athens promised in general terms to respect the freedom and autonomy of the allies, and in particular not to do various things which she had come to do during the history of the Delian League. One of those promises was not to collect *phoros*: before long Athens did resort to collecting 'contributions' (*syntaxeis*), but the sums involved were not large, and the little evidence that we have suggests that the assessment, collection and spending of the money were not left

[21] Glotz 1938 (A 47) 115; Larsen 1940 (E 39); *ATL* III 227; Meiggs 460–2; Culham 1978 (E 16). But some have argued that in the Delian League as in the Peloponnesian League a council of allies excluding the leading state counterbalanced the leader: Walker, *CAH* v¹ 40–1; Hammond 1967 (E 33) = A 54, 311–45; de Ste Croix 1972 (G 36) 298–307.

[22] Cf. below, pp. 55–6. [23] Cf. *CAH* IV² 308, 361.

[24] Ostwald 1982 (A 95); Karavites 1982 (A 71). It was suggested in *ATL* III 228 that members' autonomy was guaranteed at the foundation of the League, but Meiggs 46 doubts if the question arose then.

[25] Cf. *CAH* vi², ch. 7. The most important text is *IG* II² 43 = Tod, *GHI* 123.

entirely to Athens. In the Second League Athens did not only have to
live down the reputation of the Delian League: the danger from Sparta
was greater to Athens than to the League's largely island members, and
in those circumstances it was Athens that needed to attract allies rather
than allies that needed a leader.

The anti-Persian alliance of 481 remained in force after the foundation
of the Delian League, at any rate until in the late 460s Athens sent help to
Sparta against the Messenians by virtue of this alliance but abandoned
the alliance when Sparta dismissed her troops (Thuc. 1.102).[26] Otherwise
we hear nothing of this alliance except in late and probably fictitious
stories of its being invoked against Themistocles (Diod. XI.55.5–7; Plut.
Them. 23.6).[27] It has been argued that the Delian League was not an
independent alliance but an enterprise within the alliance of 481;[28] the
question is one which probably would not have interested contemporaries. More drastically, it has been suggested that Thucydides' account of
the League is seriously misleading, and that what really happened is that
Athens and a few strong island states banded together to attack medizing
Greeks in the Aegean, while Sparta was to attack medizers in mainland
Greece.[29] It is right to stress the difficulties in Thucydides' account, and
the early appearance of Athenian self-interestedness in the history of the
League,[30] but we do not possess evidence of a quality and quantity that
would justify us in departing from Thucydides to that extent.[31]

II. THE EARLY HISTORY OF THE LEAGUE

The chapters in Thucydides I cited above form part of his digression on
the *Pentekontaetia*, the period of almost fifty years between the Persian
Wars and the Peloponnesian War (1.89–118.2), placed there to justify his
claim that Sparta's truest reason for going to war lay not in particular
instances of objectionable behaviour by Athens but in the power which
Athens had acquired and in Sparta's fear of that power (1.23.5–6, cf. 88,
118.2).[32] After dealing with the rebuilding of Athens' walls after the
Persian Wars and with the foundation of the Delian League, he proceeds
to give a bald catalogue of events in Athens' foreign relations down to
the Thirty Years' Peace of 446/5 (98–115.1), followed by an account of
Athens' war against Samos in 440–439 (115.2–117), which is the only
near-contemporary narrative that we have of the *Pentekontaetia*; in a
separate digression he tells stories of the downfall of Pausanias of Sparta
and Themistocles of Athens (128–38).

---

[26] Cf. p. 110.   [27] For attacks on Themistocles see pp. 65–7.
[28] Giovannini and Gottlieb 1980 (E 32).
[29] Robertson 1980 (E 69); cf. earlier Meyer 1963 (E 56).
[30] Cf. below, pp. 46–8.   [31] Cf. p. 6.   [32] Cf. pp. 371–2.

Another continuous narrative is provided by Diodorus Siculus (in his annalistic account the years 478/7–451/0 are covered in XI.38–92, and 450/49–432/1 in XII.1–37), and episodes in the history of the League are mentioned in Plutarch's lives of Cimon and Pericles. On the whole, Diodorus and Plutarch write of episodes already known to us from Thucydides, though in connexion with those episodes they often supply details conflicting with his narrative or omitted from it. From the 450s we begin to have contemporary evidence in epigraphic form, largely from Athens. It seems to have been a policy of the democracy ushered in by Ephialtes to inscribe public documents on stone, and we have a number of decrees of the Assembly and other documents concerning the Delian League; in particular, from 453 we have the annual tribute quota-lists recording the one-sixtieth taken from the tribute paid by League members as an offering to the treasury of Athena.[33] Unlike our later literary sources, the epigraphic evidence informs us for the most part of matters not dealt with by Thucydides: not only does it give us details of a kind which we could not expect to find in a narrative history, but the inscriptions contain pointers to difficulties in the League about the middle of the century which Thucydides might have mentioned but chose not to mention.

From this material we cannot write anything approaching a full history of the League. Thucydides' account is a selection of events, presented in order to illustrate the growth of Athenian power. It is highly likely that League forces fought in a number of campaigns of which we know nothing whatever, but our ignorance makes it impossible to estimate how far Athens pursued the anti-Persian objectives for which the League was founded and how far and how deliberately she sought to further her own interests. We are not told how widely the policies followed by Athens were supported by the Athenian citizens, or how much support there was for Athens and the League within actual and potential member states. We are not told how widespread were the revolts and the stern responses by Athens of which some instances are reported (though for the years whose quota-lists are well preserved we have fairly clear knowledge of which states paid tribute and which did not).

Thucydides' catalogue of events begins with the capture from the Persians of Eïon, at the mouth of the Strymon: Cimon of Athens was in command, the inhabitants (non-Greek) were enslaved, and (stated only by Plutarch, but there is no reason to doubt it) Athenian settlers were sent there (Thuc. 1.98.1, cf. Hdt. VII.107, Plut. *Cim.* 7–8.2). A scholiast on Aeschines (II.31) mentions the destruction of an Athenian force at

---

[33] Cf. p. 124, and on documents concerning the League, pp. 54–6. For an inscription of the 460s see p. 46.

Nine Ways, a short distance up the Strymon, after the capture of Eïon:
presumably the Athenians were trying to found another colony there.
The next event is the capture of the Aegean island of Scyros (again
inhabited by non-Greeks), the enslavement of its inhabitants, and the
foundation of another Athenian settlement (Thuc. 1.98.2). We are told
by later writers, but not by Thucydides, that in response to a Delphic
oracle Cimon found the skeleton of the Athenian hero Theseus on
Scyros and took it back to Athens (Plut. *Thes.* 36.1–3, *Cim.* 8.3–7; Paus.
1.17.6; cf. *Ath. Pol.* fr. 4 Kenyon). Next came a war against Carystus, at
the south-east end of Euboea, which, having been sacked by the Persians
in 490, had supported them in 480 (Hdt. VI.99.2, VIII.66.2): this ended
with the Carystians' coming to terms and joining the League (Thuc.
1.98.3, cf. Hdt. IX.105). Then Naxos, one of the largest island states,
revolted and was blockaded and reduced: Thucydides comments that
'this was the first allied state to be [metaphorically] enslaved contrary to
what had been established, but afterwards it happened to the others one
by one' (1.98.4).

Depriving the Persians of their European outpost at Eïon was clearly
a proper act for the Delian League; but the Athenian colony there, and
the attempted colony at Nine Ways (finally established as Amphipolis, in
437/6), would primarily benefit Athens. Nine Ways was at an important
crossing of routes, and the area had gold and silver deposits and suitable
timber for shipbuilding. It is doubtful if the attack on Scyros was
justified as an anti-Persian measure: one Scyrian had helped the Persian
navy to locate and mark a dangerous reef in 480 (Hdt. VIII.183.3), but
that is Herodotus' only reference to Scyros. The removal of barbarian
pirates could be represented as generally advantageous; but the gain for
Athens was clear, not only in the finding of what could be revered as
Theseus' skeleton but also in the acquisition of an island which occupied
an important position on the route from the Hellespont to Athens and
which may itself have had corn to export. Presumably the settlers were
all Athenian: in the fourth century Athens was to claim Scyros as one of
her rightful possessions (e.g. Andoc. III.12). Yet it is likely that the
members of the League both approved and joined in the campaigns
against Eïon and Scyros (though 'the Athenians' are to be understood as
the subject of the verbs in Thuc. 1.98). Carystus was a fair target for an
anti-Persian League; already in the autumn of 480 the patriotic Greeks
had extorted money from it and had ravaged its land (Hdt. VIII.112,
121.1). However, it like Scyros lay close to the route from the Hellespont
to Athens, and so Athens in particular would benefit from a compliant
Carystus. We are not told why Naxos revolted. Technically it was not
entitled to withdraw from what had been founded as a permanent
alliance; it was to have been the Persians' first foothold in the Cyclades at

the beginning of the century, and was their first conquest in the Cyclades in 490 (Hdt. v.28–34, vi.96), and it could reasonably be claimed that the League could not afford to let Naxos go. The 'enslavement' of Naxos was probably similar to the subsequent treatment of Thasos: Naxos will have been forced to remain in the League against its will, to demolish its city wall, to surrender its warships (presumably, to Athens), and to pay an indemnity and tribute; we need not suppose that Athenian interference went further than that.[34]

There is no doubt about the anti-Persian nature of the next event mentioned by Thucydides, the battle of the river Eurymedon. Probably, in previous campaigns, the League had been winning over coastal cities as far as Pamphylia (on the south side of Asia Minor); when the Persians began assembling a large fleet, Cimon went with Athenian and allied ships (specially designed to carry a larger number of hoplites than usual), forced Phaselis to join the League, and continued east to the Eurymedon, where he destroyed the Persians' fleet in the mouth of the river and then landed and sacked their camp; he then proceeded further east to defeat Persian reinforcements coming from Cyprus. This was a major campaign, with two hundred Persian ships destroyed according to Thucydides, and more according to later writers (Thuc. 1.100.1; details added by Diod. xi.60.3–62, with battles first off Cyprus and then at the Eurymedon on the same day, and by Plut. *Cim.* 12–13). If the League had been recruiting members as far away as Pamphylia, and was prepared to send large forces to fight against Persia at the Eurymedon, we should expect it to be well established in the Aegean.

We should also expect a sequel to the victory at the Eurymedon. Cyprus is not far beyond the river. Greeks had settled there, dominating but not displacing the other inhabitants, at the end of the Mycenaean period; in the Archaic period Cyprus had looked south and east rather than north and west, and she had submitted to Persia *c.* 545, but by the end of the sixth century Greek culture was in favour with those who objected to Persian rule. Cyprus joined in the Ionian Revolt against Persia in the 490s, but was obliged to contribute to Xerxes' invasion of Greece in 480.[35] Pausanias had begun the campaign of 478 there, but had then turned his attention to Byzantium, and we must assume that none of the states of Cyprus joined the Delian League at its foundation. After the battle of the Eurymedon we should expect an attempt to recover Cyprus for the Greek world, and later events were to show that Athens did not forget Cyprus, but at this point the attempt seems not to have been made.

[34] *Contra* Ostwald 1982 (A 95) 38–9, supposing that Naxos 'lost control over her internal administration'. Blackman 1969 (E 10) 199–200 leaves open the possibility that Naxos was allowed to retain her ships.

[35] Cf. *CAH* ii[3].2, ch. 22*b*, iii[2].1, ch. 12, iii[2].3, ch. 36*c*, iv[2] 48 (Hdt. vii.90), 483–4; and, on Cyprus both before and during the fifth century, Meiggs 477–86.

Given that the date of the battle is uncertain and that Thucydides' narrative is highly selective, we can not be sure why the victory was not immediately followed up.

For Thucydides' next episode we return to the Aegean, and to Athens' pursuit of her own advantage. The island of Thasos revolted, on account of a dispute over trading posts and mines on the Thracian mainland, which were controlled by Thasos but coveted by Athens. The Athenians won a sea battle and landed on the island, and the large number of ten thousand Athenian and allied settlers were sent to Nine Ways (but were annihilated by the Thracians in a battle at Drabescus, to the north east). The Thasians appealed to Sparta, and Thucydides believes that the Spartans secretly promised to distract Athens by invading Attica, but Sparta herself was distracted by the great earthquake and the Helot Revolt which followed it, and no invasion of Attica took place.[36] Sparta and Athens had not yet quarrelled, and Sparta was shortly to ask for Athenian help against the helots; Thasos may have appealed to Sparta, but it is unlikely that Sparta intended to respond. Thasos was besieged, and in the third year came to terms with Athens: she was to demolish her city wall, surrender her warships and mainland possessions, presumably to Athens, and pay an indemnity and tribute (Thuc. 1.100.2–101). The colony at Nine Ways was not purely Athenian, and Athens presumably claimed that Thasos was monopolizing resources in barbarian territory from which all the League should benefit, but other members too had a *peraia* which might be threatened by such a doctrine, and this episode looks more like an extension of Athens' power than a furthering of the Leagues's objectives.

'In the third year' (1.101.3) is Thucydides' first indication of time since the beginning of his account of the *Pentekontaetia*. Diodorus groups all the events from Eïon to the Eurymedon under 470/69, and mentions Thasos under 464/3 (XI.60–2, 70.1, 5). The scholiast on Aeschines dates to the archonship in Athens of Phaidon (476/5) the Athenian defeat which followed the capture of Eïon. Plutarch (*Thes.* 36.1) dates to the same year the oracle in response to which Cimon brought back the bones of Theseus from Scyros; in *Cim.* 8, §§3–7 Plutarch deals with the capture of Scyros, and in §§7–9 reports that the archon Apsephion (469/8) invited

---

[36] There seem to have been links of *xenia* between Sparta and Thasos. A man called Pausanias son of Alexarchus was a *theoros* in Thasos in the 440s (Salviat 1979 (F 62) iv. 25 in the text between pages 116 and 117), and should have been born about the time of Pausanias' Aegean command of 478. A man called Liches son of Arcesileos was an archon in Thasos in 398/7 (Pouilloux 1954 (F 58) 266–70 no. 29.17; date, Pouilloux and Salviat 1984 (F 59) 257–8, and 1983 (C 79) 386): he is more probably a Thasian whose family has taken over two Spartan names (Pouilloux 1954, *loc. cit.*; Cartledge 1984 (F 15)) than the well-known Spartan Lichas, *geron* in 420 (Thuc. v.50.4 with Xen. *Hell.* III.2.21), still alive in 398/7 (*pace* Thuc. VIII.84.5) and appointed archon in Thasos (Pouilloux and Salviat 1983 (C 79)).

Cimon and his fellow generals to supplant the regular judges of the tragedies performed at the Dionysia. For the coercion of Carystus there is no chronological evidence. For the revolt of Naxos there is none unless we take seriously a story in Thucydides' digression on Themistocles: in his flight across the Aegean he passed Naxos while the Athenians were blockading it (1.137.2). If this is true, and if the Persian king whom Themistocles met was Artaxerxes (1.137.3), who succeeded Xerxes in 465, the revolt of Naxos can hardly be earlier than *c*. 466; but it is by no means certain that Thucydides' story should be accepted.[37] There is no direct evidence to date the battle of the Eurymedon.

The war against Thasos occupied three years (Thuc. 1.101.3), probably three archontic years. Thucydides (IV.102.3) dates the colony whose settlers were destroyed at Drabescus thirty-two years after the failure of Aristagoras in Thrace (Hdt. V.124–6), and the successful foundations of Amphipolis in the twenty-ninth year after the unsuccessful colony; the Aeschines scholiast dates the unsuccessful colony to the archonship of Lysicrates (453/2) and the successful to 437/6 (the latter confirmed by a date-table entry in Diod. XII.32.3). The scholiast can be reconciled with Thucydides if we suppose that our text gives the wrong name beginning Lysi—: the archon of 465/4, twenty-nine years by inclusive counting from 437/6, was Lysitheus (and 496/5, the date obtained if we count inclusively again, is an acceptable date for Aristagoras' failure[38]). The war against Thasos may therefore be dated 465/4–463/2, and this is compatible with what is known of Cimon's subsequent career.

It used to be normal to assign Eïon and Scyros to 476 and 475, and Carystus and Naxos to the later 470s. Plutarch did not necessarily have evidence for, or even believe in, a connexion between the capture of Scyros and Cimon's judging the tragedies, and it has been suggested that judging the tragedies may have been a reward for victory at the Eurymedon in 469.[39] More recently, however, later dates have been canvassed for some or all of these episodes. According to Diod. XI.53.1 the archon of 469/8 was not Apsephion but Phaidon or Phaion, and Diodorus might have placed the sequence of events beginning with Eïon in 470/69 because the capture of Eïon belonged to that year; Plutarch might have had evidence connecting the judging of the tragedies with the capture of Scyros and the recovery of Theseus' skeleton; Thucydides might be correct in stating that Themistocles passed Naxos while the

---

[37] Cf. p. 66.

[38] The most striking feature of Badian 1988 (B 1) is the argument that the scholiast's date is correct and the disaster at Drabescus occurred in 453/2, long after the foundation of the colony.

[39] See the tables of dates in Gomme, *HCT* I 394–6, *ATL* III 175–9. The suggestion about Cimon's judging of the tragedies was first made by Jacoby 1947 (C 56) 3 n. 1 = C 58, 147 n. 17.

Athenians were blockading it.[40] Nevertheless, the old orthodoxy is still to be preferred. Chronological arguments which rely on Diodorus' narrative dates are fragile; and it is hard to believe that Athens would have waited many years to take Eïon from the Persians, to occupy Scyros and to assert herself against Carystus, or that within months of facing the revolt of Naxos she should have felt safe enough in the Aegean to take large forces to the Eurymedon.

Three episodes not included in Thucydides' summary have to be fitted in. He tells us later that Pausanias, after his recall to Sparta in 478, returned to Byzantium, was dislodged by the Athenians and moved to Colonae, and from there was again recalled to Sparta (1.128.3, 131). Some have placed this before the capture of Eïon, since a fragment of Ephorus or a writer using him (*FGrH* 70 F 191.6) and Diodorus (XI.60.2) take Cimon and the fleet to Eïon from Byzantium,[41] but this may be simply because in Diodorus at least (XI.44.7) Byzantium is where the fleet was last mentioned, under the command of Pausanias in 478. A passage in Justin, defective at least in that it makes Pausanias the founder of Byzantium, states that he controlled it for seven years (IX.1.3): we may wonder why Athens should have tolerated his presence there for so long, but since his downfall is more easily placed in the 460s we should accept the statement and date his expulsion *c.* 470.[42]

Plutarch (*Cim.* 14.1) mentions a campaign of Cimon against Persians and Thracians in the Chersonese, between the Eurymedon and the Thasian war, and this is confirmed by a casualty list which records deaths both in the Hellespont and on Thasos, presumably in the same campaigning year (*Agora* XVII 1). The Chersonese campaign must therefore be dated immediately before the war against Thasos, and the fact that opposition to the League occurred there so late makes a long occupation of Byzantium by Pausanias less implausible. In *Cim.* 13.4 Plutarch mentions that on separate occasions Pericles and Ephialtes sailed beyond the Chelidonian Islands (south of Phaselis) and met no resistance. Pericles' voyage may be that of 440 (Thuc. 1.116.3), but that of Ephialtes at any rate must be placed between the battle of the Eurymedon and his murder at the end of the 460s.

As stated above, it is highly likely that during these years the League engaged in activity against the Persians of which we know nothing at all.

[40] All these events from Eïon onwards are down-dated by Smart 1967 (E 84); some but not all are down-dated by Meiggs 80–3, Lévy 1976 (D 48) 277–9, Milton 1979 (B 9). For a variant on the low chronology, see Unz 1986 (B 16) 69–73. I am not persuaded by Badian 1987 (E 3) 2–8 that in Thuc. I. 100.1 μετὰ ταῦτα καί means that the siege of Naxos and the battle of the Eurymedon were contemporaneous.   [41] E.g. Gomme, *HCT* I 399–400; *ATL* III 158–60.

[42] White 1964 (F 71) argued for a late date from the likely age of Pausanias and the number of his sons; see also Rhodes 1970 (C 82) 396–7; Badian 1988 (B 1) 300–4; Chronological Notes below, p. 499. For the end of Pausanias' career see pp. 100–1.

We do know that there was fighting against Persia on various occasions until *c.* 450 (below), and that by then Persia had been driven so far from the Aegean that a peace treaty either was imposed on her or later could be believed to have been imposed on her.[43] Those who joined the League as an anti-Persian organization could not complain that Athens was failing to pursue the League's objectives. But, appropriately for his own purpose, the episodes chosen for inclusion in Thucydides' catalogue can all be seen as illustrating the growth of Athenian power. Eïon became an Athenian colony, and gave Athens access to the area where Amphipolis was eventually to be founded; Scyros became an Athenian colony. Carystus was forced to join the League against its will; Naxos was forced to remain in the League against its will. The Eurymedon was a famous victory for the League, but more specifically for Athens. Athens fought against and subdued Thasos to take from it territory which Athens coveted.

This is not to say that Thucydides is wrong to represent Athens' foundation of the Delian League as an innocent matter, the acceptance of an invitation from the eastern Greeks to be their leader in a continuing war against Persia: we need not suppose that Athens had ulterior motives in accepting the invitation, or enforced her will on reluctant allies from the beginning.[44] But from the earliest years, as the League's policy developed, Athens found herself presented with opportunities to further her own interests, and, not necessarily of set purpose, she took those opportunities: the response to one situation tended to set the pattern for responses to later situations.

According to Thucydides, it was largely by the defections of the allies that Athens was compelled to become more despotic: as leader she insisted on the allies' obligations, the allies hated her for it, and so she came to fear the consequences of not retaining a tight control (1.75–7, 97.1, 11.63.1–2). After the revolt of Naxos he inserts a chapter on the tightening of Athenian control within the League (1.99): revolt often grew out of default in the provision of tribute, ships and men, since the allies did not take kindly to Athens' punctilious exaction of what was due from them (cf. VI.76.3, also Hdt. VI.11–12, on the Ionians in the 490s); Athens increasingly became a superior rather than a leader of equals, and the allies encouraged this development by deciding that it would be less burdensome to pay tribute than to take part in campaigns; thus the Athenian fleet grew at the allies' expense, and the allies were not trained

---

[43] Cf. pp. 121–7.

[44] Cf. above, pp. 36 with n. 8, 40 with n. 29. Pride in Athenian achievements, not only against the Persians but also against Greeks, is attested by the names which some men of this generation gave to their sons: Eurymedon (Thuc. III.80.2, etc.; notice also the vase inscribed Εὐρυμέδον εἰμι κυβάδε ἕστεκα, published by Schauenberg 1975 (1 146)), but also Carystonicus and Naxiades (M–L 48.27, 79).

or equipped to resist when Athens used force against them. Certainly it will have been less arduous for a small state to pay tribute than to provide and man even one ship for a long campaign regularly each summer;[45] and since from the beginning all executive power lay with Athens we may accept Thucydides' implication that ships built and manned as a charge on the tribute became Athenian ships. An ally which did not provide its own ships and men could not withdraw from a campaign of which it disapproved; even if it retained one or two warships it would have little practice in fighting, on sea or on land, and so would easily be dealt with when dissatisfaction reached the point of withholding tribute.

Diodorus places his comment on the changing nature of the League after the coercion of Thasos and Aegina (XI.70.3–4): the Athenians no longer treated the allies reasonably, but ruled forcibly and arrogantly; most of the allies, unable to bear this, began to discuss revolt amongst themselves, and some despised the League Council and 'took to organizing themselves individually' (κατ' ἰδίαν ἐτάττοντο, by which he may mean that they withdrew from the League). In Thuc. III. 10–11 the Mytilenaeans complain that the structure of the Council enabled Athens to get her own way, and she picked off the allies one by one, beginning [which is not true] with the weakest. Since Athens with the allies remaining loyal to her controlled the sea, and most members were island states or coastal states with easier communications by sea than by land, concerted revolt by a number of allies would have been hard to organize, and there is no evidence that it occurred.

In its early years, then, the Delian League was both a body fighting against Persia on behalf of the Greeks and a body through which Athens found opportunities to extend her own power: the Thasian war is the most blatant instance mentioned by Thucydides of Athens' not merely furthering her own interests but doing so at the expense of one of her allies.

According to Thucydides the Spartans were happy at the formation of the new League under Athenian leadership, since they distrusted the influence of the wider world on Spartan commanders, and regarded the Athenians as competent to take the lead and friendly to themselves. Later texts disagree. The *Athenaion Politeia*, if its text is neither emended nor given an unnatural sense to obtain agreement with Thucydides, states that Athens' taking the lead at sea was contrary to Sparta's will (23.2). Diodorus (XI.50) has a debate in which the Spartans consider going to war to recover the lead, and it seems likely that they will decide for war, but unexpectedly a member of the *gerousia* called Hetoemaridas obtains

[45] Cf. above, p. 38 with n. 18. The point was made earlier, in more general terms, by Finley 1978 (E 25) 110–14.

majority support for his arguments on the other side. Certainly no such war took place. It might be surprising if details of a debate which did not issue in action leaked out of secretive Sparta, and another contributor to this volume regards the story as an invention.[46] The *Athenaion Politeia* is not bound to have agreed with Thucydides, and there may well have been some Spartans who had supported Pausanias and who wanted Sparta to remain involved in Aegean affairs; but after the Persian Wars Sparta had trouble not only with her own commanders abroad but with her neighbours in the Peloponnese,[47] and, as long as Athens' expansion took place in the Aegean and under the command of the pro-Spartan Cimon, many may have thought that there was no cause for alarm. Spartan cooperation with Athens led to the condemnation of Themistocles (Thuc. 1.135.2–3);[48] whatever Thasos may have hoped, Sparta did not interfere with her reduction by Athens; and in 462/1 Cimon took Athenian hoplites to help Sparta against the Messenians (below). Thucydides' judgement clearly reflects the prevailing, if not the universal, opinion in Sparta.

III. THE AMBITIONS OF THE ATHENIAN DEMOCRATS

Friendship between Sparta and Athens came to an end as a result of the Messenian War which followed the great earthquake of 464: Sparta asked for help from her allies including Athens; Cimon wanted to send help but Ephialtes did not (Plut. *Cim.* 16.9–10); Cimon had his way and went to the Peloponnese, with four thousand hoplites (Ar. *Lys.* 1138–44); but the Spartans, afraid of the daring and radicalism of the Athenians, suspected that they would be persuaded by the rebels to take radical action, and so claimed that they had no further need of the Athenians and sent them home. Athens then abandoned the alliance of 481 with Sparta, and instead made alliances with Argos and Thessaly, enemies of Sparta (Thuc. 1.101.2–102). It is argued in another chapter that what aroused the Spartans' fear was the political success of the anti-Spartan Ephialtes in Athens in Cimon's absence: the Athenian soldiers, had they stayed, might have received new orders to support the rebels against Sparta.[49] The era of peaceful coexistence between Athens and Sparta was at an end, and Athens was now prepared to challenge Sparta's dominant position on the Greek mainland. In Greece Athens' new alliances, and the desire to conquer Aegina at last, drew her into the First Peloponnesian War; but at the same time she continued the fighting against Persia for which the Delian League had been founded, now prosecuting the war outside the Aegean, and she also began to look to

[46] Cf. p. 100.   [47] Cf. pp. 101ff.   [48] Cf. p. 65.   [49] Cf. p. 69.

the Greeks in Italy and Sicily, where previously she had not had any direct involvement.

Athens' expansion on the mainland, and her conquest of Aegina, are discussed elsewhere in this volume.[50] Aegina was treated in the same way as Naxos and Thasos: she had to demolish her walls and surrender her warships, and was incorporated in the League as a tribute-paying member (Thuc. 1.108.4); in 432 she was to complain that Athens was denying her the autonomy promised either in the treaty of incorporation or in the Thirty Years' Peace of 446/5, but Thucydides gives no details (1.67.2 etc.).[51] From the first of the quota-lists she is found paying tribute at the high rate of 30 talents a year. The members of the League were full allies of Athens, and she used League forces not only against Aegina (1.105.2) but also on the mainland (1.107.5; cf. the reference to Ionians in M–L 36, Paus. v.10.4). It has normally been assumed that her mainland acquisitions were not enrolled in the League but were made directly subject to Athens; but the possibility has been suggested that Boeotian Orchomenus is to be restored in the quota-list of 452.[52]

War against the Persians continued. A fleet of two hundred Athenian and allied ships was sent to Cyprus (mentioned in parenthesis, Thuc. 1.104.2). In spite of the victory at the Eurymedon, Cyprus had still not been added to the Delian League. Ephialtes had sailed beyond the Chelidonian Islands at some time in the 460s, but we cannot infer another expedition of Cimon to Cyprus in 462 from Plut. *Cim.* 15.2.[53] However, again Cyprus had to be left for future attention.

This force in Cyprus received an appeal for help from the Libyan king Inaros, who had incited Egypt to revolt against Persia, and it was decided to help. Egypt was not half-Greek, as Cyprus was, but Greeks had fought for Egyptian kings and had settled in Egypt in the seventh and sixth centuries, and many Greeks still lived there in the fifth century;[54] campaigning for the Egyptians could thus be represented as a continuation of the war against Persia for which the League had been founded, and as an act of Greek solidarity. The fact that Egypt had abundant crops of corn may also have appealed both to Athens and to some other members. So the League's forces moved on from Cyprus to Egypt, where they gained control of the Nile delta and the greater part of the city of Memphis, and laid siege to the remaining part (Thuc. 1.104).

The Persians, like the Thasians earlier, tried to induce the Spartans to

---

[50] Cf. pp. 111–16.   [51] Cf. p. 376.
[52] *IG* I³ 260. ix.9, with Lewis 1981 (E 41) 77 n. 43, and *ad loc.* See also p. 116 n. 72.
[53] As was argued by Barns 1953–4 (E 5). See p. 69.
[54] Cf. *CAH* III².3, ch. 36b. Athens' Egyptian campaign of the 450s is treated briefly in an Egyptian context in *CAH* IV² 276.

distract Athens by invading Attica, but again Sparta did not act.[55] In due course the Persians sent a large army under Megabyxus to Egypt. The Egyptians and the Greeks were driven out of Memphis, and eventually were surrounded in Prosopitis, an island in the south of the delta bounded by two branches of the river and a canal. There they were besieged for eighteen months, until the Persians drained the canal and crossed to the island. 'Thus the Greeks' cause was ruined, after six years of war: a few of the many who had gone escaped through Libya to Cyrene, but the majority perished.' Fifty further ships from Athens and the League arrived in time to join in the disaster (1.109–10).

Thucydides continues not to give precise indications of chronology; he does not use temporal expressions when moving from one field of activity to another, and it is reasonable to suppose that he has not presented each separate incident in chronological order but that the Egyptian episode has been organized in two blocks of narrative for tidiness' sake and these events may have overlapped with those reported from Greece.[56] The Thirty Years' Peace was made in 446/5, and the five-year truce between Athens and the Peloponnesians in 451; three years without attested activity separated the truce from the last events which Thucydides mentions of the fighting in Greece (1.112.1).[57] The treasury of the League had been moved from Delos to Athens by the spring of 453 (below); two inscriptions confirm that the Samians took part in the Egyptian campaign,[58] and they are said to have proposed the moving of the treasury (Plut. *Arist.* 25.3): it is reasonable to suppose that the treasury was moved in fear of Persian reprisals,[59] and to date the end of the Egyptian campaign to 454. We cannot be sure in what kind of year the six years are reckoned, but probably the campaign began in 459 (see also pp. 500–1).

An Athenian casualty list (M–L 33) lists men who died in 'the war' in Cyprus, Egypt, Phoenicia, Halieis, Aegina and Megara 'in the same

[55] Some connect with the Persian envoy Megabazus one Arthmius of Zelea, who was believed in the fourth century to be an Athenian *proxenos* whom the Athenians outlawed for bringing Persian gold to the Peloponnese (Dem. IX.41–3, XIX.271; Aeschin. III.258; Dinarch. II.24–5; cf. Craterus *FGrH* 342 F 14 (decree of Cimon), Plut. *Them.* 6.4, Aristid. II.392 Dindorf (decree of Themistocles)). Arthmius' mission is placed here by Busolt 1893–1904 (A 12) II². 653 n.3, III.i. 328 n. 1; earlier by Meiggs 508–12; it is rejected as a fourth-century fiction by Habicht 1961 (C 40) 23–5.

[56] Cf. the discussion of his dating of the Third Messenian War, p. 500.   [57] Cf. p. 120.

[58] M–L 34 has long been known. Dunst 1972 (C 129) 153–5 no. xxiv publishes an inscription recording Inaros' award of a prize to Leocritus of Samos, 'in command of the allies' sailors'.

[59] Plut. *Per.* 12.1 says that Pericles was accused of taking over the monies of the Greeks from Delos (an accusation which may be authentic despite the weaknesses of these chapters of the *Pericles* discussed by Andrewes 1978 (D 3) 1–5), and it is almost universally accepted that the treasury was moved immediately before the publication of the first quota-list in Athens, in 453. However, arguments have been advanced for a transfer in Aristides' lifetime by Pritchett 1969 (E 63) (cf. Plut. *Arist.* 25.3), and for a transfer in the late 460s by Robertson 1980 (E 69) 112–19 (cf. Just. III.6.1–4).

year', probably a year which includes all of the summer of 459: the campaign against Persia in the Levant and the campaign in Greece are being regarded as part of one and the same war. The last three items are given in what appears from Thucydides to be chronological order.[60] Probably the first three items are in chronological order too: there was fighting in Cyprus at the beginning of the season; then the forces were transferred to Egypt, and after they had established themselves there a raid was made on Phoenicia (this is not mentioned in any of our literary sources).[61]

Diodorus, mentioning neither Cyprus nor the League, has the Egyptian campaign undertaken after Inaros sent envoys to Athens (XI.71.4–6). From Thucydides and the inscription it appears that the move from Cyprus to Egypt was made at short notice: this suggests that Inaros' approach may have been made not to Athens but to the forces in Cyprus, and that the initial decision to respond may have been taken on the spot by the commander of the fleet (Ctesias, FGrH 688 F 14.36, gives his name as Charitimides, not otherwise attested); he will no doubt have consulted the leaders of the allied contingents.

Thucydides suggests that all 250 ships sent to Egypt and their crews were involved in the final disaster, in which case this was indeed a major setback. Diodorus has 300 ships voted and 200 sent (XI.71.5, 74.3); the Egyptians and Athenians defeat a first Persian expedition of 300,000 under Achaemenes (74.1–4); then Artabazus and Megabyxus take 300,000 soldiers and 300 ships (75.1–2, 77.1: there is no sign of ships in Thuc. 1.109.3–4); and when the Egyptians surrender the Athenians burn their ships but themselves withdraw under a truce (77.3–5); reinforcements are not mentioned. In the epitome of Ctesias (FGrH 688 F 14.36–9) the Greeks' original force comprises only 40 ships; Achaemenides has 400,000 soldiers (of whom 300,000 survive their defeat) and 80 ships; Megabyxus takes 200,000 soldiers and 300 ships; 6,000 Greeks survive and are taken to Persia; again there is no mention of Greek reinforcements. Those who find it hard to believe in a disaster on the scale implied by Thucydides have been tempted by Ctesias' forty ships to believe either that on that point he is right and Thucydides is wrong or that after the initial victory most of the Greek ships were withdrawn.[62] There may well be some authentic material behind the Ctesias epitome and Diodorus, but the 6,000 survivors later in the epitome point to more than forty ships, and on this point Diodorus is closer to Thucydides. The raid on Phoenicia shows that all the ships did not stay in Egypt all the time, but

[60] Cf. p. 112.   [61] See CAH IV² 144.
[62] See, against Thucydides, Westlake 1950 (E 92), Salmon 1965 (E 77) 151–8; for Thucydides, Libourel 1971 (E 43), Meiggs 473–6.

there is no reason to think that Thucydides' account is fundamentally wrong.

While they were fighting against the Persians in the Levant and against their fellow Greeks at home, the Athenians also began to take an interest in the West. An inscription whose lettering points to a date before *c*. 445[63] records an alliance between Athens and Egesta, an Elymian (non-Greek, but hellenized) city in the north west of Sicily (*IG* I³ 11): the prescript of the decree included the name of the Athenian archon, but the only letters which can safely be deciphered are the last two, *ON*. Editors used to date this 454/3, on the inadequate grounds that Diod. XI.86.2 mentions under that year a war in Sicily in which Egesta was involved;[64] there was another archon whose name has the right ending in 458/7, and that provides a better context for this further extension of Athens' interests than the time when the Egyptian campaign ended in failure and the fighting in Greece came to a halt.[65] Why Athens should have made her first alliance with a western city at this time we do not know: possibly it was Egesta which made the approach to Athens, and once more Athens accepted an invitation.

Six years of fighting in two areas had brought mixed results. In Greece, Aegina was a gain kept until the end of the League, but Athens' other acquisitions, extensive and impressive though they seemed, were more than she had the strength to retain against concerted opposition, and most of them were to be lost in 446. In Egypt a promising start led to a disastrous conclusion, when the Persians sent into Egypt forces which were too much for Athens and the allies. The alliance with Egesta was to be followed by the establishment of other Athenian contacts with the West, and ultimately by the disastrous Sicilian Expedition of 415–413, which again if it had succeeded in the short term would not have brought gains which could be retained permanently. Athens could dominate the

[63] Although this text was dated by an archon's name, it did not become normal Athenian practice to date decrees in that way until *c*. 420. The authors of *ATL*, in working on inscriptions concerning the League, accepted what was already standard doctine, that the forms of *beta, rho, sigma* and *phi* used in Athenian inscriptions changed about the middle of the fifth century: this doctrine has been subjected to a sustained attack by H.B. Mattingly, in a long series of articles beginning with E 44, E 45, E 47, who brings down to about the 420s many texts which orthodoxy places about 450; but study of texts which are securely dated, by Meiggs 1966 (C 145), Walbank 1974 (C 170, revised in 1978 (C 171)); cf. Meritt and Wade-Gery 1962 and 1963 (C 152), shows that texts which can be dated independently support the orthodox doctrine. The argument has extended from epigraphic to linguistic phenomena, with some support for later dates claimed by Henry 1978 (C 134). I shall assume that the orthodox doctrine is correct, but shall indicate when a date depends on the doctrine.

[64] See p. 159 n. 10.

[65] *há*]*ββρον* the archon of 458/7, was read by Raubitschek 1944 (C 161) 10 n. 3; *háββ*]*ον* is restored in M–L 37; in *IG* I³ Woodhead supports *há*]*β*[*ρ*]*ον* in his commentary but leaves the text unrestored. '*Αντ*]*ιφόν*, the archon of 418/17, was read by Mattingly 1963 (E 47) 267–70; this dating has been accepted by Smart 1972 (E 83), by Wick 1975 (C 176) and 1981 (C 177), and, with new photographs, Chambers, Gallucci and Spanos, *ZPE* 83 (1990) 38–63.

Aegean even against opposition, because the sea kept separate medium-to-small states apart, and as long as she kept the naval power in her own hands a large force could not be put together against her; but in the early 450s she tried expanding into areas where it was much harder for a single city state to establish its power securely.

IV. THE MID-CENTURY CRISIS

However great the disaster in Egypt, Thucydides does not suggest that the Athenians were greatly chastened. After making a truce with the Peloponnesians in 451, they turned their attention to Cyprus once more, and sent a force of two hundred Athenian and allied ships there under the command of Cimon, returned from ostracism.[66] Sixty of these were diverted to Egypt in response to an appeal from Amyrtaeus, 'the king in the marshes', still holding out against Persia (cf. 1.110.2). On Cyprus a siege of Citium was begun, and in the course of the fighting Cimon died; the League forces won a combined land and sea battle against Phoenicians, Cyprians and Cilicians, but they then withdrew from both Cyprus and Egypt (1.112.1–4). According to Diodorus (xii.3–4) the Athenians captured Citium and Marium, and laid siege to Salamis, thus prompting the Persians to sue for the Peace of Callias. After this Cyprus does not figure in the history of Greece again until the last decade of the century, though there is archaeological evidence for continuing contact.[67] Further dealings between Egypt and Athens are attested in the gift of corn to Athens by Psammetichus in 445/4. If he was hoping to obtain further intervention against Persia, he was unsuccessful.[68] There is only one more appearance of the Delian League in Thucydides' narrative before the Samian War of 440-439: the revolt of Euboea in 446, followed by the recognition of the League as an Athenian power bloc in the Thirty Years' Peace of 446/5, treated in connexion with events on the Greek mainland (1.114–115.1).[69]

But, despite Thucydides' silence, inscriptions indicate that these were momentous years in the history of the League, that after the disaster in Egypt Athens had lost ground to recover, and went further along the road of becoming more despotic by insisting strictly on the allies' performance of their obligations.

After the removal of the League's treasury to Athens (above), the Athenians claimed one-sixtieth of the tribute as an offering to Athena: this quota of a sixtieth was calculated not on the total tribute but

[66] On Cimon's return from ostracism see p. 75.

[67] Cf. *CAH* vi² ch. 11c. Excessive confidence in reconstructing the history of fifth-century Cyprus is exposed by Maier 1985 (F 49).

[68] Cf. p. 77. For the suggestion of a bid for support against Persia see Plut. *Per.* 20.3 and Busolt 1893–1904 (A 12) iii.i.500.   [69] Cf. pp. 136–7.

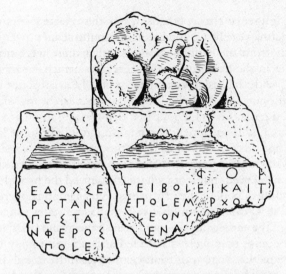

Fig. 1. Fragment of an Athenian decree (*IG* 1³ 68 = M–L 68) concerning tribute, with a relief showing tribute bags and vessels. (After B. D. Meritt, *Documents on Athenian Tribute* (1937) 4 fig. 1.)

separately on the payments of individual member states, and from 453 a series of numbered, annual lists of these quotas was inscribed on stone. We are thus able to discover how much tribute was paid by particular members in particular years; and, since there was a tendency to list together states in the same region (reinforced by the decision to organize the lists in five regional categories from 443/2, and in four from the early 430s), where the texts are well enough preserved we can infer which states did not pay any tribute at all in a particular year.[70]

We also have a number of decrees of the Athenian Assembly affecting individual members of the League or all the members, and a few documents from individual members. Athens took to publishing state documents in quantity after Ephialtes' reform of 462/1;[71] and it is noteworthy that the decrees which we have to consider are decrees of the Athenian Assembly, not of the League Council. If the Council still existed, we should expect at least such matters as the standardization of weights, measures and coinage (M–L 45) and the collection of tribute (*IG* 1³ 34) to be decided by the Council: what is said of the Council in Thuc. 1.96.2–97.1 and III.10.5, 11.4, is not explicit about its fate, but it is a

[70] The most recent edition of the quota-lists, incorporating the new fragments found in the 1970s, is *IG* 1³ 259–90. There is a detailed Register of members and their payments in *ATL* 1 215–460 (based on the texts of the lists in that 1939 volume), and there are summary tables in Meiggs 538–61 (based on the texts in *ATL* II). The relief in Fig. 1 here seems to symbolize the arrival of the tribute at Athens.   [71] Cf. p. 80.

reasonable inference that, perhaps when the treasury was moved to Athens, meetings of the Council were discontinued.[72]

It appears from the earliest quota-lists that there were considerable irregularities in the payment of tribute in the late 450s.[73] The first list, that of 453, with the late payments from small Carian states in the first column of the next list, contained about 155 entries; the rest of the list for 452, about 144; that for 451, about 143; that for 450, about 152;[74] that for 449, about 163, with an appendix containing not only some late whole-payments but also complementary payments from about twenty members whose initial payments had been incomplete. The lists are not completely preserved, but from what is preserved the probability that a member included in all of the first four survives in none of them is only 19 in 1,000; it is overwhelmingly likely that some states found later did not appear in the earliest lists, either because they were still contributing ships[75] or because they were disaffected and refused to pay when they should have paid.[76] States not found earlier than the fourth list include Andros, Ceos, Cos, Lebedos, Seriphos, Teos; altogether nineteen are attested for the first time in this list, and twenty or more which appeared in at least one of the first three lists must have failed to appear in this. States not found earlier than the fifth list include Chalcis, Cythnos, Eretria, Naxos,[77] Paros, Siphnos, Tenos; again nineteen in all are first attested this year.

There are some positive indications of trouble. An Athenian decree for Erythrae, which seems to have used the older letter-forms (*IG* i³ 14: we are dependent on a printer's facsimile of a lost copy of a lost stone), begins with offerings at the Panathenaea, and continues with regulations for a council of 120 appointed by lot; Athenian overseers (*episkopoi*) and a garrison commander are involved in setting up the council, and the garrison commander is to be involved in future years; the council swears allegiance to the people of Erythrae and of Athens and the allies; men who have fled to the 'Medes' may not be taken back, and men who have remained in Erythrae may not be exiled, without the permission of Athens; in certain circumstances men are to be exiled from the whole Athenian alliance. Presumably an anti-Athenian regime had come to

[72] Jones 1952/3 (E 38) argued against this view, and Lewis in the commentary on *IG* i³ 64.9–11 wonders if there is a sign there that the Council survived in some form.

[73] What I say about the earliest quota-lists owes a good deal to unpublished work by Lewis.

[74] Without the *c.* 18 Carian states which appear as late payers for 453 and in 450, the first and fourth lists are shorter than the second and third: 453 and 450 are the years in which Athens experienced the greatest difficulty in collecting tribute.

[75] West 1929/30 (E 91); *ATL* III 267–8; Woodhead 1974 (E 96) (but Woodhead 173–4, 177–8 thought some absences might be due to the chance of preservation).

[76] Nesselhauf 1933 (E 57) 10–13; Meiggs 109–24 (cf. Meiggs 1943 (E 51) 28–31 and 1963 (E 52) 4–9).

[77] It is highly unlikely that Naxos was contributing ships: see above, p. 43, and below, p. 60.

power with Persian support; Athens then overthrew this regime and imposed a democratic constitution on Erythrae. Here we find Athens infringing the autonomy of an ally which has rebelled by means which she was to use frequently from the middle of the century onwards, but is not known to have used before the late 450s: not merely a constitution determined by Athens, but the sending of temporary overseers and a permanent garrison, the setting of limits to the independence of the ally's law courts and the extension of some judicial sentences to the whole League, and the demand for offerings at the Athenian festival of the Panathenaea.[78]

Some editors have restored the name of the Athenian archon of 453/2 in the second line of the text, but with archontic dates rare this early the traces in the facsimile are not enough to justify the restoration. Nevertheless the tribute record suggests that a date at the end of the 450s is appropriate.[79] Erythrae is not attested in any of the first four quota-lists; its neighbour Buthia appears in the first list, with the amount lost, and in the second, with a tribute of as much as 3 talents (IG I³ 259, v.19; 260, x.5): it is a plausible assumption that in 453 and 452 Erythrae was in revolt and Buthia was paying on behalf of the dependencies which remained loyal. Neither name survives in the third and fourth lists, of 451 and 450: one or the other is probably to be restored in the third, and possibly in the fourth. In the fifth list Erythrae and its neighbours appear in a block in the main part, with the amount lost, but Erythrae can have paid little of its tribute at first, since it pays over 8½ talents among the complementary payments later (IG I³ 263, ii.13–17, v.3).

The requirement of offerings from Erythrae at the Panathenaea may not have seemed alarming, since Erythrae was Ionian in the strictest sense of that term, but before long this requirement was to be extended to all members of the League (IG I³ 34, 41–3, of 447). There is another sign of Athens' taking the place of Delos not only as the financial but also as the religious centre of the League: about the middle of the century cults of Athena and of Ion and his sons were established in allied cities, possibly on confiscated land.[80] We also see a development in the language used to refer to the allies. The decree for Erythrae calls for allegiance to Athens and the allies, in a formula which may well have

[78] The fragments in IG I³ 15 are probably not part of the same text. In an inscription from Erythrae (DGE 701 = Hill, Sources² B 116 = IEK 2) there is a property qualification for jurors (lines A 13–18): this possibly but not certainly belongs to the constitution established by Athens; the editors of IEK pp. 25–6 consider the possibility, but prefer a date before Athens' intervention.
[79] Mattingly 1963 (E 47) 271 with n. 69 originally favoured a later date, but subsequently he changed his mind (E 49, 206–7); an earlier date was preferred by Highby 1936 (E 35), especially 33–5, Accame 1952 (C 114) 119–23. Welwei 1986 (E 90) stresses that demos 'people' or plethos 'mass' in such texts as IG I³ 14 does not necessarily imply a democracy, and argues that when the Athenians interfered in the constitution of an allied state in the mid-fifth century they were not doing so on ideological grounds. [80] Barron 1964 (E 7) and 1983 (E 8).

been used since the earliest years of the League (except that before
Ephialtes' reform of 462/1 we should not expect to find the emphasis on
the *plethos*, the mass of the people), and at a later point seems to refer to
'the Athenian alliance'. Language of this kind was never wholly
abandoned (cf. *IG* i³ 101, 9–11, of 409), but before long more proprietor-
ial language was to come into use as well, with oaths of allegiance simply
to Athens (e.g. *IG* i³ 37, 43–8, and 40, 21–32, of 447–445), and references
to 'the cities which Athens rules' (restored in *IG* i³ 19, 8–9, and 27, 14–15,
of *c.* 450/49).[81]

For Miletus we have several pieces of evidence. [Xen.] *Ath. Pol.* 3.11
says that there Athens once supported the upper class, but they soon
revolted and cut down the *demos*. A Milesian decree of uncertain date,
whose beginning is lost, outlaws certain men and their descendants
(M–L 43); another decree, probably to be dated 435/4, seems to reflect a
democracy modelled on that of Athens.[82] An Athenian decree for
Miletus (*IG* i³ 21) deals with judicial matters and appoints a board of five
Athenians to work with various Milesian officials: it has the older form
of lettering; probably its prescript dated it to the archonship of Euthynus
(or perhaps Euthynous, as in *PA* 5659), and certainly that archonship is
mentioned twice in the course of the decree. Literary texts give the name
Euthydemus to the archons of 450/49, 431/0 and 426/5 (Diod. xii.3.1,
38.1, 58.1, cf. Ath. v.217A, 218B), but other texts, including a contemporary inscription, call the archon of 426/5 Euthynus/nous (*IG* i³ 369, 5):
probably Diodorus has made the same mistake for 450/49, and the decree
belongs to that year.[83]

The tribute record has been complicated by the new fragment of the
first list, first published in 1972.[84] At *IG* i³ 259, vi.19–23, we have
Milesians from Leros and Teichiussa. These were interpreted in the same
way as Buthia (above), and it was assumed that Miletus itself did not pay
in 453, so at iii.18–20 part of the new fragment was restored with a three-
line entry, Νεοπο[λῖται ἐκ]/Μιλέ[το ἐν Λευκôι]/'Ακρ[οτερίο]ι: *HHH*; but
it can plausibly be argued that it is better to see here three separate
entries, of which the second is Μιλέ[σιοι: —].[85] In the second list no
Milesians are clearly preserved, but Μιλέσιο]ι ἐ[κ —] is a possible
restoration at *IG* i³ 260, iii.2.[86] In the third list Μιλέσ[ιοι] appear, with
the quota lost (*IG* i³ 261, ii.28). In the fourth list no Milesians are

---

[81] The language used to express the relationship between the superior partner and the inferior
partners in alliances is studied by Pistorius 1985 (A 98; on these formulae, 8–77).
[82] Published by Herrmann 1970 (E 34): he dates it 437/6 on the basis of *Milet* i.iii 122.90; the later
date follows from Cavaignac 1924 (G 11) 311–14.
[83] Mattingly first championed 426/5 in E 44, 174–81; in C 144, 117 he suggests a later date for
Herrmann's decree.   [84] Meritt 1972 (C 150).   [85] Piérart 1974 (E 60).
[86] [Σερμυλ]ιέ[s], retained in *IG* i³, is unlikely to be right, since they have for some time made a
more secure appearance in the same list at ix.5.

preserved. In the fifth list Miletus is among those whose whole payment arrives late (*IG* I³ 263, v.18); she seems not to have paid in 446; she appears, paying half the tribute she paid in 449, in and after 442. The normal view is that there was a first Milesian revolt in the late 450s, after which Athens continued to tolerate an oligarchic government; and a second in the 440s, after which a democracy was imposed but the tribute was reduced. However, the Athenian decree no longer seems incompatible with a democratic constitution,[87] and it has been suggested that there was a single revolt in the 450s, followed by the establishment of democracy.[88] It now looks as if there may have been a revolt about 450, but not earlier, and the tribute record certainly does not exclude a second revolt in the 440s; we cannot tell on which occasion the Athenians imposed a democracy.

It is now clear, at any rate, that separate payment by a dependent community need not prove that the principal community was refusing to pay. In 1974 a new fragment of the second list was published, from which we learn of two communities of Phocaeans:[89] Φοκαιês παρὰ [.]ϵ[.]κο is followed immediately by Φοκαιês (*IG* I³ 260, viii.7–8; 9). In 450 there were payments from Ceos and, separately, from the city of Coresia, but in and after 449 there was a single payment from the whole of Ceos, larger than the total of the two payments in 450 (*IG* I³ 262, v.22, i.21; 263, iv.21). Nor is absence from the lists as preserved always a sign of disaffection. Sigeum is first preserved in the quota-list of 449 (*IG* I³ 263, iv.25), but there is an Athenian decree of 451/0 (*IG* I³ 17) which praises it for its loyalty, presumably because it has resisted pressure from the Persians and/or its neighbours to be disloyal.

But, although spotting defectors is a difficult exercise, except in cases where there is clear evidence of Athenian intervention, and we must continue to allow for the possibility that some members changed from ship-providing to tribute-paying about the end of the 450s, it is evident that there must have been a considerable amount of defection in these years, and that in dealing with it and trying to secure members against future trouble Athens was led to take steps impinging on what previously would have been regarded as the internal freedom of the member states.

Plutarch writes of Pericles' sending cleruchs (settlers who did not go

[87] The *prosetairoi* (religious functionaries found in a Milesian sacred law of 450/49, *SIG* 57), formerly restored in *IG* I³ 21.7, were eliminated by Bradeen and McGregor 1973 (C 121) 24–70. Details in the democratic constitution of Miletus are studied by Piérart 1983 and 1985 (E 61): it was not a carbon copy of the Athenian constitution.

[88] Gehrke 1980 (E 31). For another attempt to accommodate the evidence, see Robertson 1987 (E 70): in the 450s Miletus was divided, Athens supported the oligarchs in the city and enabled them get control of the countryside; in the 440s there was a revolt, after which Athens imposed a democracy.

[89] Camp 1974 (C 124) 314–18 no. 1.

as *apoikoi*, 'colonists', to found a totally independent state, but who retained some connexion with Athens[90]) to the Chersonese, Naxos, Andros and Thrace, and to refound Sybaris in Italy as Thurii, in order to relieve the city of the unemployed, to rectify the poverty of the people and to provide a garrison which would prevent revolt among the allies (*Per.* 11.5–6). Urban unemployment is not likely to have been a problem in fifth-century Athens, but the cleruchies did provide land for Athenian citizens at the allies' expense and serve as an informal garrison: presumably the allies which had cleruchies inflicted on them are allies which had provoked Athenian interference. Diodorus mentions cleruchies in the Chersonese, Euboea and Naxos (xi.88.3): his year is 453/2; it is his last mention of Athens in Book xi; the settlements in Euboea and Naxos are attributed to Tolmides, who was killed at Coronea in 447/6 (xii.6.2).

Again, help can be obtained from the tribute record. Carystus, in Euboea, paid 12 talents in 453 (*IG* i³ 259, ii.16: part of the new fragment), but only 7½ talents in 450 (*IG* i³ 262, i.23) and only 5 in 449 (*IG* i³ 263, iv.26) and after. Reduced tribute is likely to reflect reduced ability to pay, and so it may be inferred that the cleruchy was sent in 453/2 or 452/1, and that the further reduction of tribute in 449 was made in response to a plea that the original reduction had been insufficient.[91] Andros first appears in the quota-list of 450, with a tribute of 12 talents (*IG* i³ 262, i.19), but in 449 (*IG* i³ 263, iv.22) and subsequent years it paid only 6 talents, so we may infer that the cleruchy was sent in 450 and Andros' tribute was reduced to allow for this. Naxos is perhaps to be restored in 449, but makes its first certain appearance in 447 (*IG* 13 263, iv.35; 264, iii.25), paying 6⅔ talents, a surprisingly small sum for so large and prosperous an island. It is not likely to have remained a ship-provider after its early revolt,[92] so it may be that there was further trouble about the middle of the century, followed by the sending of the cleruchy mentioned by Plutarch and reduction of the tribute to the level attested in 447. The settlements in the Chersonese and in Thrace cannot be placed so early,[93] and the foundation of Thurii was an altogether different kind of operation,[94] but it is likely that Athens' policy of imposing cleruchies on recalcitrant allies began, in Euboea, Andros and Naxos, at the end of the 450s.[95]

It has been argued that, although the Athenians did not set out with the intention of founding an empire, from the earliest years of the Delian League they found themselves taking decisions which led to their

---

[90] On the distinction between cleruchies and colonies see Brunt 1966 (E 13) 71–82.

[91] For this sequence of events see Erxleben 1975 (E 23) 85–7.

[92] Cf. above, p. 56 with n. 77.   [93] Cf. pp. 127–9.   [94] Cf. pp. 141–3.

[95] The early cleruchies are discussed by Meiggs 121–4 (cf. Meiggs 1943 (E 51) 31–3, and 1963 (E 52) 8–9).

furthering Athens' particular interests as well as driving back the Persians from the Greek world, and to their strengthening the position of Athens within the League. The democracy of Ephialtes tried to continue the war against Persia, in Cyprus and Egypt, and at the same time to extend Athens' power in Greece itself, but the attempt to keep Egypt out of Persian hands ended in disaster, and the gains in Greece were to prove insecure. After the failure in Egypt, Athens had to cope with revolts from allies whose allegiance she must have come to take for granted: in suppressing these revolts she carried Athenian interference into areas of life where the allies' freedom had not previously been disturbed, and expressed her leadership in ways which suggest that she was beginning to think of the League not as a free alliance but as an empire which she could use as she wished. The climax of this transformation of the League was reached with the abandonment of the League's original objective, war against Persia – but that belongs to another chapter.[96]

[96] See pp. 121–7.

CHAPTER 4

THE ATHENIAN REVOLUTION

P. J. RHODES

I. ATHENS AFTER THE PERSIAN WARS

We have little enough evidence for the external history of the Greek cities between the Persian Wars and the Peloponnesian War; we have less for the internal history even of Athens. Thucydides provides information only on Themistocles: his clash with Sparta over the rebuilding of Athens' walls (1.90–2), and the story of his ostracism and his flight to the Persians (1.135–8). The *Athenaion Politeia* tells us of a period of good government in which the Areopagus was predominant (23.1–2); and of the leadership of Themistocles and Aristides, the foundation of the Delian League and the resulting provision of *trophe* (maintenance) for the Athenians (23.2–24); then follow Ephialtes' attack on the Areopagus and (probably an addition to the original text) an anecdote associating Themistocles with him in that attack (25). The aristocrats had no leader except Cimon, and the constitution became 'slacker' (26.1); in the 450s the archonship was opened to the *zeugitai* (the third of the four property classes), the *dikastai kata demous* (deme judges) were revived, and the law of Pericles was enacted, which limited citizenship to those whose parents were both Athenians (26.2–4); Pericles attacked the Areopagus and fostered Athens' naval power; to rival Cimon's generosity with his own wealth he used the state's wealth to introduce payment for jury service (27). There are short lives by Nepos of Themistocles, Aristides and Cimon, and longer lives by Plutarch of these three and of Pericles. Plutarch's *Themistocles*, after telling stories of him in Athens after the Persian Wars (20–22.3), writes at length of his downfall and his flight to Asia (22.4–31.3); *Aristides* proposes an extension of democracy and pronounces on a suggestion of Themistocles (22), organizes the Delian League (23–25.3), ends his life in virtuous poverty and does not join in the attack on Themistocles (25.3–27); *Cimon* puts his wealth to political use and takes a conservative line in politics (10), commands in the campaigns of the Delian League until he is prosecuted after the Thasian

The basic text was drafted in 1979–80; I have tried to add references to some of the substantial later bibliography. Most of the topics are treated at greater length in Rhodes 1981 (C 83).

war (6–9, 11–14), clashes with Ephialtes over support for Sparta and the powers of the Areopagus, and is ostracized (15–17.3), tries to return at the battle of Tanagra and dies on a final campaign in Cyprus (17.4–19); *Pericles* takes a democratic line, using jury pay to counter Cimon's generosity and joining in the attack on the Areopagus (7, 9), and the story of Cimon at Tanagra is followed by a digression on Pericles' prosecution of Cimon and a denial that Pericles could be the murderer of Ephialtes (10.6–8).

Themistocles, the creator of Athens' new fleet and the man responsible for the decision to fight at Salamis,[1] is not found with the fleet again after 480: Xanthippus commanded in 479, Aristides in 478, and Cimon thereafter. In various matters Themistocles and Cimon may be seen as opponents. Themistocles was responsible for the rebuilding of Athens' walls after the Persian Wars, in the face of Spartan objections, and there are other stories of his coming into conflict with Sparta, though in 480/79 he was better received there than any other foreigner (Hdt. VIII.124–5); but Cimon gave the name Lacedaemonius to a son born in the 470s,[2] and was eager to help Sparta in the Third Messenian War. The two men differed in their interpretation of Athens' recent history. The expulsion of the tyrant Hippias in 510 had been due to the Alcmaeonid family and Sparta: the pro-Spartan Cimon had married an Alcmaeonid wife about 480, and was presumably happy to acknowledge this debt; but his relative Thucydides complains that the Athenians gave the credit for ending the tyranny to Harmodius and Aristogeiton, who had murdered Hipparchus in 514 (1.20.2, VI.54–9), and the epigram on the base of the new statues of these men set up in 477/6 to replace those taken by the Persians was by Themistocles' friend Simonides.[3] There was dispute also as to whether Athens owed her salvation from the Persians primarily to the victory at Marathon, won by the army and Cimon's father Miltiades, or to that at Salamis, won by the fleet and Themistocles.[4] Themistocles was clever, and had successfully interpreted a Delphic oracle when he insisted on fighting at Salamis: Plutarch tells stories in which Cimon outdid Themistocles in cleverness (*Cim.* 5.1, 9), and Cimon interpreted a Delphic oracle commanding the Athenians to bring back the bones of Theseus, and brought a skeleton from Scyros.[5] Themistocles was responsible for rebuilding the city walls after the war, but the spoils won by Cimon at the Eurymedon paid for the building of

[1] Cf. *CAH* IV[2] 524–5, 571–6.   [2] Date: Davies 1971 (L 27) 305.

[3] On the ending of the tyranny, see *CAH* IV[2] 299–302; on defenders of the claims of the Alcmaeonids and of Harmodius and Aristogeiton see Podlecki 1966 (D 69).

[4] Pl. *Leg.* IV, 707b4–c7; Fornara 1966 (D 28) 51–3; and cf. below, p. 67, on Aeschylus' *Persae* (but a further block of M–L 26, with additional verses, renders pre-1988 descriptions of that inscription out of date).   [5] See Podlecki 1971 (D 70).

the south wall of the Acropolis (Plut. *Cim.* 13.5); and each man is credited with other public works too.[6]

Xanthippus is not heard of again after 479: since his son Pericles was *choregos* to Aeschylus in 472 he was presumably dead by then. Aristides survived, but is hard to place. In the main tradition he is consistently the rival of Themistocles, aristocratic and upright where Themistocles was democratic and cunning, and Plutarch's *Cimon* makes him an associate of Cimon (5.6, 10.8); but there are traces of an alternative version which placed Aristides on the same side as Themistocles after the war: in the story of the walls and in other stories of Themistocles, Aristides appears as his confidant, in *Ath. Pol.* 23.2–24 Aristides is the partner of Themistocles and founder of the league which provided *trophe* for the Athenian *demos*, and in Plutarch's *Aristides* (25.10), although Themistocles had been responsible for his ostracism, Aristides did not join in the final attack on him; the summary of the narrative in *Ath. Pol.* (41.2) makes Aristides the predecessor of Ephialtes in advancing the democracy, and Plutarch's *Aristides* (22.1) makes him the author after the war of a decree that the constitution should be 'common' and the *archontes* chosen from all Athenians. Before the war against Xerxes, Aristides was a rival of Themistocles;[7] after his organization of the Delian League there is no evidence of his further involvement in public affairs, and the texts linking him with Themistocles rather than Cimon are the more circumstantial and credible.

Apart from Plutarch's attribution of a democratic reform to Aristides, not mentioned elsewhere and clearly fictitious, there is no evidence that how the Athenian state ought to be governed was a live issue in the 470s. *Ath. Pol.* 23. 1–2 tells of a period of Areopagite ascendancy, saying that it was based not on any resolution but on prestige. This, too, is to be connected with the rivalry arising out of the Persian Wars: Plutarch (*Them.* 10. 6–7) cites both *Ath. Pol.*'s story that, when Athens was evacuated before Salamis and the generals were at a loss, the Areopagus provided money for the citizens, and the alternative account of Clidemus (*FGrH* 323 F 21), that Themistocles provided the money by searching men's luggage. Probably *Ath. Pol.*'s is the original version of the story, an attempt by Themistocles' opponents to give the Areopagus some of

---

[6] For instance, in the case of Cimon, the Theseum built to house Theseus' bones (on which see Barron 1972 (I 9)), the Stoa Poikile (Thompson and Wycherley 1972 (I 166) 90–4; cf. Plut. *Cim.* 4.6–7) and the Telesterion and other work immediately after the Persian Wars at Eleusis (e.g. Mylonas 1962 (κ 66) 107–13) are ascribed to him, though without positive evidence (Shear, 1982 (I 151) dates the 'Cimonian' Telesterion in the 480s). Themistocles was responsible for the temple of Artemis Aristoboule (Travlos 1971 (I 171) 121–3; cf. Plut. *Them.* 22.2–3, *De mal. Hdt.* 869 D), the Telesterion at Phyla (Plut. *Them.* 1.4), and possibly some work on the Odeon (Vitr. *De Arch.* v.9.1, with Davison 1958 (κ 21) 33–42 and 1962 (κ 22) (= Davison 1968 (J 20) 48–66, 66–9), but Themistocles is not mentioned by Travlos 1971 (I 171) 387).   [7] Cf. *CAH* IV² 343–4.

the credit for Salamis, and Clidemus' is a reply restoring the credit to Themistocles.[8] In the 470s most of the Areopagites will have been men who were appointed archons after the fall of the tyranny, by direct election from the two highest property classes,[9] and the Council of the Areopagus will thus have been a fairly distinguished collection of Athenians. It retained judicial powers of political importance, and it may – we have no evidence – on occasions have debated matters of public concern and given advice to the magistrates or to the Council of Five Hundred and the Assembly. However, there is no reason why the Areopagus should have been more powerful in the 470s than it had been in the 480s, and probably the tradition of a period of Areopagite ascendancy was built up later with the help of the Salamis story, when it was known that Ephialtes had put an end to the political power of the Areopagus, to explain why such a reform should have been necessary.

Themistocles and Cimon were rivals as individuals, and stood for different views of Athens' recent history and different views of the foreign policy which Athens ought to pursue. This rivalry culminated in the ostracism of Themistocles, and his subsequent condemnation on a charge of medism (treacherous support for the Persians). The story of his flight is told by Thucydides (1.135–8), and was repeated, with variations and elaborations, by many later writers. According to Thucydides, Themistocles when ostracized went to live in Argos, and visited other places in the Peloponnese; after the death of Pausanias the Spartans sent messengers to Athens alleging that the two men were together guilty of medism, and Themistocles on learning of this fled from Argos (Thucydides does not mention that he was prosecuted *in absentia*: according to Craterus, *FGrH* 342 F 11, the prosecutor was an Alcmaeonid). He went first to the west, to Corcyra and then to Epirus; Admetus of the Molossi refused either to surrender him to his pursuers or to let him stay, and sent him across northern Greece to Pydna. From Pydna he took a ship to Asia Minor, travelling incognito; but a storm carried the ship towards Naxos while the Athenians were besieging the city, and Themistocles had to reveal his identity to the captain and urge him not to betray him; the captain did not put in to land but kept the ship riding at anchor, and in due course brought Themistocles safely to Ephesus. Themistocles wrote to Artaxerxes, who had recently succeeded Xerxes, and set about learning Persian; after a year he went to meet the Great King, and the man who had contributed so much to the defeat of the Persian invasion of 480 ended his life as an honoured

---

[8] It appears that these two versions of the story underlie successive examples in Arist. *Pol.* v, 1304a17–24; *Ath. Pol.* solves the problem by making the Areopagite ascendancy a short-term and the development of the Delian League to Athens' advantage a long-term consequence of Salamis (with the democratic version of the story suppressed).   [9] Cf. *CAH* iv² 320.

pensioner of the Persians. Ironically, there is no firm evidence and little likelihood that he was guilty of medism at any time before his arrival in Asia Minor.

The chronology of Themistocles' flight has been endlessly discussed.[10] He is last attested in Athens as *choregos* in the spring of 476 (Plut. *Them.* 5.5), and his appearance at Olympia (Plut. *Them.* 5.4, 17.4, cf. Ael. *VH* XIII.43, Paus. VIII.50.3) should belong to the summer of that year. The most reliable detail in the story of his flight is that he met the new Persian king, Artaxerxes, who came to the throne in 465;[11] Ephorus and other later writers made Themistocles approach Xerxes, the king whom he had defeated in 480, but Thucydides' less exciting version was rightly preferred by both Nepos (*Them.* 9.1) and Plutarch (*Them.* 27.1–2). The death of Pausanias, which preceded the accusation of medism and Themistocles' flight from Argos, is more easily placed after than before 470,[12] and so supports this conclusion. The text of Thucydides takes Themistocles from Pydna past Naxos to Ephesus; but Plutarch (*Them.* 25.2–26.1), while claiming to follow Thucydides, takes him past Thasos,[13] while the Athenians were besieging that city, to Cyme (which arouses suspicion as the home of Ephorus, to which that writer gave as much publicity as he could: cf. *FGrH* 70 F 236). Thucydides gives us no dates in his sketch of the growth of the Delian League: the siege of Thasos can be dated 465/4 –463/2,[14] but that of Naxos is insecure; if we accept Thucydides' route the siege of Naxos can hardly be earlier than *c.* 466, and nothing that Thucydides says conflicts with that date, but most of those who have wrestled with the chronology of the *Pentekontaetia* have placed it some years earlier.[15] Perhaps it is wrong to assume that either Thucydides' route or Plutarch's route must be correct: it is certainly true that Themistocles in crossing the Aegean will have to take care not to fall into the hands of the Athenians, and the alternative routes may be no more than rival attempts to make of this a story with convincing details.

Ostracism entailed banishment for ten years, and we do not know how long a period elapsed between Themistocles' ostracism and his flight from Argos. Diodorus narrates the whole story under the year 471/0 (XI.54–9), and many have been anxious to believe that one episode in the story was known to belong to that year; but in this part of his history Diodorus found only one major story to tell under each year, and in view of his demonstrable errors in the 430s[16] it would be unwise to assume

---

[10] On the flight of Themistocles see in general Podlecki 1975 (D 71) 37–44; Lenardon 1978 (D 47) 108–53; maximum scepticism is displayed by Rhodes 1970 (C 82).

[11] See p. 13 n. 47.   [12] Cf. p. 46.

[13] Only one MS has Θάσον, but it is supported by Cyme as the destination, and Νάξον in the others is probably a correction made from Thucydides; see Flacelière 1953 (D 27) 6–7.

[14] Cf. p. 45.   [15] Cf. pp. 44–6.   [16] Cf. p. 7.

that he had any justification for assigning the fall of Themistocles to this year. In the spring of 472 Aeschylus produced a set of tragedies including the *Persae*, Pericles being the *choregos*. The play treats of the Persians' defeat at Salamis as experienced by the Persians at Susa: Salamis was the greatest achievement of the Athenians in the war against Xerxes, but it was specifically the achievement of Themistocles and Aristides (though neither is named in the play); at a time when Salamis was being invoked in the rivalry between Themistocles and Cimon it is hard to believe that a tragedian whose sympathies were not with Themistocles would have chosen to write a play on this theme.[17] However, Themistocles had become a controversial figure before his ostracism and remained so afterwards: we cannot say whether he was ostracized before or after the production of the *Persae*,[18] and the exact date of his ostracism must remain an unsolved problem.

By the ostracism and condemnation of Themistocles, Cimon's chief rival was eliminated. In the spring of 468 an unusual honour was paid to Cimon. Plutarch reports (*Cim.* 8.7–9) that at the Dionysia in that year the archon did not appoint the usual judges of the tragic contest but called on Cimon and his fellow-generals to act as judges: although Aeschylus was competing, they awarded the prize to Sophocles, competing for the first time. It may have been clear that Sophocles' were the better plays, but if Aeschylus was a champion of Themistocles it was politically appropriate that Cimon and his colleagues should refuse him the prize.

II. THE REFORM OF THE AREOPAGUS[19]

It is used to be thought that the *Supplices* was the earliest surviving play of Aeschylus, but in 1952 a papyrus fragment was published which shows that the tetralogy of which that formed a part won the first prize on an occasion when plays by Sophocles won the second prize, ἐπὶ αρ— (*P. Oxy.* xx.2256, fr. 3). If Sophocles competed for the first time in 468, the *Supplices* is later than that, and if αρ is the beginning of an archon's name rather than of ἄρχοντος, the only possible year is 464/3, the

---

[17] *Persae* a patriotic Athenian play, Lattimore 1943 (J 61); a defence of Themistocles, Podlecki 1966 (J 87) 8–26; possibly hostile to Themistocles, Lenardon 1978 (D 47) 121–5.

[18] Lenardon (*loc. cit.*) abandoned his earlier view (Lenardon 1959 (B 7) 29 with nn. 33–4) that the play was a defence of Themistocles after his ostracism; before his ostracism, Podlecki 1966 (J 87) 12 with 157 n. 11.

[19] This chapter was written before the appearance of Ostwald 1986 (A 96). He discusses major trials in the early fifth century and the reforms of Ephialtes on pp. 28–53; the chief difference between us is that he believes that capital sentences by the Areopagus were made subject to *ephesis* c. 500 (cf. below, p. 72 n. 31), and he therefore attaches less importance than I do to Ephialtes' removal of what remained of the Areopagus' jurisdiction in this field. For another recent study of the Ephialtic reform see Wallace 1989 (D 105) 72–93.

archonship of Archedemides.[20] *Supplices* is a play set in the heroic period, in which the fifty daughters of Danaus flee with him from Egypt, to avoid incestuous marriage with the fifty sons of his brother Aegyptus, and seek sanctuary with king Pelasgus of Argos; attempts to see in this a reflection of the flight of Themistocles from Argos[21] are implausible. However, Pelasgus is a remarkably unkingly king: he is not immediately recognizable as king at his first appearance (ll. 247–8), and throughout the central part of the play it is emphasized that the decision to accept or reject the suppliants must be taken not by the king but by an assembly of the people (ll. 365–523, 600–24). This is not required by the legend , and can hardly be accidental: the play is not crude propaganda for democracy, but it does display a sympathetic interest in the view that the *demos* ought to be sovereign.[22] How the state ought to be governed, apparently not a live issue immediately after the war, had now become one. Aeschylus in 472 had extolled the achievements of Themistocles and Aristides, and Pericles, the future leader of the democracy, had been his *choregos*; in 468 he had been passed over by Cimon and his colleagues in favour of the novice Sophocles; in 463 he gave his sympathetic attention to the theme of democracy. These three instances all point in the same direction, and Aeschylus may be ranked with the believers in popular sovereignty and the opponents of Cimon.

Shortly after the production of the *Supplices* we have the first sign of an attack on Cimon. He commanded the Athenians in their successful siege of Thasos (465/4 – 463/2), but on his return to Athens it was alleged that he had been bribed not to attack Macedon. He was prosecuted, a board of ten prosecutors being elected for the purpose; Pericles was one of the prosecutors, and the story was told by Stesimbrotus that Cimon's sister Elpinice tried to plead with him and that he was in fact the least insistent of the prosecutors (Plut. *Cim.* 14.3–15.1; *Per.* 10.6). It is said that Sparta had promised without the Athenians' knowledge to support Thasos by invading Attica, but had been prevented by the great earthquake of 464 and the outbreak of the Third Messenian War (Thuc. 1.101.1–2). Athens was still an ally of Sparta, by virtue of the alliance made when Xerxes' invasion was imminent (cf. 102.4), and Sparta appealed for help to Athens and her other allies. Thucydides reports that Cimon was sent with a substantial army (102.1); Aristophanes specifies four thousand hoplites (*Lys.* 1138–44); Plutarch tells us that this was a contentious issue in Athens, with Ephialtes not wanting to help a rival city but Cimon claiming that it would be wrong to make Greece lame or deprive Athens of her yoke-fellow (*Cim.* 16.9–10, citing Critias and Ion).

[20] See especially Lesky 1954 (J 64).
[21] Cavaignac 1921 (D 12); cf. Forrest 1960 (F 24) 239–40, Podlecki 1966 (J 87) 42–62.
[22] Cf. Podlecki *loc. cit.*

The Third Messenian War presents another of the notorious chronological cruces of the *Pentekontaetia*.[23] Thucydides, if our text is sound,
says that the war ended in the tenth year (1.103.1), but events which he
mentions before and after were less than ten years apart: apparently this
was recognized as a problem in antiquity, and behind the narrative of
Plutarch, in which Cimon twice went to the Peloponnese and twice
returned to Athens (*Cim.* 17.1–3), there may be rival accounts with
different chronologies. The Spartans were afraid of the daring and
radicalism (*neoteropoiia*) of the Athenians, suspected that they would be
persuaded by the rebels to take radical action (*neoterizein*), and so,
claiming that they had no further need of them, sent them home; the
Athenians reacted by breaking off their alliance with Sparta and making
alliances with Sparta's enemies, Argos and Thessaly (Thuc. 1.102.3–4).
Plutarch, after mentioning his prosecution and acquittal, says that when
Cimon sailed off on another campaign Ephialtes accomplished his
reform of the Areopagus, and Cimon on his return tried to upset the
reform and revive 'the aristocracy of Cleisthenes' time', but he was
attacked by his enemies, who referred to scandals concerning his sister
and to his *lakonismos* (support for Sparta), and inflamed the *demos* against
him (*Cim.* 15); then follow a passage on Cimon's friendship for Sparta
and the account of his helping Sparta against the Messenians (16–17.3);
when Sparta dismissed the Athenian army the Athenians were angry
with the laconizers and, 'seizing on a small excuse' (perhaps a pro-
Cimonian view of his dismissal by Sparta), ostracized him (17.3). In the
Pericles Plutarch links the reform of the Areopagus by Ephialtes with the
ostracism of Cimon as *philolakon* (pro-Spartan) and *misodemos* (anti-
democratic) (9.5). Cimon will not have taken his hoplites to Messenia by
sea, but probably when Plutarch writes that he 'sailed off on another
campaign' and that the reform was enacted in his absence (*Cim.* 15.2) he
is in fact referring to that expedition; and what particularly made the
Spartans fear the *neoteropoiia* of their Athenian allies will have been the
news that in Athens Ephialtes, known to have opposed the expedition,
was now in control. Hoplites as well as *thetes* stood to gain from the
reform of the Areopagus, and the absence of four thousand hoplites will
not necessarily have tipped the balance in the Assembly; but Cimon was
opposed to the reform, and, unsatisfactory as Plutarch's narrative is, his
statement that the reform occurred while Cimon was away from Athens
need not be rejected.[24]

Ephialtes is a man about whom hardly anything is known. His father

---

[23] Cf. p. 500.
[24] See, in favour of this chronology, Busolt 1893–1904 (A 12) III.i. 261 with n. 1, Hignett 1952 (D
38) 196, 337–41, Cole 1974 (D 15); arguing that Cimon's dismissal preceded the reform, Beloch
1912–27 (A 2) II.1.153, II.2.196–8, Walker *CAH* v[1] 71, 467–8, Jacoby, *FGrH* III b suppl. ii 369–70 n.
17.

was called Sophonides (a name not found on any ostraca); like Aristides he is described as upright (*Ath. Pol.* 25.1), and like Aristides he is included in a list of leading statesmen who were not rich (Ael. *VH* 11.43, XI.9, XIII.39); he once commanded a naval expedition (Plut. *Cim.* 13.4). In *Ath. Pol.* 25.3–4 he and Themistocles are said to have combined to attack the Areopagus, but 25.2 dates the reform to 462/1 and Themistocles must have left Athens long before ; 35.2 mentions the annulment by the Thirty in 404 of the laws of Ephialtes and a not securely identifiable Archestratus; Plutarch mentions Pericles as a supporter of Ephialtes (*Cim.* 15.2; *Per.* 9.5, 10.7: he will have been a little over thirty in 462/1), and the separate reform of the Areopagus attributed to Pericles in *Ath. Pol.* 27.1 is probably a distortion of this fact.[25]

We read in *Ath. Pol.* 25.2 that Ephialtes

first eliminated many of the Areopagites, bringing them to trial over their administration. Then in the archonship of Conon he stripped off from the Council all the accretions (*epitheta*) on which its guardianship of the state depended, giving some to the five hundred and some to the *demos* and the law courts.

(The trials of individuals were probably for misconduct as archons.[26]) According to Plutarch (*Cim.* 15.2),

the many were finally unleashed, and overturned the existing order in the state and the traditional observances which they had previously followed, and with Ephialtes as leader they took away from the Council of the Areopagus all but a few of its judicial functions (*kriseis*), making themselves masters of the law courts and pitching the city into undiluted democracy.

The account of *Ath. Pol.* is favourable to the reformers, while that of Plutarch is hostile; and probably the language which they use derives from the propaganda of the time: the powers of which Ephialtes deprived the Areopagus were regarded as accretions by the reformers, as part of the established order by the conservatives.[27] These powers were primarily judicial, and they had given the Areopagus a 'guardianship of the state'. This role of the Areopagus is mentioned by *Ath. Pol.* in its account of the pre-Draconian constitution (3.6), in the supposed constitution of Draco (4.4), and in the account of Solon's constitutional laws (8.4), but we are nowhere told precisely what powers it entailed. Some have supposed that it was a specific power, possibly a power of

[25] Arist. *Pol.* II, 1274a7–8 would be compatible either with separate reforms by Ephialtes and Pericles or with a joint reform.

[26] Wade-Gery 1936/7 (D 102) 269 = 1958 (A 121) 177.

[27] A fragment of Lysias (178 Sauppe, *ap.* Harp. ἐπιθέτους ἑορτάς) shows that the Areopagus was discussed in the same terms *c.* 400; Davies 1978 (A 23) 69–70 compares an inscription of the 450s (*IG* I³ 7) which defines what things are traditional for the priestly clan of the Praxiergidae.

quashing improper decrees of the Assembly, as later there was a democratic way of quashing improper decrees through the *graphe paranomon* (charge of making an illegal proposal);[28] others have thought that it was a comprehensive description of the various powers of the Areopagus as a body entrusted with the enforcement of the laws.[29] It appears from *Ath. Pol.* that the Areopagus had long been referred to in this way: perhaps this language was first used, when the laws were first written down by Draco or even earlier, to provide a comprehensive description of the Areopagus' judicial powers, and in the course of time, as circumstances altered, this description and the prestige of the Areopagites were used to justify its enforcing the laws in new ways, without explicit authority. If this is so, we can understand how these powers came to be rejected as accretions by some but defended as part of the established order by others.

But we have still to discover what powers Ephialtes took away from the Areopagus. Two possibilities may be suggested. First, the magistrates of Classical Athens were subject to frequent checks on their conduct: before entering office they had to undergo a vetting process called *dokimasia* (*Ath. Pol.* 55.2); after leaving office they had to present their accounts, and submit to a more general examination called *euthynai* (54.2; 48.4–5); while in office they had to present interim accounts each prytany (i.e. each tenth of the year), and each prytany the Assembly held a vote of confidence in the authorities (48.3; 43.4, 61.2). There are signs that *dokimasia* and *euthynai* were ancient institutions, and the body most likely to have conducted these examinations, and any other examinations that there may have been, of at any rate the principal magistrates in early Athens, is the Areopagus; such oversight of the magistrates would have given it considerable political power.[30] Secondly, Solon's laws included one on the prosecution before the Areopagus, by *eisangelia* (impeachment), of 'those who conspired for the dissolution of the *demos*' (*Ath. Pol.* 8.4: Solon is more likely to have referred to setting up a tyranny than to dissolving the *demos*, but the basic fact may be accepted); *eisangelia* was used also for treason, for taking bribes to speak contrary to the interests of Athens, and perhaps for public wrongs not explicitly forbidden by law; in Classical Athens these *eisangeliai* were tried by the Council of Five Hundred and the Assembly, or the Five Hundred and a law court. How certain charges in the early fifth century came to be tried by the *demos* has

[28] E.g. Wade-Gery 1933 (D 101) 24 with n. 3 = 1958 (A 121) 146 with n. 4.
[29] E.g. Hignett 1952 (D 38) 208–9; Cawkwell 1988 (D 14) interprets the Areopagus' guardianship of the laws as a *cura morum*.
[30] Cf. Lipsius 1905–15 (A 78) 37; Hignett 1952 (D 38) 90–1, 203–8 (not accepting *dokimasiai* by the Areopagus).

been disputed, but it is likely that until 462/1 *eisangeliai* to the Areopagus remained possible, and that Ephialtes abolished this possibility.[31]

If the Areopagus had claimed the right to quash decrees of the Assembly, this too must have been abolished: but the democratic *graphe paranomon* is not attested until 415 (Andoc. I. *Myst.* 17), and although it is possible that the earlier silence of our sources is accidental it is by no means necessary;[32] probably this is not a right which the Areopagus had claimed. By the second half of the fifth century, contested lawsuits went not to Solon's *heliaia* (a judicial session of the Assembly) on appeal from the verdict of a magistrate but to one of a number of *dikasteria* (jury-courts) after a preliminary enquiry by a magistrate: it is has been suggested that this change was made by Ephialtes;[33] but more probably there was a gradual development rather than an abrupt reform, though the new procedure will have had to be standardized, and that can hardly have been done much later than 462/1.[34] A passage derived from the third-century historian of Athens, Philochorus, states that a board of seven *nomophylakes* (law-guardians) was established at the time of Ephialtes' reform (*FGrH* 328 F 64b(a)); but the first contemporary evidence for this board comes from speeches by Dinarchus in the late 320s (F 64a), and the attribution to Ephialtes must be a mistake. One other change, however, needs to be postulated: if the judicial activities of the Areopagus had been based on its title of guardian of the laws, it must have lost that title; a purely negative measure is unlikely, but it may have been stated that in future the Council of Five Hundred and the *demos* were to be guardians of the laws. The powers which the Areopagus is known to have retained after the reform were further judicial powers, in connexion with intentional homicide, wounding and arson, damage to the sacred olive trees, and certain other religious offences (Lys. VII. *Ol.* 22; Dem. XXIII. *Arist.* 22; [Dem.] LIX. *Neaer.* 79–80; *Ath. Pol.* 57.3, 60.2).

The Areopagus was a council of ex-archons. In the sixth century the archonship had been the most important office of the Athenian state; but

---

[31] On *eisangelia* see Rhodes 1972 (D 75) 162–71, 199–205, and 1979 (D 77); Hansen 1975 (D 30) and 1980 (D 33); Sealey 1981 (D 88); Carawan 1987 (D 11). Hansen believes that *eisangelia* was a democratic institution introduced by Cleisthenes; some have thought that it was Cleisthenes who took the hearing of *eisangeliai* from the Areopagus (Lipsius 1905–15 (A 78) 179–81), or that Cleisthenes allowed prosecution before the *demos* as an alternative to prosecution before the Areopagus (Bonner and Smith 1930–8 (A 8) I 299–300), or that Cleisthenes required confirmation of the Areopagus' verdicts by the *demos* (Ostwald in *CAH* IV² 330–3). Sealey argues that *eisangelia* was regulated by custom rather than by law; I sympathize, and agree that it originated thus, but believe that a law of Solon provided for *eisangelia* to the Areopagus in cases of attempted tyranny (without necessarily providing a complete law of *eisangelia*), and that Ephialtes took away from the Areopagus the right to hear *eisangeliai*. Carawan studies *eisangelia* and *euthynai* in the light of the major trials of the early fifth century.

[32] Cf. Wolff 1970 (A 127) 15–22.   [33] Wade-Gery 1958 (A 121) 180–200.

[34] Sealey 1964 (D 87) 14–18 = 1967 (A 111) 46–52; MacDowell 1978 (A 81) 33 doubts whether the old procedure was ever forbidden.

in 487/6 sortition from an elected short list (*klerosis ek prokriton*) had replaced direct election, and in the fifth century the generals overtook the archons in prestige and importance:[35] a powerful Areopagus thus became increasingly hard to justify. The new organization given to the Athenian state by Cleisthenes required a considerable degree of participation by the citizens, both at polis level and at local level, and we may assume that the Athenians came to enjoy their share in the political process and to want a larger share.[36] Thus it need cause no surprise that the powers of the Areopagus came to be challenged. There may have been a more specific stimulus for the challenge in two decisions given by the Areopagus in the course of the 460s. The procedure of *eisangelia* would have been appropriate for the prosecution of Themistocles on a charge of medism, and according to Craterus that was the procedure used (*FGrH* 342 F 11); Cimon's *euthynai* would have been an appropriate occasion for his prosecution on a charge of taking bribes as a general, and according to *Ath. Pol.* (27.1) that was the occasion of his prosecution; both of these charges may have been tried by the Areopagus, and a trial of Themistocles by the Areopagus underlies the (implausible) anecdote in *Ath. Pol.* 25.3–4. Themistocles appears to have been innocent, and on Cimon's guilt we cannot pronounce, but Themistocles was condemned and Cimon was acquitted: if the Areopagus was consistently giving verdicts in favour of Cimon and his supporters, their opponents may well have been prompted to ask by what right it occupied so influential a position in the state.

Present-day historians have been less willing than their predecessors to ascribe to ancient politicians doctrinaire views on how their states should be governed, and have preferred to look for other explanations of their actions. What happened in 462/1 in Athens can certainly be represented as the victory of the Themistocles–Ephialtes–Pericles set over the Cimon–Alcmaeonid set.[37] The victory was marked by a change in foreign policy: Athens abandoned the friendship with Sparta of the last thirty years, and extended her ambition to the whole Greek world; some have suggested that this was Ephialtes' primary objective and that the reform of the Areopagus was incidental to its achievement.[38] But it is wrong to play down the importance of the constitutional reform. By the

[35] Cf. *CAH* IV² 333.

[36] According to *Ath. Pol.* 22.3 the institution of ostracism was used after Marathon, 'the *demos* now being confident'; on the growing confidence of the *demos* see below, pp. 90–1.

[37] On the politics of the Alcmaeonids in the fifth century, see Forrest 1960 (F 24) 233–4 (*contra* Bicknell 1972 (D 6) 73–4). The ideological aspect of the reform is played down by Sealey 1964 (D 87) = 1967 (A 111) 42–58, Wallace 1974 (D 104), Sealey 1981 (D 88), and studies cited in the next note.

[38] Cf. Ruschenbusch 1966 (D 81); Martin 1974 (D 57), especially 29–40. Ruschenbusch 1979 (D 82) argues that all constitutional changes to the end of the fifth century were made to achieve immediate objectives, particularly in foreign policy. By contrast, Thuc. v.31.6, 44.1 show foreign policy being influenced by constitutional dogmatism.

opening years of the Peloponnesian War the Athenians were proud of their democracy: the *Athenaion Politeia* of pseudo-Xenophon describes it as undesirable but effective (1. 1), and the funeral oration of Pericles takes pride in it (Thuc. 11.37); *misodemos* ('hating the people' and so anti-democratic, used of Cimon by Plutarch) is a word of abuse in Aristophanes (*Wasps* 474, of 422); Sparta had come to be associated with oligarchy (cf. Thuc. 1.19), while Athens had come to be associated with democracy and had imposed democratic constitutions on various member states of the Delian League (on Erythrae, as early as the 450s: M–L 40 = *IG* 1³ 14). Aeschylus in his *Supplices* had emphasized the powers of the *demos*; and in his *Eumenides*, in 458, he focused attention on the Areopagus as a homicide court: Athena's speech instituting the Areopagus points to the good that it will do in this role, as long as the citizens do not introduce innovations or defilements in the laws, and ends by describing the Areopagus as a 'wakeful guardian of the land on behalf of the sleeping' (ll. 681–710, esp. 704–6); later passages in the play point to a fear of civil war (ll. 858–66, 976–87). So far we have seen that Aeschylus is to be associated with the democrats, and many regard this presentation of the Areopagus as favourable to the reformers, but the allusion to the Areopagus as guardian and the warning against defiling the laws suggest rather that Aeschylus had come to regret the reform or to fear that the reformers might continue too far.[39] At any rate the *Supplices* and the *Eumenides* confirm that the powers of the *demos* and the position of the Areopagus in the state were serious issues at the time.

Ephialtes and his supporters were also hostile to Sparta, and they may have been provoked by particular decisions of the Areopagus in favour of their opponents, but they did genuinely come to think that the state ought to be run on more democratic lines; we may believe Plutarch when he says that Cimon was ostracized both because he was *philolakon* and because he was *misodemos*. The word *demokratia* may well have been coined at this time,[40] and Ephialtes may have moved the *axones* on which the laws of Draco and Solon were inscribed from the Acropolis to the new Stoa of the Basileus in the Agora, to symbolize the transfer to the people of the control of the state.[41]

[39] Cf. Dodds 1953 (J 27) 19–20 and 1960 (J 28) = 1973 (J 29), 45–63; *contra* Dover 1957 (J 30) = 1987 (A 26) 161–75), Macleod 1982 (J 74) 124–33 (= 1983 (A 82) 20–9); for Podlecki 1966 (J 87) 80–100, Aeschylus approved of Ephialtes' reform but feared further reform by Pericles.

[40] Notice δήμου κρατοῦσα χείρ in Aesch. *Suppl.* 604, and the name Democrates given to an Athenian born *c.* 470–460 (Davies 1971 (L 27) 359–60, cf. Stroud 1984 (C 168)). Against the view that the word was not adopted until late in the fifth century, see Hansen 1986 (A 57). Earlier, *demos* and *kratos* had been combined in the Great Rhetra at Sparta (Plut. *Lyc.* 6.2, Tyrt. fr. 4.9 West; cf. *CAH* III².1, 740–1).

[41] According to Anaximenes (*FGrH* 72 F 13), Ephialtes moved the *axones* and the *kyrbeis* to the *bouleuterion* and the Agora; Poll. VIII.128 substitutes the *prytaneion* (where these objects were certainly to be found later) for the *bouleuterion*. It has often been thought that this was merely a metaphorical

On his return from Messenia Cimon tried to upset the reform, but he was unsuccessful and was ostracized (Plut. *Cim.* 15.3–5, 17.3; *Per.* 9.5). The democracy had come to stay, but its enemies were not yet prepared to accept defeat. Ephialtes himself was murdered: the orator Antiphon cited this as an instance of an unsolved crime (v. *Caed. Her.* 68); Idomeneus alleged that Pericles killed him out of envy (*FGrH* 338 F 8, *ap.* Plut. *Per.* 10.7), but *Ath. Pol.* says that the killer was Aristodicus of Tanagra (25.4); either this last was an unconfirmed rumour or it was known that Aristodicus was the actual killer and assumed that some Athenian must have instigated him. The *Eumenides* in 458 shows a fear of civil war (cf. above), and at the time of the battle of Tanagra, perhaps in the following year,[42] there were rumours of a pro-Spartan oligarchic plot (Thuc. 1.107.4, 6). Plutarch tells the story that Cimon was anxious to return and fight on the Athenian side at Tanagra and was forbidden to do so, but his friends fought and died in the battle, and afterwards he was recalled on the proposal of Pericles (*Cim.* 17.4–7; *Per.* 10.1–3). We may accept that Cimon was not willing to do as Isagoras had done fifty years earlier and invoke Spartan help against his political opponents, but probably he was not recalled at the time of Tanagra and did not return to Athens until the end of his ten years of exile, though perhaps then he was not simply allowed to return but was positively recalled.[43]

Ath. Pol. 26.2–4 chronicles three laws of the 450s: in 457/6 (or in the previous year, to take effect in that year) the archonship was opened to the *zeugitai*, the third of the four property classes; in 453/2 the thirty travelling magistrates, *dikastai kata demous* (an institution of the tyranny, not then necessarily numbering thirty: *Ath. Pol.* 16.5) were revived; in 451/0 a law of Pericles limited citizenship to men who had Athenian mothers as well as Athenian fathers. Another law of Pericles is mentioned in 27.3–4: to rival Cimon's generosity from his own resources Pericles used the resources of the state to provide payment for jurors in the *dikasteria*. These laws completed the democracy established by the reform of the Areopagus. The first of them marks the penultimate stage in the process by which the archons came to be thought of as routine officials, with duties which any loyal citizen could be trusted to perform: as for most offices, all but the members of the lowest class were now

way of saying that Ephialtes placed the control of the state in the hands of the people (Wilamowitz 1893 (A 125) 145 n. 7). If the Stoa of the Basileus was built in the second quarter of the fifth century, as proposed by Thompson 1981 (I 165) 345–6, it may be that the *axones* of Draco and Solon were moved from the Acropolis to the Stoa by Ephialtes and from the Stoa to the *prytaneion* on the publication of the new code of laws at the end of the fifth century, and that Ephialtes' act was intended to have the metaphorical significance detected by Wilamowitz.

42 But see pp. 113–15, 501, placing it in the same year.

43 However, the story that Cimon was recalled early is found also in Theopompus, *FGrH* 115 F 88; and Gomme, *HCT* I 326–7, argued strongly that in the absence of good conflicting evidence it should be believed. Unz 1986 (B 16) 76–82 accepts it and argues for a revised chronology.

eligible; for a while appointment continued to be by *klerosis ek prokriton*, but by the time of *Ath. Pol.* this had given way to a two-stage allotment (8.1). *Dikastai kata demous* and payment for jurors are both responses to the development of the *dikasteria*, which Ephialtes' reform had aided; judicial business formerly handled by the Areopagus was now handled by organs of the *demos*, and it will have been necessary for him to divide the *heliaia* into separate *dikasteria* and to standardize the new procedure by which one of the archons after a preliminary enquiry referred suits to a *dikasterion*, if this had not already been done. *Dikastai kata demous* probably decided minor private suits in which the sum at issue was not more than 10 drachmae (cf. *Ath. Pol.* 53.2): such suits would often be between near neighbours, and in this way litigation would be made easier and pressure on the *dikasteria* would be relieved. Payment for jurors (at first, probably 2 obols a day[44]) enabled the poorer citizens to play their part in the judicial process and allowed the formation of the large juries, representative of the *demos*, which the Athenians preferred. If the story of a political manoeuvre against Cimon is pressed, this measure must be assigned to a time when he was in Athens, but more probably we should conclude only that the payment was introduced during his lifetime, and date it shortly after Ephialtes' reform.[45]

Pericles' citizenship law requires more discussion. The only explanation given in an ancient text is 'because of the number of the citizens' (*Ath. Pol.* 26.4);[46] but that will certainly not explain the re-enactment of the law in 403/2, after the losses of the Peloponnesian War; and if, as seems likely, bastards were never legally entitled to Athenian citizenship,[47] the effect of the law will have been to limit citizens in their choice of wives but not to limit the number of citizen sons born to citizen fathers.[48] Distinguished citizens with foreign mothers had included Cleisthenes and Themistocles, and currently included Cimon. It has been suggested that the law was a party-political manoeuvre against Cimon, but there is no indication that the law was made retrospective, and almost certainly Cimon held his last Athenian command (Thuc. 1.112.2–4) after the law had been enacted.[49] Rich aristocrats were more likely than

---

[44] Schol. Ar. *Wasps* 300, cf. 88 (emended).

[45] Hignett 1952 (D 38) 342–3, *contra* Wade-Gery 1938 (C 104) 131–4 = 1958 (A 121) 235–8.

[46] Arist. *Pol.* III, 1278a26–34 remarks that when democracies are short of 'legitimate' citizens they adopt generous criteria for citizenship, but as they come to have an ample supply of common people (*ochlos*) they adopt increasingly strict criteria.

[47] Lacey 1968 (L 90) 282 n. 15; Humphreys 1974 (L 73); Rhodes 1978 (L 120); *contra* Harrison 1968–71 (A 59) I 63–5; MacDowell 1976 (L 97).

[48] Hignett 1952 (D 38) 346.

[49] Hignett *op. cit.* 345, *contra* Jacoby, *FGrH* IIIb suppl. i 477–81; for Cimon's last command cf. p. 54 (Meiggs 1963 (E 52) 13, believing that Cimon was recalled from ostracism slightly early, placed his death in Cyprus before the enactment of the law; same chronology in Meiggs 1972 (E 53) 111, 125, 422–3, 456–7, but see Chronological Notes, pp. 501–2).

poor commoners to bring foreign wives back to Athens; but in the mid-fifth century more Athenians were going abroad than earlier, and also foreigners were probably coming to Athens as metics in large numbers, and their daughters were as accessible to the poor as to the rich. We may guess that mixed marriages had been accepted when they were few and illustrious, but were incurring disapproval as they became more frequent: Athens and her democracy were flourishing, and membership of the citizen body should be limited to those who were entitled to it by their Athenian origins. In 445/4 Psammetichus of Egypt sent a consignment of corn to Athens, which was distributed among the citizens; the gift provoked a check on the registers of citizens, and it is implausibly alleged that as many as 4,760 from a total of 19,000 were deleted (Philochorus, *FGrH* 328 F 119). We need not follow Plutarch (*Per.* 37.4) in linking this check with Pericles' law, [50] but it reflects the same attitude, that only those with a good claim to them should enjoy the benefits of Athenian citizenship: there is nothing incompatible with democracy in the law.[51]

III. PERICLEAN DEMOCRACY

The core of the Athenian state was the Athenian *demos*, the body of Athenian citizens, and under the democracy the state was run by, and for the benefit of, the *demos*. In the making of decisions all citizens were involved together: the one sovereign body was the *ekklesia*, the Assembly which consisted in theory of all adult male citizens. In the carrying-out of decisions all could not be involved together but all could be involved in turn: administration was based on a large number of boards with limited duties, and no man could hold any one civilian office for more than one year. Most of the more important lawsuits were referred to a *dikasterion* after preliminary enquiry by a magistrate: the juries in these courts were large, and as subdivisions of Solon's *heliaia* were regarded as representative of the *demos*.

It was the Assembly which enacted laws, imposed taxes and spent the proceeds of them, made alliances and declared peace and war. Any citizen present could speak in the debate, or put forward an amendment to a proposal already before the Assembly, or make a new proposal

---

[50] Hignett *loc. cit.*

[51] Patterson 1981 (D 65) argues that before 451/0 there was no law laying down the qualification for registration as a citizen, which I think possible, and that many men of non-Athenian birth on both sides had been registered, which I doubt. Walters 1983 (L 139) argues that bastards were not *ipso facto* excluded from citizenship and that the purpose of the law was to exclude the sons of citizens by slave women. Humphreys 1977/8 (D 39) 99 = 1983 (A 67) 24, sees the law's purpose as 'to prevent families based on international dynastic marriages from using their private relationships to manipulate foreign policy'. See also pp. 292, 299.

himself. The most important restriction of the Assembly's powers of decision lay in the principle of *probouleusis* (advance deliberation).[52] In Athens as in other Greek cities of varying political complexion the Assembly worked in conjunction with a smaller Council (the *boule*) which gave prior consideration to its business; cities differed in the extent to which they allowed the Council to decide matters without reference to the Assembly, and in the degree of freedom which they gave the Assembly to debate matters which were referred to it;[53] in democratic Athens all major and many subsidiary decisions were taken by the Assembly, and the restriction of the Assembly's freedom was minimal. The rule of *probouleusis* was formulated, 'It is not permitted to the *demos* to decree anything which has not been given prior consideration by the Council and has not been put to it by the *prytaneis*' (*Ath. Pol.* 45.4), and all that was forbidden by this was the taking of a positive decision on a subject not referred to the Assembly by the Council. The Council might make a recommendation of its own, in which case the Assembly was free to adopt it or amend it or reject it and adopt an alternative proposal; or it might decline to offer a recommendation, and simply invite the Assembly to debate a subject and make up its own mind, in which case proposals would have to be made in the Assembly; our evidence suggests that in the fifth and fourth centuries both bodies took their duties seriously. If a matter was raised in debate which the chairmen were not prepared to accept as covered by the Council's *probouleuma* (memorandum to the Assembly), the Assembly could call for a proposal to be presented to a subsequent meeting: in the fifth century *ad hoc* drafting committees (*syngrapheis*) were sometimes appointed to present proposals through the Council; such committees prepared the way for the oligarchies of 411 and 404, so this practice was abandoned, and in the fourth century the Council itself was commissioned to draw up proposals.

Some other limitations on its power were normally accepted by the Assembly, but might fail to work on the occasions when they were most needed (the Assembly which set up the oligarchy in 411 began by suspending all the normal safeguards against hasty decision;[54] in the 'trial' of the generals after Arginusae the *prytaneis* tried to enforce the normal rules of procedure, but 'the mass shouted out that it would be a terrible thing if any one prevented the *demos* from doing what it wanted' Xen. *Hell.* 1.7.12[55]). By 415 there existed the possibility of prosecuting the author of a decree and invalidating the decree through a *graphe paranomon*.[56] On some occasions the *demos* voted that a question might

52 On the working of *probouleusis* in Athens, see Rhodes 1972 (D 75) 52–81.
53 Cf. below, pp. 92–3.   54 Cf. below, p. 475.   55 Cf. below, p. 493.
56 Cf. pp. 70–2 with nn. 28, 32.

not be raised without a previous vote of immunity (*adeia*), so that a decision could not be taken at a single meeting of the Assembly, but one meeting would have to vote the immunity and a second to take the substantive decision.[57] Some important decisions, like that on Corinth and Corcyra in 433,[58] were spread over two days, so that the people should hear the arguments on the first day and return to vote on the second (Thuc. 1.44.1); but there seem to have been no precautions to ensure that only those who had heard the arguments took part in the vote.

In the fourth century there were four regular Assemblies in each of the ten prytanies of the year, one of the four being designated 'principal' (*kyria*) (*Ath. Pol.* 43.4–6): probably there was a time when the *kyriai ekklesiai* were the only regular Assemblies, and we may guess that the others were added between Ephialtes' reform and the end of the fifth century. For a tenth of the year at a time the fifty councillors of one tribe served as the *prytaneis*, the standing committee of the Council and the joint chairmen of the Council and Assembly; each day one of their number was picked by lot to serve as president. The mechanism was available from the time of Cleisthenes' creation of the ten tribes, but before Ephialtes' reform there is no clear evidence for these *prytaneis*, and probably the Council was not busy enough to need a standing committee, so we should perhaps attribute the institution of the *prytaneis* to Ephialtes[59] and suppose that previously the nine archons had presided.[60] Decisions in the Assembly were taken by a simple majority. On some motions, particularly some affecting a named individual, voting was by ballot and a quorum of 6,000 was required;[61] the latter requirement suggests that attendance in excess of 6,000 was possible but was not always achieved.[62] On other motions the Assembly voted by show of hands: many votes might be needed in the course of a meeting, and it is likely that an exact count was not attempted but if a vote did not produce an unchallenged majority the vote was repeated.[63]

The regular meeting-place of the Assembly was the Pnyx (south west of the Agora, west of the Acropolis); the earliest work there is dated to the end of the sixth century, and the site was remodelled at the end of the fifth century and again in the fourth.[64] The Council had its headquarters in the Agora (see below, Fig. 27): originally the excavators dated the council chamber (*bouleuterion*) *c.* 500 and the round house (*tholos*) which was used by the *prytaneis* in the second quarter of the fifth century,[65] and

---

[57] E.g. M–L 58 = *IG* i³ 52.15–19.   [58] Cf. below, p. 374.

[59] Rhodes 1972 (D 75) 16–19.   [60] Hignett 1952 (D 38) 74, 92, 98–9, 150–1.

[61] Cf. law *ap.* Andoc. 1.87 and the rule concerning ostracism as formulated by Plut. *Arist.* 7.6.

[62] On the population of Athens see below, p. 83.   [63] Hansen 1977 (D 31).

[64] Cf. Travlos 1971 (I 171) 466–76, where detailed discussions are cited.

[65] Travlos 1971 (I 171) 191–5, 553–61; Thompson and Wycherley 1972 (I 166) 20, 25–46.

it was possible to link the first with Cleisthenes and the second with Ephialtes;[66] but the appearance of re-used material in the *bouleuterion* is an embarrassment, and may indicate that that too should be dated to the second quarter of the fifth century.[67] At any rate, the buildings of the Council and Assembly belong to the half-century from Cleisthenes to Ephialtes.

If the Assembly was to discharge its duty responsibly it had to be kept informed. Documents could not be reproduced in large numbers, as they are in the modern world, and an important official of the Athenian state (who was considered to require special skill, and was therefore appointed not by lot but by election) was the secretary, who read documents aloud at meetings of the Council and Assembly (*Ath. Pol.* 54.5, cf. Thuc. VII.10). Before and after meetings, though documents could not be sent to the citizens, the citizens could go to the documents: more than any other Greek state, Athens took to inscribing, on stone, decrees of the Assembly, accounts of public expenditure and a wide range of official documents; publication on a large scale seems to have begun shortly after Ephialtes' reform, presumably by a deliberate decision of the new democracy. As has been mentioned, business for the Assembly was prepared by the Council, and the way in which the Council came to act as supervisor of the state's administration (see below) ensured that it was well informed on the day-to-day working of Athens. The Assembly was helped also by the fact that its members were not utter laymen: many of those who attended were holding some state appointment in the current year, and many more had done so in a recent year.

Greek cities had no professional civil service, and in democratic Athens much of the city's administration was entrusted to committees of citizens, usually comprising one man from each of the ten tribes. This may be illustrated from the organization of Athenian finance. The collection of a tax will have been put up for auction among rival syndicates of tax-farmers, and the contract for the year awarded to the syndicate which offered the highest yield, by the *poletai* (sellers) in the presence of the Council; the Council kept a record of the contract, with the amount due and the date fixed for payment; a few public slaves (*demosioi*) were available for mechanical tasks of that kind (*Ath. Pol.* 47.2–3). On the day appointed the money was paid to the *apodektai* (receivers) and the record of the contract was cancelled, again in the presence of the Council (*Ath. Pol.* 47.5–48.1); defaulters were pursued by the Council through another committee, the *praktores* (exacters) (law *ap.* Andoc. 1. *Myst.* 77). In the fifth century, state revenue was paid by the

[66] Rhodes 1972 (D 75) 30–1, 18–19 (using this to support the attribution of *prytaneis* to Ephialtes).
[67] This date preferred by Thompson 1981 (I 165) 345–6.

apodektai into a central treasury, and all expenditure from the treasury had to be authorized (either as a single or as a recurrent payment) by the Assembly;[68] the paying officers were the *kolakretai* (an ancient title, meaning literally 'ham-collectors'), and it has been argued that these, presumably because they were the most strongly tempted to embezzlement, held office not for a whole year but only for one prytany.[69] The work of the various committees was held together through the supervision of the Council (cf. *Ath. Pol.* 45.2, 47.1, 49.5): in the financial realm this supervision covered not only the secular officials but also the treasurers of Athena and other sacred treasurers (cf. *Ath. Pol.* 47.1), and the *taktai* (assessors: *IG* I^3 71 = M–L 69, 8–26) who assessed and the *hellenotamiai* (treasurers of the Greeks: *IG* I^3 34 = M–L 46, 16–22) who received and disbursed the tribute of the Delian League. The tribute was spent on ships for the Athenian fleet, and on payment to soldiers and sailors who were engaged in the League's wars; in the 440s and 430s tribute which was surplus to these requirements was spent on public buildings in Athens and Attica;[70] and Athens' position as capital of the League meant that citizens of member states had for various reasons to visit Athens and contribute to Athenian taxes and to the wealth of the Athenians.[71]

The state had a large number of officials – a passage in *Ath. Pol.* refers plausibly to 700 internal and (700, but this repetition of the number is a corruption) overseas officials in the fifth century (24.3) – and in addition the tribes, trittyes and demes, and other organizations within the Athenian state, had officials of their own. Almost all of the state's regular civilian appointments were made by lot, and could be held only for one year in a man's life; the Council of Five Hundred was likewise appointed by lot; in the fourth century men were allowed to serve twice as councillors, and some repetition is likely to have been needed at the beginning of the fifth century, but this concession may not have been necessary in the time of Pericles.[72] For this system to work, a large number of men had to be able and willing to devote some of their time to public service: payment for jurors (cf. above, pp. 75–6) was probably the first instance of payment to civilians to compensate for loss of earnings while engaged in public business; in due course payments for the various officials and committees were introduced;[73] the culmination was reached in the 390s, with payment for attendance at the Assembly (*Ath. Pol.* 41.3, cf. Ar. *Eccl.* 186–8, 289–311, 392). The philosophy behind this practice

---

[68] In the fourth century there was a regular allocation (*merismos*) of fixed sums of money to separate spending authorities: Rhodes 1972 (D 75) 99–101, 1979/80 (D 78) 310–11.

[69] Wilhelm 1939 (C 179).   [70] Cf. p. 126.   [71] Cf. pp. 307–12.

[72] Rhodes 1980 (A 105) 195–6.

[73] One motive for the oligarchic revolution of 411 was a desire to save money by abolishing these civilian stipends: see below, p. 475.

was that all should play their part in the running of the state: not all will have been good administrators, but the work was simple and the scope for incompetence limited, and although each year each official was new to his current post most will have been men who had held other posts in the public service in previous years. Public appointments were not, however, open to all adult male citizens: men under thirty were ineligible (cf. *Ath. Pol.* 63.3, on jurors), and so too were the members of the lowest property class, the *thetes* (*Ath. Pol.* 7.3–4).

The Council acquired not only administrative functions but judicial functions to reinforce them (*Ath. Pol.* 45.2). In the modern world, where the power of the state over the individual is large, it seems important that the courts should be independent of the other organs of the state and so able to insist that even the state must abide by the laws, but in the Greek world the power of the state was much less; in fifth-century Athens an opposition between the polis and the individual citizens who comprised the polis would scarcely have been intelligible, and the distinction between the laws and what the *demos* currently wanted had yet to be drawn. The Council was involved also, after Ephialtes' reform, in the trial of *eisangeliai*, charges of major offences against the state. Apart from the jurisdiction of the Council, most public lawsuits (on charges on which any citizen might prosecute), and private suits where the sum at issue was more than 10 drachmae,[74] now came after a preliminary enquiry by a magistrate to one of the *dikasteria* into which Solon's *heliaia* was divided: juries were of some hundreds, or even thousands, and the total list of registered jurors ran to 6,000 (Ar. *Wasps* 661–2, *Ath. Pol.* 24.3); men under thirty were excluded, but *thetes* were not. In dispensing justice as in administration the Athenians did not set a high value on expertise: litigants were expected to plead their own cases; in due course professional speech-writers are found, but not specialists in the law as such. There were no regular public prosecutors: the Council might uncover offences in the course of its administrative work (cf. Ant. VI. *Chor.* 49), and sometimes, as for the trial of Cimon (p. 68), prosecutors might be elected; but usually it was left to 'whoever wished' (*ho boulomenos*) to initiate a public lawsuit, and malicious prosecutors called *sykophantai*,[75] who made a practice of prosecuting in order to obtain the rewards offered to those who won their cases, were a well-known evil in Athens (e.g. Ar. *Ach.* 898–928). Litigants swore to keep to the point at issue (*Ath. Pol.* 67.1), and jurors swore to make their decision on the point at issue (oath *ap.* Dem. XXIV. *Tim.* 151), but it is clear from surviving speeches that the Athenian courts did not in fact observe strict

[74] The lesser private suits were judged by the *dikastai kata demous*: cf. pp. 75–6.
[75] Literally, 'fig-exposers': perhaps originally, as in Ar. *Ach.* 818–28, 904–28, denouncers of contraband imports.

standards of relevance: the courts were cross-sections of the Athenian *demos*, expressing the will of the *demos* with regard to the contestants appearing before them.

The body which met in the Assembly, and which supplied councillors and other officials, and jurors, was not the whole population of Athens but the Athenian *demos*, the adult male citizens. The exclusion of children from political power is still accepted in our own century; the exclusion of women was accepted for a long time but is not today. But even if we include women and children, as citizens in a wider sense, citizens were a far lower proportion of the total population in Attica than they are in a modern state. The *demos* could and sometimes did confer citizenship on a foreigner, but there was no general right to acquire citizenship by place of birth or by migration, and Pericles' law of 451/0, requiring a citizen mother as well as a citizen father, defined the entitlement to citizenship more strictly than before (see pp. 75–7). There were many non-citizens living in Attica, some as long-term visitors, others as permanent residents: they had to register as *metoikoi*; they had military and fiscal obligations; they had no political rights, and only such rights at law as the citizens chose to allow them. Metics, though not citizens, were still free men and women; many other inhabitants were unfree. Slaves, who were the property of their masters, to be treated almost entirely as their masters wished, were present in large numbers. The Athenian citizens were not parasitic on their metics and slaves to the same extent as the Spartiate citizens were parasitic on their *perioikoi* and helots[76] – many citizens worked on their own land or in their own workshops, often with the help of slaves – but the large-scale participation by the citizens in the running of the state was possible partly because they were not the whole population, but there was an unleisured class of non-citizens which did not share in political activity. Figures are hard to come by for citizens and even harder for non-citizens; but at the outbreak of the Peloponnesian War the total population perhaps numbered about 300,000, comprising 100,000 or more slaves, somewhat under 50,000 members of metic families and somewhat over 150,000 members of citizen families; of these last, 45,000, 15 per cent of the population, were adult male citizens over thirty years old in the three highest property classes, eligible to hold office.[77]

Apart from its use to denote the demes, the smallest units in Cleisthenes' organization, the word *demos* can refer either to the whole citizen body or to the mass of ordinary citizens as opposed to the rich and

---

[76] Cf. *CAH* iii².1, 742–4.

[77] These approximations are based on the estimates of Gomme 1933 (A 48), Ehrenberg 1969 (A 33) 30–2; but arguments for rather higher citizen numbers are advanced by Rhodes 1988 (C 84) 271–7, while Duncan-Jones 1980 (A 30) has argued for considerably higher metic numbers.

aristocratic: in Pericles' funeral oration the Athenian democracy is described as a constitution in which all citizens have the opportunity to display their merits in the service of the state (Thuc. II.37.1), while pseudo-Xenophon's *Athenaion Politeia* represents it as rule by the lower classes in their own interests (1.2–9); Aristotle, trying to define democracy, began by regarding it as a constitution in which power resides not with one or a few but with many, but added that in fact it is the rule of the poor (*Pol.* III, 1279a22–1280a6). In appointment to office, the Athenian democracy retained some bias in favour of the rich: the poorest citizens were officially ineligible, and despite the provision of stipends the poorest of those who remained will probably have found it less easy than the richer to entrust their private concerns to others and devote their time to the service of the state. The poorest citizens were not excluded from the Assembly, and distance was more likely than poverty to keep men away from its meetings (Marathon is 37 km from Athens by the shortest route, 42 km by the easiest): if the Assembly had divided on class lines the poor could regularly have outvoted the rich, but there is no evidence that this occurred. There is some evidence for opposition of rich and poor in the law courts: the stipend paid to jurors will have appealed to those who would otherwise have had difficulty in earning their living, though not to the hard-working; if the state was short of money the stipends could not be paid and the courts would not sit;[78] and when a rich man was on trial the argument might be used that continuing payment of the stipends depended on a vote of condemnation.[79]

We do not know when the property tax called *eisphora*, first mentioned in 434/3 (*IG* I³ 52 = M–L 58 B15–19), was introduced or first collected; most other taxes were indirect taxes, so that the amount which a man paid depended on his consumption rather than his wealth. The rich were called on to make further contributions to the state through the system of liturgies, acting as *choregoi* to train and finance a chorus in a festival or as trierarchs to command and finance a trireme in the navy. This system involved the payer in the life of the community, as the collection and expenditure of taxes by government agents does not; it also provided the rich payers with opportunities for competition and display, and we see from law-court speeches that men took pride in performing more liturgies, more expensively, than was actually required of them, and expected these services to be remembered to their credit when they were under attack.[80]

Any community needs leaders, though in Athens, where the compo-

---

[78] Dem. XXXIX.17, cf. XXIV.99, XLV.4.

[79] Ar. *Knights* 1357–61, cf. *Wasps* 300–6, Lys. XIX.11, XXVII.1, XXX.22, Hyp. IV.32–7.

[80] E.g. Lys. XIX.29, 42–3, XXI.1–5, 11–12, XXV.12–13; Dem. XIX.282. Aristotle, *Pol.* V, 1309a17–20, VI, 1320b3–4, expresses disapproval of ostentatious but useless liturgies.

sition of the Assembly changed from meeting to meeting and that of the Council changed from year to year, it was harder for even the most popular leader to pursue a coherent policy than in a modern parliamentary system. Thucydides writes that Periclean Athens was 'in name democracy but in fact rule by the first man' (II.65.9); Plutarch, oversimplifying, writes that 'for forty years Pericles was a leader together with men like Ephialtes, Leocrates, Myronides, Cimon, Tolmides and Thucydides, but after the defeat and ostracism of Thucydides [c. 443][81] he acquired for not less than fifteen years a continuous and single rule and predominance in his yearly generalships' (Per. 16.3). By the middle of the fifth century the decline of the archonships to routine offices, concerned largely with festivals and the machinery of justice, was complete; owing partly, no doubt, to the achievements of Cimon as general in command of the forces of Athens and the Delian League, the generals had become not only the commanders of the army and navy but also the political leaders of Athens. Whereas nearly all civilian officials were appointed by lot, and could not be reappointed, to posts which were thought to require loyalty rather than ability, it was recognized that generals and other military officials did require ability, and so these were appointed by election and could be reappointed as often as the *demos* chose to re-elect them (cf. *Ath. Pol.* 43.1, 61.1). Thus in the Periclean period the people elected their leaders: appointment as general was at the same time an acknowledgement of a man's predominance and a means of exercising and maintaining that predominance.

Constitutionally the generals were executive officers, given particular tasks by the people, inevitably allowed some discretion in the field but ultimately answerable to the people for the performance of those tasks. When they combined with the Council and other officials to swear to a treaty or to protect an honorand, this was a recognition of their importance in the state. Evidence that they had a privileged constitutional position and could require an Assembly to be called or not is limited to the period of the Peloponnesian War, but the Assembly would inevitably pay more attention to a proposal from a general or from the board of generals than to one from a private citizen or a group of private citizens:[82] the age of the politician as *rhetor* (speaker), a man who regularly spoke in the Assembly but did not regularly hold office, was still in the future.[83]

Like most Athenian boards, the generals were ten in number. Originally they had been elected, by the Assembly, one from each tribe (*Ath. Pol.* 22.2), and if Plutarch may be trusted that was still true of the generals of 469/8 (*Cim.* 8.8); by the time of *Ath. Pol.* they were elected irrespective of tribe (61.1), and our incomplete knowledge of the fourth-

---

[81] Cf. p. 141.   [82] Rhodes 1972 (D 75) 43–6.   [83] Cf. pp. 404–5, 417.

century generals suggests that this was not yet true of the generals of 357/6.[84] A fragment of Androtion (*FGrH* 324 F 38), purporting to list the ten generals of 441/0, seems to list eleven and certainly includes both Pericles and one other member of his tribe, and in some later years Pericles again had a colleague in his own tribe. Two of the generals of 357/6 were from the same tribe: almost all scholars have been convinced that in the second half of the fifth century and the first half of the fourth there was a method of appointment intermediate between the two mentioned by *Ath. Pol.*, retaining the basic principle of one general from each tribe but allowing at any rate one exception and possibly more than one.[85] How and why these exceptions were provided for has been endlessly discussed; the most helpful approach is one which starts by asking how elections in the Assembly are likely to have been conducted.[86] The Assembly voted in elections as in most other matters by show of hands, and probably a precise count of votes was not made (p. 79): if there were several candidates for the first tribe's generalship, the presiding officers (probably) would not count the votes in favour of each but would take each candidate in turn and invite votes for and votes against him; the first candidate who had a majority of votes in his favour would be declared elected. If the voters knew before they started voting who all the candidates in the tribe were, and understood that it would prejudice the chances of the candidate whom they preferred to give a favourable vote to any other candidate, it ought never to have been the case that, for instance, the second candidate was elected by a small majority but continuing the voting would have yielded a larger majority for the third. On the other hand, it might well happen that in one tribe none of the candidates secured a favourable majority: in that case, before the modification was introduced, a second vote would have been taken on the candidates in that tribe; afterwards, when the first vote had been completed, places left unfilled would be offered in the second vote to all surviving candidates irrespective of tribe. The appearance of two generals from one tribe will thus be a sign that in the first vote none of the candidates in one other tribe secured a majority. Certainly the ten

[84] In 357/6 eight of the generals were from seven different tribes (*IG* ii² 124 = Tod, *GHI* 153.20–4): it is possible that Chares should not be restored as the second name (Chabrias may have been accidentally inscribed twice and therefore deleted once), but Chares was a general in 357/6 even if he was not included in that list; see Develin 1989 (D 20) 275–6; it used to be held that in 323/2 four of the six generals whom we know were from the same tribe (Sundwall 1906 (L 130) 23–4), and if that were true it would support *Ath. Pol.* 61.1, but later prosopographical work has reduced them to two (Develin 1989 (D 20) 408; I count his 'nauarchos' as a general).

[85] *Contra* Fornara 1971 (D 29), especially 19–27, arguing that the tribal basis of appointments was wholly abandoned in the late 460s; but if that were so we should expect to find more exceptions than are reliably attested, and Hansen 1988 (D 35) points out that a (modified) tribal basis for 360 is confirmed by *P. Oxy.* 1804, fr. IV. 4–6.

[86] Piérart 1974 (D 67), cf. Rhodes 1981 (C 83) 129–32, Hansen 1983 (D 34) 119–21. References to other discussions may be found in Fornara 1971 (D 29).

generals remained constitutionally equal, and it is wrong to suppose that one of the ten was elected in a special way to a position of special authority.[87]

Pericles, though a leader of the democrats, was both rich and aristocratic. It was easier for the rich than for the poor to devote their time to political activity, and nearly all politicians were rich men. Of those mentioned with Pericles in Plut. *Per.* 16.3 (p. 85), Cimon and his relative Thucydides were aristocratic; we do not know the families of the others. Our sources suggest that Cleon, in the generation after Pericles, was the first of a new kind of politician, vulgar both in origin and in manner (e.g. *Ath. Pol.* 28.1–3), while after Pericles' death few men from the old aristocracy were active in politics.[88] It should not surprise us that the first leaders of the democracy were from families with a long tradition of political activity, but the democracy encouraged men from other families to try to rise to prominence, and as they succeeded the democracy in these new hands came to have less attraction for the aristocrats.

IV. THE IMPACT OF ATHENIAN DEMOCRACY

Athens, as we have seen, was the paradigm of a democratic state; Pericles is represented as saying in his funeral oration, 'We ourselves are an example, rather than imitators of others' (Thuc. 11.37.1). All adult males of Athenian descent were citizens, entitled to attend, speak and vote at the Assembly, which was the sovereign decision-making body. All citizens over thirty were entitled to sit on the juries, which expressed the will of the people in the more important lawsuits. All citizens over thirty except those in the lowest of the four property classes were entitled to sit in the Council and to hold most of the offices of state, and the offices were so numerous that unless most of these citizens had been willing to exercise their rights the mechanism of government would have ground to a halt. Payment for the performance of a citizen's civilian duties, to some extent made possible by the revenue which Athens derived directly from her empire, and by the prosperity which she enjoyed as head of that empire, enabled even the poorer citizens to devote time to public affairs.

The final achievement of this democracy was the deliberate work of Ephialtes and his associates. Only 160 years before Ephialtes' reform, Athens was still without written laws; the *basileus* was no longer a king but one of a college of nine annual archons; a single state had come to control the whole of Attica; but in other respects there had been little development from the primitive Athens of the dark age. The state was

---

[87] This was demonstrated by Dover 1960 (D 21) (*contra* Beloch 1884 (D 5) 274–88).
[88] Cf. pp. 404–5.

governed by the Eupatrid aristocracy, whose members provided the
archons and other officials, whose memories preserved the laws and
traditions of Athens; probably all native Athenian adult males were
citizens, and could attend the Assembly, but the Assembly met rarely and
transacted little business, and without the courage of a Thersites (Hom.
Il. II.211–77) the ordinary citizen would not venture to speak. Many of
the citizens, indeed, were less than free men: as *hektemoroi* they had to
surrender to an overlord one-sixth of the produce of their land, and they
were no doubt expected to be subservient to him in other ways too. In
other cities, farther south, there had recently been revolutions in which
aristocracies had been overthrown and tyrannies had been established;
but when Cylon had tried to make himself tyrant in Athens the attempt
had failed.[89]

Draco's production of a written code of laws, in 621/0, marked the
first step from the primitive aristocracy towards the classical democracy:
knowledge of the laws no longer depended on the memory of the ruling
families but was accessible to all; procedures for remedying wrongs were
publicly defined.[90] Several further steps were taken by Solon, in 594/3:
his three most democratic measures, according to *Ath. Pol.* 9.1, were (the
liberation of the *hektemoroi* and) the ban on enslavement for debt,
abolishing the distinction within the citizen body between overlords and
underlings; the provision for whoever wished (*ho boulomenos*) to prosecute in 'public' lawsuits, offering a chance of justice to those who were
unable or afraid to prosecute on their own account; and the institution of
the *heliaia*, the judicial session of the Assembly to which litigants might
appeal if they were dissatisfied with a magistrate's verdict. Other
measures deserve emphasis also: the use of wealth as the sole qualification for office, so that the old, closed aristocracy would in time be
replaced by a new, open class of office-holders; the institution of a new
Council, immediately independent of the old aristocracy, to prepare
business for the Assembly, and (we may guess) coupled with this a
guarantee of regular meetings for the Assembly. This was not yet
democracy, and it was not intended to be democracy – 'I gave the *demos*
as much honour as is fitting for it'; 'In this way will the *demos* best follow
its leaders, if it is neither unleashed too far nor constrained' (Solon, frs.
5–6 West *ap. Ath. Pol.* 12.1–2) – but Solon did attack some of the
inequalities of the primitive state, and try to establish a regime in which
each Athenian had his proper part to play.[91]

Nevertheless, *stasis* persisted; Pisistratus tried to make himself tyrant,
and on the third occasion, in 546, he was successful. Solon's institutions
were retained, but the tyranny had a levelling effect, since rich aristocrats
and poor commoners were alike subject to the rulers of the state, and a

[89] Cf. *CAH* III².3, 368–9.   [90] *CAH* III².3, 370–1.   [91] *CAH* III².3, 375–91.

centralizing effect, increasing the importance of Athens, where the rulers lived, at the expense of the townships of Attica. As in other cities, in due course the citizens became more conscious of their present subjection than of the old grievances which had enabled the first tyrant to seize power, and in 511/10 the Pisistratids were driven out.[92] At first the old aristocratic rivalry was renewed, but Cleisthenes, 'having previously spurned the *demos*, then attached it entirely to his own side' (Hdt. v.69.2), and by so doing he not only got the better of Isagoras but obtained enough support to defeat the Spartans when they invaded on Isagoras' behalf. The essence of his reform was a reorganization of the citizen body in ten new tribes, thirty trittyes and 139 demes; on this new structure the whole mechanism of the classical democracy was to be built, and the effect of the reform was to lessen the importance of the old organizations through which the aristocrats had remained influential, and to provide an apparatus for constitutional government at local level as well as at polis level. 'When this was done, the *politeia* became far more democratic than that of Solon' (*Ath. Pol.* 22.1); whether that was Cleisthenes' intention is another question, which need not be argued again here.[93]

Among other things based on the ten new tribes was the organization of the army; from 501/0 Athens had ten generals, appointed annually by election and capable of being re-elected. The nine archons were at that time elected (but perhaps given their particular posts within the college by lot), but in 487/6 Solon's method of sortition from an elected short list was revived; the elected offices based on the new organization came to be more important than the old offices appointed by lot.[94] Cleisthenes' apparatus of government required a considerable amount of participation by the citizens, and as they worked the machinery the *demos* 'grew in confidence' (*Ath. Pol.* 22.3, cf. 24.1). After the Persian Wars the forward-looking Themistocles was worsted by Cimon, who built up Athens' power in the Aegean but whose attitudes and style in domestic politics were those of a conservative aristocrat; the Areopagus, thanks to the decline of the archonship no longer a council of the most important men in Athens, gave verdicts in Cimon's favour; and so Ephialtes was prompted to challenge the prominence of the Areopagus in the state, and to usher in the classical democracy. For the author of the *Athenaion Politeia* the development was still far from complete: further moves are attributed to Pericles (26–7);[95] things became much worse with the rise of more vulgar leaders after Pericles' death (28);[96] at the end of the fifth century there were two oligarchic interruptions but the democracy was restored (29–40),[97] 'since when it has continued to the present day,

[92] Cf. *CAH* IV² 301–2.   [93] Cf. *CAH* IV² 321–4.   [94] Cf. *CAH* IV² 333.

[95] But on the alleged reform of the Areopagus by Pericles see above, p. 70.

[96] Cf. below, p. 404.   [97] Cf. below, p. 484, and *CAH* VI² ch. 2.

always adding to the power of the masses' (41.2). There were changes during the century after Pericles' death, some of them affecting the character of the democracy,[98] but in comparison with the earlier constitutional changes they were minor adjustments, and we may regard the *politeia* of the Periclean period as the classical form of the Athenian democracy. Both in Aristotle's *Politics* (II, 1273b35–1274a21) and in *Ath. Pol.* (9.2) it is insisted that Solon should not be supposed to have intended all that was later built on his foundations; but nevertheless we can see how the various changes briefly chronicled above contributed to the finished product.

Why should it have been in Athens that this democracy made its appearance? Thanks to the early synoecism of Attica, Athens was much larger than most Greek *poleis*, but it was not in other respects atypical. Though it had taken the lead at the end of the dark age, it was overtaken during the Archaic period by the cities of the Isthmus and the Peloponnese. The political changes which we have noticed in Athens are paralleled in other cities. Written texts of laws were published elsewhere (the oldest surviving law, from Dreros, in Crete, is of the second half of the seventh century: M–L 2). Other cities experienced a transition from aristocracy through tyranny to a more broadly based constitution (notably Corinth, where, as in Athens, there was a reorganization of the citizen body after the fall of the tyranny: Nic. Dam., *FGrH* 90 F 60.2; Phot., Suda, πάντα ὀκτώ). Other cities had guaranteed meetings for the citizen Assembly (e.g. Sparta, in the Great Rhetra). At the end of the sixth century Athens was not strikingly different from other cities, but in the first half of the fifth she developed as the others apparently did not.

The beginnings of the difference are to be sought in Cleisthenes' organization and its consequences. Perhaps because of the sheer size of the Athenian state, much greater than would have been approved by fourth-century philosophers,[99] Cleisthenes' new tribes and demes, if not his trittyes, came to be accepted as authentic political units to an extent which no one could have predicted; involvement in political activity at the local level, which required comparatively little courage and effort, gave the citizens the taste for political activity on a higher level.[100] Further contributions were made by the Persian Wars. *Ath. Pol.* (22.3) links the first use of ostracism with the confidence of the *demos* after Marathon, and their achievement in repelling a Persian invasion almost

---

[98] On the democracy of the fourth century, which did not in fact grow ever more extreme, see Rhodes 1979/80 (D 78). Koerner 1974 (D 42) stresses even more than I would Athens' departures from 'democracy' in the fourth century.
[99] E.g. Pl. *Rep.* IV, 422e–423c, *Leg.* V, 737c–e, Arist. *Eth. Nic.* IX, 1170b30–2, *Pol.* VII, 1326a5–b25.   [100] Cf. above, p. 73.

unaided must have considerably enhanced the confidence of the Athenian hoplites.[101] When Xerxes passed through Thermopylae the Athenians evacuated Attica, an experience which will have added to their solidarity if not to their confidence. By the time of Xerxes' invasion Athens had a fleet of two hundred triremes, requiring a total crew of about 40,000 (Chalcis, with its Athenian cleruchs, manned twenty, and the Plataeans supplied some men for the fleet at Artemisium but not at Salamis, but most of the sailors must have been Athenian citizens). Athens' contribution amounted to more than half of the whole Greek fleet; the next largest was the Corinthian contingent of forty ships; the Aeginetans contributed thirty ships from a fleet which, if we emend 46.1 to save Herodotus' arithmetic, comprised forty-two in all (Hdt. VIII.1–2, 14.1, 43–8).[102] Salamis was as great an achievement for the Athenian *thetes* as Marathon had been for the hoplites; and after the invaders had been defeated the Athenians won further successes in the campaigns of the Delian League. If earlier in various cities there had been a 'hoplite revolution', Athens was now ripe for a *'thetes'* revolution', and the importance of the *nautikos ochlos* (mass of sailors) was used to explain the Athenian democracy by pseudo-Xenophon (*Ath. Pol.* 1.2) and others (e.g. [Arist.] *Ath. Pol.* 27.1).

Ephialtes' reform was not in fact a *'thetes'* revolution' (see p. 69): probably there was no conscious opposition between hoplites and *thetes* on this issue, but ordinary Athenians of both classes could respond to proposals that the government of the state should be placed effectively in the hands of the *demos*. The proposals came from above: Athens before the reform had as broadly based a government as any other Greek city, and we may doubt whether there was a spontaneous demand for more power from the ordinary citizens; the democratic leaders of the first generation were aristocrats, and it was only in the following generation that new men rose to political prominence (cf. p. 87). The opponents of Cimon may have been provoked by verdicts of the Areopagus in his favour, but the *Supplices* of Aeschylus shows that the constitutional principle of the power due to the *demos* had begun to be discussed. When invited to take control of its own affairs, the *demos* accepted the invitation.

Hitherto, the basic distinction in Greece had been between constitutional governments and tyrannies; when Herodotus writes (VI.43.3) that in 492 Mardonius deposed all the tyrants in Ionia and established 'democracies' in the cities, he probably does not mean that the new constitutions were of a kind which would have been considered

---

[101] Cf. Hdt. v.78 on the moral effect of the *isegoria* (freedom of speech) which followed the ending of the tyranny.   [102] See Burn 1962 (A 11) 441–2.

democratic in the second half of the fifth century. The earliest sign of a different analysis is in Pindar, *Pyth.* 11.86–8 (written perhaps in 468[103]), which distinguishes the rule of a tyrant, of 'the turbulent army' and of the wise (plural). In the debate which Herodotus (III.80–4) insistently but implausibly sets in sixth-century Persia, the rival claims of democracy (the word *demokratia* is not used here, but the cognate verb is used in VI.43.3 with reference to the debate), oligarchy and monarchy are advanced; and from the second half of the fifth century onwards the merits of government by the many, by the few and by a single ruler were endlessly discussed. Although the threefold division became a standard part of the Greek conceptual framework, there was of course a continuous progression from the absolute rule of a small clique to a comparatively egalitarian democracy, and not all Greeks would draw the line between oligarchy and democracy in the same place. Pericles in his praise of democracy in the funeral oration credits Athens with more complete equality (of opportunity, not of achievement) than she in fact possessed (Thuc. II.37.1); Athenagoras championing democracy in Syracuse speaks of a regime more like that envisaged by Solon, in which it is the function of the wise to give counsel and of the many to listen and judge (Thuc. VI.39), whereas Socrates claims that in Athens, on political as opposed to technical matters, any citizen is considered equally capable of giving good advice (Pl. *Prt.* 319b–d). When Aristotle attempts to list kinds of oligarchy and democracy there is no perceptible difference between his most moderate oligarchy and his most moderate democracy, and he adds that an oligarchic constitution can be administered in a democratic spirit and a democratic in an oligarchic spirit (*Pol.* IV, 1292a39–1293a34); his most extreme democracy is the kind in which the state's revenues allow it to make payments for public service and the poor are enabled to exercise the rights which the constitution gives them (1292b41–1293a10).

By this criterion of Aristotle the democracy of Periclean Athens, although it retained a property qualification for office, was an extreme democracy. We are rarely able to give a detailed account of the government of other cities, whether they styled themselves democratic or oligarchic, but the following may be identified as matters in which an oligarchic state might differ from democratic Athens. All native Athenian free adult males had a minimum of political rights, as members of the Assembly and potential members of juries – whereas in the oligarchies of 411–410 and 404–403 the poorest citizens had no rights; in federal Boeotia and in the separate cities of Boeotia there was a property qualification for membership of the 'four councils' which wielded the

---

[103] E.g. Bowra 1964 (J 9) 410. Others have argued for a date in the 470s; see especially von der Mühll 1958 (J 79) (setting out the problems and arguing for 475), Lloyd-Jones 1973 (J 71) 117–27 (tentatively accepting Bowra's date).

sovereign power (*Hell. Oxy.* 16.2); in Sparta only the *homoioi* ('equals') were members of the Assembly.[104] Though the Council and the magistracies were not open to all members of the Assembly, it was the Assembly which exercised the sovereign power in democratic Athens, and all members could take an active part in its proceedings – while the extreme oligarchy of summer 411 was based theoretically on a Council of four hundred and a hoplite Assembly, but under this regime the Assembly never met; in Sparta the most important issues, at any rate in foreign policy, were referred to the Assembly, but the members' freedom of debate was limited, and much of the government of the state proceeded without reference to the Assembly. In Athens the large number of offices, appointment to civilian offices by lot and the ban on reappointment, and the provision of stipends for office-holders, ensured that the constitution was 'administered in a democratic spirit', that offices were not only theoretically open to but were actually held by a high proportion of the members of the Assembly – whereas in Sparta ephors were elected for one year from the whole Assembly and could not be re-elected, but members of the *gerousia* (council of elders) were appointed for life from a privileged group of families.[105] In the larger and more complex states of the modern world the use of representative institutions and of permanent civil servants means that a far lower proportion of the citizen body is directly involved in government than in Periclean Athens; but in modern forms of democracy a far higher proportion of the total population comprises enfranchised citizens, entitled to participate both as voters and as candidates in the election of representatives, as well as to seek employment as civil servants.

Athens and Sparta came to be regarded as the leading exponents of democracy and oligarchy respectively. When she had the opportunity to interfere, Athens imposed democratic constitutions on member states of the Delian League, while Sparta encouraged oligarchies in the Peloponnesian League (see p. 74); this polarization was fostered by the clash between Sparta and Athens in the Peloponnesian War (Thuc. III.82.1). How closely other Greek democracies imitated the Athenian model it is hard to say.[106] Probably in most states which regarded themselves as

[104] On the kind of sub-citizen status which included no political rights, see Mossé 1979 (A 92), Lotze 1981 (L 96) 177–8.   [105] On the government of Sparta see *CAH* III².1, 740–4.

[106] For Cleisthenic tribes and Athenian-style preambles to decrees in fifth-century Miletus see *SGDI* 5496 = Sokolowski *LSAM* 45, Herrmann 1970 (E 34) (publishing another inscription), Gehrke 1980 (E 31). For a year divided into prytanies and Athenian-style preambles in fifth-century Lindos see *SIG* 110 n. 4 = *DGE* 78 = Blinkenberg 1941 (C 117) 212–14 (appendix to no. 16), *SEG* IV.171, Accame 1938 (C 112). See in general Lewis 1984 (A 77) 56–8. Ostracism, instituted in Athens by Cleisthenes (*CAH* IV² 334–8), is found also in Argos, Megara and Miletus (Arist. *Pol.* v, 1302b18–19, Schol. Ar. *Knights* 855: no date), and in Syracuse (Diod. XI.86.5–87: *petalismos* used for a short time in the 450s, in imitation of Athens). Recently one *ostracon* which may have been used in an ostracism has been found in Argos (*BCH* 110 (1986) 764–5 no. 3) and one in Megara (*HOPOΣ* 5 (1987) 59–73). That there was ostracism in Ephesus, alleged in many works of reference, depends on an unwarranted inference from Heraclitus 22 B 121 D–K, by Guhl 1843 (F 28) 71 with n. 2.

democratic the Assembly was open to all citizens, without a property qualification, and was the effective sovereign body.[107] How far these constitutions were 'administered in a democratic spirit' is more doubtful. Appointment by lot, and restrictions or a total ban on reappointment, were appropriate for maintaining equality not only within a citizen body but also within a ruling class; but no doubt they were widely used in democratic states. The claim has been made, and rebutted, that 'Pay for public office is not attested for any Greek (or Roman) city other than Athens . . . Lacking imperial resources, no other city imitated the Athenian pattern.'[108] Certainly pay for office was introduced in Athens in the time of the Delian League, and the connexion between the League and Athens' ability to provide pay was seen by ancient writers (e.g. *Ath. Pol.* 24); but Athens continued these payments in the fourth century, though the League was no more and in the first half of the century she was far from affluent;[109] Aristotle in *Politics* does not write as if pay was peculiar to Athens, there is evidence for pay in the Boeotian federation and Rhodes, and, given the concentration of our literary evidence on Athens, the absence of specific evidence for pay in other democracies may not be significant. Other cities were much smaller than Athens: they will not have had the large number of potential office-holders which Athens had (in fifth-century Erythrae men were allowed to serve in the Council of a hundred and twenty one year in four: M–L 40 = *IG* I³ 14, 12), and could not have afforded the large number of stipends which Athens paid; but no doubt they made do with fewer offices, and with single officials or smaller boards where Athens used boards of ten, and it is not incredible that some of the other democracies should have provided appropriately modest schemes of pay for office and so should have involved some of the less wealthy citizens in the running of the state.

Even so, the provision of pay may well have been more of a strain for some of the other states that attempted it than it was for Athens. In Athens the rich were expected to make substantial contributions to the expenses of the state, through the payment of taxes and the performance of liturgies, and jurors were sometimes told that if their stipend was to be paid they must condemn a rich man accused before them (see p. 84), but after the sixth century we hear no more of demands for the cancellation of debts and the redistribution of property. In many other places, life was

[107] But if *DGE* 701 = Hill *Sources*² в 116 = *IEK* 2 belongs to the democracy imposed on Erythrae by Athens (cf. below), it is striking that a property qualification was fixed for jury service (see p. 57 n. 78).

[108] Finley 1973 (L 39) 173, cf. Finley 1960 (A 38) 48; *contra* de Ste Croix 1975 (A 108).

[109] Assembly pay was added in or after 403 (*Ath. Pol.* 41.3). Hansen 1979 (D 32) argues that fewer offices were salaried in the fourth century than in the fifth. The argument depends largely on silence, and I am doubtful, but see Lewis 1982 (D 53).

less stable. All too often, the establishment of a democratic regime was accompanied by the exile of the rich oligarchs and the confiscation of their property, and from the middle of the fourth century demands for social revolution became increasingly frequent.[110] Part of the reason for Athens' freedom from such troubles may be that, even in the fourth century, she was able to make the payments which the *demos* wanted without having to confiscate the property of the rich.

Constitutional government was an achievement of which the Greeks were justly proud. Herodotus (VII.104.4) represents the exiled king Demaratus as saying to Xerxes that the Spartans 'are free men, but not utterly free: for they have the law as a master, and they fear that much more than your subjects fear you'. If barbarians submitted to autocratic monarchies which the Greeks would not have tolerated, that showed that they were inferior creatures.[111] The Athenians, like other Greeks, denied both personal and political freedom to slaves, and denied political freedom to immigrants, as men who lived within their state but did not belong to it, and to women; but subject to these limitations they did come to see political freedom as the right of all, not only of the rich or well born. The influence of that discovery has not been limited to Classical Greece.

[110] See Asheri 1966 (L 2) 60–119; Fuks 1966 (L 49); Harding 1974 (C 43) 285–6. Aristotle, *Pol.* V, 1305a3–7 mentions the imposition of burdensome liturgies as a practice which might provoke the rich to combine against a democracy.

[111] Cf. Hippoc. *Aër.* 16, Arist. *Pol.* III, 1285a16–19, VII, 1327b18–23.

CHAPTER 5

MAINLAND GREECE, 479–451 B.C.

D. M. LEWIS

I. FROM 479 TO 461

There is no reason to doubt that the Hellenic alliance had taken some form of oath to punish medizing states, though the versions least affected by later propaganda contain an escape clause which would allow interpretation (Hdt. VII.132 'those who had not been forced', paraphrased as 'voluntarily' by Diod. XI.3.3). But while Leotychidas and the Peloponnesians on the other side of the Aegean were still contemplating a wholesale expulsion of the medizers of northern Greece (Hdt. IX.106.3[1]), Pausanias, in the aftermath of Plataea, was already faced with interpreting the programme in the light of realism and military necessity. A few miles from the battlefield, Thebes still held out. After ten days he turned his force on the city, but its walls provided a substantial obstacle and he may not have wished to proceed by a prolonged siege (it will have been at least well into September). The medizing party is said to have lost 300 men of its 'first and best' in the battle, a substantial number for a narrow oligarchy. A settlement was reached by which the city, no doubt already throwing the blame on a small group (Thuc. III.62.3–4; contrast Hdt. IX.87.2), and with earlier services to the Greek cause to claim (Hdt. VII.202, 222; Plut. *De mal. Hdt.* 864–7), simply handed over the principal medizers, who were later executed (Hdt. IX.86–8). It seems likely that it was at this point that Thebes and other Boeotian cities became or reverted to being the hoplite democracies which seem to have been the norm later in the century.[2] Very little else can be asserted about Boeotia in the next twenty years. The numismatic evidence may suggest that Thebes lost her superiority and that Tanagra may from time to time have tried to claim some form of ascendancy.[3] Of the two Boeotian states with an unblemished record, Plataea, still an Athenian ally, acquired a recognized position as a shrine of Greek freedom, but we hear little about Thespiae, except that she seems to have tried to expand her

---

[1] *emporia* is puzzling here; perhaps it was thought that the Ionians would be happier in coastal cities. [2] See p. 133.

[3] Kraay 1976 (C 190) 110; Fowler 1957 (C 184).

population (Hdt. VIII.75.1); links with Athens are also possible here (cf. p. 116 n. 74).

The advantages of a city wall will thus have been well in mind when, in the autumn, friction first appeared among the victors. Athens had had some kind of wall-circuit at least since the first half of the sixth century,[4] although it had played no visible part in strategic thinking up till now; Mardonius had removed virtually all there was on his final withdrawal (Hdt. IX.13.2; Thuc. 1.89.3). Its rebuilding and improvement was thus an urgent matter for a state which was henceforth likely to use much of its military manpower by sea, and Themistocles' view that it should be put in hand immediately was supported even by Aristides, so far more associated with hoplites than with the fleet. The operation, however, prompted disquiet among those of Sparta's allies who could already see that the rise of the Athenian fleet had changed the balance of power in Greece; only the Aeginetans are named as raising objections (Plut. *Them.* 19.2), but the Corinthians may have felt the same (cf. Thuc. 1.69.1). Sparta was persuaded to press Athens to stop building her walls, on the excuse that it might create a base for a future Persian invasion, but, by means which rapidly passed into legend (Thuc. 1.89–93, with a host of later variations), Athens carried her point and built the walls. On this, as on so much about the rise of Athenian power in the fifth century, opinions differed as to how hostile Sparta had been to Athenian moves. We may suspect that there were differences of opinion in Sparta as well.

Spartans had commanded at the two great victories of 479, Plataea and Mycale. These victories pointed forward to the two main directions in which they could be followed up, the punishment of the medizers of northern Greece and the liberation of the eastern Greeks. The commanders now changed roles. Pausanias, who had already discovered that the punishment of medizers was not straightforward, was given the fleet in 478, and his later actions prove that he himself saw his and Sparta's future field of action beyond the Aegean; his activities in 478 are discussed elsewhere (p. 35). Leotychidas, whom we have already seen associated with projects for northern Greece, moved to the mainland.

The logical date for his Thessalian expedition is 478, and this gets some slight confirmation from a dubious story that Themistocles proposed to burn the Greek fleet while it was wintering at Pagasae after the retreat of Xerxes (Plut. *Them.* 20.1–2), but reasons have been found to suspect that the sequence of events does not end until 476, and another school of thought defers it to 469.[5] Herodotus' account (VI.72) is that Leotychidas could have subdued the whole of Thessaly, but was bribed to desist. After he was discovered in the act with a sleeve full of silver, he was brought before a Spartan court, his house was demolished (cf. Thuc.

---

[4] Vanderpool 1974 (I 172).   [5] See Chronological Notes, p. 499.

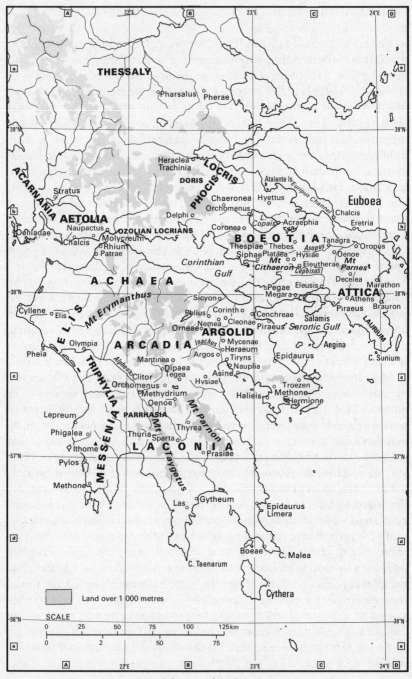

2 Central Greece and the Peloponnese

v.63.2–4), and he died in exile in Tegea. Pausanias (III.7.9), in the second century A.D., says he won several battles and that the bribery was by the Aleuadae of Larissa, already known to us as the principal medizers; Plutarch (De mal. Hdt. 859c) names two tyrants actually deposed by Leotychidas, Aristomedes and, probably, Agelaos.[6] Neither name is known for this period; it has been guessed that Aristomedes is of Pherae and, with greater plausibility, that Agelaos belonged to the principal family of Pharsalus (Michel 1281, cf. Tod, GHI 147.34). The Aleuadae certainly survived, though with diminished influence. Our evidence for what happened next is almost entirely numismatic.[7] Before this time, the dominant coinage had been that of Larissa, on the Persian standard. We now have two quasi-federal groupings, both using the Aeginetan standard, one claiming, for the first time, the name of Thessaly. There is some movement of states between them, and Pharsalus stands alone. That she, at any rate, started to look towards Athens is suggested, e.g. by the activity of her citizen Menon in support of Cimon at Eïon in 476 (Dem. XXIII.199).

Obviously, we are not in a position to distinguish between what Leotychidas found it difficult to do and what he was bribed not to do, and we can hardly speculate about the nature of the opposition to him at home. Since the uncontradicted story in Herodotus' day was that he owed the throne to a false oracle, his position can never have been strong.

Even less can be said with certainty about relations with Delphi and its Amphictyony. Of the process by which Delphi's defeatist attitude and dubious actual record[8] in the Persian invasion was pushed into the background we hear nothing, and can only guess that some individuals may have lost power there. Delphi remained a major Greek shrine and received one of the three main Greek war-memorials (Hdt. IX.81.1; M–L 27), as well as dedications from individual states (Hdt. VIII.122[9]). Another late story (Plut. Them. 20.3–4) describes an argument between the Spartans, who wanted to expel medizing states from the Amphictyonic Council, and Themistocles who argued that this would leave too few states in control of it. Since we can, on the basis of later representation, calculate that about two-thirds of the twenty-four Amphictyonic votes were held by medizers, the question will certainly have been raised, but presumably it was decided that it would be sufficient if the actual representatives were more respectable. Fairly shortly after the war we

---

[6] This is now seen to be hardly an emendation for the Agellos of the better MS.

[7] Herrmann 1922, 1924–5 (C 186–187); Franke 1970 (F 26); Kraay 1976 (C 190) 115–16. Martin 1985 (C 194) 36–8 shows the dangers of drawing political conclusions. For a survey of the non-numismatic evidence see Larsen 1960 (F 43).

[8] See CAH IV² 540–2, 564–5. That Delphi's 'medism' has been exaggerated is argued by Parker 1985 (K 73) 317–18.   [9] Gauer 1968 (I 68) passim.

find the Amphictyones honouring the glorious dead and taking action against the wicked (Hdt. VII.213, 228–4; ?Paus. X.19.1).[10]

If we take the early date for Leotychidas' Thessalian expedition, there is no reason to place any Spartan activity north of the Isthmus after 476. On the other front, similarly, Spartan official activity ceases after the allies' refusal to accept Dorcis in succession to Pausanias in late 478 or early 477 (see p. 35). Here, however, there is evidence that opinions were divided. Pausanias, in a private capacity, retained a strong interest in overseas ventures. How widely in Sparta his opinion was shared is uncertain. Thucydides' account of his end shows some Spartans personally sympathetic to him (1.134.1), but the main evidence for Spartan resentment at the loss of hegemony to Athens lies in a story dated by Diodorus (XI.50) to 475/4, but probably attached by Ephorus to his account of Aristides' organization of the Delian League. According to this, there was a serious possibility that Sparta would contest the naval hegemony with Athens and the move to war was surprisingly averted by the skill of one Hetoemaridas, a member of the *gerousia*. The consultative procedure described has always interested constitutional historians because of its similarity to a sequence of events in the third century,[11] but it seems likely that the story was invented or expanded at a later date when it became fashionable to project the theme of Spartan hostility to Athens backwards. Thucydides seems to have no knowledge of it, and is firm that the Spartans were happy to let the Athenians continue the naval war (1.95.7).

The operations of Pausanias raise further chronological problems. It is clear that he stood his trial in Sparta for his conduct in 478 almost immediately. He was acquitted on the major charge of medism (Thuc. 1.95.5, 128.3), though the story of his medism became more and more elaborate (Thuc. 1.128.4–130; a variant in Hdt. v.32). However, Thucydides does not date his later private venture, in which he held Byzantium for some time, was expelled from there by the Athenians, and moved to Colonae in the Troad, remaining there until he was recalled to Sparta by the ephors (Thuc. 1.128.3, 131.1–2). I hold that this sequence roughly covers the rest of the decade, but certainty is impossible.[12]

After his return from Colonae, the ephors, after delays and uncertainties, felt that they had accumulated sufficient evidence to proceed to extreme action against him. To the original charge of medism was now added a charge of plotting with the helots. Thucydides was told enough to enable him to endorse the charge and to accept that Pausanias' activities had been revolutionary. If this is true and to be given a rational

---

[10] It may be that it is in this period that the Spartans expelled the otherwise unknown tyrant Aulis of Phocis (Plut. *De mal. Hdt.* 859d), despite the loyalty of Phocis to the Greek cause, but the episode may belong to the early 440s (Thuc. 1.112.5).

[11] Plut. *Agis* 8–9; Jones 1966 (F 37) 168–70; Forrest 1967 (F 25) 11.

[12] See Chronological Notes, p. 499.

basis, the only plausible line[13] is that Pausanias had come to see that Sparta's manpower did not offer a sufficient base for the concept which he had of Sparta's role, but, even in Thucydides, we are moving so close to romance that it is not rational to distinguish between fact, accusation and embroidered accusation.[14] Pausanias died, having taken refuge in the sanctuary of Athena of the Brazen House and been starved out there (*c.* 466). The Spartan authorities proceeded to use what they thought (or said) that they had discovered to discredit the Athenian Themistocles, now ostracized and living in Argos (see p. 65).

At what point Plistarchus, for whom Pausanias had been the regent, attained his majority is uncertain, but it may not have been all that long before his death in, apparently, 458. Whenever Leotychidas went into exile, he was succeeded by a grandson, Archidamus, who will have taken time to make his mark. It is possible that the importance of the previous royal generation is exaggerated for us by the way Herodotus told his story, but the doubts and troubles about Leotychidas and Pausanias, together with the youth of their successors, will certainly have done much to shift the power-balance at Sparta away from the kingship in the direction of other centres of power in the state.[15]

We must now retrace our steps to discover why Sparta should be particularly sensitive at this time to possible plots with the helots and to Themistocles' presence in Argos. Specifically, we are attempting to find out what lies behind Thucydides' judgement (1.118.2) that one of the factors which inhibited the Spartans from interfering with the growth of Athenian power in the fifth century was that they were in part prevented by wars of their own.

In 494 (or possibly a few years earlier[16]), Cleomenes of Sparta at the battle of Sepea had knocked out Argos as an effective opponent in a hoplite war by a victory which is said to have cost the Argives six thousand men. Thereafter, Argos was forced to reorganize her citizen population by the absorption of persons described by Herodotus as slaves (VI.83), more probably members of perioecic communities (Arist. *Pol.* 1303a6; Plut. *Mor.* 245F[17]), 'until the sons of the slain grew up' and

13 Lotze 1970 (F 47) 270–5.

14 Rhodes 1970 (C 82); Westlake 1977 (C 108).

15 For the weakness of the fifth-century kingship, see, against de Ste Croix 1972 (G 36) 138–49, Lewis 1977 (A 76) 43–8.

16 The double oracle of Hdt. VI.19 and 77 only fixes the year if it was made up after the event, which there is no particular reason to assume. On the battle itself, see *CAH* IV² 364.

17 As argued by Gschnitzer 1958 (A 53) 69–81; Forrest 1960 (F 24) 222–5. Lotze 1971 (F 48), followed by Adshead 1986 (F 1) 37, argues that the new citizens did not come from outlying communities, but had been inferior within Argos itself. As evidence accumulates for the classical Argive constitution (see e.g. *SEG* XXIX 361, showing the Temenidai not in the tribe of their ancestor Hyllus, but in the new tribe Hyrnathioi, for which see Nilsson 1951 (K 67) 73–5), I find it increasingly hard to believe that such a drastic reorganization took place without the admission of substantial new elements to the state. For this, the aftermath of Sepea still seems the most likely date. A slightly different view in Andrewes 1990 (F 4).

expelled the 'slaves' to Tiryns (Hdt. *loc. cit.*). For Herodotus, the sons of the slain had still not grown up in 481 (VII.148). He can hardly be thinking precisely, since Sepea will not have wiped out all male Argives over the age of one, and it remains an open question whether the expulsion of the slaves is earlier or later than 481. That there is a king and a *boule* at Argos then (Hdt. VII.149.2) hardly proves the matter either way. If those expelled to Tiryns were *perioikoi*, no argument can be drawn from the presence of Tirynthians at the battle of Plataea, brigaded with Mycenaeans (Hdt. IX.28.4, 31.3), and consequently in the lists of those who had fought the Persian War at Delphi (M–L 27) and Olympia (Paus. V.23.2).

Despite Sepea, Sparta's position had not remained unchallenged. That there was a Messenian revolt in 490 which delayed the Spartan arrival at Marathon was asserted by Plato (*Laws* 698e) and has been believed by many scholars who have adduced flimsy supporting evidence.[18] Some helot trouble in the early fifth century may be inferred from Thuc. I.128.1, which has had less attention, but, if we believe that 35,000 helots accompanied the Spartans to Plataea in 479 (Hdt. IX.28.2), the Spartans had them well in hand at that time. More seriously, Cleomenes in 490, after his withdrawal from Sparta (*CAH* IV² 366), had caused alarm at home by organizing the Arcadians and persuading them to convert their traditional oath to follow the Spartans wherever they might lead[19] to one to follow him personally. The centre of his activity was in the extreme north of Arcadia at Nonacris, where they swore by the waters of the river Styx, but it was surely more widely extended. The only manifestation of it which we find is that Hegesistratus, an Elean seer escaping from Sparta in the 480s, found Tegea on bad terms with Sparta at this time (Hdt. IX.37.4).[20]

It is easier to use the names of Arcadian states as counters in a historical game than to form any idea of the physical and social realities which underlie the names. Tegea, the first substantial community to come into contact with Sparta (*CAH* III².3, 355) will always have had a focus in the cult of Athena Alea which goes back to Mycenaean times;[21] we have no means of telling when it coalesced, first politically and then geographically,[22] into a single city from the nine demes of which, we are told, it was originally composed (Str. VIII.3.2, p. 337). Mantinea, northwards in the same valley, is less visible in the sixth century, except with Demonax the lawgiver, once described as *basileus* (*P. Oxy.*

[18] Jeffery 1949 (C 135) 26–30 on M–L 22; Wallace 1954 (F 70); Huxley 1962 (F 35) 88; but see den Boer 1956 (B 3); Pearson 1962 (C 77) 421 n. 56.

[19] de Ste Croix 1972 (G 36) 108–10; Peek 1974 (F 57) = *SEG* XXVI 461; Cartledge 1976 (F 13).

[20] See Adshead 1986 (F 1) 30–2. For the coins which have been associated with Cleomenes, see below, p. 105.   [21] Callmer 1943 (F 12) 24–5.

[22] Information about synoecisms is collected by Moggi 1976 (F 53).

1367 = Hermippus fr. 82 11 Wehrli); its synoecism, from five demes (four
in Xen. *Hell.* v.2.8), is said to have been under Argive influence (Str. *loc.
cit.*), and an older site retained the name of Ptolis (the city) until a very
late period (Paus. VIII.8.4). It is normal to attribute this Argive-
influenced synoecism to the 470s, but perhaps one should not rule out
earlier periods of Argive influence in Arcadia, even as early as 600 (Diod.
VII.13.2). Some stimulus to political unity in both cases will have been
given by their appearance in the Homeric Catalogue of Ships (*Il.* 11.607).
In any case, by 480, we find a force at Thermopylae consisting of 1,000
Tegeates and Mantineans (half each), 120 from Orchomenus, and 1,000
from the rest of Arcadia (Hdt. VII.202). At Plataea there were 1,500
Tegeates and 600 Orchomenians (Hdt. IX.28); the Mantineans arrived
late, as we shall see, and there is no mention of a general Arcadian force.
It seems fairly clear which Arcadian communities are approaching or
have reached a polis-organization.[23]

A polis-organization is possible without synoecism (cf. Sparta, Thuc.
1.10.2). The one fixed point in the development of synoecism is provided
by Elis, further west, where the synoecism is dated after the Persian Wars
by Strabo (VIII.3.2, p. 336) and precisely to 471/0 by Diodorus'
chronological source (XI.54.1). Even here there were still no walls in 401
(Xen. *Hell.* III.2.27), though the city spread into suburbs and fine
gymnasia. At both Tegea and Mantinea, the synoecized site was on fairly
open ground, with no acropolis or obvious natural defences; presumably
they both had a wall-circuit from a fairly early date,[24] though the first
Arcadian city wall attested in literature happens to be that of the much
stronger Orchomenus (Thuc. v.61.4–5).[25] It is fashionable to associate
synoecisms with democratic movements;[26] Elis at least has some very
democratic-sounding institutions in the early fifth century (*DGE* 410.8,
412.4 (Hill, *Sources*[2] B124)[27]). But the reasoning for associating democracy and synoecism is unclear, and it seems more likely that the initiative
towards settling in a city and building town houses will have come from
the owners of large estates who wished to keep up with the urbanizing
trend of greater cities. At Mantinea it appears to be the landowners who,
in 385, after the Spartans broke up the synoecism, at first resent the need
to tear down their houses in the city (Xen. *Hell.* v.2.7). Democracy, not
certainly visible at Mantinea before 421 (Thuc. v.29.1), and the 'unplea-

---

[23] For other aspects of the character of Arcadia see Adshead 1986 (F 1) 21–2.

[24] Mantinea had a wall in 385, and Scranton 1941 (I 149) 57–9 argues that some of the surviving
polygonal masonry is earlier than that, though it may have been preceded by a wall only of mud-
brick (cf. Paus. VIII.8.7–8 for mud-brick in the pre-385 wall). For Tegea see Bérard 1892 (F 5) 547–8.
On the general probability of both walls being early, see Winter 1971 (I 179) 30 n. 60, 33 with n. 68,
58.   [25] See Winter 1971 (I 179) 31 n. 64.

[26] Most recently Adshead 1986 (F 1) 95–8. For criticism of this prevalent view see O'Neil 1981 (F
56).   [27] See Jeffery 1961 (C 137) 218–20 for dates and discussion.

sant demagogues' of the early fourth century (Xen. *loc. cit.*) may be a later development after the synoecism, and the Mantinean democracy was not always of a radical type (Arist. *Pol.* 1318b21).

These centralized Peloponnesian states are regularly found indulging in minor imperialisms of their own, attempting to incorporate or subjugate neighbouring rural communities. Elis had in effect reduced Lepreum to tributary status well before 431 (Thuc. v.31.2), and absorbed other parts of Triphylia (Hdt. iv.148.4; Str. viii.3.30, p. 355). It seems unlikely that the engagement in western Arcadia between Mantinea and Tegea in 423 (Thuc. iv.134) was the first attempt either city had made to extend her influence in that direction (both already have allies), though this particular episode in which the Mantineans had established a permanent fort (Thuc. v.33) does not antedate 431 (Thuc. v.29.1). There is no particular reason to associate such expansionism with either oligarchic or democratic governments, and Sparta, the *hegemon* of the Peloponnesian League, may not have taken a continuous interest in it.

Despite the evidence for 490 and the 480s (above, p. 102), both Tegeates and Mantineans joined Leonidas at Thermopylae in 480 (Hdt. vii.202), and 'all the Arcadians' and the Eleans were at least included in the force which went to the Isthmus (Hdt. viii.72). In 479 the position was slightly different. The Tegeates were well represented at Plataea with 1,500 hoplites (ix.28) and fought well (ix.70–1) in close alignment with the Spartans. But, although Plataea, with its lengthy preliminaries (*CAH* iv² 599ff), was eminently a battle for which it was difficult to be late by accident, both the Eleans and the Mantineans arrived after the victory (ix.77). They blamed themselves vigorously, the Mantineans made a gesture of pursuit of the departing Persians, and both states exiled their generals when they got home. The delay even cost the Mantineans their place on the lists of the victorious Greeks at Delphi (M–L 27) and Olympia (Paus. v.23.2), though the Eleans were included, doubtless because of their control of Olympia. Disloyalty to the Peloponnesian League has been inferred by some scholars, but it is not clear that anything more is involved than caution in the leaderships in the cities about a distant and dangerous battle.

The main evidence about Spartan troubles in the Peloponnese after 479 lies in a list of five battles which they won under the auspices of the seer Tisamenus (Hdt. ix.35; Paus. iii.11.7–8). The first is Plataea, the second at Tegea against the Tegeates and the Argives, the third at Dipaea against all the Arcadians except the Mantineans, the fourth against the Messenians at Isthmus,[28] the fifth at Tanagra against the Athenians and Argives. We shall see that Tanagra was in 458 and that Isthmus was after

[28] This place is unknown, and the temptation to emend it to Ithome or to add Ithome was felt very early, to judge from Pausanias' text.

465. The date of Tegea is much less certain. As for Dipaea, the recent consensus[29] has been to put it after 465 in the period of the Helot Revolt, since the Spartans fought it with much reduced numbers (Isocr. VI.99). This seems improbable. Dipaea is securely placed in the valley of the Helisson (Paus. VIII.30.1), far to the north of any likely movement between Laconia and Messenia. An engagement there will only make any sense if the Spartans are on the offensive, unlikely after the revolt, and on a route to or back from Mantinea which will avoid Tegea.[30] If the force is small, perhaps we should think in terms of something like a raid to support pro-Spartans in Mantinea.

This does suggest that Mantinea's loyalty was again in doubt after 479. The only literary evidence which could support this is the undated synoecism under Argive influence, since she was absent from the battles of Tegea and Dipaea and there is positive evidence of her loyalty to Sparta at the time of the Helot Revolt (Xen. *Hell.* v.2.3).[31] More positive evidence for activity at Mantinea may come from the substantial series of coins labelled *Arkadikon* which proclaim Arcadian unity (Fig. 2). Their dating and interpretation has varied.[32] It used to be thought that they were festival issues of no political significance, but this is hard to square with the demonstration that three separate mints were at work, and we can hardly overlook the fact that the predominant denomination is the triobol on the Aeginetan standard, known from Thuc. v.47.6 as a standard Peloponnesian soldier's ration allowance. It now seems hard to refer the beginnings of the issue to Cleomenes' activities in 490, and the start, at a single mint,[33] seems to fall after 480. At a later stage this mint is joined by two others. Though the evidence for identifying these mints is somewhat tenuous, there is a reasonable case for referring one of them to Tegea, and it is not implausible to see Mantinea in the third, which long survives the other two, perhaps until 418. If Mantinea returned to the Peloponnesian League at the time of Dipaea, Sparta may have tolerated the survival of a claim to an Arcadian entity there.

Tegea's dissatisfaction seems to have been longer lasting,[34] though we

---

[29] Wade-Gery 1958 (A 121) 84 with n. 3; Andrewes 1952 (F 2) 3–4; Forrest 1960 (F 24) 229.

[30] Cf. Andrewes, *HCT* IV 32.

[31] Synoecism in itself is not necessarily anti-Spartan. At Elis, after the punishment of the dilatory generals of 479, there seems no reason to find hostility to Sparta. Elis falls into a period of political obscurity (we do not even hear of any Elean force in action till 435, Thuc. 1.27.2) and cultural glory, as she embarks on the rebuilding of the temple of Zeus at Olympia (see p. 189); if we could trust Pausanias (v.10.2), this would be an assertion of supremacy in her own area.

[32] See Wallace 1954 (F 70) 33–4; Williams 1965 (C 199); Caltabiano 1969/70 (C 182); Kraay 1976 (C 190) 97–8.　　　[33] Clitor for Williams, but perhaps Orchomenus should be considered.

[34] Besides the battles of Tegea and Dipaea, we have to fit in Simonides fr. 122 (see Page 1981 (J 82) 278–9 n. LIII) for men who saved Tegea from destruction (perhaps the battle of Tegea seen in a different light) and what looks like the conclusion of the whole sequence, Polyaenus II.10.3, Cleandridas' capture of Tegea with the aid of laconizing *aristoi*. Since Cleandridas was active well after 445, the later this last is put the better, and it may well belong even to the 450s.

Fig. 2. Silver coin of the Arcadian League, about 465 B.C. (After *British Museum Catalogue of Coins* Peloponnese pl. 31, 18; cf. Kraay 1976 (C 190) no. 289.)

do not know its causes. She had indeed lost her argument at Plataea that she was entitled to the left wing as the most honourable place after that of the Spartans (Hdt. IX.26–28.1), but the post she was given, next to the Spartans, was nearly as honourable and one which we find her occupying later (Xen. *Hell.* IV.2.20). Other motives are more likely, perhaps a conflict of interests in western Arcadia; for later Spartan sensitivity here, compare Thuc. V.33.1. In any case, the presence of Argives at the battle of Tegea warns us that wider issues were involved.

Argos had been neutral in 480 and 479; Herodotus' account assumes that this neutrality might amount, if occasion served, to actual medism (VII.148–52, IX.12). The limits of her influence at this point may be defined by those of her neighbours, some of them at times her subjects, who appear on the Greek side: Mycenae by itself (VII.202, with 80 men) and grouped together with Tiryns (IX.28, 400 men), Epidaurus (eight rising to ten triremes, VIII.1, 43; 800 men, IX.28), Troezen (five triremes, VIII.1, 43; 1,000 men, IX.28, and providing a naval base, VIII.42.1), Hermione (three triremes, VIII.43; 300 men, IX.28); all these duly appear on the Greek victory lists. It looks as if Argos has lost all influence east of the river Inachus. We learn without surprise that one of the Argive grievances against Mycenae was its claim to the cult of Hera (Diod. IX.65.2), and there is slight, but positive, epigraphic evidence (*SEG* XIII 246) that Argos had lost control of the Argive Heraeum in this period. The uncertainty in this direction, as we have seen (above p. 102), is the nature of Tiryns in 480–79. It is assumed here that the 'slaves' had already been expelled to Tiryns and that the Argive government was already one of 'the sons of the slain', naturally hostile to Sparta.[35] The main remaining uncertainty about what Argos controlled is in the north, where the small town of Cleonae had importance for her as the means of controlling a panhellenic festival, the Nemean Games.[36] Mycenae is

---

[35] For an alternative view, in which the aristocratic leanings of 'the sons of the slain' incline them to Sparta and which defers their counter-revolution until about 468, see Forrest 1960 (F 24) 225–7.

[36] Lewis 1981 (E 41) 74; Adshead 1986 (F 1) 35, 59–61. See also her study (4–7) of the geographical position of Cleonae and Nemea.

found asserting a claim to Nemea as well (Diod. *loc. cit.*), and the position
of Cleonae was certainly at issue in this period (see p. 109). But Cleonae
does not seem to have taken part in the Persian War and, alone of the
panhellenic sanctuaries, Nemea received no Greek victory dedication.
Cleonae was certainly in Argive control in 465 (Str. VIII.6.19, p. 377), and
it looks as if Argos held on to it practically without a break. Of Orneae,
in the same general area, we hear nothing in this period.

The long-term aim of any Argive regime will have been to rebuild the
city's manpower and territorial control, although short-term political
considerations may have modified this, as when the 'slaves' were ejected.
The process which followed is summarized by Pausanias (VIII.27.1): the
Argives were in continual risk of subjection by Sparta until they
strengthened Argos' population by destroying (or incorporating?)
Tiryns, Hysiae, Orneae, Mycenae and other unimportant towns of the
Argolid; this gave them greater security from the Spartans and greater
power with their neighbours.[37] The process envisaged here was a long
one; Orneae was still independent in 418 (Thuc. v.67.2) and not
demolished until 416 (Thuc. VI.7.1–2).

According to Herodotus (VI.83), it was the slaves at Tiryns who, some
time after their expulsion from Argos, took the initiative in attacking
their masters, urged on by a seer from Arcadian Phigalea; a long war
followed, finally won by the Argives. This certainly ended the independence of Tiryns. Some of the inhabitants may have been incorporated
into the Argive population (Paus. II.25.8, VIII.27.1); some certainly
moved on to the coastal town of Halieis (Hdt. VII.137.2; Str. VIII.6.11, p.
373[38]). We can hardly fix the dates, and it is perfectly possible that the
final capture of Tiryns is to be put relatively late, after the other events in
this period in which Argos is involved.[39]

Argos' efforts at recovery and Tegea's independent line are both in a
sense anti-Spartan. Cooperation between Argos and Tegea is twice
attested: Argos helped Tegea at the battle of Tegea (Hdt. IX.35); Tegea
helped Argos in the capture of Mycenae (Str. VII.6.19, p. 377). We shall
see reason to date the latter after 465. But the visible contacts between
Argos and Sparta are more contradictory. The battle of Tegea was a
battle against Sparta, but when, after Pausanias' death, the Spartans and
Athenians sent missions to arrest Themistocles, living in ostracism at
Argos (see p. 65), Themistocles did not think he could rely on Argive
resistance to the demand and fled from the Peloponnese (Thuc. 1.135.2–
136.1). The views so far adopted in this volume (pp. 45, 66) put this event
around 466.

[37] περιοίκους can hardly be technical here; what *perioikoi* would be left? See Andrewes 1990 (F 4).
[38] On the text see Aly and Sbordone 1950 (C 1) 245–6, and Baladié 1978 (C 8) *ad loc.*
[39] See Chronological Notes, p. 500.

According to Thucydides, Themistocles, though living at Argos, had been making visits to the rest of the Peloponnese. It has been assumed[40] that there is a hint to be taken here, that these visits are to be associated with anti-Spartan, democratic, synoecisms in the Peloponnese and, in particular, with trouble for Sparta in Arcadia, and that it was these local activities which prompted Spartan action against him. It is a shade disquieting that the copious ancient tradition about Themistocles shows no signs of having taken the hint and gives him no specific anti-Spartan activity at this time, despite the various scraps suggesting earlier hostility to Sparta.[41] But, even if we discount the anti-Spartan nature of the Elean synoecism and are agnostic about the date of that at Mantinea, there does seem to be enough trouble in Arcadia, at any rate, for the Spartans to hold against Themistocles and for them to be in a generally sensitive mood. Whether their suspicions of Themistocles in Argos were firmly grounded or general, they could support them with evidence (true or false) about his correspondence with Pausanias and felt that they could ask for Athenian support in removing him; they had, after all, acquiesced in the Athenian expulsion of Pausanias from Byzantium (p. 100).

If the Spartan–Athenian move against Themistocles is to be dated around 466, it would seem unlikely that any further major events in the Peloponnese intruded before the Helot Revolt, generally and rightly dated in 465,[42] at least on the assumption that the battle of Dipaea and therefore that of Tegea antedated that revolt. Argos may have been sufficiently daunted by the battle of Tegea to be unwilling to resist Spartan demands, at least with pressure from Athens added.

The earthquake at Sparta which sparked off the revolt was certainly substantial; late sources speak of 20,000 dead (Diod. XI.63.1), all but five houses destroyed and 'all the ephebes' killed (Plut. *Cim.* 16.4–5). Opinions differ about the long-term effect on Spartan manpower and the contribution of the earthquake to the situation of 425 when the capture of 120 Spartiates was a major disaster (see p. 415); it must surely be true that a loss of citizen women will have had serious demographic effects.[43] The young king Archidamus, grandson of Leotychidas, was said to have behaved well in the emergency and to have seen the importance of military readiness (Diod. XI.63.5–7; Plut. *Cim.* 16.6). For Thucydides,

[40] Gomme, *HCT* I 408–9, 437; Andrewes 1952 (F 2); Forrest 1960 (F 24); Adshead 1986 (F 1) 86–103. But see O'Neil 1981 (F 56).

[41] The episodes of Athens' walls, the projected burning of the Greek fleet, the expulsion of medizers from the Amphictyony.   [42] See Chronological Notes, p. 500.

[43] The fullest recent argument is that of Toynbee 1969 (A 115) 346–52, criticized by Cartledge 1979 (F 14) 221–2. That the Spartiate population fell steadily is not in dispute, and I am not out of sympathy with Cartledge's discussion of other factors (see particularly 307–17, and compare Hodkinson 1986 (F 31)); the question is how great a push the earthquake gave the decline. See also Cawkwell 1983 (F 16) 385–90.

the revolt which followed was predominantly Messenian, though joined
by two perioecic communities, Thouria in the lower Pamisus valley of
Messenia and Aethaea, which we cannot place; the rebels immediately
established a base on Mount Ithome, the last stronghold of independent
Messenia (see *CAH* III².3, 328). Herodotus gives us a Spartan disaster at
Messenian Stenyclarus in which 300 Spartans were wiped out (IX.64.2)
and a victory at Isthmus (IX.35.2[44]). Diodorus and Plutarch seem to
presuppose more activity by the Laconian helots and even a projected
attack on Sparta itself. That there was a serious threat to Sparta would
follow from the Athenian claim that Cimon had saved Sparta when it was
under heavy Messenian pressure (Ar. *Lys.* 1137–44 with scholia[45]).
Plutarch (*Cim.* 16.8–17.3) accepted this and the consequences that
Cimon led two Athenian expeditions to Sparta during the war, but
Thucydides only describes one expedition by Cimon (see below), and it
seems slightly more likely that Aristophanes is exaggerating the services
which it performed. It is clear, at any rate, that the war was largely fought
in Messenia, that it had its elements of open warfare, and that the
Spartans only slowly drove the Messenians back to their base on Ithome.

Sparta was not without support. We hear of help from Aegina (Thuc.
II.27.2, IV.56.2) and Mantinea (Xen. *Hell.* V.2.3); the Plataeans (Thuc.
III.54.5) presumably came with the Athenians. Neither Elis nor Corinth
is attested, and the situation could have been worse. Despite their
hostility to Sparta in the previous decade, Argos and Tegea made no
attempt to intervene. It was more important to Argos to use Spartan
preoccupation as an occasion for a final settlement with Mycenae, which
was destroyed after a siege (Diod. XI.65; Str. VIII.6.10, p. 372) with
Tegeate help (Str. VIII.6.19, p. 377). We have suggested (above, p. 107)
that the Argive capture of Tiryns also belongs to this period.[46]

Corinthian neutrality has been inferred from Plut. *Cim.* 17.1–2, a
passage which certainly attests aggressive Corinthian behaviour both to
the north against Megara and to the south against Cleonae (see above,
p. 107). The first evidence for Corinthian activity after the Persian Wars
suggests an attempt to strengthen her grip over her colonial dependencies in north-western Greece.[47] Thucydides (1.103.4) goes further than
Plutarch and attests an actual war in the 460s between Corinth and

---

[44] See Cartledge 1979 (F 14) 219 for a suggestion about the location.

[45] The version is adopted by Spartans in 369, Xen. *Hell.* VI.5.33.

[46] Strong arguments have been produced (Amandry 1980 (K 1) 235–40) for supposing that the
Argive decision to reshape the Heraeum site had already been taken around 460 in the euphoria at
regaining control of the Argolid. The archaeological evidence shows that work there long
antedated the burning of the temple in 423 (Thuc. IV.133.2), and there is unpublished epigraphic
evidence pointing to a similar conclusion.

[47] Graham 1964 (A 52) 128–30; for Leucas see Plut. *Them.* 24.1.

Megara, perhaps made possible by Spartan preoccupation. It has been argued[48] that Plutarch's story about Cleonae and events at the beginning of major hostilities in 459 suggest that Corinth had for some time been building influence at the expense of Argos, that she had been backing Mycenae and showing considerable interest in the area to the east of the Argolid; in these activities she had the support of Sicyon and Epidaurus. For her, then, as for Argos, there were interests to be pursued close to home, but it would be surprising if she had not made even a token gesture to help Sparta.

By 462, the main problem remaining for the Spartans was the Messenian position on Ithome, defended, apparently, by stockades which they found it hard to deal with. Athenian skill in dealing with such defences had been demonstrated at Plataea and Mycale (Hdt. ix.70.1–2, 102.2–4), and Thucydides (1.102.2) gives this as the principal reason for asking Athenian help. Whether the Athenians had any obligation to come is unclear.[49] The debate at Athens and the relationship of Cimon's expedition to Athenian internal politics are discussed elsewhere (pp. 68–9). The expedition was authorized, and Cimon came to Sparta with a large force (4,000 hoplites in Ar. *Lys.* 1143, if that passage refers to this occasion; see above). However, before any substantial success was achieved, the Spartans, 'suspecting Athenian daring and *neoteropoiia*', dismissed them, alone of all the allies, saying that they had no further use for them. In chapter 4, the reference to *neoteropoiia* is taken to be the revolutionary spirit manifested in the reforms of Ephialtes; it has also been held[50] that the Athenian troops were visibly coming to doubt whether the Messenians were really the revolted slaves they had been sent to subdue. The rebuff was a turning-point in Greek history, precipitating a major change in Athenian policy which we discuss in the next section.

Some emend Thuc. 1.103.1 and place the end of the Messenian War in 461 and 460.[51] We are here accepting the text and ending the war in 456/ 5, but, like Thucydides, we record it here. The terms agreed were notably favourable, testimony to Spartan desperation as well as to their obedience to a Delphic oracle 'to release the suppliant of Zeus of Ithome'. The occupants of Ithome and their families could leave the Peloponnese freely; they could only be seized if they returned to it; they would then become the personal property of their captor. The Athenians could find a use for them (see p. 117), and they will return to the narrative, formally known as Messenians.

---

[48] Lewis 1981 (E 41) and, quite independently, but with a greater stress on the Nemean Games, Adshead 1986 (F 1), 67–85.

[49] The alliance against the Mede was still in force (Thuc. 1.102.4); nothing follows from the epexegetic ξυμμάχους at 102.1.

[50] de Ste Croix 1972 (G 36) 179–80.   [51] See Chronological Notes, p. 500.

II. THE 'FIRST PELOPONNESIAN WAR'

'As soon as the Athenians returned home, they renounced the alliance they had made with the Spartans against the Mede and became allies of the Argives their enemies, and both of them made the same oaths and alliances with the Thessalians' (Thuc. 1.102.4). Thucydides did not need to stress that in the Persian Wars Argos had pursued an ambiguous neutrality and Thessaly had medized. After his 'footnote' about the end of the Messenian War, he continued:

The Megarians too joined the Athenians in alliance, leaving the Spartans, because of their border war with Corinth. The Athenians acquired Megara and Pegae and built for the Megarians the long walls from the city to Nisaea and garrisoned them themselves. And it was not least on account of this that the Corinthians first conceived their violent hatred for the Athenians.

It has been suggested[52] that this new grouping was defensive, that Athens now realized that Sparta was basically hostile to her, now learnt that the Spartans had considered helping Thasos in 465 (p. 44; Thuc. 1.101.1–2),[53] and looked for the kind of help which would be useful; Argos would provide hoplites, Thessaly cavalry, Megara a position on the Isthmus to impede Spartan action. This view seems hardly likely. Sparta was still, on our view, involved with the Messenians, and the Athenians would hardly have embarked on the Cyprus campaign which developed into the Egyptian expedition (p. 50) if substantial trouble were expected on the mainland.

It seems more reasonable to suppose that Athenian policy was expansionist, and that the Spartan alliance and memories of 480–479 would no longer be allowed to stand in the way of implementing policies which had been in many minds for many years. Athens' initial wish will have been to have a final, long-delayed, settlement with Aegina (see *CAH* IV² 365–7). Aegina was on good terms with Sparta (see p. 109) and probably a member of the Peloponnesian League; we shall see that her independence was a prime concern for Corinth. Megara wanted security from Corinth. Argos wanted self-respect and at least the re-establishment of her position in her own area; we have argued that Corinth had been meddling in it. Corinth seems to be the main target of the new alliance. This will not hold for Thessaly, but there are indications that some Thessalians, perhaps the Aleuadae, had been angling for Athenian support for some time.[54] The attraction for Athens may have been cavalry, but there may also have been ideas in Athens about exercising pressure in Boeotia.

[52] Jeffery 1965 (I 81) 52; de Ste Croix 1972 (G 36) 182–3.
[53] This rumour, apparently unknown in 462, cannot have gained currency at Athens before this point.   [54] Jeffery 1965 (I 81) 52 n. 49.

The timing of what follows presents problems which we discuss elsewhere.[55] Spectacular diplomatic action was not, at Athens, always followed up militarily, and, on our view, there is nothing to fill 460 except the take-over and securing of Megara. The Long Walls to Nisaea were only a fifth of the length of the Athenian Long Walls to the Piraeus (Thuc. IV.66.3 against II.13.7), but will have taken time to complete. Corinth was being warned off, and a positive threat to her was created by the occupation of Pegae on the Corinthian Gulf. There may still have been some uncertainty at Athens as to how far and how fast the new policy should go, and its claims were matched against those of older commitments.

It is after all noteworthy that the change in internal politics at Athens led only to the abandonment of Cimon's Spartan policy, and not also to slackening of the Persian War, with which he was equally identified. The Eurymedon campaign (p. 43) had not liberated the Greeks of Cyprus, and the Thasian revolt (p. 44) had inhibited a further move in this direction. In 459 an Athenian and allied fleet of 200 ships lay in Cypriot waters. It did not stay there long; its further moves, successes and ultimate defeat are described in chapter 3.

However, the new alliance got to work on the mainland as well in 459. The first move may have been on a small scale, and was in the interests of Argos. An Athenian force landed at Halieis, now occupied by the exiled Tirynthians, and was caught and defeated by a combined force of Corinthians, Epidaurians and Sicyonians,[56] demonstrating their interest in the Argolid. The Athenian navy did better, winning a naval battle over 'Peloponnesians' (presumably the same combination) at Cecryphalea, between Epidaurus and Aegina. A much greater battle followed, off Aegina itself, in which both Athens and Aegina were supported by allies. The Athenians captured seventy ships and, under Leocrates, laid siege to Aegina. They had established naval superiority in the Saronic Gulf, but the Corinthians and their allies were determined to save Aegina, the capture of which would seal that superiority. They slipped a small force across to Aegina, but placed their main hopes on an invasion of the Megarid. They seized the heights of Geranea to the north of Megara, and invaded the plain. They could not believe that the Athenians had the strength to help the Megarians, with so much effort already committed against Aegina and in Egypt; if they did try, that would relieve the siege of Aegina. Thucydides' brief narrative takes on a warmer glow. 'But the Athenians did not move the force at Aegina, but the oldest and the youngest of those left in the city arrived at Megara, under the command of Myronides.' These reserve forces (probably those from 18 to 20 and 50

---

[55] See Chronological Notes, pp. 500–1.
[56] The Sicyonians, not in Thucydides, are attested by *SEG* XXXI 369.

to 59), presumably with the Megarians, fought a drawn battle. The Corinthians withdrew, which was in the circumstances tantamount to a defeat, and the Athenians set up a trophy. The Corinthians, heavily criticized by their elders at home, returned twelve days later and started to set up their own trophy. They were beaten off. A largish group, losing their way on the march home, found themselves trapped in a quarry and were wiped out by a combination of hoplites and light-armed troops. Corinth had had a bad year, and we hear little more of her for some time.[57]

It is likely that the Megarian Long Walls had shown their value in this campaign, and the Athenians now embarked on long walls of their own, a project, nearly five times as large, which shaped the strategy of the rest of the century. Themistocles had said (Thuc. 1.93.7) that, if Athens were hard pressed by land, it would be more important to hold on to Piraeus than to Athens itself. The Long Walls, a shorter one covering Phalerum, a longer Piraeus, eliminated the need for such a choice. The Athens–Piraeus–Phalerum complex would henceforth be as near to an island (Thuc. 1.143.5, [Xen.] *Ath. Pol.* 2.14–16) as anything on the mainland could be. We can say little about the details of this great enterprise, destroyed in 404. Leake in 1841[58] saw well-built foundations, over $3\frac{1}{2}$ metres thick (see p. 208, Fig. 25).

The walls would hardly have been started now, had it not been thought possible that the conflict would widen and that Sparta would come in, even though she was still involved at Ithome.[59] Sparta did come into the war in 458, but curiously sideways.[60] For Thucydides (1.107), there was no original Spartan intention of attacking Athens at all. Sparta was provoked by a Phocian attack on her supposed mother-city Doris into an expedition into central Greece. The expedition was large, involving 1,500 Spartans (presumably including *perioeci*) and 10,000 allies, and some scholars[61] have been unwilling to believe that it can have had the limited objective of protecting Doris. They have appealed to Plutarch (*Cim.* 17.4), in whose manuscripts Delphi rather than Doris is the object of aggression, or to Diodorus (xi.81.2–3), where, in a later stage of the account, a desire to promote Theban interests is relevant. This is not Thucydides' story, and it is unwise to underestimate what

[57] Athenian casualties in 459 will also have been very heavy. Now that a parallel text to M–L 33 has appeared (*SEG* xxxiv 45), it is no longer safe to regard that text, with its 170-odd dead, as an exceptional monument for the tribe Erechtheis alone. Simple multiplication by ten would be dangerous, but the total surely ran well into four figures.   [58] Leake 1841 (D 46) I 417.

[59] The continuation of the Messenian War is presumed, not only from the text of Thuc. 1.103.1, but from the absence of Archidamus in 458. [Xen.] *Ath. Pol.* 3.11 will hardly bear the weight some have put on it.

[60] For recent argument that Sparta did not play an aggressive role in the war, see Holladay 1977 (F 32), Lewis 1981 (E 41); and, against Salmon 1984 (F 61) 420–1, Holladay 1985 (F 33).

[61] E.g. Walker, *CAH* v¹ 79–80.

Sparta might do from motives of religion and sentiment.[62] We follow Thucydides, assuming only that he has antedated the period at which the Spartan allies reached 10,000.[63]

Having settled with Phocis, the Spartan commander, Nicomedes, regent for Plistoanax son of Pausanias, found himself in a difficulty. The expedition had presumably come by sea across the Corinthian Gulf, but that way of return was thought likely to be blocked by an Athenian naval squadron. The alternative route, through the Megarid, was also blocked by the Athenians, not only in Megara, but watching the difficult roads across Geranea.[64] He decided to wait in Boeotia and see what might turn up; no eagerness for a clash with Athens is visible. Thucydides does not say, but one of the sources of Diodorus (XI.8.1.1–3) did, that at this point the Thebans prevailed upon the Spartan force to enlarge their wall-circuit and give them control of the Boeotian League. In Boeotia, Nicomedes was approached secretly by Athenians, hoping to abolish Ephialtic democracy and stop the building of the Long Walls; the two are obviously thought to be interconnected. Aeschylus' *Eumenides*, produced that spring, had spoken with foreboding about the possibility of civil war at Athens (861–6).[65] Thucydides does not say that Nicomedes was impressed, but the fact that he moved as far east as Tanagra perhaps suggests that he was.[66]

At Athens the Ephialtic strand of policy which in 462 had advocated the trampling of the Spartans now gained full control. The Spartans were fostering plotters against democracy and they were cut off from home; such an opportunity might never recur. The Athenians themselves crossed the border to Tanagra in full force; a thousand Argives and some Thessalian cavalry came to help, as well as other allies, described by the Spartans in their victory dedication (M–L 36) as Ionians; not only naval forces, as at Aegina, but land allies from the Delian League were now being employed against Greeks. The force, 14,000 in all, outnumbered the Spartans and their allies, only now perhaps rising to 11,500. The battle seems to have lasted two days (Diod. XI.80, with some confusing details[67]). The facts most remembered were that the Thessalians changed sides, no doubt for reasons of internal politics,[68] and that losses on both sides were heavy.[69] The Spartans

---

[62] Doris could have been important as the basis for Spartan representation on the Amphictyonic Council; see Zeilhofer 1959 (F 73) 36–8, 43–4; Daux 1957 (A 22) 104–5; Roux 1979 (F 60) 4–9.

[63] See Reece 1950 (E 67).   [64] See Hammond 1973 (A 54) 435.

[65] But Macleod 1983 (A 82) 25–7 shows that this is not necessarily a reference to contemporary events.   [66] For Tanagra, see p. 96, but we can hardly be sure what is going on there.

[67] The confusion of Diodorus' narrative of Tanagra and Oenophyta is sorted out by Andrewes 1985 (C 7).

[68] Jeffery 1961 (C 137) 375, with text of a Thessalian victory dedication, on which see also Larsen 1960 (F 43) 241–2. A new gravestone of a man from Atrax who died in the battle (*SEG* XXXIV 560; Hansen, *CEG* 2.637) is notably ambiguous.

[69] The Argives may have lost as many as four hundred of their thousand (M–L 35; Clairmont 1983 (K 17) 136–8).

certainly in a sense won (cf. Hdt. IX.35.2), but Diodorus (XI.80.6) makes the battle a draw and followed by a four-month truce. Such a truce makes slightly better sense of Thucydides' account, by which the Spartans went home through Geranea and the Isthmus, pausing only to chop down trees in the Megarid. They had certainly not conducted themselves as if they had instructions to make war on Athens.

Diodorus' truce has been connected with an unsolved problem about Cimon. Plutarch (*Cim.* 17.4–9) has an elaborate story of how he, though in ostracism, had wished to fight on the Athenian side at Tanagra. The *boule* had decided to reject the offer, but he encouraged his friends to fight gallantly and remove the suspicion that they were pro-Spartan. This influenced the Athenians to recall him and he immediately made peace between Athens and Sparta. This is very close to, though not the same as, a fragment of Theopompus (*FGrH* 115 F 88), by which the Athenians recalled Cimon to make peace, when he had not yet completed five years of ostracism. I am more inclined than the author of chapter 4 (p. 75) to accept the recall, but, since, in Plutarch, it appears to belong to the winter after the battle and Plutarch, at any rate, seems to be thinking of the armistice of 451 (below, p. 120), Diodorus' armistice after Tanagra appears to be something different.

If the Spartans had had enough for 458, the Athenians had not.

On the sixty-second day after the battle, they made an expedition against the Boeotians under the command of Myronides, and, beating the Boeotians in battle at Oenophyta, they gained control of Boeotia and Phocis, took down the walls of Tanagra, took the hundred richest of the Opuntian Locrians as captive, and finished their own long walls. And after this the Aeginetans too came to terms with the Athenians, taking down their walls, surrendering their ships, and agreeing a tribute for the future.   (Thuc. 1.108.2–4)

We have no idea where Oenophyta was, and Thucydides' order may be more logical than chronological.[70] To these gains of 458 we can perhaps add the port of Naupactus on the north coast of the Corinthian Gulf, taken from the Ozolian Locrians (Thuc. 1.103.4).[71]

Athenian control now extended far beyond the original naval alliance, but we can hardly assess either the amount of strength it brought Athens

[70] Diodorus' order (XI.82.5–83) is: siege of Tanagra and destruction of its walls, general ravaging of Boeotia provoking the Boeotians to battle, capture of all Boeotian cities except Thebes, gaining control of the Opuntian Locrians and taking of hostages, a further move resulting in control of the Phocians and taking hostages from them. To this campaign he adds what appears to be the same campaign against Pharsalus which appears in Thuc. 1.111.1; no commander is named there, but Myronides is not impossible for it.

[71] For those who maintain the manuscript text of Thuc. 1.103.1 (see Chronological Notes, p. 500), the only limiting factor for this acquisition is the end of the Messenian War, 458 then becomes the most likely date, and the connexion will be with the Athenian fleet, estimated by Diodorus (XI.80.1) at fifty ships, which Nicomedes had been expecting in the Corinthian Gulf. Those who maintain Thucydides' strict order and emend 1.103.1 have to assume an Athenian *periplous* to the Corinthian Gulf in 461 or so (even before the accession of Megara had given Athens Pegae), which has left no trace except this capture of Naupactus.

or how the control actually worked. The new territories entered into some form of alliance with Athens (they provide troops at Thuc. 1.111.1); it has generally been assumed that they were differentiated from the members of the Delian League.[72] Theban speakers in Thucydides twice (III.62.5, IV.92.6) attribute Athenian success in Boeotia to Boeotian *stasis*, and Pericles said (Arist. *Rhet.* 1407a2) that the Boeotians were like holm-oaks; as they knocked each other down as they fell, so did the Boeotians by fighting each other. That suggests that the *stasis* is between cities. We have seen slight numismatic evidence for Tanagra's claims to hegemony after 479 (p. 96) and an assertion by Diodorus that Sparta backed renewed Theban pretensions in 458 (p. 114). But, if this is the *stasis* in question, it is not obvious that Athens took sides in it. It was Tanagra's walls which Athens demolished after Oenophyta, and Diodorus (XI.83.1), generally disbelieved, asserts that Thebes remained independent. The problems are, if anything, worse at the level of party or constitutional *stasis*. There are two main pieces of evidence. Aristotle (*Pol.* 1302b25) speaks of a time after Oenophyta when democracy at Thebes was destroyed by its disorder and anarchy which won the contempt of the wealthy, and a fifth-century Athenian speaks of a time when Athens unsuccessfully backed 'the best men' in Boeotia ([Xen.] *Ath. Pol.* 3.11). There is little point in trying speculative combinations;[73] Athens will have backed whatever groups seemed likely to support her,[74] perhaps without regard to their ostensible political colour, and may have changed policy from time to time. She could, for example, have started by allowing a Theban democracy to retain its walls. By 447 Athenian control was weak in north-western Boeotia, and exiles had seized at least Orchomenus and Chaeronea (Thuc. 1.113.1).

The fall of Aegina, the last event to be attributed to 458, perhaps gave most pleasure in Athens. The 'eyesore of the Piraeus' was now under control, her fleet, a threat to Athens for fifty years, had gone for good, she was indistinguishable from any other member of the Delian League. This had been achieved in the teeth of a now quiescent Corinth, and Athens was now supreme in the Saronic Gulf, a supremacy to be confirmed, at dates which we cannot fix, by the acquisition of Troezen (Thuc. 1.115.1) and, for a time at any rate, Hermione (*IG* I[3] 31).

Thucydides' main narrative gives us no events for the campaigning season of 457.[75] We need not regard it as a totally blank year. The

---

[72] The view that *IG* I[3] 9 records a treaty with the members of the Delphic Amphictyony and belongs to this year is rejected by Roux 1979 (F 60) 45–6, 239–40. It has been suggested that at least Orchomenus may have paid tribute in the strict sense in 452 (Lewis 1981 (E 41) 77 n. 43), and it would also be possible to restore Acraephnia in *IG* I[3] 259.111 20 of 453.

[73] See Larsen 1960 (F 42A) 9–10 with 17 n. 2; Buck 1979 (F 11) 148–50; Demand 1982 (F 20) 34–5.

[74] Cf. the Thespian *proxenoi* of *IG* I[3] 23, one of whom is called Athenaios; his family's connexions with Athens will have been of long standing.

[75] For this unorthodox view, see Chronological Notes, p. 501.

tightening of Athens' grip on Boeotia and Phocis will not have been a small matter, and there is also Troezen to be considered. There will also have been uncertainty about Spartan intentions. The story in Plutarch about Cimon's recall (see above, p. 115) could imply the expectation of a Spartan invasion of Attica in spring 457, and it may not be coincidence that this also seems to be the most likely year for a Persian mission to Sparta (Thuc. 1.109.3). Thucydides' story is that the King sent one Megabazos to Sparta with money to persuade the Peloponnesians to invade Egypt; he did not succeed and some of the money was wasted.[76] Either Sparta did not fancy facing the Megarid again or she remained unwilling to fight Athens in any whole-hearted manner.[77]

Thucydides' next item, to be dated to the summer of 456, is Tolmides' circumnavigation of the Peloponnese. His account is brief. He only mentions three stopping places; the burning of the Spartan dockyard, the capture of Chalcis, a Corinthian settlement west of Naupactus, a landing at Sicyon and a victory here. Since he uses the word *periplous* (circumnavigation) and two of the three stops are in the Gulf of Corinth, we can believe that, whatever damage was intended to Sparta on the way, one of the main objects of the expedition was to carry the war there. Diodorus (XI.84) provides more detail. Tolmides, wishing to compete with Myronides' glory, advocated the ravaging of Laconia. He was given fifty ships and a thousand hoplites, which he succeeded in increasing unofficially to four thousand.[78] He took Methone in Laconia,[79] but withdrew at the Spartans' approach. He captured Gytheum, burnt the Spartan dockyards there, and ravaged Laconian territory. He then moved to the mouth of the Corinthian Gulf, won over Zacynthos and Cephallenia, and then moved to Naupactus. He captured this too and settled in it Messenian notables, just released by the Spartans at the end of the siege of Ithome, which happened at the same time.[80]

Since the Spartans had a fleet of at least sixteen ships in 480 (Hdt. VIII.43), they are likely to have had a formal fleet-base, presumably already at Gytheum (cf. Cic. *de Off.* III.11.49), at least as early as this.[81] We

[76] Diodorus (XI.74.6) expresses a Spartan refusal in even firmer terms. For Arthmius of Zelea who 'brought the Median gold to the Peloponnese', see p. 51 n. 55.

[77] If the Spartans did anything this year, besides sitting it out at Ithome, it will have been a raid against Argos, repelled at Oenoe with Athenian assistance. So Jeffery 1965 (I 81) 56–7, antedating Tolmides' expedition. But the battle of Oenoe is not easy to believe in; see Andrewes 1975 (E 1) 9–16 (the topography revised by Pritchett 1965–85 (A100) III 2–12, 46–50); Francis and Vickers 1985 (E 27 and 1 64).   [78] This is an unparalleled and implausible proportion of hoplites to ships.

[79] Presumably Messenian Methone, as in Thuc. II.25.1. Methana in the Argolid cannot be totally excluded and would give better geographical order, but there is more geographical confusion later.

[80] Most of Diodorus' account is not paralleled elsewhere. Schol. Aeschin. II.75 and Paus. I.27.5 add Boeae and Cythera to Tolmides' achievements. No other source has Thucydides' Chalcis, and only Pausanias picks up the battle at Sicyon. Only the burning of the Spartan dockyard is common to virtually all accounts.

[81] For Gytheum, see Str. VIII.5.2, p. 363, Edgerton and Scoufopoulos 1972 (F 21).

have seen no particular reason to assume any Spartan naval activity in this war (the crossing of the Corinthian Gulf in 458 is unlikely to have involved naval vessels), but evidently Gytheum was thought a worthwhile objective. It may have been thought, rightly or wrongly, that some Persian gold was going into an effort to repair the losses of Sparta's allies in the Saronic Gulf. Any circumnavigation of the Peloponnese would involve landing somewhere in Laconia, and few Athenians are likely to have felt inhibitions about doing damage while they were there.

Given that Tolmides' fleet will have had to land from time to time, there is nothing implausible about the stops at Zacynthos and Cephallenia which Diodorus gives him. We may be more doubtful that they were actually won over in any permanent sense; we know next to nothing about either in this period. The remaining two stops in Thucydides are definitely hostile, the capture from Corinth of Chalcis in a useful position covering the approaches to the narrows of the Corinthian Gulf,[82] and the attack on Sicyon, which we now know to have been in the war from the first (above, p. 112). Simply because of Thucydides' silence, there has been reluctance to believe Diodorus' account that it was Tolmides who settled the Messenians in Naupactus; his view that he now captured it as well certainly runs against Thucydides. But one should not multiply Athenian incursions into the Gulf unnecessarily, and provisionally we should accept this occasion for the settlement.[83]

'Provisionally' in this case has more than its usual force. An inscription connected with the settlement has remained unpublished for more than twenty years. All we know of it[84] is that it lays down the arrangements under which the Messenians and the native Naupactians should live together under the protection of Athena Polias, no doubt representing her city; the continued existence of a Naupactian community, invisible in Thucydides, had already been deduced from M–L 74 (cf. *SEG* xix.392). The Messenians of course also honoured Zeus of Ithome, whose suppliants they had been (Paus. iv.33.2). The wall-circuit was large, but even so the suburbs spread outside it (Thuc. iii.102.2–4); at least once (*ibid.*) it was too large for the inhabitants to guard themselves. Before the capture of Pylos (p. 414) brought reinforcements, the largest Messenian hoplite force we hear of is 500 (Thuc. iii.75.1); we can envisage a population of four or five thousand, dedicated to maintaining the Messenian name and available for a range of Athenian projects. They may not have been all that ready to settle down on the useful plain of

[82] Cf. Thuc. ii.82.3. At some time Athens captured another Corinthian foundation, Molycreum, closer still (Thuc. iii.102.1).

[83] There is even reason to wonder whether Tolmides did something to secure the adhesion of Achaea, mentioned by no one; see below, p. 119.

[84] Mastrokostas 1964 (F 50) 295.

their new home. At least once we hear of them on a piratical expedition (Thuc. IV.9.1).[85]

Athens now had a potentially firm grip on Corinth's western gateway. We do not know whether she attempted to exercise it by putting a blockade squadron into Naupactus, as she did in the Archidamian War (p. 399).

The next group of actions in mainland Greece which Thucydides describes (I.111) all seem to belong to one campaigning season; it is uncertain whether it is 455 or 454.[86] First comes a Thessalian expedition, led, according to Diodorus (XI.83.3-4), by Myronides. Diodorus says, plausibly enough, that the Athenians wished to punish the Thessalian behaviour at Tanagra (p. 114), but also alludes to the main motive in Thucydides. Here it is a Thessalian exile, Orestes, son of Echecratides, *basileus* of the Thessalians, whose request for reinstatement initiated the expedition. With Boeotian and Phocian troops the expedition moved against Pharsalus, but achieved nothing against the Thessalian cavalry. Orestes presumably came from Pharsalus and his exile is likely to be connected with the Thessalian change of sides at Tanagra; we can say little more.[87]

Not long after, Pericles took a thousand Athenian hoplites on a naval expedition in the Corinthian Gulf. This was not a circumnavigation of the Peloponnese, but started from Pegae in the Megarid.[88] The first target was again Sicyon; again there was a successful battle with no long-term results.[89] Pericles moved on to the west. The first stop was in Achaea. Thucydides' language does not suggest that these were Athens' first dealings with Achaea, certainly in her control in 446 (Thuc. I.115.1, IV.21.3). Plutarch did not read him thus and no one gives Pericles credit for the acquisition; it should perhaps be added to Tolmides' achievements (see above, p. 118, n. 83). With Achaean help Pericles crossed the Gulf to Acarnania and unsuccessfully besieged Oeniadae, at the mouth

[85] Pausanias (IV.25) has a long and involved story of how they almost at once captured the Acarnanian town of Oeniadae and held out there for more than a year. There are too many implausibilities in it to make it profitable to try to isolate a kernel of truth. Basically, it belongs to the patriotic literature of revived Messenia; cf. *CAH* III².3, 352 n. 44.

[86] See Chronological Notes, p. 501.

[87] The view of Morrison 1942 (F 54) 60-3, that Orestes and Echecratides were Aleuadae of Larissa and that Pharsalus was attacked not for itself, but because it was the key to Thessaly, depends on an interpretation of Theocr. XVI.34 which I do not find compelling.

[88] The ships had perhaps been left by Tolmides (Anderson 1954 (F 1A) 81). Thucydides gives no number. There are a hundred in Plut. *Per.* 19.2-3, fifty in Diod. XI.85 (Diodorus describes the expedition twice; XI.88.1-2 is a better version).

[89] In Diod. XI.88.2 the Spartans send help to Sicyon. Plutarch makes much more of the Sicyon episode, and says that Pericles penetrated far inland and that the battle was at Nemea. He or his source has probably confused the sanctuary of Nemea with the river of that name, but see Lewis 1981 (E 41) 78.

of the Achelous;[90] we may guess that it had some affinities with Corinth.[91] Further operations in mainland Greece were curtailed by bad news from Egypt (p. 52). A pause in Thucydides' account is marked by a brief sentence (1.112.1): 'later, after a gap of three years, a five-year truce was made with the Peloponnesians', perhaps in winter 451/0.[92]

The preoccupations of Athens during these three years have been discussed in chapter 3 (pp. 54-60). Here it is only relevant to remark that, if the Peloponnesians made any serious attempt to profit by Athenian weakness or reverse any of Athens' gains, it has left no mark on the record, and that there is no reason to assume that Athens made any territorial concessions in the Five Years' Truce. The picture seems to be one of Corinthian exhaustion and Spartan quietism. Those who hold Sparta to be fully committed to the war can explain her inaction by the impossibility of passing the Megarid.[93] Those who hold that she had never been enthusiastic[94] can more easily contemplate the possibility that Sparta was unwilling to profit by Athenian lack of success against Persia; the spirit of 480-479 could still be invoked.[95] If it were argued at the time of the making of the truce that Athens must have her hands free for the Persian War, the argument would sit well in the mouth of Sparta's old friend Cimon, surely back from ostracism by 451, if not earlier (above, p. 75). That Cimon made the truce is stated by Diodorus (XI.86.1) and could be read into a confused passage of Andocides (III.3); as we have seen (p. 115), it is hard to disentangle this truce from one made after Tanagra.

A more permanent arrangement was a Thirty Years' Truce between Sparta and Argos (Thuc. v.14.4, 22.2, 28.2), probably made in 451.[96] We have heard nothing of Argos or indeed anything beyond the coast of the Peloponnese since the battle of Tanagra,[97] and have little evidence to elucidate Argive preoccupations. What we do have is remarkable, a text from the middle of the century (M–L 42; see also SEG xxx.354) in which a federal structure appears to link Argos with at least two states in Crete and in which physical intervention by Argos in Crete is thought possible. It is not inappropriate to end this chapter with such a reminder of the extent of our ignorance, once we leave the main line of Thucydides' narrative.

[90] Diodorus' inferior version makes him win over all the Acarnanians except Oeniadae; that is in direct conflict with Thuc. II.68.8. The attitude of Oeniadae to Athens is distinguished from that of the rest of Acarnania at Thuc. II.102.2, but its hostility may only start now. For Paus. IV.25 see n. 85.

[91] Grundy 1911 (C 39) 347-54; Lewis 1981 (E 41) 77.

[92] Argument about the date turns on whether the Spartans broke the Truce in 446, and certainty is impossible; see e.g. Gomme, HCT I 413. Good judges have thought it possible that there was a dislocation in Thucydides' text and that the Truce came before the three blank years (Gomme, HCT I 325, Bengtson 1977 (A 4) 212), but such procedure is very dangerous.

[93] de Ste Croix 1972 (G 36) 187-95.   [94] See note 60.   [95] Lewis 1977 (A 76) 62-3.

[96] It has not quite run out in summer 421 (Thuc. v.28.2). No other states are mentioned, and it is hardly clear whether any of Sparta's allies were involved.   [97] But see p. 119 n. 89.

CHAPTER 6

THE THIRTY YEARS' PEACE

D. M. LEWIS

I. THE PEACE OF CALLIAS

Thucydides' account of the Fifty Years contains no statement of any kind about a cessation of hostilities between Athens and Persia. That is, by any standards, a serious omission of a matter directly relevant to the development of the empire (cf. Thuc. III.10.4): it is the nature and completeness of his excursus which should be questioned rather than the fact that the Persian War came to an end. It is clear that Athens abstained from further offensive action against Persia after Cimon's last expedition. Nothing in Book I of Thucydides suggests that Athens was known to be in a state of war with Persia in the 430s, and in the early years of the Peloponnesian War Athens appears to be feeling for Persian help without any suggestion that peace itself was an issue.[1]

The only sources which fill the gap with any clarity are derived from Ephorus. Of these, Aristodemus 13 may be safely neglected. In Diodorus (XII.4) the King is moved by the defeats in Cyprus to desire peace. A mission to Athens from the Persian commanders is followed by an Athenian embassy headed by Callias son of Hipponicus and by a settlement. The terms reported are that all the Greek cities of Asia should be autonomous, that the Persian satraps should not come within three days' journey of the sea, that no long ships should come beyond Phaselis and the Blue Rocks,[2] and that the Athenians should not attack the King's territory (*chora*).[3]

It is not clear in Diodorus where Callias went: he could certainly be read as if the mission went no further than Cyprus. But Herodotus (VII.151) speaks of an Argive embassy to Artaxerxes in Susa as coinciding with the Athenian embassy under Callias which was there on other business (ἑτέρου πρήγματος εἵνεκα); his language suggests that Callias'

---

[1] Thuc. II.7.1, Ar. *Ach.* 61–125; Meyer 1899 (A 87) 71–2, 77.

[2] These are just inside the Black Sea. See, against Wade-Gery 1958 (A 121) 213–14, Oliver 1957 (E 58).

[3] The attempt of Meister 1982 (E 54) 29–31 to show that Ephorus, working from a tradition which had these events in the 460s, had wrongly transposed them, is unconvincing.

mission would be well known to his readers.[4] We should therefore accept that the negotiations took place in Susa.

Herodotus expresses himself indirectly. Thucydides has failed to recount the negotiations in their place; he is similarly silent about the renewal of the Peace with Darius II, now virtually certain (see p. 422), and VIII.56.4, a passage which strongly implies a previous limitation on the King's movements by sea,[5] is the nearest he gets to referring to a definite arrangement. We are therefore faced with an absence of direct contemporary evidence, and the silence is not fully broken until 380. In that year, Isocrates (IV.120) makes an unfavourable comparison between the King's Peace negotiated by Sparta in 387/6 and the Peace which the Athenians had made:

One may see the greatness of the change most clearly, if one were to read out and compare [one word, παραναγνοίη] the treaty of our time and those now inscribed. It will appear that then it was we who were defining the border of the King's empire, assessing some of his tributes and preventing him from using the sea. But now it is he who governs Greek affairs and gives orders as to what each shall do, and is practically establishing billeting officers in the cities.

Thereafter, there is a flood of similar passages[6] in which the comparison with the King's Peace is stated or implied, which vary in the terms which they report. These all come from Athenian orators; we have already seen what the Athenocentric Ephorus said.

By the third quarter of the fourth century this Athenian propaganda was provoking a reaction. Some unknown muddler may have said (Plut. *Cim.* 13.4) that it was the battle of Eurymedon which had forced the King to make peace; Callisthenes (*ibid.*) said that the King's acceptance of territorial limits was purely *de facto*, through fear. As we have seen, Isocrates implies the existence of a written text in 380. Theopompus (*FGrH* 115 F 154) knew such a stela, but said it was a forgery, since it was in the Ionic letters introduced officially in 403/2; it is unfortunately unclear whether he was denouncing a treaty with Artaxerxes or that with Darius II.[7]

These remained minority views, and Plutarch (*Cim.* 14.5) treats the fact that Craterus, at the end of the fourth century, included a text of the Peace in his collection of decrees as conclusive. But no topic in fifth-

---

[4] It has been argued again recently (Walsh 1981 (E 88); Meister 1982 (E 54) 22–4; even more vigorously Badian 1987 (E 3) 2) that these missions should be dated shortly after Artaxerxes' accession in 465/4; it is not explained why the Argives should then be worried that Artaxerxes might think them enemies, which makes good sense in 450/49 after they had been allied to Athens for a decade (Meyer 1899 (A 87) 75).   [5] Andrewes, *HCT* v 134–5.

[6] Bengtson 1962 (A 3) 64–9 is the most convenient collection; add Theopompus *FGrH* 115 F 153 (*ibid.* pp. 29–30).

[7] Wade-Gery 1958 (A 121) 205–7; Connor 1968 (C 21) 77–87; as it happens, M–L 62 = *IG* 1³ 402 provides an Athenian official text of imperial interest in Ionic letters as early as 432.

century history has provoked more continuous debate. The silence of Herodotus and Thucydides, the variety of the reported terms,[8] the alleged belief of the unknown source of Plut. *Per.* 12.3 that war was continuing at the time of the debate on the Acropolis buildings have all been pressed into repeated attempts to demonstrate that the Peace was not authentic. Most recently, the wrong dating of Hdt. VII.151 and the implications of Plut. *Cim.* 13.4 have been used to shift the argument to the 460s, either along the lines that the Peace genuinely belonged after Eurymedon but was short-lived[9] or that the tradition put it after Eurymedon but was false.[10] Even these views are not totally new, and on all the topics so far discussed I find myself in total agreement with Eduard Meyer's defence of the Peace in 1899.[11] To fuss about the details involves the dangers of losing sight of the main fact. The war did come to an end.

But there is now much factual detail not available to Meyer which needs to be explored. First, there is the evidence of the quota-lists (Fig. 3).[12] The fifth list (its number is preserved: *ATL* I and II List 5 = *IG* I³ 263), the first of a new assessment period, reflects the collection of spring 449. The maximum number of entries is 188 names in 199 lines, but there are some double entries and more two-line names than usual; the true figure will be approximately 163.[13] This represents a rise of about 14 names over the average for the first assessment period, and it is likely that most of the 21 to 23 names attested in it for the first time are in fact appearing for the first time: the most important are Acanthus, Erythrae, Hestiaea, Iasus, Cythnus, Paros, Siphnos, Tenos, possibly Naxos, Eretria, and Chalcis; by contrast, 28 states disappear for a time after the first assessment period, though some of them will still be paying, through larger units. Whatever the explanation for the earlier absences (see pp. 56–9), the problem has now been settled. After this list, it is more difficult to see clearly. If we make the universal assumption that the list at the top of the reverse of the first stela was labelled the ninth list[14] and reflects the collection of spring 445, we only have two lists (*ATL* I and II Lists 7–8 = *IG* I³ 264–5, henceforth A and B) to cover the collections of 448, 447 and 446.[15] There can be no doubt that A and B belong to consecutive years; they are linked by close similarities of order and by payments in B complementary to shortfalls in A. The difficulty is

8 On these see Thompson 1981 (E 85).   9 Walsh 1981 (E 88).
10 Meister 1982 (E 54).   11 Meyer 1899 (A 87) 71–82.
12 For fuller discussion, see M–L 50, Meiggs 1972 (E 53) 153–4, 599.
13 *ATL* III 30–1.
14 *IG* I³ 266; it is not certain whether 'ninth' should actually be read (Lewis 1954 (C 138) 25–9; McGregor 1962 (C 140) 267–75).
15 The attempt of Pritchett 1964, 1966, 1967 (C 158–160) to find space for the eighth list on the back of a lost block attached to the top of the stela has been disproved by a new fragment of the top, Meritt 1972 (C 150) 403–5.

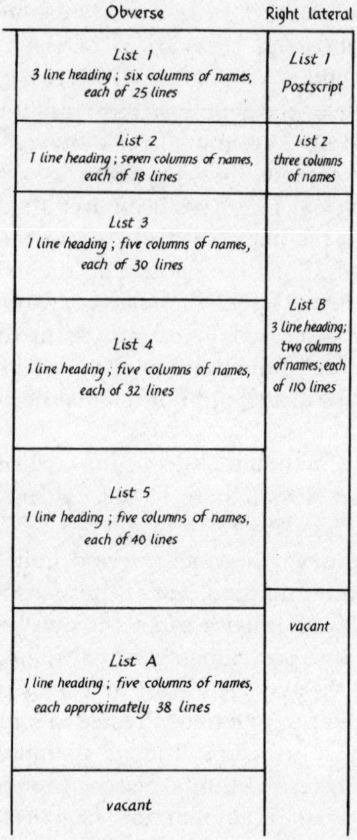

	Obverse	Right lateral
	List 1 *3 line heading ; six columns of names,* *each of 25 lines*	*List 1* *Postscript*
	List 2 *1 line heading ; seven columns of names,* *each of 18 lines*	*List 2* *three columns* *of names*
	List 3 *1 line heading ; five columns of names,* *each of 30 lines*	*List B* *3 line heading;* *two columns* *of names; each* *of 110 lines*
	List 4 *1 line heading ; five columns of names,* *each of 32 lines*	
	List 5 *1 line heading ; five columns of names,* *each of 40 lines*	
		vacant
	List A *1 line heading ; five columns of names,* *each approximately 38 lines*	
	vacant	

Fig. 3. Layout of Athenian tribute-list stela I.

to know whether they are the lists of 448 and 447 or of 447 and 446. If they are the lists of 447 and 446, there is no possibility that the stela explained the gap for 448.[16] If the missing year was 448, there is a strong temptation to relate this to the Peace of Callias; it has for example been held that there is no list because tribute was in theory only payable while war with the barbarian was in progress.[17] If, on the other hand, A and B belong to 448 and 447, the range of possibilities is slightly increased, because there is space unaccounted for above the ninth list. There could have been an explanation of the absent list of 446; there might have been a very short quota-list, reflecting widespread withholding of tribute after

[16] Though uncertainty *may* have been shown by the omission of the numeral in the heading of A.

[17] Support for this has been sought in Thuc. 1.96.1; see Wade-Gery 1958 (A 121) 227; Wade-Gery 1945 (E 87); *ATL* III 230–1, 277–9, but see de Ste Croix 1972 (G 36) 311–12; the view that there was no record of quotas in 448 because the whole tribute was allocated, e.g. for a temple to Athena Nike (M–L p. 135, Meiggs 1972 (E 53), 154), seems less probable.

the battle of Coronea (p. 133); it has even been held that Athens, in that crisis, gave up her claim for the year.[18]

Interpretation about what is going on inside Lists A and B themselves can be deferred (p. 129). At a minimum there seems to be some considerable dislocation of the system of receiving and recording tribute in these years, which are likely to be years of crisis. I prefer the solution by which no tribute was paid or payable in 448 and in which attempts to restart collection in 447 were not well received, but clearer evidence would be welcome.

Certain aspects of the start of the Periclean building programme are clearer and relevant.[19] It is quite certain that the first year of the published accounts of the building of the Parthenon was 447/6 (IG I³ 436; the date deduced from IG I³ 449); some preliminary discussion will have taken place. The building programme can be seen in various aspects (see p. 139). One aspect was certainly that of a group of dedications (ἀναθή-ματα) to the gods for the achievements which were past (Dem. XXII.76 = XXIV.184; Plut. Per. 12.1); it will not be irrelevant that part of the decoration of the Parthenon involved contests of Lapiths and Centaurs, Greeks and Amazons, Gods and Giants, all symbols of a triumph of civilization over barbarism.[20] It seems hard to believe that the Parthenon did not have something of the nature of a victory dedication from the first.[21]

Thought will have been given to the cost of such a programme. The hardest figure we possess for the ultimate cost is that for the gold and ivory cult statue designed by Phidias, between 700 and 1,000 talents (M–L 54B = IG I³ 460). Some very high figures used to be believed, resting on a reference to 'thousand-talent temples' in Plut. Per. 12.2, and a figure of 2,000 talents for the Propylaea (Harp. s.v. προπύλαια ταῦτα[22]); comparative study of better documented building operations[23] seems to show that these figures are much too high. The most likely interpretation of a text of 433 (M–L 58A.3–4 = IG I³ 52) seems to be that at some earlier stage a decision had been taken to fund expenditure of 3,000 talents and then think again.[24]

[18] Accame 1938 (C 113) 413.

[19] No attempt is made here to use the evidence of Plut. Per. 17 on the summoning of a panhellenic congress to discuss the rebuilding of temples destroyed by the Persians; see Seager 1969 (E 81); Bosworth 1971 (E 11); Walsh 1981 (E 88).   [20] See pp. 177, 215–17.

[21] The point is made even more clearly for those who believe that a temple to Athena Nike (Victory) was planned in the early 440s (M–L 44 = IG I³ 35), but the dating of the text rests on epigraphical considerations which not all accept (see Mattingly 1982 (I 108) 381–5, but scepticism is made more difficult by Tracy 1984 (C 169) 281–2).

[22] For the text, see Keaney 1968 (I 87).   [23] Stanier 1953 (I 157).

[24] The view of ATL III 326–8 (cf. Wade-Gery and Meritt 1957 (D 103) 182–8) by which fifteen annual payments of precisely 200 talents were planned is over-elaborate (see M–L p. 159); it seems simpler to suppose that the hellenotamiai were to turn over their annual surpluses until the target figure was reached.

There is a further point of interest in the building accounts. Earlier accounts, certainly for the bronze statue of Athena Promachus (*IG* I³ 435), show the source of the funds as the *kolakretai*, Athens' civic treasurers. By contrast, the main source of the funds for the Parthenon, the chryselephantine statue and the Propylaea, is always the Treasurers of Athena: the *kolakretai* do not appear; the *hellenotamiai* only seem to contribute that which is properly Athena's, the quota of one-sixtieth of the tribute. In 440 (M–L 56 = *IG* I³ 363) we find the Treasurers of Athena paying the costs of suppressing the Samian revolt. It appears to follow that the *hellenotamiai* now have no reserve, that the League reserves transferred from Delos were given to the Treasurers of Athena, and that the basic contention of Pericles' critics in Plut. *Per.* 12, that the building programme was financed by the money contributed by the allies, was correct.[25] The merging must have taken place before 447/6.[26]

It may now be clearer why this chapter has shown so little patience with the conventional criticisms of the Peace of Callias. The League treasury has been appropriated; a building programme, showing strong signs of being a victory dedication and perhaps expected to cost 3,000 talents, has been started. The only conclusion which can be drawn is that the Athenians were confident before starting work on the Parthenon that the Persian War was over, by mutual consent. Beside this conclusion, the details are relatively unimportant. We can have no sure view as to whether the King was forced to the indignity of oath-taking; we cannot be sure how authentic was the text which Isocrates could read and which Theopompus disbelieved.[27] It may be the case that no great parade was made of the details; Demosthenes even asserted in 343 (XIX.273) that Callias had been fined 50 talents for taking bribes in his embassy, and the abandonment of Cyprus at least will have been a bitter pill to swallow. Only after the King's Peace would the achievement really be proclaimed, at a time when Athens had little else to be proud of.

Some terms of the agreement can perhaps be deduced from the history of the following years. The King does not seem to have renounced his claim to the tribute of Ionia.[28] There is some reason to believe that the

[25] Despite the scepticism of Gomme 1953/4 (G 15) 16–17 and *HCT* II 31–2, this contention (Stevenson 1924 (D 91); *ATL* III 337) appears to be sound.

[26] A papyrus scholiast on Demosthenes appears to date the decision, on Pericles' motion, to 450/ 49, and is the basis of the financial scheme worked out by *ATL* and Meritt and Wade-Gery 1957 (see n. 24). Accepting it produces grave chronological problems: see below.

[27] In Thuc. VIII.58.1 an agreement is made for the King, and he does not swear it himself. That it could be asserted that Artaxerxes II had sworn the King's Peace (Tod, *GHI* 118.10–11) perhaps does not make it true; see Badian 1987 (E 3) 27. The second part of that article and Holladay 1986 (E 36) represent a welcome willingness to accept informality, though I have reservations about both.

[28] See Thuc. VIII.5.5, 6.1 and Murray 1966 (A 93). For Isocrates' claim that the Athenians were to assess some of his tributes, see Wade-Gery 1958 (A 121) 211–13; *ATL* III 275; Cook 1961 (F 18) 16–17; Murray, *op. cit.* 155–6.

cities of Ionia were to be deprived of fortifications,[29] perhaps some that Athens gave up her right to establish settlements or colonies there.[30] That the restrictions on naval movements existed in some form seems to follow from Thuc. VIII.56.6; the restrictions on military movement by land are more mysterious.[31] It is not to be expected that the arrangements would be honoured at all levels; we shall find at least one satrap engaged in subversion from time to time (pp. 143, 398).

There can be no certainty about the chronology. It is hard to believe that the Peace was known when tribute was paid in spring 449 (p. 123). If we omit Plutarch's Panhellenic Congress,[32] it might just be possible for Callias to return and for the decision to be taken about the financing of the building programme before the end of the archon-year 450/49, as the papyrus commentary on Demosthenes[33] requires, but not all will think this source worthy of such respect.[34]

II. THE EMPIRE ESTABLISHED

In the years immediately following the Cyprus expedition, Thucydides reports only one pair of events, a Spartan expedition to Delphi, which entrusted the shrine to the Delphians, followed by an Athenian counter-expedition handing it over to the Phocians.[35] This would be in line with the Athenian alliance with Phocis (p. 115), and Sparta, which had an Amphictyonic vote, seems to be making an anti-Athenian move while debarred from direct action against Athens by the Five Years' Truce.[36]

It seems that much else was going on to occupy Athens. If the events of the late 450s had created an empire, techniques of control had to be created. We have tentatively argued that 449 saw the conclusion of an arrangement with Persia and the merging of the League treasury with that of Athena. Plutarch (Per. 11.5), in the general context of Pericles' provision for the demos, speaks of his cleruchies, 1,000 settlers to the Chersonese, 500 to Naxos, 150 to Andros, 1,000 to Thrace 'to live with the Bisaltae', others to the foundation of Thurii. Later (19.1) he gives more detail about the Chersonese, Pericles' most admired expedition.

[29] Wade-Gery 1958 (A 121) 219–20; Lewis 1977 (A 76) 153; contra Meiggs 1972 (E 53) 149–51, Brunt 1966 (E 13) 92 n. 54, Cawkwell 1973 (E 14) 54 n. 3.

[30] It has, however, been argued that there is evidence for colonies at both Erythrae and Colophon after the Peace; see ATL III 282–4; Meiggs 1972 (E 53) 162–3; Bradeen and McGregor 1973 (C 121) 98–9.   [31] Wade-Gery 1958 (A 121) 215–19; Andrewes 1961 (G 5) 16–18.

[32] See p. 125 n. 19.   [33] See p. 126 n. 26.   [34] See Chronological Notes, pp. 501–2.

[35] Thuc. 1.112.5; more details in Plut. Per. 21.2–3, where the Phocians have Delphi in the first place, Schol. Ar. Birds. 556, where Philochorus (FGrH 328 F 34) is said to have dated the Athenian expedition in the third year after the Spartan one; in view of Thucydides' language, 'year' has often been emended to 'month'; Hdt. 1.51.3–4 and Plut. De mal. Hdt. 859d may be relevant (see p. 100).

[36] For the Spartan vote, see Roux 1979 (F 60) 4–9, who also (44–6, 239–40) discusses the relationship of IG I³ 9 to these events; see also Sordi 1958 (F 66); Zeilhofer 1959 (F 73) 45–50.

The Chersonese had been subject to a prolonged period of Thracian raids, and Pericles not only strengthened the cities' population with his thousand Athenian settlers, but fortified the isthmus from sea to sea. For these events, the quota-lists provide some clarification and dating, since, as shown above (p. 60), reductions in tribute can provide valuable clues. To start with the Chersonese, in 453, 452 and 451, the main unit is the Cherronesitai, paying 18 talents, though Alopeconnesus also seems to have been named in 451. For 450 we have no evidence. In 449 the Cherronesitai pay 13 talents, 4,840 drachmae, Alopeconnesus 3,240 drachmae. In 446 (on the dating adopted here) the Cherronesitai are joined at least by the Limnaei and Elaeus, and after 445 we can see fairly regularly that the peninsula is divided into six paying units, never paying more than 2 talents, 2,500 drachmae in all before the outbreak of the Peloponnesian War. It is a reasonable inference that Pericles' campaign and resettlement belongs to 447. This is also the most likely year for the casualty list M–L 48, in which 28 Athenians, including the general Epiteles, died in the Chersonese, 12 at Byzantium, 19 in 'the other wars', with an epigram on those who died by the Hellespont. That the sharp reduction in tribute is due entirely to the settlement of Athenian citizens cannot be affirmed; there may have been a more careful assessment of the area's resources and an allowance for services which we cannot identify.[37]

On the evidence of reduced tribute, Plutarch's cleruchy to Naxos should be before spring 447, since her tribute does not vary thereafter, and the cleruchy to Andros precisely between spring 450, when she pays 12 talents, and spring 449, when she pays 6. More complex problems are raised by Lemnos. Settled by Athenians before the foundation of the League,[38] she is found paying 9 talents in 451. By 446, the tribute is entered to two states, Hephaestia and Myrina, and the total of the two never exceeds 4½ talents. Though there is no direct evidence (Thuc. VII.57.2 and Paus. 1.28.2 may be relevant), it has been held[39] that the settlement was reinforced, possibly in 450, by new settlers from Athens and that the tribute was reduced to compensate. It does not seem a sensible solution to create a community composed entirely of Athenians, some of whom were liable to tribute and some not, and our understanding of the position remains unclear.

It has been held that the Athenians drew a rigid distinction between a colony (ἀποικία), which became a new state, and a cleruchy, which did not. This seems unlikely, since there are variations in terminology in the texts which cannot be explained away, and fluidity in nomenclature and in practice, for example, in what legal cases went to Athens, is to be

[37] See *ATL* III 45–6; Kahrstedt 1954 (F 39) 15–23; Brunt 1966 (E 13) 79; Meiggs 1972 (E 53) 160.
[38] See *CAH* IV² 298–9.
[39] *ATL* III 290–4; Ehrenberg 1952 (E 21) 146–9 = 1965 (A 32) 250–3; Brunt 1966 (E 13) 80–1.

expected.[40] It is from a text about an *apoikia*, Brea, that we get our most detailed information of what went on at a settlement (M–L 49 = *IG* I³ 46; *IG* I³ 47 is a similar text). The colony is to set out within thirty days of the passing of the decree. There will be a founder and a board of ten to distribute the land, except that already held by gods. The religious duties of the colonists to Athens are prescribed, and defence by their neighbours is arranged. Those currently away from Athens on an expedition can join if they arrive in Brea within thirty days of their return. There seems to be some discussion of qualification for joining on the basis of the Solonian property classes; it is unclear whether the aim is to provide for poor *zeugitai* as well as *thetes* or to block the possibility of richer absentee landlords.[41]

We have already spoken of the confused picture provided by the lists of 447 and 446 (or 448 and 447). The list of 447 is well preserved, but below average in terms of number of names. At least ten states made short payments, and it is particularly attractive to link a confused pattern at Byzantium with the casualties there. A case can be made for saying that partial payments and absences are more frequent in the Hellespont than elsewhere, which fits the epigram on M–L 48. Eight states seem to have paid late, including three substantial island payers, Cythnus, Carystus and Ceos, and, above all, Mende (including Scione) with its 15 talents. The influence of Potidaea, the Corinthian colony absent from all lists until after the Thirty Years' Peace, is to be suspected.[42]

The greater part of the list for the next year (*ATL* I and II List 8 = *IG* I³ 265) follows the order of its predecessor very closely indeed, but it also has a substantial appendix, which seems to have recorded back payments and supplementary payments from the previous year as well as supplementary payments for the current year. Three entries, very abnormally, record payments in the field, one, from Abdera, at Eïon, two at Tenedos. These were presumably Athenian bases of the year. It has been held[43] that payment in the field was more widely spread and that many of the partial payments and absences of this year really represent such payments, belatedly reported to Athens. However, such a pattern would in itself suggest extensive military operations, and a simpler view is to be preferred.[44] Athens was attempting to reimpose the payment of tribute after a year's gap and met with considerable resistance, eventually

---

[40] *ATL* III 284–6 argue for a rigid distinction, but see Ehrenberg 1952 (E 21) = 1965 (A 32) 245–53; Brunt 1966 (E 13).

[41] The name Brea seems to be Celtic for a settlement. The colony was mentioned in literature (Steph. Byz. s.v.; Cratinus F 426 K–A), but, beyond the fact that it was in the Thracian area, its situation is uncertain. Letter-forms place the text in the 440s, and it may have been the settlement among the Bisaltai mentioned by Plutarch and abandoned after the foundation of Amphipolis; M–L pp. 132f; Meiggs 1972 (E 53) 158–9; but see Asheri 1969 (E 2).

[42] Reasonable doubts are also possible about the presence of Miletus, Colophon and Aegina.

[43] *ATL* III 59–60.

[44] Wade-Gery 1945 (E 87) 226–8; Meiggs 1963 (E 52) 16–18; M–L p. 135; Meiggs 1972 (E 53) 156.

quelled. By the time the books were closed for 446, the number of defaulters was much reduced. Precision about the continuing absentees is impossible: there may still be trouble in the Hellespont and the Thraceward area, and there is no evidence that Aegina, which had made a short payment in 449, had resumed payment.[45]

It is tempting to link the tighter collection of the second list with a preserved decree which lays down the procedure for the despatch of tribute in some detail (M–L 46 = IG i³ 34). Its proposer was called Cleinias, and this could be the father of the great Alcibiades, killed at Coronea in spring 446. The identification would provide a firm *terminus ante quem*, but the decree has no clear early letter-forms, and difficulty has been found in a casual reference which puts on the same footing as offences about tribute offences concerning the despatch of 'the cow and the panoply'; it is argued that this became a universal obligation only in 425 (see p. 421); debate about the date is likely to continue.[46] The substantial point which turns on it is the spread of Athenian officials in the empire, since the opening clause seems to imply that 'the magistrates in the cities', who may be, but are not necessarily, Athenians, and the 'supervisors' (ἐπίσκοποι), who are, are fairly widespread. On the orthodox dating of the Miletus Decree (above, p. 58), we have already seen such a board in action.

Athenian magistrates appear, even less equivocally, in a decree which is even more controversial in its dating (M–L 45). We have fragments of six copies of a decree ordering the use of Athenian coinage, weights and measures and forbidding the coinage of silver by allied cities. The decree itself provides for its exhibition in the Agora of each city, and this will be done by the Athenians if the city does not. This seems to have happened at Cos, where a copy has been found in Attic lettering and dialect. If it had been found at Athens, it would certainly have been dated to the early 440s, and many would prefer to date the decree then; before the Cos fragment was found, it was assumed that the decree did not long precede a parody of it in 414 (Ar. *Birds* 1040–1). Prolonged study of the decree itself and of the coinages which it should have affected has led to no agreed result.[47]

---

[45] The fragmentary decree IG i³ 38 may reflect trouble with Aegina. That the patchy record in Thrace, particularly at Argilus, is connected in some way with the colony at Brea (p. 129) is a plausible speculation.

[46] Besides M–L 46 and the literature cited there, see Mattingly 1970 (C 143) 129–33; Meiggs 1972 (E 53) 166–7; Schuller 1974 (E 78) 212–13.

[47] For the coinages see Robinson 1949 (E 71); Barron 1966 (C 181) 50–93; Erxleben 1970 (E 22) 66–132; Carradice, ed. 1987 (A 16). It now looks as if coinage in northern Greece was uninterrupted until the Chalcidic revolt or the arrival of Brasidas. A surprising deviation by Chios into electrum coinage (Barron 1966 (C 181) 86–7 and 1986 (E 9) 96–7) is at present counter-balancing evidence for an early date for the decree, but N. M. Hardwick tells me that he has a different view of the relation of this electrum issue to the Chiote silver. For recent general treatments of the dating problem, see Schuller 1974 (E 78) 211–17; Lewis 1987 (E 42); Mattingly 1987 (E 50).

To forbid the allies to coin their own silver is clearly a political act of a fairly demonstrative nature.[48] Insistence on the use of Athenian coinage is scarcely less so, but administrative convenience will also have been relevant. The growth of Athenian power produced inter-state monetary transactions on a scale hitherto quite unknown in the Greek world. The advantages of a uniform system of exchange in these transactions will have been obvious.[49] Electrum was accepted as tribute in 453 (*IG* I³ 259 postscript 10–13), and there may have been later payments in it,[50] but the 74 Lampsacene staters and 27⅙ Cyzicene staters which were acquired by the Parthenon commissioners in 447 remained unused throughout their accounts. Life would be much easier for Athenian financial officials and commanders if they were working with one coinage only, and it has been plausibly suggested[51] that the Athenians recoined the whole contents of the Delian League treasury when they took it over. Similar arguments will apply to the weights and measures, rather neglected in modern scholarship. Whether Athens was making special concessions to individual states about the amount of corn they would be allowed to import from the Black Sea (M–L 65 = *IG* I³ 61.34–6, *IG* I³ 62) or acquiring provisions, an agreed standard would be helpful.[52] We need not imagine any intention of creating a common market or of interfering extensively in private transactions. This line of thinking supports an early date for the decree; by 418 the Treasurers of Athena are disbursing electrum (M–L 77 = *IG* I³ 370.14–15).

Thucydides (1.77.1) presents an Athenian embassy at Sparta in 432 defending itself against criticisms of Athenian conduct in legal matters, and a war-time author ([Xen.] *Ath.Pol.* 1.16) says that the Athenians are blamed for forcing the allies to sail to Athens for lawsuits. The complications of what may have happened in commercial cases lie beyond our present scope;[53] it is doubtful whether Athenian provisions here should be thought of as instruments of empire, except in so far as the right to proceed in particular courts is included among the privileges given to particular foreigners. More straightforwardly, we have references (M–L 52 = *IG* I³ 40.71–6, cf. *IG* I³ 96.6–8) in which cases involving particular penalties, death, confiscation of property, loss of citizen rights, exile, seem to be transferred to Athens; one literary reference from war-time (Antiphon v.47) casually asserts that no city can inflict the

[48] Finley 1965 (A 41) 22–4, and 1973 (L 39) 168–9.
[49] Parallel difficulties will readily occur to the reader. I have in mind the elaborate testing of grades of silver at Persepolis (Cameron 1948 (A 14) 200–3) and the difficulties which the fourth-century administrators of the rebuilding of the Delphic temple got into with exchange rates (*CID* II, 62, IIA. 5–13; see Bousquet 1985 (C 118).
[50] See Eddy 1973 (E 19), arguing that such payments seem to be confined to the periods before 446 and after 430 and suggesting that this is the effective period of the Coinage Decree.
[51] Starr 1970 (C 197) 64–72, important for the whole question.
[52] An excellent treatment along these lines in Martin 1985 (C 194) 196–207; see also Lewis 1987 (E 42). [53] de Ste Croix 1961 (E 76) 95–112; Gauthier 1972 (L 57) 157–65.

death penalty without Athenian consent. These restrictions seem to come in during our present period; in the first reference, of 446/5, Chalcis is told that she can conduct her own legal procedures, except in cases involving exile, death and loss of citizen rights; these are to be transferred to Athens 'according to the decree of the *demos*', and it is easier to think that this is a general decree which has already been made for all the cities rather than a decree particular to Chalcis.[54]

This is not a simple assertion of dominance. Except in the rare cases where an entire population was expelled, Athens managed to control her subjects through her sympathizers. Identified with the ruling power, they would need all the protection they could get. As it happens, we have no fifth-century evidence for the violence sometimes visible in the milder atmosphere of the fourth-century confederacy,[55] but we cannot doubt that some occurred. From about 450 we find Athenian decrees for foreigners providing that, if they get killed, the punishment will be the same as if an Athenian gets killed; more precise texts suggest that the city in which the event occurred was liable to a fine of 5 talents.[56] More subtle action could be undertaken through the courts in the cities,[57] and the most effective protection which Athens could offer her friends was to limit the penalties which could be inflicted on them there.[58] She could not contemplate a situation in which a squadron might arrive at a town and enquire for the Athenian *proxenos*, only to learn that he had been executed the previous week for, say, impiety.

For us, these developments can only be dimly seen. We are fleshing the bare, chaotic figures of the tribute quota-lists with inference from the institutions which we see developing. As Athens moved to consolidate her control in the changed circumstances after the end of the Persian War, there will have been recalcitrance, more or less severe. In 447 thirty-one Athenians died, at Byzantium and in the 'other wars' (M–L 48), in what may have been little more than street-fighting. Friends who were prepared to accommodate themselves to the realities of power were found almost everywhere; those who were not had gone into exile. Athenian magistrates and, doubtless, garrisons were placed here and there. Cleruchies added stability to the situation as well as satisfying land hunger at home. Whatever the dating of the Cleinias Decree or the Coinage Decree, it still appears that most of the essential tools of

---

[54] For general decrees applying to the whole empire, cf. M–L 65 = *IG* i³ 61.13–16, 41–46. de Ste Croix 1961 (E 76) 268–80 is the best treatment of the legal instruments of empire; cf. Schuller 1974 (E 78) 48–54.

[55] The Athenian *amphictyones* driven out of the temple of Delian Apollo and beaten (Tod, *GHI* 125.136–7); an Athenian *proxenos* killed on Ceos, even before more extensive disorders (Tod, *GHI* 142.33–40).   [56] Meiggs 1949 (E 51A); de Ste Croix 1961 (E 76) 268.

[57] Cf. Thuc. III.70.3–5 for political litigation, direct and indirect.

[58] This is essentially the explanation offered by [Xen.] *Ath.Pol.* 1.16.

Athenian control were in use by 446. It is of course the fate of controls to produce more recalcitrance waiting for an opportunity.

III. 446 B.C.

Although Athens had made her attempt to bolster the Phocian position in Delphi (above, p. 127), most effort was going into sustaining her naval empire. Such control as had been exercised over the Locrians by the taking of hostages (p. 115) had been dropped or had become ineffective, and, by the spring of 446,[59] former exiles were once more in control in north-west Boeotia, notably at Orchomenus and Chaeronea. Something needed to be done. Pericles was later said to have been sceptical (Plut. *Per.* 18.2–3), but Tolmides took a thousand Athenian hoplites, supported by an allied force on which we have no detail (Phocian cooperation at least may be inferred), and moved on Chaeronea, seizing some of its inhabitants and leaving a garrison there. As he withdrew, doubtless without some of the allies with whom he had been operating, he was caught near Coronea by a mixed force from Orchomenus, the Locrians, Euboean exiles, doubtless plentiful in Boeotia at the time, and 'others of the same mind', under the command of one Sparton (Plut. *Ages.* 19.2), presumably from his name, a Theban. Tolmides himself and other Athenians, notably Cleinias father of Alcibiades, were killed; the rest were captured.[60] In order to recover the prisoners, the Athenians agreed to evacuate Boeotia completely; Plataea, Eleutherae and Oropus remained under their control. The exiles returned, and the cities once again became autonomous.[61] There will have been scores to settle and thinking to do about the future; no Boeotian activity is visible for the rest of the year. How soon the federal constitution described in the *Hellenica Oxyrhynchia* and alluded to by Thucydides was reorganized or established we cannot tell. It is noteworthy that for the rest of the century the only coinage in Boeotia is that of Thebes.[62]

The Euboean exiles had seen what could be done, and revolt spread. On the chronology of the quota-lists adopted here, the cities of Euboea paid their tribute normally at the Dionysia of spring 446,[63] but they went into revolt fairly rapidly thereafter. We hear nothing of the cleruchies

[59] See Chronological Notes, p. 502.

[60] The casualty list which bears an epigram generally attributed to Coronea seems to have had a maximum of 850 names, say 550–850 (Bradeen 1964 (C 119) 21–9; Clairmont 1983 (K 17) 164 is not quite certain that the name-lists belong to the epigram). If this was 446, there will have been many other casualties in places other than Coronea, and the Athenian reaction presupposes that the proportion of those captured among the thousand was large. Thuc. III.67.3 suggests that the Boeotians had casualties too. [61] For all this, see Thuc. I.113, III.62.5, 67.3, IV.92.6.

[62] For more detailed discussion of these events, see Buck 1979 (F 11) 150–60. The evidence for the city and federal constitutions comes mostly from *Hell. Oxy.* 16 (11); it will be discussed in *CAH* VI², ch. 9. [63] Chalcis is not certain, but likely.

established by Tolmides (p. 60); we do hear of the massacre of the crew of an Athenian ship at Hestiaea (Plut. *Per.* 23.3). Presumably the exiles found sufficient discontent to exploit towards their own return and a breaking of ties with Athens; at Chalcis the movement could be identified with the landed aristocracy of the *hippobotai*.

Pericles had already crossed to Euboea with an Athenian army when even worse news came. Megara had revolted, with support from Corinth, Sicyon and Epidaurus; most of the Athenian garrison there had been killed, though Athenian forces held out at the ports of Nisaea and Pegae. There is no word here of Megarian exiles being active or of any change of constitution; simple resentment of Athens seems to have been the driving force.[64] This was a strategic disaster. Control of the Megarid was a substantial inhibition to any Peloponnesian move north of the Isthmus.[65] The Five Years' Truce had expired or was expiring, and a Peloponnesian invasion of Attica was expected. Pericles rapidly returned from Euboea, and a counter-move against Megara was devised.[66] Andocides (grandfather of the orator) took three tribes, won a victory over the Megarians and based himself on Pegae.

He was cut off by the arrival of a Peloponnesian force, which must have come through Megara itself, and which rapidly penetrated into Attica as far as Eleusis and the Thriasian Plain. He was forced to extricate himself by a long, circuitous, but apparently undisturbed, march through Boeotia; his movements are only known from the gravestone of Python, a Megarian who died in Athens, claiming to have guided his march (M–L 51).

The Peloponnesian force was commanded by Plistoanax son of Pausanias, not the elder king, Archidamus; we can only speculate about the reasons.[67] Plistoanax was well under thirty,[68] and was provided with advisers, notably Cleandridas (see p. 105; Plut. *Per.* 22.2[69]). We have no information about the size of his force, but it seems to have been a full

---

[64] For discussion of the Megarian revolt and campaign see Legon 1981 (F 45) 192–9. He treats Megara as an oligarchy throughout; I would be inclined to make the opposite assumption. Megara was clearly a democracy in 424 (Thuc. iv.66). There had been a democratic coup some time before this; the question is whether it had instituted the democracy or intensified it. de Ste Croix 1972 (G 36) 243 n. 25 argues from Ar. *Ach.* 755 that Megara was more oligarchic than democratic in 426/5; this will not bear much weight. Either Megara revolted as a democracy in 446 and remained one, with Spartan tolerance, or became one before 424, with Spartan indifference. In view of Sparta's general preference for oligarchies (cf. Thuc. 1.19, 144.2), I find the first alternative slightly easier; the Megarian democracy had proved its reliability.   [65] de Ste Croix 1972 (G 36) 190–5.

[66] This counter-move is not in Thucydides, but Ephorus had it (Diod. xii.5) and M–L 51, on which the text chiefly depends, confirms him. Since it appears from Diodorus that Ephorus had the order – revolt of Megara, Spartan invasion of Attica, battle of Coronea, revolt and suppression of Euboea, Thirty Years' Peace – confirmation is certainly needed.

[67] Andrewes *ap.* White 1964 (F 71) 140 n. 3; de Ste Croix 1972 (G 36) 142; Lewis 1977 (A 76) 46 with n. 138.   [68] White 1964 (F 71) 140–1.

[69] de Ste Croix 1972 (G 36) 197 n. 95 suggests that he was ephor this year.

league levy; no military difficulty is mentioned (Thuc. II.21 is slightly fuller than 1.114.2; cf. V.16.3). Nevertheless, he went no further than the Peloponnesian invasion sixty years before, which had broken up for rather more public reasons (*CAH* IV² 308, 361), and went home.[70] Contemporaries were quite clear what had happened. Plistoanax and Cleandridas had been bribed. Details of their punishment are given variously, but both went into exile, Plistoanax to Arcadia, Cleandridas to Italy.[71]. On the Athenian side, Pericles' claim at an audit that he had spent 10 talents 'on necessary purposes' was famous in the 420s (Ar. *Clouds* 859) and presumably already bore the interpretation we find later. Money may well have passed, but there was surely also some talk about the lines which a more permanent settlement between Athens and the Peloponnesian League might take. The real mystery is what Pericles said to induce his opponents to abandon the protection they were in effect providing for the Euboeans.[72]

With the principal threat disposed of, Pericles returned to Euboea. Plutarch (*Per.* 23.3) says he took 5,000 hoplites and fifty ships. The latter detail is surprising, since there is no reason to think that the Euboeans had any substantial naval force; it might suggest that the loyalty of one or more of the remaining naval allies was not beyond doubt. The revolt collapsed. There was no forgiveness for the Hestiaeans, held to have committed murder (p. 134). They were expelled, going by agreement to Macedonia (Theopompus *FGrH* 115 F 387), and were totally replaced by a new settlement of Athenians (2,000: Theopompus *loc.cit.*, 1,000: Diod. XII.22.2);[73] one of the new settlers, Hierocles, had been active in producing oracles during the crisis (M–L 52 = *IG* I³ 40.64–7; Ar. *Peace* 1047). The other cities were allowed terms. At Chalcis, the *hippobotai* were expelled (Plut. *Per.* 23.4), but otherwise Athens was merely politely firm. A very well-preserved text (M–L 52 = *IG* I³ 40) gives us the terms of the oaths to be exchanged. The Chalcidian oath was to be sworn by all of military age; failure to swear would involve loss of civic rights and confiscation of property. The expressions of loyalty required were extreme, and the loyalty was only to Athens; uniquely in such texts, there is no mention of Athens' allies.[74] In return for loyalty, the Athenian Council and jurymen promised the continued integrity of Chalcis, due legal procedure in dealing with the state and its citizens, and a hearing when it was asked for. The oaths exchanged with Eretria were identical

---

[70] Diodorus (XII.6.1) says that much land was ravaged and a fort besieged. On the topography of the campaign see also Hammond 1973 (A 54) 433–4.

[71] Busolt 1893–1904 (A 12) III 1, 428 argued that Plistoanax was condemned to death; see de Ste Croix 1972 (G 36) 198.   [72] See de Ste Croix 1972 (G 36) 197–200.

[73] For the regulations governing the new settlement see *IG* I³ 41 and McGregor 1982 (C 141).

[74] Meiggs 1972 (E 53) 179, 579–82.

(*IG* I³ 39). Hostages had already been taken and would for the present be kept (*IG* I³ 40.47–52[75]). The clause defining the limits of Chalcis' own jurisdiction we have already seen (p. 132). The most difficult clause (lines 52–7) maintains Chalcis' right to tax the foreigners in Chalcis, except those taxed by Athens or given immunity by her. Discussion of this has been linked with the question of whether there was now new Athenian settlement at Chalcis. The weight of the evidence seems against it, at least in the form of a cleruchy, of which we have no clear contemporary trace. But, when we eventually get evidence for the tributes of Chalcis and Eretria after 446, there has been a fall, and it is tempting to believe that the Athenians used the land of the *hippobotai* for something.[76] Assignment to various gods, leasing (cf. *IG* I³ 418), perhaps even simple sale, are not to be excluded, and the events of 446 will have produced exiles to whom Athens owed a debt and a home.[77] The Chalcis Decree ends with an injunction to the generals to keep a watch on Euboea. Athens had had a severe fright, and was glad to perform the sacrifices recommended by Hierocles' oracles. The generals were given that task as well, and required to find the money for them.

A contemporary poem is harder to interpret in detail, but should not be forgotten. *Pythian* VIII[78] is Pindar's last dated poem, for an Aeginetan who won at Delphi in late summer 446 (did the Phocians still maintain the control which the Athenians had given them?). That the poem ends with hope for the freedom of Aegina is clear, and it is scarcely less clear that Pindar takes pleasure in the fact that the Athenian disturbers of the peace have been taught a lesson. But the victor seems to be warned against dangerous thoughts; tranquillity, external and internal, is recommended.

Peace negotiations between Athens and Sparta now continued. Callias seems to have been the principal negotiator again (Diod. XII.7, which adds an unknown Chares; perhaps also Andocides, cf. Andoc. III.6). He was perhaps already Spartan *proxenos* at Athens.[79] The nature of the negotiation may have been unfamiliar. On our evidence, this is the first generation which had to face the problems of regulating peace outside the framework of an alliance or permanent friendship. The arrangements took their name (*spondai*) from the libations which reinforced the oath-taking, and seem to have been developed from the short periods of truce already used during major festivals (cf. e.g. *IG* I³ 6.B 8–47). The Argives

---

[75] See Garlan 1965 (A 44) 332–8.

[76] Cf. Ael. *VH* VI.1, though this probably refers to the cleruchy of 506 (*CAH* IV² 308).

[77] *ATL* III 294–7; Brunt 1966 (E 13) 87–9; Meiggs 1972 (E 53) 566–9; Erxleben 1975 (E 23). For the Chalcis Decree in general, see Balcer 1978 (E 4).

[78] Wilamowitz 1922 (J 110) 439–45; Wade-Gery 1958 (A 121) 250–2, 265–6; Lloyd-Jones 1982 (J 72) 158–62.

[79] Cf. Xen. *Hell*. VI.3.4, where his grandson stresses his own role in making peaces with Sparta.

had sought such arrangements with Sparta in 481 (Hdt. VII.149.1), in effect a guarantee that Sparta would not attack them for a generation, but the first which we hear of are the Five Years' *spondai* between Athens and Sparta in 451 (Thuc. I.112.1) and the Thirty Years' *spondai* between Sparta and Argos in 451/o (Thuc. v.14.4, 28.2; Bengtson 1962 (A 3) no. 144). The Athenians felt later, and rightly, that they had been under the heavier pressure to make peace (Thuc. IV.21.3), and made further territorial concessions, handing over Nisaea and Pegae, the two ports of Megara, Achaea and Troezen.[80] Otherwise each side kept what it held. The essential clause was that neither side was to make an armed attack on the other, if the latter was willing to go to arbitration.[81] Lists of allies were appended to the treaty, which allowed for the possibility of further adhesions to either side, but Athens seems to have been barred from full alliance with Argos. Whether anything was said explicitly in the treaty about the autonomy of the allies on either side, either generally or specifically about Aegina (cf. Thuc. I.67.2), remains unclear; there was a clause in the Peace of Nicias providing for the autonomy of certain cities, provided they paid Athenian tribute (Thuc. v.18.5), and there may have been one here. The duration was fixed at thirty years. Events would show that the treaty was very far from watertight, but deficiencies of detail in the drafting were less important than the unlikelihood that the arbitration clause would work.

To say that Sparta thus recognized the Athenian empire is to make a point which appears in no ancient source (even Thuc. I.69). It seems that the Spartans felt that they had done well to confine Athens to her proper sphere, and, although Plistoanax and Cleandridas went into exile,[82] there is no trace at Sparta of doubt about the Peace. Athens had renounced meddling on the mainland, and the freeing of the Megarid and Boeotia had made Attica much more vulnerable to invasion if there was future misbehaviour. To maintain pressure of a type which would threaten the naval empire would be beyond Sparta's powers and aspirations. The Peace may well have said something to clear Spartan consciences about such clear interests as Aegina and Potidaea. In effect, the dualism of Cimon's aspirations, Sparta to dominate by land, Athens by sea, was being accepted on both sides.

There is little sign of dissatisfaction among Athens' Aegean allies, and Athens seems to have made adjustments in the light of the new situation. Tribute was paid in spring 445 on the basis of a new, conciliatory, assessment. About thirty states have their tributes reduced, and in some

---

[80] For the terms of the Peace, see Bengtson 1962 (A 3) no. 156; de Ste Croix 1972 (G 36) 293–4.

[81] Thuc. VII.18.2; de Ste Croix 1972 (G 36) 259; I am less confident than the latter that this was a single sentence in the original.

[82] The trial seems to have been some months after the Peace; Gomme, *HCT* III 664.

cases the reduction is unequivocal. The states of Rhodes, for example, were paying in the late 440s about three-fifths of their tribute before the Peace. In other cases, there may be compensation for Athens. Potidaea appears for the first time as a tribute-payer; we know that she continued to receive magistrates from Corinth. Given the relations between Athens and Corinth before 446, the standard view[83] that she had been a ship contributor up to this point does not seem attractive; that she started to pay has something to do with the Peace. But there are reductions elsewhere on the Pallene peninsula which precisely balance the new 6 talents from Potidaea; we cannot tell what is going on. Only three rises break the pattern. The most noticeable is Thasos, jumping from 3 to 30 talents. In the general context this can hardly be punitive. It has generally been supposed that she has had land or mines restored to her;[84] it may rather be that money which she had been paying as indemnity is now being paid as tribute.[85]

In terms of actual payment record the picture is quiet. There are minor puzzles. Euboea may have taken time to settle, and there is only one recorded payment, from the Cenaeum peninsula, in the lists of 445 and 444. A case has been made for renewed trouble in Miletus, where there is no recorded payment in 445, 444 or 443, but it is not totally cogent.[86] A practically unique entry shows the Lycians and their co-contributors paying 10 talents in 445. But, compared with what one might have deduced from the literary evidence (Thuc. 1.96, 11.13), tribute is not very large. A strong case can be made[87] for supposing that the actual collection was only 376 talents in 443, which compares well with the calculation of 388 talents which can be made for 432.

IV. AFTER THE PEACE

Whether because of the condemnation of Plistoanax and Cleandridas or for other reasons as well, the Athenians may not have been confident that the Peace would hold. The evidence for their doubt lies in Pericles' sponsorship of a middle Long Wall (see p. 208, Fig. 25), not finished until 443 (Pl. *Gorg.* 455e; Plut. *Per.* 13.7–8; the date from *IG* I³ 440.127). The events of 446 had shown an awkward gap in the strategic theory which had built the Long Walls. With Euboea in revolt, Athens had had nowhere to send its flocks, even if there had been more time for preparation, and the Spartans had actually arrived at a time when the main land force was out of the city. The middle wall would at least meet

[83] *ATL* III 267–8.
[84] Nesselhauf 1933 (E 57) 114; *ATL* III 259.   [85] Meiggs 1972 (E 53) 85–6.
[86] Earp 1954 (E 17); Barron 1962 (E 6); Meiggs 1972 (E 53), 563–5; Piérart 1969, 1974, 1983, 1985 (E 59–61); Robertson 1987 (E 70; see p. 59 n. 88).
[87] M–L p. 88.

such a difficulty as the latter, since it would make it possible to concentrate the wall garrison, a more economical use of troops than manning the Phaleric Wall. Progress was apparently slow (Cratinus F 326 K–A), as the danger receded, and we have no evidence that the wall was ever used.

Meanwhile the Acropolis building programme continued, evidently without much interruption from external events.[88] We have already considered the dedicatory aspects of the Parthenon. As it developed and Phidias' chryselephantine statue took shape, aspects of Athena became stressed which went far beyond her traditional role in Athens.[89] Most accounts of Athena's cult,[90] by assuming that the robe offered to Athena at the Panathenaea continued to go to the old olive-wood statue, leave virtually no cult function for the new temple and statue; the evidence, however, seems to suggest[91] that major parts of the cult were boldly transferred to the new statue. The goddess created was very much one of that generation, and the lines between Athena herself and her city are very blurred.[92] To say that the Athenians built the Parthenon to worship themselves would be an exaggeration, but not a great one. Pericles, as the Funeral Speech (p. 396) makes clear, would probably have accepted that the polis was the true object of devotion; one aspect of his polis is the nature of the relationship between its citizens.

The unknown source of Plut. *Per.* 12.4ff[93] attributes to Pericles economic motives for the building programme, a desire to promote employment and stimulate economic activity as a whole, a strange foreshadowing of the Keynesian 'multiplier'. The suspicion must be that these motives are anachronistic, but they are as hard to match in later ancient theory as in the Classical period. They make no appearance in [Xen.] *Ath. Pol.* 1.13, where they might be expected, and, although Aristotle (*Pol.* VII.1313b18ff) is prepared to discuss building programmes as a way in which tyrants keep their subjects busy and poor, he never contemplates democratic building as a way of making the *demos* busy and rich. When Xenophon in the 350s (*Vect.* 3.12–13) advocates public building, it is to provide income, not work. The specific point made by Plutarch is that Pericles wanted the *demos* to have its share in the fruits of empire, but did not wish it to get it in idleness. Anti-democrats made it a principal charge against Pericles that he made the *demos* idle (Pl.

[88] Burford 1963 (I 38) 28–32.
[89] Herington 1955 (K 39) ch. 7, but see Harrison 1957 (K 38).
[90] E.g. Simon 1983 (K 85) 66.   [91] Lewis 1979–80 (K 57).
[92] This would be particularly the case if the Panathenaic procession on the Parthenon frieze depicted ordinary Athenians (so Brommer 1977 (I 27) 145–50; Simon 1983 (K 85) 58–72), a view argued against by Boardman 1977 (I 18).
[93] Meiggs 1963 (D 58) 42–3; Meiggs 1972 (E 53) 139–40; Andrewes 1978 (D 3); Ameling 1985 (C 2).

Gorg. 515e); this is a defence, but we cannot fix its date. One ground for believing that the passage is relatively early is the fullness and precision of the list of trades involved; one would not have thought that they would all have suggested themselves to a rhetorician of any very late date. What proportion of citizens were engaged in them is perhaps another matter.

For Plutarch the building programme lies at the centre of a political struggle. There is enough earlier evidence to confirm that Cimon's political successor was his son-in-law or brother-in-law, Thucydides son of Melesias of Alopeke,[94] a shade older than Pericles. His father had had no political or military career that we know of, but had an international reputation as a wrestling master; all his known pupils are Aeginetans, which will at times have caused him embarrassment over his city's foreign policy. Thucydides, unlike Cimon, was more a politician than a general, though he could be described as a man of many friends, inside and outside Athens (Pl. *Meno* 94d). Plutarch gives an anachronistic oligarchic colouring to his political stance, which is contrasted with Pericles' lavishness towards the *demos* in providing spectacles, employment in the fleet, cleruchies and the building programme. Pericles' enemies (vague at Plut. *Per.* 12.1, explicitly Thucydides at 14.1) are said to have attacked the programme as a misappropriation of allied funds and excessively lavish in itself; with money compulsorily contributed to the war, the Athenians were gilding and embellishing the city like a wanton woman, bedecking her with expensive stones and statues and temples costing a thousand talents. Pericles' reply was that no account need be rendered to the allies, provided that they received the defence that they were paying for; if the city had what was needed for the war, she was entitled to use the surplus for creating an eternal glory and the economic advantages which we have already considered.

There are certainly suspicious details in this. It is presupposed, apparently, that the war is still on, which is a point against the Peace of Callias for its critics and against the debate for its supporters; the point might be mitigated by shifting the debate to the origins of the building programme, not implausibly. There is certainly rhetorical exaggeration in Pericles' reply that the allies did not contribute horses, ships or hoplites. Yet the core seems reasonable enough. We have seen that the charge that the programme was financed from the League treasury is true, and the complaint about the luxury of the new statues and buildings might fit with what has been suggested above about the innovations in the cult of Athena. These are credible issues, and Thucydides may well have taken a different view from Pericles over relationships with the

[94] Wade-Gery 1958 (A 121) 239–70; Davies 1971 (L 27) 230–3.

allies. There is less reason to believe that he had a distinguishable attitude on relations with Sparta.

The course of the debate cannot be plotted in detail. It ended with Thucydides' ostracism, apparently in spring 443, and Pericles' position as leading man in Athens was apparently unchallenged thereafter.[95] The precise date rests only on Plut. *Per.* 16.3; Pericles had fifteen years of annual generalships after the ostracism.[96] Surviving ostraca of Pericles are very rare, and such evidence as we have, mostly from unpublished ostraca, suggests that Thucydides' supporters tried to concentrate their votes, not against him, but against Cleippides, only known from literature as general in 428.

Other events can be associated with the year 443. It seems that, for no very obvious reason, the quadrennial assessment of tribute was brought forward one year, and the list of 442 shows some tightening of the book-keeping. Organization of the lists by tribute districts is now formalized, though there had been a considerable move to geographical order earlier, and for two years the *hellenotamiai* employed a second secretary; the poet Sophocles was their chairman for 443/2, and the spelling of foreign names is improved.

More substantially, the archon-year 444/3 is the year of the final foundation of Thurii, on the instep of Italy, under Athenian auspices [Plut.] *Mor.* 835c).[97] Since the destruction of the great city of Sybaris in 510, the remnants of its population and the area around it had had a chequered history, which we cannot recover in detail.[98] The situation becomes clearer from 452 (Diod. xi.90.3–4 and, for the later developments, xii.10–11; for the numismatic evidence see Kraay 1976 (c 190) 173–4; see Fig. 4). Under an unknown Thessalos, there was then a refoundation with citizens drawn from Laos and Posidonia. Suppressed again by Croton, the exiles appealed to Sparta, which paid no attention, and to Athens. In 446/5 Athens assumed responsibility, and refounded Sybaris by sending ten ships; the coins of the new Sybaris have a very Athenian Athena on their obverse. Further trouble followed over the privileges claimed by the descendants of old Sybaris, who were expelled (Diod. xii.22.1). In 444/3 the settlement was renamed Thurii and given a democratic constitution with ten tribes (Arcas, Achaeis, Eleia, Boeotia,

---

[95] The nature of his constitutional position is discussed in ch. 4.

[96] This is not evidence that he failed to be elected in 444/3, as maintained by Wade-Gery 1958 (A 121) 240.

[97] See Wade-Gery 1958 (A 121) 255–8; Ehrenberg 1948 (E 20); Smart 1972 (E 83) 138–9 with n. 71.

[98] See *CAH* iii².3, 184. Diod. xi.48.4 attests some kind of continuance in the time of Hieron. For coinage at Laos (cf. Hdt. vi.21), see Kraay 1976 (c 190) 172–3, who also argues (p. 176) for a move to Posidonia. Van Effenterre 1980 (F 22) 193–5 considers the possibility that M–L 10 is later than 510. For an extreme view of a continuously prospering Sybaris, see Vickers 1985 (c 198) 36–7.

Fig. 4. Silver coins of Sybaris and Thurii. (*a, b*) stater and diobol of about 450 B.C.; (*c*) drachma with bull of Sybaris but the name now in Ionic letters and Athena head obverse, about 445 B.C. after refoundation by Athens; (*d*) drachma type changed about 440 B.C.; (*e*) stater with the new name, about 440 B.C. (After Kraay 1976 (C 190) nos. 584–7, 728.)

Amphictyonis, Doris, Ias, Athenaeis, Euboeis, Nesiotis), which made no provision at all for old Sybarites. The Athena head remained on the coins. Among the colonists, at once or eventually, were Herodotus and the family of the orator Lysias (originally Syracusan, but in exile at Athens); Protagoras is said to have written the law code (Heracl. Pont. *ap.* D.L. IX.8.50), and Hippodamus, the Milesian town-planner and political theorist, also went there; he was surely responsible for the grid-plan of the city which Diodorus describes.

Diodorus has only one refounding expedition, where modern scholars, on the evidence of the coins, have two, and it is not certain where his details belong. If he is correct in associating the sending of heralds to the Peloponnese to invite settlers with an expedition led by Pericles' seer Lampon and Xenocritus, there is no ground for distinguishing two types of Athenian thinking in the ventures. The only change was that the original Sybarites proved indigestible. What began with Athens asserting her position as a great Greek power in refounding a famous city turned into an altogether new foundation, one of mixed origins, but in which the Athenians were the largest identifiable element (cf. Diod. XII.35.2). Although many other states were represented, this is not necessarily a sign of pure panhellenism; those who went from the Peloponnese or from Boeotia may well have felt politically, as well as economically, uncomfortable at home. Their gratitude to Athens wore thin later (Diod. XII.35, cf. Thuc. VII.33.5, VIII.35.1), but they were taking part in a project in which Athens' interests were all-important. The colony was a cultural and political gesture, and may have had economic motives as well; the plentiful timber supplies of Italy could have been in view.[99] That Athenian interest in the West was increasing in this period is likely enough; the original Athenian treaty with Rhegium on the toe of Italy seems to be near Thurii in date.[100]

But the first event after the Thirty Years' Peace thought worthy of report by Thucydides is in 440, a war between Samos and Miletus about Priene. This bordered the Samian possessions on the mainland, but was an independent state, paying a regular tribute of one talent to Athens until 441. Miletus' tribute may have been interrupted (see p. 138), but she was paying again in 442. Samos had remained a ship contributor, under an oligarchy. The claims and counter-claims are obscure for us,[101] but the Milesians got the worst of the war and, supported by individual Samian democrats, denounced the Samians to Athens. Athens' case for intervention was rather curious. Since her allies had sworn to have the same friends and enemies, it could be held that wars within the empire were against their oaths. The Peloponnesian League had never interpreted the oath in that sense, but the Athenians now did. 'Fighting each other' is given by Hermocrates at Thuc. VI.76.3 as one of the pretexts used by Athens for subjecting her allies; this is the only instance we know, and it may have been preceded by a Samian refusal to accept Athenian arbitration (Plut. Per. 25.1).[102] An Athenian fleet[103] of forty ships went to Samos, took a hundred hostages, depositing them on Lemnos, and set up a democracy supported by an Athenian garrison. Samos retained her fleet.[104]

Some Samians fled to the mainland and applied to Pissuthnes, the satrap of Sardis, for help. They raised 700 mercenaries and, coordinating their plan with the Samian upper classes, crossed to Samos by night. An attack on the *demos* was largely successful, the hostages were daringly rescued from Lemnos (a round trip of 640 km or so), and Samos was in revolt. The Athenian garrison and magistrates were handed over to Pissuthnes.[105] An expedition was prepared against Miletus, evidence both for the height of feeling among the Samians and their scepticism

[99] Cf. Meiggs 1982 (L 99) 124–5.

[100] This and a treaty with Leontini in Sicily were renewed together in 433/2 (M–L 63–4), but the date of the original treaty with Leontini, probably earlier, is harder to fix; see Lewis 1976 (C 139).

[101] See Meiggs 1972 (E 53) 428: the position of Marathesium, paying tribute for the first time, probably, in 442.   [102] de Ste Croix 1972 (G 36) 120–1.

[103] Commanded by Pericles, according to Diod. XII.27.1 and Plut. Per. 25.2.

[104] On this part of the story see Schuller 1981 (E 79). For the chronology, see p. 502.

[105] For the implications of Pissuthnes' activities see Lewis 1977 (A 76) 59.

about the power of Athens to interfere. Athenian response was, however, swift. Chios and Lesbos were summoned to help and a force went to Caria to watch for any mobilization of the Phoenician fleet. With a force of 44 ships, Pericles caught a Samian fleet of 70 ships returning from Miletus and won a victory. Reinforced by 40 more ships from Athens and 25 from Chios and Lesbos, the Athenians landed and started a siege. At this point, reports of the approach of the Phoenician fleet grew stronger,[106] and Pericles took 60 ships towards Caria. In his absence the Samians broke out and did much damage to the remains of the blockading squadron and their camp; for fourteen days they controlled their home waters and replenished their supplies. On Pericles' return the siege was resumed. Further reinforcements, 60 ships from Athens, 30 from Chios and Lesbos, created an overwhelming force, and, though the siege continued for some months, the Samians at last surrendered. Their walls were demolished and their fleet handed over to Athens, and they agreed to repay the cost of their subjection by instalments; it is, however, by no means clear that Athens continued her attempt to impose democracy.[107] There had indeed been no sign that democracy at Samos had deep roots; her sailors had fought well. If an oligarchy remained, it was one without a fleet which had been forced to give up mainland adventures. A settlement of exiles is later found at Anaea on the mainland opposite.

One of the clearest indications of the incompleteness of Thucydides' account of the Fifty Years is that the four hundred words which he devotes to this episode contain no hint of an important event which he refers to elsewhere (1.40.5, 41.2). The Peloponnesian League congress met and was divided in its opinions as to whether to help the Samians; all we know of the debate is that the Corinthians claimed to have spoken against intervention and for the right of a great power to chastise its own allies. It has been held[108] that, if the course of events was the same as that in 432 (see below, p. 378), such a League meeting would have been preceded by a decision of the Spartan Assembly that there was a *prima facie* case for war. That is perhaps an extreme view, but it is reasonably clear that Sparta at least thought that the opinion of her allies should be tested. It should be even clearer that news of such a meeting will not have encouraged Athenian belief in the durability of the Thirty Years' Peace.[109]

That the Samians had come near to taking the command of the sea

---

[106] It is in fact not clear that it was ever mobilized at all (*ibid.*).

[107] On the fragmentary epigraphic record of the treaty (M–L 56 = *IG* I³ 48) see also Fornara 1979 (E 26), Bridges 1980 (C 123). On the constitution of Samos after 439, see Meiggs 1972 (E 53) 193–4 and Schuller 1981 (E 79) (democracy), Will 1969 (E 94) and Quinn 1981 (E 64) 13–19 (oligarchy).

[108] Jones 1952–3 (E 38); cf. de Ste Croix 1972 (G 36) 200–3.

[109] The Peloponnesians were mentioned in the treaty between Samos and Athens (*IG* I³ 48.7); we cannot tell how.

from Athens (Thuc. VIII.76.4) is an exaggeration, but the situation had been dangerous. Nevertheless, the possible intervention from Persia and the Peloponnesians had not happened, and the Lesbian and Chian fleets had answered Athens' call. The Samians had been virtually isolated. Only Byzantium, in an episode of which we know nothing whatever, had joined the revolt and returned to allegiance; she may have been moved by the change of sides by her mother-city Megara. The Athenian empire had survived.

The Samian revolt is the latest event described by Thucydides before the sequence which started in 435 and led to the outbreak of war. The impression of a historical lull is heightened by a sheer accident; the tribute quota-lists of 438, 437, 436, most of 435 and half of 434 have been lost by the weathering of the stone. From the missing years, two events emerge which, in their different ways, illustrate Athenian self-assertion.[110]

The first, the foundation of Amphipolis, has a clear date, the archon-year 437/6 (Diod. XII.32.2; Schol. Aeschin. II.31, cf. Thuc. IV.102.3). Athenian eyes had long been fixed on the area where the river Strymon came down to the sea in a great bend. Now, after the failures of 476 (pp. 41–2) and 465 (p. 44), the dream became a reality. Hagnon, who had already served in the Samian War, drove out the Edonians, built a wall from river to river and founded a great city. The Strymon crossing was in itself worth controlling, and by 424 the city was already a vital interest for Athens (Thuc. IV.108.1), for its supplies of ship timber and its financial resources (that is, principally, the gold mines of Mt Pangaeum). Ten thousand settlers had been thought appropriate in 465, and we should think of a similar number now, but we have very little information about how they were made up. The Athenian element was not large (Thuc. IV.106.1), and otherwise we only hear specifically of settlers from Argilus (Thuc. IV.103.3);[111] the dialect was the Euboean form of Ionic (Tod, *GHI* 150), and doubtless Chalcidians from Thrace were strongly represented. We have next to no information about the constitution.[112]

More shadowy is Pericles' expedition to the Black Sea, briefly

---

[110] It is tempting to add a third. At some time before 431, Athens intervened in north-west Greece in a local quarrel between Ambracia and the Acarnanians, sending thirty ships under Phormio; some Ambraciots were sold into slavery, and an alliance was made between Athens and the Acarnanians (Thuc. II.68.2–9). Ambracia was a Corinthian colony with very close ties to her mother-city (Graham 1964 (A 52) 138–40), and Corinth had been the only great power in the area. There is no clear way to date the episode, but the early 430s seem most likely (Meiggs 1972 (E 53) 204).

[111] Argilus was always hostile to the colony, and presumably lost land to it, since its tribute drops from 1 talent in 437 to 1,000 drachmae in 432. (It is probably a stone-cutter's error which shows it paying 10½ talents in 453; *contra*, Meiggs 1972 (E 53) 159 n. 3.)

[112] *IG* i³ 47 may be an Athenian decree relevant to the foundation. For recent excavations see *Archaeological Reports* 1976–7, 92; 1978–9, 29–31; 1980–1, 33; 1981–2, 41; 1982–3, 44–5; 1983–4, 48–9; 1984–5, 47–8.

Fig. 5. Silver coin of Amisus, renamed
Piraeus. (After E. Babelon, *Traité des
monnaies grecques et romaines* (1901–19) II
pl. 185, 11; cf. B. V. Head, *Historia
Numorum* (1911) 496.)

described by Plutarch (*Per.* 20.1–2).[113] With a large fleet, splendidly
fitted out, he attended to the needs of the Greek cities in a friendly way
and showed the greatness of Athenian power to the barbarians around
and their kings. The only detail is that he left thirteen ships at Sinope
with Lamachus, who assisted in driving out the tyrant Timesileos;[114] six
hundred volunteer Athenian settlers went to Sinope to take over the
property of the tyrant's faction. We have no idea where else Pericles
went, though there is a strongish case for an Athenian settlement at
Amisus (Theopompus *FGrH* 115 F 389, Appian *Bell. Mithr.* 83; fourth-
century coins with an owl on the reverse (*HN²* 496) (Fig. 5) show it
renamed Piraeus). The corn supply from the Black Sea seems to have
been reliable thereafter and in the fourth century Athenian relations with
the Spartocid dynasty of the Crimea had long been good (see *CAH* VI²,
chapter 11*j*), but there is no particular reason to associate the expedition
with the accession of Spartocus in 438/7 (Diod. XII.31.1).

A contemporary (Ion fr.16 *ap.* Plut. *Per.* 28.7) reports that, after the
Samian War, Pericles said that it had taken Agamemnon ten years to
capture a barbarian city, but that he had defeated the first and most
powerful of the Ionians in nine months. The remark was not likely to be
well received by panhellenists (cf. the comment of Cimon's sister
Elpinice at Plut. *Per.* 28.6), and makes few appearances in the modern
literature. The year 446 had been a bad one, but in the ten years thereafter
Athens under Pericles had squashed a major revolt in the empire,
founded two great cities, dedicated the most splendid of temples with a
cult-statue of unparalleled splendour at the Great Panathenaea of 438
(Schol. Ar. *Peace* 605), and sailed on the track of the Argonauts. Pericles
was not a modest man, and there was nothing little about his ideas.

---

[113] The approximate date of the expedition is not now in doubt, despite the attempt of *ATL* III
114–17 to date it around 450. Besides arguments from the age of Lamachus, it is now virtually
certain that an Athenian casualty list of the 430s listed casualties 'in [Sin]ope' (ἐν [Σιν]όπει) (new
fragment of *Agora* XVII 17 in Clairmont 1979 (C 126) 123–6 and 1983 (K 17) 178–80; Clairmont's view
that the stone was not inscribed until 431 is not convincing, but it certainly cannot go back into the
440s).

[114] Timesileos seems to have gone to Olbia; see Vinogradov 1981 (F 69) (*SEG* XXXI 701).

CHAPTER 7

SICILY, 478–431 B.C.

D. ASHERI

After the battle of Himera in 480 (see *CAH* IV² 771–5), Sicily was once again divided into four main political blocs. The western corner of the island was the 'epicracy', or dominion, of Carthage, with major centres at Panormus, Solus and Motya, and no territorial changes despite the Greek victory. The Elymian enclave, with its main cities of Segesta, Eryx and Entella, also remained subject to Carthage, though culturally hellenized, and Greek Selinus, while aspiring to neutrality, remained subservient to Carthage as well. Although Punic Sicily flourished throughout the fifth century, Carthage itself was notably absent from Sicilian affairs. Greek Sicily also remained divided into its three epicracies under their respective ruling dynasties: the Deinomenids at Syracuse, the Emmenids at Acragas and the Anaxilads at Rhegium. To these three all other Siciliote cities were subject; Syracuse controlled Naxus, Leontini, Catana and Camarina; Acragas dominated Gela and Himera; and Messana was united with Rhegium. The determining force was no longer the Greek–Punic antagonism of the 480s, but the maintenance of the balance of power between the two main epicracies, the Syracusan and the Acragantine, the latent rivalry between them suddenly erupting in unexpected 'wars'. The Sicel (and Sican) heart of the island, separated from, yet connected with, the Greek coastal fringe by a large hellenized belt, remained unaffected by fifth-century changes, whereas the hellenized Sicel zones, especially the part subject to Syracuse in eastern Sicily, were to play a role in an extraordinary though unsuccessful attempt at autonomy.

A useful collection of sources (literary, epigraphic and numismatic) on Sicily in this period is included in Hill, *Sources²*, *Index* v, pp. 361–4; for sources and bibliography on ancient sites see Manni 1981 (H 11); evidence from archaeology and air photography, indispensable and invaluable today, will be found in section H of the Bibliography. The main narrative is to be found in the Sicilian chapters of Diodorus Siculus (XI.38, 48–9, 51–3, 59, 66–8, 72–3, 76, 78, 86–92, XII.8, 26, 29–30), mainly following Timaeus' *Histories* (Books XI–XII; see fragments in *FGrH* 566). Diodorus' dates should often be taken as approximate, owing to his habit of bringing together under the same year several events belonging to a longer period. The relevant odes of Pindar (*Ol.* I–VI, XII; *Pyth.* I–III; *Nem.* I, IX; *Isthm.* II), with their scholia, and Bacchylides (*Epin.* III–V), as well as a few fragments of Aeschylus and Simonides, reflect the opinion of foreign court guests on their hosts and on some of the historical events mentioned in this chapter. Pausanias' description of Sicilian dedications at Olympia and Delphi and his data on Sicilian victors at panhellenic games add valuable information.

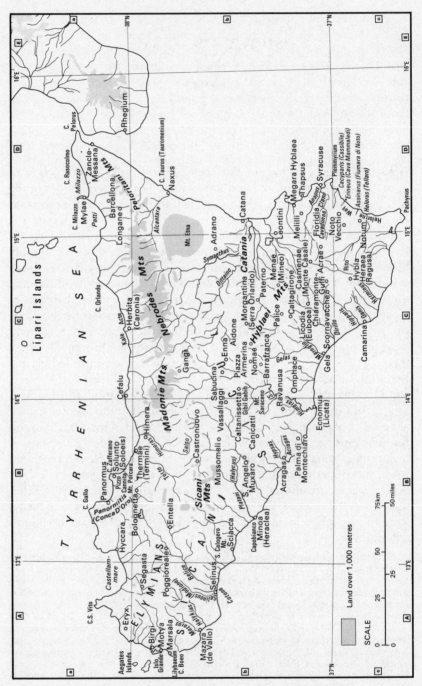

3. Sicily

Unquestionably, the central event of the period is the fall of the three Greek tyrannies and the subsequent disintegration of their respective epicracies. Yet its lasting effect was practically confined to the internal affairs of the cities concerned. All major trends and structures of Sicilian and Western history remained basically unaffected. Economic and cultural prosperity, hellenization, the tendency towards the creation of blocs and new epicracies, the drive of the latter to annexe the hellenized Sicel belt, and, on a more comprehensive scale, the struggle for hegemony on the Tyrrhenian Sea and the irreversible Etruscan decline – such historical trends, though some of them temporarily halted by the fall of the tyrannies, all emerged stronger than ever within a couple of decades. Continuity prevailed over change in fifth-century Sicily. The democracies had to conform to the rules of the game laid down in the age of the tyrannies and determined by the given framework of economic and political interests and powers.

I. SICILY IN THE AGE OF HIERO

After Gelon's death in 478/7, his brother Hiero ascended the Syracusan throne, according to the alleged Deinomenid rule of succession from brother to brother. Hiero's younger brother Polyzalos was married to Gelon's widow Damarete (the daughter of Theron of Acragas) and received the governorship of Gela, at the time under Syracusan sovereignty. Polyzalos then gave his daughter from a previous wife to Theron, thereby cementing relations with Acragas and the Emmenid dynasty (*FGrH* 566 F 93; Hill, *Sources*[2] B 101). Tensions between the two Deinomenid brothers must have arisen immediately. Though much pleased to be addressed publicly by Pindar, his greatest court poet, as the '*basileus* who governs Syracuse' (*Pyth.* III.70) or the '*tyrannos*, leader of the people' (*ibid.* 85), Hiero himself never used an official title or put his own name on coins. Rather, he always signed himself modestly 'Hiero, the son of Deinomenes', adding tactfully 'and the Syracusans' on official dedications (M–L 29), and his coins were always 'of the Syracusans'. Polyzalos was a different character. He pompously dubbed himself 'The One who is Lord (Ϝανάσσων) over Gela' on the base of the famous Delphic Charioteer (Hill, *Sources*[2] B 101), and manifestly resented his second-class position in the state. When Hiero tried to get rid of him by sending him to war in Italy, Polyzalos returned to Gela victorious at the head of a great army and joined forces with Theron. War between Syracuse and Acragas was prevented, according to one version of the story, at the last moment through the good offices of a common friend of Hiero and Theron, the poet Simonides of Ceos. The crisis passed, Polyzalos kept Gela, and the Grand Alliance between the Deinomenids and the Emmenids was saved (*FGrH* 566 F 93; cf. Diod. XI.48.3–8).

Hiero's next problem was how to achieve Syracusan control over the eastern and northern coasts of Sicily. The area was largely Sicel, with four important Chalcidian cities peacefully coexisting with their hellenized neighbours: Naxus, Catana and Leontini on the eastern area, and Himera, a dependency of Acragas, on the northern coast. Hiero soon decided to resume Gelon's policy of mass-deportation and resettlement. In 476 the entire population of Naxus and Catana was transferred to Leontini; Naxus apparently remained depopulated, while Catana was resettled with 10,000 Dorian colonists and renamed Aitna. Chromios, a brother-in-law of Gelon and an old partisan of the Deinomenid cause, was appointed *epitropos* of Aitna until Hiero's son, Deinomenes, came of age (Diod. xi.49.1–2; Pind. *Pyth.* 1; *Nem.* 1, IX, with scholia). The event was celebrated by a series of tetradrachms and drachms, of which only single specimens have survived, showing on the reverse a seated Zeus 'Aitnaios' holding thunderbolt and sceptre and a Syracusan quadriga on the obverse. Contemporary sources are full of the praises of court poets. Pindar calls Hiero 'Aitnaios' and 'the renowned Founder of Aitna', and dedicated to Chromios two Nemean odes. Pindar was fond of the idea of a Dorian community in Aitna 'living in freedom according to the laws of Hyllos' rule' (*Pyth.* 1.61), and even the Ionian Bacchylides was enthusiastic about 'well-built' Aitna (fr. 20C.7), and the Athenian Aeschylus contributed a drama, *The Aitnaean Women*, written specially for the occasion (*Vit. Aesch.* 9). However, for a view of the less glorious side of mass-deportation we must turn to later sources. Four main points clearly emerge from Diodorus' account of the foundation of Aitna (probably derived from Timaeus): the Chalcidians were forcibly deported; Catana was resettled by Hiero's 'own colonists', 5,000 from Syracuse and as many from the Peloponnese;[1] lots were distributed in the newly delimited territory of Aitna, after it had been much enlarged through expropriation of neighbouring Sicel lands; and finally, the unflattering assumption was made that the real aim of the enterprise was to create a ready base of loyal supporters and establish a Founder-cult of Hiero. In any case, contrary to official expectations, Aitna had but a short and precarious life. It began with an eruption of nearby Etna,[2] an ominous event that greatly impressed both Pindar and Aeschylus, and ended in 461 with an outbreak of a different kind (see below, pp. 161f).

[1] According to Schol. Pind. *Pyth.* 1 62 (120) b, settlers were brought from Gela, Megara and Syracuse (but Megara ceased to exist *c.* 483). Evidence on Arcadian immigrants is relatively solid for the first half of the century, e.g. Hagesias of Stymphalus (Pind. *Olymp.* VI), Phormis of Maenalus (Paus. v.27.1ff), Praxiteles of Mantinea (see below, n. 8), and others (see Guarducci 1953 (H 23) and 1959–60 (C 132) 270).

[2] In 475, according to Thucydides' informants (III.116.2); the *Marmor Parium* mentions an eruption (the same or a previous one?) under the year 479/8 (see *FGrH* 239 A 52).

Theron of Acragas was not to be outdone. He too must found, or at least refound, a city, preferably a Chalcidian one. Himera was under his sway, harshly governed by his son Thrasybulus. In the same year that Aitna was founded, some harassed citizens of Himera secretly complained to Hiero, a fatal *faux pas* that was immediately revealed to Theron and branded subversive. The 'plotters', who were many, were promptly arrested and either put to death or exiled. No better opportunity to 'refound' Himera could have been hoped for. Accordingly, all the confiscated houses and lands of the dead or banished plotters were granted to a group of settlers, mainly Dorian, who had been enrolled by Theron for this purpose. Surprisingly enough, Diodorus tells us that the new settlers lived on good terms with the surviving citizens of Himera until the end of the century (XI.48.6–8, 49.3–4). If so, Himera, with its mixed Ionian–Dorian population and dialect, and its mixed cults and institutions, provides us with a remarkable example of peaceful coexistence in a century marked by cruel episodes of ethnic antagonism.[3] By now, all Sicilian coastal cities were Dorian: in two of them, Himera and Messana, lived Chalcidian communities, and the inland Leontini became an internment camp for all the surviving Ionians.

With the colonization of Aitna and Himera in 476, Messana found itself surrounded. Left since the battle of Himera without Carthage, his major ally, Anaxilas managed to survive by quickly switching to Gelon's side and giving his daughter in marriage to Hiero (Schol. Pind. *Pyth.* 1.58); but he could not afford to conduct an independent foreign policy. Inasmuch as Hiero's best friends in southern Italy were Epizephyrian Locri and the scattered Sybarite communities, Rhegium and Croton, both substantial powers, found themselves in the grip of Syracuse. Hiero's dream of supplanting Rhegium on the Tyrrhenian Sea was realized soon after Anaxilas' death around 476 when a delegation from Campanian Cumae asked Hiero for help against the Etruscans. A Syracusan fleet put in immediately at Cumae, joined with local forces to fight a naval battle, in which many Etruscan ships were destroyed, and delivered Cumae from danger (Pind. *Pyth.* 1.71 with scholia; schol. to *ibid.* II.1; Diod. XI.51). It was presumably in connexion with this famous battle (474 B.C.) that an abortive attempt was made to garrison the island of Pithecussae (Ischia), opposite Cumae, with Syracusan military settlers (Str. V.4.9, p. 248). With Cumae and her new colony at Naples both friendly to Hiero, the southern Tyrrhenian Sea was gradually becoming a Syracusan lake.

---

[3] Probably in the same year another plot was crushed by Theron; two Emmenids in exile, Capys and Hippocrates, first occupied Camicus, a Sican town (the legendary capital of Kokalos, located on Mt S. Calogero near modern Sciacca) and then fought to the last near Himera (*FGrH* 568 F 2; Schol. Pind. *Ol.* II 95).

Fig. 6. Bronze helmet of Etruscan type dedi-
cated by Hiero at Olympia. 'Hiero, son of
Deinomenes, and the Syracusans [dedicate] to
Zeus, from the Tyrrhenian spoils at Cumae.'
(M–L 29; after W. Hege and G. Rodenwaldt,
Olympia (1936) 27, fig. 12.)

Hiero and his court poets made the most of the battle of Cumae. Part
of the spoils was promptly sent as offerings to Olympia and Delphi. At
Olympia three bronze helmets (M–L 29; *SEG* XXXIII 328) have been
found bearing inscriptions in archaic Syracusan script: 'Hiero, the son of
Deinomenes, and the Syracusans – to Zeus, from (the spoils of) the
Tyrrhenian at Cumae' (Fig. 6). At Delphi a golden tripod and a Nike
were later dedicated by Hiero beside the tripod offered there by Gelon
after the battle of Himera (Ath. VI.231f; cf. Bacch. III.17–19). The
panhellenic myth of Greeks fighting barbarians was revived. Simonides,
in a well-known, but possibly partly spurious, epigram (Page, *Epigr. Gr.*
Sim. XXXIV), represented the sons of Deinomenes as 'conquerors of
barbarian nations who offered the Greeks a mighty allied hand for
freedom'. Pindar for once was less enthusiastic: his own prayer in 470
was that 'the Phoenician and the Tyrrhenians' war-cry keep quiet at
home: it has seen what woe to its ships came of its pride before Kyme'
(*Pyth.* 1.72 f). All this looks like a well-orchestrated plan on the part of
Hiero to emulate Gelon and even surpass him in feats of arms, display of
wealth, and panhellenic propaganda. This, of course, is not to say that
the battle of Cumae was an insignificant event. On the contrary, modern
scholars have rightly considered it the turning point in the Etruscan
decline; but this decline was not yet perceptible to Hiero's generation.
And Hiero's panhellenic propaganda, though formally justifiable by the
fact that Dorian Syracuse fought with Chalcidian Cumae against the
Etruscans, was obviously intended also to obscure the memory of less
pleasant facts, as Gelon's refusal to give a 'mighty allied hand' to the
Greeks against the Persians (*CAH* IV² 772) and Hiero's own policy of
dechalcidization and doricization in Sicily.

Hiero's control over the Tyrrhenian coast as far as Cumae remained firmly in his hands until the end of his life. After Anaxilas' death in about 476, the overlordship over Rhegium and Messana was entrusted to Micythos, a former liegeman of Anaxilas, who ruled honestly as *epitropos* of his master's sons (Hdt. vii.170.4; Just. iv 2.5; Diod. xi.48.2). However, as soon as they came of age (*c.* 469/8), Micythos was honourably dismissed through the direct intervention of Hiero, and after rendering an impeccable account of his administration, he retired to spend the rest of his life at Tegea in Arcadia (Hdt. *loc. cit.*; Paus. v.26.2–5; *DGE* 794).

Apart from these crises, the Concert of Greek Sicily was successfully orchestrated by Hiero until his major partner Theron died in 472. Hiero's last years were certainly not his happiest. The fall of the tyrannies at Acragas, Gela and Himera must have had repercussions within the Syracusan epicracy, perhaps in the form of increased oppression; but evidence is ambiguous and lacks a precise chronological setting. Epicharmus' picture of night watchmen (*peripoloi*) giving a good beating to a suspected vagabond in the streets of Syracuse (fr. 35 Kaibel) is no more than a picturesque scene from the night life of any ancient city. But regular employment of spies and delators under Hiero seems well attested. Aristotle may have preserved a Syracusan term, *potagogides*, for women-spies(?); he also mentions the 'eavesdroppers' (*otakoustai*) despatched by Hiero to report the utterances and sentiments of people in town (*Pol.* v.1313b11). Even such devices, however, are not peculiar to tyrannies; democracies too had their sycophants, and Aristotle himself was aware that Hiero's model for his eavesdroppers might have been borrowed from Persia. Yet at Syracuse they aroused dread and suspicion even at the tyrant's court.

Nevertheless, Hiero's court was pre-eminently a *salon* of literary men. It probably developed as such during the years of the tyrant's illness. Almost all his guests were great poets imported from Greece and Ionia: Pindar, who settled in Sicily long enough to make friends and enemies at court and to dedicate to Sicilian tyrants and magnates one-third of his extant poems; Aeschylus, whose *Persians* was performed at Syracuse in 471 (another instance of panhellenic propaganda) (*Vit. Aesch.* 18), and came to Sicily for a last time after 458 to settle and die at Gela; Simonides of Ceos, to whom are also ascribed odes in honour of Theron's brother Xenocrates and Anaxilas (or his son Leophron); Simonides' nephew Bacchylides and the Ionian Xenophanes of Colophon. Two of his guests were certainly Sicilians: Epicharmus and Phormis.

A valetudinarian despot like his elder brother, Hiero suffered for years from gall-stones. In about 474/3 his illness was alarming enough for Pindar to send him a consolatory letter (*Pythian* iii); and in 470 the poet compared Hiero with Philoctetes, the wounded hero (*Pyth.* 1.50). At last, in 467 the tyrant died; he was buried in Aitna and accorded heroic honours (Diod. XI.66.4; Str. VI.2.3, p. 268). To his son Deinomenes, by then governor of Aitna, he left the task of dedicating at Olympia the offerings he had vowed for his victories (Paus. VI.12.1, VIII.42.8). With Hiero's death, the age of archaic tyranny in Sicily came to an end. After him, *le déluge*. As was the case with many archaic tyrants, Hiero's appraisal by his contemporaries and later generations was ambivalent. Inevitably, to his court poets he was a wise and just king, never jealous of nobles, a generous host, the blessed leader of armies, the first in opulence and glory, and even a man of letters. Later authors display mixed feelings. The Timaean tradition as retained by Diodorus had much good to say of Gelon, but not of Hiero, who is depicted as violent and avaricious, unbeloved by his subjects and a stranger to sincerity and nobility of character. A different appraisal was expressed by Xenophon, who wrote a fictitious dialogue between Hiero and Simonides on the happiness of tyrants and their subjects. Later, Plutarch (*Mor.* 551F) favourably compared Hiero and Pisistratus, both of whom, he says, maintained 'good order' (*eunomia*), promoted husbandry, and taught the people sobriety and industry. The comparison of Hiero with Pisistratus implies that in later centuries, at least some archaic tyrants could be judged by their actions, without the modern need to classify them sociologically as 'restorers' or 'revolutionaries'. Hiero, like Gelon – but unlike Pisistratus – was indeed a champion of the old good order, and the Deinomenids were remembered as such when their rule was contrasted with the years of democratic anarchy preceding and following them. Theirs was a military monarchy, the rise and fall of which never entailed an economic revolution of any sort; as a result, both agrarian and commercial classes were left to thrive. It was truly a golden age for Syracuse, and even allowing for the high price in human suffering, it was a golden age for most of the Western Greeks as well.

II. THE FALL OF THE TYRANNIES

As we said earlier, the central event of Sicilian history during the period in question is the fall of the three great dynasties within a decade (471–462) and the consequent disintegration of their respective epicracies. Acragas was the first to meet this fate for the simple reason that Theron was the first of the great established tyrants to die without leaving a worthy successor. In 472 his son Thrasydaeus ascended the throne. Having demonstrated his unfitness as governor of Himera, in the first and only year of his reign at Acragas he provoked a pointless war with Syracuse by conscripting an alarming host of some 20,000 citizen levies and mercenaries. He was easily defeated by Hiero on the river Acragas. Subsequently expelled by the citizenry, he fled to Megara, in central

Greece, where he was put to death in 471. Peace was soon restored between free Acragas and Syracuse, a decisive step which saved the infant republic. Tyranny thus helped to bury itself. Following an exhaustive war against Thrasydaeus' mercenaries, the citizenry finally forced them to evacuate their quarters in town and to withdraw to Minoa, some 32 km west of Acragas. A few years later the mercenaries were also dislodged from Minoa by a joint Acragantine and Syracusan attack. This spelled the end of the Emmenid dynasty and the beginning of the end of all tyrannies in Sicily.[4]

The fall of the Emmenids marked not only a radical constitutional change in the city state of Acragas, but also the dissolution of the entire Acragantine epicracy. This happened not because the new republic was anti-imperialistic, but because it was paralysed by its domestic troubles and unable to maintain control over its foreign dominions. The result was that two important subject towns, Gela and Himera, were gradually transformed into autonomous republican city states. Although Gela was already free when the Syracusans petitioned its help in 466, its citizens were still engaged in a protracted war against their mercenaries, who had withdrawn to such strongholds as Omphace and Cacyrium in the hellenized Sicel hinterland north west of Gela. Only after the liberation of Syracuse could the latter aid Gela in this struggle, and only then were the Geloans who had been deported to Syracuse by Gelon able to return to their homeland. Himera, too, was free by 471. Later on, Pindar joyfully invoked Saviour Tyche, 'the daughter of Zeus the Liberator' in his ode in honour of Ergoteles, a Himeraean Olympic victor, apparently performed in 466.[5] In 466 that city, like Gela, was able to aid the Syracusan revolt. Some exiles returned to Himera, while the local mercenaries left, eventually settling in the territory of Messana.[6] Recent excavations provide evidence of a new urban plan at Himera, which supplanted an earlier one. However, the chronology of the finds is too vague to enable us to verify whether the new plan is to be referred to the restructuring of the city state after liberation or to the Dorian resettlement of 476 (see above, p. 151)[7]. While Gela retained long after

[4] The liberation of Acragas was probably celebrated with offerings to Delphi (see the story in Ael. *VH* II.33). Before the final attack on Minoa, an Acragantine expedition against Crastus (an unidentified Sican town in the centre of Sicily, possibly halfway between Acragas and Himera (modern Kassar?), and allegedly the birthplace of Epicharmus) provoked a war between Acragas and her former subject-cities Gela and Himera (*P. Oxy.* IV 665 = *FGrH* 577 F 1), the context of which is hopelessly obscure.   [5] See Barrett 1973 (H 32).

[6] This is one plausible interpretation of a confused passage of Justin (IV.3.1). On the settlement of mercenaries in the Messenian territory see below.

[7] The reckoning of the Himeraean era of 'good regime' in Diod. XI.49.4 is similarly ambiguous: if the right reading is 58 years (as in all MSS), the era must open in 466 (to end with the Carthaginian sack of 409); if corrected to 68 years, it opens in 476, the year of Theron's resettlement, when Himera became a Dorian–Chalcidian mixed city.

Fig. 7. Silver coins of (*a, b*) Himera, didrachm and tetradrachm, about 465 B.C.; and (*c*) Aitna, tetradrachm, about 475–470 B.C. (After Kraay and Hirmer 1966 (C 192) figs. 66–7, 33.)

liberation the coinage types established by the tyrants, Himera rejected the Acragantine symbols and adopted new ones, especially a river-goddess pouring libation over an altar. A coin of Himera with a biga and the name of Pelops has been thought to celebrate Ergoteles's Olympic victories (Fig. 7*b*).

The liberation of Syracuse, like that of Acragas, had to await the death of her established tyrant and the revolt which his harsh successor provoked. When Hiero died in 467 his brother Thrasybulus seized power; Polyzalos must have been dead at that time. But Gelon had a son, next in line to the throne after Thrasybulus, who had to be awarded some governorship or command. His disappointment gave rise to a dynastic crisis. Wider discontent at Syracuse is ascribed to Thrasybulus' violent character and to his execution or exiling of many citizens in order to confiscate their property. At last the Syracusans revolted, chose their own leaders and seized the suburbs outside the walls of Achradina. Military aid, infantry, cavalry and even ships promptly arrived from the free cities of Acragas, Gela and Himera, as well as from pro-Punic Selinus and the Sicels. Basing himself on the fortified island of Ortygia and in the walled quarter of Achradina, Thrasybulus tried to resist with an army of mercenaries and a force of colonists from Aitna, but after his defeat on land and sea he was forced to leave with his garrison. He was given permission to retire to the friendly town of Epizephyrian Locri in southern Italy, there to spend the rest of his life as a private citizen (Diod. XI.67–8).

The end of tyranny at Syracuse precipitated the immediate dissolution of the Deinomenid epicracy in eastern Sicily. Again, as in the case of Acragas, it was not out of the love of liberty for all that the nascent republic of Syracuse assisted in the break-up of its own dominions, but out of the imperative need for loyal allies in the fierce fight for its own liberty. A general autonomistic movement spread from city to city, calling for liberty (rather than 'democracy'), repatriation of the deported or exiled 'Old Citizens', enlistment of 'New Citizens' to swell the popular ranks, and redistribution of land. This programme appears to be a restoration of the *status quo ante* rather than an innovative plan. At first, armed violence raged everywhere; the garrisons and governors found themselves besieged in their own quarters and acropolis by the rebellious citizenries. Later, a 'Common Resolution' (*koinon dogma*) was endorsed by most cities, according to which the 'Old Citizens' were entitled to return and partial rights were conferred upon veterans and immigrants who had been naturalized in their respective cities by the tyrants. The garrisons on active service were required to leave the cities and settle in the territory of Messana, the only city in Sicily still governed by tyrants (Diod. XI.72–3, 76).

Five autonomous, republican city states grew up within a few years on the ruins of the Syracusan epicracy: Syracuse itself, Catana, Naxus, Leontini and Camarina. All started new issues of coins, usually rejecting types associated with tyranny (with the exception of the Syracusan quadriga, which gradually lost its former political meaning) and adopting new types with gods or local river-deities. The republic of Syracuse was left with her own city territory on the south eastern corner of the island and with her colonial outposts at Acrae and Casmenae. The Dorian colony of Aitna was attacked by a host of armed Sicels under the leadership of Ducetius – the first appearance of this remarkable personage, whose career we shall treat at length in the next section – in cooperation with a republican army from Syracuse. The Aitnaeans were ejected, and the original Catanaeans came back from Leontini, where they had been confined since 476. Aitna again became Catana, a

Fig. 8. Silver *litra* of Camarina, after 460 B.C.
(*British Museum Catalogue of Greek Coins* Sicily 33.)

Chalcidian city; the territory was delimited anew, with the Sicels recovering their confiscated lands while the returning Catanaeans redistributed their own portion among themselves. Clearly, free Syracuse preferred an anti-Deinomenid Chalcidian–Sicel population on the banks of the Simeto to a Dorian base of potential followers of a new tyrant. The ejected Aitnaeans removed to Inessa, a Sicel township on the slopes of Etna west of Catana (it is variously located in the area of Civiti or Paternò), taking with them the bones of Founder Hiero from his desecrated tomb. At Inessa a new Aitna grew up near the Sicel township, and some form of coexistence had to be worked out by both communities, possibly more along the lines of the peaceful Chalcidian model than on the coercive Syracusan one. A coin of Aitna with the head of Selinus replacing the Syracusan quadriga on the obverse has been hesitantly attributed to the new Dorian settlement at Inessa.

Naxus too must have been restored by its original population returning from Leontini. At any rate, Thucydides mentions that the town existed in 425. A new urban plan, consisting of straight streets and long rectangular blocks with boundary stones at the crossroads, can plausibly be attributed to the resettlement at this time, since nothing about a Deinomenid foundation at Naxus is known from extant sources. Leontini, relieved at last of its surplus population of deportees, now looked forward to a new era of prosperity. On the southern coast, Camarina was soon restored. After standing deserted since Gelon deported the population to Syracuse in about 485, the deportees and their descendants came back to their former houses and lands. A number of additional colonists joined the resettlement, and two new quarters, unearthed by recent excavations, had to be erected to the east and west of the original town to house the enlarged population. In 456 (or 452) this 'newly peopled seat' had already become a town that 'nourishes the people' (Pindar's words), boasting of an Olympic victor of its own, the first since 528 B.C.[8] After a period of twenty-five years without any

---

[8] Praxiteles of Mantinea, who calls himself 'Syracusan and Camarinean' on an inscription from Olympia (Hill, *Sources*[2] B 100), vaguely datable in the second quarter of the fifth century, was possibly an Arcadian who settled first at Syracuse under the Deinomenids and then joined the colony of Camarina. For a different, and widely accepted, view of this inscription, see Jeffery 1961 (c 137) 160–1, 211.

coinage, Camarina now started minting silver *litrae*, showing on the reverse Athena, the chief goddess of the city (a temple of Athena is among the excavated remains) (Fig. 8).

Besides these eight cities, all autonomous since 466–461, four others should be mentioned. Two of them were never restored (Megara Hyblaea and Euboea), while the history of the other two, Messana and Selinus, developed almost independently. Messana remained united with Rhegium until the sons of Anaxilas were expelled in 461 under unknown circumstances. This was the last Sicilian dynasty to leave the stage after thirty-three years of rule. There are signs of Chalcidian revival at Messana after 461. The old city name Zankle reappeared temporarily on a famous tetradrachm (Fig. 9*b*),[9] and members of the old 'Zanclaean' population prospered again in the next decades, as shown in the case of two Olympic victors, Leontiscus and Symmachus, who were apparently of that stock. However, all this does not amount to a 'rechalcidization' as in the case of Catana. On the contrary, Messana remained predominantly Dorian, and may even have absorbed a mass of discharged mercenaries, including many Dorians from the Peloponnese, according to the 'Common Resolution' (see above, p. 157). Even Anaxilas' hares, the coinage symbol rejected by Rhegium in favour of its mythical founder Acastus, were retained by Messana throughout the fifth century.

Selinus, as we have said, was a world apart. Lying within the Punic sphere of influence, the vicissitudes of its history in the fifth century appear to be almost totally unrelated to the main trends of Greek Sicilian history. In 466 Selinus sent aid to the rebellious Syracusans, a step certainly not unwelcome to Carthage, and soon started minting a new series of tetradrachms portraying the local river-god and the Syracusan quadriga. Relations with post-Emmenid Acragas eventually improved, especially after the mercenary base at Minoa was broken up. The story of how Empedocles of Acragas drained the malarial marshes around Selinus and was subsequently worshipped there as a god may serve as an instance of the friendly relations between these cities. Sporadic border wars coupled with intermarriage rights (*epigamia*) typify the kind of relationship prevailing in the fifth century between Selinus and the Elymian hellenized city of Segesta.[10] Generally speaking, Selinus pros-

[9] Two symbols on this coin have been unconvincingly interpreted on the lines of the symbolic crosses on the Union Jack: a 'Chalcidian' Poseidon holding a 'Messenian' thunderbolt, or, alternatively, a 'Messenian' Zeus wearing a 'Chalcidian' chlamys. See Lacroix 1965 (C 193) 24–5 with nn.

[10] A war between Segesta and Lilybaeum, dated in 454/3 by Diodorus (XI.86.2), has been transformed by some scholars into a war between Segesta and Selinus, on the ground that Lilybaeum did not exist before 396 (see Diod. XXII.10.4). The Temple G inscription from Selinus (*IG* XIV 268 = M–L 38) has been referred to this hypothetical war, although on palaeographical grounds it is datable at any time between *c*. 460 and 409. On the *epigamia* of Selinus and Segesta see Thuc. VI.6.2.

Fig. 9. Silver tetradrachms of (a) Messana, about 460 B.C.; (b) Zancle,
about 460 B.C.; (c) Selinus, about 450 B.C. (After Kraay and Hirmer
1966 (C 192) figs. 52, 53, 186.)

pered during this century and even expanded beyond the city walls over
the northern Manuzza area, where aerial photography has revealed
streets laid out on a grid-plan, though slightly differing in orientation
from the famous sixth-century axial plan of the walled area (see *CAH*
III².3, 168 Fig. 28). Selinus was a mixed city. A well-known fifth-century
inscription (M–L 38) recording a great victory over an unnamed enemy
gives us some idea of the local pantheon, with its Megarian and Laconian
deities as well as a Heracles who might well be a Phoenician-hellenized
Melqarth. Perhaps owing to such non-Greek contacts, the art of Selinus
was more inventive than elsewhere in Sicily. Its achievements in the fifth
century are best illustrated by the famous metopes of Temple B, which is
in itself a masterpiece of the new classical Dorian architecture.

By the close of this revolutionary decade, the coasts of Greek Sicily were again dotted with autonomous city states, as in the late colonial period prior to the rise of the tyrannies. Most cities had now regular urban plans, either new or renewed, new residential quarters beyond the walls, and magnificent temples. Despite all the turmoil, the decade was also a period of growth and expansion of the new republics, and a significant chapter in ancient urban history.

III. THE SICEL MOVEMENT

The autonomistic movement could not be confined to the urbanized Greek coast. During the years when the Greek towns were practically paralysed by intestine strife and political change, the notion of autonomy spread endemically into the rural Sicel interior where the indigenous population felt secure enough to establish an independent entity of its own and even to expand at the expense of the hellenized belt stretching around the heart of the island. In other words, the Sicel movement took advantage of the void created by the crumbling epicracies, and in the first stage also exploited the Greek cities' need for allies in their own struggle against tyrants and mercenaries. At Syracuse, the moderate faction of the so-called *chariestatoi* (fair-minded) citizens apparently fancied for a time that Ducetius, the Sicel leader, might be manipulated, but, as soon as these hopes were banished and a more radical form of democracy prevailed, a joint effort with Acragas was made to stamp out the Sicel political entity. The Sicel interlude, though doomed to failure, lasted about two decades (*c.* 461–440).

Ducetius' immediate goal in 461 was probably nothing more than the recovery of confiscated land in the vicinity of Catana. But the result was that a centre of Sicel autonomy arose in the redeemed land in the western part of the plain, between the slopes of Etna and the hills of Caltagirone. It was the traditional area of Sicel and Chalcidian cooexistence, strongly hellenized from Catana and Leontini at first, and later on from Gela and Syracuse as well. A couple of years later (459/8) two memorable events show the first signs of consolidation and expansion: the foundation of Menainon and the conquest of Morgantina. A hilly village named Menae, the birthplace of Ducetius (commonly located at modern Mineo, east of Caltagirone), was first enlarged and then removed to the plain[11] – a typical act of synoecism in a mountainous area, giving birth to a polis of Greek type, with Ducetius (the only occasion on which he is called *basileus*) as its Founder. Then followed the conquest of Morgantina, an important Sicel township almost unanimously located on the Serra

---

[11] Diodorus may have referred twice to the same event, first as the foundation of Menainon (in 459/8; XI.78.5), and secondly as the transplantation of Menai (νεας MSS, in 453/2; XI.88.6).

Orlando ridge (near Aidone).[12] Recent excavations have revealed the extent of hellenization in this site. Since about 560 it was a mixed town, with an acropolis (the hill of Cittadella), city walls and regular buildings, but no archaic temples of Greek type. Some Chalcidians and Dorians lived apparently in the town, but the population was predominantly Sicel, to judge from the evidence of burial architecture and funerary rites. Like a few other Sicel townships, Morgantina had apparently been reluctant to join the autonomous Sicel entity, and had to be annexed by force.

The events of 459/8 can plausibly be viewed as the second phase in the growth of the Sicel movement as well as of Ducetius' personal leadership. A third phase was inaugurated by Ducetius' foundation in 453/2 of a sacral and administrative capital at Palice, an ancient Sicel site usually located at Lake Naftia (not far from Mineo). It is a volcanic site where in antiquity two jets of acid water shot high into the air from two craters in the lake. A *temenos* of two Sicel deities, called the Brothers Palikoi – probably personifications of the jets themselves[13] – had been built and used from time immemorial for worship, for taking solemn oaths, and as an oracle. More recent, and possibly of Greek origin, was its use as an asylum for runaway slaves. Near this *temenos*, Ducetius founded the Sicel capital. A town of Greek type, Palice was enclosed with strong walls and its surrounding territory portioned out among the settlers. Some traces of it may have been identified in aerial photographs of the so-called hill of Rocchicella (to the east of the lake), and parts of what might be the city walls have been excavated. They are poor remnants, indeed, of such a 'remarkable city', as Diodorus calls it. Though only for a short time (*c.* 452–440), Palice became the political and sacral centre of a Sicel 'League', *synteleia* or *koinon*, as Diodorus calls it. Of course, these two hellenistic federal terms could hardly have been current among the fifth-century Sicels, who in any case would have preferred a Sicel word. The hellenistic terms imply the existence of a compulsory state organization, mainly for military and fiscal purposes. A common Sicel army is in fact mentioned by Diodorus in connexion with the *synteleia*, and a number of so-called 'barbarized' coins, minted on Greek models around the middle of the century, belong to a number of sites, all within the autonomous Sicel area. The official *raison d'être* of Ducetius' *synteleia* was the notion of a 'common peoplehood'. We are told, in fact, that most townships 'which were of the same people [*homoethneis*]', with the exception of one

[12] An alternative location in the area of Caltagirone has been suggested on the ground that Morgantina appears in the treaty of Gela (424) as a dependency in an area disputed by Syracuse and Camarina (Thuc. IV.65.1).

[13] Innumerable etymologies have been suggested for *Palikoi*, from the Greek one (πάλιν ἱκέσθαι = 'those who come back') already known to Aeschylus (fr. 6 Radt), to the more serious, Italic, ones proposed by modern scholars (see e.g. Bello 1960 (H 49), Croon 1952 (H 53)).

Hybla in the region of Catana, were gathered by Ducetius into his *synteleia*. 'Common peoplehood' is not to be understood in racial terms; most townships were mixed anyway, and even the Sicel–Dorian double city of Inessa–Aitna was forced to join, after the local governor (Hiero's son Deinomenes?) was slain in 451 B.C.

In that same year the Sicel League was at its zenith; a year later it went to pieces. An uncontrolled, expanding Sicel statehood could not be tolerated by either Syracuse or Acragas, both of which had watched passively for a decade, and at times utilized, the growing movement. During the same decade, the moderate faction at Syracuse had been gradually yielding to more radical, democratic, and imperialistic, elements – a significant change which should not be viewed as a reaction to the rise of Ducetius, who never posed a threat to Syracuse in any way comparable to that posed by Carthage at the beginning and the end of the century. Rather, this radicalization was a result of inner social and constitutional developments. When in 451/0 Ducetius laid siege to Motyon, probably a hellenized Sican stronghold then held by an Acragantine garrison,[14] the Syracusans joined the Acragantines in despatching aid to the besieged. In the ensuing battle Ducetius won the day,[15] and the Syracusan general, a certain Bolkon, blamed for the defeat and charged with having had secret dealings with Ducetius, was promptly tried and executed. But the following summer, a strong Syracusan army attacked Ducetius at Nomae[16] and in the fierce battle that ensued the Sicels were in turn routed. Most of the survivors scattered, seeking refuge in the surrounding Sicel strongholds, and leaving Ducetius with only a handful of followers. The Acragantines meanwhile reconquered Motyon.[17] This was the end; Ducetius begged for refuge at Syracuse where he was tried before a General Assembly, which, persuaded by the moderate 'fair-minded' elders, spared the

[14] It has been tentatively located at Vassallaggi, west of Caltanissetta, where an excavated site has an urban plan of Greek type, walls, an archaic shrine, terraced houses and a rich necropolis showing Rhodian–Cretan influence probably transmitted through Gela or Acragas.

[15] A bronze shield from Olympia inscribed in Ionic letters (*SEG* xv 252) has been restored to give the meaning that it was dedicated from 'the spoils of Acragantines *and* Syracusans' (Συρακοσ[ίων καὶ] Ἀκραγαντίνων λάφυρα) by an unnamed victorious enemy of both who in the mid-fifth century could hardly be anyone else but Ducetius. However, the text could also be read as a dedication *by* the Syracusans *from* Acragantine spoils (Συρακόσ[ιοι ἀπὸ] Ἀκραγαντίνων λάφυρα) and referred in that case to the war of 446 B.C. (see below).

[16] Nomae has been tentatively located on the slopes of Monte Navone (between Piazza Armerina and Barrafranca), mainly because the site is surrounded by several hilltops suitable for Sicel strongholds. One of the summits, Montagna di Marzo, has traces of a regular plan of Greek type identifiable by air photography, and graffiti (in both Sicel and Greek letters) on vases of Attic type; see Mussinano 1966 and 1970 (H 61–62).

[17] Pausanias (v25.5) mentions a statuary group dedicated by the Acragantines after a war against *Motya*, and conjectures that the artist was Calamis (active in the first part of the fifth century). The suggestion that *Motyon*, not Motya, should be understood, seems acceptable, though it does not solve other difficulties aroused by the passage.

suppliant, and voted by acclamation to exile him with a pension to Corinth, the mother-city of Syracuse, on condition that he never return to Sicily.

Without its leader, the Sicel movement was apparently immobilized for some years. But Ducetius' story was not yet at an end. Contrary to all agreements, but undoubtedly with full Syracusan connivance and secret cooperation, Ducetius came back to Sicily in 446 on the plea that he had been instructed by an oracle to found a city at Kale Akte, the 'Fair Shore' on the northern coast where half a century earlier the scheme of a pan-Ionian colony under Zanclaean auspices failed to materialize (see *CAH* iv^2 762–3). A contingent of Greek colonists from mainland Greece, joined by Sicel settlers led by a certain Archonides, ruler of Herbita (a hellenized Sicel township, probably to be located in the area of Kale Akte[18]), participated in the enterprise. Some traces of the original urban plan of the colony have been identified in aerial photographs of land near modern Caronia (between Capo d'Orlando and Cefalù). Founder for the third time of a hellenized Sicel polis, Ducetius became once more a useful and tractable agent of Syracuse. The whole Kale Akte affair, in fact, looks like a Syracusan plan to plant a staunchly loyal Sicel–Greek base on the Tyrrhenian coast, too vital an area to be left to others, whether the cities of the Strait or Acragas. Understandably enough, the plan created a furore at Acragas, which had, since the sixth century B.C., regarded the coast of Himera as its own sphere of influence. After charging Syracuse with blatantly permitting Ducetius to return, Acragas declared war, provoking a dangerous confrontation between two blocs of cities. As it turned out, the sole outcome was a single battle on the southern Himeras (Salso) river, won by Syracuse. Greatly encouraged, Ducetius was allowed to pursue his colonial enterprise undisturbed and even to make a last attempt at reviving the movement. But soon afterward (440) he died of an illness. The Syracusans then decided to revert to their old policy of subjugating the hellenized Sicel territory in eastern Sicily. One pocket of heroic resistance at Trinacie (presumably another name for Palice[19]) was cleared out by a Syracusan army. The Sicel capital was destroyed, the inhabitants sold into slavery, and the choicest spoils offered at Delphi,

---

[18] Herbita has been variously located on the north coast (at S. Stefano di Camastra) or inland (at Nicosia or near Gangi, in the mountainous area south west of Cefalù). A later namesake of this Archonides founded Halaesa Archonidon in 403 (Diod. xiv.16.1–4), located at Castel di Tusa (on the coast, to the west of Cefalù).

[19] Trinacie, a Greek symbolic name possibly alluding to the synoecism of all Sicily as the final goal of the movement, is said by Diodorus (xii.29.2) to have occupied the 'first place' among Sicel cities, an expression well suited for Palice. In the ancient summary of Diodorus' Book xii, ἐπὶ Πικηνοὺς (*scil.* Π<αλ>ικηνοὺς) refers to the Syracusan attack on Trinacie. Others read Πι<α>κήνους or Πι<α>κίνους, the inhabitants of Piacus, a Sicel site known from its late fifth-century bronze coinage and tentatively located at Mendolito, near Adrano, on the south-western slopes of Etna.

but no self-evident mark of the struggle and victory was left on Sicilian coinages. These were stirring days for Syracuse. Its old epicracy was coming to life again on an oblong tract of Sicel land, protruding to the north west of her own territory, from the hills of Caltagirone to the slopes of Etna. Most Sicel townships in this area became tributary, some of them garrisoned and others formally declared 'allies'. Only at the very heart of the island, and on the northern coast, did an autonomous Sicel reserve survive. The Chalcidian cities on the east coast, which had become free thanks to the nascent republic of Syracuse a quarter of a century earlier, suddenly found themselves surrounded by a new Syracusan epicracy and reduced to the precarious status of an ethnic enclave.

Ducetius' movement, judged by its ultimate results, was an utter failure. Though born out of the ashes of the old Deinomenid empire, it became instrumental in the birth of yet another epicracy. Its transient successes were totally dependent on the silent or conniving support of Syracuse, and only as its puppet did Ducetius have a chance of achieving any degree of autonomy for his own people. By and large, Ducetius understood the rules of the game and worked within the given framework of the existing political powers; but he made his own blunders and his movement had no deep roots and feelings. Further-more, archaeology, numismatics and aerial photography have amply documented the high degree of hellenization and urbanization of the area affected by the Sicel movement. In fact, we may confidently state that without the full assimilation of the Greek notions of statehood and urban life, the Sicel movement would never have seen the light. Ducetius' models were Gelon and Hiero, not Kokalos or Hyblon of old. Both attraction and resistance to Hellenic culture, assimilation and artificial revival of national traditions, interacted within the movement, among elites and masses alike. Thus, ironically, the Sicel movement's most enduring result was the furtherance of Sicel assimilation into the cultural Siciliote *koine* of the late fifth century B.C. All non-Greek Sicilian vernaculars had disappeared as written languages by the end of the century.

IV. DEMOCRACY AND CULTURE AT SYRACUSE AND ACRAGAS

The three decades following the fall of the tyrannies were crucial to Syracuse's constitutional and socio-economic development and its rise to the rank of a major hegemonic power in the West. After Thrasybulus and his garrison left Syracuse in 466, there was protracted strife between two classes of citizens, whom Diodorus (presumably following Timaeus) termed the 'Old' and the 'New'. The 'Old' were the victims of tyranny, excluded and dispossessed, mostly living in the suburbs outside the walls of Achradina, and some returning exiles. The 'New' were the élite which had been created under tyranny – veteran soldiers, 7,000 of them still left in town, immigrants from the Peloponnese, wealthy people who had been deported to Syracuse from towns razed to the ground (such as Megara Hyblaea and Euboea) and could not be repatriated. The 'New' had been installed by the tyrants in the walled quarters of Ortygia and Achradina and presumably assigned land in the countryside. The restoration of the *ancien régime* as conceived by the 'Old' citizens implied a thorough reversal of the situation, including the exchange of quarters, properties and political rights, a programme evidently unacceptable to the 'New'. Entrenched in their respective quarters, 'Old' and 'New' citizens started a war of nerves and attrition that went on for years. In 463 an assembly of the 'Old' deliberated on the establishment of 'democracy' and a cult of Zeus the Liberator, with an annual festival of Liberty. They also voted to reserve all magistracies for themselves to the exclusion of the 'New' citizens. A true civil war ensued, with blockades and attacks on land and sea. It was finally won by the 'Old' in 461, thanks mainly to an élite corps of 600 *epilektoi*.[20] At this stage some compromise must have been made, the 'Old' probably agreeing that the restoration of property be made by legal means and that the 'New' be assigned other land and houses in compensation. In fact, Syracusan courts became so busy with claims to confiscated property that the belief that Greek forensic oratory was actually born of such trials was seriously credited in antiquity.

It was out of these changes that the new institutions of republican Syracuse – the General Assembly, the Council, the board of *strategoi* – took shape. Typical elements of radical democracy, such as sortition and payment for office, were never introduced at Syracuse, but a variant of Athenian ostracism, called *petalismos*, came into use for a short while, allegedly after a certain Tyndarides made an abortive attempt at tyranny in 454. Imperial ambitions were aroused along with the rise of democracy, as usually occurred in ancient maritime city states. In 453 two admirals, first Phayllus then Apelles, were sent with a fleet to the Tyrrhenian Sea to ravage the Etruscan coast and the islands of Elba and Corsica,[21] a reminder to all concerned that the new democracy was not loath to adopt Hiero's Tyrrhenian policy. Then, in 440, Ducetius' death

---

[20] Theories that this élite corps became later an oligarchic 'council' or vigilante cabal (see especially Diod. XI.86.5 on Tyndarides, 454 B.C.); a picked body of six hundred in summer 414 (Thuc. VI.96.3, 97.3); *epilektoi* under Hermocrates in 413 (Diod. XIII.11.4); oligarchic *synedrion* of Six Hundred in 317 (Diod. XIX.4.3, etc) are largely unwarranted. For a battle between Syracusans and mercenaries in the (otherwise unknown) 'plain of Glaukoi' (?) see *P. Oxy.* IV 665 (*FGrH* 557 F 1).

[21] Whether Phayllus' name should be read on an inscription from Selinus (*SEG* XII 411) and identified with the Syracusan admiral is still a matter of dispute; see now Giuffrida Ientile 1983 (H 75) 68–9 with n. 33.

gave Syracuse a golden opportunity to re-establish its epicracy on land. The next year the Syracusans were capable of building one hundred triremes, besides doubling their cavalry and increasing their infantry. Democratic Syracuse was rapidly becoming a major power in the West, as it had been under its great tyrants, an achievement that, at this point, did not even cost it very much, for Syracuse was now simply taking advantage of Etruscan decline, Sicel disorientation, and Carthaginian self-imposed isolation.

Under democracy, Syracuse was on the verge of becoming the greatest city state in the Greek world and a centre of Hellenic culture. With some 20,000 citizens and a total population of a quarter of a million, Syracuse was a 'megalopolis' (Pindar's term) by fifth-century Greek standards, 'in no way smaller than Athens' (as Thucydides put it), including a prosperous community of Phoenician merchants with vessels in port and houses in town, and a growing number of Etruscan and Sicel slaves. The four quarters of Syracuse – Ortygia on the island with its archaic temples, Achradina on the mainland opposite with its large and regular streets, Temenites outside the walls with its old theatre, probably built up under Hiero, and a fourth suburb, later named Tyche – were densely populated (see below, Fig. 40). The famous quarries north of the unwalled suburbs, on the still empty plateau of Epipolae, were in full use both for building stone and as prisons.

Summing up the general situation at Syracuse at mid-century, Diodorus writes that 'a multitude of demagogues and sycophants was arising, the youth were cultivating cleverness in oratory, and, in a word, many were exchanging the ancient and sober way of life for ignoble pursuits; wealth was increasing because of the peace, but there was little if any concern for concord and honest conduct'.[22] In this moralistic vein later Greek historians perceived the changes from Deinomenid culture, with its ostentatious architecture, court poetry and the politically innocuous comedies of Epicharmus, to a democratic, written and more sophisticated culture. With the remarkable exception of the choral lyric, an import from mainland and Aegean Greece, and comic theatre, literature and science made their first appearance in Syracuse after the fall of its tyranny. The mime of Sophron gradually evolved from Epicharmus' comedy as a genuine creation of Doric Sicily. The art of persuasion and the theoretical study of rhetoric, traditionally 'first invented' by Corax and Tisias of Syracuse, attained a high level of excellence thanks to the genius of Gorgias, a recognized master of his art before he visited Athens in 427 B.C. Finally, in the field of historiography, Sicily did not lag far behind Ionia. Antiochus of Syracuse, a younger contemporary of Herodotus active in the third quarter of the fifth century, was the author

---

[22] XI.87.5 (tr. Oldfather).

Fig. 10. Silver decadrachms of Syracuse, about 465 B.C. (After Kraay and Hirmer 1966 (c 192) figs. 78–9.)

of the first continuous *History of Sicily*, beginning with the mythical king Kokalos and ending with the year of the Congress of Gela (424/3 B.C.), and of a great treatise *On Italy*. Writing in Ionic, the dialect of historiography at that time, his wide interest lay in the history of the Greek as well as the non-Greek West. Yet this new written culture did not oust fine arts. It was the Syracusan engravers working at the mint under democracy who achieved an unsurpassed mastery of sculptural design. The best known example is the first issue of a bullion silver decadrachm (Fig. 10), once wrongly identified with the gold 'Damare-teion' struck, according to Diodorus, immediately after the battle of Himera (see *CAH* IV² 775), but now connected by most numismatists with the final liberation of Syracuse in 461 B.C.

Acragas, the second greatest city in Sicily, continued to be the major rival of Syracuse. Its new regime after 472/1 was at first an oligarchy of wealthy citizens. An Assembly of the 'Thousand' was established and then abolished by Empedocles (by what authority we do not know) just three years after it had been set up. A less narrow oligarchy developed. Anecdotes about Empedocles, deriving in part from Timaeus, imply the functioning at his time of a Council and magistrates, the existence of factions, the plundering of public funds alongside the use of judicial means to prevent illegalities of any kind. But Acragas never became a 'democracy' of the Syracusan, let alone the Athenian, type. However, for two generations, until sacked by the Carthaginians in 406 B.C., Acragas was an affluent plutocratic republic.[23] A recent calculation (De Waele 1979 (H 5)) puts the population of Acragas in the fifth century at about 20,000 within the walls and 100–150,000 outside, including Sicans and slaves. 'A most beautiful city', as Pindar called it, with its parallel streets

[23] See *CAH* III².3, 166, Fig. 27; *CAH* IV² 777, Fig. 84.

Fig. 11. Silver tetradrachm of Acragas, about 460–420 B.C. (After Kraay and Hirmer 1966 (C 192) fig. 170.)

running the length from the slopes of Rupe Atenea and the acropolis down to the hill of the temples, Acragas was engaged for decades in erecting its colossal Olympieum, which was never finished.[24] Two new Doric temples, conventionally called the temples of Concord and Hera, rose on the southern slope, beside the four already standing on the eastern crag. No less famous than the temples were the monumental tombs (including some for horses which had won at Olympia), the artificial lake, and the luxurious houses and villas. Fine specimens of Western Greek art, such as the well-known ephebos and the recently restored warrior, fictile busts and lion-head spouts decorated public buildings and streets. The coinage of fifth-century Acragas is remarkable for its beauty and size, especially the famous tetradrachms with the original types of eagle and crab (Fig. 11). The economy flourished, in part owing to export of wine and olives, mainly to Carthage. But values had also changed since the beginning of the century, as Pindar noted when comparing the good old days with the more vulgar money-minded present. Tales of Acragantine luxury and effeminacy, of neglect of military duties, as well as descriptions of public festivals and great marriages abound and testify to the image of fifth-century Acragas in later minds.

Letters and sciences flourished as well. Whether Carcinus, the tragic poet often mocked by Aristophanes, was an Acragantine by origin is still a matter of dispute; he flourished at Athens, and his son Xenocles attained the level required to win against Euripides at Athens in 415 with a tetralogy. Deinolochos, a comic writer, may have been an Acragantine. Music was the art of Midas, and later of Metelos, who became Plato's teacher. A local school of medicine is represented by Acron, a physician and the son of a physician, and, of course, by Empedocles, by far the greatest representative of almost every branch of learning in post-Emmenid Acragas. Philosopher, poet, mystagogue and healer, Empe-

[24] See *Pls. to Vol.* IV, pl. 266 and pp. 189–90 here.

docles derived the fullest benefit from such visiting men of letters as Pindar and Simonides, as well as from the new open atmosphere which prevailed in the city and all over Sicily. He is in fact associated with both western and eastern philosophers – Pythagoras, Parmenides, Xeno-phanes, Anaxagoras – and their schools, thereby bringing to his native city some of the most vigorous intellectual influences of the time. A good citizen involved in local politics and remembered as a 'democrat', he wrote a long poem on the invasion of Xerxes, and Aristotle considered him the inventor of rhetoric. He in fact delivered, and possibly also wrote, many discourses on the most pressing problems of his day. A great intellect, and a peculiar mixture of mysticism and science, Empedo-cles was both venerated and dreaded by his countrymen; significantly, he was finally exiled from his motherland.[25]

Lesser cities, too, flourished economically and culturally. Besides their silver coinages, which have often been mentioned above, most cities now also issued bronze pieces to replace silver *litrae* for minor denomina-tions; this is in itself a sign of expanding local circulation. Himera boasted a Pythagorean of her own, a certain Petron, said to be of Dorian origin, but bearing a name that may point to the Sican (or Elymian) township of Petra in western Sicily. The school of Pythagoras of Rhegium influenced much Sicilian sculpture, and the Himeraean painter Demophilus became a teacher of Zeuxis of Heraclea. Leontini produced Gorgias and his brother Herodicus, a physician of renown. Another physician, and a disciple of Empedocles, named Pausanias, was a Geloan. Olympic laurels, which had been the monopoly of the tyrants and their capitals, were now won by the lesser free cities of Himera (five), Messana (two) and Camarina (two) – an accurate indicator of both change and continuity, considered in terms of wealth, life-style, and cultural values.

[25] For a revised view of constitutional developments at Acragas, and of Empedocles' role, see my article in *Athenaeum* 78 (1990) 483–501.

CHAPTER 8a

ART: ARCHAIC TO CLASSICAL

J. J. POLLITT

I. STYLE AND ICONOLOGY

Archaic Greek art, with roots stretching back to the Geometric style of the eighth century B.C., had been concerned with forms whose effectiveness was judged not so much by the degree to which they simulated one's optical experience of the surrounding world as by the degree to which their internal properties of harmony and clarity expressed an essential idea. Archaic artists did not so much imitate nature as create analogues for it. They did this by dissecting the components of natural phenomena into their fundamental geometric forms and then recomposing these forms according to principles of *symmetria*, the commensurability of parts. Works of representational art resulting from this process may not have looked exactly like their counterparts in nature, but they were not intended to. What was expressed by such familiar products of the Archaic style as the *kouroi*, for example, was more in the nature of an *eidos*, simultaneously a 'form' and an 'idea', than an imitation. Until well on into the Hellenistic period an interest in defining underlying structures through works of art, structures which evoked immutable ideas, continued to be of great importance in Greek art, but from the fifth century B.C. onward this interest was increasingly combined with a desire to record a wider range of natural appearances. To a great extent it is the interplay between traditional idealism and a new empiricism that gives the art of the Classical period its distinctive character.

Naturalism, the desire to represent both one's actual sensuous experience of nature and also the social and physical setting of one's everyday life, first played an important role in the Greek artistic tradition during the innovative era between about 520 and 480 B.C. The supplantation at this time of the self-contained perfection of mature Archaic Greek art by an experimental naturalistic style is most strikingly illustrated in Athenian red-figure vase painting. The simple shift about 525 B.C. from painting figures in black to reserving them on a reddish

Some account of the art of the Classical period will be found in the forthcoming *Pls. to Vols. V and VI*. In the following notes reference is made to easily accessible illustrations in standard works and a few monographs. See also Bibliography, Section 1.

ground with only anatomical details painted in black stimulated, or perhaps was stimulated by, a new interest in the expressive qualities of single figures as opposed to those of a tapestry-like pattern made up of many figures. And with this intensified focus on individual figures in painting came a new concern for how they looked as they moved and acted in space. The invention of the technique of representing foreshortened figures by Greek artists of the late Archaic period was from both a technical and conceptual point of view one of the most profound changes ever to have occurred in the history of art. It marks the beginning of a long series of phases, lasting up to the twentieth century, in which the artist's role as a recorder of passing sensuous phenomena, and his mastery of the means of making his records exact, came to rival in importance his role as a narrator of stories and ideas. In the works of the great red-figure Pioneers of about 510 B.C., such as Euphronius, Euthymides and Phintias, one senses the excitement that seems to have accompanied experimentation with foreshortened forms. As they strove to outdo one another in their attempts to capture particularly difficult views of the body's movements in space (folded knees seen from the front, the bottom of twisted feet, etc.), naturalistic representation seems for a brief (and in the overall context of Greek art, rare) time to have been the principal aim of their art.

What is documented in vase painting was almost certainly also true of mural and other forms of large-scale painting. Pliny (*HN* xxxv.56) credits a painter named Cimon of Cleonae with the invention of *katagrapha* or *obliquae imagines*, almost certainly a reference to foreshortened forms. What little evidence there is for Cimon's date suggests that he was active in the late sixth century B.C. He may have been a metic who worked in Athens.

Another aspect of the new naturalism of late Archaic vase painting was a gradual democratization of subject matter. Black-figure painters of the Pisistratan era, perhaps echoing the taste of Pisistratus himself, had favoured scenes from the world of myth and heroic legend. Their successors in the first phase of red-figure, by contrast, showed an increasing fondness for scenes which reflected the everyday experience of the average citizen, such as athletes in the gymnasium, music teachers with their pupils, and symposia. While many of these subjects, particularly those of athletes, may have been chosen in part because they offered opportunities for cultivating the new interest in anatomical detail and foreshortening, it is also possible that social and political changes contributed to their popularity. The overthrow of the tyranny in Athens and the creation of the Cleisthenic democracy may have created an atmosphere in which it was both desirable and profitable for painters to depict the common man busily involved in familiar, unpretentious aspects of civic life.

Still another feature of the move toward capturing familiar experience in art was an interest in conveying emotion through facial expression. The grimace of the giant Antaeus on Euphronius' crater in the Louvre[1] or the wince of pain on Patroclus' face as Achilles binds his wounds on the Sosias Painter's cylix in Berlin[2] herald a new category of artistic expression which was to be a major preoccupation of Greek artists for half a century.

Because sculpture is a slower, more intractable medium that lends itself less readily to rapid experimentation than does vase painting, its naturalism in the late Archaic period is perhaps less obvious. Relief sculptures, which are closely tied to the conventions of painting, show it most clearly (e.g., the athletes' base in the National Museum in Athens),[3] but a naturalistic trend is also detectable in venerable forms of Archaic free-standing sculpture, like the *kouros*. *Kouroi* had always provided an opportunity for experiments in the representation of anatomy, but the purpose of early and mature Archaic *kouroi* was essentially symbolic and/ or iconic rather than naturalistic. The naturalism of the latest Archaic *kouroi*, such as Ptoon 20 (National Museum, Athens) or the Strangford *kouros* (British Museum), seems, by contrast, to be an end in itself and to clash with the rigid, 150-year-old format of the type. Abandonment of the type around 480 B.C. and its replacement by figures like the 'Critian boy' (Acropolis Museum, Athens), which allowed for the representation of internal movement, seems to have been an inevitable step.[4]

In one way the naturalism of the late Archaic period was distinctly untypical of the Greek artistic tradition as a whole. From the Geometric period onward every successive style of Greek art has regularly been disciplined by strict canons of formal order. Hence it is not surprising that the pervasive, free-wheeling but seemingly directionless humanism of the decades around 500 B.C. should eventually, in the Early Classical period (*c.* 480–450), have been subjected to such discipline. Some cause seems to be required, however, to explain the particular forms which the new discipline took. That cause, in all likelihood, was the series of crises, from the Ionian Revolt of 499 to the battle of Plataea in 479, which constitute the Persian Wars.

The conflict with the Persians, as Herodotus and Aeschylus make clear, was as much a moral as a military one. By restraining the

---

[1] Robertson 1975 (I 140) 214–30; Boardman 1975 (I 17) 29–36.
[2] Boardman 1975 (I 17) figs. 23, 50.1; *Pls. to Vol. IV*, pl. 149.
[3] Boardman 1978 (I 18A) fig. 242, cf. 241.
[4] Boardman 1978 (I 18A) figs. 147 (Critian boy), 180 (Ptoon 20), 182 (Strangford).

competitiveness and aggressiveness with which they had traditionally approached one another, the allied Greek city states had overcome an enormous and seemingly irrational power that had threatened them with extinction. The religious and moral significance of this achievement from the Greek point of view was most forcefully expressed in the *Persae* of Aeschylus (especially lines 807–29) where the Persians' defeat was depicted as punishment for their *hybris* and the Greeks' victory as the fruit of their self-restraint. Moderation and self-control, in other words, came to be viewed as divinely sanctioned virtues, and those who spurned them did so at the risk of divine vengeance. Morality became a matter of attitude as well as action.

The sober cultural atmosphere created by this new moral self-consciousness had a deep influence on the art of the Early Classical period. It inspired a new simplicity and austerity of form, particularly in the use of ornament, which have led some to refer to the sculpture of the period as the 'severe style', and it also led to a strong interest in expressing states of consciousness and their moral implications in art. Further, the fact that the Persian conflict as a historical event, as a particular moment of time and change, seemed to have a deep religious significance and be important in some cosmic process, appears to have provoked a general interest in the significance of change, whether physical, emotional or historical.

Nowhere are these traits more vividly and movingly exhibited than in the greatest monument of the period, the temple of Zeus at Olympia (470–457).[5] The austere, unadorned features of Heracles and Athena on its sculptured metopes have the strength and spareness of the temple's Doric columns. Their style represents an extreme rejection of the decorative ornateness of Archaic art and of the Oriental heritage which was at the root of much of that ornateness. It was an appropriate, perfect style, however, for the serious, at times meditative, atmosphere of the metopes, in which Heracles' changing states of consciousness, his weariness, anxiety and steadfastness, for example, are explored as he passes from youth to advancing states of maturity.

In the sculptures of the two great pediments of the temple, the use of expressions of consciousness to bring out the moral significance of narrative subjects is developed within two particular categories which Early Classical artists (and the critics, like Aristotle, who later wrote about them) seem to have considered fundamental – character (*ethos*) and emotional reaction (*pathos*). The quiet foreboding of the east pediment forces the viewer to enter into the minds and characters of Pelops, Oenomaus and others and to share the moral consternation of the 'old seer' (figure N) as he ponders their fate. In the elemental clash of the west

[5] Ashmole and Yalouris 1967 (I 5); Ashmole 1972 (I 6) chs. 1–3; Boardman 1985 (I 20) ch. 4.

pediment the civilized restraint of the Lapiths, in whom only a trace of *pathos* betrays itself in facial expression, is pitted against the barbaric abandon of the Centaurs in such a way that the moral clash of the Persian Wars is re-enacted in symbolic form. The west pediment also offers examples of another distinctive stylistic trait of Early Classical Greek art: the representation of physical motion by diagrammatic patterns of composition which, by isolating obvious stopping points in a particular motion (like the back-swing of a discus thrower), convey the nature of an entire movement. In ancient art criticism such patterns were called *rhythmoi*.

The features that give the Olympia sculptures their special force – surface severity, concern with change through time, study of character and emotion, clear definition of motion – pervade, naturally, other works of the period, either singly or in combination. An extreme of surface severity is apparent not only in original sculptures like the Charioteer of Delphi,[6] but also in what were apparently particularly admired works that are now preserved in Roman copies – the 'Aspasia' type, for example, and the 'Hestia Guistiniani'.[7] *Ethos* and *pathos* seem to have been principal features of the paintings of Polygnotus of Thasos, whose elaborate *Sack of Troy* and *Underworld* are described by Pausanias (x.25–30).[8] On extant monuments character and emotion are captured with unusual vividness on the two great cups in Munich by the Penthesilea Painter, one representing the story of Achilles and Penthesilea and the other that of Apollo and Tityus.[9] In a sense almost all the best works of Early Classical sculpture and vase painting can be said to convey *ethos* through their evocation of an atmosphere of noble awareness. This quality is particularly apparent, for example, in the two bronze warriors found in the sea off the southern coast of Italy near Riace. Even though the original context of the Riace bronzes and the meaning of the group to which they presumably belonged are uncertain and debated, their embodiment of character (or perhaps two distinct characters) is unmistakable.[10]

The emergence of *rhythmoi* can be seen in the figures from the east pediment of the temple of Aphaea at Aegina (about 480 B.C.),[11] and their culmination appears in works like the bronze striding god from Artemisium (National Museum, Athens).[12] Exceptionally clear, almost textbook, examples of *rhythmos* are again preserved in Roman copies of

[6] Chamoux 1955 (I 44); Boardman 1985 (I 20) fig. 34.
[7] Robertson 1975 (I 140) 191–3; Boardman 1985 (I 20) figs. 74–5.
[8] Robertson 1975 (I 140) ch. 4, IV; cf. Barron 1972 (I 9).
[9] Arias *et al.* 1962 (I 4) pls. 168–71; Boardman 1989 (I 21) fig. 80.
[10] *Due Bronzi* 1985 (I 63); Boardman 1985 (I 20) figs. 38–9.
[11] Robertson 1975 (I 140) 165–7; Boardman 1978 (I 18A) fig. 206.
[12] Robertson 1975 (I 140) 196–7; Boardman 1985 (I 20) fig. 35.

famous lost originals – the Tyrannicides of Critius and Nesiotes, for example, and the Discobolus of Myron.[13] In vase painting examples of it are abundant.

All of these features can be seen as aspects of an effort to impose a new order, clarity and certitude on the experiments in naturalism that had characterized the late Archaic period. The severe style brought a canonical form of sorts to the desire for more 'real-looking' anatomy and drapery. Categories of *ethos* and *pathos* brought definition and signifi- cance to the raw, if powerful, emotional expression that was present in the works of artists like the Sosias and Kleophrades Painters; and *rhythmoi* imposed order and definition on the changing appearance of figures in motion that had so captivated the painters who invented foreshortening. In the sense that it marks a reassertion of the desire for archetypal forms that had long characterized the Greek artistic tradition, the art of the Early Classical period can be seen as a reaction to the naturalism of the immediately preceding decades. The range of exper- iences for which archetypal forms were deemed necessary, however, had been expanded.

Because time and change took on a new significance in the Early Classical period, so too did the landmarks that mark the course of change, important historical events and personalities. Although extant monuments do not document the fact particularly well, literary sources make it clear that historicity first became a significant element in Greek art at this time. Actual portraits of historical personalities, especially political and military leaders like Themistocles and Miltiades, began to appear,[14] and the creation of at least one very detailed historical painting, a mural by Micon and Panaenus in the Stoa Poikile in Athens represent- ing the battle of Marathon, is documented (Paus. 1.15.3; Ael. *NA* VII.38).

After 450 B.C., with the Persian threat in full recession and the politics of Greece dominated by the long struggle between the Athenian and Spartan alliances, the spirit of *sophrosyne*, moderation, that had pervaded the thought of the previous thirty years yielded to a new intellectual climate in which the extremes of idealism on the one hand and pragmatism on the other were juxtaposed and often kept in a state of tension. The art of the High Classical period reflects this changed atmosphere. In one way it pushes forward the Early Classical period's interest in the perception of change, and in another it reasserts the timeless feeling of mature Archaic art.

The story of High Classical Greek art is for the most part the story of Athenian art, and it is in the great monuments of the Periclean building

[13] *Pls. to Vol. IV*, pl. 141; Robertson 1975 (I 140) 185–6, 340–1; Brunnsåker 1971 (I 33); Boardman 1985 (I 20) fig. 60.
[14] Robertson 1975 (I 140) 187–8, pl. 62d; Richter 1984 (I 133) 210–12, 166–9.

programme that the emerging dual nature in the art of the time is most apparent. With its carefully calculated *symmetria*, its pervasive 9:4 proportion, the Parthenon carries on the ancient Greek quest to express formal perfection, to express a kind of *eidos*. On the other hand its well-known refinements take into account the uncertain, subjective, fluctuating nature of sense experience.[15] Partly by compensating for optical distortion, partly, perhaps, by exaggerating the effects of curves, and partly by creating a tension between what one expects to see and actually does see, the refinements of the Parthenon force one to dwell on the uncertain nature of one's own perceptions and to ponder the relationship between the ideal and the actual.

The same dual nature appears in the style of the sculptures of the Parthenon, tentatively in the metopes, with full maturity in the frieze, and with a hint of mannered exaggeration in the pediments.[16] The idealism of these sculptures – the simple geometry of their faces, their serenity, the youthfulness (symbolizing timelessness) that pervades their forms, and, in the frieze, the bestowal of divine attributes on the ordinary Athenian citizen – has always been recognized. Along with it, however, there is a new manner of handling the texture and movement of drapery and hair which relies on indistinctness, on a sense of fleeting impression, for its effect. The clear, patterned forms of Archaic and the simple solidity of Early Classical drapery are replaced by irregular eddies, furrows and shadows. The flickering, transitory impressions that these forms make, like the effects of the Parthenon's architectural refinements, have to be grasped and given compositional unity by the viewer, and his subjective reactions become the interpreter of their meaning.

The way the Parthenon sculptures bring together two fundamental modes of perception, intuitive perception of the ideal and sense perception of passing phenomena, and hold them in harmony may reflect the influence of, or at least in a spontaneous way run parallel to, a similar dualism in philosophical speculation during the fifth century B.C. One tradition, characteristic of most of the pre-Socratics but most obviously of the Pythagoreans, accepted the perceived universe as having objective reality and adopted an essentially idealistic position by maintaining that its underlying truth could be demonstrated by mathematics and geometry. A second, relativist tradition, developed among the Sophists with Protagoras as its chief exponent, argued that subjective experience is the only certain reality and that men's personal impressions or perceptions were thus the 'measure of all things'. That these philosophical currents might have had an influence on Pericles and the

[15] Dinsmoor 1950 (I 60) 164–9; Coulton 1977 (I 51) 108–12.
[16] Brommer 1963, 1967, 1977, 1979 (I 25–7, 29); Robertson 1975 (I 140) ch. 5; Berger, ed. 1984 (I 11); Boardman 1985 (I 20) ch. 10; Boardman and Finn 1985 (I 22).

circle of intellectuals and artists, including Phidias, who were associated with him is not entirely far-fetched, since Pericles is known to have had close contact with contemporary philosophers. (He was a patron and friend of Anaxagoras and on at least one occasion sought the advice of Protagoras.) In contemporary literature of a not strictly philosophical nature it is clear that this juxtaposition of idealism and pragmatism of various sorts was also 'in the air'. It is at the heart of Sophocles' *Antigone* (with something like Parthenonian idealism getting its most famous paean in the third stasimon), and it colours the picture of Athenian life that Thucydides puts into the mouth of Pericles in the Funeral Speech of 431.

Although a fusion of idealism with a subjectivism that dwelt on passing impressions would always characterize Classical, and much of Hellenistic, art, it can be argued that, after the outbreak of the Peloponnesian War and the great plague, the balance tipped somewhat toward the latter quality. Capturing impressions seems to have become an end in itself in much of the art of the last three decades of the fifth century. In Greek painting, for example, a second revolution occurred which was as influential in its long-range effects as the invention of foreshortening in the late sixth century B.C. Graphic perspective (the illusion of spatial depth through the diminution of forms as they recede into it) and shading (the illusion of corporeal mass through the modulation of light and shade) were both developed for the first time in this period. Tradition attributed the invention of the former to a Samian painter named Agatharchus, who worked in Athens, and of the latter to an Athenian named Apollodorus, known as the *skiagraphos* (shader, or shadow painter), but other widely admired artists like Zeuxis undoubtedly also played a role in the development of these techniques. Surviving contemporary monuments preserve only the barest hints of these achievements (vase painting, with the partial exception of white-ground lekythoi, could not be adapted to shading at all and only in a rudimentary way to perspective), but Etruscan funerary paintings and Macedonian tomb paintings dating from late in the next century document the direction in which Greek painting now began to move.[17]

In Greek sculpture of the later fifth century B.C. this fascination with the effects of impression comes out most clearly in the continuing development of the style of rendering drapery (variously known as the 'wind blown', 'flying', or 'wet' drapery style) that had begun to evolve in the Parthenon sculptures. The style was already fully developed in the pediments of the Parthenon (finished 432) and underwent an increasingly mannered transformation, aimed sometimes at evoking a sense of excitement and sometimes at producing a soothing, elegant, calligraphic

[17] Robertson 1975 (I 140) chs. 4.VI, 6.IV–V, 7.IV–V.

effect, in monuments designed later in the century like the Nike temple parapet (c. 425–420),[18] the Nike of Paeonius at Olympia (c. 420),[19] and the frieze of the temple of Apollo at Bassae (c. 400).[20]

Vase painting in the second half of the fifth century largely loses a distinct stylistic development of its own and tends to mirror the reigning styles of the monumental arts. Artists like the Achilles Painter and the Cleophon Painter, for example, absorb the style of the Parthenon frieze, while later in the century artists like the Eretria Painter, the Meidias Painter, and others adopt the wind-blown drapery style.[21] Whether the painters who adopted the latter borrowed it from sculpture or whether it had an independent existence of its own in large-scale painting is difficult to decide, but the importance attached to the perfection of line and contour in the art of one of the major painters of the time, Parrhasius (Pliny, *HN* xxxv.68), perhaps suggests that the style had a separate development in mural and easel painting.

What relationship, if any, this reigning calligraphic style in the later fifth century bore to the historical climate in which it was created is a puzzling question. Thucydides conveys the feeling of an increasingly dark era of Greek history, with war, plague and civil strife generating harshness and despair. Yet the art of the period conveys a feeling of carefree, airy, cosmetic elegance which can be paralleled in other arts (for example, the rhetoric of Gorgias, the ornate 'new music' of Timotheus of Miletus, and some of the choral hymns in the dramas of Euripides). It may be that ornamental elegance was not so much an effect of as a reaction to the temper of its time. The pursuit of fantasy as an escape from an increasingly threatening, oppressive and burdensome world has parallels in other cultures.

The glitter of creations like the Nike temple parapet, in any case, did not altogether eclipse a more sombre side in the art of the late fifth century. It is there, as one might expect, in works of funerary art like the white-ground lekythoi[22] and a remarkable series of grave stelae.[23] The latter, judging by their style and high quality, were probably the work of sculptors who had learned their trade in the palmier days when the Parthenon was being built and who, in this troubled period, had to take whatever modest commissions came their way. The most striking example of a new subdued atmosphere, however, is found in the Erechtheum,[24] the last of the great structures conceived for the Periclean

---

[18] Robertson 1975 (I 140) 349–50; Boardman 1985 (I 20) figs. 129–30.

[19] Robertson 1975 (I 140) 287–9; Boardman 1985 (I 20) fig. 139.

[20] Robertson 1975 (I 140) 356–9, pl. 119c,d.   [21] Boardman 1989 (I 21) ch. 5.

[22] Robertson 1975 (I 140) 324–6; Bruno 1977 (I 34); Boardman 1989 (I 21) ch. 4.

[23] Robertson 1975 (I 140) 363–72; Boardman 1985 (I 20) 183–5.

[24] Paton *et al.* 1927 (I 122); Dinsmoor 1950 (I 60) 187–95; Berve and Gruben 1963 (I 13) 182–6; Lawrence 1973 (I 95) 164–6.

building programme on the Athenian acropolis. This complicated temple was still being worked on when Athens was compelled, at last, to surrender to Sparta. It was designed to house those ancient, mysterious and numinous forces which the Athenians in the heyday of the Parthenon may have been inclined to subdue or suppress but which, in their travail and disillusionment at the end of the fifth century, they must have felt it was important to placate. Along with the ancient wooden image of Athena and the altars and tombs of early heroes and kings, it enshrined, like a great reliquary, snakes, a miraculous tree, a miraculous pool, a sacred rock, and other holy tokens. For all its jewel-like surface elegance, the Erechtheum was really a shrine to the same irrational forces that haunted Euripides in the *Bacchae*.

The foregoing analysis of the stylistic and conceptual development of High Classical Greek art is, as already noted, essentially an interpretation of the art of Athens. Given the nature of the art and literature which survives for study, this Athenian bias is inevitable, and it is natural to wonder whether such bias distorts our picture of Greek art as a whole during the second half of the fifth century B.C. What evidence there is from outside Athens (mainly sculpture from Olympia, Bassae, and the islands, and vase painting from Corinth and Boeotia) suggests, however, that this is not the case. It is known from inscriptions and literary sources that many of the artists who worked in Classical Athens were not Athenian citizens. Presumably many of them moved on after a time, carrying the style of Phidias and his pupils with them. In any case, it does appear that the art of other areas of Greece was widely, and fairly rapidly, 'athenianized' at this time. The one artist of great importance who to some degree seems to have remained aloof from Athens and to have cultivated his own distinct style was Polyclitus of Argos.[25] His interest in developing a perfect canon of proportions probably had a closer spiritual link to the art of the Archaic and Early Classical periods than it did to the art of Phidias. But Polyclitus too was clearly an idealist, and if the seeming stylistic progression from his Doryphorus to his Diadumenus that one can detect in Roman copies has any validity, his idealism may have gradually taken on an Athenian cast.

II. ARTISTS AND PATRONS

Artists as a group were never accorded the reverence and adulation in antiquity that has come to them in post-Renaissance times, and the idea of the artist as an inspired visionary, to the degree that it existed at all in the ancient world, belongs to late Hellenistic and Roman literature. Yet even when these facts are taken into account, it can still be argued, on the

[25] Robertson 1975 (I 140) 328–40; von Steuben 1973 (I 158); Boardman 1985 (I20) 205–6.

basis of literary sources which deal with the careers and work of Classical artists, that the emergence of sculptors and painters as figures of some social prominence in the Greek world, figures who were appreciated for their intellects and strong personalities as well as their skill, first occurred in the fifth century B.C.

A relatively early case in point is Polygnotus of Thasos. His widespread reputation is attested by the fact that, according to Pliny (*HN* xxxv.59), the Amphictyonies awarded him free food and lodging, presumably in recognition of his remarkable paintings at Delphi. This was an honour normally awarded to such prominent figures as victors in the Olympic Games. He also moved in prominent social circles. Gossip preserved by Plutarch maintained that Elpinice, the sister of Cimon, was Polygnotus' mistress and that he used her portrait for the face of one of the Trojan Women in a mural in the Stoa Poikile (Plut. *Cim.* 4). Even if that story was only gossip, it is very likely that he was a friend and follower of Cimon. Plutarch relates that he would not take payment like a 'common workman' for his paintings in the Stoa Poikile but did them as a patriotic offering to Athens (where he had attained citizenship), an anecdote that conjures up the picture of a man of pride, zeal, and perhaps also a certain amount of power.

While Cimon's patronage of Polygnotus is a possibility, Pericles' patronage of Phidias is a fact beyond doubt. As *episkopos* of the whole Periclean building programme, Phidias must have become a man of considerable influence and perhaps also wealth. He was prominent enough to be the object of an attack by Pericles' political enemies, and when this attack ultimately forced him to leave Athens (he was charged with embezzling gold designated for the Athena Parthenos), he quickly received the most important commission that a sculptor of the period could aspire to, the assignment to make the great chryselephantine image for the temple of Zeus at Olympia. In addition to being an intimate of Pericles, it is fair to assume that Phidias was on close terms with the circle of intellectuals whom Pericles befriended, Anaxagoras and Protagoras, for example, and that he exchanged ideas with them. He himself must be considered one of the prominent intellectuals of the age, and through the medium of his own sculptures and of those, like the architectural sculptures of the Parthenon, which bore the stamp of his influence, his ideas had a lasting effect on the ancient world and continue to be felt even now.

Other scattered anecdotes relating to artists who worked somewhat later in the century also evoke a picture of prominent reputations and of strong, often contentious, personalities. The services of Agatharchus were considered so valuable by Alcibiades that he locked the painter in his house in order to force him to finish a work (Plut. *Alc.* 16).

Agatharchus may have had as vivid a personality as the man who locked him up. He is said to have written a treatise on graphic perspective (Vitr. *De Arch.* VII. *praef.* 11), of which, as already noted, he was considered the inventor. He also boasted about his ability to paint with unusual rapidity. His successor and apparent rival Zeuxis countered this boast with the sober declaration that his own paintings took him a long time, implying that the most obvious result of Agatharchus' quickness was carelessness (Plut. *Per.* 13). Humility, as this anecdote suggests, was no more typical of Zeuxis than of the rivals whom he taunted. According to Pliny, 'he acquired such great wealth that he showed it off at Olympia by having his name woven into the checks of his cloaks in gold letters. Afterwards he decided to give away his works as gifts, since he felt that no price could be considered equal to their true worth'; and he was so pleased with one of his paintings, a picture of Penelope, 'that he wrote beneath it a verse which as a result has become famous: "You could criticize this more easily than you could imitate it"' (*HN* xxxv.62–3). Equally flamboyant was Zeuxis' contemporary and rival Parrhasius. 'No one ever made use of his art more insolently than he,' Pliny records, 'for he even laid claim to certain cognomens, calling himself the "Habrodiaitos" [lover of luxury] and in some other verses the "Prince of Painting", claiming that the art had been brought to perfection by him' (*HN* xxxv.71). The verses referred to by Pliny may be those recorded by Athenaeus (543D–E), in which Parrhasius describes himself as the 'foremost practitioner of art among the Greeks' and claims that 'the clear limits of this art have been revealed by my hand'. Along with this kind of vanity and flamboyance, there is even a hint, if late sources can be trusted, of contempt for public opinion among the artists of the era. Lucian describes Zeuxis as reacting in disgust when people were dazzled by the subject matter of his *Centaur Family* but were oblivious to the painting's technical excellence (*Zeuxis* 3), and Aelian depicts Polyclitus as taunting visitors to his workshop for their lack of sound judgement (*VH* xiv.8).

Even if these are simply amusing anecdotes invented in later centuries, they do point to an important fact about at least some of the prominent artists of the fifth century, that they were literate, self-conscious theoreticians who were concerned with defining and explaining the principles of their art. The foremost figure in this respect was clearly Polyclitus. His *Canon*, written to explain the system of proportions (*symmetria*) which was the basis of the perfect beauty of his sculptures, seems to have been a quasi-philosophical work strongly influenced by Pythagoreanism.[26] The *Canon* was the most famous but not the only example of such a treatise. Ictinus, the architect of the Parthenon (along

[26] Pollitt 1974 (I 128) 14–23.

with a certain Carpion, perhaps an error for Callicrates), is said by Vitruvius to have written a treatise about the temple (VII. *praef.* 12); Agatharchus, as already noted, wrote on perspective; and a number of painters in the fourth century also wrote about their art (*CAH* VI², ch. 13*e*).[27] The philosophical overtones that can be detected in the fragments and descriptions of Polyclitus' *Canon* make it probable that the work was something more than simply a workshop manual designed to instruct pupils, and it is likely that this was true of other artists' writings as well. Like Vitruvius' *De Architectura*, which is descended from them, their purpose, at least in part, was probably to demonstrate that the artist was an important, thoughtful functionary in his culture and deserved to be taken seriously.

To a degree they achieved their aim. Many Classical artists, of course, laboured in obscurity and were no doubt thought of simply as craftsmen. This was obviously the case with those obscure but gifted sculptors who carved the frieze of the Erechtheum and whose names, otherwise unknown, are recorded in the building accounts of the temple. But when we read Isocrates, writing not in late Antiquity but only a few decades after the end of the fifth century, claiming that his own speeches had no more similarity to conventional courtroom speeches than the art of Phidias had to figurine making or the art of Zeuxis and Parrhasius had to sign painting (*Antid.* 2), it is clear that these artists at least had become celebrities in their own time.

[27] Pollitt 1974 (I 128) 23–4.

CHAPTER 8*b*

CLASSICAL CITIES AND SANCTUARIES

R. E. WYCHERLEY

The Greek city was a creation of the Archaic period, in architectural form as in political, religious and social life. The fifth century was a time of continued development and of refinement. This was still strongly concentrated in the temple, and in the Doric and Ionic orders. In other elements of the city there was a good deal of what one might call non-architecture. Many activities took place under the open sky on a piece of ground demarcated for the purpose. The city centre, the Agora, was a loose aggregation of mostly simple buildings around an open square. Buildings specifically designed were slow in making their appearance and attaining a complete form. The ubiquitous and adaptable stoa supplied the deficiency to some extent. Houses were unpretentious; and though the best of them were well built and commodious, their outward treatment gave no architectural distinction to the narrow streets. Next to the major temples, the city walls were the most impressive works of architecture.

Cities old and new were built on an endless variety of sites – around an acropolis or on one side, on a terraced slope, on a ridge or spur, headland or peninsula, on ground which rose theatre-like from a harbour, occasionally even on level or featureless ground; and the way in which the architectural elements were adapted to their setting varied enormously. Many old cities, especially in Greece proper, kept the irregular, loosely-knit form which they had attained by expansion, gradual or spasmodic, around acropolis, Agora or, on some sites, age-old shrines. Of course fine effects were obtained even in these, in general aspect and in siting of particular monuments, notably the walls. But we now have evidence to show that from the Archaic period onwards more deliberate planning, based on a rectangular pattern, was applied both in the east and in the west. In the fifth century we see in this art too a refinement of methods. Hippodamus of Miletus, who for Aristotle and others was the master city-planner, lived through almost the whole of the century.

There was no dramatic change in materials and methods of construction, such as might have altered the character of Greek architecture and

184

enlarged its scope. The use of stone for the main structure of temples had already been fully developed. Tools and equipment remained simple and even rudimentary; but this was compensated by extreme care and delicacy in handling, shaping and fitting.

The blocks were laboriously hewn out in the quarries with pick, chisel and wedge (not by saw till much later) to the approximate size and shape. On Pentelicum they were slid down the mountain-side on ramps by means of sledges. Then they were loaded on strong waggons or occasionally rollers, and drawn slowly by bullock teams, which for the biggest loads comprised many yokes. On the site the stones were more accurately shaped; some finishing touches, notably the fluting of columns, were not given till they were in position and safe from serious damage. Curiously, in our period we do not find the truly gigantic blocks used in the colossal Archaic temples, nor monolithic columns except on a small scale. The architrave blocks, set on top of the columns, in the Archaic temple of Artemis at Ephesus and Temple GT at Selinus, weighed forty tons or more. Such heavy stuff was raised by means of 'ramps, levers and massed manpower'.[1] By the end of the sixth century simple cranes were in use, but they would not take such enormous loads. In some major fifth-century temples the architrave consisted not of single massive blocks but of lighter slabs set side by side. Even in the colossal Olympieum at Acragas, the architrave, because of its peculiarly complex construction, did not require blocks of more than fourteen tons.

Marble was used on a bigger scale in the fifth century, for whole temples and occasionally other buildings. White or off-white marble was used; coloured stone did not come into favour till much later. 'Stones white, sound, unspotted' are specified in an Attic building inscription.[2] Athens was favoured above all other cities in her plentiful supplies. The western cities in particular were at a disadvantage. For sculptural adornment, limited supplies were sometimes brought from a great distance or even transported by sea. For the sculpture of the temple of Zeus at Olympia, Parian marble was used; the temple was built of a shelly local stone, given a finish resembling marble, as were many temples, by the use of a fine white stucco.

Most cities could draw on quarries of serviceable stone at a moderate distance, but the builders sometimes went further afield for a better stone; for example Corinthian *poros* was taken to Delphi. We find a variety of limestones in use, greyish or creamy or yellowish, neither extremely hard nor very soft. These, the common Greek building stones,

---

[1] Coulton 1977 (I 51) 48, 84; cf. Martin 1965 (I 106) 200–21.
[2] *IG* II² 1666; cf. R. E. Wycherley, *BSA* 68 (1973) 351.

are what can properly be called *poros*, though the term is not very clearly defined by our ancient authorities.[3] The use of very hard, intractable limestones, as found in the Acropolis rock for example, becomes comparatively rare in this period; the use of rough conglomerate, mainly in massive foundations, begins in the latter part of the fifth century and becomes common later. Metal – iron and lead – was used for dowels and clamps; iron bars were occasionally inserted as reinforcements for architraves. Roof timbers supported tiles of fine baked clay, rarely of marble. Baked brick was exceptional. The commonest material of all was still unbaked, sun-dried brick, used over a stone socle in all houses, some public buildings and even in massive fortification walls. Athens was a city not so much of marble or any kind of stone as of mud-brick. This does not mean poor flimsy construction. Unbaked brick is a very serviceable material, strong, durable and not unsightly if well maintained, protected from the elements by tiles above and a coat of white lime-plaster on its face. Still, conservatism and economy in material and methods imposed limitations on Classical Greek architecture, bonds which were not burst until the Roman period.

Much has been written recently on 'the economics of temple building', though the evidence, largely from inscriptions, is far from complete.[4] Money and manpower set strict limits. At Acragas in the course of the century a series of temples was built; at Athens a great building programme was carried out in the second half of the century. Very few cities could build on this scale; most had to be content with two or three major temples, very seldom as large as the Parthenon, and numerous modest shrines. Commercial prosperity under enlightened leadership provided the conditions for ambitious building; some temples and stoas were victory monuments, to which the spoils of war might contribute; in good times pious, public-spirited or ostentatious citizens might be expected to make contributions.

The procedure for bringing into being a great temple or other important building was normally as follows, in a democratically governed city, or under enlightened tyranny. A proposal was passed in the Assembly. A small supervisory commission of *epistatai* was set up. An architect was appointed, sometimes more than one. Work of various kinds was put out on contract piecemeal; there were no great building firms who would take on the whole job. Specifications were drawn up. As regards plans and drawings, evidence is slight and not clear; probably at some points it was a case of *solvitur aedificando*, in our period. *Peradeigmata* or prototypes were made of elements which had to be accurately reproduced in numbers. As the work gradually proceeded

[3] Bradeen and McGregor, eds. 1974 (A 9) 179–87.
[4] Burford 1969 (I 40) and 1965 (I 39). On the epigraphical evidence see Scranton 1960 (I 150).

there were annual scrutinies of the expenditure, submitted to the Assembly.

The architect[5] was no mere designer at the drawing-board but a man with practical ability and experience, an engineer. The closeness of his relation with the builders varied from site to site. The design of a temple was of course largely determined by tradition and convention, and sometimes by special circumstances; but there was still room for originality, for variation and experiment, for a constant striving towards the idea of perfection, in the proportions of the temple as a whole and of its constituent parts, in the relation of particular elements to one another in form and dimension, in the treatment of the details of the orders, in the use of the so-called 'refinements'. The western architects had ideas of their own, more particularly in the Archaic period. Quite apart from certain buildings of exceptional plan, the great fifth-century architects such as Ictinus were by no means merely reproducers of a stereotype.

The profession was an honourable one, practised by men of good standing and education, but our authorities seem to imply that it did not carry the prestige of the leading sculptors. Occasionally a sculptor performed the function of architect too. We know the names of some scores of architects, but are told very little about them. Remuneration was not very high. Some, we see in the inscriptions, were paid not much more than their best craftsmen.

Of the workforce many were unskilled labourers; some were carters, and of these some were no doubt provided by the farmers who supplied the teams of oxen. Even at the lower level large hordes of workmen would not be available; the skilled workers in stone, wood and metal were apt to be in short supply, and few cities if any would have enough in more or less permanent residence for a big sustained programme. Work was intermittent, and in pursuit of it craftsmen commuted over a wide area. Athens was a kind of clearing-house, and so were the great international sanctuaries. Changing political conditions created complications, with the result that work sometimes proceeded in spasmodic fashion.

The Doric and Ionic orders, fully developed in the sixth century, attained perfection by the middle of the fifth. The simple single curve of the Doric capital then attained its most subtle form and so did the volute superimposed on the convex *echinus* of the Ionic capital. The Doric frieze of triglyphs and metopes was still 'petrified carpentry',[6] though the relation of the classical ornamental forms to their structural prototypes, beam ends and so forth, is a matter of dispute. The junction of Doric

[5] Coulton 1977 (I 51); cf. Clarke 1963 (I 46).
[6] Lawrence 1973 (I 95) 99; cf. Coulton 1977 (I 51) 60–4, 130–1. On Doric design in general see Coulton 1974, 1975, 1979 (I 48, 49, 52); Winter 1976, 1978 (I 180, 181).

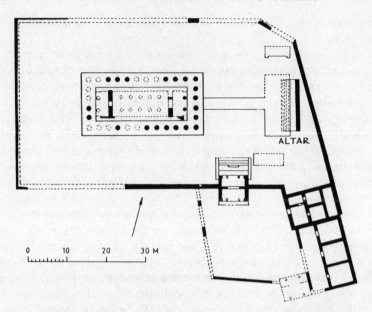

ALTAR

0   10   20   30 M

Fig. 12. Plan of the fifth-century sanctuary of Aphaea on Aegina. (After Bergquist 1967 (1 12) plan 3.)

friezes at the corners of a building created difficulties, solved by ingenious manipulation of the widths of triglyphs and metopes. Ionic on the other hand had problems with its capitals at the corners, where two adjacent faces required volutes; and this may have been a factor in the creation of the Corinthian capital, which avoided the difficulty by having four faces all alike. Corinthian was not a wholly new order; other elements remained as in Ionic. The invention was attributed to Callimachus, the sculptor of the late fifth century who was called 'katatexitechnic', a word which implies that he wasted his art on over-elaborate detail. Known to us first at remote Bassae, the Corinthian capital was still used in a somewhat tentative fashion, mainly for interiors, even in the fourth century, and finally came into its own in the Olympieum in the second.

Of particular temples, one can hardly do more here than mention several which represent the norm and one or two which deviate from it in notable fashion. As a typical example of a well-developed Doric temple of the beginning of the fifth century we may take the temple of Aphaea (a local goddess associated with Artemis) at Aegina. The sanctuary was enlarged and given a more regular form (Fig. 12). Built of local limestone, the temple had a long *cella* divided by two rows of columns, with an entrance porch on the east consisting of two columns between the side walls and a similar porch at the back (without door); and a *pteron*, peristyle or outer colonnade of six columns by twelve (*Pls. to*

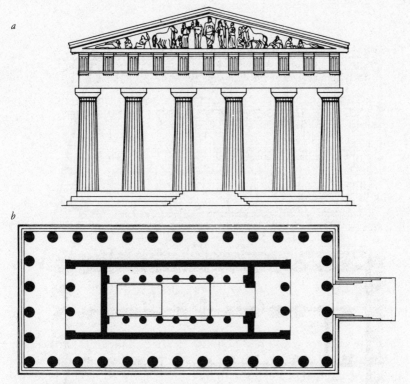

Fig. 13. Temple of Zeus at Olympia, east elevation (*a*) and plan (*b*). (After Coulton 1977 (1 5 1)
figs. 45a, 46a.)

Vol. IV, pl. 116). The great temple of Zeus at Olympia, built in the 460s,
has a similar plan on a grander scale (Fig. 13).

Athenian buildings, including the Parthenon and the Hephaesteum,
will be considered in chapter 8*c* below. Meanwhile we may note that in
some great Doric structures Ionic details were incorporated to give
variety and mitigate severity. The Ionic style itself is seen at its most
delicate in the Erechtheum; here the idea of placing a band of ornament
round the top of the column shaft may represent one step towards the
creation of the Corinthian capital.

The great series of Doric temples in the west continues at Paestum,
Selinus (*CAH* IV² 754–6), and above all Acragas.[7] At the last-named city,
superb sites were found on the ridges to the north and south (*CAH* IV²
777, Fig. 84). Most of the Acragantine temples were of normal type, with
variations; but the Olympieum, begun early in the fifth century and

---

[7] De Waele 1980 (1 57) gives a careful study of the temples of Acragas and Paestum (1 58).

a

b

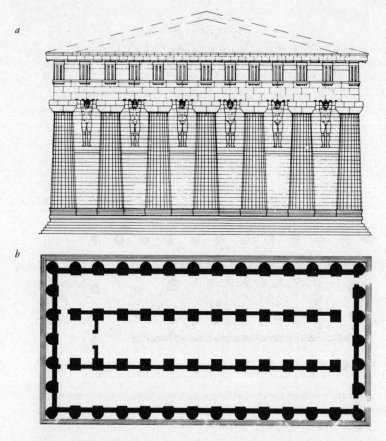

Fig. 14. Temple of Zeus Olympius at Acragas, west elevation (*a*) and plan (*b*). (After Coulton 1977 (I 51) figs. 28b, 29b.)

never finished, besides being the only temple of our period which vies in size with the archaic colossi, was very unusual in form and construction. Both inner supports and outer columns were built into continuous walls, and on ledges between the outer columns were placed Telamones, giants who helped to carry the great weight of the architraves (Fig. 14) (*Pls. to Vol. IV*, pl. 266).

Among western buildings of the late fifth century the unfinished temple at Segesta is of peculiar interest. It raises the whole question whether a peristyle could stand in its own right, without an inner structure; in any case it shows the structural independence of the peristyle. Of a possible *cella* there are only a few uncertain traces.[8] Some have suggested that the Segestans merely provided a handsome frame

[8] Burford 1961 (I 37).

for a very simple shrine, which may not have been that of a Greek deity –
Segesta was the capital of the Elymi, a Sicilian community which aspired
to Greek culture. However, the colonnade was built in the best tradition
of Doric architecture, with refinements, and pediments were added; on
the whole it seems likely that an interior structure was planned and even
begun. The columns did not receive their fluting, and bosses for leverage
were left on some blocks. We see on this site as on some others how a
peripteral temple was built from the outside inwards.

The chief architect of the Parthenon, Ictinus, created at Bassae, on a
superb terraced mountainside in Arcadia, a temple of Apollo which,
although at first glance it appears to be orthodox Doric, has several
unusual features (Fig. 15). It has a north–south orientation instead of the
usual east–west. The interior has two rows of Ionic columns, with
unorthodox capitals and bases, engaged in short walls, with a continuous
sculptured frieze above. The back end of the *cella* is marked off from the
rest by a single column standing between the southernmost pair and is
entered by a door at the southern end of the eastern side, thus forming a
kind of separate shrine. A curious capital (Fig. 16), now lost and known
only from drawings, is thought to have belonged to the single central
column, though it is suggested that the column on either side of this may
have had similar capitals. On an underlying moulding in the shape of an
upturned bell, inner and outer volutes rise on all four sides from a ring of
acanthus leaves. We have here the prototype of the Corinthian capital, in
a somewhat tentative form.

For reasons of expense few sanctuaries received large temples. More
modest shrines still took the form of a simple *cella* with a columnar
porch, as in the so-called treasuries, with the columns either *in antis*
(between the projecting side walls), or prostyle, standing in a row in
front. But of the innumerable sanctuaries found in any large city the
majority had no temple at all. All that was needed was the demarcation of
a piece of ground as *hieron*.[9] This was commonly done by means of simple
marker-stones carrying a minimal inscription; such *horoi* have been
found in large numbers and in great variety and were an important part
of the urban scene. There might be a solid wall and it might have a
propylon or columnar gateway. Every shrine needed an altar and this
might be a plain stone or something more ornamental, perhaps set on a
platform approached by steps – the magnificent altars which were
elaborate works of architecture in themselves belong to a later date. A
certain area might be designated as an inner sanctum, with its own
entrance and limited access, the rest of the sanctuary being more freely
available to worshippers. Some shrines had a third area one degree more
remotely attached, and used for various purposes, athletics for instance,

---

[9] Bergquist 1967 (i 12) is still relevant for our period; further, Tomlinson 1976 (i 169).

a

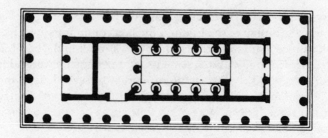

b

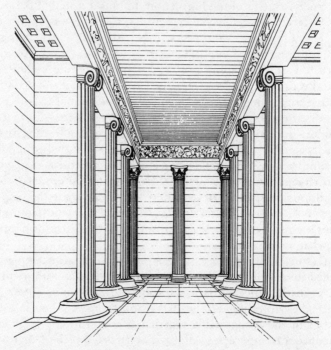

Fig. 15. Temple of Apollo Epicurius at Bassae, plan (*a*) and interior of *cella* (*b*). (After Coulton 1977 (1 51) figs. 49, 50.)

or even cultivation. We find a peculiar example in south-eastern Athens, known not from remains but from details given in an inscription.[10] In this sanctuary were shrines of the heroic king Codrus, and of a pair of ancient deities Neleus and Basile. Nothing is said of a temple, but we hear of *ikria*, wooden stands presumably for viewing the ceremonies. An extensive piece of ground was leased to a tenant for growing olive-trees – a useful source of revenue for maintenance of the cult; and this tenant had the right to use the water from an even wider catchment area.

When we come to sanctuaries architecturally more developed we find

[10] *IG* 1³ 84; Wycherley 1960 (1 183).

Fig. 16. Corinthian capital from the temple of Apollo
Epicurius at Bassae, restored. (After D. Watschitzky,
JÖAI 37 (1948) 53, fig. 5.)

great variety in component elements and arrangement, in accordance
with the nature of the site and the requirements of the cult. The greatest
sanctuaries, especially those which, though they belonged to a particular
city, had assumed a panhellenic character and drew worshippers and
funds from a wide area, attained a complex form in course of time,
without a formal plan. They might include any of the following elements
– an additional temple of the major deity, multiple altars, reflecting the
complexity of the cult; shrines of associated deities and heroes, with
altars or occasionally a temple; quarters for priestly officials; dining-
rooms; store-rooms; 'treasuries' (small temple-like buildings commonly
erected by particular cities); and, for a variety of purposes, stoas; all
embedded in a wealth of sculptural monuments, dedications of many
kinds. A theatre and a stadium might be added if the cult so required.
Olympia had a large *prytaneion* and a curious old *bouleuterion*, in fact all the
elements of a city except the residential. Yet even this great sanctuary
remained simple and open in plan in the fifth century (Fig. 17),
dominated by the temples, the archaic Heraeum (in which Zeus too was
worshipped), and the splendid new temple of Zeus. Handsome buildings
for the use of the athletes and distinguished visitors were not added till
later ages. At Delphi a comparable assemblage of monuments was
differently arranged (Fig. 18). The temple stood high up on the hillside
on a terrace. The processional way ascended in a zig-zag to the east front
and the altar, and was lined with treasuries and sculpture. Above were
yet more monuments, and the theatre, and still higher was the stadium.

The stoa played a vital part in Greek life and architecture.[11] Already in
the Archaic period architects realized that the colonnade not only
provided a useful and ornamental addition to a building but was also
important as an adjunct to an open space – agora, shrine, gymnasium and

[11] Besides Coulton 1976 (I 50) note Martin 1951 (I 105) 449–502.

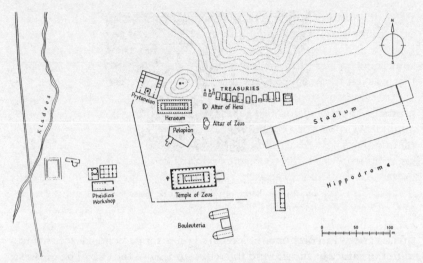

Fig. 17. Plan of the sanctuary of Zeus at Olympia, fifth century B.C. (After Herrmann 1972 (K 40) 158, fig. 111.)

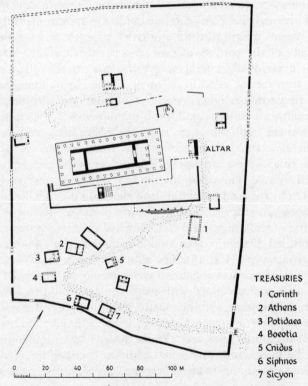

TREASURIES

1 Corinth
2 Athens
3 Potidaea
4 Boeotia
5 Cnidus
6 Siphnos
7 Sicyon

Fig. 18. Plan of the sanctuary of Apollo at Delphi, early fifth century B.C. (After Bergquist 1967 (I 12) plan 12.)

so forth – putting a roof over a limited part of that space and giving it ornamentation and partial definition. Archaic stoas were already remarkably well developed and varied in form. Again the fifth century had something to add without introducing a high degree of elaboration – that was left to the Hellenistic period.

The stoa consisted of a wall and a row of columns; the ends too were normally short walls or else a short row of columns; or the end walls might leave room for a column in front, giving a prostyle effect; or again they might make a return along the front of the building. The addition of a second storey belongs to a later period. The depth of the stoas varied greatly. Beyond a certain point a second row of columns was needed and the interior row could conveniently be made Ionic, contrasting with the outer Doric. Two-aisled stoas are found already in the Archaic period. We also have an early example, in the shrine at Delos, of the L-shaped stoa, a type which may have helped to suggest the pi-shaped stoa, and the more complex rectangular arrangements found, from the fourth century onwards, especially in the Ionian type of agora. The most effective way of creating a finished and satisfying architectural design out of a simple colonnade was to bring forward a section at either end of the front and give it a temple-like façade. The earliest and best example is the Stoa of Zeus at Athens, late in the fifth century (Fig. 29). It had few successors; for the most part the stoa remained a simple basic type. Sculptural adornment was applied very sparingly, but occasionally we find handsome *acroteria* on the roof. On the other hand the stoas frequently served as the setting and background for notable free-standing statues. A few had paintings on their walls.

Occasionally a colonnade was placed on either side of the central wall, giving the effect of two stoas back to back. Much more commonly rooms were built behind the colonnade, to serve as offices, dining-rooms for officials, or shops. The uses of the stoas cover the whole range of Greek political, religious and social life; and the same stoa might be used for different purposes at different times. In the case of the largest political and religious gatherings, including theatre audiences, the main activities would take place in the open and an attached stoa would be used as occasion arose. But a sufficiently spacious stoa could be the regular meeting-place of a court or council. Seats were sometimes built along the foot of the walls and rows of wooden benches could be added. Even stoas which were used for such august purposes were available between times as *leschai*, for casual social needs, for sitting and strolling and talking. And if the talker was a Zeno, the nucleus of a school might be formed. Some eccentrics more or less took up residence. Diogenes the Cynic, according to his namesake (VI.2.22), pointing to the Stoa of Zeus said 'The Athenians have provided me with somewhere to live.'

In the above account 'stoa' has been assumed to mean an independent free-standing colonnade. This is its usual meaning in ancient authors and it is probably best to confine oneself to this. But the name is occasionally applied to a colonnade attached to a major structure. Taking the widest significance, one might properly say that Greek architecture is decidedly 'stoic' in character, if the adjective had not been appropriated by those who set up their school in the most famous of all stoas.

Greek architects were not well equipped to provide roofed halls for very large assemblies. All they could do was to extend the principle of the two- or three-aisled stoa, introducing row upon row of columns, obstructive to movement and vision. The Telesterion or hall of initiation at Eleusis, repeatedly enlarged in the sixth and fifth centuries, was a building of this type; and so was the Odeum of Pericles (Fig. 19). The most ingenious and successful example was the Thersilium at Megalopolis in Arcadia, which had room for ten thousand; but this was not built till after 371 B.C. In due course the theatre came to be used for political as well as festal gatherings. The Greeks in our period had no equivalent of the basilica. Law courts met in stoas and other buildings not designed for the purpose or in an unroofed enclosure. A council of several hundreds could meet in a spacious stoa; but a fairly satisfactory *bouleuterion* or council house was devised by placing a small theatre-like arrangement within a rectangular hall which needed only four or five supports for the roof. We find this type already in the fifth century at Athens (Fig. 27), but it reached full development in the Hellenistic period.[12]

The theatre of Sophocles and even Euripides was still not a work of fine architecture but a simple adaptation of a suitable site (Fig. 19).[13] It consisted of three parts, the orchestra, the flat dancing-place – and acting-place; the *theatron* proper, the auditorium, normally provided by shaping a convenient adjoining slope; and, facing it across the orchestra, the *skene*, whose name, meaning 'tent' or 'booth', betokens its essential simplicity. All three elements even in the latter part of the fifth century were somewhat rudimentary and makeshift in form; only in the fourth were they given a truly monumental character and combined into an effective architectural whole. In the fifth century the orchestra was of hard earth – stone paving comes much later; in the auditorium *ikria*, wooden benches on wooden uprights, were used, though the provision of stone seating was begun; and the *skene* was a simple and adaptable structure mainly of timber. There may have been a low wooden platform for the use of the actors when dramatically desirable, but nothing like the later *proskenion*, a high stone-built structure. Renewed investigation in

[12] McDonald 1943 (I 100).
[13] Hammond 1972 (I 73); cf. Taplin 1977 (I 162) appendixes B and C. For a controversial view see Anti 1947 (I 2) and Anti and Polacco 1969 (I 3).

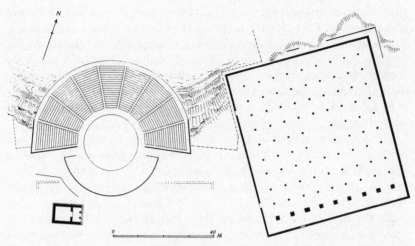

Fig. 19. Athens, the theatre of Dionysus and Odeum, late fifth century B.C. (After Travlos 1971 (1 171) 389, 540.)

the theatre of Dionysus at Athens[14] in recent years has led Greek archaeologists to conclude that the first massive stone scene-building was not erected till the fourth century, at the same time as the later temple of Dionysus, of whose shrine the theatre was a huge appendage. It must be freely admitted that the history of the theatre throughout is full of doubts and problems; in particular, under repeated elaborate reconstructions it is extremely difficult to discern the form of the theatre in its earlier periods. At present we can only attempt to assess its place in the scheme of the city. Even though architecturally undeveloped, a great theatre, on a fine site, ingeniously adapted to hold an audience of many thousands, would still be one of the city's most impressive features.

Any place provided for people to watch a spectacle was called *theatron*. The stadium was a greatly elongated version of the type, such that the athletes could run a stade in a straight line; it was even slower than the theatre in achieving a fully built-up form. To the end the great stadium at Olympia consisted of simple embankments with stone seating for only a few. At Athens Lycurgus reconstructed the stadium in the fourth century, but one hardly imagines that even he provided seating on the scale later provided by Herodes Atticus.

Being of such great length the stadium was normally located along with the cemeteries in the suburbs of the city or on the fringe. So were the gymnasia, which were originally extensive athletic and military training grounds, used in course of time for more academic pursuits. A gymnasium was commonly attached to the shrine of a local deity or hero

14 Kalligas 1963 (1 86); Travlos 1971 (1 171) 537–9.

and contained shrines of Hermes and other appropriate deities. It usually acquired stoas, a simple bath-house and a palaestra or wrestling-ground. These last two elements could also exist independently – Athens is said to have had many palaestras by the end of the fifth century, used by sophists and other teachers as well as athletes. From the fourth century we find gymnastic buildings in the form of a handsome colonnaded court with rooms attached, and a simple version of this arrangement may have existed earlier.

Aristotle tells us that the city wall should be an ornament as well as a defence (*Pol.* VII.10.8). Of course the two things were not separate. A fine-looking wall was a crowning element in the architecture of the city; at the same time it was a deterrent to an attacker even before its strength was put to the test.

By the fifth century nearly all cities had an outer fortification, not merely an acropolis, citadel or strong point. An old acropolis might still form part of the defences, as an inner line or bastion. It was not indispensable, however, and a new town might have no distinct acropolis; but a dominant hill might be included in the defences to give them greater strength and prevent an attacker from occupying it. On some sites there was an acropolis in the sense of 'high town', even though it was not a separately fortified citadel. Outlying defences were sometimes provided in the shape of border forts, watch towers or cross-walls.

The building of the city wall was the biggest job which a city had to undertake. Athens and other cities had boards of *teichopoioi* who were responsible.[15] Architects were appointed and work entrusted in sections to numerous contractors. Constant maintenance and repair was needed and improvements from time to time to keep pace with advances in methods of siege and assault. This process continued energetically in the fourth century and reached its climax in the Hellenistic period.

In this as in other things the Greek architects were glad to let nature build for them, and in planning the line went out of their way to take advantage of natural strength. Thus large areas not required for habitation or public purposes were sometimes included. The system of defence in the fifth century remained simple, with towers, curtain walls between, and fortified gates. Important gates were planned as *dipyla*, with an inner and outer opening, a small court between and towers at the corners. Complicated outworks were not employed in the fifth century. The highly elaborate defence-works at the eastern tip of the wall at Syracuse and a similar structure on the north at Selinus, formerly attributed to Dionysius of Syracuse, are now thought to be still later.[16]

[15] Inscriptions provide much interesting evidence; see Maier 1959 (I 101).
[16] Lawrence 1946 (I 94) and 1979 (I 96) s.v. index.

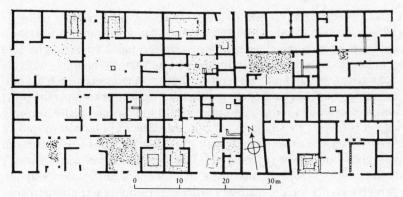

Fig. 20. Houses at Olynthus, fourth century B.C. (After Robinson *et al.* 1929–46 (1 141) VIII (1938) pl. 94.)

Only the finest walls were built of well-shaped masonry throughout. More often there was a massive rubble core, embedded in clay. The total width varied considerably on either side of 3 metres. Unbaked brick was still often used for the upper parts of city walls; it was quite satisfactory provided that the stone socle was high enough to prevent attackers from reaching it easily with picks.

The style of the masonry varies and does not provide a precise criterion for date. Polygonal masonry is still sometimes found in the fifth century. Roughly shaped stone (i.e., not merely in the core) indicates that the wall is of lesser importance, or hastily constructed, rather than that it is very early. Ashlar masonry, perfectly rectangular and well-smoothed on the face, was not entirely suitable for fortifications. A style which was favoured because while it had an elegance of its own, it gave the appearance of rugged strength, is what is called 'trapezoidal'; in this the upper and lower edges of the great blocks are horizontal, but the sides depart noticeably from the vertical, giving an effect somewhere between polygonal and ashlar. The face of the blocks is commonly 'rusticated' – left somewhat rough, though shaped with care, or decorated with simple grooves and striations. In some walls the upper part is treated with greater precision than the socle.

On many sites these great walls seem to be an appropriate extension of the rock on which they stand; on some they are the only immediately visible evidence that a city once stood here.

In no department of our subject has the available material increased so greatly during the last half century as in the study of classical Greek houses. Most notably, at Olynthus during the 1930s a large part of the town was excavated, including numerous residential blocks in which the plans of individual houses were clearly preserved (Fig. 20). Except that they conform to a strictly rectangular street plan, one may reasonably regard these as fairly typical of the houses of moderately well-to-do Greek citizens in this period. Each is about 18 m square and built round a small courtyard normally set in the southern part. There might be a simple colonnade on one or more sides but nothing comparable with the monumental peristyles of Hellenistic Delos. An entrance porch led into the courtyard. The space of the colonnade on the north side of the court was often extended across almost the whole width of the house, forming what was called a *pastas*, on to which opened the main rooms. In spite of the strict regularity of general plan, the arrangement of the rooms in individual houses varied endlessly. The principal room was the men's dining-room or *andron*, which can sometimes be identified by its layout, with plastered floor and a raised border – most floors were of hard clay. Though the evidence is slight, we can assume that most houses had an upper storey. The material was stone for the lower walls and unbaked brick for the rest; and of course timber for upper floor, roof and pillars, and terracotta for tiles.

This solid block of evidence is now supplemented by more scrappy material from other sites, notably Athens itself, mainly on the fringes of the Agora region, and from scattered sites in Attica. The Athenian houses were not, of course, uniform in size and they were apt to be irregular in outline since the Athenian streets were highly irregular; but in mode of construction and in general character they are similar to those of Olynthus.

There were simple houses at Athens and no doubt at other cities, consisting of no more than two or three rooms huddled together. At the other end of the scale, the house of the wealthy Callias must have been better than any we know from remains; colonnades in the courtyard could accommodate sophistic seminars, as we see in Plato's *Protagoras*.

The old idea that the builders of the Parthenon lived in domestic squalor is not now tenable. Thucydides (II.65.2) tells us that some Athenians had comparatively costly establishments in the country. Two substantial farmhouses have recently been excavated, one between Mt Aigaleos and Mt Parnes to the north west, one at Vari in southern Attica (Fig. 21).[17] The former is of the late fifth century, the latter of the fourth. They are solid rectangular structures, not being subject to the vagaries of town streets. They are indeed more spacious than most town houses, but with no suggestion of architectural luxury. The basic plan is the same, with a courtyard of larger dimensions towards the south side and the principal rooms opening on it through a colonnade on the north.

The common house-type could be adapted for various purposes, as inn, school or factory. The Prytaneum was essentially a large house with accommodation for official dining and the cult of Hestia, goddess of the

[17] Jones *et al.* 1962 (I 84) and 1973 (I 83).

Fig. 21. Reconstructions of the Attic farmhouses beside the Dema wall (*a*) and at Vari (*b*), by J. E. Jones. (After *AAA* 7 (1974) 311, fig. 5; cf. Jones 1975 (182), Jones *et al.* 1962 and 1973 (1 84, 83)).

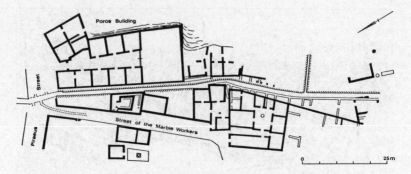

Fig. 22. Houses west of the Areopagus at Athens. (After Boersma 1970 (I 23) 253.)

hearth.[18] Here again we do not find buildings specially designed for their purpose. We now have a good example of industrial quarters at Thoricus and elsewhere in southern Attica, where the processes of silver-working were carried out,[19] besides the houses of marble- and bronze-workers on the streets leading from the Agora at Athens.

The better grade of house in the late fifth century was not without architectural character, but this would be apparent mainly in the interior. The house presented a plain unadorned face to the street, with perhaps a simple entrance porch. The ordinary streets of Athens (Fig. 22) and no doubt of many old cities were notoriously narrow, mean and dirty. Surfaces were of hard earth, which might be fortified by layers of gravel. Stone paving was only used at particular points for some special purpose. Drainage and sanitation were primitive; the well-built and efficient stone drain which took the effluents of the Agora region at Athens to the Eridanus stream was exceptional.[20]

Domestic water was provided mainly by wells and by cisterns, commonly bottle-shaped, which collected the rain. Fountain-houses were constructed in public places, with spouts and cisterns, sometimes adorned and protected by a columnar façade (*Pls. to Vol. IV*, pl. 195);[21] these were fed by springs usually on or near the spot, rarely by long pipe-lines, still less by imposing aqueducts.

Finally we must consider the art of city-planning. Though we now know that its origins stretch far back into the Archaic period, and to the western cities as well as Ionia, we can still believe that Miletus, and in particular Hippodamus, played an important part. At Miletus itself traces of rectangular planning have now been found in the pre-Persian city. Of Hippodamus we are told more than of most Greek architects –

[18] Miller 1978 (I 113).
[19] Mussche *et al.* 1963– (I 117) and 1974 (I 116); cf. Jones 1975 (I 82).
[20] Thompson and Wycherley 1972 (I 166) 194–7.
[21] B. Dunkley classifies types in *BSA* 36 (1935–6) 142–204; cf. Wycherley 1962 (I 184) 198–209; Thompson and Wycherley 1972 (I 166) 197–203.

he was a man of striking personality, with notable views on things political as well as architectural; yet we cannot precisely define his contribution to the art of *poleodomike*. Aristotle's statement (*Pol.* II.5) that he 'discovered the division [*diairesis*] of cities' is not literally true. Another word which is used of his work is perhaps more significant – *nemesis*, allocation. We can probably assume that he improved methods of working out a plan and adapting it to the contours, and determining sites for the different elements. Orientation, size of blocks, width of streets and so forth had to be taken into account; but above all the city had to be given that quality of *kosmos* which made it a convenient place to live in and which in Greek eyes gave it beauty.

Hippodamus is associated with four cities which are of importance for our subject, Miletus, Piraeus, Thurii and Rhodes. There is no need to take Rhodes from him on the grounds of extreme old age; octogenarians have done great work in many fields. One may assume that he was born early in the fifth century and that in his youth he saw the rebirth of Miletus and was no doubt moved and inspired by the way in which a plan was created for the growth of a great city, with ample provision for all its elements, notably the Agora, even though centuries rather than decades would be needed for its full realization. 'He cut up Piraeus,' says Aristotle, presumably meaning that he produced a plan for the whole peninsula. We may assume that he did this job in the 450s, when he was in his thirties, under Pericles. He was commemorated at Piraeus in the name of the Agora, Hippodameia. The evidence for the plan of the harbour town is extremely scrappy; there are traces of rectangular streets, but not with the same orientation throughout the whole complicated site.[22] In 443 Hippodamus went to Italy with the colonists who founded Thurii and, though we are not told so, it is natural to assume that he took an active part in planning the new city. Diodorus tells us (XII.10) that is had three streets running one way, four the other; and this can be assumed to mean main streets, with lesser streets between.

Before proceeding to Rhodes, we may take a brief look at Olynthus in northern Greece, which, in the latter part of the fifth century, expanded enormously. The old town, on the south hill, was irregular, with two streets converging towards the northern tip of the hill and others running across. The new town occupied a much more spacious plateau to the north, with an extension on the lower ground to the east. Its rectangular plan represents a complete regularization of the informal arrangement which we noted on the southern hill. Long 'avenues' ran north to south, of which one was given added width at the expense of neighbouring houses. Numerous cross streets then divided the area into

[22] Judeich 1931 (I 85) 430–56; Wycherley 1976 (in I 129 s.v. Peiraeus) and 1978 (I 187) 261–6.

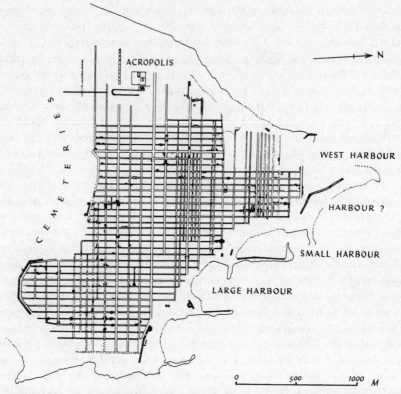

Fig. 23. Plan of Classical Rhodes. (After G. Constantinopoulos, *AAA* 1 (1970) 55, fig. 1.)

long blocks, each occupied by ten houses divided into two rows of five by very narrow alleys, which probably only served for drainage.

Rhodes provides a climax. In 408 the three ancient cities of the island decided to build a federal capital. They had a superb site (Fig. 23), a challenge for any architect, on the peninsula at the northern tip of the island. 'The city was founded', says Strabo (XIV.2.9), 'by the same architect as Piraeus'; and this probably means that the Rhodians brought in the venerable Hippodamus to provide a master plan.[23] Though remains are very scrappy, the overall plan has been largely recovered by adding to their evidence that of the medieval walls and streets and extensive features revealed in air photographs. A single unified street plan was applied to the whole peninsula, and excavation, though limited,

[23] Abandoning the view given in 1962 (1 184) 17, I put the case for giving Rhodes to Hippodamus in 1964 (1 185); Burns 1976 (1 41), in a very good assessment of the work of Hippodamus, concurs, as does McCredie 1971 (1 99). For further bibliography, notably the important work of J. R. Kondis and G. Constantinopoulos, see 1 129, 758.

has shown that certain streets were given additional width. The Agora was probably near the main harbour, the central of three, on the east side, where foundations of a temple of Aphrodite have been found. From this the ground rises gradually to west and south west, giving a theatre-like effect, till it culminates in a plateau on the western side of the peninsula. The stadium was effectively placed on the eastern scarp of this hill, with a gymnasium nearby; and the theatre must have been in the same area too, though only a small odeum of Roman type has been found. Temples were splendidly placed on the ridge above, looking over the town. Finally a magnificent wall, of whose foundations bits have been found here and there, surrounded the whole; this, as usual in planned Greek cities, took a course independent of the rectangular plan in accordance with natural features. Thus it contrasts curiously with the massive fortifications of the Knights of St John, long stretches of which take the line of ancient streets.

We need not doubt that the basic plan under which this great development took place was that of Hippodamus. Though the extant remains are mainly of later date, it is very unlikely that there were two successive plans and that the original was abandoned and obliterated.

We still know far too little of fifth-century *poleodomike* to speak in terms of general principles. Rectangular planning was normal, but there was room for freedom and imagination in its application for each site. Hippodamus is still an elusive figure. Perhaps we shall do him some justice if we think of him as Capability Hippodamus. He defined the possibilities of sites. He pointed the way and took the first steps towards the creation of the most beautiful city in the world (Strabo XIV.2.5, p. 652).

REBUILDING IN ATHENS AND ATTICA

R. E. WYCHERLEY

When the Persians had withdrawn, the Athenians returned to find their city mostly in ruins. Rebuilding and new building during the rest of the fifth century fall into three phases, though these are not entirely distinct (Fig. 24). In the earlier years, concern was mainly with housing and defence. There must have been much refurbishing of shrines and public buildings; the erection of major temples had to wait. Several important but modest public buildings were undertaken, notably the Tholos and the Stoa Poikile. Whatever is the truth about the 'oath of Plataea' (see p. 206), by which the Greeks are said to have sworn not to rebuild the shrines destroyed by the Persians, peace with Persia (440 B.C.) seems to have led to the phase of far more ambitious temple building at Athens, including the great programme of Pericles. Already in the 440s there are signs that the Athenians had undertaken more than their resources would permit; in the next decade with the inevitable onset of war the difficulties increased. Yet even after the outbreak of war in 431 the impetus was not wholly lost, and the architectural achievements of the troubled decades of the late fifth century, though not on the scale of the Parthenon, are varied and considerable. The work cannot have been confined to the years of uneasy peace following 421, though these no doubt provided occasion for the revival of activity and the completion of abandoned work. One obvious difficulty in years of invasion or occupation of Attica would be transport from the quarries.

For the most part we can only give general historical circumstances. Even at Athens precise dates and contexts are often difficult to determine and open to dispute and revision. Most of the leading figures of the century were concerned in some way with building.[1] But when a particular person is mentioned in such a connexion it is not always clear what part he played. He may have provided general inspiration and guidance, as Pericles undoubtedly did; he may have made a proposal in the Assembly, sometimes acting on behalf of a major statesman; he may have contributed money from his own resources. Through committees

[1] Especially Boersma 1970 (I 23). Even the Persian sack does not provide such a clear and agreed dividing line as one used to think.

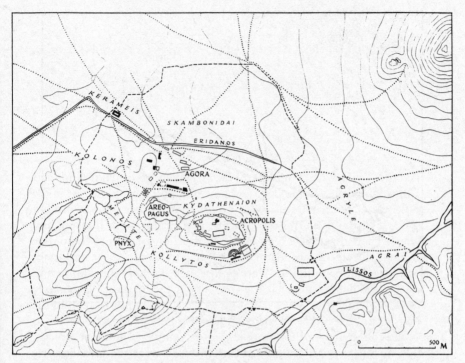

Fig. 24. Athens in the late fifth century B.C. (After Boersma 1970 (I 23) plan VI.)

and contracts many others were involved, and through Council and Assembly the whole people.

After 479 the Athenians might have built a largely new city, perhaps at Piraeus. This would probably have been to the liking of Themistocles – 'He thought Piraeus more useful than the upper city,' says Thucydides (1.93.7). Instead they restored the old city of Athens without any radical change of character. In the end they had it both ways; continuing to develop Piraeus as harbour town, they made it a complete duplicate *asty*, planned on modern Hippodamian lines.

Inevitably the first concern would be the roofs over their heads. We have already noted examples of the houses they built. The streets of the old town remained, with a few special exceptions, narrow and irregular. Travlos computes that there may have been some 6,000 houses within the main city wall.[2]

The provision of defences was almost as urgent. Thucydides describes how the Athenians threw up their walls in great haste, in fear and defiance of the Lacedaemonians, incorporating gravestones and other

[2] Travlos 1960 (I 170) 72. On the extent of the walls see *ibid.* 47–8 and 1971 (I 171) 158–61. New sections, constantly coming to light, are reported annually in *Arch.Delt.*

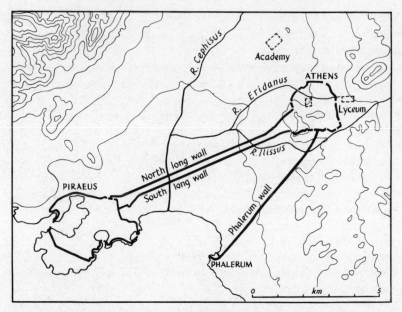

Fig. 25. Athens, Piraeus and the Long Walls. (After Boersma 1970 (I 23) 157.)

miscellaneous material. In spite of this, the walls were powerful enough, constructed in the technique described above, with unbaked brick on a stone socle. 'The *peribolos* [circuit] was extended in all directions,' says Thucydides (1.93.2); this implies an early outer city wall, but because of the lack of archaeological remains the very existence of this is still disputed. By contrast, the line of the Themistoclean wall can now be determined with great precision. It enclosed a large area on all sides of the Acropolis, taking in some outlying communities or suburbs. There were over a dozen gates; the main entrance, the great Dipylon or double gate on the north west, took its characteristic form at this time, and some other important gates were similar but simpler. The fortification of Piraeus, begun earlier by Themistocles, proceeded more deliberately; but though Thucydides says that the wall was built of stone masonry throughout, the scanty remains show that this was so only in certain sections. Lastly, towards the middle of the century, the two circuits were joined into a great defensive system by the Long Walls (Fig. 25). First, two legs were built, one running west-south-west to Piraeus, the other south west to Phalerum. A third, closely parallel to the first, was added later.

What happened on the Acropolis in the earlier phase is not clear. It is commonly believed that in place of the great archaic temple of Athena a simple makeshift shrine – *cella* or treasury – was contrived; full reparation was not made till late in the century. On the more southerly site, where the Parthenon was to stand, work on a large Doric temple was rudely interrupted by the Persians and probably not renewed on a big scale till after the middle of the century.[3] Architectural members from the temples badly damaged by the Persians were incorporated in the reconstructed north wall of the Acropolis to serve as a kind of memorial of the destruction. From about 460 the western part of the hill was dominated by Phidias' colossal bronze Athena Promachos.

On the site of Athens' largest temple, the Olympieum to the south east, construction had been abandoned after the fall of the tyrants, partly because the project was associated with their hated names, and partly, we can imagine, because it was too grandiose for the resources of the city. Great column drums, intended for the temple, were built into the Themistoclean city wall near by. The cult was carried on of course, and we have to assume some makeshift arrangement; it was to be several centuries before large-scale construction was resumed and completed, under royal and imperial patronage.

In the Agora the altar of the Twelve Gods (*CAH* iv² 296) continued to be a main focus of religious life, but it was not given a handsome new form till late in the century. The temples on the west side, of Apollo Patroos and the Mother of the Gods, were not replaced by new shrines till much later, even though Calamis produced a notable new statue for Apollo and Phidias for the Mother.

A curious example of the *deisidaimonia* of the Athenians, their scrupulous piety in small matters as in great, can be seen in the middle of the Agora. On this spot the cult of an unnamed hero must have existed from an early date. Now the miscellaneous small offerings were carefully gathered together and placed in a receptacle specially prepared for the purpose, a circular pit constructed of reused blocks.[4]

Some distance west of the Agora, on the street leading to the Piraeus Gate, remains of a shrine were found a few years ago, consisting of a temple and an altar in an enclosure. An inscription shows that it belonged to Artemis, and it is a reasonable assumption that it is the shrine of Artemis Aristoboule (giver of best counsel), founded by Themistocles near his house in the deme Melite (Fig. 26). The temple is very simple and small, a square *cella* with projecting side walls forming a porch. The remains belong chiefly to what appears to be a fourth-century

[3] Carpenter 1970 (I 42) has a building phase under Cimon. Bundgaard 1976 (I 36) ch. 8 makes the predecessor of the Periclean Parthenon post-Persian. Neither of these ideas has won much support. Cf. also Knell 1979 (I 90) 6–11.

[4] Thompson 1958 (I 163) 148–53. For this and comparable features see Thompson and Wycherley 1972 (I 166) 199–21.

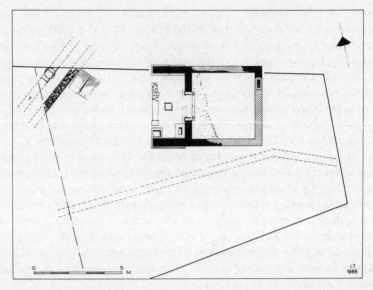

Fig. 26. Sanctuary of Artemis Aristoboule, Athens. (After Travlos 1971 (I 171) 122, fig. 164.)

reconstruction. No doubt Themistocles would think of the shrine as a kind of victory monument; Plutarch (*Them.* 22.1) says that the people were offended by his presumption in founding it himself.[5]

In various ways the Athenians celebrated their great victories in monumental fashion. The prompt replacement of the statues of Harmodius and Aristogeiton, which the Persians had carried off from the Agora, by a new pair made by Critius and Nesiotes, may be seen in this light (*Pls. to Vol. IV*, pl. 141). Cimon, besides restoring the shrine of Theseus, after defeating the Persians at Eïon in Thrace in 476/5, dedicated three Herms in a stoa (*Aisch.* III.183–5; above, pp. 41–2).[6] Nothing has been found of this building, but there is reason to believe that it stood on the north side of the Agora, in the same region as the much more famous and splendid Poikile or Painted Porch. To this a number of architectural fragments have been attributed, and recently a little of the foundation has been found and identified with probability.[7] The stoa has been dated about 460 B.C., and this would agree with our knowledge of the artists concerned. It also bore the name Peisianakteios, after one Peisianax, an associate of Cimon, connected with the building in some way which we cannot define. Pausanias (1.15) describes the great

[5] Threpsiades and Vanderpool 1965 (I 168); Amandry 1967 (I 1).

[6] For this elusive monument see Threpsiades and Vanderpool 1963 (I 167); Wycherley 1957 (I 182) 103–8; Thompson and Wycherley 1972 (I 166) 94–6.

[7] H. A. Thompson, *Hesperia* 19 (1950) 20–35; Meritt 1970 (I 109); Thompson and Wycherley 1972 (I 166) 90–4; T. L. Shear, *Hesperia* 53 (1984) 5–19.

paintings – a contemporary battle of Athenians and Lacedaemonians at Oenoe in Argive territory (above, p. 117 n. 77); Theseus and the Amazons; the capture of Troy; and, most famous of all, Marathon. The arrangement of the pictures, which were probably painted on boards affixed to the walls, is disputed. The most notable artists of the day were employed, Micon for the Amazons, Polygnotus, the greatest of all, for Troy, and Polygnotus or Panaenus or Micon – our authorities differ – for Marathon. Standing in the Agora, readily visible to all, the paintings were amongst the most renowned and conspicuous sights of Athens. The stoa played a great and varied part in the life of the city. It served as picture gallery, *lesche* (lounge for meeting and talking), occasionally law court, eventually philosophical seminar. In it was an altar – we do not know of what deity. Most public buildings had religious associations and housed some cult or other.

In the time of Cimon and even Pericles the official buildings, concentrated in the Agora, remained architecturally unpretentious (Fig. 27). In the sixth and early fifth centuries the Athenians had endeavoured to make modest provision for the instruments of government, especially in the time of Cleisthenes. One may assume that some of the old buildings were refurbished and continued in use, notably the *basileios*, a stoa of modest size and basic type, with interior columns, at the north end of the west side, used by the archon who retained the title of *basileus*, king, and for the display of copies of laws inscribed on stone; and the 'Old Bouleuterion' or Council House, a square hall towards the south end of the west side, spacious enough to hold the Council of Five Hundred in a kind of covered theatre. Late in the fifth century a 'New Bouleuterion' was added immediately to the west; and henceforth the old building and the new between them must have accommodated the Council, the archives, and the associated shrine of the Mother of the Gods (see also above, pp. 79–80).

By contrast, the rambling old building like a large house at the south corner, thought to have been occupied by officials and committees, was replaced after a few years by a compact circular structure with a conical roof and six interior supports; the irregular form of the old building was still apparent in the shape of the precinct in which its successor stood. We have here one monument whose identification is absolute and not surmised; no one doubts that this was the Tholos or Skias, where the *prytaneis*, the committee of fifty, deliberated and dined, and official weights and measures were kept. With it was associated a cult of Artemis. The Tholos was at the very heart of Athenian life; and with repeated refurbishing retained its peculiar and unexplained form throughout antiquity.

Another pre-Persian building which long remained in being is the

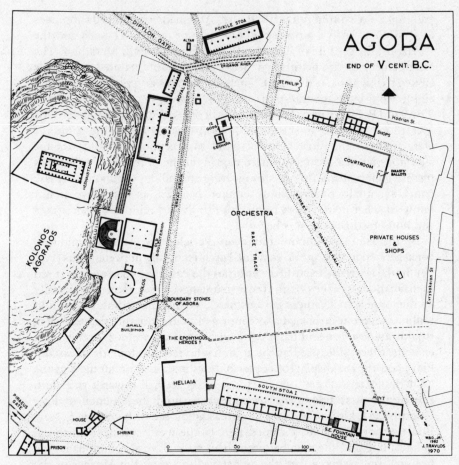

Fig. 27. Plan of the Athenian Agora at the end of the fifth century B.C. Courtesy of the American School of Classical Studies.

large well-built square enclosure at the west end of the south side, which is very reasonably supposed to have been used by a principal law court. The democratic courts were a dominant element in Athenian life in our period, and one might have expected to find buildings specifically designed and handsomely constructed in keeping with their dignity; but in fact arrangements remained simple and even makeshift. Not only the Poikile but even the Odeum or music-hall built under Pericles was pressed into service. We hear in various contexts of what is called *perischionisma* or the roping-off of a more or less suitable area.[8] In the latter part of the century another rectangular enclosure, less solid in construction, shown to have been a law court by the discovery of

[8] Wycherley 1957 (I 182) 163–4; Thompson and Wycherley 1972 (I 166) 34, 50, 87, 130, 159.

forensic paraphernalia in a room attached to it, was built in the north-eastern sector of the Agora. This, and another added to it later, were to be replaced in the fourth century – perhaps in the time of Lycurgus, who devoted much attention to the architectural improvement of various public buildings – by a large peristyle court. Simplicity of form and lack of a specific design make it more difficult to recognize the remains of law courts even when they are unearthed.

The *ecclesia* continued to meet in a kind of primitive theatre on the slope of the Pnyx hill to the south west of the Agora. Towards the end of the fifth century, surprisingly, the auditorium was reconstructed by means of an embankment with a slope which ran contrary to the natural contours. The Assembly clung to this spot and, except for particular occasions, it was to be long before they fully realized the advantages of meeting in the theatre of Dionysus.

The old South-east Fountain House, a rectangular building with basins at either end and columns in the middle section of the north side, continued to provide the main supply of water for the Agora area.[9] It was not till early in the fourth century that it was supplemented by the architecturally more impressive South-west Fountain House, with an L-shaped columnar façade, fed by the same underground aqueduct which brought water from sources to the east of the city.

In the time of Pericles the Agora was still a spacious open square, with buildings of modest character loosely distributed along the edges. In the latter part of the century two large stoas were built on the west and south sides; but they were quite different from one another and did not go far towards giving the Agora any unity or completeness of plan.

The long south stoa had a double Doric colonnade and a row of rooms behind. It was built of limestone, with unbaked brick, of which a little has survived, in the upper part of the walls. There is evidence that the rooms were designed as offices and dining-rooms for some of the numerous boards of magistrates. Till we come to this building, magistrates' offices too are difficult to identify, since they have no readily recognizable characteristics. Two buildings to the south west of the Agora, dated in the middle of the fifth century, both comprise a long quadrilateral with a courtyard at one end and a row of rooms on either side of a corridor at the other. One has been very tentatively called *strategion* and assigned to the board of ten generals; the other too was at one time thought to contain magistrates' offices, but on various evidence a good case has now been made for making it the *desmoterion* or jail, the scene of Plato's *Phaedo* (Fig. 28).[10]

[9] This *may* be the elusive Enneakrounos; see Travlos 1971 (I 171) 204; Thompson and Wycherley 1972 (I 166) 198–9.

[10] E. Vanderpool, *Illustrated London News* June 1976; Wycherley 1978 (I 187) 46–7 (here note also the Mint, south east of the Agora).

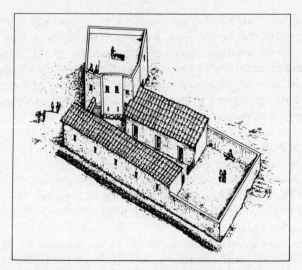

Fig. 28. The 'Prison of Socrates', south west of the Agora, Athens, reconstruction by J. E. Jones. (After Wycherley 1978 (1 187) fig. 16.)

In the stoa towards the north end of the western side of the Agora, identified as belonging to the shrine of Zeus Eleutherios or Soter, god of Freedom or Saviour, the architect's aim was obviously to produce something architecturally superior to a straight colonnade, and he did it, as we have seen, by adding temple-like wings (Fig. 29). The outer order was Doric, the inner Ionic. The materials used were nicely varied – limestone of a harder and a softer kind in the foundations; brown Aeginetan limestone for the walls and for the triglyphs; Pentelic marble for the rest of the façade and for the inner columns; both Pentelic and the darker Hymettian in the steps. Fine marble Victories were used as *acroteria* on the roof. This is one stoa which has something of the architectural distinction of a great temple. Though he had many shrines under many names in various parts of Athens and was honoured along with his daughter on the Acropolis, while the Olympieum lay largely derelict Zeus had no worthy temple. The embellishment of the stoa offered some compensation. Pausanias (3.2) saw Zeus's statue in front of the building, where it had been joined by the generals Conon and Timotheus and the emperor Hadrian. In the fourth century Euphranor adorned the walls with paintings: of the Twelve Gods; of Theseus, Democracy and Demos; and a battle of Athenian and Lacedaemonian cavalry at Mantinea. Thus, though not built for the purpose, it came to rival the Poikile as a picture gallery. In general function one may think of it as a large extension of the *basileios*; and in typical Athenian fashion the

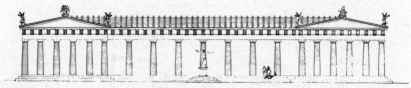

Fig. 29. Restoration of the façade of the Stoa of Zeus, Athens. (After H. A. Thompson, *Hesperia* 6 (1937) 54, fig. 34; cf. Coulton 1976 (I 50) fig. 8.)

modest old building, with wings now added, continued to stand for centuries beside the handsome new one.

But of course the glory of Athenian architecture was concentrated in the creations of the Periclean building programme. By the middle of the century the Athenians were devoting much thought to the building of worthy shrines of the gods, which would at the same time be a visible symbol of the achievements and the power of the city (Fig. 30). Actual work on the Parthenon began in 447 B.C., and for sixteen years the complicated processes of erecting the temple and giving it elaborate sculptural adornment were a major concern. Each year resources were allotted and progress and accounts were scrutinized.

Much preparatory work had already been done. Early in the century the Athenians had planned and begun to build a large temple, similar to the Parthenon but somewhat smaller and simpler. It was in this temple that Pentelic marble was first used in huge quantities. With extension and adjustment the massive foundations could still be used, and some material from the super-structure could be incorporated. To enlarge the flat summit area of the Acropolis, extensive terracing had been carried out to the south, with retaining walls ranging from the ancient Cyclopean wall to the ultimate fortification built in the time of Cimon. For the Parthenon which we know, the guiding spirits were Pericles and Phidias. With a number of technical assistants of course, Phidias made the great gold and ivory statue of Athena which the temple was designed to contain. Furthermore, 'He managed everything for Pericles,' says Plutarch (*Per.* 12.3), 'he was the overseer (*episkopos*) of everything, even though the various works required great architects and artists.'[11] How much truth there is in this and just what it means we cannot say precisely; at least we can be sure that Phidias gathered about him and directed a school of first-rate sculptors. His relation to the three architects named by our authorities, Ictinus, Callicrates, and one Carpion who is otherwise unknown, cannot be clearly defined.

From inscriptions, supplemented by the evidence of the building itself, we can give the stages by which the Parthenon came into being. As

[11] Drerup 1981 (I 62) gives a synopsis of problems of old and new.

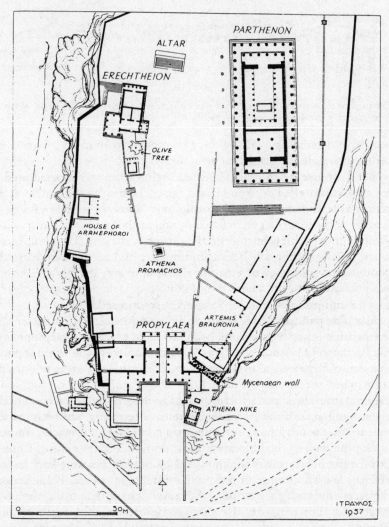

Fig. 30. Plan of the Acropolis, Athens. (After Travlos 1971 (1 171) fig. 21.)

usual, the outer colonnades were built before the inner structure, though presumably with gaps through which material could safely be taken. Everything from steps and pavement to tiles, except for roof timbers, *cella*-ceiling and doors, was of Pentelic stone. The metopes and the frieze were carved on stones which were part of the fabric. The former were carved on the ground, the latter possibly in their position, though this is disputed. The metopes naturally came earliest and in them the perfection and harmony which we see in the later elements has not been fully attained. The cult statue was dedicated in 438/7, by which date the temple must have received its inner colonnades and roof; the pedimental sculpture, free-standing statues though still intimately related to the architectural setting, required another five years.

The plan speaks for itself. It is entirely regular and represents a moderate elaboration of the basic form of the peripteral temple. It is octastyle, with eight columns at either end; the inner Doric colonnade was in two storeys and continued round the back of the statue; the rear chamber, probably a treasury, opening onto the rear porch, contained four tall Ionic columns.

The Parthenon illustrates in their most subtle form the refinements which are found in the best Doric architecture and more rarely in Ionic – the upward curve of horizontal lines, the curve and inward tilt of column shafts, the thickening of corner columns. These are so slight as to be barely perceptible; but they enhance the beauty of the building; some give it greater stability in appearance as in fact; the curvature of the platform assists drainage. These features were thought worth while even though they added greatly to the labour of the carving and laying of many of the stones.

The approach to the Acropolis has always been from the west, and one can assume that from time immemorial a propylon, a gate with a porch inside and out, stood at this end. There are traces of such a gateway built earlier in the fifth century with a distinctly different orientation from its successor.[12] The great Propylaea which Mnesicles built for Pericles in the 430s, when the workforce of the Parthenon was free for other tasks, was more than a simple entrance to the Acropolis. As the plural form of the name suggests it was a complex building. The central element was still essentially a propylon; but on either side of the main gateway, through which the processional road ascended, were two doors reached by steps – the inner porch was at a higher level. In the deep outer porch, behind the façade of six Doric columns, were three Ionic columns on either side of the roadway. To the north-west corner a wing was attached, in the form of a temple-like building facing south through a façade of three Doric columns. A similar façade was built at the south-west corner, facing north, but the structure behind it was much curtailed. The north-west wing was eventually a *pinakotheke* or picture-gallery, though it may have been intended for a dining-room. There is evidence in the stones that wings on the north east and south east were planned in the form of halls which might have served as store-rooms, but these were never built. It is unlikely that there was ever any idea of adding elaborate sculpture which might have competed with the Parthenon; but to the east and to the west and in the interior stood a number of statues of great

[12] Dinsmoor 1980 (161) finds several building phases, the last *after* 480 B.C., and gives the plan as a simpler version of the central Mnesiclean building. He gives a full bibliography of the Propylaea.

religious and artistic importance. Old shrines clustered thickly on the site, no doubt an embarrassment at times to the architects and planners. Somewhere down below were sanctuaries of Aphrodite Pandemos (of all the people), Ge Kourotrophos (nurturer of youth), and Demeter Chloe (green) (Paus. 1.22).[13] On the bastion which jutted south-westward was Athena Nike (victory), of whom we shall see more; and adjoining the south-west wing were Hermes Propylaeus (with whom were associated the Charites or Graces) and Hecate Epipyrgidia (on the tower), for both of whom Alcamenes made famous statues. The way in which minor shrines could cling to the great buildings like limpets is vividly illustrated by the remains at the foot of the southernmost column of the east porch, an altar and statue base of Athena Hygieia (health), who cured a workman seriously injured during the construction of the Propylaea. The ground to the south east was sacred to Artemis Brauronia, and the shrine was embellished with a stoa facing north with a rectangular hall at either end; the shrine of the goddess at Brauron itself in southernmost Attica was given a comparable stoa.

The great Doric temple, which stands miraculously preserved on the hill overlooking the Agora from the west, was under construction at the same time as the Parthenon, probably in the middle 440s; there was, however, a break of over twenty years before the sculpture and other details were finally completed. Modern scholars have installed various deities in this temple, but though the problem has not been settled outright there is now general agreement that it is the Hephaesteum, in which Hephaestus and Athena were worshipped together. An inscription recording accounts from 421 to 415 B.C. is thought to refer to the making and erection of their bronze statues, which were probably by Alcamenes.[14] Above the lowest step, which like the foundation is of limestone, the whole of the upper structure is of marble; except that most of the sculpture and certain other details were of Parian, the stone was Pentelic. Examination of the foundation has revealed that the inner colonnade, which, probably in imitation of the Parthenon, was carried across the east end of the *cella*, was an afterthought, not part of the original plan. The sculptural decoration seems to be a curtailment of the scheme which we see in the Parthenon; there were pedimental groups, of which very little survives, metopes at the east end, supplemented by four round the corner on the north side and four on the south; and friezes

---

[13] The topography of the area is still very unclear and remains unidentifiable.

[14] *IG* I³ 472. Harrison 1977 (I 74), in her reconstruction of the statues, maintains that Athena and Hephaestus cannot have stood in the existing temple and that this was occupied by Eucleia (possibly Artemis). Her theory rests on very disputable sculptural evidence, and is contradicted by Pausanias, who places Eucleia south west of the Agora (1.14.5); and not a trace of another temple has been found. Brommer 1978 (I 28) gives a different reconstruction and keeps Athena and Hephaestus in the existing temple.

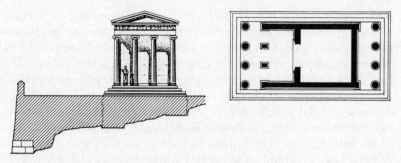

Fig. 31. The temple by the Ilissus at Athens, elevation and plan. (After Travlos 1971 (1 171) 116, fig. 156.)

over the front of the back porch of the inner structure, but not as in the Parthenon along the sides. On a more modest scale than the Parthenon, the Hephaesteum still gave a touch of architectural distinction to the Agora. From their dominant site Athena and Hephaestus presided directly over the life of the centre of their city. By contrast the spacious city sanctuary of the Eleusinian deities, diagonally opposite on the slope south east of the Agora, remained content with its simple pre-Persian temple.

Doric was the dominant order in fifth-century Athens, but in the latter part of the century Ionic was used to design buildings which offered a wonderful contrast. Incidentally an Attic type of column-base was developed, with a concave moulding between two convex. We find it in the little temple built outside the city on the south bank of the river Ilissus (Fig. 31). Although this was completely demolished by the Turks to provide material for a fortification, by great good fortune we know much more about it than about many which have left solid remains, since Stuart and Revett, who examined it before the destruction, left a full account with fine drawings.[15] It was amphiprostyle, with a columnar façade at both ends. To what deity it belonged is not clear, possibly the Mother of the Gods, more probably Artemis Agrotera (huntress). A very similar temple was built, probably in the 420s (but see above, p. 125 n. 21), in the old shrine of Athena Nike on the south-western bastion of the Acropolis, now enlarged and reconstructed. The time was not entirely appropriate for an offering to the goddess of victory, but a long-standing debt was handsomely paid with a temple which on a small scale is an example of Attic Ionic at its best. This too was amphiprostyle and had sculpture in the pediments and not only on its own frieze but also on

[15] Stuart and Revett 1762 (1 159) ch. 2. The temple has commonly been dated just after the middle of the century and associated with *IG* i³ 35 (M–L 44), but some recent writers have disputed this and brought the date down to the 420s. See Boersma 1970 (1 23) 75; Picon 1978 (1 125); Miles 1980 (1 111). W. A. P. Childs supports the earlier date in *Ath. Mitt.* 100 (1985) 207–51.

the outer face of the balustrade which was erected around the bastion.

Though they gave precedence to the Parthenon, we can assume that the Athenians always intended to build, on the northern part of the Acropolis, a direct replacement for the great archaic temple of Athena. It says much for their piety, their resources and their persistence that in troubled times they fulfilled this obligation so handsomely. The Erechtheum was highly peculiar in plan, besides having different ground levels in different parts. It was built of Pentelic marble, in the last two decades of the fifth century. The eastern façade was normal, with six prostyle Ionic columns, behind which was a broad *cella*. The western façade consisted of a low wall on which stood four columns *in antis*. This part of the temple contained two *cellas* side by side behind a vestibule, but it is doubtful whether this arrangement goes back to the original construction. A large columnar porch, facing northwards, was somewhat awkwardly attached on the north-west corner; at the corresponding point on the south was the small Caryatid porch, with female figures in place of columns. Capitals, bases and other decorative elements were elaborate and delicate; the frieze which ran round the building was of dark Eleusinian stone, with figures of white marble attached. Besides the shrine and ancient statue of Athena Polias and the altar of Erechtheus which has provided a convenient name, the temple contained a whole series of altars and curious cult-spots; their distribution about the complex building is conjectural.[16] Yet others occupied the ground to the west – the grave of Cecrops, the altar of Zeus of the Hearth, the sacred olive tree, the little temple of Pandrosus, and the house of the priestesses known as Arrhephoroi. Religious complexity may account in part for the exceptional form of the building, but we cannot know what was in the minds of the architects.

The Acropolis was now crowned by three splendid buildings. Each had its own independent character. The Parthenon was dominant, but the Propylaea was something more than a mere prelude and the Erechtheum provided a contrast and a foil. They rose above a great host of sculptural monuments of many kinds; these stood in no particular order, except that they tended to accumulate along the roads leading eastward from the Propylaea in the direction of the temples and along the north side of the Parthenon to its east end. On the south slope, adjacent to the theatre, a shrine of Asclepius was added to the primitive shrines towards the end of the fifth century, but did not receive a temple till the fourth.

Temple building was by no means confined to the *asty*, the city proper. Piraeus, as we have seen, was developing rapidly; the harbour town had

<hr />

[16] For the internal arrangements and a suggested distribution of the various shrines see Travlos 1971 (I 171) 213. Much uncertainty remains, however.

many shrines, and some had temples, but we know very little about them. Solid evidence of temple building comes from several country demes, by a curiously devious route. By the Roman period a number of temples in these districts had fallen into a state of dilapidation; from several of them, architectural members were brought into the city for reuse and some of these have been found in excavations.[17] One large temple was completely transferred, block by block, each marked with letters to ensure that it was correctly placed. This is the building which, although it can be dated in the fifth century, stood eventually on foundations of Augustan date in the middle of the Agora. Its place in Pausanias' account (1.8.4) leaves no doubt that it belonged to Ares, for whom Alcamenes made the statue. In extreme contrast with the Hephaesteum, the remains consist of scores of scattered blocks, but there is enough to show that the temple was very similar in dimensions and general plan. The material was Pentelic marble with a peculiar greenish tinge – Pentelic was by no means entirely monotonous in character. Where the temple originally stood is not known. It is very difficult to find a site within the city, or a reason for the transference if that is where it stood; a probable suggestion is that it came from Acharnae, north of the city, which had a notable shrine of Ares.

Criteria of style in architecture are admittedly not so precise as in other arts; but Dinsmoor detects in this building the work of the architect of the Hephaesteum, and to the same hand he ascribes the temples of Poseidon at Sunium and of Nemesis at Rhamnous in eastern Attica.[18] The former is the temple whose columns still crown the southern cape. Pausanias (1.1.1) wrongly assigns it to Athena, but in fact the scanty remains of this shrine lie some distance further north.

The temple of Poseidon was peripteral, six by thirteen like many others and, like several others in this region, it was built of a milky white marble, not so fine as Pentelic, peculiar to south Attica. Beneath it are remains of a temple of the early fifth century, unfinished when it was destroyed by the Persians. At Rhamnous too there was a pre-Persian temple, a simple *cella* with Doric porch; but in this case the replacement, a Doric peristyle of comparatively modest size, was built on a distinct site a little further north;[19] another leading pupil of Phidias, Agoracritus, made a notable cult statue of the goddess. Two other temples originally built in south Attica in the fifth century provided material for building in the city itself in Roman imperial times. Ionic elements from the temple of Athena at Sunium, a building of unusual plan, with columns only along

[17] Thompson and Wycherley 1972 (I 166) 162–7.
[18] Dinsmoor 1950 (I 60); cf. Wycherley 1978 (I 187) 69; Knell 1973 (I 89) distinguishes two architects.
[19] See now M. M. Miles, *Hesperia* 58 (1989) 135–249.

the east front and south side, have been found in the southern part of the Agora and assigned tentatively in their later use to the 'south-west' temple which may have housed an imperial cult. Doric columns from the peripteral temple of Demeter and Kore at Thoricus were probably incorporated in the façade of the 'south-east' temple, which was perhaps dedicated to the same deities. The temple at Thoricus was never finished; and it has been noted that in column drums from the Agora the fluting has been begun at top and bottom with the meticulous care of a fifth-century craftsman but completed somewhat carelessly, presumably by his successors of the first century A.D.

To return to the city, in conclusion, on theatre, stadium and gymnasium one can add hardly anything to what has been said in the previous section, though they played a vital part in the life of the city, especially in our period. The Odeum of Pericles formed an impressive appendage to the theatre; the theatre itself remained structurally very simple. 'The Academy', says Plutarch (*Cim*. 13.8), 'formerly waterless and parched, he made a well-watered grove, equipped with clear running tracks [*dromoi*] and shady walks'; he is speaking of Cimon, who also had plane-trees planted in the Agora. The further architectural development of all these elements belongs to a later time, the age of Lycurgus, statesman, finance minister and tireless builder.

CHAPTER 8d

PANHELLENIC CULTS AND PANHELLENIC POETS

N. J. RICHARDSON

I. THE PANHELLENIC FESTIVALS IN THE FIFTH CENTURY B.C.

Many of the innumerable ancient Greek festivals included athletic and cultural contests. By the fifth century B.C. a few of these gatherings had achieved much more than a purely local prestige and significance. Pindar and Bacchylides often give long catalogues of the victories of an athlete or his family at places all over Greece, but Pindar distinguishes these from the 'common festivals', where athletes 'contested against all the Greeks together' (*Isthm.* IV.30–1).[1] By this time, a special group of four festivals had come to be distinguished from the rest, the Olympian, Pythian, Isthmian and Nemean Games, and it is for victories at these that the majority of our surviving epinician poems were composed. These were known as 'crown games' (*stephanitai*), because the prizes were not objects of material value but simply crowns, at Olympia of wild olive, at Delphi of bay, and at Nemea and Isthmia of fresh and dry celery respectively (at least, in Pindar's time).[2] Such crowns were given at some other festivals, but at the majority prizes of greater utility were offered.

These four festivals were in origin very different in size and significance from each other. The Olympic Games, which were held in honour of Zeus, in the district of Pisa beside the river Alpheus, seem to have acquired a wider importance quite early in the Archaic period. Since lists of Olympic victors were kept from the first Olympiad in 776 B.C. onward, they could later be used to provide a convenient chronological framework for the entire Greek world. These games took place every four years, in August or September, at the hottest and dustiest time of year for both athletes and spectators. The original race was the *stadion*, a sprint of approximately 200 metres, and other contests were added gradually during the following centuries.[3] There was a tradition (Philostr., *De Gymnastica* 5) that originally the athletes ran to the altar of Zeus, and the victor kindled the flame on the altar for the sacrifice (cf. also Schol. Pind. *Ol.* 1.149e). If this is true, it shows very clearly the

---

[1] For Pindar's lists and the festivals he mentions, see Kramer 1970 (K 52) 3–63.

[2] On Isthmian crowns see Broneer 1962 (K 8) 259–63.

[3] For a convenient list see Bengtson 1972 (K 3) 35–6.

religious purpose of the earliest form of the festival. It is now known from archaeology that until the stadium was rebuilt in the fourth century B.C. it lay very much closer to the altar of Zeus, with its western end open, and within the sacred enclosure.[4] The fact that it was later rebuilt outside the sanctuary proper suggests that the old religious ties had been loosened by that time, but in Pindar's day they were still strongly felt (cf. *Pls. to Vol. III*, pl. 304(*b*)).

The Pythian Games at Delphi began as a purely musical event. The original contest was said to have consisted simply in the singing of a hymn to Apollo. After the First Sacred War, in the early sixth century B.C., the festival was reorganized by the Amphictyonic League, with the addition of further musical competitions, and subsequently of athletic contests. These games also took place every four years, in late August in the third year of each Olympiad, and the Pythiads were reckoned from 582 B.C.[5] Because of the prestige of Delphi they ranked second in importance after Olympia in the Classical period.

The Isthmian and Nemean Games also took their classical form in the early sixth century, the Isthmian probably in 582, the Nemean in 573. Both were held every two years, in April or May and in July respectively. The Isthmian Games were administered by Corinth, and were probably reorganized on their new scale after the fall of the Cypselids. They were in honour of Poseidon, and owed their popularity to Corinth's position as a meeting-place for mainland Greece, and as a flourishing port. The Nemean festival, in honour of Zeus, was officially controlled by Cleonae, but its earliest foundation was linked in legend with the expedition of the Seven against Thebes, led by Adrastus of Argos, and Argos probably had a hand in its organization. It may have been intended to rival the activity of Cleisthenes of Sicyon, who had banned the cult of Adrastus, and who had helped to reorganize the Pythian Games.[6] There was a similar rivalry between Olympia and Corinth in the tradition that no Elean was allowed to compete at the Isthmus (Plut. *Mor.* 400E; Paus. V.2.2). This exclusion was said to date from the time when the Eleans had refused to erase the names of the Cypselids from their offerings at Olympia, after the fall of the dynasty.

Although the early history of the Nemean festival is obscure, it seems likely that Argos exercised some kind of general influence over the sanctuary throughout this period, rather than taking control of Cleonae and Nemea around 460 B.C.,[7] or after the destruction of the temple of Zeus, at the end of the fifth century.[8] Already in 468 we hear of Mycenae

---

[4] Cf. Mallwitz 1972 (I 102) 180–6, Romano 1981 (I 144) 116–41; *Pls. to Vol. III*, pl. 304.

[5] Cf. Gaspar 1900 (J 41) 1ff. For a recent, unconvincing attempt to argue for 586 as the date of the first Pythiad see Miller 1978 (K 62) 127–58.

[6] McGregor 1941 (K 59) 277–8, Jeffery 1976 (A 69) 137.

[7] Cf. Bölte 1922 (F 8) 726 with references *ad loc.*

[8] Cf. Miller 1977 (I 115) 9–10, 1981 (I 115) 51–2, with references to earlier reports.

claiming against Argos the right of sole control of the games (Diod. XI.65.2), and this seems to imply some form of Argive control at this period.

It is clear from inscriptions, and from the order in which Pindar lists the festivals in his victory catalogues, that the Isthmian Games ranked as more important than the Nemean.[9] But throughout the Classical period both these festivals attracted competitors from a less wide area than the other two sanctuaries.

The gods in whose honour these festivals were held were panhellenic deities, and in gathering at their sanctuaries the Greeks felt very strongly the bonds of a common religion and culture. Only those of pure Greek birth could compete in the games in the Classical period. A sacred truce, which extended over the whole Greek world, prevailed for a period before, during, and after these festivals. This was not strictly speaking an armistice, but was probably designed in the first place to guarantee safe conduct to those visiting the festivals.[10] But by the fifth century B.C. Olympia's role as a panhellenic sanctuary came to assume a much greater significance, especially in the period after the Persian Wars. It had already come to be used as a place for debate between cities when a dispute arose, for arbitration, and for the publication of treaties. It became also a place where orators, philosophers and literary men could display their talents, by speeches or recitation of their works. It was said that Herodotus read parts of his history here, in the *opisthodomos* of the temple of Zeus (Lucian, *Herod.* 1). Gorgias appealed for unity against Persia here in 408, and Lysias and Isocrates composed speeches for delivery at Olympia in the early fourth century. Cities also dedicated war trophies here, as they did at Delphi. This, however, may have had a divisive rather than a unifying effect, if the defeated enemy were fellow-Greeks, as was often the case. The temple of Zeus itself is said by Pausanias (v.10.2) to have been built by the Eleans from the spoils of a war with their neighbours. One must beware of equating religious and cultural unity with political cohesion, which was always a very fragile reality for the Greeks at the best of times. Nevertheless, it is clear that they did see Olympia as representing an idea of this kind. As Lysias says when praising Heracles for his legendary foundation of the Olympic Games: 'he thought that this gathering would become for the Greeks the origin of their mutual friendship' (XXXIII.2). Certainly from a religious point of view Olympia came to be seen as the Greek sanctuary *par excellence*. Phidias' great statue of Zeus represented for many the most impressive embodiment in visual form of the Greek idea of divinity, and

---

[9] *IG* I³ 131.12, I² 606, 829 (= I³ 893, 1022), II² 3128, Thummer 1969 (J 104) II.115. At some stage in transmission the books of Isthmian and Nemean odes must have been transposed in the collection of Pindar's epinicians: cf. Irigoin 1952 (J 55) 100.

[10] Rougemont 1973 (K 79) 75–106.

Olympia's supremacy is most memorably expressed by Pindar, at the opening of *Olympian* I (3–7):

> But if to sing of contests
> You long, dear heart,
> Look no further for another star
> Shining by day through the barren ether
> Warmer than the sun: nor shall we tell
> Of any gathering mightier than Olympia.

Although Delphi never achieved the same reputation as Olympia for political neutrality, as the 'navel of the earth' it could claim to be in another sense the religious centre of Greece, and as the chief oracular sanctuary in the Classical period it also exercised a powerful political influence. Our view of the Pythian Games at this period depends largely on Pindar's Pythian odes, and Pindar's own special connexions with Apollo and Delphi are evident. No other deity is portrayed so vividly and sympathetically in his poetry. But, although this may reflect Pindar's personal bias as a poet, we can gain through him a view of Delphi as a focus for the cultural ideals of Greece, which is surely also an expression of what many Greeks of this time must have felt.

The poems of Pindar and Bacchylides demonstrate in another import-
ant way the unifying force of these great festivals, in that so many of them were composed for Sicilian patrons. The Persian Wars and their aftermath coincided with a serious threat to the Greeks in Italy and Sicily from the attacks of the Etruscans and Carthaginians. Pindar's first *Pythian* expresses most clearly the sense of an urgent need for unity between Greeks of the motherland and their western colonies. The Sicilian tyrants were at the height of their power and wealth at this time, and their victories at Olympia and Delphi were an essential medium for increasing their prestige. The rivalry with which they competed in these contests, and also in enriching the sanctuaries with treasuries and other splendid monuments, must have helped to give the Greeks a greater sense of unity in the face of external dangers.

II. THE RELIGIOUS CHARACTER OF THE GAMES

Nowadays competitions of any kind take place in a purely secular setting, and the idea of connecting sport with religion seems particularly odd. There is a sense of ceremony and of a contrast with everyday life, but usually no more than that.

For the Greeks, however, the religious context was essential. The competitions formed part of the festivals in honour of gods and heroes.

The gods themselves took pleasure in contests, and to compete at a god's sanctuary was a special way of honouring him. The poet of the *Homeric Hymn to Apollo*, in his vivid description of the Delian festival, reminds Apollo of how all the Ionians 'give you pleasure as they commemorate you with boxing, dancing and singing, whenever they institute your festival' (149–50). Lucian describes the gods as 'overseers of the games' (*Pro Imag.* 19). As the Phaeacians in the *Odyssey* hold special contests to entertain Odysseus, and Achilles in the *Iliad* institutes funeral games to honour his dead companion Patroclus, so the games of the historical period were celebrated against an imagined background of divine and heroic spectators.

But the gods were not merely detached observers. They could also favour individual competitors. The Greeks viewed life in general very much in competitive or 'agonistic' terms, and all success was a divine gift. We see them in action in the *Iliad*, both in war and also in war's image, in the contests of Book XXIII. Plutarch calls Greek athletics an 'imitation and preparation for war' (*Mor.* 639DE), although by his time athletic and military training diverged (cf. Plut. *Philopoemen* 3.2–4). As Pindar says to the victor Arcesilas, king of Cyrene:

> Forget not, while you are sung of
> In Aphrodite's sweet garden at Cyrene,
> To set God as the cause
> Over all things.   (*Pyth.* V.23–5)

Many athletic festivals were believed to have been originally instituted to commemorate the death of a legendary figure of the past. In fact, the ancient commentators on Pindar state that all ancient games were originally of this character (Schol. Pind. *Isthm.* init.). At Olympia the games were in honour of Pelops and commemorated his victory in the chariot race with king Oenomaus of Pisa, by which he won the king's daughter Hippodameia as his wife (Pind. *Ol.* 1.67–88). But they were also said to have been founded by Heracles, and Pindar gives a list of the victors on this first occasion when they were held (*Ol.* x.24–77). One tradition ascribed to Heracles the foundation of the Nemean Games, too, after he had killed the Nemean lion (Schol. Pind. *Nem.* init.). But the usual version was that they were in memory of the child Opheltes, who was killed by a snake at Nemea when Adrastus' army stopped there on the way to attack Thebes. Likewise, the Isthmian Games commemorated the death of the child Melicertes (or Palaemon), son of Ino. The Pythian Games, although not in honour of a hero, could also be described as funeral games, as they marked Apollo's killing of the serpent Python.

We have already seen that the original race at Olympia was a religious event, being run to the great altar of Zeus, where the chief sacrifice of the festival took place. This altar stood near the precinct of Pelops and the temple of Hera, which existed long before the temple of Zeus was built. These religious landmarks formed the central cult area of the sanctuary. In *Olympian* I (90ff) Pindar speaks of the honours paid to Pelops at his tomb, beside the altar of Zeus, and of the contests which are held in their honour nearby.

Likewise at Isthmia one can still see the starting lines of the stadium that was used in the Archaic and Classical periods (*Pls. to Vol. IV*, pl. 203). These lie right next to the later sanctuary of Palaemon, and near the temple of Poseidon.[11] It has also recently been suggested that the earliest stadium at Nemea lay quite near the temple of Zeus, unlike the later one.[12]

In addition to the heroes in whose honour the games were held, there were others who could be associated specifically with these contests. The great model for all athletic achievement (but especially for boxing, wrestling and the *pankration*) was Heracles, whose own exploits (*athla*) had, in Greek belief of the late Archaic and Classical periods, earned him a place among the gods.[13] But the Dioscuri were also patrons of athletes, Castor specifically of horsemen and Polydeuces of boxers, and they too had their alternating shares of immortality. Pindar is also fond of mentioning the athletic and other exploits of Iolaus, the nephew and companion of Heracles, who shared a festival with Heracles at Thebes.[14]

More generally, the achievements of living athletes are seen by the epinician poets in the context of both the recent historical past and also the remoter past of legends. The heroes whom they mention were often worshipped by the athletes' communities, or regarded as their ancestors. For Pindar and Bacchylides past and present are inseparable, and the present only has meaning in the light of the past. It is not really possible in these poets to separate history from mythology, and for this reason it is misleading to speak of their use of myths, as if these were extraneous to the main subject matter of their poems. The historical event which they celebrate has greater significance by virtue of its relationship with the heroic age when men and gods were on closer terms. Living athletes in turn come closer to divine status as a result of their god-given success. This is confirmed most dramatically by the numerous legends which rapidly sprang up about the supernatural exploits and deaths of famous athletes of the sixth and fifth centuries B.C., and the fact that some of them were actually worshipped as heroes after death.[15]

---

[11] Cf. Broneer 1973 (I 31), esp. 46–66, 137–42, and Romano 1981 (I 144) 53–70. *Pls. to Vol. IV*, pl. 203.   [12] Cf. Romano 1977 (I 143) 27–31. See also Miller 1983 (I 115) 80–2.

[13] Kramer 1970 (K 52) 108–38.

[14] *Ol.* IX.98–9; *Pyth.* IX.79–83, XI.55–61; *Nem.* III.36–9; *Isthm.* I.14–32, V.32–3, VII.9.

[15] Cf. Fontenrose 1968 (K 30) 73–104, Harris 1964 (K 36) 110ff, Pouilloux 1954 (F 58) I.62–105.

III. THE ORDER AND DEVELOPMENT OF THE FESTIVALS[16]

1. Olympia

The Olympic festival lasted for five days in the fifth century B.C. (Pind. *Ol.* v.6). It was held in the month Parthenios or Apollonios, at the full moon, once every forty-nine or fifty months, and was preceded by a sacred truce of a month. The centrepiece of the ceremonies was the sacrifice of a hecatomb on the altar of Zeus, which was itself composed of ash from the victims (Paus. v.13.8). The exact order of the athletic events is not known for certain. According to Pausanias (v.9.3), up to 472 the equestrian contests were held on the same day as the other events, but thereafter the *pentathlon* (running, jumping, discus, javelin and wrestling) and horse-races took place before the sacrifice, and the other contests after it (cf. also Xen. *Hell.* vii.4.29). The boys' contests preceded the men's (Plut. *Mor.* 639A), the foot-races were all on the same day, and the wrestling, boxing and *pankration* were also on the same day (Paus. vi.6.5, 13.3, 15.4). The last event was the race in armour.

At the end of the sixth century the list of contests was as follows: *stadion* (single lap foot-race), *diaulos* (double lap), *dolichos* (long race), *pentathlon*, wrestling, boxing, *pankration*, boys' foot-race, boys' wrestling, boys' boxing, race in armour, four-horse chariot-race, horse-race. To these were added the mule chariot-race in 500 and the mares' race in 496, but both of these were discontinued in 444. In 408 a two-horse chariot-race was introduced.

The contests were preceded by a procession from Elis to Olympia, and a ceremony at which athletes and officials swore an oath to observe the rules of the games, and they were followed by victory celebrations, with processions and banquets.

The overall control of the festival was in the hands of a board of Elean judges. The number of these was increased from one to two in 580 B.C. (Paus. v.9.4), and some time later, probably during the fifth century, it was raised to nine, and soon after to ten. (The dates in Pausanias are unfortunately corrupt.) In inscriptions from before the Persian Wars these judges are called *diaitateres*. In 476, however, Pindar uses the term *hellanodikas* (*Ol.* iii.12; cf. *Inschr. v. Olympia* No. 2 = Jeffery 1961 (C 137) 220 No. 15, 475–50 B.C.); and Pausanias also refers to them as *hellanodikai* when speaking of the change to nine (v.9.5). It is possible that the name was introduced at this time in recognition of the increased national prestige of the games.[17]

The judges exercised a strict disciplinary authority over the athletes,

---

[16] Cf. Gardiner 1910 (K 33) 194–226, Bengtson 1972 (K 3) 32–56.

[17] Cf., however, Hellanicus, *FGrH* 4 F 113, Arist. fr. 492.

and had power to impose heavy fines for breaches of the rules. An unpublished inscription of the late sixth or early fifth century mentions offences, in particular the breaking of fingers in a wrestling match, and also bribery. Punishments include beating, provided that this is not on the head, and fines are mentioned. It is notable that offenders are called *mianteres* (defilers), a word which again reminds one of the religious character of the occasion. There is also mention of 'the Eleans and their alliance', and this suggests that Olympia may already have been controlled by a league of Elean communities at this period.

The main changes at Olympia during the fifth century are linked to the political development of Elis.[18] After the Persian Wars the Eleans, who had arrived too late to fight in the battle of Plataea, banished their oligarchic leaders (Hdt. IX.77). The scattered communities of Elis were then concentrated in a newly founded city of Elis (Diod. XI.54.1, Str. VIII.3.2, p. 336). This city was designed with special consideration for the preparations for the festival at Olympia, with spacious training-grounds for horses, several gymnasia, and the headquarters of the *hellanodikai* (Paus. VI.23–4). After a war in which they gained control over some of their neighbours (cf. Hdt. IV.148, Str. VIII.3.30, p. 355), the Eleans built the temple of Zeus at Olympia. This is thought to have been finished soon after 457 (cf. Paus. V.10.4). It was some time before the temple housed the great statue of Zeus by Phidias, which was not finished until the 420s. Phidias' workshop, and some of the materials and tools which he used when working on the statue, have been found at Olympia.[19]

Towards the middle of the fifth century a new stadium was built, which replaced the previous one of the mid-sixth century. This was in use until some time in the fourth century, when the surviving stadium was constructed. This lay for the first time outside the bounds of the *Altis*, the sacred enclosure proper.[20]

During the Peloponnesian War the Olympic Games continued to be held. Elis at first sided with Sparta, and in 428 the Mytilenaeans presented their case against Athens to the Peloponnesian alliance at Olympia, after the festival (Thuc. III.8ff). But a dispute with Sparta over the Elean control of Lepreum led to the formation of an alliance between Elis and Argos in 421, and the next year the Eleans and Argives allied themselves with Athens (Thuc. V.31, 47). At the games of 420 the Spartans were forbidden to compete or sacrifice, because they had not paid the fine imposed by the Eleans for an alleged breach of the Olympic truce, and the festival was conducted in the presence of a garrison for fear

---

[18] Cf. Swoboda 1905 (F 67) 2392–2401 and Hönle 1968 (F 34).
[19] Cf. Mallwitz 1972 (I 102) 211–34, 255–66, Herrmann 1972 (K 40) 128–57.
[20] Cf. Mallwitz 1972 (I 102) 180–6, Herrmann 1972 (K 40) 105ff, 159, 164–5, Romano 1981 (I 144) 116–41, and Koenigs in Mallwitz 1981 (I 103) 366–8.

of a Spartan attack. The Spartan Lichas, the wealthiest man in Sparta, was also beaten by the Olympic officials for ignoring the regulation debarring the Spartans from taking part (Thuc. v.49–50).

After the battle of Mantinea, Elis seems to have adopted a neutral position. But at the end of the war Sparta took her revenge. Elis was invaded by Agis, defeated, and forced to give up her dependent territories. However, she was allowed to retain control of the administration of the Olympic festival (Xen. *Hell.* III.2.21–31).

2. Pythia

The Pythian Games were held in the Delphic month Boukatios (August–September), under the control of the *Hieromnemones*, who were the twenty-four representatives chosen by the twelve peoples of the Amphictyonic League to run its affairs. In addition to looking after the upkeep of the sanctuary, the *Hieromnemones* were responsible for the proclamation of the sacred truce and the general administration of the festival.[21] The musical contests always remained important, and consisted in those for singing to the cithara, cithara-playing and flute-playing (Paus. x.7.2–4; cf. Pind. *Pyth.* XII). The athletic contests were similar to those at Olympia, with the addition of a *diaulos* and *dolichos* for boys. The race in armour was added in 498. The horse-races were always held in the plain of Crisa below Delphi. It has recently been argued on archaeological grounds that the existing stadium was not built before the late fourth or early third century B.C., and that before this date the athletic events were also held in the plain.[22] The temple of Apollo whose ruins can now be seen was built in the fourth century B.C. to replace the one built in the late sixth century and completed by the Alcmaeonids (cf. Pind. *Pyth.* VII.7–9). The gymnasium and palaestra are situated near the temple of Athena Pronaia and date from the late fourth century.[23]

3. Isthmia

The Isthmian Games included the usual athletic and equestrian contests. Chariot- and horse-races were especially prominent here, perhaps because of Poseidon's patronage of horses. There was also a special foot-race of four laps called the *hippios*, which was not run at Olympia, and there were by the fifth century B.C. separate competitions for youths as well as men and boys. Musical contests are not attested before the third century. The temple of Poseidon was built around the middle of the fifth

---

[21] Cf. Roux 1979 (F 60) 57–8.
[22] Cf. Aupert 1979 (I 8), esp. 17–31, 52–4, 164–5, 180. See also Miller 1981 (I 114) 504–6 for criticisms.   [23] Cf. Courby 1927 (I 53), and Jannoray 1953 (I 80).

century, and replaced an earlier temple of the seventh century. The early stadium nearby was replaced by one outside the sanctuary, probably in the late fourth century or thereafter.[24]

4. Nemea

The Nemean Games took place on the twelfth day of the Nemean month Panemos, under the control of officials known as the *hellanodikai*, who wore dark robes to commemorate the legendary funereal origin of the festival. The main attraction seems to have been the athletic contests, although there was also a chariot-race. The origin of the *pankration* is traced by Bacchylides to Heracles' victory over the Nemean lion (XIII.46–57). There was a *hippios* race, as at Isthmia, and many events for boys and youths. The boys' *pentathlon* was not introduced until the fifth century B.C. (Schol. Pind. *Nem.* VII init.). The stadium, which has recently been excavated, dates from the second half of the fourth century B.C.[25] But a block which appears to come from the starting-line of an earlier stadium was built into the threshold of a later building near the temple of Zeus (above, n. 12). The earliest temple was probably built in the sixth century. It was destroyed at the end of the fifth, and rebuilt only in the later fourth century.[26] Nine buildings of the early fifth century have been discovered, which appear to be treasuries as at Olympia and Delphi, and also what is thought to be the *temenos* of a hero, which may perhaps be the sanctuary of Opheltes (cf. Paus. II.15.3).[27]

IV. THE ATHLETES: BACKGROUND AND CAREERS

The late sixth and fifth centuries were a golden age for Greek athletes. This was the time when aristocrats and tyrants vied for the most coveted prizes, those in the chariot- and horse-races, and our picture of athletes in general at this period is very much influenced by the wealthy patrons for whom Pindar and Bacchylides wrote many of their poems. But, contrary to what is often believed, athletic success was by no means confined to the wealthy amateur at this time.[28] By the fifth century there were enough festivals to keep an athlete perpetually busy, and those who were successful from an early age could devote a large part of their lives to training and competition, and probably also look forward to a prosper-

---

[24] Cf. Broneer 1971 (I 30) and 1973 (I 31) 46–66.

[25] Cf. Miller 1975 (I 115) 169–72, 1976 (I 115) 193–202, 1977 (I 115) 22–6, 1978 (I 115) 84–8, 1979 (I 115) 93–103, 1980 (I 115) 198–203, 1981 (I 115) 65–7, 1982 (I 115) 36–7; and Romano 1981 (I 144) 71–114.

[26] Cf. Hill 1966 (I 75) and Miller (above, n. 25).

[27] Cf. Miller 1978 (I 115) 67–78, 1979 (I 115) 83–5, 1981 (I 115) 60–5.

[28] Cf. Young 1984 (K 91). See also Kyle 1987 (K 56) 102 ff.

ous retirement. We already hear of a number of famous athletes in this period who came from humble backgrounds, for example Glaucus of Carystus, who was said to have been a ploughboy, and whose success as a boxer earned him the praise of the poet Simonides (fr. 509 *PMG*), or the runner Polymestor of Miletus, in the early sixth century, who was said to be a goatherd, or the cowherd Amesinas in the fifth century.[29] We are told that Alcibiades avoided entering for other events at Olympia, apart from the chariot-race, because 'he knew that some of the athletes were of low birth, came from small towns, and were of poor education' (Isocr. XVI.33-4).

To get some idea of the number of festivals available throughout Greece, one need only consider the extraordinary career of Theogenes of Thasos, in the early fifth century. He was said to have won over 1,300 athletic victories, and never to have been defeated at boxing during a career of twenty two years. Apart from his success as a boxer, he had a number of victories in the *pankration*, and also won the long-distance race at Argos and at Phthia in Thessaly.[30]

One should also take account of the scale of prizes at some of the games, and of other rewards to athletes by their home cities. At Athens, victors in the Panathenaea received amphorae of olive oil as prizes (cf. *Pls. to Vol. IV*, pls. 204-5). An inscription of the fourth century B.C. lists these prizes. The largest, for the winner of the chariot-race, was 140 amphorae (*IG* II^2 2311.55-6), and those for some of the other athletic contests were also considerable (e.g. probably 100 amphorae for the winner of the stadion). An amphora of olive oil was worth at least 12 drachmae at this time, and probably considerably more than this, and the daily wage of a skilled workman was only about 1-1$\frac{1}{2}$ drachmae. This gives some idea of the scale of such prizes in financial terms.

Although the crown games did not offer such material rewards, athletes could expect these on their return home. By the time of Solon such rewards seem to have been already considerable at Athens, as he is said to have restricted the amounts given to victors at Olympia and Isthmia to 500 and 100 drachmae respectively (Plut. *Solon*. 23.3, D.L. 1.55). Plutarch (*loc. cit.*) also informs us that at this time 500 drachmae was the equivalent of the annual yield from the estate of the top Solonian property class, the *pentakosiomedimnoi*.

The sixth-century poet and philosopher Xenophanes pours scorn on the honours and rewards given to Olympic victors, saying that their achievements really were of no value to their communities by contrast with his own intellectual contribution (fr. 2 *IEG*).[31] He lists these

[29] Cf. Moretti 1957 (K 64), nos. 134, 79, 261.
[30] Cf. Pouilloux 1954 (F 58) 62-105; Harris 1964 (K 36) 115-16.
[31] Cf. Bowra 1953 (J 6) 15-37, Marcovich 1978 (J 77) 16-26.

rewards as a seat of honour at festivals (*proedria*), meals at public expense (i.e. σίτησις ἐν πρυτανείῳ), and expensive gifts, and these practices are confirmed by later evidence.[32] Criticisms like those of Xenophanes also recur later, most notably in a speech from Euripides' *Autolycus* (fr. 282 N²).[33] But there were other honours which Xenophanes does not mention: the statues of athletes, with which Greek sanctuaries and public places began to be crowded from the sixth century onwards;[34] the public inscriptions recording their exploits, and in the case of rulers the issues of coins struck to commemorate their equestrian victories (*Pls. to Vol. IV*, pl. 214); the celebrations, often very extravagant, both after victory and on their return home, when they were escorted in a grandiose triumphal procession by their fellow citizens, and thanksgiving was offered to local gods and heroes; the victory songs themselves; and finally the fact, already mentioned, that some athletes came to be regarded as heroes, and worshipped after death.

Such extravagant honours, and the resentment and criticism which they aroused, should be borne in mind when we read the frequent references in Pindar and Bacchylides to the risk of envy (*phthonos*) to which the successful athlete was always vulnerable. When Pindar solemnly warns his patrons that they have reached the limits of success available to men, we should take his words at face value. Pythagoras was said to have advised men to compete at Olympia, but not to win, because of the danger of envy (Porph. *VP* 15); and in a famous comparison of life to the Olympic Games he said that athletes were like men possessed by a desire for rule and leadership, and by a mad lust for glory (Iambl. *VP* 58).

Political and athletic ambitions were, in fact, often inseparable. There is a story that Glaucus of Carystus ended his life as governor of Camarina in Sicily (Schol. Aeschin. *In Ctes.* 190, Bakker *Anecd. Gr.* 1.232).[35] Another famous athlete, Phayllus of Croton, was the only representative of the western Greeks to send aid to the battle of Salamis, and he came with his own ship (Hdt. VIII.47). We do not know whether or not he was wealthy by birth: like Glaucus he may have risen to prominence by his athletic prowess.

A salient example of the political use of athletic success is provided by Alcibiades. In the debate at Athens about whether to mount an expedition against Sicily, he defended his credentials as an advocate of this project and a potential leader by claiming that he had brought exceptional honour to Athens through his personal success at the Olympic Games in 416 B.C. He had entered seven chariots, and had been

---

[32] For fifth-century Athens, cf. Bowra 1953 (J 6) 30–4, and *IG* I³ 131.11–18, Pl. *Ap.* 36d.

[33] Cf. also Finley and Pleket 1976 (K 29) 113–32.

[34] Cf. Gardiner 1910 (K 33) 70, 77, 86ff.   [35] Dunbabin 1948 (A 29) 416.

placed first, second and fourth, a unique achievement. This in his view had led the rest of Greece to have a far higher opinion of Athens' power, instead of supposing her to have been ruined by the expenses of the war (Thuc. VI.16). Thucydides himself comments that Alcibiades' expenditure on his race-horses had really overstrained his resources, and he was hoping to recoup his fortunes in Sicily. His ostentation was, in fact, a chief cause of popular mistrust of his ambitions and of the fear that he was aiming at tyranny, which led to his later expulsion from Athenian politics (Thuc. VI.15.3–4).

It is significant that at Sparta the only king who had ever won a victory in the chariot-race at Olympia, down to Herodotus' time, was the renegade Demaratus, who ended his life as an exile in Persia (Hdt. VI.70). The Spartans feared such successes.[36]

Horses and chariots were a heritage from the epic age of heroes. Cimon, son of Stesagoras, who was winner of the Olympic chariot-race three times in the late sixth century, and was killed by the sons of Pisistratus, was buried together with his victorious horses (Hdt. VI.103). This reminds one of the funeral of Patroclus, and of the horse-burials of the Mycenaean and Geometric periods. Race-horses were usually ridden by professional jockeys, but a wealthy owner, or one of his family, could drive his own chariot (cf. Pind. *Pyth*. v, *Isthm*. I and perhaps *Pyth*. VI). Cimon is also a good example of the political use of these contests, since he allowed Pisistratus to be proclaimed as victor on the second occasion when he won, and was then permitted to return from exile (Hdt. *loc. cit.*).

After the equestrian contests, we can possibly get some idea of the popularity of other events by considering the order in which Pindar's poems were arranged by the Hellenistic scholar Aristophanes of Byzantium. Boxing, wrestling, *pankration* and *pentathlon* are placed next, and after them the foot-races. Boxing, wrestling and *pankration* were always favourite sports. They were all very demanding, and one could even be killed in these contests. The most brutal, to our view, was the *pankration*, which has been called 'unarmed combat converted into a scientific sport'.[37] It was perhaps rather like a combination of wrestling and boxing, in which only biting and gouging were forbidden (cf. *Pls. to Vol. IV*, pl. 208). Yet as many as eight odes of Pindar celebrate pankratiasts, and Philostratus called it 'the fairest of all contests' (*Imag.* II.6).

One of the leading themes of Pindar's poetry is that of the inheritance of natural ability from one generation to another. In fact, athletic success did tend to run in families in ancient Greece.[38] An outstanding example in the fifth century was the family of Diagoras of Rhodes, the subject of *Olympian* VII, which celebrates his boxing victory of 464. His three sons

[36] Cf. Bowra 1953 (J 6) 25–6, but see also Plut. *Lyc.* 22.4, and de Ste Croix 1972 (G 36) 354–5.
[37] Cf. Harris 1964 (K 36) 106.   [38] Harris 1964 (K 36).

and two of his grandsons all won victories at Olympia in boxing and the *pankration*, and one of the sons, Dorieus, had a succession of triumphs at all four major games as well as elsewhere. Dorieus also had a notable political and military career. Exiled from Rhodes to Thurii in the Peloponnesian War, he commanded a fleet against Athens in 410, was captured and condemned to death, but was then spared because of his athletic fame. Later, when Rhodes sided with Athens, Dorieus was captured by the Spartans, who showed their lack of tolerance by putting him to death.

Another family praised by Pindar was that of the Oligaethidae of Corinth. In *Olympian* XIII, for Xenophon's victories in the foot-race and *pentathlon* in 464, Pindar says that they have already won sixty victories at Isthmia and Nemea in the past (96–100), and he alludes to a host of successes at other festivals throughout the Greek world (1–2, 13–14, 29–46, 101–13).[39]

Epinician odes sometimes include compliments not only to the athletes and their families, but also to their trainers.[40] By the fifth century training was already a specialized and professional affair, which went with the development of theories about diet and health. One tradition connected the concentration on a meat diet for athletes with Pythagoras (D.L. VIII.12, Porph. *VP* 15), while another put this innovation later, in the early fifth century (Paus. VI.7.10). By Euripides' time the development of such a regime had evoked the criticism of athletes as gluttons, which later became a commonplace (Ath. 412D ff), and we find frequent protests against athletic training as not conducive to a balanced state of health (e.g. Hippoc. *De Alimento* 34, Pl. *Rep.* 403e8ff). There was a saying that training made athletes shine like the columns of the gymnasium but it also made them as solid as the stone of which these were made (cf. Plut. *Mor.* 133D)!

These games were not open to women as competitors, although they could enter chariots as owners in the men's races at Olympia. Women had their own athletic contests on other occasions.[41] At Olympia, for example, unmarried girls ran races in the stadium at the ancient festival of Hera (Paus. V.16.1). Pausanias also tells us that at Olympia married women were not even allowed to watch the games, with the exception of the priestesses of Demeter Chamyne (VI.20.9, V.6.7). Some modern scholars believe that this ban extended to unmarried girls also, but Pausanias' text states that they were allowed to be spectators, and Pindar seems to envisage girls, probably at Cyrene, watching the contests which he mentions at *Pythian* IX.97–103.

[39] Cf. Barrett 1978 (J 4) 1–20.
[40] Cf. Harris 1964 (K 36) 170–8; Gardiner 1910 (K 33) 122–32; Kramer 1970 (K 52) 64–107.
[41] Cf. Harris 1964 (K 36) 179–86.

V. POETS AND PATRONS

The epicinian ode was a specialized variety of the hymn to a god or a hero, and it was a late development in the history of Greek choral lyric song. The first who is recorded as having composed such songs in praise of athletic victors was Simonides of Ceos (c. 557–468). Very few fragments of these poems survive (*PMG* 506–19).[42] Simonides composed these songs on commission and for payment, and he enjoyed the patronage of several of the most powerful rulers of his time. Hipparchus is said to have persuaded him to come to Athens by offering rich gifts and fees, and he also spent some time in Thessaly, supported by the Aleuadae and Scopadae. During the Persian Wars he was again at Athens, where he was friendly with Themistocles, and he ended his life at the court of Hieron of Syracuse. Simonides very quickly acquired a reputation for greed and for a mercenary attitude to his art (cf. Xenophanes 21B21D–K[6], Ar. *Peace* 697–9, Arist. *Rhet.* 1391a8, 1405b24, Callim. fr. 222, etc.). Such an attitude is criticized by Pindar (*Isthm.* 11.1–11), and the ancient commentators assume that he has Simonides in mind, but we do not know if this is so.[43]

There was a legend later that a victorious boxer refused to pay Simonides the whole of his fee for a poem, telling him to ask the Dioscuri for the rest, because he had spent so much of his song in praise of these deities. At the victory feast they appeared at the door and asked to speak to Simonides. When he came out they had disappeared, but the house then collapsed, killing all inside (*PMG* 510). This story does at least suggest that Simonides was capable of devoting only a minor part of his poem to direct praise of his patron. Some of the surviving fragments also seem to show that he did not always adopt a very serious attitude towards the occasion of the poem (507, 514, 515). Once, however, he indulged in a remarkable hyperbole, when he said of Glaucus of Carystus that 'even the strength of Polydeuces would not have raised a fist against him, nor the iron son of Alcmene' (509). Again, he may not have been entirely serious here!

This new type of praise poem was very rapidly developed into a highly elaborate and complete art form by Simonides' successors Pindar and Bacchylides. Pindar is said to have been born in 518 B.C. at Cynoscephalae in Boeotia (Suda s.v. Πίνδαρος, *Scholia vetera in Pindari carmina*, ed. Drachmann, 1.1.1).[44] Of his seventeen books of poems only the four books of the epinician odes survive, together with a larger number of fragments of other types of poetry. We thus possess at least forty-four

---

[42] Cf. Fränkel 1975 (J 39) 434–6, and Bowra 1961 (J 8) 308–17. See also Barrett 1978 (J 4) 1–20.

[43] Cf. Lefkowitz 1981 (J 63) 50–3.

[44] Cf. Lefkowitz 1981 (J 63) 57–66, 155–7 for traditions about Pindar's life.

complete poems of Pindar. The last book, containing the Isthmian odes, is defective at the end. These poems are said by Eustathius to be 'more human, less mythological and less obscure than the rest', and hence were more popular in later antiquity (*Scholia Pindari*, ed. Drachmann, III.303–9–11).

Pindar's earliest surviving datable poem, *Pythian* x, was composed in 498 when he was only twenty, and his last, *Pythian* VIII, over fifty years later in 446. He wrote for patrons from many parts of the Greek world. His longest poem, *Pythian* IV, is dedicated to Arcesilas, king of Cyrene, as is *Pythian* v, but he wrote many poems for Sicilian patrons, especially Hieron of Syracuse and Theron of Acragas, and also a substantial number for Aeginetan victors. The Olympian and Pythian odes are, for the most part, securely dated by ancient records, whereas the Nemeans and Isthmians are not.

Bacchylides of Iulis in Ceos was the nephew of Simonides. His exact dates are uncertain, but he was composing in the same period as Pindar, sometimes for the same patrons and in competition with him.[45] In his fifth ode he celebrated Hieron's success at Olympia in the horse-race of 476, the subject of Pindar's first *Olympian*, and in the fourth Hieron's chariot victory of 470 at Delphi, the theme of Pindar's first *Pythian*. The third commemorates his chariot victory at Olympia of 468. As he calls Hieron a ξένος (guest-friend) in *Ode* v(11) he had presumably already visited him in Sicily by 476. *Odes* VI and VII, for Lachon of Ceos, are dated to 452 by a papyrus fragment of the Olympic register (*P. Oxy.* 222.ii.18). There was also a tradition that at some stage Bacchylides was exiled from Ceos to the Peloponnese (Plut. *Mor.* 605C).

Of Bacchylides' work we possess the remains of at least fourteen epinician odes and six dithyrambs, found in 1896 on two papyrus rolls, together with a number of fragments of other poems.

Like Simonides these poets worked on commission, and they frequently allude to the hospitality and generosity of their patrons.[46] Sometimes the poet himself was present at the performance of his work, but he could also send a poem to be performed at the victor's home. Some of the shortest songs seem to have been intended to be sung at the place where the victory was won (e.g. *Ol.* XI; *Pyth.* VI), but more often they were performed after the athlete returned home, sometimes at the door of his house (*Nem.* 1.19ff; *Isthm.* VIII.1ff) or at a temple (*Pyth.* XI.1ff). Although designed primarily for performance by a chorus of young

---

[45] Cf. R. C. Jebb, *Bacchylides* (Cambridge, 1905) 1–26; Severyns 1933 (J 98); Maehler 1982 (J 75) 1.6–9.

[46] On conditions of composition and performance of epinician poems, cf. Fränkel 1975 (J 39) 429–33, and Bowra 1964 (J 9) 161–2.

men, they could also be sung individually, for example by a member of the victor's family on later occasions (*Nem.* IV.13–16). The songs were intended as artistic heirlooms for the family of the athlete, preserving his memory for all time to come. A special copy might even be kept in a temple in the victor's city, as was said to have been done with *Olympian* VII (*Scholia Pindari*, ed. Drachmann, 1.195.13–14).

Epinician poems regularly contain statements made in the first person singular.[47] Since the time of the ancient commentators there has been debate as to whether these refer to the poet himself, to the chorus who are to sing the song, or even to the victor. Some instances can, however, only refer to the poet (e.g. *Pyth.* III.63–79), and in general one may assume that this is the case, unless there are strong grounds for doubt. The poet does not introduce himself merely for advertisement, but rather to add authority to what he says. As the Muses' spokesman (Pind. *Paean* VI.6), he is entitled to a special respect, both in praising and in giving advice. By alluding to his personal relations with his patron, or the victor's city, he also gives greater validity and immediacy to his praise. Such personal references can be regarded as an epinician convention, but this in no way detracts from the genuineness of what the poet says of himself on such occasions.

About the musical aspects of these songs, or how they were danced, little is known. There are frequent references to accompaniment by either the lyre, or lyre and flutes together. The terms Dorian, Aeolian and Lydian are sometimes used with reference to the song (*Ol.* XIV.17; *Nem.* VIII.15; probably *Ol.* 1.102), or the instrument (*Ol.* 1.17, V.21; *Pyth.* II.69; *Nem.* III.79), or the dance (*Ol.* III.4–6; *Pyth.* VIII.20); but the precise meaning of these terms in such cases is uncertain. For dancing, we possess some brief statements in late sources, according to which in triadic songs the *strophe* was sung as the dancers circled in one direction, the *antistrophe* as they circled in the opposite direction, and the *epode* while they stood still.[48] We are also told that Greek dancing in general was mimetic, expressing in its movements or poses character, emotion and action (Arist. *Poet.* 1447a27–8; Pl. *Leg.* 655d; Plut. *Mor.* 747A–8D). But it is hardly possible to reconstruct what this may have meant for epinician song.

VI. THE POEMS

These epinician odes are composed in a literary language which combines an overall colouring of Doric (the traditional dialect of choral

---

[47] Cf. Lefkowitz 1963 (J 62) 177–253.
[48] Cf. Färber 1936 (J 36) II.14–19; Mullen 1982 (J 80) 21–31, 225–30.

lyric poetry) with the language of epic, and also a number of Aeolic features.[49] They are written in either Doric (what is now know as dactylo-epitrite) or Aeolic metres, with the exception of *Olympian* XIII, which mixes Aeolic with dactylo-epitrite.[50] They are usually triadic in structure, i.e. composed in groups of *strophe*, *antistrophe* and *epode*, but occasionally monostrophic, with a single stanza repeated several times. The shortest is only fourteen lines (Bacchyl. II), the longest 229 (Pind. *Pyth.* IV). Modern texts use a different line-numbering system for Pindar from that of ancient editions and commentaries. The Alexandrian scholars divided the lines into shorter metrical lengths, and it was Gottfried Hermann, followed by Boeckh, who first established that Pindar was composing in longer metrical periods than those of dramatic lyric poetry.[51] Pindar's metrical structures are elaborate, and in the case of his Aeolic poems difficult to analyse. He differs significantly from Bacchylides in his tendency to avoid a correspondence between breaks in metrical and sense structure. In Pindar, word-end seldom coincides with the end of a *colon* or metrical phrase, and his sentences often run over the end of a period, *strophe* or triad. This kind of enjambment creates a counterpoint between sense and rhythm, which carries one forward, and gives much greater flexibility and variety to his poetry. This is especially marked in the poems of his maturity, although in his last works (e.g. *Pyth.* VIII; *Nem.* XI) there is again a tendency towards structural simplification, which goes with a remarkable compression and powerful simplicity of language.

Although their language owes much to earlier epic and lyric, Bacchylides' vocabulary is usually traditional, whereas Pindar aims constantly at originality. He uses words far more sparingly than Bacchylides, and his expression is often elliptical, with abrupt, dramatic transitions and vivid, complex imagery. These features make him at first sight difficult to follow, but they also give his poetry great power and directness. Pindar aims to give an impression of the freedom and spontaneity of inspiration, but his technique is really very sophisticated, and he is more self-conscious about his art than any earlier Greek poet. Bacchylides' style is smooth and easy. It has great charm, but seldom achieves real intensity (cf. [Longinus] *Subl.* 33.5). He is at his best in extended narrative, as in the story of *Ode* V of Heracles' descent to Hades, or of Croesus' rescue from the pyre in *Ode* III. His dithyrambs are dramas in miniature, full of life and colour. By contrast, Pindar's narrative is rapid and impressionistic. He approaches well-known stories at a tangent, concentrating on a particular scene or moment, and leaving the audience to fill in the rest for

[49] Cf. Forssman 1966 (J 38); Nisetich 1980 (J 81) 26–31; Maehler 1982 (J 75) I.9–12.
[50] Cf. Dale 1969 (J 19) 41–97, and Nisetich 1980 (J 81) 31–9; Maehler 1982 (J 75) I.14–23.
[51] Cf. Hermann 1809 (J 53) and A. Boeckh, ed. *Pindari Opera* (Leipzig, 1811–21).

themselves. This was a new and striking development in the history of Greek narrative style, whose repercussions were felt much later, especially in Hellenistic poetry.

In their basic content epinician poems can seem quite predictable, and some modern scholars have wrongly labelled everything in this type of poetry as purely conventional. The poet's primary aim is clearly to praise the victor and commemorate his achievement. This often leads to praise of his family or city, or both, and references to the exploits and fame of his ancestors. These may develop into a 'mythical' narrative. Alternatively the narrative element, which is a regular but by no means indispensable ingredient of the poem, may spring from some other aspect of the occasion, for example the place of the victory with its associated legends, or from some general reflection, stimulated by the victory. Such gnomic reflections are another regular element, and they usually serve as structural pivots for a transition from present to past or vice versa. Other recurrent motifs are (as in hymns) the opening invocation, and prayers for future success and prosperity, which can effect a transition, or alternatively conclude the song.

Although these constituents seem simple enough in essence, the possibilities for thematic and structural variation are very wide, and there is always a tension between the poet's inspirational freedom, which strives to escape from set rules and patterns, and the sense of a need to fulfil the primary task of praise, which is the poet's debt (*chreos*) to the victor, and to keep a proportion between the parts of the song. Pindar speaks of the 'ordinance' (*tethmos*) of epinician song, which imposes obligations and limits on him (*Nem.* iv.33–4; *Ol.* vii.88; *Paean* vi.54–7), and he often refers to the need for proportion (*metron, kairos*) and brevity (*Ol.* xiii.47–8; *Pyth.* i.81–4, iv.247–8, 286, ix.76–9; *Nem.* x.19–20; *Isthm.* i.60–3, vi.56–9).

From these diverse materials the poet constructs an elaborate, highly wrought work of art, which invites comparison with other refined forms of craftsmanship, such as architecture and sculpture, and the arts of weaving, embroidery and jewellery (cf. *Ol.* vi.1–4; *Pyth.* vi.7–17, vii.3; *Nem.* iv.81, v.1–3; *Pyth.* iii.113; *Nem.* vii.77–9, viii.14–15; fr. 179 Snell, etc.; cf. also the frequent use of terms such as *poikilos* and *daidallein*). But the stability of the visual arts is combined and contrasted with the mobile quality of the spoken word, which is free to fly over earth and sea, and outlasts all material monuments.

An important technique for welding this material together is that of thematic or verbal repetition. Pindar often uses ring composition, whereby a poem, or part of a poem, is framed by a series of recurring themes, usually repeated in reverse order. This is a fundamental device of early Greek poetry, especially narrative song. But Pindar frequently uses less obvious patterns of imagery or ideas, sometimes repeated in the same metrical position, in order to give shape and direction to his subject matter. These patterns are infinitely variable and not easy to analyse. It is dangerous to overstress their significance, but they contribute to the overall effect of the poem.

The opening invocation may be very brief, but it can also develop into a small preliminary hymn. (Pindar actually uses the word προοίμιον at *Pyth.* 1.4, VII.2; *Nem.* II.3; and ὕμνου προκώμιον at *Nem.* IV.11).[52] Occasionally (e.g. *Ol.* XIV) the whole poem is in hymn form. Whereas Bacchylides often has a simple invocation of the Muses or Fame, Pindar's proems are elaborate and varied. Sometimes he will invoke well-known deities, at others the victor's city or the place of the victory. But he can also begin with a material object or element, which is seen as endowed with divine power, such as water and gold (*Ol.* 1) or the lyre (*Pyth.* 1), or else with what would now be called an abstract idea, which he sees as divine, such as Truth (*Ol.* x.4), Fortune (*Ol.* XIII), Wealth (*Pyth.* v) or Quiet (*Pyth.* VIII).[53] Pindar can invest these divinities with exceptional powers, as in his invocation of Theia (Divine Lady), the mother of the Sun (*Isthm.* v.1ff), who is said to be the source from which gold derives its value, and the origin of all human success in contests on land or sea. In his frequent references to such abstract ideas as Time, Truth or Law, Pindar seems to be looking for principles at work in the world on a higher and more philosophical plane than that of the traditional Greek gods (cf. *Ol.* II.17, x.53–5; frs. 33, 169, 205 Snell).

In his treatment of the Olympian gods Pindar adopts an explicitly critical attitude to traditional stories, rejecting those which he sees as straining credulity or being offensive from a moral point of view (*Ol.* 1.25ff, IX.28–41, etc.). Sometimes he will seem to accept the familiar version, only to surprise his audience by replacing it suddenly with one of his own. In *Pythian* III, for example, he appears to be referring to the raven which brought news to Apollo of the infidelity of Coronis, but then he says that it was Apollo's own omniscience which persuaded him of the truth (27–30). This device draws attention dramatically to the poet's innovation. His gods are dignified and can appear remote. But there is also a tendency to stress their nearness, both in legendary narrative and also in the poet's references to his own personal connexions with particular gods and heroes, for example Apollo (*Pyth.* VIII.67–9; *Paean* VI.1–18) or the Mother of the Gods and Pan (*Pyth.* III.77–9), or the hero Alcmaeon (*Pyth.* VIII.56–60). Pindar's allusions to the mystery cults of Demeter and Persephone, and to the doctrines about life after death and reincarnation which had developed around these, also show a

[52] Cf. Schadewaldt 1928 (J 91) 269–81.
[53] Cf. Fränkel 1975 (J 39) 481–8 and Bowra 1964 (J 9) 84–8.

concern for the personal implications of religious belief, at its most crucial point (*Ol.* II.53–83, frs 129–31, 133, 137).

This paradoxical sense that the divine world is immeasurably separate in its eternal nature from the human, but that man can nevertheless come very close to the gods, is expressed in the proem to *Nemean* VI (1–7):

> Single of men, single of gods is the race. From a single
> Mother we both draw breath. But a total difference of power
> Keeps us apart: for the one is nothing, whereas the brazen
> Heaven remains a sure
> Foundation for ever. And yet somehow we resemble
> In greatness of mind or in nature the immortals:
> Although we know not by day or during the night-time
> To what line
> Fate has written that we should run.

All success demands and is counterbalanced by effort and suffering, but song, as the 'mirror for fine deeds' (*Nem.* VII.14) is the reward for labour, both now and in the future, with its promise of glory. The divine radiance of victory brings men joy and peace (*Pyth.* VIII.95–7). Their celebrations echo the gods' life of feasting, music and pleasure, and after physical death poetry offers immortality to a man's name. Pindar's eschatology occasionally goes further, suggesting that those who have lived exceptional lives on earth will eventually enjoy a special fate after death with the heroes in the Island of the Blest (*Ol.* II.61–83). Bacchylides also describes how Apollo rescued Croesus from death, carrying him off to live with the Hyperboreans, 'on account of his piety, because he sent the greatest dedications made by any mortal to holy Pytho' (III.58–62). The rulers to whom these poems are addressed are praised for a similar magnanimity in the use of their vast wealth (Bacchyl. III.10–22, 63–6; Pind. *Ol.* II.90–100). By implication, such greatness of achievement, and the benefits it brought to one's fellow-men, could offer hopes of a heroic fate beyond the boundaries of this life.

VII. AFTERMATH

Epinician poetry reached its peak of development very rapidly, and there were no worthy successors to the three great poets of this genre. Songs in praise of athletes continued to be composed. Two short fragments survive of a poem attributed to Euripides, celebrating Alcibiades' chariot victories of 416 B.C. at Olympia (*PMG* 755–6).[54] But this was an exceptional occasion, and we do not have any other surviving poems of this type. The great age of the epinician is the period immediately after the Persian Wars, when for the first time in the historical period the

[54] Cf. Bowra 1970 (J 7) 134–48.

Greeks were drawn together in a unity which found one of its most significant forms of expression in the panhellenic festivals. The threats from abroad also gave a special impetus to the old form of education, which linked musical culture and athletic training. At the time of the Peloponnesian War we see this system breaking down, and this breakdown coincided with the destruction of the brief and fragile ideal of Greek unity. The athletic festivals continued to flourish throughout later antiquity, but never again do we find that unique combination of physical achievement and musical celebration (*athla* and their *apoina* of song) which flowered in Greece in such a memorable way, in the course of the fifth century B.C.

CHAPTER 8e

ATHENIAN CULTS AND FESTIVALS

WALTER BURKERT

I. CONTINUITY AND CHANGE

Although what follows concentrates on the fifth century, it has to be seen in a larger perspective. Religious ritual is conservative and may survive for uncounted generations; its authority, for Greeks, is simply traditional custom, *nomos*. It shapes society, but it is also affected by all changes on the political, economic or intellectual level. From the earliest times on, ritual activity concentrates on special occasions that stand out from everyday life and serve as markers in the flux of time – the festivals. The basic elements of these are simple: processions, dances, vows and prayers, animal sacrifices with feasting, and contests (*agones*) of various kinds; yet special variants and combinations make up a system of impressive complexity, characterizing the group or city concerned as well as the gods and heroes addressed in the cult.

The rituals of Greek polis festivals contain elements of great antiquity. Particular traits of animal sacrifice as found especially in the Athenian ceremony of 'ox-murder', Buphonia, have been traced to the palaeolithic period,[1] and the women's festival of Thesmophoria has been credited with a 'stone age' character, too. We are on firmer ground in stating that the linguistic form to designate festivals in Greek, especially the suffix *-teria*, had been established by the Mycenaean epoch. The form of months' names derived from festivals, with the suffix *-(ter)ion*, is secondary, but still common to Athens and the Ionians from the islands and Asia Minor and must thus go back to the beginning of at least the first millennium. In fact there is a common stock of festivals characteristic of Ionians and Athenians which points to a common heritage: Apaturia (Hdt. 1.147), Lenaea, Anthesteria. No less characteristic is the division of the population into four *phylai* (tribes), each headed by a *phylobasileus* (tribal king); after the reform of Athenian *phylai*, the *phylobasileis* still continued to exist with their religious obligations and privileges. There must have been in addition a single *basileus* (king) for the polis as a whole; when yearly election of the magistrates had been

---

[1] Meuli 1946 (κ 60); Burkert 1972 (κ 12) 20–31, 153–61.

introduced, the *basileus* was one of them, second in rank after the archon, with his chief duty to take care of the traditional festivals (Arist. *Ath.Pol.* 57).[2] The priesthoods of individual gods in their several sanctuaries were the prerogative of certain noble families, including those of the cult of Athena Polias and Erechtheus-Poseidon on the Acropolis, of which the Butadai were in charge.

When the Athenian laws were codified by Solon, the calendar of festivals and sacrifices formed part of them. This was no obstacle to further expansions and additions. By the middle of the sixth century the two festivals called 'great' surpassed all the others in splendour: the Panathenaea at the beginning of the civil year in summer and the 'Great Dionysia' in the spring; the archon was responsible for both. The Eleusinian Mysteries, supervised by the *basileus*, equally rose in prominence.

The revolution of 510 which paved the way towards a more equal distribution of civil rights (*isonomia*) did not intentionally change the established system of cults. There were additions, especially the ten heroes of the *phylai*; there was increased public control of the finances of cults, with various bodies of elected officials in charge of the treasuries, expenditures and emoluments of sanctuaries. Sometimes special taxes were raised to finance a specific cult.[3] For the dithyrambic choruses, tragedy and comedy at the great festivals, especially the Dionysia, *choregoi* were selected from among the rich citizens who derived prestige from conspicuous expenditure.

New impulses for change came through the historical events, the crisis of the Persian Wars with devastation of city and citadel and the ensuing victory which brought an enormous increase of power, wealth and influence and made Athens the centre dominating the Greek world. The programme of rebuilding launched by Pericles was almost exclusively concerned with the public sanctuaries. Only then did the Acropolis lose its function as a fortress and become the centre of state religion exclusively. The Hephaestus temple above the Agora and the Poseidon temple at Sunium still remain as well-known survivals of this epoch.

During these years, about the middle of the century, political and social change was faced with a most profound challenge on the intellectual level in what is commonly called the sophistic movement. Independent thinking had developed in small coteries of men who read and wrote books, the 'pre-Socratics'; now the consciousness of possible progress in knowledge and organization of life spread to a larger public, with men such as the 'natural philosopher' Anaxagoras and the 'sophist'

---

[2] The old hypothesis that the *basileus* by title and function was a continuation of the Mycenaean king has been disproved by Linear B: a Mycenaean king was called *wanax*.

[3] Schlaifer 1940 (K 83) 233–41.

Protagoras leading the ranks. Their teachings shook the very foundation of established religion, the *nomos*, the authority of the forefathers. The traditional way of speaking about gods in the form of anthropomorphic myth was soon found to be unacceptable past remedy. But also the cults were felt to be old-fashioned; the 'Buphonia' became proverbial for the ridiculous attitudes of a hoary past (Ar. *Clouds* 985).

The crisis led to polarization, which becomes manifest in a surge of trials on the charge of 'impiety' (*asebeia*); this now was found not only in sacrilegious acts, but in teachings and beliefs.[4] Both Anaxagoras and Protagoras were affected. In 399 a later victim was to be Socrates.

The surprising fact is that the crisis of modernism did not destroy the system of cults either at Athens or anywhere else. This was not due to any spirited defence of traditional religion but rather to unreflective experience which found the religious forms of common life simply irreplaceable. Many will have concurred with the matter-of-fact position of Pericles, who stated that we believe in the existence of immortal gods on account of the honours which they receive, and of the good things they bestow on us (Plut. *Per.* 8, 9) – who would risk putting this to the test? Or witness Thucydides' description of the fleet setting sail for Sicily (VI.32): a trumpet calls for silence, and the traditional prayers and vows are pronounced in unison, led by the sonorous voices of heralds; mixing-bowls are set up all along the piers; all the soldiers and the officials of Athens pour libations to the gods; even the onlookers join in the vows, and only when they have finished the libations with the sacred song, the *paian*, do the ships begin to move. Who could exclude himself from such an event? Even if the gods were found to deny their help, as in this case, there was nothing left but to try again.

After the constitutional crisis of 411, restorative trends become noticeable. Among other ancestral laws, the revision and publication of which was organized, there was a comprehensive calendar of sacrifices to be set up in the 'Porch of the King' in the Agora; the huge task of compilation was entrusted to a certain Nicomachus who worked on it for about ten years; he was accused of accumulating more sacrifices than the city could possibly afford, but his work on the code was brought to a successful conclusion.[5] About the same time a new form of antiquarian literature was inaugurated which persisted for some generations: local chronicles dealing especially with mythical traditions in relation to Athenian institutions, cults and festivals, called *Atthides*.[6] We must not assume too much undisturbed continuity and scrupulousness in the performance of old rituals, but much of the religious system of the polis

---

[4] Derenne 1930 (J 22); Rudhardt 1960 (D 80); Fahr 1969 (K 26).
[5] *IG* I³ 239–40; *LSS* 10; *LSCG* 17; Lys. xxx; Dow 1960 (D 22).
[6] Beginning with Hellanicus *FGrH* 323a; *FGrH* 323–9; Jacoby 1949 (C 57).

is seen to continue down to the Roman conquest and even beyond to the end of the pagan world, with the temples of the fifth century still presenting their gorgeous façades for the same festivals. Many Athenians would go on to experience their home as the place 'where the mystery hall is opened in sacred ceremonies, where . . . the high temples and images of gods are standing, where there are the most sacred processions of the blessed gods, sacrifices adorned with beautiful wreaths for the gods and feasting at various times of the year, and especially the joy of Dionysus in spring' (Ar. *Clouds* 302–11).

II. NOTE ON THE SOURCES

The character of our sources changes with the general development. Much of the documentation still consists in the material remains of cults in the sanctuaries as recovered and analysed by archaeology. But the growth of literacy led to the greater regulation of religion, for laws, including *leges sacrae*, were published in the form of inscriptions under the pressure of the democratic system. There are fragments of sacrificial calendars prior to 480 (*IG* I³ 230–2) and the regulations for the 'precinct governors' of the Acropolis, the 'Hekatompedon inscription';[7] there are similar regulations from the following epoch, e.g. from the Agora (*IG* I³ 234 = *LSCG* 1) and from the Eleusinium (*IG* I³ 6 = *LSS* 3); then comes the big codification of Nicomachus (above, n. 5). Individual demes published their *leges sacrae* too, such as Scambonidae (*IG* I³ 244 = *LSCG* 10) and Paeania (*IG* I³ 250 = *LSS* 18).[8] Similar codifications from the fourth century are relevant for the earlier period, too, such as the calendar of Erchia (*LSCG* 14) or the convention of the 'Salaminioi' (*LSS* 19).

The fifth century saw the outburst of Athenian literature which has remained classic, especially tragedy and comedy. Tragedy, freely moving in the sphere of myth, tends to refer to local cults by telling their 'causes' (*aitia*). We find vivid representations of the Areopagus and the cult of the Semnai in Aeschylus' *Eumenides*, of Colonus Hippius in Sophocles' second Oedipus play, of Acropolis cults in Euripides' *Erechtheus*;[9] there are many shorter references to other local traditions. Comedy takes religious practice for granted in passing remarks and sometimes brings it live on stage, though in a parodistic vein, for example, the drinking contest of the Anthesteria (Ar. *Ach.* 1085–234), the women's gathering at the Thesmophoria (Ar. *Thesm. passim*), and even the chorus of Eleusinian initiates (Ar. *Frogs* 316–459).

Historiography as inaugurated by Herodotus has invaluable accounts

---

[7] *IG* I³ 4; Jordan 1979 (к 44).   [8] Mikalson 1977 (к 61).
[9] C. Austin, *Nova Fragmenta Euripidea in Papyris Reperta* (Berlin, 1968) 39.

of *nomoi* and of various incidents connected with cults and festivals. Attic prose writing, which came into being in the last third of the fifth century, rhetoric as well as historiography, has allusions to and brief accounts of religious institutions; again, fourth-century authors supply much information that is valid for the fifth century as well. But for detailed knowledge of Athenian cults and festivals we depend primarily on the 'Atthidographers' (above, n. 6), fourth-century authors of Attic chronicles, although these survive only in fragments, mainly in commentaries to Attic poets and orators.

A word needs to be said about iconography as a source for the understanding of Athenian cults.[10] Attic painted pottery was produced in large quantities, and among the thousands of often conventional pictures there are some clearly depicting religious ceremonies, processions, sacrifices and dancing. They are not numerous, except for Dionysiac scenes, and interpretation is often difficult. One class of jugs belongs to the Choes festival at the Anthesteria,[11] another group of characteristic representations has women worshipping a very primitive image of Dionysus; these have come to be called 'Lenaean vases',[12] but on insufficient evidence. A few interesting pictures of the Dionysiac ship waggon still belong to the sixth century, as does a unique representation of the *phallophoria*.[13] On the whole, fifth-century art is less concerned with group action. A celebrated exception is the Panatheniac frieze encircling the *cella* of the Parthenon,[14] a unique self-representation of the Polis at her 'great' festival in the presence of her heroes and her gods.

III. THE CYCLE OF THE YEAR

Greek calendars are composed of lunar months that shifted from year to year, unlike the dates computed by the Julian calendar in modern chronology. The Athenian year begins in summer after harvest, with the first month, Hekatombaion, roughly corresponding to July. This and the following months are each named after a festival: Metageitnion, Boedromion, Pyanepsion, Maimakterion, Posideon, Gamelion, Anthesterion, Elaphebolion, Munichion, Thargelion, Skirophorion. It is not only the similarity to other Ionian calendars that testifies to the antiquity of the system; another indication is the fact that by the sixth and fifth centuries some of the festivals implied in month names (Hekatombaia, Boedromia, Elaphebolia) had become quite insignificant in comparison with other festivals, celebrated in the same month, that had risen to

---

[10] A critical assessment in Rumpf 1961 (K 82); Metzger 1965 (I 110).

[11] Van Hoorn 1951 (K 88).

[12] Frickenhaus 1912 (I 65); Pickard-Cambridge 1968 (J 85) 30–4; Burkert 1972 (K 12) 260–2.

[13] Pickard-Cambridge 1968 (J 85) figs. 11–14; Simon 1980 (K 84) 284. Deubner 1932 (K 23) pl. 22; Pickard-Cambridge 1962 (J 84) pl. IV.   [14] Brommer 1977 (I 27).

special splendour – Panathenaea in Hekatombaion, Mysteria in Boedromion, and Dionysia in Elaphebolion. It is interesting to note that most
names of months refer to festivals of Apollo and Artemis, except for the
four winter months from Maimakterion to Anthesterion, three of which
include the ancient festivals of Dionysus, the rural Dionysia, Lenaea, and
Anthesteria in turn.

Yet there is no single system determining the calendar of festivals in
the well-documented period, but a conglomerate of various circles,
correspondences and oppositions that make a complex rhythm of life.
There are the seasonal changes between winter storms (Maimakteria),
spring blossoms (Anthesteria) and summer heat; there are the main
agricultural events: sowing, reaping and vintage; there is the political
symbolization of dissolution and a new beginning surrounding the New
Year festival; there are the celebrations of the phratries and of cult
associations of women. Moreover, responsibility for different cults
rested with the *basileus*, the archon, certain priestly families, and in some
cases with members of private cult organizations; furthermore, the
demes, 139 altogether, had traditional cults of their own, each marked by
its own peculiar stamp and paralleling the cults of the city.

The New Year festival already had a special standing in the ancient
Near East. At Athens it culminated in the Panathenaea on the 28
Hekatombaion, but the preliminaries began almost two months in
advance. The rituals concentrated on the main cults of the Acropolis, of
Erechtheus, the aboriginal king who was most closely associated with
Poseidon in cult, and his protecting deity, the 'Athenian' goddess,
Athenaia, Athena,[15] who for the citizens is just 'the goddess', ἡ θεός. The
approaching end of the year brought with it the need to clean the temple
and to wash the garments of the goddess: Kallynteria, 'Making tidy', and
Plynteria, 'Washing', are performed by women, and since the image of
the goddess was veiled and the temple closed to visitors, this was a day of
ill omen.[16] There follows a strange nocturnal ceremony, Arrhephoria,
when two girls who have been living for almost a year in the service of
the goddess on the Acropolis, and have taken part in the weaving of
Athena's *peplos*, are dispatched from the citadel by the priestess through a
special passage close to the precinct of Aphrodite, carrying on their
heads in baskets objects purportedly unknown to them as well as to the
priestess. This ritual of the *arrhephoroi* or *errhephoroi*[17] seems to reflect the

[15] Whether the goddess got her name from the city or vice versa is an old controversy. Word
formation is in favour of *Athenai > Athenaia*. Burkert 1985 (κ 16) 139.

[16] For the date of Plynteria there are conflicting testimonies, Mikalson 1975 (D 59) 160f, 163f; the
calendar of Thorikos (*SEG* XXXIII.147, lines 52–3) has Skirophorion, not Thargelion. The Plynteria
procession is to be kept distinct from the Palladion procession, Burkert 1970 (κ 11).

[17] *errhephorein* is the form used in Attic inscriptions since the third century B.C.; the literary texts
have *arrhephoros*; the word should mean 'dew-bearer'; Burkert 1966 (κ 10).

structure of puberty initiations, the seclusion of 'virgins' ending in an encounter with Aphrodite, generation and birth. There is a corresponding myth about the daughters of Cecrops, the first king on the Acropolis: they opened a secret basket at night against the goddess' instructions, discovered the earth-born divine child Erichthonius (= Erechtheus) encircled by a snake, and jumped panic-stricken to their deaths from the Acropolis rocks. Later, by the middle of Skirophorion, at the ceremony called *Skira*, the priest of Erechtheus and the priestess of Athena leave the citadel in procession and proceed towards the frontier on the way to Eleusis; two days later the 'Heralds' (*Kerykes*) perform that proverbially old-fashioned sacrifice, the 'ox-murder', Buphonia, right on the Acropolis, in honour of 'Zeus of the City', whence the festival was called Dipolieia. By an elaborate trick the sacrificial bull was made responsible for his own death: several animals were driven around a table filled with vegetable offerings, and the one which first touched the food was slain immediately; but the ox-slayer had to flee in his turn, and there followed a mock trial in the *prytaneion* at which the participants had to shift the 'guilt' of killing the ox from one to another, until the knife itself was found to be the murderer and thrown into the sea. This curious 'comedy of innocence' may be of special antiquity, as analogies in Siberian hunters' costumes suggest (above, n. 1). It acts out and playfully overcomes the antinomy inherent in all sanguinary sacrifice: killing for food becomes a ritual to honour a god. This uncanny act falls into the gap separating the old year from the new and in a way links Athens with Eleusis: myth has Erechtheus perishing in the first Athenian war against Eumolpus of Eleusis, while his widow became the first priestess of Athena (above, n. 9).

Hekatombaion, the New Year's month, once more recalls disorder with the festival of Kronia – analogous to the Roman Saturnalia – when slaves are treated to a feast and may revel freely through the town. This has an air of the past golden age, when Kronos was king, before Zeus took over by force. Normal order is finally restored with the Panathenaea, the festival of Zeus's formidable daughter. There are no longer perplexing or scurrilous rites, but the normal elements of festivals in stately parade. After an all-night festival (*pannychis*), the day begins with a torch-race from the grove of Academus through the city gate and the market-place up to the Acropolis to light a fire on the altar of Athena; there follows the great sacrificial procession towards the goddess displaying the new garment (*peplos*) – later it was hoisted like a sail on a ship waggon –, the enormous feast, and contests (*agones*), with both musical and sports events. An archaic feature is the *apobates* ceremony, when men in light armour jumped from chariots at full speed and continued with a foot-race; this was said to have been invented by

Erichthonius and seems to symbolize the king taking possession of the land. Panathenaic victors received amphorae filled with olive oil as a prize, the special product of Attic soil granted by Athena and her father. The Panathenaea, especially its sports events, was celebrated on a large scale every fourth year; the intention had been, in 562, to create a panhellenic festival equivalent to the Olympic Games. This plan had failed; but with the new glory acquired through the Persian Wars the festival was to represent Athens itself, bound to the goddess by a divinely sanctioned, civilized order.

While the second month seems to have no major festival, Boedromion and Pyanepsion (roughly September/October) contain celebrations concerned with agriculture and the fertility of the soil as autumn sowing approaches. The mysteries on 19/20 Boedromion are taken to reflect the gift of grain brought to Eleusis by Demeter, even if the emphasis comes to be more and more on death and afterlife. It is the hierophant of Eleusis who proclaims at the beginning of the next month, 5 Pyanepsion, the 'Festival before sowing', Proerosia (LSCG 7), with special sacrifices which are to guarantee good crops; similar sacrifices will accompany 'Sprouting' (Chloaia), 'Shooting of stalks' (Kalamaia) and 'Blossoming' (Antheia) of the corn. But it is also in this connexion that the festival of women, Thesmophoria, takes place in Athens on 10–13 Pyanepsion: sacrificial pigs are thrown into crevices or subterranean receptacles,[18] and the putrefied remnants of the last year, hauled up again, are put on the altars and later mixed with the seed, the clearest case of agrarian magic in Attic ritual.

Pyanepsion also had a festival associated with vintage, which could not be fixed in the calendar. At the Oschophoria, vine twigs with grapes (oschoi) were carried in procession towards a sanctuary of Athena Skiras at Phalerum; there was a race of the ten phylai as well, but the texts seem to be confused, and the details are controversial.[19]

Maimakterion, the month of winter storms, had a purification festival, Pompaia, about which not much is known. With Posideon, the series of Dionysus festivals begins. The 'rural Dionysia' were held in the villages at different days during the month; most conspicuous were those in the Piraeus. A he-goat was led to sacrifice, and a wooden phallus was carried in procession. From an Athenian perspective these festivals had a flavour of peasant simplicity and ribaldry, Dionysiac vitality erupting from the frozen structures of winter and orderliness. There was also a strange ceremony called Haloa, of the 'threshing-floors'(?), when women met in secret and were said to indulge in licentious behaviour.

The festival of Lenaea in the next month, Gamelion, must have been

---

[18] Wrongly connected with skira by Deubner 1932 (K 23) 40f, cf. Burkert 1985 (K 16) 242–3.
[19] See Jacoby's commentary on FGrH 328 F 14–16; Kadletz 1980 (K 46).

Fig. 32. Festival at a pillar image of Dionysus from an Attic red-figure stamnos by the Dinos Painter, about 420 B.C. (Naples, Museo Nazionale 2419; *ARV²* 1151, 2; after E. Pfuhl, *Malerei und Zeichnung der Griechen* (1923) fig. 582.)

one of the old and characteristic Dionysus celebrations; many Ionian cities call the corresponding month Lenaion. *Lenai* is a name for Bacchants. But hardly any details are known. The so-called Lenaean vases (Fig. 32) have women mixing wine and dancing in front of a primitive image of Dionysus, made for the occasion and consisting of a simple mask suspended from a column with a cloth wrapped around to indicate a garment, adorned with wreaths and branches but without hands or feet; but the attribution to either Lenaea or Anthesteria remains unclear (above, n. 12). State management of the Lenaea was introduced in 440 when it was made a second occasion, besides Dionysia, for the staging of comedies.

Much more is known about the Anthesteria, the festival which gave its name to the following month. This, too, is shared with Ionia, and it is thus correctly called the 'older Dionysia' (Thuc. II.15.4). The name suggested 'flowers' to the Greeks, but the main subject was the new wine that had been stored during the winter and was tasted for the first time in spring. Thus the first day of the festival, 11 Anthesterion, is 'Opening the jars', Pithoigia. Offerings were brought to the little sanctuary of 'Dionysus in the Marshes', ἐν λίμναις, which was opened only in the evening of this day and during the next. This, the 12th of the month is called Choes, 'Jugs', from the vessels employed in a drinking contest: in private meetings and in official banquets each participant had to empty one *chous* – more than two litres – of wine, beginning at a trumpet signal,

Fig. 33. Attic red-figure *chous*, late fifth
century B.C. (London, British Museum E
536; after Van Hoorn 1951 (K 88) fig. 93.)

and the winner received a prize. Children who had entered their fourth
year were made to take part and offered a little jug of wine, together with
other presents, as shown in representations on surviving *choes* vases.
Children who died before they had reached the age of four were given a
chous in their tomb, usually a miniature copy (Fig. 33). The drinking
contest was a merry occasion that appealed to Aristophanes (*Ach.* 1085–
234), but it was surrounded by strange taboos. The entire day of Choes
was considered unclean, apotropaic twigs were hung at the doors, the
doorposts were painted with fresh pitch; each guest at the gatherings had
not only a *chous* of his own, but also a separate table, and silence had to be
observed during the drinking. Uncanny presences filled the streets,
masked people mocking at others from carts; tradition wavers between
calling them *keres*, harmful ghosts, or *kares*, strangers, or even forgotten
original inhabitants of the countryside.[20] Legend explained that the first
Choes had been held when Orestes, the polluted murderer, had stayed
with the king of Athens; hence the 'day of defilement' with its taboos,
and avoidance of the common table. Another mythical account of the
strange mixture of merry-making and uneasiness is the tale about the
violent death of the first cultivator of the vine, Icarius, or even of the
wine-god Dionysus himself, represented by the wine sacramentally
consumed in the ceremony. The following night saw one of the most
startling rituals – at least from a modern point of view – a 'sacred
marriage', the wedding of Dionysus to the 'queen' of Athens, the wife of

[20] Burkert 1972 (K 12) 250–5.

the *basileus*, in a building called an 'ox-shed' (*boukolion*) in the market place. Some vase paintings seem to allude to the wedding procession,[21] while the revellers brought their *choes* to the sanctuary 'in the Marshes' for a last offering to Dionysus. What 'really' happened in the *boukolion* is left to the imagination. The last day, of 'Pots', Chytroi, took its name from a special meal cooked in earthenware pots, a stew of 'all kinds of cereals and honey'. None of the priests tasted it,[22] as none of the Olympian gods was invoked on this day but Hermes Chthonios, 'of the Underworld'. The uncanny aspect of the festival is prevalent in these details, yet myth explained that the meal of 'Pots' and the sacrifice to Hermes had first been held by the survivors of the great flood, when they had reached firm ground again. The eery visitors are chased away: 'Out with you, *keres* [or *kares*]!' There were games and musical contests organized at the Chytroi, and there was a ceremonious and joyful festival of 'swinging' for children, traced by myth, though, to the sad event of Icarius' daughter Erigone hanging herself. On the whole, the Anthesteria seem to have retained a popular character for a long time without too much interference and organization on the part of the polis. Later in the month there were the 'Little Mysteries', held at Agrae near the river Ilissus, and the 'greatest festival of Zeus' (Thuc. 1.125.6), the Diasia, in the same region. This was for a chthonian Zeus, Meilichios, honoured with holocausts, but according to local custom the animals to be burnt were made of pastry.

Elaphebolion must once have been the month of Artemis the 'huntress of deer', *elaphebolos*, but from the sixth century onwards it was dominated by the 'great' festival newly introduced and second only to the Panathenaea in lavish equipment, the 'City Dionysia'. The god who had his sanctuary installed at the south slope of the Acropolis had been brought from Eleutherae. The central procession which mirrored the advent of the god seems to have been basically a larger replica of the rural Dionysia, with he-goat and phallus, but the magnificence of the festival was manifested in choruses honouring the god, dithyrambs in which all ten tribes competed, with a bull for a prize, and the three days of tragic performances including satyr play, to which, since 485, a day of comic performances was added. Music and poetry finally got the better of ancient ritual.

The festival of Munichia, which gave its name to the following month, was to honour Artemis installed at Munichia, the hill close to Piraeus. It was overshadowed, as it seems, by the parallel cult of Artemis of Brauron, transferred to the Acropolis by Pisistratus. The festival of Thargelia in the next month received more attention, when the first

---

[21] Deubner 1932 (κ 23) pl. 18, 2; Simon 1980 (κ 84) 279.
[22] Accepting the text of Theopompus *FGrH* 115 F 347b, Burkert 1972 (κ 12) 264f.

bread produced from the new crops, called *thargela*, was offered to Apollo. This was connected with a much-discussed scapegoat ceremony: two men, noted for their ugliness or other physical defects, were chosen. They were adorned with strings of figs, one with white ones, the other with black, representing women and men respectively; thus attired they were chased out of town, carrying with them bad luck and uncleanness. Even if the more drastic procedures attested for other places – stoning, throwing from a cliff, even burning – seem to be absent from Athens, the inhumane selfishness inherent in such forms of 'purification' seems not to be to the credit of ancient ritual, even if it may mirror biological strategies.[23]

'The good luck that has come from these sacrifices' was the general justification of worship on which Nicomachus and his accuser would agree (Lys. xxx.19). Piety was found to pay. As Euripides puts it, Athena is bound to help her polis of which she is 'Mother, Mistress and Guardian' because of the 'honour of the many sacrifices'; yet for the participants this meant at the same time 'the songs of the young, the hymns of the choruses, the cries resounding all night with the dance of the virgins from the airy hill' (Eur. *Heracl.* 770–83). The *pannychis* on the Acropolis at the Panathenaea was an unforgettable experience of a cult filled with joy and life which defined the identity of Athens.

IV. POLIS RELIGION: CULTS DEFINING IDENTITY

The social function of ritual, which has received much interest in this century, is so evident in Greek religion that we rather lose sight of its 'truly religious' dimension. To begin with the nucleus of society: the concept of 'family' is commonly expressed in Greek by 'hearth' (*hestia*), which is at the same time a goddess who claims first offerings from all the meals. The newborn baby is carried around the hearth at the Amphidromia and thus integrated into the cult community of the family. The question asked in order to establish citizenship in the examination of candidates for the archonship takes the form: 'Where is your Apollo Patroos and your Zeus Herkeios?' (Arist. *Ath. Pol.* 55.3); to know the god of the phratry and to have a household protected by Zeus is to know one's place in the city. Individual families had special cults which defined their status; some had claims to public priesthoods. Legitimate citizenship is conferred by the 'brotherhoods', *phratriai*, who meet at the Apaturia festival in Pyanepsion; the father has to present his child at the age of three, and later his grown-up son, to the meeting and pays for a sacrificial meal; marriage is validated in a similar way. Illegitimate sons have a mythical model in Heracles; the gymnasium of Heracles at

Fig. 34. *Krateriskos* from Brauron. (Brauron Museum; after L. Kahil, *Antike Kunst* Beiheft 1, pl. 6, 3.)

Kynosarges is open to them. The status of women finds various expressions in ritual. Women have special goddesses by whom they swear, they have their own festivals at which they may leave their apartments and gather 'according to the ancient customs' (*LSCG* 36.11). The most important of these is Thesmophoria when women live together for three days in temporary barracks, forming, as it were, their own state with elected presidents; men are strictly excluded. The strange ritual of throwing pigs into subterranean caves has been mentioned as a kind of agrarian charm. The second day was a day of 'fast', Nesteia, made shorter by mutual jesting. The last day included a sacrifice for 'beautiful offspring', Kalligeneia, with an opulent meal. The crucial changes in a woman's life, from girl through marriage to matron, were dominated by Artemis; virgins had to be 'consecrated' to Artemis of Brauron or Munichia before marriage (Craterus *FGrH* 342 F 9); serving as 'bears' (*arktoi*), of Artemis at Brauron, they probably had to spend some time in seclusion, with games and dances,[24] until they were restored to their normal state at the festival of Brauronia.

The polis, as the more comprehensive community, had its own 'common hearth', *koine Hestia*, established as a centre for the magistrates and the members of the Council dining together; there was also a temple of Apollo Patroos and of the Mother of the Gods in the market-place. But the supreme authority rested with the goddess of the Acropolis, Athena. There were on the Acropolis two signs of divine action, created

[24] Kahil 1965 (K 47), 1977 (K 48); Brelich 1969 (L 16) 240–79.

at the foundation of Athens according to myth, Poseidon's little 'sea' of salt water and Athena's olive tree; there was the wooden image of the goddess (*xoanon*) which received the new garment at the Panathenaea. Athena was also Ergane, 'wool-worker', as well as patroness of olive trees, but over against these more female and peaceful aspects the sixth century had already stressed the warlike features of the goddess: Athena striking down a giant was the recurrent subject woven into the *peplos*, and it was shown in the pediment of the Pisistratean temple. The fifth century added the huge statue of Athena Promachos, 'fighting in front', and temple and priesthood of Athena Nike, 'victory' (*IG* I³ 35–6). That the most sumptuous and beautiful temple was dedicated to Athena the Virgin, Parthenos, seems a contrast; it was probably to stress the untouchable, impregnable character of the goddess and her city. It is unclear, however, which form of the cult was installed at the Parthenon; all the old and venerable rituals pertain to Athena Polias finally housed in the Erechtheum.

Erechtheus, who in cult appears to be identified with Poseidon, but distinguished from him in myth, is a peculiar case in so far as there seems to be a 'loser' on both levels: Erechtheus was crushed by Poseidon, Poseidon lost Athens to Athena. In more general terms the paradox is that the female, the goddess, is triumphant while the male partner represents the vanquished, the 'chthonian' principle. This structure is widely attested and probably quite old; it arose from ancestor cults and sacrifices and was to reinforce the dominating order in a patriarchal society; the vanquished powers below have to be reconciled lest they should thwart aggressive domination in the upper world. Thus Erechtheus is 'appeased' at the Panathenaea (Hom. *Il.*2.550f).

Zeus, as everybody knew, was the supreme god; his altar held the highest spot on the Acropolis where the rites of the Dipolieia were performed. He had, in addition, his precinct outside the city walls as Olympius, where the huge temple, begun by Pisistratus, was left uncompleted until Hadrian (see *CAH* IV² 295–6). According to Draco's code, oaths were to be sworn by Zeus, Poseidon and Athena, in that order. Yet since Athena was the favourite daughter of Zeus, a sequence Zeus–Athena–Poseidon–Demeter was equally established for Athenian oaths.

The need to take oaths was the strongest means of linking the gods to justice as required in everyday behaviour. For penal laws as codified in Draco's *thesmoi*, special religious forms were established by tradition: different courts were tied to certain cults and provided with corresponding myths. Most prominent was the Areopagus with the worship of the 'Venerable' avenging goddesses, the Semnai called 'Eumenides' in the play of Aeschylus; according to him the court was set up for Orestes, while others said Ares himself was put on trial there for having slain Halirrhothius, son of Poseidon, who had tried to rape his daughter (Hellanicus *FGrH* 323a F 22); in both cases myth stresses the possibility that there may be 'justified' homicide. Involuntary homicide is the speciality of the courts 'at the Palladium', where a sacred image of armed Athena, allegedly brought from Troy, was worshipped by the clan of the Buzygai and ceremoniously escorted to Phalerum for a bath once a year (above, n. 16). A third court with a mythical background was at the Delphinium, a sanctuary of Apollo. However, the court that handled most legal proceedings in the fifth century, the Heliaia, established on the basis of the Cleisthenean system of *phylai*, was far less dominated by ritual and tradition, although of course purifications and oaths were included in the proceedings. In a similar way the general assembly of citizens, the *ekklesia*, was a rational organization; but it had still to gather in a 'clean' place, purified by the *peristiarchoi* through the slaughter of piglets and the burning of incense, and it could be stopped by a 'sign of Zeus', *diosemia*; the Athenians, though, were less prone to heed such signs than the Romans were. Most important, however, was ritual connected with warfare, consisting in various sacrifices when leaving the city, crossing the borders and engaging in battle;[25] it was the gods who granted victory.

Three factors contributed to shaping and to some extent transforming this system in the course of the fifth century: the evolution of democratic government, patriotism born of the victory over the Persians, and the emergence of empire. All these had their effects on the organization and reorganization of cults.

A most revolutionary measure initiated by Cleisthenes was the creation of ten new, totally artificial *phylai*. This had to find religious sanction at once: ten local heroes, out of a list of one hundred names (Arist. *Ath. Pol.* 21.6), were selected by the Delphic oracle and assigned to give the names to the tribes (the 'eponymous heroes').[26] Some already had individual cults, such as Cecrops on the Acropolis, Hippothoon at Eleusis, and Ajax at Salamis; others, such as Antiochus, seem to have become prominent only then; yet as it was the god of Delphi who proclaimed that it was 'better and more profitable' to worship them, innovation soon became tradition.

An anti-tyrannical stance was strengthened with a cult of Harmodius and Aristogeiton, the so-called tyrannicides, established in the Agora in 477/6.[27] The more conservative though anti-Pisistratid families found their ideal hero in Theseus, the democratic king. The Theseus myth had become popular by the end of the sixth century, presenting, as it were, an

---

[25] Burkert 1972 (K 12) 77f; Pritchett 1979 (A 101) vol. III.   [26] Kron 1976 (K 53).
[27] Thompson and Wycherley 1972 (I 166) 155–61.

Athenian contrast figure to Dorian Heracles. But Theseus was not included among the tribal eponymous heroes, which left the door open to assign him a special position. In 475, when Cimon conquered the island of Skyros, he discovered the relics of Theseus, as predicted by the Delphic oracle, and solemnly brought them to Athens; a spendid heroon was built in the Agora, admired for centuries; funeral banquets and games were instituted on 8 Pyanepsion; the Theseia remained one of the major festivals in Athenian tradition.

A contrary move to accord worship not to a hero of the past but to the living 'people' themselves, Demos, was made by the middle of the century.[28] An image of Demos by Parrhasius (Pliny, *HN* xxxv.69), admired by later antiquity, may have been votive in character. If Demos is divine, he is not to be checked by human laws, and even gods will tactfully avoid censuring him.

The rising influence of craftsmen among the citizens over against the old aristocrats is to be seen in the superior rank granted to Hephaestus, the god of smiths and potters. The Hephaestus cult plays a peculiar role in Athens. A crude and probably very ancient myth made Hephaestus, pursuing Athena, the father of Erechtheus–Erichthonius, the earth-born king. But only by 420 was a splendid festival, Hephaestia, organized (*IG* i³ 82 = *LSCG* 13) with a torch-race in honour of the god of fire, after his temple, dominating the west side of the Agora, had been completed; it is still well preserved (see above, p. 218). It housed statues of both Athena and Hephaestus. Both Athena and Hephaestus were addressed in the festival of the smiths, Chalkeia, which marked the beginning of weaving the Panathenaic *peplos*. Craftsmanship seemed to balance warlike prowess.

The anguish and triumph of the Persian Wars was nothing less than a religious experience. Many will have concurred with the word of Themistocles: 'Not we have accomplished this, but the gods and the heroes' (Hdt. viii.109.3). The defeat of the barbarians was readily ascribed to their destruction of Greek temples everywhere. The tomb of the men who fell at Thermopylae was invoked as an 'altar' by Simonides (fr. 531 *PMG*), and later Pericles would put all the men who fell for the city on a level with the immortal gods (Plut. *Per.* 8.9). There were special festivals instituted in memory of Marathon (6 Boedromion), Salamis (16 Munichion) and Plataeae (3 Boedromion); as for Marathon, the Athenians had taken a vow to sacrifice one goat for each Persian killed, and we have the word of Xenophon (*An.* iii.2.12) that by his time they had not yet come to close the account. Themistocles demonstrated his singular position by founding a cult of Artemis Aristoboule, goddess of 'best counsels' (Plut. *Them.* 22). There were unforeseen incidents to be

---

[28] Kron 1979 (D 45).

memorialized as well: the cult of Pan the goat-god, on account of a vision which appeared to the long-distance runner Philippides on his way to summon Spartan help at the time of Marathon (Hdt. VI.105); the cult of Boreas, the north wind which badly damaged the Persian fleet (Hdt. VII.189) (he, incidentally, was a son-in-law of Erechtheus): and even the cult of Pheme, 'rumour', that miraculously spread to announce the victory of the Eurymedon (Aeschin. 1.128; 11.145).

The myth of Theseus fighting the Amazons, the perversely dangerous females from the fringe of 'Asia', was applied to Athens fighting the Eastern threat. This is reflected in the imagery of Attic poetry, but it attained official sanction with the dedication of Amazon statues, wrought by the foremost artists of the day, in the most splendid temple of Asia, the Artemisium of Ephesus.[29] Needless to say, the propagation of the cult of Athena Nike, with the beautiful temple to the right of the entrance to the Acropolis, was to express similar feelings of triumph. Nike was also seen alighting on the right hand of the chryselephantine statue of Athena Parthenos.

This celebrated image by Phidias set up in the Parthenon established a new level of lavish magnificence; the similar and still more famous image of Zeus at Olympia followed suit. It was to outdo the huge golden Apollo of Delos.[30] The sanctuary of Delos, which had developed into a centre of the 'Ionians' at the time of Pisistratus and Polycrates, had been the obvious headquarters for the anti-Persian alliance. When these and the treasury had been moved to Athens, the construction of the Parthenon began. The *hellenotamiai* now officiated 'from Panathenaea to Panathenaea'. As the alliance developed into imperial rule, the allies were made to participate in the Athenian cults, in both the 'great' festivals, supplying a phallus for the Dionysia and a cow and a panoply for the Panathenaea; they were also required to contribute first-fruit offerings to Eleusis, where huge silos were built to hold the incoming grain (*IG* I³ 78). The tribute paid by the allies, talent by talent, was carried through the orchestra of the theatre when large crowds would be present for the Dionysia (Isocr. VIII.82); Athena received her share, to be assessed and controlled 'from Panathenaea to Panathenaea' (*IG* I³ 52A.27). The goddess would allow the funds to be used, among other things, for the building programme. Imperialism is approaching cynicism, without giving up the ritual frame of administration.

The last cults to be introduced in the fifth century, though, were not the result of pride and imperial control. As a belated consequence of the disastrous plague, Asclepius, the god of healing, was brought from Epidaurus to Athens in 420. The snake representing the god was carried on a waggon, and Sophocles received it in his house until the sanctuary

---

[29] P. Devambez in *LIMC* I (1981) 640–4.   [30] Fehr 1979 (E 24).

was completed. The festivals of Asclepius were thoughtfully integrated with the celebrations of the Mysteries in autumn and Dionysia in spring. The sanctuary occupied a prominent place on the south slope of the Acropolis; however, the other Asclepius sanctuary in the Piraeus seems to have enjoyed greater popularity for a while. The last addition was the cult of the Thracian goddess Bendis, interest in whom had been aroused by the campaigns in the north and by the employment of Thracian mercenaries in the Athenian armed forces.[31] This festival brought the uncommon spectacle of a torch-race on horseback. The image of the goddess was thoroughly hellenized, but the quest for new gods was beginning to reflect uncertainties of identity.

V. DIVINATION

While the functional and practical aspects of religious activity in ancient cults are easily observed – the use and abuse of prestige and influence, the display of social roles, the greedy hopes for 'all good things' – there is another, more irrational side that tends to be obscured because it may appear as sheer superstition. Although there was an absence of revelation, of a sacred scripture and a theologically trained clergy, it was still believed that there were ordinances and counsels of the gods to be observed directly, through various 'signs' such as 'sacrifices, the flight of birds, chance utterances, dreams' (Xen. *Hipparch.* 9.9). In the countless uncertainties and anxieties of everyday life, in the private suffering of disease and in the common danger of war, divination of all kinds was a momentous factor in making decisions.

The interplay of experience and tradition had long led to specialization: on the one hand there were the established oracles, above all the Pythian sanctuary at Delphi; to consult it was complicated, costly and time-consuming, but its prestige remained paramount for generations. On the other hand there were charismatic individuals, 'seers' (*manteis*), who claimed special skills in interpreting the signs sent by the gods. They usually relied on family tradition, but they had begun to use books by the sixth century. Some were found to be especially successful and acquired riches and influence. Their greatest responsibility was to determine the correct time to engage in battle. Victory was thought to belong no less to the seer than to the military commander: the Delphic monument celebrating Aegospotami represents Lysander accompanied by his *mantis* (Paus. x.9.7).

The enactment and development of cults in Athens constantly involved dealings with oracles and seers. Each major change in ritual had to be approved by Delphi; the impulse to establish new cults, but also

[31] *IG* i³ 136 with arguments for a date 413/12; *LSS* 6.

injunctions against their establishment, often came from seers. In order to have counsel permanently available, the *demos* appointed different kinds of 'expounders', *exegetai*, who either belonged to the Eleusinian Eumolpids, were selected by Delphi, or were chosen by the *demos*.[32]

Divination had played its part in overthrowing the tyrants. While Hippias was collecting oracles of Musaeus, the Alcmaeonid opposition had Delphi pronounce in favour of the liberation of Athens (no. 79).[33] The eponymous heroes of the tribes were selected by Apollo (no. 80). Probably about the same time Athenians began to build their own, still well preserved, treasury at Delphi[34] and to send, at irregular intervals to be determined by special 'signs', a sacred embassy to Delphi to offer sacrifice and to bring back sacred fire from Apollo's hearth. While we today suspect that the Delphic priests judiciously foresaw a Persian victory, contemporaries credited the defeat of the barbarians to Apollo; the tithe of the booty taken from the Persians was dedicated at Delphi in the form of splendid monuments. The Athenians especially erected monuments for Marathon and placed votive offerings from Salamis both in their treasury and in a special hall constructed beneath the temple terrace at Delphi. At that time Athens was granted *promanteia*, privileged access to the oracle. Thus Delphi was consulted with regard to the transfer of Theseus' bones (no. 113), the colonies at Thurii (no. 132) and Amphipolis (no. 133); there were regulations issued for families such as the Praxiergidae (no. 124 = *IG* I[3] 7) and surely on many more occasions. One oracle that acclaimed the *demos* of Athens as an 'eagle in the clouds' (no. 121) naturally enjoyed popularity with the Athenians. By the beginning of the Peloponnesian War, though, Apollo's attitude had changed, and the god clearly took a stand against Athens (no. 137). The oracle authorizing the cult of Bendis (no. 30) was brought from Dodona, the oracle of Zeus second in importance to Delphi. Yet in 404 a new Delphic oracle forbade the annihilation of Athens (no. 171).

The crowd of private seers in a city such as Athens must have been considerable. They were present at every sacrifice, and the officials had to heed them (Arist. *Ath.Pol.* 54.6). We know of two men, Lampon and Diopeithes, who rose to such prominence that they were repeatedly attacked in comedy. Lampon was active in the foundation of Thurii, and was even considered one of the 'founders' (*oikistes*) of the colony. He predicted that Pericles would prevail over his adversary Thucydides from the portent of a one-horned ram that had been found (Plut. *Per.* 6.2), while Anaxagoras explained the prodigy rationally through his

[32] Oliver 1950 (D 62); Clinton 1974 (K 19) 89–93.

[33] The numbers following refer to the collection of Delphic oracles in Parke and Wormell 1956 (K 72) II; these numbers are also given in the more recent catalogue of Fontenrose 1978 (K 31) (Concordance 430–5).

[34] On its controversial date, Robertson 1975 (I 140) I 167f.

knowledge of anatomy. Lampon was elected to sign important state treaties in 421 (Thuc. v.19.2, 24.1); he cooperated with Eleusis and the Delphic oracle in bringing about the decree about first-fruit offerings (*IG* 1³ 78). Diopeithes had a decree passed which threatened with prosecution for *asebeia* those who 'did not believe in the divine things or taught about things in the sky' (Plut. *Per.* 32.2); tried on this charge Anaxagoras had to leave Athens. The 'divine things' were, primarily, the 'signs' by which the gods would give their directives; in the view of a man like Diopeithes, this was the very foundation not only of piety, but even of religion. The central role such signs played in Athenian religious practice must not be underestimated.

VI. THE MYSTERIES

The festival of Eleusis, which was known simply as 'the Mysteries', is as fascinating as it is elusive. Mysteries are initiation ceremonies with the obligation to silence, and the secrecy was strictly and deliberately kept throughout pagan literature. Yet the Mysteries were open to the public: 'whoever among the Greeks wishes is initiated' (Hdt. VIII.65.4), and the huge Telesterion built by Ictinus, the architect of the Parthenon, held more than 3,000 *mystai*. The administration of the Mysteries was in the hands of the Athenian authorities, but the priestly functions inalienably belonged to the two families of the Eumolpids and the Kerykes. In investigations and lawsuits involving the Mysteries the non-initiated were bidden to leave the court; the majority would be those who 'knew'. The ephebes regularly took part in organizing and protecting the procession from Athens to Eleusis; it started at a special sanctuary above the Agora, the Eleusinium. When Diagoras, called 'the atheist', provocatively violated the secret of Eleusis, he was pursued through the whole Athenian empire, yet he escaped.

Philosophically inclined writers spoke about the 'two gifts' Demeter brought to Eleusis, grain and the Mysteries. Both were intimately linked, as the same myth about the rape of Persephone and Demeter's visit to Eleusis had to account for both. According to a late gnostic writer, an ear of corn was shown by the hierophant at the climax of the secret festival (Hippol. *Haer.* v.8.39). Yet the point of the nocturnal celebration, whatever its symbols, gestures and words might have been, was to arrive at 'better hope' for a life after death. This is already present in the earliest text, the 'Homeric' hymn to Demeter, and it persisted to the end of antiquity. The promise seems to have been general, with different possibilities of interpretation.

We are well informed about the general programme (*IG* II/III² 1078 = *LSCG* 8) and some details of organization. At some time participation in the 'Lesser Mysteries' in spring was made a prerequisite

(Pl. *Gorg.* 497c). On 15 Boedromion the candidates assembled at Athens. There were purifications, including bathing in the sea, and the sacrifice of piglets, one for each person. Some kind of verbal explanation and instruction that prepared for what was to be 'seen' on the concluding night must have been part of the proceedings. The main event was the procession on the 'sacred way' to Eleusis, some 30 km from the city, on 19 Boedromion. Priestesses carried 'holy things' in closed baskets (*kistai*, while the crowd chanted the rhythmical cry '*Iakch' o Iakche*'; this was soon understood as the invocation of a special *daimon*, Iakchos. With the arrival at the Eleusinian sanctuary the fast was broken, and after sunset the really secret rites began. We have some allusions: 'wandering to and fro', terror in the dark, and sudden 'amazement' (Plut. fr. 178 Sandbach); the Telesterion opened to admit the crowd, there were things 'done' by the hierophant and the priestesses, presumably in the dark, dimly lit by the torches of the torchbearer (*daduchos*); at some point a huge fire blazed up in the middle, 'under' which the hierophant was seen officiating. Persephone was called from the dead and somehow 'appeared', the hierophant exhibited the ear of corn, and proclaimed the birth of a divine child. The construction of the Telesterion gives some guidance to imagination, with steps rising on all four sides for the onlookers, and the *anaktoron*, a small rectangular building slightly off-centre with a door at its side, where the hierophant had his throne. 'Thrice fortunate he who has seen these *orgia*,' the shouts proclaimed. Yet we remain outside the circle of those who 'knew'. Dances outside the building must have followed throughout the night, and there were bull sacrifices which guaranteed a copious feast even here.

The Mysteries became part of the prestige of Athens and retained their authority, and their identity, for about one thousand years. They make strange company in the age of Euripides and Socrates. It remains for us to speculate how the Greeks succeeded in this very special festival in finding sense and 'better hopes' against the apparent senselessness of death.

VII. PRIVATE PIETY

A pious man is one who is seen performing sacrifice and is known to make use of divination: these are the criteria by which Xenophon (*Mem.* I.1.2) tries to disprove the charge of *asebeia* against Socrates. Sacrifice, primarily animal sacrifice accompanied by libations and incense, goes together with prayers or rather vows which, if fulfilled, lead to votive dedications. All these activities involve spending property; the problem of whether the rich have better access to the gods begins to be discussed in this period.

State cult and private worship are not to be seen as contrasts; they are parallel and often intertwined. Like each private household, the city observes rites in honour of Hestia, Apollo and Zeus. A very wealthy and pious man such as Nicias made lavish dedications at Delos and Delphi, but every Athenian could go to the Acropolis to offer a humble gift to the goddess. The inscriptions and material remains from the Acropolis attest numerous, varied, and simple votives at this time.[35] The state cult would guarantee a rich meal to the citizens, at the Panathenaea, for instance; at the Apaturia and the Anthesteria, family celebration and public cult practically coincided. Each major business contract was sealed by oaths in a sanctuary. No merchant dared to engage in sea-faring without vows to the appropriate gods. The work of the peasant was obviously dependent upon Demeter and Dionysus. In sickness everybody would turn to the gods. Pericles installed a cult of Athena Hygieia on the Acropolis when a good craftsman, incidentally wounded in the construction of the Propylaea, had recovered (Plut. *Per.* 13.13). This cult was meant to bring together the goddess and private needs more closely; it was soon overshadowed, however, by Asclepius.

There were countless minor sanctuaries installed by associations, families, or even individuals on special occasions. About 400 B.C., Archedemus, 'seized by the nymphs', adorned the cave of Vari south of Athens with inscriptions and reliefs (*IG* I² 778–80), solving, as we would put it, a private identity crisis through ritual activity. Beautiful offerings connected mainly with marriage, it seems, survive from the small precinct of 'the nymph' on the south slope of the Acropolis.[36] The cult of nymphs, goddesses of living water, was popular everywhere, as was Hermes: pillars of Hermes (Herms) were set up in both town and countryside to mark crossroads and neighbourhoods – vase paintings often show private sacrifices in front of them. Local associations, observing the cult of Heracles with substantial feasts, spread over the whole of Attica. There were still more groups celebrating Dionysus, Bacchic *thiasoi*, not always easy to distinguish from simple drinking parties.

It is perhaps more interesting that even women could be called together for private Baccheia (Ar. *Lys.* 11). Conspicuous was the cult of Adonis, the dying god beloved by Aphrodite. From Phoenicia the cult had spread to Greece by the time of Sappho, but it never received official status in the cities. The women raised a shrill lament over the death of the god from the roofs of their houses in early summer, disconcerting for men and men's business (Ar. *Lys.* 389–96).

Another foreign god who became notorious was Sabazios, a Phrygian variant of Dionysus. In certain Dionysiac *thiasoi*, the mythical singer

[35] *IG* I² 401–760; Raubitschek 1949 (C 162); Graef and Langlotz 1933 (I 70) nos. 1330–417.
[36] Travlos 1971 (I 171) 361–3.

Fig. 35. Lead puppet in a box, from the Ceramicus cemetery, Athens. (After *Ath. Mitt.* 81
(1966) Beilage 1; cf. Kurtz and Boardman 1971
(K 54) p. 46.)

Orpheus was claimed as an authority, books of Orpheus were presented,
and through a special and partially secret mythology startling doctrines
about metempsychosis and the divinity of the human soul were circu-
lated in radical opposition to the prevailing system of values; a special
form of 'life' was demanded; a totally new kind of spirituality could be
seen to be on its way. It is not clear, though, to what degree any
permanent groups or 'sects' or 'Orphics' were established; the cult was
promoted rather by itinerant 'purifiers' (*orpheotelestai*), who offered
initiations as a cure for various practical needs. But some suspicion
about private mysteries and new gods began to grow among the public.
Some of this is seen in the picture drawn of the Socratic circle in the
Clouds of Aristophanes in 423, and fun turned to hysteria with the
mystery scandal of Alcibiades in 415, which resulted in numerous
executions.

The trends towards the end of the century are not moving in any one
direction. There is rational detachment, there is a quest for a new
philosophical religion, there is scrupulous conservatism, there is growth
even of sheer superstition. While scientific medicine launched theoretical
attacks on healing by magic, amulets were provided even for Pericles
when struck by the plague (Plut. *Per.* 38.2), and from the end of the
century comes the oldest *defixio* found at Athens, a puppet pierced and
buried in the Ceramicus to harm an enemy (Fig. 35);[37] this was meant to
be serious. Intellectuals were developing new concepts of pure divinity,
all-powerful, all-knowing and without human shape, passions or needs,
yet practical manipulation remained a strong element in the piety of the
man in the street. There was growing complexity, but a radical break did
not come for centuries.

[37] Trumpf 1958 (K 87); Jeffery 1955 (C 136) 67–76.

CHAPTER 8f

ATHENIAN RELIGION AND LITERATURE

B. M. W. KNOX

I. INTRODUCTION

In the context of modern Western thought a title which associates these two words raises expectations that the text so introduced will discuss the influence exercised on written works of the imagination by the doctrines of a religious establishment and the adaptation or critique of those doctrines by the writers of the works. For fifth-century Athens, however, the terms 'religion' and 'literature' (neither of which has a satisfactory equivalent in ancient Greek) serve to designate activities which differ significantly from their modern counterparts.

Literature, for us, is something written and to be read, but, though there were undoubtedly books and readers in fifth-century Athens, the principal medium of literary communication was not written text but public performance. The Homeric epics were recited by trained specialists who excelled in dramatic presentation; epinician odes for victories won at the great athletic games were sung by a dancing chorus at the victor's home; dithyramb, tragedy and comedy were competitive events mounted at the city's expense in the huge theatre of Dionysus. All this is not to say that there were no books or readers in fifth-century Athens; the evidence, literary and pictorial, suggests widespread literacy and even, in the final decades of the century, a book trade. But there can be no doubt that for most Athenians the message of the poets, lyric, epic and above all dramatic, was conveyed not by the written word but by the word spoken and sung.

For the fifth-century Athenian audience the dominant literary phenomenon was the drama. Epic was a voice from the far past; lyric and choral poetry a fading tradition, associated with the aristocratic and tyrannic regimes of the Archaic period. But tragedy and comedy, though their origin can be traced at least as far back as the era of Pisistratus, owed the splendour of their fifth century achievements to the democracy which had played so crucial a role in the defeat of the Persians. The festivals which were the occasion for these dramatic performances, the Dionysia and Lenaea, were high points of the civic calendar; they were also ceremonial days in the city's religious calendar, for the performances were a celebration of the god Dionysus.

By the fifth century the cult of Dionysus was widespread in Greece, but it was only at Athens that it gave birth to the theatre. The nature of the process which gave rise to this unique development is unfortunately far from clear. In literary treatments of the Dionysiac myth (the *Bacchae* of Euripides chief among them), as well as on black- and red-figure Athenian pottery, the Dionysiac cult is portrayed as an ecstatic religion which released the worshippers from the bonds of constraint imposed by civilized life. It appealed especially to the women, confined as they were in Greek society to the house and the daily round of household duties; it sent them out to dance, dressed in fawnskins, on the hills among the pine trees as Maenads, the mad women of Dionysus. The god brings a temporary return to nature, to communion with the creatures of the wild and an assumption of their innocence and strength. None of this, however, is reflected in the organization of the festivities which in fifth-century Athens bore the name of the god, Dionysia, and his female devotees (*lenae*), the Lenaea. To judge from the cult aspects of the dramatic festivals, Dionysus seems to have come to Attica not as a spirit of the wild forest but as a fertility god, with power over the agricultural crops on which the city's life depended. This is how he appears in the *Acharnians* (241–83) of Aristophanes, where Dicaeopolis, proud beneficiary of a separate peace, celebrates the Rural Dionysia (*ta kat' agrous*), a festival held in December, which, it seems likely, was thought to promote the growth of the autumn sowing. Dicaeopolis' daughter carries a basket containing offerings to the god (a cake with gravy ladled on it), slaves follow carrying *phalloi* on poles and Dicaeopolis brings up the rear chanting a ribald hymn to Phales, companion of Dionysus (it contains what look like crude insults aimed at individuals). All these features recur in the magnificent preliminaries to the dramatic performances at the City or Great Dionysia, which were held in March–April. The basket carrier (*kanephoros*) was of noble birth and her basket was of gold, the sacrifices included a bull and other offerings besides, *phalloi* were carried and, though we have little direct testimony to their appearance, the revellers of the procession almost certainly indulged in the satiric songs characteristic of Athenian processions. This procession, *pompe*, was the prelude to a four-day religious holiday (shortened to three days during the Peloponnesian War). The statue of the god was brought in and seated to watch the dramatic performances; the theatre was purified by the sacrifice of a pig and libations poured by the generals; public business (except in emergencies) was suspended and prisoners released on bail for the duration of the festival.

Drama emerged from a context of ritual celebration and remained even in its developed form an act of worship, honouring the god in his precinct. The origins of modern European drama offer a striking parallel: the key role played by the dramatic presentation of the Easter service, the trope known as *Quem quaeritis* – the words the angel addresses to three Maries at the tomb. But the surface aspects of the parallel draw attention in fact to the total dissimilarity of the two cases. The Christian play was based on a sacred book, interpreted with incontestable authority by an organized supranational priesthood, a powerful hierarchy exerting immense spiritual influence and backed by impressive economic resources. In Greece no such priestly organization existed (priests were for the most part technicians of ritual sacrifice presiding over local and family cult); there was no holy book, no fixed sacred history, no ethical code based on divine revelation. For their vision of their gods and the relation of those gods to human life and morality the fifth-century Athenians still relied on the poets, Homer and Hesiod in particular. All through the Archaic period the problem of the connexion between these Olympian deities and human ideals of justice and morality was a theme for the poets. Heraclitus and Xenophanes criticized Homer and Hesiod in harsh terms but Theognis appealed for understanding – 'Dear Zeus, I wonder at you . . . how can your mind bear to treat the wicked and the good man alike?' (375–8); Solon tried to justify the ways of Zeus to man by the slowness of justice which may fall on the sinner's descendants. Theology, in fact, was in Greece the business of the poets before it became the concern of the sophists and fourth-century philosophers, and Attic tragedy which dramatized, in a religious context, the central myths of the Greek past, stories of heroic action locked in a pattern of divine prophecy and intervention, assumed the same prerogative and burden. The relation between 'religion' and 'literature' was a phenomenon unique in the history of the West.

The performances staged at the two festivals were a celebration of the god; the celebrant was the city of Athens, the polis itself. The organization and financing of the dramatic festivals was the responsibility of the city's annually elected magistrates and the Dionysia was a demonstration to the Greek world of Athenian imperial power and of that cultural supremacy which made Athens, in Pericles' proud phrase, 'the education of Greece'. Unlike the Lenaea, celebrated in December, when stormy weather on the Aegean restricted the audience to native Athenians, the Dionysia, which marked the opening of the sailing season, attracted visitors, private and official, from all over the Greek world. Once arrived, they saw the tribute from the cities of the Delian League displayed in the theatre, watched the orphaned sons of Athenian battle casualties, now fully grown and equipped with arms by the state, paraded in the theatre to receive the blessings of the people, and heard

Fig. 36. Satyr player from an Attic red-figure cup by
Makron, about 490 B.C. (Munich, Antikensammlungen
2657; ARV^2 475, 267; cf. Boardman 1975 (1 17) fig. 314.)

the proclamation of decrees honouring foreigners and citizens who had
distinguished themselves by service to the Athenian state.

After these preliminaries the huge audience (the theatre could probably hold some 14,000 people) sat through the performance of twenty
dithyrambs, three sets of three tragedies, each followed by a satyr play,
and five comedies (the number was cut to three during the Peloponnesian War). The dithyrambs were lyric poems sung and danced by a
chorus of fifty which danced in a circle; ten choruses of boys and ten of
men (representing the ten Athenian tribes) competed for prizes. We have
very little idea of the nature of these dithyrambic poems. Their lyric style
was proverbially exalted and ornate and we have reason to believe that
by mid-century the music became more important than the words. This
event, however, was the one most calculated to rouse the partisan
emotions of the audience, for the ten different choruses of boys, like
those of men, represented the ten Athenian tribes in competition for a
prize. The three tragic poets had a day each for the presentation of three
tragedies; they were followed by a satyr play. This, as its name indicates,
had a chorus of satyrs, the grotesquely phallic companions of Dionysus
in myth and art (Fig. 36); it presented the mythic material in tones
ranging from light-hearted to burlesque. The comic poets offered one
play apiece; during the war when there were only three comedies instead
of five, they came last in the day, after the satyr play.

The planning for the festival had begun long before. One of the first
tasks of the incoming eponymous archon was to assign *choregoi* for the
tragic and comic contests – one for each competing poet; the *choregoi* for

the dithyrambs seem to have been elected by the members of the tribes. The *choregos* was a wealthy citizen who assumed responsibility for the training of the chorus, its costumes and salaries, as well as the salaries of trainers and musicians. This form of imposed public service (the Greek name for it has become our word 'liturgy') was standard practice in democratic Athens; the same procedure was used to provide for other state and tribal ceremonies and, in an emergency, to finance the equipment, maintenance and repair of warships. A citizen might appeal against his selection for such expensive honours, name someone wealthier who could better afford it, and even offer to exchange property with him if he challenged that estimate. But such attempts at evasion were uncommon; the *choregia* was regarded as a privilege as well as a duty, as is clear from the fact that though resident aliens could serve as *choregoi* for the Lenaea, only citizens were called on for the Greater Dionysia. The post conferred conspicuous public honours. The *choregos* of the tribe victorious in the dithyrambic contest received, as the representative of his tribe, a tripod, for which he built a monumental base, inscribed with his name, that of the tribe, the flute-player, the poet and the archon; there was a whole street of such monuments and one, that of Lysicrates (334 B.C.), is still standing in Athens. The *choregos* had a place of honour in the splendid procession with which the festival began; Alcibiades used to wear a purple robe for it (Ath. XII.534C) and Demosthenes had prepared a gold crown and a gold-embroidered cloak for the occasion. Furthermore, fulfilment of this liturgy could be cited in the courts as testimony to the speaker's democratic loyalty and public spirit (cf. Lys. XXI.1–5, XIX.29).

The actors were paid by the city and assigned by the archon, who also selected the poets for the occasion. We have no account of how this was done; presumably aspirants read their scripts to him. The prizes at the contest itself, for the poets and later for the actors, were assigned by judges who had been selected through an elaborate system of sortition designed to eliminate personal influence (though they were certainly subject to another form of influence, the audience reaction to the performance). In this respect, as in every detail of its organization, the theatre of Dionysus reflected, like the law courts and the Assembly, the egalitarian spirit of democratic Athens.

II. TRAGEDY

Plays produced in such a thoroughly civic context could be expected, their mythical content notwithstanding, to reflect social and political concerns and this is indeed the case, though in tragedy specific contemporary allusions were avoided. In six of the extant plays of

Aeschylus, for example, the outcome of the tragic action determines the fate not just of individuals but of a city (or, in the case of the *Persians*, an empire). But this political element, far from clashing with the solemn religious note and deep moral concern characteristic of Greek tragedy, combines with it and is in fact often inseparable from it, just as, in the real life of the cities, it was sometimes difficult, if not impossible, to distinguish clearly the political from the religious. The oracle at Delphi, for example, was the voice of Apollo, who expressed the will of his father Zeus, but it was at the same time a powerful arbiter in relations between the Greek states on matters involving both peace and war. At Athens the new temple on the Acropolis, the Parthenon, was a shrine of the city's patron goddess Athena; in its inmost recesses were stored the Athenian war reserves, the tribute from the allies. And in the mythical tales which the poets shaped to form a dramatic vision of the Greek past, the gods were manifest in the patterns of the action even when they were not actually represented on the stage.

The earliest tragedy we have, Aeschylus' *Persians* (produced in 472), is an anomaly: it is set, unlike the plays which accompanied it, not in mythical time but in contemporary reality. It deals with events which everyone in the audience had lived through and presents to a people seated among the burned-out ruins of their city an idealized vision of the war which shows no trace of hatred or contempt for the defeated invader, gives no hint of the disunity of the Greeks and the fact that many of them had fought on the Persian side. It mentions no Greek leaders by name and makes no allusion to their partisan quarrels, past and present. What it does is to create a dramatic world resonant with the poetic and religious values inherent in the great myths which were the normal basis of tragedy. Though the Greeks, and Athens in particular, are given full credit for their endurance and courage, the glory for the great sea battle is ascribed to heaven – 'some power divine', says the Persian messenger, 'has destroyed our host, weighing down the scale with unequal fortune' (345–6).

The divine motive is not so much partiality for the Greeks as anger against Xerxes, who has overstepped the limits of human power by building a bridge across Hellespont; his destruction of the temples and the divine images in Greece is one more proof of his impious folly. This simple scheme of transgression and punishment is however darkened by a theological complication which will recur in sinister emphasis throughout Aeschylean drama: Xerxes is as much a victim as sinner, for he has been tempted to ruin. 'What mortal man', sings the chorus early in the play, 'shall escape the cunning deceit of a god? . . . For, fawning kindly on him at first, Delusion leads a mortal astray into the nets . . .' (94ff).

In *Seven Against Thebes* (467) the fate of a city hangs in the balance as the decisive assault is launched against its walls. The city is saved, but its defender Eteocles dies killing his brother; heroic defender of the city though he may be, he is also the heir to a father's curse and a tainted heredity reaching back over generations. The nature of his motivation when, at the climax of the play's great central scene, he decides to face his brother at the seventh gate, is complex. But one thing seems certain: his action is the final manifestation of a curse imposed on Laius as punishment for his failure to obey Apollo's command: 'Die without issue; save the city' (*Sept.* 747–8). Aeschylus here used the trilogy (the two preceding plays, now lost, were called *Laius* and *Oedipus*) to show the working of the divine will over three generations, its culmination the extinction of the male line of Laius. He was to exploit trilogic form for similar ends again, but on a grander scale and with a more reassuring denouement, in the *Oresteia* of 458.

The *Suppliants* (probably produced between 465 and 459) is the first play of a trilogy which traced the story of the daughters of Danaus from their acceptance as suppliants at Argos, through the defeat of Argos by their Egyptian suitors and the forced marriage which followed, to their murder of their husbands on the wedding night. The refusal of marriage, an obsessive theme of their lyric odes in the first play, seems to be specifically reproved by the goddess Aphrodite in a fragment of the last play (Mette 125), a speech which celebrates the universal power of Eros. The political element is not absent, since the king of Argos has to face the danger involved in sheltering suppliants whose enemies may attack his city – as indeed they do, successfully; the king's pious action ends in disaster for him and his city. How this religious problem is resolved we do not know exactly, but the *Suppliants* is remarkable for its solemn lyric evocations of the power of Zeus and the impenetrable mystery of his will. 'What the desire of Zeus may be is not easy to track down . . . The paths of his mind stretch dark and tangled, impervious to sight' (*Suppl.* 87–90).

In the *Oresteia* (458) the themes of the earlier plays are combined with new elements to produce the intricate patterns of a dramatic world which recognizes no distinction between the theological and the social, the mythical and the historical. The curse on the house of Atreus is also the operation of a primitive system of justice by vengeance; its guarantors are the Erinyes, terrifying spirits of vengeance personified, who, in the dilemma posed by Orestes' murder of Clytemnestra, champion the rights of the mother against the husband, of the blood bond which is the tribal warrant for private vengeance against the marriage bond which is the city's affirmation of the domination of the male. Against the Erinyes stands Apollo, who claims to speak for a Zeus whose inscrutable will, hymned by the chorus of the *Agamemnon* in some of the greatest lines in Greek poetry, manifests itself through human crime and suffering to an end which is unforeseen even by Apollo: the reconciliation of the Erinyes with the city which, through the court of the Areopagus convened by Athena, has decided against them, the reconciliation also, as the closing words of the trilogy proclaim, of all-seeing Zeus and Destiny.

The trilogy is also a charter myth of the Areopagus and it was produced at a time when the democratic leaders Ephialtes and Pericles had recently stripped that august body of its political power, confining its sphere of action to the judicial. The question of Aeschylus' stand on this controversial reform has been much debated but no agreement has been reached and it seems likely that the original audience did not think of the play in such terms at all. Aeschylus spurs the audience to think and to sympathize; he does not tell them what to think. He shows them the roots of their contemporary institutions in the mythical past, emphasizes the continuity of their history with the age of gods and heroes and, leaving the question of Ephialtes' reforms open (but in such a way that partisans on either side can feel the dignity of their position enhanced), he presents his fellow citizens with a vision of advancing Athenian progress and power. 'Time as it flows onward', says Athena to the Erinyes, 'will bring ever more honour to these citizens' (853–4). But it is honour that has to be won, like the acquittal of Orestes, through that struggle and suffering which are the will of Zeus 'who has set mortal men on the road to right thinking, laid down this law to hold good: Learn by Suffering' (*Ag.* 176–7).

Prometheus Bound is so anomalous a play in so many respects that doubts of its Aeschylean authorship, first expressed over a hundred years ago, are still widespread. There is a fair measure of agreement, however, that it is a fifth-century tragedy and it is certainly one which must figure in any discussion of religion. Its characters are all gods, Titans or sea nymphs with the single exception of Io, a human victim of Zeus, changed into a heifer by his jealous wife Hera. The play's delineation of Zeus as a merciless tyrant seems a world away from the reverent brooding on the mysteries of his will so characteristic of the other plays. Zeus, however, is presented to us always from the standpoint of his opponent; and we know that in the lost second play, *Prometheus Released*, a reconciliation takes place between the two great adversaries. And even in the first play, as Prometheus prophesies the eventual birth of Heracles, his deliverer, from the line of Io, we note that characteristic Aeschylean sense of the mystery of the will of Zeus, working through apparent evil to good.

One of the counts against the authenticity of *Prometheus Bound* is the author's apparent familiarity with sophistic rhetoric and even sophistic teaching, for the long speeches which detail the Titan's gifts to mankind have been thought to reflect the influence of Protagoras' famous book on the development of human civilization. Since Aeschylus died in 456 B.C., such influence is, in his case, hardly possible but the younger dramatists, Sophocles, whose first production at the Dionysia was in 468 and Euripides, whose début was in 455, were certainly exposed to and affected by the questioning, critical attitudes and the new ideas of the men, all of them non-citizens, who dominated Athenian intellectual circles in the last half of the century. The older poet, Sophocles, shows the impact of sophistic thought in a strong reaction against it: the famous first stasimon of *Antigone*, for example, certainly betrays acquaintance with Protagorean teaching and sketches in unforgettable lines man's conquest of his environment; but it concludes with a reminder that he cannot conquer death, a warning that his ingenuity may lead to evil as well as to good, and a solemn injunction to respect the justice of the gods. This tension is a constant in Sophocles' tragic vision: an admiration for human greatness is combined with sorrow for its inevitable fall. The confident note of the last scene of the *Oresteia*, the city launched on its forward course under divine protection, is never heard again.

Unlike his predecessor who, born when Hippias was tyrant, saw the establishment of democracy and defended it at Marathon and Salamis, Sophocles had grown up in the expanding Athens of the Delian League, which became an empire. He had seen the fulfilment of Athena's prophecy in the *Eumenides*, had indeed played his own part in Athens' spectacular advance by serving in high office, civil and military. But in the plays we still possess (most of them dating from the last thirty years of his long life), the polis, the high point of man's march to civilization in the *Antigone* stasimon (*Ant.* 355–6), is no longer the place of judgement and reconciliation as in the *Oresteia*. The polis in Sophocles is seen as a problem rather than a solution. In *Ajax*, *Philoctetes*, *Antigone* and *Oedipus at Colonus*, for example, the hero bitterly opposes the representatives of the polis (or of the *stratos*, the polis in arms) and in all four cases the spokesman for the polis, the Atridae, Odysseus and Creon, are, to say the least, unsympathetic characters. And in two of the plays, *Ajax* and *Antigone*, the grounds for opposition to the community are religious: they are the defence of a dead man's right to burial.

In the case of Ajax we are left in no doubt that his actions and attitudes are hateful to the gods, for the goddess Athena in person makes this clear; nevertheless his right to burial is vindicated against the savage sentence of the two kings. Antigone is never so explicitly disowned by the gods though she considers herself abandoned by them (*Ant.* 922–3) and they allow her to die; yet they assert the rightness of her action through the prophet Tiresias and avenge her, as she prayed they would (*Ant.* 927–8), by the destruction of Creon's wife and son. Though both plays shed an ambiguous light on the character and situation of the hero, they strongly suggest that there are some areas of conduct for which the polis cannot prescribe, some spheres in which a higher religious law prevails. But the will of the gods in Sophocles is never clearly spelled out; usually it manifests itself through prophecies, divine pronouncements which, neglected or misinterpreted, are understood too late to affect action. The will of heaven is a mystery. 'Since the gods conceal all things divine', runs a fragment of a lost Sophoclean play, 'you will never understand them, not though you go searching to the ends of the earth' (fr. 919 *TGrF*).

There are some aspects of the religious element in Sophoclean tragedy which seem to stem from sources darker and deeper than the final Aeschylean vision of civic order based on divine reconciliation. The focus of his tragedy is often not the community but the lonely, stubborn protagonist who defies it, recalcitrant to the end, impervious to persuasion or threat; in the harsh but magnificent intransigence of Antigone, the vindictive wrath of Ajax, the suicidal obstinacy of Philoctetes and above all in the terrifying curse old Oedipus pronounces on his son we can feel something of the awe and terror inspired by hero-cult, the sacrifices made on the hero's grave (real or supposed) to placate and avert his wrath. But hero-cult is not the only archaic belief that finds expression in Sophoclean tragedy; there is also a remarkable insistence on a primitive taboo which is repudiated by both Aeschylus and Euripides, implicitly in the *Oresteia* and explicitly in the *Heracles*. This is the idea of pollution: the ineradicable and communicable impurity of the man who has shed blood. In Aeschylus, Orestes is particularly tainted, since the blood is his mother's; he is instructed by Apollo to purify himself by means of sacrifices and at Athens makes the claim to Athena that his hands were clean when he sat in supplication at her image. The claim is dismissed by the Erinyes but accepted by Athena and the court; no further mention of pollution is made. In Euripides' *Heracles*, the hero, in a fit of madness sent by Hera, has murdered his wife and children; invited to Athens by his friend Theseus he is reluctant to accept because of the pollution which makes him an outcast from society. Theseus not only urges purification by sacrifice (*HF* 1324) he also, in a line which 'though stated in pious terms exhibits a new rationalistic spirit',[1] rejects the doctrine that pollution could affect the elements. At the end of the play, when Heracles hesitates to take his hand – 'I am afraid I may smear your garments with blood' (pollution literal as well as symbolic) – Theseus replies with a contemptuous dismissal of such fears: 'Wipe it off,

[1] G. W. Bond, ed. *Euripides, Heracles* (Oxford 1981) on ll. 1232–4.

don't hold back. I don't care' (*HF* 1400). But Sophoclean tragedy does not treat this matter so lightly. When Creon comes out of the palace to find the blind Oedipus wandering in the light of day, he reproves his servants fiercely for allowing such an unholy object to remain uncovered. Oedipus makes no objection to this estimate of his condition: he begs to be expelled from Thebes without delay, to be sent to the wilderness where no one will speak to him (*OT* 1436–7). Many years later, at Colonus, when he has come to realize that he bears no moral responsibility for the actions that have made his name a byword and at a moment when he knows he is now being guided to his resting place by the gods who will, in fact, call him by name in the last moments of his life (*OC* 1627–8), he still feels the pollution strong upon him. He asks for the hand of Theseus, who has restored his daughters to him. But this is followed at once by a shocked renunciation. 'But what am I saying? How could I, a man born for misery, wish to touch one with whom there lives no strain of evils?' Theseus makes no demur to this; the contrast with the Euripidean scene, produced some years before, may be deliberate. Oedipus goes still polluted in the eyes of men to his hero's grave. In this, as in so many other aspects of his drama, we can find justification for Dodds' perceptive estimate, that Sophocles was 'the last great exponent of the archaic world view'.[2]

To air on the stage such a radical rejection of belief in pollution as the words Euripides gave his Theseus was a bold gesture, for such belief was widespread and deep rooted; it is reflected in Athenian judicial procedure and legal oratory. But this was not the only aspect of popular religion which was exposed to criticism in Euripidean drama; even more radical and frequent is the attack on prophecy, which in Sophocles is always vindicated, and on human prophets, who in Sophocles are always presented in an aura of respect, even reverence. Euripidean characters are apt to dismiss human soothsayers with scornful contempt (e.g. *Hel.* 744–57, *IA* 956–68), but even divine prophecy does not escape unscathed. In the *Ion*, Apollo, the prophetic spokesman of Zeus, is apparently unable to foresee the failure of his plan to palm his son by Creusa off on Xuthus, revealing the truth to Creusa only when Ion reaches Athens (*Ion* 71–2); furthermore, the god's oracle tells Xuthus a plain lie.

A sceptical attitude towards prophecy, however, was by no means rare in the last half and especially in the last years of the fifth century. Thucydides remarks acidly of the many prophecies made about the length of the war that only one was correct. And Aristophanes in *Birds* (959–91) and *Knights* (996–1095) makes outrageous fun of professional prophets and their wares. The Euripidean presentation of Apollo in *Ion*,

[2] Dodds 1951 (J 26) 49.

however, is a different matter; whether it is to be taken as a serious indictment of Apolline prophecy or a light-hearted handling of the god's peccadilloes appropriate for a play which in many respects foreshadows Menandrian comedy, it goes far beyond the norms of popular scepticism. But this does not mean that Euripides was an atheist, still less that his tragedies denied the existence of the gods, as Aristophanes claimed in jest (*Thesm.* 450–1), and some modern critics have claimed in all seriousness. A dramatist who wants to demonstrate the non-existence of gods does not create such impressive stage presences as the Aphrodite of *Hippolytus*, the Poseidon and Athena of *Troades*, the Lyssa and Iris of *Heracles*, and above all, the Dionysus of *Bacchae*.

Bacchae is not only a Dionysiac Passion Play – a powerful enactment of the religion's central mystery, the tearing apart of the god-substitute – it is also an exploration of the varieties of experience offered by the god and the wide range of reactions to his cult. It exposed the audience to the time-serving pliancy of old Cadmus, the hollow professionalism of Tiresias, the revulsion charged with prurient curiosity of Pentheus, the god's smiling passivity and merciless revenge, Agave's deluded exaltation and her cruel awakening to reality, the paradisial innocence of the Maenads in the pine-woods and their ferocity when disturbed and, above all, the revelation, in the magnificent poetry of the choral odes, of the Dionysiac ecstasy, the abandon of the barefoot night-long dances (862ff), the savage 'joy of the living flesh devoured' (*omophagon charin* 138, tr. E. R. Dodds). This fascination with religious phenomena is characteristic of Euripides; it surfaces elsewhere in the exquisite prayer to Artemis of Hippolytus, whose total abstinence from sexual intercourse is a singular rarity in the pre-Christian world, and in the innocent trust in Apollo of Ion the Delphic temple servant and the charming naivety of his morning song as he cleans the approaches to the shrine. Gods are ubiquitous on the Euripidean stage; five of the extant plays (and one of the lost) have their prologues delivered by gods (in *Alcestis* and *Troades* two gods appear), and in nine of the extant and two of the fragmentary plays a god appears in majesty at the end to settle accounts, offer explanations and predict the future.

These last-minute epiphanies have been severely criticized ever since Plato made the sarcastic comment that the tragic poets, when they are at their wits' end, fall back on the machine and bring in the gods on high (*Crat.* 425d). It may be that at the time Plato was writing, such divine appearances had become a tiresome routine, but it is remarkable that Aristophanes, who does not miss many Euripidean targets, makes no similar complaint in the *Frogs*. In Euripides, in fact, the *deus ex machina* is much more than a convenient device for rescuing the protagonists from impossible situations and the dramatist from contradictions. Unlike

Sophocles, whose play endings are often enigmatic (*Electra* is not alone in this), Euripides seems to have felt the need to compensate for the abandonment of trilogic form by reinserting his dramatic excerpt in the mainstream of myth. This could only be done by a character who foretells the future and so the prophet is usually a god. But these gods do more than explain and prophesy; they also give directions for the burial of the dead (*Andromache*, *Electra*, *Antiope*, *Erechtheus*) and establish religious rites: the cult of Hippolytus at Troezen (*Hipp.* 1423ff), of Artemis Tauropolos (*IT* 1450ff) and the Hyakinthides (*Erechtheus* fr. 65, 74ff, Austin) in Attica.

The gods are a solid reality in Euripidean drama: Euripides' place of honour among the atheists in the ancient doxographic tradition must be due to reliance on passages quoted out of context. For the role these gods play in the government of the universe and human life is discussed by Euripidean characters with a freedom and sophistication which owes much to the philosophical speculation of the age. Hecuba's address to Zeus in *Troades* is a celebrated example: 'O you', she says 'that are the earth's support and also have your seat upon the earth, whoever you may be, for knowledge is beyond our conjecture, Zeus, whether you are nature's law of necessity or the mind of man...' (*Tro.* 884–6). Sometimes the characters reprove the gods for their cruelty or neglect; similar sentiments are to be found in the other dramatists too but in Euripides they are expressed with a particularly uncompromising vehemence. 'Great god though you are', says Amphitryon when he sees no hope for the wife and children of Heracles, son of Zeus, 'I, a mortal, surpass you in manly virtue... You must be a stupid god or unjust right through' (*HF* 342, 347). In other plays the gods are called on to show themselves morally superior to men, in particular, to show mercy. So Cadmus appeals to Dionysus, 'Gods should not be like mortals in their passion' (*Ba.* 1348), and Hippolytus' old servant to Aphrodite, 'gods should be wiser than mortals' (*Hipp.* 120). Needless to say, both appeals fall on deaf ears and though the children of Heracles are saved from the tyrant Lycus, they are reserved for something worse – to be killed by their own father.

Euripides' gods are utterly indifferent to human ideals of morality and justice. Sophocles' Athena in *Ajax* exacts a terrible payment from the hero for his neglect but she bases her conduct on an ethical claim – that the gods love those who are wise in heart (*sophronas*) and detest evildoers (*Aj.* 132–3), and the intervention of Heracles in *Philoctetes* is beneficent, for Philoctetes will win not only health but glory; furthermore Heracles speaks not only of himself as a model for the hero in his pursuit of excellence (*Phil.* 1418–22), but of mankind's duty to show reverence for things divine (1441–3). In *Antigone* the gods, through their prophet Tiresias, show their approval of her action, and even Oedipus, whose destiny in *Oedipus Tyrannus* seems to raise unanswered questions about divine justice, is welcomed by the gods in the last play (*OC* 1627–8). But in Euripides the gods demand only one thing of mortals: submission. Aphrodite cites no justification for her destruction of Hippolytus and Phaedra other than his neglect of her rites; Dionysus has no mercy on Cadmus, who tried, at the last moment, to join in his worship. And Athena in *Troades* turns against the Achaeans whom she has so far favoured; for one man's crime against her left unpunished she joins Poseidon to destroy the whole Achaean fleet. This play in fact presents the ironic spectacle of a series of Achaean atrocities which would be enough, in human eyes, to justify the destruction at sea which awaits them; the prologue shows, however, that their punishment has nothing to do with the sacrifice of Polyxena or the appalling murder of the child Astyanax; the Achaeans will be paying with their lives simply because a goddess considers herself insulted. It may be that some subtle theological point is being made here – the apparently random coincidence of divine action with human expectations of justice – but no such explanation offers itself for the inflicting of homicidal madness on Heracles after the completion of his labours for mankind, or for the destruction of Hippolytus and Phaedra. Their deaths in fact are explained as incidental products of an eternal struggle between Aphrodite and Artemis (*Hipp.* 1327–34), which will produce yet another human victim when Artemis, in her turn, destroys a favourite of Aphrodite (*Hipp.* 1420–2). These gods are like those of the *Iliad*, who bargain for the fate of men and cities in their private quarrels (*Il.* IV.30–63); Euripides rejects all that his predecessors since Homer had done to reconcile the Olympian gods and human ideas of right and wrong. The gods exist, his tragedies seem to say, but they are the amoral, elemental forces which, locked in eternal conflict both outside and inside us, rule the tragic universe in which we live.

There is another fifth-century poet who appears on the list of 'atheists' – Critias, the uncle of Plato, the leading spirit of the Thirty Tyrants. From a play called *Sisyphus* our ancient authority (Sextus Empiricus) quotes forty-two lines of a speech which clearly reflect radical rationalist thought. It is cast in the form of a sophistic *Kulturgeschichte*, starting with the original state of lawless chaos and proceeding to the invention of laws and punishments. When, however, the laws were evaded by criminals who acted in secret, some clever man invented fear of the gods, so that evildoers would have something to fear even if not found out. He introduced the idea of an immortal spirit who hears and sees everything, who even knows human intentions. So he 'concealed the truth with a false tale, locating the gods where they would cause most fear, in the sky, the source of thunder and lightning. So, I imagine, someone first persuaded men to think that there was a race of gods' (Snell, T. 19 *TGrF*).

The attribution of this fragment to Critias is disputed; it may belong to a satyr play called *Sisyphus* which we know was a Euripidean title.[3] But whoever wrote it, the assumption that it reflects the sentiments of the poet is of course unjustified. There is a similar speech in the Euripidean satyr play *Cyclops*; the speaker expresses utter contempt for the gods, Zeus in particular. If this speech were a fragment without context, such remarks as 'To eat and drink your fill from day to day – that's what Zeus is, to men who can use their heads' (*Cycl.* 337–8) would certainly have earned Euripides a place in the ancient (and some of the modern) handbooks as a forerunner of the Cyrenaics and Epicurus. But in the play the Cyclops is blinded by Odysseus, and Sisyphus, the arch-trickster and liar of Greek myth, whose punishment in Hades was proverbial, is not likely to have escaped unscathed in a play produced in the theatre of Dionysus.

Cyclops, like *Sisyphus* (whoever its author may have been) was a satyr play, a burlesque appendage to the tragic poet's offspring of three serious plays. *Cyclops* is our only complete specimen but the papyri have given us large sections of Sophocles' *Ichneutae* (*The Trackers*) and smaller fragments of the satyr plays for which Aeschylus was famous in antiquity. From this material there emerges a picture of an extraordinary dramatic form: the enactment of a mythical action by characters whose would-be tragic dignity is undercut by the antics of a chorus of ithyphallic satyrs, creatures compounded of insatiable greed, carnal lust and abject cowardice. This might seem, at first sight, to be a relic of some original Dionysiac ritual, piously preserved, but in fact there is good evidence that it was introduced into the festival around the beginning of the fifth century by Pratinas, who, Pausanias (II.13.6) tells us, was Aeschylus' only rival in this remarkable genre. Whatever its origin, it became the exclusive domain of the tragic poets and though the performance of a satyr play after the three tragedies must have provided a psychological transition to the comedy which followed, comedy and satyr play belong to different spheres.

III. COMEDY

In satyr plays the dancers of the chorus wore not only horse tails and a mask which combined a snub nose with baldness and a beard but also tights made of animal-skin equipped with a prosthetic phallus (Fig. 37). In comedy the phallus, 'made of leather, hanging down, tipped with red, thick, a laugh for the children', as Aristophanes describes it (*Clouds* 358–

---

[3] Cf. Dihle 1977 (J 23) 28–42.

Fig. 37. Clay figure of a comic actor. (Berlin, Staatliche Museen 8823; after M. Bieber,
Die Denkmäler zur Theaterwesen im Altertum
(1920) pl. 69; Bieber 1961 (1 15) fig. 133.)

9), was usually (though not always) attached to the costume of the actors
as well. In satyr plays the poet played off the tragic pretensions of the
mythic world of the actors against the gross animality of the chorus; in
comedy there is no such contrast, it is a world of here and now. The
creatures of the comic poet move through the landscape not of the
mythical past but of fifth-century Athens – the Pnyx, the *ecclesia*, the
Agora, the Acropolis, with occasional excursions to Hades and Cloud-
cuckoo-land. But though the Athenian setting is familiar, what happens
in it on stage soon leaves reality far behind: an Athenian landowner
makes a separate peace with Sparta, another flies on a giant dung-beetle
up to Olympus to complain to Zeus about the war; the women of Athens
and Sparta force their men to make peace by declaring a sex-strike; two
Athenian adventurers organize the birds to cut the gods off from the
smoke of sacrifice and so force Zeus to surrender his sovereignty. In the
course of these extravaganzas many Athenians seated in the audience
were outrageously slandered and lampooned: prominent statesmen and
literary figures appeared travestied on stage and subjected to scurrilous
abuse. Even the gods did not escape the comic poet's unwelcome
attentions; the trio of gods who come to negotiate in *Birds* include a
gluttonous Heracles and a barbarian Triballian god, both of them a great
embarrassment to the chief of mission Poseidon. And Dionysus in *Frogs*
is presented in his own theatre as a coward and buffoon. Furthermore, in
keeping with the phallus on the actor's costume, the proceedings were

enlivened throughout by explicit sexual and excretory jokes.

About the origins of this remarkable performance we know no more than we do about the origin of tragedy; in both cases what little information we have is contradictory. Why tragedy was called goat-song (*trag-oidia*) no one has ever explained satisfactorily, but *komos* song makes a kind of sense, for *komos* is the Greek word for a revel, a riotous celebration. There were many such occasions in the Greek festival calendar at which personal lampoons and parody would be the natural media of spontaneous entertainment, but we do not know of any specific occasion which could have given rise to the dramatic structure which meets us in Aristophanes; a core consisting of an *agon*, a contest between two adversaries, and a *parabasis*, a choral address to the audience, embedded in a series of lively scenes enclosed by a prologue and a danced exodus.

Comedy was first included in the programme of the Dionysia in 486 B.C. (before that, according to Aristotle, there had been productions by 'volunteers' (*ethelontai*: *Poet.* 1449 b 1–2); it was not introduced at the Lenaea until much later (in or about 442). The only complete plays which have come down to us are all the work of one man, Aristophanes, and they were all produced between 424 (*Acharnians*) and 388 (*Plutus*); of the comedies of his predecessors and competitors we have only fragments. Coming so late in the history of the genre Aristophanes' work may have been atypical: his plays reflect a literary sophistication which, one suspects, was not characteristic of his rivals; his masterly parodies of Euripides, for example, speak of an intimate knowledge of his target that may have provoked one of his competitors to coin the remarkable verb-form *euripidaristophanizon*, suggesting that he was as much fascinated as repelled by the phenomenon he attacked. Sophisticated and literary he might be, but he was competing in a field where what counted was the laughter of the audience. Though he complains about the third prize given to *Clouds* (*Clouds* 518–25), he managed to combine the low notes with the high successfully enough to win first prize with *Acharnians* (425), *Knights* (424) and *Frogs* (405); and a second prize with *Wasps* (422), *Peace* (421) and *Birds* (412).

The tragic poets found religious and ethical problems immanent in the myths with which they worked; they embodied these universal themes in dramatic patterns which expressed contemporary concern. But though tragedy could also address social and political issues in general terms, it avoided specific issues currently under debate and above all specific personal allusions. Comedy had less to say about theology and theodicy but it took for its raw material the events of the day and the personalities of the hour. The *Acharnians*, produced in a city which had suffered and was still enduring shortages and inconvenience caused by the annual

Spartan invasions, celebrates a hero who makes a separate peace and enjoys on stage all the delicacies and comforts that the audience can only dream of; he exonerates the Spartans of responsibility for the war, asserting, in an outrageous travesty of Athenian war aims, that Pericles declared war because the Megarians stole two whores belonging to his mistress Aspasia; he finally exits in drunken high spirits, clutching two accommodating ladies of the night, while Lamachus, the general, comes back from a battle with a twisted ankle and a broken head (he had fallen in a ditch), to lament his lot in Euripidean lyric clichés as he is carted off to the doctor. *Knights*, produced in the following year, is a full-scale attack on Cleon, the political leader, who, like Pericles before him, maintained such a hold over the popular Assembly that he was in effect in control of Athenian policy. In the play he is a Paphlagonian slave in the house of a foolish old man called Demos, but the slave is in fact the master, since Demos is the dupe of the Paphlagonian's flattery and is kept stupidly content with handouts. Two other slaves, whose 'Spartan cake made at Pylos' the Paphlagonian had taken credit for, learn from an oracle that the leather-seller (Cleon) is to be succeeded by a 'blood-sausage seller' – a figure which of course appears at once 'as if sent by a god' (*Knights* 147). Reluctant at first to enter politics because of his lack of education, but persuaded that even the little he has is a disadvantage, he takes on Cleon and proves victorious in the *agón* of vulgar abuse, wild accusation and disgusting flattery which follows (at one point they both vie for the privilege of having Demos wipe his fingers on their heads after he has blown his nose (*Knights* 910–11)).

Like *Acharnians*, *Knights* is a massive comic offensive against the current Athenian leadership and its policies. And yet both plays won first prize. And neither play seems to have undermined popular support for the war or for Cleon, its chief promoter, who was elected one of the ten generals not long after the performance of *Knights*. Nor is there reliable evidence for attempts at retaliation by the powerful figures who were targets of the comic poets.[4] To be singled out for abuse in comedy was evidently something to be expected if you were noteworthy in any way; it was not to be taken to heart. Comedy was the licensed clown of Athenian democracy; in its proper place and time its civic and religious duty was to release its audience from restraints and inhibitions like the god in whose precinct it was performed. For an hour or two at the end of the day comedy had licence to turn the world upside-down. Its plots defy

---

4 Aristophanes claims (or rather his character Dicaeopolis does) that he was dragged before the *boule* and abused because of his comedy *Babylonians* (*Ach.* 377–82), but we have only his word for it; and that has to be weighed against the fact that later in the same play, speaking in his own person through the chorus, he announces that the Great King believes that Athens will win the war because they have Aristophanes to advise them and that the Spartan claim to Aegina is simply a manoeuvre to gain possession of that valuable asset – Aristophanes.

reality: Dicaeopolis' separate peace, the sausage-seller's conquest of power, Trygaeus' ascent to heaven to end the war, Pisetaerus' defeat of the Olympians and, above all, the revolt of the women led by Lysistrata, are all events so utterly impossible that their presentation on stage constitutes no threat whatsoever to established institutions.

It was, however, possible for the comic poet to make a momentary exit from his fantasy world and speak on social themes in a serious tone. In the *parabasis*, a long and elaborate lyric unit in which the chorus addresses the audience directly, the poet sometimes has his chorus discuss matters which lie outside the bounds of the comic plot. In one section of this structure, the *epirrhema*, a harangue in trochaic tetrameters spoken in character (young aristocrats in *Knights*, fierce old men in *Wasps*, and so on), the chorus offers advice to the Athenians. Their recommendations have usually nothing to do with the themes exploited in the play proper; they consist for the most part of unobjectionable championship of old-fashioned morals and patriotism. In one play, however, *Frogs* of 405, the chorus of mystic initiates calls on the Athenians to restore their civic rights to those who had been penalized for their participation (or suspected participation) in the oligarchic coup of 411. We have it on the authority of Dicaearchus, a pupil of Aristotle, that this advice was so welcome to the Athenians that they took the unprecedented step of giving the comedy a second performance. But this example is the exception that proves the rule: the proper function of comedy was not to advise but to be outrageous. It is the safety-valve of the emotional pressures generated by life in the polis and, like the reign of the Lord of Misrule in medieval England or the freedom granted to slaves at the Roman Saturnalia, it offers a utopian vision of revolution which serves to reinforce the solidity of the existing order.

Comedy's treatment of the gods is no more radical in intention than its abuse of individuals. It is not to be wondered at that gods suffered at its hands the same indignities as men, for the gods, outside philosophical circles, were regarded, sometimes with fear and sometimes with affection, as human beings on a more majestic scale; their passions – love, hate, pride and anger – were no different from ours, only more dangerous. From fear and reverence for the gods, even for Dionysus himself, comedy brought the worshipper a momentary dispensation. But the medium of release – the actors with their grotesque masks and phallic appendages, the dancers with their deliberately vulgar choreography – was itself a ceremony of worship of the god. 'The man is dancing', runs a fragment of the comic poet Phrynichus (κ9), 'and all's well with the god.'

CHAPTER 8g

SOCIETY AND ECONOMY

J. K. DAVIES

The only statement which can be made with security about Athenian society and economy in the Periclean period is that they were evolving rapidly but unsystematically. Since very much the same can be said of our scholarly understanding of those processes, the reader should be warned that this section must needs be more provisional than most, and is likely to date rapidly even so.

It may be helpful to explain why. Earlier generations of scholarship on the subject were (in broad terms) split between two approaches. Some adopted an antiquarian approach, organized according to the sector of economic activity or to the legal status and socio-economic functions of population groups.[1] This approach served essentially as a backdrop to the political, military, artistic and intellectual history of Athens and the rest of Greece. Others, more interpretatively inclined, became enmeshed in the unending debate between those who saw the Greek (including the Athenian) economy as essentially agrarian and undeveloped, based upon the largely autarkic farm plus family (*oikos*), and those who consciously or subconsciously saw the city states in Hanseatic terms, with a corresponding emphasis on capital, innovation, and market-oriented production and competition.[2] The post-war debate, having belatedly absorbed Hasebroek's fundamental attack of 1928 (A 60) on the latter view, came to be dominated by the late Sir Moses Finley. For present purposes the salient features of his approach were three. The first was methodological, comprising the claim that economic or social institutions and practices cannot be seen in isolation but must be interpreted as integral parts of the general fabric of a society and its value-systems. Thus seen, even innovations like banks, or loans on the security of an identified portion of a property-holding (*apotimemata*), were not what they *prima facie* seem to be, inventions to help capital accumulation or economic growth, but social instruments developed to help meet costly obligations such as liturgies, dowries, or interest-free loans (*eranoi*) to

[1] E.g. Tod 1927 (L 134); Michell 1940 and 1957 (L 101); Ehrenberg 1951 (L 34); an approach deriving ultimately from Boeckh 1840 (L 8).
[2] Surveys of the debate in Oertel 1925 (L 105); Gernet 1933 (L 58); Will 1954 (L 144); Pearson 1957 (L 114); Humphreys 1970 (L 71); Musti 1981 (L 103) 3ff. Recent exponents of each view are Starr 1977 (A 113) and Gschnitzer 1981 (L 63).

friends in need.[3] The second feature of Finley's approach, at once methodological and substantive, was the assertion that the analysis of such a society needed to be 'monocolore', i.e. that there was a single system, an ensemble, or a predominant pattern to be detected, and that whatever did not fit that pattern was a 'rare exceptional practice', 'on the margins'.[4] Thirdly and substantively Finley claimed that the prevailing ideology of Greek – indeed of ancient – society was that of its top social echelon. Its economic attitudes were those of a non-innovative agrarian society which erected 'a wall between the land and liquid capital' and made little of entrepreneurship or growth. Its social attitudes likewise linked landholding with citizenship, status with descent, and dignity with leisure. For Finley, therefore, Aristotle's *Ethics* and *Politics*, or the social writings of Xenophon, accurately reflected a cultural–psychological framework within which the town was a centre of consumption, not of production, all echoes of the Hanseatic city-state model were to be firmly rejected, and the economy was embedded in society.[5]

Such views always had their critics,[6] and reassessment is now gathering pace. Ancient agronomic techniques and strategies, ever more intensively studied, are being seen as both more complex and more rational than hitherto. Settlement and landholding patterns, at last the object of serious attention within the Attic landscape, are being seen to have generated specific aspects both of the economy and of public finances. The conceptual distinctions between economy, society and polity, or between polis as central place and polis as polity imposed upon landscape, are being used more confidently. Notions that the Athenian economy, not to mention the wider Greek economy, was a compound of contradictions, whether of structure or of representations, are being broached,[7] though their implications have yet to be digested. Fiscal demands, or the social imperatives of prestige spending, emerge as generating a system of economic and social interaction which was *sui generis* and eludes glibly applied labels. Other approaches from other newly adjutant disciplines, ranging from palaeobotany to historical demography, are already under way, so that the debate about ancient economic and social model-building looks set to continue well into the currency of this volume and may yet change its mode of discourse radically. What follows here, therefore, is highly provisional.

Aristotle built his mytho-historical generative model of the polis up from the association of man, woman and slave in accordance with nature

[3] Finley 1952 (L 36) 38–52; Finley 1953 (L 37).
[4] References in Davies 1975 (L 28) 101.
[5] Best in Finley 1973 (L 39) and 1977 (A 40).
[6] E.g. Frederiksen 1975 (L 47); Davies 1975 (L 28); Thompson 1982 (L 133).
[7] E.g. Vernant 1965 (A 117) (slavery); Humphreys 1970 (L 71) 23 (role of the state).

within an *oikos* (household) (*Pol.* 1.1252b). It is tempting to follow suit, for obvious reasons. The *oikos* was the context of action and emotion for all Athenians and most non-Athenians, for much of their time. It was the context of much significant cult-practice, ranging from the everyday through *rites de passage* to such ancestor worship as was practised.[8] It was a centre of affective life, though a life clouded by the ideology and reality of homosexuality, by disparities in age, education, or expectations between husband and wife, and by a severely practical view of marriage which saw it mainly as an instrument of child creation and property transfer.[9] It was above all the context of most human labour, whether 'outside' in the fields or with the flocks or 'within', washing, weaving, carding, spinning, cleaning, cooking or nursing: though not self-sufficient, the *oikos* was certainly in this period still the primary unit of production, storage and consumption.

Yet the difficulties of applying Aristotle's model are extreme. In part it is a matter of access. Classical Athens has yielded no private archive like the Zenon archive, the Paston letters or the Montaillou records.[10] The only substitute, the law-court speeches, do indeed contain much incidental information and a few illuminating passages such as Lysias I or Lysias XXXII.11ff, but they are set pieces, written for those who could pay for them, and emerge almost by definition from a context where relationships have broken down, so that they cannot be seen as a direct reflection of normality. The same is true for comedy and even more so for tragedy, where one can detect preoccupations and ideologies rather than analytic portraits of reality.[11] Secondly, it is a matter of the rate of change in our understanding, especially in affairs of law and of female/male relationships within the household. The more the study of the Athenian legal system emancipates itself from presuppositions derived from Roman law, the more appropriate it becomes to locate court cases within an integrative social system, to take seriously the role of juries in forming and reflecting social norms, or to see law making as a continual process of accommodating norms to social reality.[12] Though this last perception is at odds alike with the Athenian assumption that their fundamentally static laws remained 'Solonic' and with the traditional modern approach of presenting Athenian law as a synchronic corpus, yet the need for recodification from 411/10 onwards (see below, pp. 484–5) suggests

[8] Rose 1957 (K 77); Theophr. *Char.* XVI. with Humphreys 1979 (L 74) 559.

[9] Dover 1978 (L 32) and Golden 1984 (L 60) on homosexuality; cf. below, n. 13.

[10] One fifth-century letter survives from an Athenian context (Wilhelm 1904 (C 178)); a few brief messages on potsherds in *Agora* XXI B1–B9 (with *SEG* XXVI 67). Household accounts were cast (Ar. *Clouds* 19–20; Plut. *Per.* 16.5–6); none survives.

[11] Humphreys 1979 (L 74) 561ff = Humphreys 1983 (A 67) 18ff.

[12] Consider the evolution from MacDowell 1963 (D 55), Harrison 1968–71 (A 59) and MacDowell 1978 (A 81) to Osborne 1985 (L 107), Humphreys 1985 (L 75, L 76) and 1986 (L 77).

what isolated evidence confirms, that substantive law was changing comparatively fast in this period, yielding precisely the sort of 'promiscuous heap of legislation' which Aristotle was later to deplore (*Pol.* 1324b 5–6). A comparable change is affecting our ways of describing male–female relationships, as it becomes ever clearer how far previous study of Athenian society has yielded descriptions based almost entirely on male-created documentation and biased accordingly towards the actions and attitudes of men.[13] Techniques for redressing the balance, created in the last twenty years, are beginning to let us see, for example, what the public (male) / private (female) division meant, both generally and in the use of space within the house, what (considerable) powers went with a dowry, or what roles in production and wealth creation, not least managerial, within and outside the house were assumed by women.[14] An eventual systematic treatment of the female–male relationship as a component of Athenian society will probably obliterate much current Athenian social history, but its chronological focus will have to be the semi-visible century from 430 to 320 rather than the near-darkness of the Periclean period.

A third and closely related difficulty arises from the imprecision of Athenian terminology. The term *oikos* denoted at once 'family' or 'lineage', 'household' and 'property-unit', and could shift its meaning even within the same legal text (e.g. Dem. XLIII. 75). In each area of meaning it competed with other terms such as *genos* ('lineage' or 'issue'), *ousia* ('beingness', 'property'), *oikia* ('house' or 'building', but a virtual synonym of *oikos*), or *kleros* ('allotted estate', 'property-holding inherited as a unit'), even apart from other property terms such as *chorion* or *agros*.[15] Behind this linguistic oscillation lay a political ambiguity, in that the polity's fiscal or military or political relationship was not primarily with the *oikos* but with the individual male person, albeit one whose role in the polity and obligation towards it (his *telos*) varied with the size of the *oikos* he commanded.

The fourth difficulty, closely linked to the third, was the demographic instability of *oikoi*. Athenian law and custom had long since come down in favour of partible inheritance and of a prioritized capacity to inherit among all members of the bilateral kindred up to a specified degree. Of

[13] The general bibliography on 'women's studies' grows exponentially. Germane to the specific context are Wolff 1944 (L 145); Lacey 1968 (L 190); de Ste Croix 1970 (L 121); Thompson 1972 (L 132); Schaps 1975 (L 126); Pomeroy 1976 (A 99); Fisher 1976 (L 43) 5ff; Schaps 1977 (L 127); Gould 1980 (L 61); Isager 1981 (L 78); Humphreys 1983 (A 67), esp. chs. 3–4; Just 1985 (L 86); Powell 1988 (A 99A) 337–82; Foxhall 1989 (L 45); Just 1990 (L 87).

[14] Respectively Humphreys 1977–8 (D 39) and Walker 1983 (I 175); Foxhall 1989 (L 45) 32ff; Pomeroy 1990 (C 78A).

[15] Conspectus in Pritchett 1956 (C 156) 261–76; Osborne 1985 (L 106) 15–22; MacDowell 1989 (L 98). Finley's promised study of property terminology in Greek authors (L 36, 246 n. 9) never appeared.

the two possible 'strategies of heirship'[16] reactive to such customs and to a likely low life expectancy, one, that of family limitation, increased the risk of patriline discontinuity. Solon's inheritance law, permitting adoption in such cases and requiring the archon to ensure that *oikoi* do not become empty, went against the interest of collaterals in consolidating property, was often evaded in practice by the adoption of close kin, was administered only with difficulty (as the numerous known suits contesting adoptions bear witness), and must derive from an interest perceived by the central polity, probably for military needs, in retaining the maximum number of minimally viable *kleroi*. The other strategy, that of maximizing family size, must have predominated in fifth-century Athens if the evidence for population increase can be trusted (below, pp. 296 ff). In the absence of any significant degree of long-term co-ownership of property among kin,[17] it presumably led to repeated property division like that of Bouselos' estate among his five sons in just this period (Dem. XLIII.19). Even if we allow for subsequent intra-family inheritance from brother to brother, or from uncle to nephew annulling some such divisions, it has to be conceded that, ideal though it may have been, the notion of the family *oikos/kleros* descending intact through the generations can rarely have been a reality. At best the well-attested use of family given names in alternate generations will have provided a certain cognitive and emotional continuity.[18]

A fifth difficulty is that the *oikos* was very likely in retreat, socially and economically, in the Periclean period. Economically an increasing amount of production was being carried on outside the *oikos* framework. Admittedly, some contexts, such as the potters' workshops or blacksmiths' forges depicted in some genre red-figure paintings,[19] may have been quasi-*oikoi*, with slaves resident as family members and with no spatial differentiation between residence and workplace. However, by now some slaves were certainly separated from their owners, 'living apart' (χωρὶς οἰκοῦντες), especially in the newly urbanized areas of Athens and Piraeus (below, p. 298) and in effect forming *oikoi* by themselves. Still further removed from tradition were the larger-scale *ergasteria* (workshops) of slave craftsmen and labourers which are well attested in the silver-mining area and in Athens and Piraeus. By the time we see them, in the speeches of Lysias (XII.8 and 12), they are spatially separate from the *oikia* and could be far larger than any household known from Classical Greece.

Socially, too, the *oikos* was being ever more weakened by circumstances or circumscribed by political action. Since 510, Cleisthenes'

[16] Sallares 1991 (L 123) 204–5.   [17] Biscardi 1956 (L 6) collects what evidence there is.
[18] Humphreys 1980 (K 42).
[19] Webster 1972 (I 177) 8–9, 248; Osborne 1987 (L 108) 114–15 (street of herm-sculptors).

restructuring of the polity, the outlawing of tyranny, the unpredictable effect of the ostracism law, and the growth in public finances had combined to ensure that *oikos* could not again overshadow *polis*. Pericles' citizenship law of 451/0, restricting the citizen's choice of wife to women born of citizen-status parents (chapter 4 and p. 299 below), reinforced that message, as did the official use of the demotic or tribal affiliation rather than patronymic. So too did the laws of the 450s which formalized, and thereby specified and restricted, the powers and privileges of certain aristocratic *oikoi* in respect of various cults and festivals (below, p. 300), as did the laws of various dates from Solon onwards which emphasized public funerary rituals while severely curtailing the costs and the likely social impact of all private commemoration of the dead.[20] Even the physical dispersal of many thousands of citizens abroad in the colonies and cleruchies of the 440s (above, pp. 127 ff) will have weakened the effective everyday solidarity of many *oikoi*.

These facts and movements created a paradox. The *oikos* carried much the same sort of fundamental social load as households and families carry in most complex agrarian societies, and was enshrined as such in law and ideology. Yet the more specifically segmented and circumscribed it was as part of the polity, the more artificial and unstable it became. Either as a result, or as the consequence of parallel but independent movements in society, social action tended to become the province of larger or more fluid units. To these we now turn.

Central in the spectrum of these larger units was the deme. Settlement in nucleated villages had clearly long been the norm in the Attic landscape,[21] though the size of settlement varied enormously according to the extent of the territory, the ruggedness, fertility, and ecological diversity of the terrain, and differential access to resources and communications. Not all of these units were of equal antiquity. Some, such as the so-called 'twelve cities of Cecrops', were Mycenaean foundations, others dated from the internal colonization of Attica in the ninth and eighth centuries, while yet others, such as the settlements in the mining area which were less dependent on agriculture, were undergoing rapid growth in just our period.

To describe the demes thus is to view them as natural realities, emanating from the logic of humans exploiting a landscape. However, like *oikoi*, they had also come to function as the segmental components of a polity. The landscape was split up among them; the citizen body

[20] Jacoby 1944 (K 43); Richter 1961 (I 130) 37f; Kurtz and Boardman 1971 (K 54); Stupperich 1977 (I 161); Humphreys 1980 (K 42).

[21] Osborne 1985 (L 106) and Whitehead 1986 (D 108) have transformed scholarly understanding of this level of Athenian society. On settlement patterns cf. also Osborne 1987 (L 108) 63f; Halstead 1987 (L 64); Hodkinson 1988 (L 68).

comprised precisely those who were listed on the deme registers; and all, most importantly, were on the same level constitutionally. Even what had by now become the built-up walled area of Athens was composed of a number of demes, which were long-established villages in their own right and remained demes, each with its own corporate life. In stark contrast to some Hellenistic and much medieval experience, there was no city corporation as such and no formalized relationship between city and country, while the privileged position of the urban centre was reduced to a minimum.[22]

These demes were miniature republics, issuing documents, handling finances, copying the institutions of the wider polis, enjoying political life of probably a highly personal kind (to judge from later speeches such as Dem. LVII), and running some cults and festivals such as the rural Dionysia. All the same, demes as incorporated segments of the polity were only two generations old in 450: indeed, though they had clearly taken root by then, yet to judge from the use of demotics the degree to which men (especially those of aristocratic pretensions) identified with their deme varied and was a socio-political issue in this period.[23] Furthermore, demes did not manage all local cults or control all matters of local importance, for some at least of the latter remained with the older-established and more shadowy *phratriai* (brotherhoods), whose role, importance, and relationship to the demes in the Periclean and later periods are very hard to assess. The problem is partly to establish how far they too reflected any sense of locality. Some phratries do seem to have been roughly coterminous, socially and geographically, with demes, while the membership of others was already scattered through several demes by 508/7. Some, again, were – or had been – dominated by a single lineage which may have given its usually patronymic name to the larger unit, and even well into the fourth century the procedures of admission to a phratry continued to coexist with, and to influence, deme decisions on admitting members to the deme register.[24] In this respect they went on being live organizations, with their own cults, lands and revenues, which fulfilled certain limited social functions of ceremonial, of *rites de passage*, and of community membership. Their affairs were worth regulating in the mid-fifth century if the law compelling them to admit certain categories to membership is rightly so dated,[25] and other evidence shows them generating sub-groups (*thiasoi*, cult-fraternities) within themselves for reasons not at all clear.

[22] Humphreys 1972 (L 72), especially on the contrast with Alexandria.
[23] Whitehead 1986 (D 108) 71.
[24] Wade-Gery 1931 (L 138); Jeanmaire 1939 (L 82) 133–44; Latte 1941 (L 92); Andrewes 1961 (D 1); Lewis 1963 (D 50); Thompson 1968 (L 131); Davies 1981 (D 18) 106f; Ito 1981 (L 79); Ito 1983 (L 79A); Ito 1988 (L 79B).
[25] Philochorus *FGrH* 328 F 35, with Andrewes 1961 (D 1).

Apart from demes and phratries, three other subdivisions of the citizen body need notice. One group was vestigial: the four 'Ionic' tribes of which the phratries were (or had been made) segments still survived on paper, with tribal officials called *phylobasileis* (tribal kings) active in cult but little else. Almost as unimportant, surprisingly, were the thirty trittyes (*CAH* IV² 312ff) which were used for certain military and cultic purposes but otherwise seem not to have taken root in society, probably because a citizen's profile of affiliations was complicated enough without them.[26] In contrast, the ten Cleisthenic tribes had taken root in spectacular fashion. Whereas there is good reason to suppose that they were created as entities to bring together men from various areas of Attica, to promote the cohesion of a (by Greek standards) exceptionally large polity, to avoid recourse to formal or informal perioecic status for outlying villages, and to reduce the danger of regional polarizations, by the mid-fifth century these functions had been supplemented by others. They were at once brigading units for the army; mobilization mechanisms for the navy; bases for competing teams of runners, singers and dancers at various festivals; constituencies for elections to magistracies, *imprimis* the ten generals; constituencies for the selection by lot of administrative officials of all kinds, from the grandiose and international-sounding *hellenotamiai* to the most humdrum market supervisors; and cult-groups of limited but real significance.[27] In these ways both the 'natural' units (the demes) and the 'artificial' units (the new tribes) into which they were grouped had come to function not merely as formal segments of the polity but also as communities with identities and lives of their own, bearing a genuine functional load.

Even so, however – such were the intricacies of Athenian society– they were inadequate by themselves. Complementary to them (or neutralizing them), less segmented, more fluid, and perhaps more immediately reflective of social needs, there had developed an untidy network of informal groups. For some the focus was a cult, especially of gods or aspects of gods who had not (yet) been adopted by the polity, exercised though it was in the fifth century to bring as many such cults as possible under public supervision and control. For others the focus was a network of kinship relationships, visible to us above all when mobilized for support in legal contexts.[28] For others again the focus was a person, whose *philoi* or *hetairoi* (friends, companions) the group members were. Mostly aristocratic in ethos, sometimes with a core of kinship, these quasi-Masonic groups encapsulated such vestigial patro-

[26] *Phylobasileis*: Sokolowski 1962 (C 165) no. 10A.31–46. Trittyes: *IG* I³ 1117–31, with Traill 1986 (D 98A) 93–113 (military); *IG* I³ 255 and 258.30 (cult).

[27] For specific aspects, Jordan 1975 (D 41) (navy); Davies 1967 (D 17) (festivals); Kron 1976 (K 53); Rotroff 1978 (K 78) 205 n. 46; Kearns 1985 (K 49) (cults).

[28] Osborne 1985 (L 106) 127–53; Humphreys 1986 (L 77).

nage relationships as had survived the advent of large-scale public pay in the 460s and 450s. They may sometimes have been purely social, as the *synousiastai* (companions) of Lysias VIII are represented as being, while others, such as the *kakodaimonistai* of an early fourth-century Hellfire Club (Lys. F 53) may have strayed onto the louche and hybristic borderline of cult. Yet others, such as those which surface in the 440s round Thucydides son of Melesias (Plut. *Per.* 11.2), in 415 (Andoc. 1) or in 411 (Thuc. VIII.54.4), were potentially if not actively political, usually in an oligarchical direction.[29] It may not be chance that such groups became visible in a period when both polity and society were changing fast, since they could evidently provide the support 'towards lawsuits and magistracies' (Thuc. VIII.54.4) which an earlier generation had found in kin groups or in locality groups, but their roots lie well back in the symposiac culture of the Archaic period whose values they tended to share.

Socially, then, effective action was transcending the boundaries of *oikos* and locality, and had probably long done so for the better-off minority. Economically the same was true. For the peasant whose estate, though maybe consisting of scattered plots, lay within the boundaries of one deme, deme life corresponded to reality. For those caught in 508 with property in two or more demes,[30] it did not. Moreover, irrespective of whether land in Attica was freely alienable in this period or of whether a market in land really existed,[31] the normal workings of inheritance, of dowry, and of the occasional public sale of confiscated land by the *poletai* (sellers) in the two generations since 508 can only have reinforced the tendency to own property in several demes. By 414 such a pattern of ownership had come to predominate in the property holdings (mostly, significantly, of the better-off) which were being sold off by the *poletai* after the Hermokopidae and profanation affairs of 415.[32]

What is more, other aspects of the economic behaviour of the upper or propertied class will have strengthened the process of detachment from locality.

(1) As is now being belatedly appreciated, the *poletai* documents of 414 reveal the ownership of much real property overseas. The processes of acquisition are far from clear, since some of the estates concerned are much too large to be the *kleroi* of cleruchs or colonists (nor are they in the right places), but the movement must be assumed to have been in train from the mid-century on.[33]

(2) The urban growth of Athens and Piraeus in the fifth century must

---

[29] Calhoun 1913 (D 10); Sartori 1957 (D 84); Connor 1971 (D 16); Aurenche 1974 (D 4); Strauss 1987 (D 93) ch. 1; Millett 1989 (L 101A).   [30] Whitehead 1986 (D 108) 75f.

[31] Fine 1951 (L 35); Finley 1953 (L 37); Cassola 1965 (L 22); Bourriot 1976 (L 12), 727ff.

[32] M–L 79: *IG* I³ 421–30: Lewis 1966 (D 51).   [33] Davies 1981 (L 30) 55–60.

have accommodated freedmen, slaves and foreigners at least as much as citizens. The resultant demand for accommodation from those who could not legally buy or own real property provoked investment in landlord-owned *synoikiai* (multiple dwellings), built inevitably where the demand was and not where the landlord's deme was, as well as investment in the new-style standard 'estate' houses of Piraeus which may or may not have been owner-occupied.[34]

(3) Of other forms of land exploitation, quarries seem to have remained a matter of small-scale concern and local ownership, but the silver mines at Laurium presented a very different picture. However imperfectly the rate of coining reflected the rate of extraction of ore, and however obscure the routes by which the investment in land, labour and installations was recouped by individuals, nevertheless the epigraphic documentation from 367/6 onwards confirms the meagre fifth-century evidence in requiring the inference that citizens from all over Attica who had capital to spare came to own land or installations in the mining area.[35]

(4) Lastly, and notwithstanding Thucydides' statement that in 431 most Athenians lived in the countryside (II.14.2), there seems to have been a clear tendency among politicians and the wealthy towards the acquisition of a town house[36] for obvious reasons of convenience.

To some extent such transformations, occurring within a settled, hitherto village-based agrarian society, were part of a long-term evolutionary process not confined to Greece or indeed to the Mediterranean seaboard. What multiplied their effect and their visibility was demographic change and change in the pattern of settlement. They were independently generated, the latter above all by military requirements and by the consequences of successful empire-building, but they interacted with the changes already sketched ever more extensively from the early fifth century onwards. The first of these inputs was population growth, where the fact is clear enough but the figures remain opaque and controversial in spite of much recent work.[37] It will be best simply to

[34] Graham 1966 (I 71); Thompson and Wycherley 1972 (I 166) 173–85; Davies 1981 (L 30) 51 n. 25; Hoepfner and Schwandner 1986 (I 77): Pesando 1987 (L 115A).

[35] Momigliano 1932 (L 102) (fiscal arrangements); Crosby 1950 (C 127); Hopper 1953 (L 69); Crosby 1957 (C 128); Mossé 1962 (D 60) 85–96; Hopper 1968 (L 70); Lauffer 1979 (L 93); Osborne 1985 (L 106) 103–26.

[36] Davies 1981 (L 30) 53–5. Add, for the fifth century, houses of Callias III of Alopece in Piraeus and Melite (Davies 1971 (L 27) 260), of Ischomachus in the city, with an estate in the country (Xen. *Oec.* 11.14ff), and of Themistocles of Phrearrhioi in Melite (Plut. *Them.* 22.2).

[37] Basic thread of debate in Gomme 1933 (A 48); Gomme, *HCT* I 246f; Jones 1957 (D 40) 161–80; Gomme 1959 (A 50); Meiggs 1964 (A 86); Patterson 1981 (D 65) 51–56; Hansen 1986 (A 56); Garnsey 1988 (L 54) 113–17; Sallares 1991 (L 123) 51–60.

state the limits of uncertainty. The two fixed points for our purposes are 508/7 and 431. In and after the former year the adult male citizen population, having probably suffered both diminution and supplementation, seems to have been reckoned at the time as being of the order of 30,000.[38] What multiplier is then applied to yield a total head count within citizen families is debated: a multiplier of three would yield 90,000, of four 120,000. To that figure – already implying a high population per arable km[2] – it would be imprudent to add substantially, since such free non-citizens as were resident in Attica in 508 may have been largely incorporated in the citizen body as *neopolitai*,[39] and since the then slave population cannot even be guessed at.

Two generations later, in spring 431, Pericles was made by Thucydides to claim that Athens had available 13,000 (citizen) hoplites of military age, an unspecified number 'in the garrisons' and a further 16,000 as a reserve force of 'oldest and youngest' and such *metics* (resident aliens) as were hoplites (II. 13.6–7). Since we hear of 3,000 metic hoplites later the same year (II.31.2), and since there were also 1,000 (citizen) cavalry (II.13.8; Ar. *Ach.* 225) besides the 200 horse-archers and 1,600 archers (who may not all have been citizens), on these figures there were at an absolute minimum 27,000 adult male citizens who were of military age (18–59) and of hoplite status or above in 431. However interpreted or emended, such figures are incompatible with a static citizen population, even if we note a later reference to an ambition to 'heavy-arm the thetes', presumably via cleruchic land-assignments (Antiphon F 61). Short of emendation or of forced interpretation of the texts, we must assume a steep rise in citizen numbers since 508/7. Such indirect or qualitative evidence as there is for the fifth century confirms the assumption.

What may matter even more is the size of the non-citizen population. If many or most metics were migrants escaping from landless poverty on Aegean islands and elsewhere, behind the 3,000 or more who had hoplite status in 431 will have stood at least enough to equal or exceed the 10,000 known from 317.[40] Likewise, when Xenophon implies that before the Spartan occupation of Decelea in 413 there were over 10,000 slaves in the silver mines (*Vect.* IV.24–5), other more specific numbers (IV.14–15) give substance to his suspiciously round figure, as does Thucydides' figure (VII.27.5) of 20,000 for those who deserted, probably in 413 itself after the Spartan occupation of Decelea. To seek further precision on slave numbers in the mid-fifth century is futile, since the degree to which

[38] Meiggs 1964 (A 86), based on Hdt. v.97.2 and VIII.65.4. Doubts in Hansen 1986 (A 56) 26.
[39] Whitehead 1977 (L 141) 143–7; Davies 1977–8 (L 29); *CAH* IV[2] 304.
[40] Whitehead 1977 (L 141) 97f; Duncan-Jones 1980 (A 30); Hansen 1981 (A 55) 23.

Athens was or became a slave society is again best examined from within
a later chronological period.[41] Nevertheless, we are left with an impression (it is no more) of a massive and rapid increase in the total population
of Attica, largely due to immigration whether forcible or voluntary.
Directly or indirectly, the process had far-reaching consequences, which
can only be sketched here.

First and simplest, and in increasingly pointed contrast to Sparta,
there crystallized an atmosphere of openness and of receptivity to
foreign influences. It was perceptible as much in language ([Xen.]
Ath. Pol. 2.8), or in cult, as reflected by the importation and semi-
naturalization of foreign gods,[42] as in the taste for imported foodstuffs
and manufactured goods which the comic poets caricatured but illumi-
nated.[43] Thucydides could make Athenian openness into a motif of the
Funeral Speech (II.39.1), not unjustly, for the fifth-century Athenian
source material shows very little trace of xenophobia.

A second consequence was the urbanization of Athens and of Piraeus.
The two developments were separate but parallel, contemporary and
interdependent, each combining a deliberate act of planned creation with
the cumulative effect of thousands of individual decisions. At Athens the
deliberate act was the building of the Themistoclean wall in winter
479/8[44] for military and political reasons. Once created, albeit as
Fluchtburg, the circuit became the locus of two processes, (a) infill
between the closely adjacent nuclei of the existing villages wholly or
partly enclosed within it (Kydathenaion, Melite, Boutadai, Skamboni-
dai, Kollytos and Kerameis) (see p. 207, Fig. 24), and (b) the more
intensive use of existing housing stock.[45] Though there were still vacant
parts of the city in 431, they could not accommodate all the then country
population (Thuc. II.17.1 and 3): we must assume that most of the
intramural area had been developed, if only as a *barrio*.

Likewise at Piraeus the planned act is datable, the organic process not
so. The latter had already yielded a substantial settlement by 508 if its
likely later quota of councillors (8) reflects Cleisthenic circumstances, so
that its fortification by Themistocles, in 493/2 and very soon after 479
(Thuc. 1.93.3–8), and initial layout (*IG* i³ 1101–15) were far from being

[41] From the rapidly moving bibliography a basic orientation relevant to the present period in
Ehrenberg 1951 (L 34) 165–91; Jones 1957 (D 40) 10–17, 76–9; Finley 1960 (L 38); Mossé 1962 (D 60)
179–215; Vidal-Naquet and Carrière-Hergavault in L 23; Jameson 1977–8 (L 80); Mossé and
Mactoux in L 24; Brockmeyer 1979 (L 17) 105ff; Garlan *et al.* in L 52; Finley 1980 (A 42) 67ff, 93ff; de
Ste Croix 1981 (A 109) 133–74; Wiedemann 1981 (L 143); Finley 1982 (L 42); Wood 1983 (L 146);
Osborne 1985 (L 106) 111; Hansen 1986 (A 56) 30f; Wood 1988 (L 147); Garlan 1988 (L 50).
[42] Notably Bendis (*IG* i³ 136), Isis, and the various cults attested in the silver-mining area.
Ehrenberg 1951 (L 34) 268–70; Nilsson 1967 (K 69) 831–9; Lauffer 1979 (L 93).
[43] Hermippos F 63 K–A; Ehrenberg 1951 (L 34) 136–40.
[44] Thuc. 1.89.3–93.6; Boersma 1970 (I 23) 44–6, 154 no. 7; Lawrence 1979 (I 96) *passim*.
[45] Pritchett 1956 (C 156) 268 (*synoikiai*); Kolb 1984 (I 93) 77ff; Roberts 1984 (A 106) 17ff.

ex nihilo. The difficulty lies in dating the various subsequent plannings and public works in the port and in blending them with Hippodamus' career, so that at present little but a general picture of demographic consolidation in the mid-century can be inferred.[46]

A third consequence was the evolution of 'metic' status and the redefinition of citizen status, processes which were certainly linked in time and political climate. The fixed point has to be Pericles' citizenship law of 451/0, which provided that any man who was not born of citizen father and mother should not participate in the city (*Ath. Pol.* 26.4).[47] If we leave aside consequential problems of detail, such as the subsequent status of bastards or the practical difficulty of defining a citizen woman in the absence of any formal process of recognition within the deme,[48] the main debate has been whether the law was directed (1) against the foreign wives of aristocrats such as Cimon, or (2) more broadly against the rapid enlargement of the citizen body as demes adlected (corruptly or otherwise) the sons of Athenian women by non-Athenian men, or (3) more broadly still against the usurpation of citizen privileges by non-Athenian men. *Ath. Pol.*'s own explanation ('because of the number of the citizens'), for what it is worth, suggests (2) or (3), as does a tradition that in 445/4, on the occasion of a distribution of corn gifted by the Egyptian king, 4,760 men were convicted as improperly enrolled.[49] So too does a consideration of the growing value of citizen status, both within and outside Attica, once Ephialtes' revolution had enhanced access to magistracies, courts, command positions, pay for public office and windfall distributions. The close parallel is with the gradual separation of Roman citizen status from Latin status in the early second century B.C., which likewise reflected the growth after the second Punic War in the importance and privileges of Roman citizen status within Italy.

The law of 451/0 was significant in two further respects. As a public enactment it was one of a series of laws and decrees of the Periclean period which showed the polity intervening in the affairs of its constituent parts. Whether in specifying the powers and duties of individual

[46] Gomme, *HCT* I 261–70; Martin 1951 (I 105) 358–61; Boersma 1970 (I 23) 37f, 46–50; Martin 1974 (I 107) 106–10; Kolb 1984 (I 93) 116ff; Hoepfner and Schwandner 1986 (I 77); Traill 1986 (D 98A) 17f (deme-quota); Garland 1987 (L 51) 58–61. It would help considerably if we knew when the local government of the town was taken out of the demesmen's hands and replaced by a 'demarch to Piraeus' appointed by the Assembly (*Ath. Pol.* 54.8), but we do not, and cannot safely infer from the creation by the Thirty of ten 'archontes of Piraeus' (*Ath. Pol.* 35.1, 39.6) that the change predated 404.
[47] Whitehead 1977 (L 141) 149–51, Rhodes 1981 (C 83) 331–4, and Patterson 1981 (D 65) are now the basis for discussion; see also Walters 1983 (L 139), and above, pp. 76–7, 292.
[48] Harrison 1968 (A 59) 61–78; Humphreys 1974 (L 73); MacDowell 1976 (L 97); Rhodes 1978 (L 120); Walters 1983 (L 139) 316–20; Hansen 1986 (A 56) 73–6.
[49] Philochorus *FGrH* 328 F 119; Plut. *Per.* 37.4; Whitehead 1977 (L 141) 151.

gene, such as the Kerykes and Eumolpidae (*IG* 1³ 6c) or the Praxiergidae (*IG* 1³ 7), or in issuing general rules about what phratries or (as in 451/0) demes could and could not do, the state was regulating, or transmuting into written public form, what had perhaps hitherto been custom and practice, and thereby was reaffirming its primacy, or sovereignty if the word can be safely used.[50] Secondly, as a statement of political values (whether generally agreed or as a product of controversy we do not know) the law of 451/0 enshrined the Athenian polity's preference for maximizing equality among the members of a clearly defined citizen body rather than permitting the emergence of a spectrum of statuses with permeable boundaries. It is not far-fetched to see it as a reaffirmation of the decision of 508/7 not to envisage *perioikoi* or other kinds of *isopoliteia* within Attica, or even of the Solonian decision not to allow Athens to become a society of serfs and serf-masters.

Given such a reaffirmation, and given the influx which has to be presumed, the status of the largely immigrant, free, non-citizen residents of Attica was having to be regularized, in ways only patchily visible.[51] We have again one fixed point, in that the term 'metic' was being formally used for them before 460 (*IG* 1³ 244c, line 8), possibly in the 470s if the Themistoclean measure quoted in Diod. XI.43.3 as giving them tax-exemption can be trusted: that its informal use, which goes back into the late sixth century, is noticeably frequent in late Aeschylus[52] suggests that their growing presence and status was on the current agenda. Since other components of the status, e.g. participation in public festivals such as the Panathenaea (by 458), the ability to act as *choregos* at the Lenaea (not before 440), liability to infantry service (by 431), or deme-residence designation (by 414) are mostly in place by 431 (with the notable exception of the metic tax), its crystallization must have been a process of the Periclean period. However caustically, one has to admire the Athenian polity's ability to have the best of both worlds, by attracting the metics' skills and manpower while tapping their wealth for public benefit and continuing to deny them access to landowning or to the political process.

A fourth and last major consequence of population growth was a significant extra pressure on food supply. That the pressure was felt is generally agreed, but the responses to it are a matter of much current debate. The traditional view has been that, as in the fourth century, so *a fortiori* in the fifth century when population levels were higher, much grain came to be imported from overseas; that the routes of Athenian expansion abroad from the early sixth century (Sigeum) and the early

---

[50] Philochorus *FGrH* 328 F 35, with Andrewes 1961 (D 1). This is not the place to broach the broader debate about the usefulness of the concept of 'sovereignty'.

[51] Whitehead 1977 (L 141) 140–54.   [52] *IG* 1³ 1357; Whitehead 1977 (L 141) 34f.

fifth century (Lemnos, Imbros, Scyros) through to the developed *arche* (Black Sea, Egypt, Thessaly, Sicily) were directed at least in part to controlling first the routes and then the sources of supply; and that every effort was made to manipulate the shippers and traders in ways favouring Athenian interests. Simultaneously, it is argued, emigration was being encouraged, especially of the landless, or little-landed, to Athenian colonies and cleruchies.[53] More recently, however, doubt has been cast on the calculations purporting to show a large annual gap between the likely production of cereals in fifth-century Attica and the likely demand. Instead, it is now argued, the demand for imported corn developed only in the post-Persian War period, while the increased need was met as much by expedients such as (i) the intensification of land use, which used all available land including the marginal or 'last' lands (*eschatiai*); (ii) the increased use of human or animal fertilizers, irrigation and cereal / pulse / legume rotation (or alternation) rather than bare fallowing; (iii) the integration of cereal cropping with animal husbandry and arboriculture in complex interlocking ways; (iv) the use of all available labour (family, slaves, hired hands) to maximize the yield of the market-gardening end of primary production; and (v) the adoption of new and more productive strains of crops.[54] Since this is currently one of the fastest moving areas of ancient historical studies, no statement here can have long-term validity. A sensible interim response is to recognize in broad terms that the Periclean strategy of retreat behind the Long Walls in 431, so far from reflecting a weakened commitment to Attica and its productive capacity in the face of readily available imports, placed in jeopardy that primary sector of the economy into which much effort, investment and innovation had been committed in the previous fifty years.

The various developments which have just been described impinged upon Attica as an entity, and are not best seen at the level of *oikos* or deme. Together with the large nucleus of non-agricultural non-citizen workers in the silver-mining area, the two evolving large towns, Athens and Piraeus, complementary in function and deliberately linked physically since the 450s, represented a new pattern of settlement, superimposed upon the older pattern which had been locally and agriculturally determined. At the same time, the growth in non-citizen numbers, whether slave or free, had prompted a sharpening of status divisions

[53] Select references to *communis opinio* in Garnsey 1985 (L 53) 62 n. 1; also Seager 1966 (D 86) and Reed 1980 (L 119) (shippers and traders); M–L 49 = *IG* i³ 46.43–6 (colonies, with Andrewes 1978 (D 3) undermining Plut. *Per.* 11.6); Brunt 1966 (E 13) and Gauthier 1973 (E 30) (cleruchies).

[54] Ehrenberg 1951 (L 34) 77–82 (i); Lewis 1973 (L 94) 210–12 (i); Pečírka 1973 (L 115) (i); Jameson 1977–8 (L 80) (iv); Burford Cooper 1977–8 (L 19) (iv); Sartre 1979 (L 125) (i); Foxhall and Forbes 1982 (L 46) (ii), (iii); Wood 1983 (L 146) (iv); Owens 1983 (L 110) (ii); Garnsey 1985 (L 53); Osborne 1985 (L 106) (i); Halstead 1987 (L 64) (i); Garnsey 1988 (L 54) 89–106; Hodkinson 1988 (L 68) (ii), (iii), (v); Sallares 1991 (L 123) (i), (ii), (iii), (iv).

such that the local or segmental divisions of the citizen body came to be secondary to the collective of all 'Athenian men'. We therefore now need to identify a third level.

It was this wider stage which provided the locus for certain forms of purposive economic and social behaviour. That some forms were old-established, while others were of recent growth or were still emergent, led to tensions which Aristophanes above all was to document in the ensuing decades; indeed it is hard to stand back from his portrayal of the 'new' music, the 'new' education, etc. far enough to judge how much represented a real long-term shift in behaviour or *mentalités* and how much was evanescent froth. It may be clearest to begin with what is palpable innovation, and then to try to measure its impact on existing patterns of action.

Three economic innovations stand out: the market, the new types of capital accumulation, and the escalation of the public economy. The formative stages of the emergence of the market have already been traced in general Greek terms (above, p. 42). How far it had by now advanced in Periclean Athens is debatable, for we lack evidence which could help, such as a dated sequence through the fifth century of quantified mintings of small denomination Athenian coinage, and have instead evidence which helps less than it should. Plutarch's report that Pericles sold the yearly produce of his estates in bulk and bought what was needed from the Agora (Plut. *Per.* 16.4) gives no hint of its credentials, is placed within an anachronistic context of 'just wealth' and restrained money making, and leaves opaque the (to us) primary question whether Pericles' behaviour was typical or *avant garde*. Likewise, though at Piraeus Pericles' corn-stoa and the layout of the Agora itself[55] must reflect market activity, there is notably little fifth-century evidence of comparable buildings in or near the Athenian Agora.[56] We are, strangely, on safer ground with the evidence from Old Comedy, which overwhelmingly depicts a retail market in fully developed form by the 420s, and which has to be taken at face value even if Aristophanes was right in 425 to make Dikaiopolis contrast the hucksters of the Agora with the domestic mode of production in his deme:[57] that a special set of officials, the 'market supervisors', was well established by then is proof

[55] Boersma 1970 (I 23) 74, 213 no. 87; Martin 1974 (I 107) 104.

[56] The South Stoa of the late fifth century (Boersma 1970 (I 23) 89f, 219 no. 97) is the first likely candidate, but the credentials of its commercial use are uncertain (Thompson and Wycherley 1972 (I 166) 76 n. 216). General survey of the skimpy evidence, *ibid.* 170–3, with Ussher's note on Ar. *Eccl.* 686. Nothing relevant can be safely predicated of earlier buildings of uncertain character (e.g. Boersma 1970 (I 23) 226–32 nos. 109–20), and other fifth-century stoas (of the Herms; Poikile; Basileios) had political-administrative, not commercial, uses.

[57] Ar. *Ach.* 33–6; but is this economic reality or literary *topos*? Cf. Ehrenberg 1951 (L 34) 113–20 for the general picture.

enough.[58] The least that can be said is that by the 420s, if not several decades earlier, increased purchasing power, urbanization, and the growth of an under-class without access to landownership (though not without access to land-leasing[59]) had generated a significant retail market sector.

The second area of economic innovation, capital accumulation, can be sketched more briefly, for its newer forms (banks, bottomry loans) have been noticed already (above, p. 24), and its older forms (hoards; interest-bearing loans;[60] and interest-free loans (*eranoi*) allowing the small cash resources of individuals to be pooled for a single larger-scale demand) were well established by the Periclean period. The problem is to decide what such ways of putting private capital to work amount to. The fact of their development makes Athenian society capitalist only in the minimal structural sense that certain customs and institutions would not have functioned unless capital sums could be assembled – up to 2,000–3,000 drachmae for a dowry in high society or for a bottomry loan. These are large sums even for an economy which was generating its millionaire equivalents and into which the Laurium mines were injecting new bullion at a substantial rate. Yet they were all assemblages for one occasion or one enterprise rather than for enterprises of indefinite duration, for repeated activity, expected to deliver a periodic dividend to shareholders, of which there is no trace now or later in Athenian society. Likewise, in the motivational sense, the profit-seeking deployment of capital was a palpable fact, ranging from the small-time loan shark to the nabobs who bought slaves and set them to work in the silver mines in the expectation of a steady income from their *apophorai*.[61] It was certainly not they whose ideas lay behind Aristotle's principled disapproval of unlimited money-making in *Politics* I. Here as elsewhere we must accept that the same society encapsulated incompatible value-systems within itself. There did not have to be a single predominant pattern, and the rapidly shifting society of mid-fifth century Athens is precisely the wrong place to find such a pattern.

There remains the public economy. The title of August Böckh's *Staatshaushaltung der Athener* notwithstanding, there is debate whether 'public economy' is the right phrase, for it could be taken to imply that both in analytic terms and in terms of contemporary perceptions there were clear divisions between 'community' and 'polity', or between

---

[58] For the *agoranomoi*, *Ath. Pol.* 51.1, with Rhodes *ad loc*.

[59] *IG* I³ 252 (lease); *IG* I³ 422.200, 213 (*misthosis*); Lys. VII.4–10 (metics leasing land); *IG* II² 10 (metic *georgoi*). In general Osborne 1988 (L 109).

[60] Note M–L 53 = *IG* I³ 248 for (not quite certainly interest-bearing) loans by a deme (Rhamnous) to individuals in the 440s; *IG* I³ 258, with Behrend 1970 (L 5).

[61] References to loan-sharks (*obolostatai*) in Ehrenberg 1951 (L 34) 233; to *apophorai* in Andoc. 1.38 and Xen. *Vect.* IV.14–15. In general Thompson 1982 (L 133).

'society' and 'the state', but it is not transparent that fifth-century Athens knew such distinctions. The idea structure was rather that all citizens were basically shareholders in a company – οἱ μετέχοντες τῆς πολιτείας, 'those who have a share of the polity'.[62] The argument whether all had an equal share or held shares proportional to their merits (wealth, strength, military capability or whatever) served indeed to differentiate egalitarian from selectivist views of the community, and was to resurface violently in 411, but the four Solonian *tele* (not quite 'property-classes') were a long-established way of bridging the divergence by encapsulating the principle 'from each according to his means'. Hence not only did differential obligations derive from differentiated resources, but also their performance (as also that of the specialized subset, liturgies) was an honour, not a tax or a statutory requirement imposed by 'the state' as a conceptually separate entity: that the political entity which we call 'Athens' was called in Greek 'the Athenians' is not chance. Given that essential principle, it was only those outside the polity, who had no share in it, who needed to differentiate between society and the polity; those within shared in good things (distributions of silver or of corn, for example), in power, in obligations, and in catastrophes alike.

It is this value-structure which makes it so hard to decide which activities and transactions count as part of the 'public economy', for even payments to jurors or to magistrates could be seen as the (re)distribution to shareholders of some of the income of community activity. So too, at the extreme, could the gains of empire be thus seen, ranging as they did from the territories overseas which became cleruchic land assignments to the monies accruing via tribute and booty which ultimately became Athene's property and were either used on prestige display projects (especially the temples) or kept as a massive reserve. Even if we cannot take as contemporary or reliable the framework of debate on these monies which is presented in Plutarch's *Pericles*,[63] 'economy' and 'public economy' appear to be as much welded together conceptually in the phrase *emmisthos polis* ('the whole city in receipt of public pay') as they are inseparable operationally when we try to assess the multiplier effect deriving from the influx of these monies. Paradoxically, the conceptual separation which *was* perceived lay within what we would call the public economy, between 'public monies' proper (δημόσια) and 'sacred monies' (ἱερά). It may be best to acknowledge that a clear reconstruction of fifth-century Athenian thought and practice in this area is not yet to hand.[64]

All the same, a shift both functional and conceptual is unmistakable. Functionally, by the 450s if not earlier, the scale of monies passing

---

[62] Patterson 1981 (L 113), quoting *Ath.Pol.* 26.3 and Thuc.II.40.2.

[63] Plut. *Per.* 12, with Andrewes 1978 (D 3).

[64] Cf. meanwhile Lewis 1990 (A 77A). The word ὅσιος, itself fifth-century official Attic (*IG* I³ 52.16, 253.13), provides yet a further category.

through the hands of the administrators of collective bodies, from *hellenotamiai* to demarchs, had become such as to rupture any sense of continuity with household management: genuine taxes, with tax-farmers to match, had proliferated by the 420s,[65] and publicity, audit, accountability, new and larger management groups, and fierce penalties for defalcation had become the norm.[66] Conceptually, too, the language about public revenues attributed to Pericles in spring 431 (Thuc. II.13.3) reveals the shift completed, while most scholars agree that by then the Athenian citizen hoplite soldiers had followed their poorer counterparts in the fleet by no longer serving by property class from their own resources (albeit with a ration allowance) but instead by being assimilated to mercenaries in their relationship to the state as paymaster.[67]

Lastly, social innovations, which are if anything even more elusive: at least three, however, are salient, clearly influencing action and discourse at the political level. First, for all citizens and many non-citizens, there was more opportunity for participating in large crowd activity. Festivals such as the Dionysia or the Panathenaea which provided spectacle, colour, drama and mass participation gained ground and new resources; juries, the Council of Five Hundred, and above all the Assembly itself daily and visibly reinforced awareness of the existence and cohesion of the collective of 'all Athenians', to the point where those who chose not to participate became thereby, and paradoxically, exposed.[68] Secondly, the skills needed in order to command attention and respect in such contexts were shifting the nature and composition of the political class away from the gentlemanly virtues and towards a professionalism in oratorical, fiscal and administrative affairs which both increased the gap between the politicians and the rest and stimulated the need to bridge it, *imprimis* by self-presentation as 'friend of the people'.[69] Thirdly, that professionalism, together with the sheer impetus of Athenian fiscal and military resources, was rendering Athens' wealthy élite larger, wealthier, and more open in recruitment. Indeed, the one single paradox which makes Athenian society so hard to encapsulate in a brief description is that that élite, outward-looking, ambitious, not fundamentally at loggerheads with itself or its common people, and busy through the Periclean period in consolidating Athenian domination in the Aegean and beyond, co-existed with, and emerged from, a society which remained (like its landscape and polity) small-scale, complex, intricate, and embedded in agrarian rhythms.

[65] Ar. *Ach.* 896; *Wasps* 658–9; *Peace* 850; *Eccl.* 1007; Plut. *Alc.* 5; Andoc. 1.133–4 for tax-farming. Böckh 1886 (L 9) I 405–14 remains the best systematic treatment.

[66] Recent surveys by Tolbert Roberts 1982 (D 98) and Ober 1989 (D 61) 327ff.

[67] Pritchett 1971–85 (A 101) I 7–29; Rhodes 1981 (C 83) 306.

[68] Thuc. II.40.2; Carter 1986 (L 20).

[69] Kennedy 1963 (J 57); Connor 1971 (D 16).

CHAPTER 8h

ATHENS AS A CULTURAL CENTRE

M. OSTWALD

I. THE ECONOMIC AND SOCIAL BACKGROUND

'Because of the greatness of our city there is an influx of all things from the entire world, with the result that the enjoyment of goods produced at home is no more familiar to us than the produce of other men' (Thuc. II.38.2). Pericles could not have spoken these words before the second half of the fifth century. The Persian Wars, and especially the Persian occupation in 480/79 B.C., had destroyed whatever splendour had made Athens attractive to foreigners in the sixth century.[1] The buildings on the Acropolis, including the Old Temple of Athena erected under Pisistratus and the Old Parthenon, a marble structure to which an earlier poros temple may have given way shortly after Marathon, and the vibrant archaic sculptures of *kouroi* and *korai* which archaeologists have recovered for us, were no longer visible after the Persian holocaust. With the exception of Simonides of Ceos, who briefly returned to Athens about the time of Marathon, and of Pindar, who is said to have received some training in Athens late in the sixth century and celebrated the Pythian victory won by the Alcmaeonid Megacles shortly after his ostracism in 486 (*Pyth.* VII),[2] we know of no literary or intellectual figure whose visit is recorded. There was no interruption in the production of tragedy at the City Dionysia, and comedy was added in 486; whether they lured a significant number of foreign visitors to Athens we do not know. The Panathenaic festival, however, is likely to have continued to attract some competitors and visitors from abroad,[3] and there was no break in the manufacture and painting of Attic vases, whose superb craftsmanship and artistry guaranteed continued export, especially to Etruria.[4]

The victories at Salamis and Mycale had raised the prestige of Athens to equal that of Sparta among the Greeks. Yet it was not until the successes of the Delian League under Cimon's leadership in the 460s that

---

[1] Thompson 1981 (D 95) 343–55, esp. 344–5.   [2] See Lesky 1966 (J 65) 184–5 and 190–1.
[3] The evidence needs to be treated with caution since it comes exclusively from the spread of the so-called 'Panathenaic' amphorae, whose production continued without major disruptions after the sixth century; see especially Gardiner 1912 (I 66A) 179–93, esp. 184–7; Amyx 1958 (I 1A) 178–86, esp. 180–3; Boardman 1974 (I 16) 167–77.   [4] Webster 1972 (I 177) 286–95.

political prominence laid the foundation for a new cultural resurgence, and it was not until the treasury of the League was transferred from Delos to Athens in 454 that, with the beginning of imperial rule, Athens became the focal point of cultural activity in the Hellenic world.

The groundwork for this had been laid by Themistocles' creation of the Athenian navy and of Piraeus as its harbour in the late 480s. Though primarily motivated by military considerations, these achievements could not fail to have a stimulating effect on the development of trade. According to Diodorus (XI.43.3),

> he persuaded the people to construct each year twenty new triremes to add to the fleet, and to grant metics and skilled craftsmen tax exemption, so that large numbers should come to the city from overseas from all quarters and provide a handy supply of more skills; for he judged both these policies to be conducive to building up a sea power.

Although the historical accuracy of some of these statements is open to doubt,[5] there can be no question that Themistocles' naval policy opened the gates to many foreigners who knew that there would be a place for them not only in the construction of the fleet but also in the reconstruction of Athens after the Persians had left. That they were made to feel welcome is attested by friendly references to metics in the plays of Aeschylus.[6] Few obstacles seem to have been put in the way of their settlement in Athens, if our evidence, which comes mainly from the fourth century, can be taken as a guide to their status in the fifth. They had to pay a special tax, the *metoikion*, they needed a *prostates* to represent them at law, they did not have the right to hold magistracies and attend meetings of Council and Assembly, and they could not acquire land or houses without special privilege. But they enjoyed the protection of the law and could engage in lucrative activities such as manufacture and industry, commerce and banking, and they freely mingled with all layers of Athenian society.[7]

When the one-sixtieth part of the tribute paid by the allies went no longer to Delian Apollo but to Athena, the influx of foreigners and with it Athenian prosperity will have increased still further. Evidence for this may be seen in the enactment of Pericles' citizenship law of 451/0 B.C., only a few years after the transfer of the League treasury from Delos to Athens, which henceforth reserved citizen rights to offspring of two Athenian parents.[8] Whatever its purpose may have been, this law would not have been enacted if the influx of metics had not been regarded as

---

[5] See Whitehead 1977 (L 141) 148–9.   [6] Whitehead 1977 (L 141) 35–6.

[7] Whitehead 1977 (L 141) 148–59; Austin and Vidal-Naquet 1977 (L 4) 99–101; Lévy 1987 (L 93A) 47–67.

[8] Arist. *Ath. Pol.* 26.4; Plut. *Per.* 37.2–5; Ael. *VH* VI.10, Suda s.v. δημοποιηυός. For a full discussion, see Patterson 1981 (L 113); cf. also Walters 1983 (L 139) 314–36.

constituting a significant threat to the rights of Athenians (see above, pp.299–300). The measure did not, however, affect the right of foreigners to reside in Athens, and it did not appreciably stem further immigration. Absolute numbers cannot be computed, but if we can trust the Old Oligarch (1.12) their numbers were large and they enjoyed the same freedoms as did native Athenians. According to recent calculations they constituted about 40 per cent of the free population of Athens at the outbreak of the Peloponnesian War,[9] which may have been close to fifty thousand men, women and children. This ratio is corroborated for the period 409–405 by the accounts of the construction of the Erechtheum, which shows that metics contributed about 39 per cent to the workforce, while citizens contributed only 24 per cent and slaves 19 per cent.[10] Less indicative of specific numbers, but, nevertheless, attesting that they were considerable, are two occasions, one toward the end of the Peloponnesian War and the other soon thereafter, on which metics are said to have been enticed by the promise of citizenship to fight alongside Athenian citizens. The first of these was before the battle of Arginusae, the other when Thrasybulus rallied some nine hundred of them to his side against the Thirty, promising them *isoteleia* (taxation equal to that of an Athenian citizen) and trying unsuccessfully to obtain citizen rights for them after his victory.[11] However liberally they were treated in social and economic matters, access to political life was made difficult for them.

Since metics were barred from ownership of land, trade, commerce and industry were the main occupations in which they engaged. Again, most of our evidence comes from the fourth century,[12] but for the fifth century the Erechtheum accounts inform us that metics worked as sculptors in stone, woodcarvers, carpenters, sawyers, joiners, painters, gilders, and as unskilled labourers, while we learn from the decree of 401/0, which rewarded foreigners who had helped liberate Athens from the Thirty (*IG* II² 10B), that there were among them several farmers, a cook, a carpenter, a muleteer, a builder, a gardener, an ass driver, an oil merchant, a nut seller, a bath maker (?), a baker, a fuller, hired workers, a statuette maker, etc. As far as industrialists are concerned, we know most about Cephalus, who was enticed by Pericles to leave his native Syracuse for Athens. He lived there peacefully for thirty years and grew prosperous from a shield factory which employed 120 slaves (Lys. 11.4, 19). The respect he commanded and his high standing in Athenian society are vividly portrayed at the opening of Plato's *Republic*, where he is host in

[9] Duncan-Jones 1980 (L 33) 101–9. More cautious and agnostic about numbers is Hansen 1981 (A 55) 19–32, esp. 23–4.
[10] *IG* I³ 474–9 as interpreted by Randall 1953 (L 118) 199–210, esp. 201–3.
[11] Xen. *Hell.* 1 6.24, Diod. XIII.97.1; Xen. *Hell.* 11.4.25 and Arist. *Ath. Pol.* 40.2 with Osborne 1982 (D 63) 26–43.
[12] See Whitehead 1977 (L 141) 116–21, and Lévy 1987 (L 93A) 55–60.

his home in the Piraeus to Plato's brothers Glaucon and Adeimantus, members of an old aristocratic family, to Cleitophon who was to become prominent in Athenian politics on the side of Theramenes, to the Sophist Thrasymachus of Chalcedon, and of course to Socrates.[13]

The career of Cephalus' son Lysias illustrates how far a metic could be involved in the social and cultural life of Athens, and even in its political life – short of becoming a citizen, even though he may have enjoyed Athenian citizenship for a brief span after the overthrow of the Thirty.[14] Not only did he write forensic speeches, many on political issues, to be delivered by Athenian clients in law courts which, as a metic, he could not address in person, but he actively supported the opponents of the Thirty from his refuge in Megara by supplying them with money, weapons and men. Of his extant speeches only his prosecution of Eratosthenes (XII) seems to have been delivered by Lysias himself, and that during the brief period in which he enjoyed citizen rights.

Other instances of participation by metics and foreigners on the fringes of political life in Athens are less constructive. According to Thucydides (VI.28.1), metics figured prominently in denouncing participants in the desecrations on the eve of the Sicilian Expedition in 415, and there is evidence that at least four rich and well-connected aliens were implicated in the parodies of the Mysteries at that time.[15] Some political assassinations are attributed to foreigners: if the story is true that Ephialtes was killed by Aristodicus of Tanagra, we are almost certainly dealing with a hired killer;[16] this is not likely to have been the case with the men credited with the murder of Phrynichus upon his return from the embassy to Sparta in the autumn of 411: the fact that Thrasybulus of Calydonia, Apollodorus of Megara, and some others were publicly honoured for their deed under the restored democracy shows that they were believed to have acted in the best interest of Athens and not for personal gain.[17] A further selfless political act in the interest of Athens is attributed by Thucydides (VIII.92.8) to Thucydides of Pharsalus, a *proxenos* of Athens, who interposed himself between the troops of the Four Hundred and their hoplite opponents in the Piraeus in 411/10. Evidently, metics and other foreigners were capable of feelings for Athens which matched or even surpassed those of many citizens.

The influences exerted by two known metics on the political life of

---

[13] The bronze-seller Sosicrates, who is recorded as *choregos* in comedy for *c.* 400 without patronymic or demotic, may well have been another prominent metic; see *Hesp.* 40 (1971) 256 (no. 4).

[14] The most reliable information on Lysias' life comes from his speech *Against Eratosthenes* (XII); less reliable, though more detailed, is [Plut.] *X orat.: Lysias* (= *Mor.* 835C–836D).

[15] Teucrus, Cephisodorus, Hephaestodorus and Poulytion; see Aurenche 1974 (D 4) 109–10 and 113.

[16] Arist. *Ath. Pol.* 25.4, cited by Plut. *Per.* 10.7–8. Ant. v.68 says that the assassin was never found, cf. Diod. XI.77.6.   [17] Lys. XIII.70–3; Lycurg. *Leoc.* 112; M–L 85 with pp. 262–3.

Athens were of a more indirect nature. Anaxagoras of Clazomenae and Aspasia of Miletus, both closely associated with Pericles' personal life, are said to have made considerable contributions to his policies. Anaxagoras spent at least twenty years (probably the years 456/5–437/6) at Athens.[18] What prompted him to move there when he did is difficult to surmise, since Athens did not yet have any tradition of philosophical activity. Indeed, Anaxagoras is said to have transplanted philosophy from Ionia to Athens and the earliest Athenian philosopher, Archelaus, is said to have been his pupil.[19] Under what circumstances his close relationship with Pericles developed is also unknown. Certain is that it existed and that Anaxagoras' influence on the statesman was believed to be so great that political opponents sought to undermine Pericles' authority by prosecuting Anaxagoras for impiety.[20] We are equally ill-informed about the circumstances under which Aspasia became Pericles' mistress in the early 440s. Had she come from Miletus alone in order to take up residence in Athens or had Pericles brought her there? If the former, what had attracted her to Athens? We cannot answer these intriguing questions. Her political influence on Pericles is attested primarily by Plutarch (*Per.* 24, 25.1), who makes her responsible for Athens' siding with Miletus against Samos in 441, and it is parodied by Aristophanes' account of the cause of the Peloponnesian War (*Ach.* 526–32). It is also indicated by the tradition that, as in the case of Anaxagoras, Pericles' political enemies veiled an attack on him by prosecuting her for impiety (Plut. *Per.* 32.1, 5).

The number of transient visitors from abroad attracted to Athens during the heyday of empire will have been greater than that of foreign residents. The arrangements for the payment of tribute alone will have brought many allies to the city, especially at the time of the Great Panathenaic festival when the amount of tribute would normally be assessed, and at the annual celebration of the City Dionysia in late March–early April when it was collected and, according to Isocrates (VIII.82), publicly displayed in the theatre.[21] The occasions were well chosen for their propaganda value: great throngs of foreigners came to Athens to attend the games and recitations of the Panathenaea and the performances of tragedy and comedy at the City Dionysia (see above, p. 261). There was also other business which brought foreigners to Athens throughout the year: the Athenians had reserved to themselves jurisdiction in many cases involving their subject allies, compelling them

---

[18] Mansfeld 1979 (J 76) 39–69 and 1980 (J 76) 17–95.
[19] Anaxagoras 59 A 7 (D–K).   [20] Mansfeld 1980 (J 76) 76–84.
[21] For the assessment, see [Xen.] *Ath. Pol.* 3.5; M–L 69 with commentary; for the collection, see Ar. *Ach.* 504–6 with scholion on 504; M–L 46 and 68. In general, see Meiggs 1972 (E 53) 234–54, esp. 237 and 240, and Will 1972 (A 126) 181–3.

to present themselves for trials in Athens. The economic effects of this are summed up by the Old Oligarch (1.17–18):

Further, the Athenian people derive the following profit from the fact that trials for allies are held in Athens. In the first place, the revenue from the 1 per cent tax in the Piraeus increases; secondly, if anyone has lodgings to let he will do better; so will anyone who can let a team or a slave for pay; also town criers are better off for visits from the allies. In addition, if the allies did not come for their trials they would show respect only to those Athenians who sail out to them, generals, trierarchs and ambassadors. But as it is, each individual ally is compelled to be deferential to the Athenian people, inasmuch as he recognizes that he has come to Athens where judicial proceedings are in the hands of none other than the people, which is the law at Athens. He is compelled to petition in the courts and to grasp the hand of anyone who comes in. So for that reason the allies have rather become slaves of the Athenian people.

Several of the foreign ambassadors who came to the imperial city on behalf of their own states found kindred spirits among the Athenians, especially among the upper-class intellectuals. We are best informed about Gorgias' embassy to Athens in 427 in order to request help for his native Leontini against Syracuse. The influence of this visit is immortalized by the dialogue which Plato named after him, and, in addition, we learn that he gave public performances (*epideixeis*) of his rhetorical skills and made some money by instruction to young Athenians.[22] Similarly, Prodicus of Ceos is said to have not only impressed the Council with his power of speech when he came as an ambassador, but also enriched himself by public performances and private instruction (Pl. *Hp. Ma.* 282c). In the case of Hippias we are told only that he was sent by his native Elis on many embassies, especially to Sparta (Pl. *Hp. Ma.* 281ab), but that does not exclude the possibility that he also visited Athens in an official capacity. His influence there is attested by two Platonic dialogues which bear his name and by Xenophon's report of a discussion in which he got involved with Socrates (*Mem.* IV.4.5–25); his admiration for the intellectual life of Athens is eloquently expressed in Plato's *Protagoras* (337d).

The most constant and visible impact of transient strangers upon Athens, however, has been left by traders who brought to Athens the goods of which Pericles boasts in the passage with which we opened this section. 'Whatever delicacies there are,' says the Old Oligarch (2.7), 'in Sicily or Italy, in Cyprus or Egypt, in Lydia, Pontus, the Peloponnese, or any other land, are all concentrated in Athens because of her control of the sea.' Mock-heroic dactyls from a comedy produced by Hermippus in the 420s tells us what these delicacies were (fr. 63 K–A):

[22] Diod. XIII.53.1–5, cf. Thuc. III.86.3; Pl. *Hp. Ma.* 282b.

from Cyrene sylphium stalks and oxhides, from the Hellespont tunny and salt-
fish, from Italy salt and ribs of beef . . . Syracuse offers port and cheese . . . from
Egypt sailcloth and raw materials for ropes, from Syria frankincense. Fair Crete
sends cypress wood for the gods, Libya plentiful ivory to buy, and Rhodes
raisins and figs sweet as dreams; from Euboea come pears and big apples; slaves
from Phrygia, mercenaries from Arcadia. Pagasae provides slaves with or
without tattoos, and the Paphlagonians dates that come from Zeus and shiny
almonds . . . Phoenicia supplies the fruit of the date-palm and fine wheat-flour,
Carthage rugs and cushions of many colours.

Through her empire and control of the sea the world had indeed come to
Athens' doorstep.

II. RELIGION AND EMPIRE

The religious consequences of the ties of common Ionian kinship which
made the allies willingly acquiesce in Athenian leadership at the
founding of the Delian League (Thuc. 1.95.5, 96.1) were skilfully
exploited by Athens after the transfer of the League treasury from Delos
to Athens in 454 to secure imperial control over the allies. Athena now
replaced Apollo as recipient of the tribute, which was assessed every
fourth year at the Great Panathenaea and was annually collected at the
Great (or City) Dionysia (see above, p. 261). Sanctuaries to 'Athena
mistress of Athens' (*Athena Athenon medeousa*) appear in Samos, Cos,
Chalcis and probably Colophon as an affirmation of both kinship and
dependence, and a shrine to the sons of Ion 'from Athens' as the
eponymous progenitors of the four Ionian tribes is found in Samos.[23]
Participation in the religious aspects of the celebration of the two great
festivals is expected of the allies. After their revolt had been crushed in
453/2, the people of Erythrae were obliged to contribute only grain to
the Great Panathenaea; but six years later, by the time Cleinias proposed
his decree on the collection of the tribute, all allies were required on pain
of penalty to despatch a cow and a panoply.[24] The same requirement in
the decree authorizing the establishment of a colony at Brea *c.* 445
implies, and its repetition in Thudippus' decree of 425/4 makes explicit,
that this contribution was envisaged as being made by colonists to the
mother-city: its purpose was, therefore, to tighten the bond between
Athens and her subject allies.[25] A similar purpose was served by the
obligation to send a phallus to the celebration of the Dionysia which,
though it is attested only for the colony at Brea, may well have been
imposed also in other colonies.[26]

Late in the Archidamian War, the first-fruit offerings (*aparchai*),

[23] Barron 1964 (E 7) 35–48; Meiggs 1972 (E 53) 295–6.   [24] M–L 40.2–4, and 46.41–3.
[25] M–L 49.11–12, and 69.55–8. Cf. Schol. Ar. *Clouds* 386.
[26] M–L 49.12 with Herter 1938 (K 41) 1704. Cf. for the fourth century the decree in S. Accame, *La
lega Ateniese del secolo* IV *a. C.* (Rome, 1941) 230, lines 2–6.

offered to Demeter and Persephone at Eleusis by the Athenians 'according to ancestral custom and the oracle from Delphi', became obligatory also for the allies, and at the same time other Greeks are invited to despatch them.[27] Clearly, this constitutes an attempt not only to tie the allies more closely to Athens but also to give the Eleusinian cult a panhellenic dimension with Athens at the centre. The success of the attempt is attested by Isocrates' report (IV *Paneg.* 31) that first-fruits were still being sent to Eleusis by most Greek cities in the fourth century.

The religious life of Athens was also enriched, spontaneously and less fostered by political pressures, by the importation of cults on the part of foreign settlers who had made the imperial city their home (see above, pp. 261–2). The oldest and best known of these importations is the cult of Bendis, a Thracian goddess brought by Thracian settlers into the Piraeus.[28] She must have been privately worshipped by Thracian metics as early as the Periclean period (Cratinus, fr. 85 K–A), but her official recognition by the state is not likely to have come until the early days of the Peloponnesian War, stimulated perhaps by the attempt of Athens to cultivate good relations with the Thracian potentate Sitalces (Thuc. II.29).[29] It will have been about this time that a temple to her was erected at Munichia (Xen. *Hell.* II.4.11). A festival in her honour in which Athenians also participated was inaugurated on the grand scale on which we know it from the opening of Plato's *Republic* (I, 327a, 328a) with a torch-race on horseback and nocturnal festivities about 413/12.[30]

The cult of Asclepius, on the other hand, does not seem to have come to Athens either to satisfy the religious needs of metics from Epidaurus or as a result – however remote – of empire. Although because of its late arrival we cannot relate the introduction of this cult specifically to the plague, its appearance can only have been motivated by the need to cope with disease in some form. Like the cult of Bendis, it had its first home in Attica in the Piraeus where it was brought from Epidaurus (see above, pp. 261–2). About its foundation there, however, less is known than about its early history in Athens. We learn from a fourth-century inscription (*IG* II² 4960) that in 420/19 a certain 'Telemachus brought it here on a chariot, coming inland from Zea at the time of the Great Mysteries, and took it to the Eleusinium, having sent for [the sacred image of] the snake from its home in accordance with the oracles.' The 'home' can only be Epidaurus, the great centre of Asclepian worship in the Peloponnese, and the mention of Zea as the point of departure for Athens may mean no more than that it had landed there from Epidaurus

[27] M–L 73 with Meiggs 1972 (E 53) 302–4.

[28] For the history of her cult in Athens, see Pečírka 1966 (C 155) 122–30; for its substance, Nilsson 1967 (K 69) 833–4.

[29] Nilsson 1960 (K 68) 55–80, esp. 67–9; Ferguson 1944 (D 25) 96–104, esp. 98.

[30] *IG* I³ 136 with Bingen 1959 (C 116) 31–44. According to a scholion to Pl. *Rep.* 327a it was celebrated on 19 Thargelion.

on its way to Athens. However, since there was an Asclepian sanctuary at Zea which enjoyed a greater reputation in the early fourth century than its counterpart at Athens,[31] it may well have been established shortly before Telemachus brought the cult to Athens.[32] When the Kerykes refused to accommodate the god in the Eleusinium, the tragedian Sophocles, who was also a priest of the healing Hero Amynos, received him in his house, pending the completion of the sanctuary on the south slope of the Acropolis in 414/13.[33] Votive offerings indicate the popularity of the cult in the late Roman period.

There must have been other imported cults that were accorded official recognition by the state in the fifth century, even though no record of them has been preserved. We may infer this from the resistance offered by the guardians of the established forms of worship to the newcomers; we encountered this phenomenon in the refusal of the Kerykes to give Asclepius shelter in the Eleusinium, and it is reflected on a grand scale in Euripides' *Bacchae*, where the official recognition of the cult of Dionysus in Thebes is the issue.

The state, however, could not inhibit the entrance of private cults into Athens from abroad, especially from the east, and could not stamp them out by refusing to recognize them. Some such cults as those of Adonis and the Mother of the Gods will have been integrated into the religious life of Athens well before the outbreak of the Peloponnesian War. But the hardships of war, breeding as they do hopes for personal salvation, will have engendered more private cults than memory has preserved. If we are to draw inferences from the few of which we know, such as the cult of Sabazios, a Phrygian divinity parallel to Dionysus, or the mysteries of the Thracian goddess Cotyto, both of whom came to Athens in the last third of the fifth century,[34] they found their devotees primarily among women, slaves and members of the lower classes. Probably they were imported by sailors and other transients milling around the Piraeus, not by metics who brought their native forms of worship with them.

III. THE VISUAL ARTS

The two literary versions of the oath alleged to have been sworn by the Greeks before the battle of Plataea bound them not to rebuild any of the sanctuaries burned down or laid waste by the Persians but to leave them

[31] The Piraeus sanctuary must be the one in which Plutus is to be cured of his blindness in Ar. *Plut.* 653–747, since it is close to the sea (656). For the sanctuary at Zea, see Kutsch 1913 (K 55) 25–6 and 36–7, and Wycherley 1978 (I 187) 265.

[32] Possibly between 422 and 420, since in Ar. *Wasps* 122–3 (422 B.C.) Philocleon is sent for a cure to the Asclepius sanctuary on Aegina.

[33] *IG* II² 4960, *Etym. Magn.*, s.v. Δεξίων, *Vita Sophoclis* 11, with Kutsch 1913 (K 55) 16–28 and Walton 1935 (J 106) 167–89, esp. 170–4. Cf. Wycherley 1978 (I 187) 181–2, and Beschi 1967–8 (I 14) 381–436.   [34] Nilsson 1967 (K 69) 835–6; Burkert 1985 (K 16) 178–9.

for future generations as a memorial of Persian impiety.[35] Regardless of whether this part of the oath is authentic or not, it is true that the temples of Attica were left in ruins for a whole generation. No attempt was made to rebuild them until the 440s, when the Peace of Callias formally terminated hostilities against Persia and when, upon the rejection by the rest of the Greek world of an invitation to meet in Athens to deliberate about the problem of restoring them, the Athenians at the instigation of Pericles decided to embark on an ambitious programme of rebuilding their own ruined shrines.[36] This, however, did not mean that the task of reconstruction was not taken in hand sooner: there was nothing to prevent the rebuilding of secular structures destroyed by the Persians and nothing to inhibit the construction of new shrines to gods or heroes. Foreign workmen are likely to have been employed in this enterprise from its very inception, but the participation of foreign artists is not attested until the 460s, when Cimon occupied the centre of the stage in Athens.

Before we come to that, however, it will be convenient to discuss the most extensive and most conspicuous renovation of this period. No other part of Attica underwent more profound changes in character in the wake of the Persian Wars than the Piraeus. Themistocles had designated it to replace Phalerum as the main harbour of the city during his archonship in 493/2, but its growth not only as a naval base but as a crucial commercial centre of the Mediterranean had to await the end of the Persian Wars and the establishment of Athenian hegemony among the Greeks. To organize it in a manner befitting its new importance, Hippodamus of Miletus, the most renowned town planner of antiquity, was invited to design it (see above, p. 203). Our determination of when the invitation was extended depends on the interpretation we give to the phrase 'about the time of confrontation with the Medes' (Schol. Ar. *Knights* 327), which may range from soon after the battle of Plataea in 479/8 to the Peace of Callias in 449; the fact that Hippodamus lived long enough to plan the city of Rhodes in 408/7 (Str. xiv.2.9) makes the latter the more likely date. According to the most detailed account of Hippodamus' activities which has come down to us (Arist. *Pol.* ii.8, 1267b22–1268a14), he was not only the inventor of the art of town planning, but developed it on a theoretical basis that included well-articulated views on the nature of the good society (or 'best constitution', as Aristotle calls it) and on certain mathematical principles.[37] This

---

[35] Diod. xi.29.3; Lycurg. *Leoc.* 81; cf. Isocr. iv *Paneg.* 155–6; Paus. x.35.2; Cic. *Rep.* iii.9.15. The clause does not appear in the epigraphical version in Tod, *GHI* ii. 204.21–51. The genuineness of the oath was disputed by Theopompus, *FGrH* 115 F 153; Siewert 1972 (F 65) 102–6 believes this clause to be a later insertion.

[36] See ch. 8c above.

[37] Ar. *Pol.* ii.8, 1267b28 says that he wanted to be 'an expert on all of nature'; Hsch. and Photius, s.v. Ἱπποδάμου νέμησις, call him a μετεωρολόγος.

theoretical penchant is reflected in his design of the Piraeus: he divided it into different sectors according to function, providing each sector with a rectilinear set of streets arranged in the grid pattern already known in his native Asia Minor. Thus, certain areas were reserved for public use and others for private, and different public areas were assigned different functions: emporium, port, agora, etc., and provided with different buildings: club-houses, gateway, etc. In short, he adapted his general principles to the local conditions and functions of the Piraeus.[38]

There are further ways in which Hippodamus left a mark on Athens. We are told by a late commentator on Aristophanes' *Knights* (schol. on 327) that he settled in the Piraeus and had a house there. Since foreigners were barred from the acquisition of real estate, this may mean that he was given Athenian citizenship, which is corroborated by the general belief that he was the father of the Archeptolemus who was prominent in Athenian politics as an advocate of peace with Sparta in the late 420s and was condemned to death together with Antiphon as one of the leaders of the Four Hundred in 411/10.[39] The father fared better than the son. His participation in the settlement of Thurii in 444/3, along with other luminaries such as Protagoras of Abdera and Herodotus of Halicarnassus, suggests his active support of Periclean policies and may even indicate membership in the Periclean brains-trust; it is virtually certain, though not explicitly attested, that the planning of the colony was his work.[40] His eccentric appearance, his long flowing hair, his taste for expensive ornamentation worn with cheap but warm clothes, which served him in both winter and summer (Ar. *Pol.* 11.8, 1267b25–8), may have prefigured the attire affected by young Athenian aristocrats in the 420s.

Considering the intensity of the building activity in Athens after the Persian Wars and especially after 450, it is astonishing how little we know about the architects responsible for their design. Only a few names have come down to us, in most cases without indication of their provenance; only in the case of Metagenes of Xypete and Xenocles of Cholargos, who finished the Telesterium at Eleusis, does the demotic give us assurance that they were native Athenians. For the rest, no more than the circumstantial evidence that only works in Attica are known to have been their design suggests an Athenian origin.[41] But foreigners

---

[38] See McCredie 1971 (I 99) 95–100.

[39] Ar. *Knights* 794–5, cf. 327 with schol.; Lys. XII *Eratosth.* 67; [Plut.] *X orat.* 833F–834A.

[40] Hsch. s.v. Ἱπποδάμου νέμησις; Schol. Ar. *Knights* 327; Diod. XII.10.7.

[41] Only Ictinus is said to have also worked outside Attica, sc. on the temple of Apollo at Bassae: see Paus. VIII.41.9, where his work on the Parthenon is also mentioned; cf. also Plut. *Per.* 13.7 and Str. IX.12 and 16. He is also credited with beginning the design of the Telesterion at Eleusis (Str. IX.12; Vitr. VII *praef.* 16), which was continued by Coroebus (Plut. *loc. cit.*, cf. *IG* I³ 33, line 26). Callicrates was an architect of the Parthenon, constructed the Long Walls connecting Athens with the Piraeus (Plut. *loc. cit.*), and designed the Nike temple on the Acropolis (*IG* I³ 35 with Meiggs 1972 (E 53) 496–503). To Mnesicles only the Propylaea are attributed (Plut. *Per.* 13.12; Harp. s.v.

were called in to help decorate the new buildings with paintings and sculptures.

Our knowledge of them depends entirely on literary records which have come down to us.[42] Practically no originals of their works have survived, although we can occasionally catch a glimpse of them in the case of painters in imitations on vase paintings, and in the case of sculptors in Roman copies and on coins. The earliest foreign painter on a monumental scale of whom we know is at once reputed to be the greatest and most seminal. Polygnotus' migration from his native Thasos to Athens is almost certainly related to Cimon's military successes in the northern Aegean in the 470s and 460s, since it cannot be an accident that his most important works in Athens were displayed in buildings closely associated with Cimon's exploits. The earliest of these is the shrine built to house the bones of Theseus, which Cimon brought back from his expedition against Scyros soon after 476/5. It was adorned with at least three paintings, one of which, depicting Theseus' visit to Poseidon and Amphitrite on the sea-bed in order to convince Minos that he was Poseidon's son, was the work of the Athenian painter Micon, whose work is often associated with that of Polygnotus. The artist of the other two paintings, representing Theseus' participation in the fight against the Amazons and in the battle of Lapiths and Centaurs, is not identified by Pausanias (1.17.6), but recent research has persuasively established that they are the work of Polygnotus.[43] Micon and Polygnotus also collaborated on the sanctuary of the Dioscuri (Anaceum), which was probably erected in the Cimonian period. Micon's contribution showed the voyage of the Argonauts to the land of the Colchians and Polygnotus' marriage of the Dioscuri (Paus. 1.18.1). What connexion, if any, this shrine may have had with Cimon's achievements is not known. But Polygnotus' most celebrated work at Athens, *Troy Taken*, was painted for a stoa built in Cimon's honour by his brother-in-law Peisianax. By the fourth century, the renown which Polygnotus' art had given it caused its name to be changed from 'Peisianacteum' to 'Painted Stoa' (Stoa Poikile).[44] A close personal bond between Polygnotus and Cimon is indicated by the report that unlike Micon, who painted the famous battle of Marathon and an Amazonomachy for the Peisianacteum, Polygnotus refused to accept pay for his work, in which, we are told, the Trojan Laodice was given the features of Cimon's sister Elpinice, who counted

Προπύλαια ταῦτα). An unnamed Athenian architect is believed to have been responsible for the temple of Hephaestus on the Agora, of Poseidon at Sunium, of Ares at Acharnae, and of Nemesis at Rhamnous (see Dinsmoor 1950 (I 60) 179–82). But Miles 1981 (I 112) 207 now attributes Hephaestus, Poseidon and Nemesis to three different architects.

[42] Conveniently collected in Overbeck 1868 (I 120).

[43] Barron 1972 (I 9) 20–45, who assigns to Polygnotus also a fourth picture in the Theseum, representing Theseus' return from the dead. For Polygnotus' activity in the Theseum, see Harp s.v. Πολύγνωτος as emended by Valcken.   [44] D. L. VII.1.5; Suda s.v. Πεισιάνακτος στοά.

Polygnotus among her numerous lovers (Plut. *Cim.* 4.6.7). The reward
for this generosity was the grant of Athenian citizenship. But Polygnotus does not seem to have made much use of it: after Cimon's death no
more is heard of his residence in Athens.[45] His work, however,
continued to exert a profound influence on several Athenian vase
painters.[46] His departure did not end the relations of his family with
Athens: a generation later his son or nephew Aglaophon was commissioned by Alcibiades to paint two pictures to celebrate his triumphs
at the great Games, one showing personifications of the Olympian and
Pythian Games crowning him, and the other a seated Nemea holding
him in her lap.[47]

There was at least one other foreign painter whose employment
brought Alcibiades considerable notoriety. Alcibiades enticed Agatharchus of Samos to come into his house and then confined him in it, despite
his protests, until he had decorated it with his paintings.[48] Little else is
known of Agatharchus' work, except that he is said to have been the first
to paint scenery for the (presumably posthumous) performance of
Aeschylean tragedy, and to have written a book on the subject which
stimulated Anaxagoras and Democritus to formulate theories on
perspective (Vitr. VII.*praef.* 11).

The context of an anecdote related by Plutarch (*Per.* 13.7) suggests
that Agatharchus also participated in the Periclean building programme
and that he was a fast and facile worker. He was criticized on that score
by his contemporary Zeuxis, who had come to Athens as a young man
from Heraclea (probably the one on the Siris in southern Italy) in the
430s (Pl. *Prt.* 318b). His social background gave him easy access to the
upper-class intellectual circles of the city, and he was well known among
the friends of Socrates.[49] Aristotle speaks of him as a superb craftsman
but inferior to Polygnotus in conveying character (*Poet.* 25, 1461b12–13;
cf. 6, 1450a27–9). Remarkably little is known about the paintings he did
in Athens. One of the earliest and most famous, an Eros crowned with
roses, was done for the temple of Aphrodite;[50] an unusual composition
of a family of Centaurs, in which pride of place went to the female, it is
said by Lucian (*Zeuxis* 3–7) to have been sunk with a cargo of art which

[45] The paintings in the Cnidian Lesche in Delphi, described in great detail by Paus. x.25–31, are
probably to be dated between 458 and 447 (see Lippold 1952 (1 97) 1630 and 1634). His appointment
by the Amphictyones as *proxenos* on this occasion (Pl. *HN* xxxv.59) and his appointment as *theoros* in
Thasos in 444 B.C. (*IG* xii.8.277, line 44) suggest that he had returned to his native Thasos.
[46] Robertson 1979 (1 139) 122–35, and 1975 (1 140) 1.252–70.
[47] Ath. xii.534D. The Nemea is attributed by Plut. *Alc.* 16.7 to Aristophon, Polygnotus' brother
and either father or uncle of Aglaophon; but chronological considerations make Aglaophon the
more likely artist. Paus. 1.22.6 saw this picture in the Pinakotheke.
[48] [Andoc.] iv. *Alc.* 17; cf. Plut. *Alc.* 16.5 and Dem. xxi. *Meid.* 147.
[49] Xen. *Mem.* 1.4.3, *Symp.* iv.63; Pl. *Prt.* 318b, *Gorg.* 453c.
[50] Ar. *Ach.* 991–2 with schol., cf. Suda s.v. ἀνθέμων.

Sulla shipped from Athens to Rome in 86 B.C., though a copy could still be seen in Athens; and a picture of Helen allegedly adorned the stoa for barley meal.[51]

Of a further painting of his we hear in an anecdote which pits Zeuxis against his chief rival Parrhasius, who had come to Athens from Ephesus, where he had been trained by his father Euenor (Pliny, *HN* xxxv.60, Harp, s.v. Παρράσιος). Zeuxis requested Parrhasius to remove the curtain concealing a cluster of grapes which he had painted for a stage set so true to nature that birds flew up to pick at it; Parrhasius had to decline, because the curtain was painted – by Parrhasius himself (Pliny, *HN* xxxv.65). Their rivalry was also expressed in poetic form: Parrhasius' claim, in one of the epigrams with which he often signed his work, that he had reached the limits of art was answered by Zeuxis in an epigram challenging him to prove his point (Page, *Epigr. Gr.* 490–3, 496–9). Parrhasius was conspicuous in Athens through his extravagantly elegant attire (Ath. xii.543c–e) but he was also enough of an intellectual to be sought out by Socrates for a discussion of the problem whether internal beauty and ugliness can be portrayed in visual art (Xen. *Mem.* iii.10.1–5). We know only of a few of his works that they were done in Athens: he is said to have painted a 'Prometheus Bound' for the temple of Athena (which of her temples, we are not told), and a picture which showed the Athenian *demos* with all its contradictory qualities – 'moody, angry, unjust and fickle, but at the same time open to entreaty, merciful and compassionate; exultant, lofty, humble, savage and timid'.[52] Probably Athenian were also the picture of Hermes, to which he is said to have given his own features, and a painting of Theseus.[53] His earliest works in Athens of which we hear were designs for a battle of Lapiths and Centaurs and some other scenes for the shield of Athena Promachus, which were executed in relief by the Athenian engraver Mys (Paus. I.28.2).

We should expect foreigners to be well represented also in that branch of Athenian painting of which the greatest number of examples have survived, most of them recovered through archaeological finds; there must have been numerous foreigners among the potters and painters active in imperial Athens. Yet this remains an assumption incapable of proof. In terms of style, little difference can be detected between Athenian and foreign workmanship or artistry.

Some debt to Ionia might seem plausible in the light of East Greek influence in other arts, but stylistically it is impossible to prove, except in the matter of the

---

[51] Eust. *Il.* xi.631, possibly a copy of the Helen he was commissioned to paint by the people of Croton for the temple of Hera Lacinia, see Ael. *VH.* iv.12, Cic. *Inv. Rhet.* ii.1, Pliny, *HN* xxxv.64 and 66.   [52] Sen. *Controv.* x.5.34; Pliny, *HN* xxxv.69.
[53] Themistius ii.29c–d; Plut. *Thes.* 4, and *De Glor. Ath.* 2 (= *Mor.* 346B).

maeander and square patterns which had a very long history in East Greece, are met in Athenian black figure rarely, but only appear regularly in red figure from about 500 . . .[54]

Moreover, the influence of Polygnotan compositions on Athenian vase painters is unquestionable, and three vase painters even borrowed his name.[55] Apart from that, and in the absence of any literary evidence, we only have foreign-sounding names to go on, with which potters and painters signed their products. Such names appear on Attic vases from the sixth century on, probably in the wake of Solon's encouragement of foreign artisans to settle in Athens (*CAH* III².3, 384). Lydos was active in Athens as a black-figure painter *c.* 560–*c.* 530, Skythes as a red-figure vase painter in the late sixth century. From the early fifth century on, the name of the potter Brygos and his painter may betray a Phrygian origin, and the fact that the potter Pistoxenos twice signs his name as '*Pistoxenos Syriskos*' may point to Syrian ancestry.[56] But the cogency of arguments from names is weak and has been doubted by R. M. Cook:

There is nothing in inferences from names, that for example Skythes and Brygos were Scythian and Phrygian slaves; foreign ethnics and personal names were naturalized in Archaic Greece . . . . But though in most schools of pottery foreign influences are visible at one time or another, there are not so many signs of painters trained and matured in a foreign tradition . . . [Normally] the vase-painters of any city appear to have been brought up in the local tradition of that city, and the odds are that they were born there. Signatures very rarely help.[57]

This brings us to the contribution of sculptors from outside Athens to Athenian sculpture in the fifth century. Here we are faced with the problem of defining what constitutes a non-Athenian, especially in the case of Myron and Alcamenes. We know that Myron came from Eleutherae, a small town on the borders between Attica and Boeotia, the control of which changed hands several times but never seems to have been incorporated into Attica (Str. IX.2.31). While it is clear that it was considered Athenian territory in the fourth century (Xen. *Hell.* V.4.19), that was probably not the case in the fifth.[58] But, whatever the political status of Eleutherae may have been in Myron's lifetime, he will, like his son and pupil Lycius, have been of Boeotian stock (Ath. XI.486D) and

[54] Boardman 1975 (I 17).

[55] Robertson 1975 (I 140) I 253–7, 261, 327; Cook 1972 (I 47) 179–82; Boardman 1989 (I 21) 11–12, 62.

[56] For these names and several others, see Boardman 1975 (I 17) 9, 59–60, 113–14; Robertson 1975 (I 140) I 130–1, 230, 261; Webster 1972 (I 177) 6, 14, 19–20, 23, 35–8, 53.

[57] Cook 1972 (I 47) 271.

[58] Chandler 1926 (D 14A) 1–21, esp. 9–12; Wallace 1979 (F 69A) 124–6, with bibliography on p. 126, assumes continuous Athenian control from the seventh century on; cf. also Ober 1985 (G 32) 223–4.

will for that reason qualify as a non-Athenian, even if a passage in
Pausanias (VI.13.2) suggests that he may have enjoyed Athenian citizenship. Although he probably lived into the Periclean age, stylistically his
work belongs to the generation preceding it.

Myron's medium was bronze and his works were made for places as
far apart as Samos and Messana, Ephesus and Acragas, Argos, Aegina,
Boeotia and Athens. He was most renowned for his statues of victorious
athletes at the Olympic Games. Four of his works are known to have
been in Athens, all on the Acropolis: a statue of Erechtheus (Paus.
IX.30.1), a Perseus shown after he had beheaded Medusa (Paus. 1.23.7;
Pliny, HN XXXIV.57), the famous group of Athena with Marsyas picking
up the flute which she had discarded (Pliny, HN XXXIV.57; Paus. 1.24.1);
and finally his bronze heifer, celebrated by no fewer than thirty-six
poems in the *Greek Anthology*.[59] His son Lycius may have worked on the
Acropolis about the same time. Near the temple of Artemis Brauronia,
where Myron's Perseus was displayed, Pausanias (1.23.7) saw a bronze
boy holding a basin for lustral water (*perirrhanterion*) which he attributes
to Lycius, and epigraphical evidence assigns to Lycius two equestrian
statues near the Propylaea, dedicated by the cavalry to commemorate its
victory over the Lacedaemonians in 446 B.C. (*IG* I² 400; cf. Paus. 1.22.4).

The question whether or not Alcamenes, the star pupil of Phidias, was
an Athenian is posed by conflicting evidence: Pliny (*HN* XXXVI.16–17)
not only makes him an Athenian but attributes to his Athenian
citizenship victory in a contest with Agoracritus of Paros; other late
authors, however, make the island of Lemnos his home (Suda s.v.
'Ἀλκαμένης; Tzetz. *Chil.* VIII.333–9 (Leone)). The conflict can be
resolved by assuming either that he was born of Athenian parents who
had been settled on Lemnos by Miltiades or that he was one of the
Athenian cleruchs who were despatched by Lemnos between 450 and
446.[60] In any event, whether born as an Athenian citizen or not, it seems
clear that Alcamenes was attracted to Athens by the wider scope it
offered for the development of his art. On the Acropolis, a statue of
Hecate Epipyrgidia by him near the Nike temple was admired for
showing three images of the goddess attached to one another (Paus.
II.30.2), and some modern scholars believe that the statue of Hermes at
the Gate (Propylaios), which was ascribed to the famous Socrates (Paus.
1.22.8), may in fact be Alcamenes' work.[61] A marble statue of a woman
with a child pressed against her skirts which was found on the Acropolis
is possibly identical with the statue of Procne and Itys which, Pausanias

[59] See Overbeck 1868 (I 120) nos. 550–91.
[60] Robertson 1975 (I 140) I 284–5 with n. 228.
[61] Robertson 1975 (I 140) I 286, cf. Harrison 1965 (I 73A) 122–4, and Willers 1975 (I 177A) 33–47.
On the possibility of two Alcameneses in the fifth century, see Barron 1984 (I 9A).

tells us (1.24.3), was dedicated by Alcamenes on the Acropolis and is almost certainly his work. The drapery of this statue bears such a close resemblance to that of the Caryatids at the Porch of the Maidens of the Erechtheum that it has been suggested that the latter, too, may have been designed by Alcamenes.[62] Outside the Acropolis, Alcamenes' most important work was the cult statue of Hephaestus – and presumably also of its companion piece, Athena – for the temple of Hephaestus which was completed on the north-west corner of the Agora between 421 and 415 (*IG* i³ 472).[63] To the theatre of Dionysus he contributed a gold-and-ivory statue of the god (Paus. 1.20.3). His statue of Aphrodite, which could be seen in the 'Gardens' outside the city, was probably an early work, because we are told that his master Phidias put the finishing touches on it (Pliny, *HN* xxxvi.16; Paus. 1.19.2). Finally, an image of Hera in a temple on the road to Phalerum was attributed to Alcamenes (Paus. 1.1.5). Most closely related to Athenian history, however, was a monument by him in the sanctuary of Heracles in Thebes. It represented Athena and Heracles and was set up by Thrasybulus and his followers in gratitude for Theban aid in the overthrow of the Thirty Tyrants in 404/3 B.C. (Paus. ix.11.6).

A more genuinely foreign sculptor to come to Athens to be a pupil (and become a beloved) of Phidias was Agoracritus of Paros (Pliny, *HN* xxxvi.17; Paus. ix.34.1). Their relationship was so close that Phidias is said to have passed off some of his own work as that of Agoracritus. One of these may have been the marble statue of the Mother of Gods in Athens which is attributed to Phidias by Pausanias (1.3.5) and Arrian (*Peripl. M. Eux.* 9), but to Agoracritus by Pliny (*HN* xxxvi.17). Pausanias (1.33.2–3, 8) also attributes to Phidias the only other important work of Agoracritus in Attica, the cult image of Nemesis in Rhamnous, adding the incredible story that its marble was brought from Paros to Marathon by the Persians with the intention of carving a trophy out of it. Pliny's attribution of this statue to Agoracritus (*HN* xxxvi.17) is based on the no more likely story that it was originally carved as a statue of Aphrodite for which Agoracritus competed with Alcamenes. When the Athenians awarded the prize to Alcamenes on the grounds that he was their fellow-citizen, Agoracritus called his work 'Nemesis' and sold it on condition that it would not be displayed in Athens. Later authors confirm that the statue bore the signature of Agoracritus, although some assert that it was affixed by Phidias, who wanted his beloved to get credit for it. No doubt it belongs to Agoracritus; local tradition, as has been wisely pointed out, prefers a great name to a lesser for its works of art.[64]

---

[62] Robertson 1975 (I 140) I 286 and 345; cf. Knell 1978 (I 89A) 9–19.

[63] Cic. *Nat. D.* 1.30.83, Val. Max. viii.11. est. 3.

[64] See Overbeck 1868 (I 120) nos. 834–43 with Robertson 1975 (I 140) I 351–2 and n. 145. Cf. Pétracos 1981 (I 123) 227–53. On Agoracritus and his statue of Nemesis, see Despinis 1971 (I 56).

It is fitting to close this section with a brief mention of two minor sculptors who are associated with the name of the statesman who did more than anyone else to make Athens the cultural centre that it was in the fifth century. Styppax of Cyprus is credited with one work only, a bronze boy in the likeness of one of Pericles' slaves, blowing to fan the flames to roast entrails. According to Pliny, Pericles was responsible for its dedication to Athena who, when the slave had fallen from the top of the Parthenon in the construction of which he was working, revealed to Pericles in a dream the drug which would cure him.[65] Two sculptures on the Acropolis are attributed by Pliny (*HN* xxxiv.74) to Cresilas of Cydonia in Crete: one, a wounded warrior, is often identified with a bronze statue of Diitrephes smitten by arrows, which Pausanias (1.23.3–4) noted in the Propylaea without mentioning the artist's name; the other was a statue of Olympian Pericles which, according to Pliny, was worthy of its title in that it added nobility to a man already noble. Many copies of it were made in antiquity, of which several survive.[66]

IV. LITERATURE

The contributions to fifth-century Athenian culture by non-Athenian poets and prose writers were immeasurably greater than the surviving remains indicate. The work of only two major foreign authors active, at some time or another, in Athens has had a manuscript tradition of its own strong enough to have been preserved in a form coherent and intelligible to us: the historical work of Herodotus and some thirty speeches of Lysias out of the 233 which were known as genuine in later antiquity. Apart from Simonides and Pindar, whose connexion with Athens early in the fifth century is tenuous at best, only stray notices of non-Athenian poets and their works have come down to us through the learned literature and lexica of late antiquity, and only rarely do we find fragments of their productions cited by excerptors such as Athenaeus and Stobaeus. The impact of Attic tragedy and comedy was apparently so strong that it obliterated all but a few traces of other kinds of poetry, even when it had come from the pen of Athenians, just as the superior quality of Aristophanic comedy deprived other comic writers of a manuscript tradition of their own. And yet we know that Athens was hospitable to poets of all genres of literature and from all parts of the Greek world in the fifth century, just as she had been in the past and was to be in the future, except that the topical, parochial, and political nature of comedy tempted no foreigners to compete with native Athenians.[67]

Tragedy, the most characteristically Athenian form of literature in the

---

[65] Pliny, *HN* xxxiv.81, cf. xxii.44. For a different version, see Plut. *Per.* 13.13, where the Propylaea is given as the scene of the accident.

[66] See Richter 1965 (I 131) I 102–4, with figs. 429–43; and 1984 (I 133) 173–5.

[67] Since the ancient evidence for the following is too scattered to permit detailed annotation, we shall refer the reader to its discussion by Lesky 1966 (J 65) and in Schmid and Stählin 1934–48 (J 92).

fifth century, owes its origins to an assimilation of art forms first developed in the Dorian Peloponnese. From the beginning, it never closed its doors to foreigners wishing to compete in the tragic contests at the City Dionysia. In fact, it was a foreigner, Pratinas of Phlius, who first introduced satyr plays into the tragic contests at Athens, winning on one occasion – probably between 499 and 496 – the first prize over the Athenians Aeschylus and Choerilus. Some of his tragedies were posthumously staged by his son Aristias, who not only won the second prize with them after Aeschylus' Theban tetralogy in 467, but also wrote victorious tragedies of his own.[68] Another innovation, the precise nature of which is not known but which was concerned with the length of the plays produced, was introduced before the middle of the fifth century by Aristarchus of Tegea, who produced seventy tragedies in the course of his long life but won only two victories.[69] Two foreign playwrights were the only tragedians besides Aeschylus, Sophocles and Euripides to be admitted into the Alexandrian canon of great tragedians. The lesser-known of these is Archaeus of Eretria, who was renowned for his satyr plays and competed with Sophocles and Euripides from the early 440s on, but is credited with only one victory.[70] His older contemporary, Ion of Chios, has a special claim to fame, not only because he was one of the most versatile writers of all Classical antiquity, but also because he knew and wrote about his encounters with some of the most prominent Athenians of his time. Moreover, his is one of the few cases in which we have some firm dates.

Ion was born in Chios within the decade 490–480, and Aristophanes' *Peace* (834–7), first performed in 421, refers to his recent death, presumably in Athens. His first tragic victory in Athens fell within the eighty-second Olympiad, that is, between 452 and 449, and he won the third prize in 428 at the contest which Euripides won with his *Hippolytus*. All in all ten tetralogies of his were known, and on one occasion of unknown date he celebrated a double victory in the tragic and dithyrambic contests of the City Dionysia by treating every Athenian citizen to a jar of Chian wine, a testimony of his wealth. Of his tragedies little more than some titles have come down to us, but the elegance and smoothness of his style are praised by as sensitive a critic as the author of *On the Sublime* (33.5), although he regards it as inferior to the fiery genius of Sophocles. This judgement is confirmed by his dithyrambs, elegies, epigrams and solo lyrics, of which a larger number of sometimes extensive fragments has survived. Nothing remains of his hymn to *Kairos* (the decisive moment), whom he called the youngest child of Zeus, and which will have prefigured the love of personification of

---

[68] Lesky 224 and 231–2; Schmid and Stählin 1.2.82–3 and 178–82.
[69] Schmid and Stählin 1.2.514.   [70] Lesky 411; Schmid and Stählin 1.2.520–1.

abstract concepts which spread from the late fifth century on throughout the Greek world. A stray remark (Schol. Ar. *Peace* 835, Suda s.v. διθυραμβοδιδάσκαλοι) that he also wrote comedies is of doubtful validity, and his work on the *Foundation of Chios*, which has been regarded as an epic by some scholars, is more likely to have been a prose work.

Ion's most original prose work is at once his most interesting for the historian. His *Epidemiai* (Travels) constitutes the earliest collection of autobiographical anecdotes of which we know in Greek literature and remained unique throughout antiquity. From it we learn that Ion was present at a banquet given in Athens by Laomedon at which Cimon reminisced about his experiences at Sestus and Byzantium, telling how he let the allies choose the rich ornamentation taken from the booty of the Persians, while he kept the Persian prisoners for the Athenians, realizing a substantially larger amount from their ransom (Plut. *Cim.* 9). If the banquet took place about the time that Cimon advocated help for the Spartans at Ithome (*ibid.* 16.10), Ion was still a young man of seventeen or eighteen years of age. What attracted him to Athens can only be guessed; but his presence at the banquet and his later munificence in distributing wine to all Athenians indicate provenance from a wealthy upper-class family. On another occasion, he encountered Aeschylus at the Isthmian Games (Plut. *Mor.* 79E), and during the Samian War in the late 440s he attended a banquet given by the Chian *proxenos* of Athens in honour of Sophocles, a general at that time, at which the poet employed his 'strategic' skills to plant a kiss on the boy who was pouring the wine (Ath. XIII.603E–604D). It will have been in the course of the same war that he encountered Socrates and the philosopher Archelaus on the island of Samos (D. L. II.23). All this shows that Ion was welcomed with open arms by the artistic and intellectual élite of Athens; how much time he spent there we do not know, but there must have been several visits of longer or shorter duration. His affection for Athens was such that his son Tydeus paid for it with his life during the Spartan occupation of Chios in 412/11 (Thuc. VIII.38.3).[71]

No epic poetry worthy of note was written in the Greek world in the fifth century, and none at all in Athens; but the only two practitioners of this genre who are of any interest seem to have had a tenuous relationship to Athens. Choerilus of Samos must have been active in the last third of the fifth century, if the report is true that Lysander retained him in his retinue in the hope that he would celebrate his feats (Plut. *Lys.* 18.7). The improbable story that he fled from slavery in Samos to be befriended by Herodotus may somehow be connected with the fact that

[71] In general, see Lesky 409–11; Schmid and Stählin 1.2.514–21 and 674–6; A. von Blumenthal, *Ion von Chios* (Stuttgart–Berlin, 1939); West 1985 (J 108); and Dover 1988 (J 34).

his epic poem on the Athenian victory over the Persians showed close resemblances to passages in Herodotus' narrative. The Athenians are alleged to have been so happy with the poem that they paid Choerilus one stater for every line of the work and had it recited along with the Homeric epics at the Panathenaic festival. Regardless of whether this tradition is reliable, there is no doubt that Choerilus was the first to reject heroic legends and to take historical events as the theme of his epic, doing for epic what Phrynichus' *Capture of Miletus* and Aeschylus' *Persians* had done for tragedy.[72] A contemporary of his, Hegemon of Thasos, is named by Aristotle (*Poet.* 2, 1448a12–13) and Athenaeus (IX.406E) as the first writer of parodies, and we know that these included travesties of both epic and tragic poetry. Since mock-heroic poetry is as old as the *Battle of Frogs and Mice* (*Batrachomyomachia*), attributed to Homer in antiquity, Hegemon's originality probably consisted in writing parodies to the exclusion of any other form of literature. We are told that he was reciting his *Battle of the Giants* (*Gigantomachia*) in Athens when the news of the Sicilian disaster reached the theatre; the audience was so enthralled by his performance and so full of laughter that they did not leave their seats, 'in order not to show the spectators from other cities how hard they were taking the disaster' (Ath. IX.407A–B). On an earlier occasion, Alcibiades is said to have come to Hegemon's rescue: Hegemon, summoned to Athens to appear as a defendant in a lawsuit, enlisted the help of Alcibiades; Alcibiades complied by marching into the Metroon to expunge the record of the indictment, and no one dared to offer resistance (*ibid.* 407B–C). A very funny epic parody of his is preserved which tells how he defended himself against his detractors in Thasos by explaining that poverty drove him to go abroad to make a living by reciting his poetry (*ibid.* XV.698D–699C).[73]

Poetry sung to the accompaniment of flute or lyre by individuals or choruses was more appreciated than composed by the Athenians. Its most common form, the dithyramb, a choral composition originally sung to the accompaniment of a flute in honour of Dionysus, is said to have been given a literary form by Arion of Methymna on Lesbos, who lived at the court of Periander at Corinth in the late seventh and early sixth centuries (Hdt. 1.23).[74] Lasus of Hermione, one of the favourite poets of the Pisistratids, may have introduced it to Athens; it was first admitted for competition at the City Dionysia to be sung by a chorus of men in 509/8, when another foreigner, Hypodicus of Chalcis, won the first prize (*Marm. Par.* ep. 46). After that, the only foreign dithyrambic poets competing in Athens before the Cimonian age were the three great

[72] Lesky 304–5; Schmid and Stählin 1.2.542–6.
[73] Lesky 417; Schmid and Stählin 1.4.473–4.
[74] For the following, see Pickard-Cambridge 1962 (J 84) 1–59.

figures of the late Archaic age, Simonides, Pindar and Bacchylides, all of whom seem to have made their mark in dithyrambic contests within the decade following the battle of Salamis (see above, pp. 237–9). Some of the fifty-six victories with men's choruses which Simonides claims for himself in an epigram ascribed to him (Page, *Epigr. Gr.* 181–4) will have been won during his stay in Athens during and immediately after the Persian Wars, and one of them will have been the victory won at the age of eighty with a chorus of fifty men in Athens in 477/6, which another epigram (Page, *Epigr. Gr.* 185–90) celebrates. Pindar wrote not only victory odes for Megacles' victory at the Pythian Games in 486 B.C., and for Timodemus' at the Nemean Games some time before Salamis (*Pyth.* VII; *Nem.* II), but we also possess a substantial fragment of one and intelligible scraps of another dithyramb performed in and in honour of Athens (frs. 75 and 76–8 Snell) in the 470s, in which he praises the Athenians for having 'laid the resplendent foundation of freedom'. And two of Bacchylides' dithyrambs, the *Io* and the *Theseus*, were composed for performance in Athens, probably soon after the end of the Persian Wars.[75]

The dithyrambs composed by Ion of Chios seem to have adhered to the traditional pattern of narrative poetry sung to the accompaniment of the flute by a chorus of fifty men or boys with or without responsive singing of strophe and antistrophe by one half of the chorus to the other. Innovations and changes introduced in the second half, especially in the last quarter, of the fifth century are almost exclusively by non-Athenians: Cinesias is the only exception of whom we know.[76] The contemporary evidence for this movement, which soon affected all choral lyric poetry, comes from the hostile reception given to it by old comedy and by Plato, who disliked its unconventionality, its changes of keys, its experimentation with increases in the number of strings of the cithara, its confused and contorted tunes, the abandonment of strophic structures in favour of lyric solos (*anabolai*) sung by professionals, its neologisms and fanciful imagery, and so forth.[77] The most valuable comment appears on a fragment from Pherecrates' *Chiron* (fr. 145K), in which battered Music complains to Justice of the insults she has had to endure. Melanippides of Melos is chastised as the first culprit. His dates are problematic, since the Suda, probably mistakenly, also mentions an earlier poet of the same name as the grandfather of the later, who is thought to have been active from *c.* 480 B.C. to his death at the court of Perdiccas of Macedonia (*c.* 450–413). He is credited with having introduced lyric solos into the

---

[75] Severyns 1933 (J 98) 56–69. According to Isocr. xv. *Antid.* 166, Pindar was honoured by the Athenians with his appointments as *proxenos* and with a gift of 10,000 drachmae; according to Paus. 1.8.4, a statue of him was set up in the Agora.

[76] Schmid and Stählin 1.4.495–7.   [77] Schmid and Stählin 1.488–90.

dithyramb. Fragments of a *Danaides*, a *Marsyas* and a *Persephone* have survived, but it is not sure whether these were dithyrambs.[78] Phrynis of Mytilene is the next foreigner on Pherecrates' list. He is known as a composer of new-fangled *nomoi*, choral compositions sung to the accompaniment of a cithara, rather than of dithyrambs, and he won the cithara contest at that Panathenaea of 456. He was outdistanced, however, by his pupil Timotheus of Miletus, who is the third and last foreigner to be rebuked by Pherecrates.[79] Timotheus, who lived from *c.* 450 to *c.* 360, composed *nomoi* as well as dithyrambs and other forms of choral lyric. His reception was initially not favourable, even though it was probably in Athens that he won a victory over his master Phrynis (fr. 802 *PMG*). But he was successful with his *nomos The Persians*, for which his friend Euripides is said to have written the prologue and which may have influenced a scene of Euripides' *Orestes*. If so, it will have been performed before 408. Some 250 verses of *The Persians* were discovered in 1902 inscribed on a papyrus of the fourth century B.C., which is not only the oldest literary papyrus to survive from Classical antiquity but also gives us an insight into his peculiar art.[80] That Philoxenus of Cythera, a younger contemporary of Timotheus, was known in Athens is shown by a reference to his style as early as Aristophanes' *Clouds* (335 with schol.) and by a parody on his famous dithyramb *Cyclops* as late as Aristophanes' *Plutus* (290 with schol.). It was the *Cyclops*, incidentally, which first treated the love of the Cyclops for Galatea, which was later celebrated in the eleventh idyll of Theocritus.[81]

Foremost among the prose writers attracted to Athens in the fifth century is one of the foremost writers of Greek prose of any period, Herodotus of Halicarnassus. What attracted him to Athens can only be conjectured: it may have been merely part of his passion for travel, it may have been the intellectual climate of the Periclean age, or it may have been a desire to visit the focus of resistance against the Persians in the previous generation. In view of the prominence given to Athens in his narrative, it is surprising how little about his relation to Athens has been preserved in the ancient traditions about his life. The most detailed account, that in the Suda (s.v. ʿΗρόδοτος), mentions his birth in Halicarnassus – presumably in the mid-480s – his exile in Samos, his return to his home to help overthrow the tyrant Lygdamis, and his participation in the Athenian settlement of Thurii, where he is said to have spent the rest of his life. It says nothing about his travels and nothing about his stay in Athens. For the latter we depend on a few

[78] Pickard-Cambridge 39–42.

[79] Pickard-Cambridge 43, Lesky 414, Schmid and Stählin 1.4.491–2.

[80] The classic edition is that of von Wilamowitz 1903 (J 109). In general, see Lesky 415–16, Schmid and Stählin 1.4.503–14, Pickard-Cambridge 48–51.

[81] Lesky 415; Schmid and Stählin 1.4.497–500; Pickard-Cambridge 45–8.

scraps of information which tell us that 'he was honoured by the Athenian Council for having read his books to them' in 445/4 (Eus. *Chron.* Olymp. 83.4), that 'on the motion of Anytus, he received from Athens a gift of ten talents' (Diyllus *FGrH* 73 F 3), and that Thucydides was reduced to tears by one of his lectures (Marcellin. 54).[82] That Thucydides attended lectures by Herodotus in Athens is chronologically improbable, since he will have been no more than ten to fifteen years old in the 440s, and after that Herodotus settled in Thurii. But when we combine this story with the dated tradition that Herodotus was honoured for his reading, it remains credible that Herodotus visited Athens and delivered lectures in the mid-440s; the fact that he was publicly honoured is corroborated by the tradition, whose general accuracy is guaranteed by a name associated with it, that he received a gift from the state. However, the sum of ten talents is somewhat high to deserve credence, unless we assume, without support from any ancient source, that in addition to his readings Herodotus had performed other meritorious services for the city.

The 'books' from which he read at that time cannot have been his work in the form in which it has come down to us. At least they cannot have included the narrative of the Persian Wars now to be found in Books VI–IX, because these books contain references to events which did not take place until the late 430s.[83] That he lectured on his travels and on the people and places he had encountered is suggested by a number of comparisons of foreign with Athenian phenomena. The fact that he compares the size of the outer circuit wall of Ecbatana with the circumference of Athens (1.98.5) and that he gives the Attic equivalent to the Persian cubic measure *artabe* (1.192.3) may indicate that he lectured on Persia; his comparison of the distance of Heliopolis from the sea with that of the altar of the Twelve Gods in Athens from Pisa and the temple of Zeus at Olympia (II.7.1) may show that his lectures included Egypt; and that he talked about his travels to Scythia is intimated by his comparison of the shape of the Tauric peninsula (the Crimea) with the peninsula on the point of which Sunium is located (IV.99.5). These analogies make sense only to an audience as intimately familiar with Athens and Attica as only the Athenians can have been, and permit the inference that foreign peoples and places constituted his main interest at the time he appeared in public before an Athenian audience.

Was Herodotus already interested in 'history' in the sense in which we, following in his footsteps, understand the term, when he lectured in

[82] On Herodotus and Athens, see Jacoby 1913 (C 55) 226–42; Kleinknecht 1940 (C 61) 241–62; Strasburger 1955 (C 97) 1–25; Fornara 1971 (C 32) 37–58.

[83] E.g., the expulsion of the Aeginetans from their homes (VI.91.1), the Peloponnesian War (VI.98.2, VII.137.1, IX.73.3), the Theban attack on Plataea (VII.233.2).

Athens? Certainly, the fact that traces of only geographical and ethnographical lectures have survived does not mean that he had nothing to say on the history of the places he had visited. On the contrary, it is unthinkable that his accounts of Persia, Egypt and Scythia should not have included what he had seen and heard about important events which these places had experienced in the past and which we find embedded in his narrative. But it is questionable whether the conception of the work as a whole, integrating as it does the Persian Wars with the events in different parts of the world that led up to it, which constitutes Herodotus' claim to the title of 'father of history',[84] was already present in his mind when he visited Athens. In the absence of any evidence, it is plausible that this conception was stimulated by his stay in the city, which had roused itself from the rubble in which the Persians had left it to become an imperial and cultural centre second to none in the Greek world.

Herodotus is even more reticent about himself and his life than is Thucydides, and this reticence extends also to the names of his informants. The crucial role played by the Athenians in the battles of Marathon, Artemisium, Salamis and Mycale makes it *a priori* likely that a large number of his informants were Athenians, who would supply him also with accounts of earlier events in Athenian history, such as the Cylonian revolt (v.71), the tyranny of Pisistratus and his sons, its overthrow, and the establishment of the Cleisthenean democracy (1.59–64, v.55–97). The Athenians are more frequently mentioned as a source of information than any other Greek people and are exceeded only by the Egyptians.[85] To identify individual informants is impossible even in those cases where individual experiences are related, such as Dicaeus' vision on the Thriasian plain (viii.65) or the exploits of Sophanes of Deceleia (vi.92.2, ix73–4). However, there is so much detailed and often intimate information on a number of noble families that the inference is inevitable that Herodotus had free access to members of the upper classes and enjoyed their confidence. The complexity of the relationship of Pisistratus to the Philaidae, the family of which Miltiades and Cimon were members, is such that one is tempted to assume that Herodotus learned of it from a family member, who also showed him the tomb of Miltiades' father, Cimon (vi.34–41, 103.2–4, 136.3). He is so well informed about the history of the Alcmeonids (vi.125–31) and so anxious to clear them of responsibility for the traitorous shield signal given to the Persians at the time of Marathon (vi.121–4) that close personal connexions between him and one or more of their number have

---

[84] On this point, see especially Jacoby 1913 (c 55) 467–86. Fehling's arguments (c 29A), contrived to deny that claim, are unconvincing, despite their occasional insights; see c 18A.

[85] See the list in Jacoby 1913 (c 55) 398–9.

been inferred. A similarly cordial relation to the Kerykes seems implied by the details he knows of their ancestor Callias under the tyrants (VI.121–2). He knows what the Gephyraei believe about their own provenance and what other Athenians believe about it (V.57.1). Further, the numerous anecdotes told to undermine the moral qualities of Themistocles (VIII.4.2, 57–8, 112.1, 124.1–2) may come from descendants of Athenians prominent at the time of Salamis who opposed the policies of the man who made Athens a naval power. Yet hostile and complimentary strands are so tightly interwoven with one another that we must assume that Herodotus integrated the family traditions he had learned with more general population traditions current about the past.[86]

Herodotus' work has often been interpreted as an encomium on Athens, on democracy, on the Alcmeonids, and on their most illustrious scion, Pericles.[87] Of Herodotus' respect and admiration for all of these there can be no doubt, but his admiration was neither blind nor confined to Athens, and above all it did not make Herodotus an apologist for Athens *tout court*.[88] Herodotus recognized that the deployment of sea power was the single most decisive factor in the victory of the Greeks over the Persians, to whom they were inferior in manpower and in materiel. It is for realizing this fact, for acquiescing in the abandonment of their city to be ravaged by the Persians (VIII.40.1) and for relinquishing the command of the allied navy to the Spartans lest divisiveness undermine Greek survival (VIII.3) that Athens is praised as the 'saviour of Greece' (VII.139). But the preface to this praise: 'At this point, I am constrained by hard facts to state publicly a judgement which will be invidious to the majority of mankind; none the less, I shall not hold back what seems to me to be true' (VII.139.1), shows that it is not a panegyric nor a defence of Athenian policy at the time of writing, but a fact about the past which contemporaries did not like to hear. Moreover, Herodotus' admiration for Athens did not make him blind to the fact that the Spartan contribution to the victory was no less decisive. Even though their stand at Thermopylae was doomed to failure, the fact that it was made under the command of Leonidas gave an example to the rest of the Greeks which evoked Herodotus' unbounded admiration (VIII.204 and 220). Further, it is at Plataea, not at Salamis, that the Greeks won 'the noblest victory of any that we know', a victory credited to the leadership of the Spartan Pausanias (IX.64.1).

Similarly, Herodotus' praise of the Athenian democracy is no simple encomium on a particular form of government or on a particular state. In

---

[86] For an excellent discussion, see Thomas 1989 (A 114), esp. pp. 171–3 on the Philaidae; 247–51 and 264–81 on the Alcmeonids; 109 and 252 with n. 34 on the Gephyraei; and 206 n. 37 and 224 on Themistocles.   [87] E.g., Harvey 1966 (C 45) 254–5.

[88] Strasburger and Fornara (above, n. 82).

fact, he never praises democracy as 'democracy', but applauds it where he does under names which suggest his admiration of a particular aspect of it. In the Constitutional Debate in Persia, he praises it as 'government by the people which has the fairest name of all, political equality (*isonomie*)' (III.80.6); and he extols its Athenian variety as 'right of free speech' (*isegorie*), which the Athenians acquired after they had expelled the tyrants. But that does not mean that he is blind to its shortcomings. Some of these are summed up in Megabyxus' statement in the Constitutional Debate that 'there is nothing more devoid of insight or more prone to arrogance (*hybris*) than a useless mob' (III.81.1), and another in Herodotus' comment on Aristagoras' success in Athens after his failure at Sparta to enlist support for the Ionian Revolt that 'it seems easier to hoodwink many than one, since he was unable to hoodwink one man, the Lacedaemonian Cleomenes, but managed to do so in the case of thirty thousand Athenians' (V.97.2). However, Herodotus does not praise *isegorie* for its own sake but as having given Athens the freedom (*eleutherie*) which she had not enjoyed under the tyranny and through which a great city became even greater (V.78, cf. 66.1). The winning of this freedom for themselves enabled them later 'to choose that Greece should survive free' and thus 'to arouse the entire rest of the Greek world which did not medize and to repel the King of Persia with the help of the gods' (VII.139.5).

There is no need here to demonstrate that for Herodotus the issue in the Persian Wars was the affirmation of freedom against the threat of slavery. But it must be pointed out that, whatever Herodotus' own attitude toward democracy may have been, he praised *isegorie* only for having given Athens that liberty which enabled her to lead the Greeks in the fight for their freedom, even if initially the Spartans regarded the newly won Athenian freedom as a challenge to their own supremacy in Greece (V.91.1). Nevertheless, the Athenians had no monopoly on freedom. The most rousing treatment of this theme is put into a Spartan context, when the exiled Spartan king Demaratus explains to an incredulous Xerxes that the Spartans, 'though free are not free in every respect: law (*nomos*) is master over them, and they fear it far more than your subjects fear you' (VII.104.4). What this means is strikingly illustrated by the behaviour of the Spartans Sperthias and Boulis at the Persian court (VII.134–6, esp. 135.3). Evidently, love of freedom is Herodotus' primary concern; whether it was exemplified in *isegorie* or in obedience to the law was of secondary importance to him.

There can be no doubt that Herodotus was aware of the prominent role the Alcmeonids had played and were still playing in the history of Athens. The fact that the birth of the most prominent Alcmeonid of his own time, Pericles, was prefigured by his mother's dream of giving birth

to a lion is neither ominous nor complimentary, but simply indicates that
Pericles was a man to be reckoned with (vi.125–31). Herodotus' defence
of the family against the charge of treason at the time of Marathon
(vi.121–4) is often taken as a sign of partiality for them. But since there is
little other evidence for such partiality, Herodotus may simply have
found it difficult to believe that a family which had rendered such
outstanding service to the state in the past could have been responsible
for the shield signal which, he knows, was given to the Persians.
Moreover, the common opinion that this defence is evidence for an
Alcmeonid source for Herodotus, though probable, does not rest on
firm foundations: Herodotus may well have learned of the charge from
sources hostile to the Alcmeonids and may have rejected it on the basis of
his judgement of what this prominent family would or would not be
capable of doing.

Our difficulty in this regard is due to Herodotus' failure to mention
even a single Athenian informant by name. But we know from other
sources the name of one prominent Athenian with whom he must have
established a close personal relationship, the tragedian Sophocles. The
external evidence for this consists in the opening of an epigram quoted
by Plutarch (*Mor.* 785 B): 'Sophocles composed a song for Herodotus at
the age of fifty-five' (Page, *Epigr. Gr.* 466–7), which was evidently
written as a dedication to accompany the song. Since Sophocles was
born in 497/6, the date of this occasion will be *c.* 442/1, at a time when
other considerations suggest Herodotus' presence in Athens. This is also
the time in which Sophocles wrote his *Antigone*. It has long been seen
that the passage in that play, in which Antigone explains her preference
for her brother by arguing that, once one's parents are dead, he alone is
irreplaceable, whereas a husband or child is not (904–24), depends on
Herodotus' story about the wife of Intaphernes (iii.119, 3–6). Unlike
Herodotean echoes in his later plays, the parallels between Antigone's
arguments and those of the wife of Intaphernes are so close that they
have been taken to corroborate the personal contact between tragedian
and historian which is suggested by the fragmentary epigram.[89]

To go beyond this to assert that Herodotus' view of the historical
process owes something to Sophocles is a plausible conjecture incapable
of proof. Yet it seems true that both authors see the same kind of factors
involved in the human situation which makes them share a similar tragic
view of life. To demonstrate this similarity in detail would take us
beyond the scope of our present task. On a superficial level, this can be

[89] Jacoby 1913 (C 55) 232–7. Among the later parallels are: Soph. *El.* 417–27 and Hdt. 1.108.1–2;
Soph. *OC* 337–41 and Hdt. 11.35.2–4. Of these the former may have been produced still in
Herodotus' lifetime, if Fornara's arguments for his death *c.* 414 (1971 (C 32A) and 1981 (C 32B)) can
be accepted.

seen in the importance of dreams, oracles, prophecies and warnings which influence the lives of legendary heroes in Sophocles and those of historical figures of an ascertainable past in Herodotus; it is further manifested in the prominence given by both authors to concepts such as *hybris* (offensive pride), *tisis* (vengeance), *dike* (justice), *phthonos* (jealousy, envy), and *ate* (moral indifference leading to ruin) as motivations for human conduct.[90] But, in a more profound sense, Herodotus shares with Sophocles more than with any of the other great tragedians a keen awareness that men are placed into situations in which, however reasonably they act, their actions will inevitably have consequences which recoil against them and those close to them in kinship, friendship or citizenship.

A very similar view of the human condition is taken by Herodotus both in working out the theme of his work as a whole and in innumerable details in his narrative which serve as building blocks for his structure.[91] History is enacted by persons whom character, family, and social and political mores and traditions have placed into situations with which they cope as reasonably as they can according to their lights, but cannot control the outcome of their actions. A decision once made is subject to the inexorable laws of an external necessity, a force which, though divine, can be communicated to men by gods, especially by Apollo and his oracle, but is apparently not determined by them. In Herodotus, the fate of a great individual is usually identical with the fate of his people; his doom is their doom. This is the thread that holds together the large issue central to the work, the wars between Greeks and barbarians from the first major encroachment of non-Greeks upon Greek territories to the re-establishment of a natural boundary – the Hellespont – between them. While the tragic setting is not sustained with equal intensity throughout the work, it is hinted at in the discovery on the part of all the major figures involved in the conflict that certain limits are set to human existence and that good fortune is never constant: Croesus discovers that his wealth does not constitute happiness when he attacks Persia; Cyrus learns it when, buoyed by 'his belief in his more-than-human birth and good fortune in war' (1.204.2), he attacks the Massagetae; Cambyses' mad lust for expansion is checked by the Ethiopians, Darius' by the Scythians, and Xerxes' by the Greeks. The meaning of these discoveries and their inevitability is punctuated by more genuinely tragic structures within the work which show the human agent placed into a situation in which he is constrained to act in a way which is bound to lead to failure because he does not realize until it is too late the limits which his humanity has set for him.

The similarities between the tragic view Herodotus takes of historical

[90] Schmid and Stählin 1.2.569–72.   [91] Cobet 1971 (C 18).

events in their large movement as well as in innumerable subsidiary details and Sophocles' treatment of the human condition is so striking that we are entitled to wonder whether they result from discussions between these two men. We have no way of telling either whether Herodotus had developed it sufficiently by the time he arrived in Athens in the 440s to transmit it to Sophocles or whether his friendship with Sophocles made him see the information he had gathered on his travels in a new way, which became the organizing principle of the work as a whole when, a decade or so later, he prepared the work for publication in Thurii. In any event, it is unlikely that two such similar conceptions of human life should have developed in complete isolation one from the other. An argument which would favour Sophocles' influence on Herodotus is that he was working in a tradition of tragedy which had been well established in Athens at least since the days of Aeschylus. We know of no similar tradition to which Herodotus could have been exposed before his arrival in Athens. That he did leave a mark on Athens is amply attested by Aristophanes' *Acharnians*.[92]

The tragic view does not divide men into saints and sinners, but presents them objectively as frail creatures placed into situations in which their decision will subject them to transcendent laws that will reveal the limits of their humanity and lead to failure or even ruin. For Herodotus, cities, states and peoples operate under the same kind of constraint, and this, as we have seen, is one of the reasons why his admiration for Athens or for Sparta cannot be unconditional. He tells us at the opening of his work that he will deal with cities both great and small, since 'cities which were formerly great have for the most part become small, and those which were great in my own time were formerly small', and this leads him to the knowledge that 'human happiness never remains constant' (1.5.4). It is inconceivable that a man holding these views was unaware of or indifferent to the events going on in his own contemporary world, dominated as it was by the imperial policy of a city which the sequel of the Persian Wars had catapulted from comparative insignificance at the time she first enters Herodotus' narrative to a greatness that set her on a collision course with Sparta.[93] Whether Herodotus approved or disapproved of Athens' imperial policy we do not know. But he is likely to have recognized it as an inevitable consequence of the role Athens had played in the Persian Wars, and his knowledge of human affairs made him foresee the conflagration to which it was leading.

Herodotus' migration from Athens to Thurii, where he seems to have spent the rest of his life, used to be seen as prompted by his support of

[92] Cf. Ar. *Ach.* 523–9 and Hdt. 1.1–4. Further parallels are cited by Jacoby 1913 (C 55) 232.
[93] Fornara 1971 (C 32) 59–91.

Periclean policy. More recently it has been suggested that he was motivated by disenchantment with Pericles for hiding imperial designs under the pretext of the panhellenic policy advocated in the guise of the Congress Decree, and that he sought fulfilment of his panhellenic ideal in the new colony.[94] However, it is more likely that he left Athens and did not return to his native Halicarnassus because he knew that both places would be embroiled in the conflict that was sure to come. Thurii was far removed from the scene where the action would take place and it would give him the intellectual and social ambience in which he could live out his days as a keen observer of human life.

Herodotus' achievement as a historian is highlighted by comparing his work with that of two other foreign prose writes who were attached to Athens during his lifetime. Strictly speaking, Stesimbrotus of Thasos was not a historian but an intellectual of sorts who lectured and taught in Athens, probably in the 430s, on Homeric criticism (and perhaps also on mystery cults) and charged money for it. His presence in Athens can be inferred from Xenophon's report (*Symp.* III.6) that Nicias' son Niceratus attended his lectures on Homer, and by his own assertion that he had seen Pericles.[95] However, he also wrote a work entitled *On Themistocles, Thucydides and Pericles*, which can be regarded as historical in the same sense in which the *Epidemiai* of Ion of Chios can so be regarded. Yet whereas Ion's work was autobiographical and included descriptions of his encounter with prominent men, Stesimbrotus seems to have written scurrilous political propaganda against Athenian statesmen whose oppressive imperial policies led to a confrontation between Sparta and Athens. Since, with the exception of one fragment (F 10a), our knowledge depends exclusively on Plutarch's lives of *Themistocles, Cimon* and *Pericles* we do not know how Thucydides, son of Melesias, figured in his narrative. Themistocles and Pericles are viciously attacked for their personal conduct, but a gentler treatment was reserved for Cimon, whose lack of intellectuality and sophisticated Attic rhetoric is more than compensated by his penchant for Spartan nobility and sincerity (F 4, cf. 5 and 7).

The work of Hellanicus of Lesbos shows an entirely different approach to history. Unlike Stesimbrotus, he was not interested in the lives of prominent men at all, to say nothing of their private conduct, and, unlike Herodotus, his works seem to have been less the result of travel and of reports of what he had ascertained on them or of a curiosity about the interrelation of events and their meaning as a whole. Rather, his chief concern seems to have been to bring order into the chaos of conflicting legends about the mythical past and to establish a clear record of the events of a less remote past so as to extract from them a reliable

---

[94] Strasburger 1955 (C 97) 23–5.   [95] Jacoby *FGrH* 107 F 10a with comment on T2.

chronicle of known human history in the foremost Greek and non-Greek lands. There is no external evidence that he ever visited Athens, but it is inconceivable that he collected the materials for his *Atthis*, the earliest local history of Attica ever to be written, anywhere other than at Athens, just as we have to assume visits to Thessaly, Boeotia, Argos, Sparta and Arcadia to account for the little we know of the contents of his works on those regions. Modern scholarly opinion on the life and works of Hellanicus depends almost exclusively on the work of Felix Jacoby, which, though highly hypothetical and in need of revision, has as a whole remained unchallenged for over seventy years.[96]

There can be little doubt that his *Atthis* was the last of Hellanicus' known published works and that he took Athenian history down to at least 407/6 B.C. (F 25–6), but presumably to the end of the Peloponnesian War. In it, the legendary past received heavy emphasis: the first of its two books was entirely devoted to the establishment of a list of the kings of Athens, while the second probably covered the period from the establishment of the annual archonship in 683/2 to the end of the fifth century. Its most remarkable feature, if Jacoby's interpretation of the very skimpy fragments is right, is that he was the first historian to use the official archon-list as his chronological framework, supplementing it with whatever information he could glean from written sources or the oral tradition current in Athens, and reporting events annalistically under the year in which each occurred. Although this method drew the censure of Thucydides (1.97.2) for its inaccuracy and excessive brevity, it became the backbone of chronology for all subsequent writers of Athenian history. The writers of the local history of Athens who built on his work in the fourth and third centuries were all Athenians. It is all the more remarkable that the man who taught them how to use their material should have been a foreigner from Lesbos.

We shall end this brief sketch on the impact of foreigners on Athenian literature in verse and in prose by a few observations on language. We are told by the Old Oligarch (2.8) that the Athenians 'from hearing every dialect have adopted one peculiarity from one and another from another; whereas other Greeks retain their own patterns of speech, ways of life, and manner of dress, that of the Athenians is a blend of elements taken from all Greeks and barbarians'. The surviving literary and inscriptional texts do not put us into a position to assess the accuracy of this statement; its minimum meaning will be that no dialect sounded strange to the Athenian ear. Nonetheless, we do know from comedy that the peculiarities of Spartan, Megarian and Boeotian speech could be a source of general amusement, intelligible though they were. Similarly, we must

---

[96] Jacoby 1913 (C 54) 104–53; *FGrH* 4 (1923) and 323a (1954), especially 'Introduction' in III b suppl. 1.1–21; and 1949 (C 57), esp. 223–5.

assume that literature conventionally written in a dialect other than Attic was perfectly comprehensible to the Athenian listener: he was as attuned to the Doric of dithyrambic poetry as he was to the Ionic of the prose of Herodotus or of the Hippocratic treatises. In fact, the origin of tragedy made it imperative for Athenian writers to give a Doric cast to the lyrical passages they wrote for their choruses.

For obvious reasons, however, public speeches, whether composed for the law courts or for some other occasion, were written in pure Attic. There is nothing remarkable about that if we consider that the earliest extant speech writers, Antiphon and Andocides, were born and raised in Athens. But it is noteworthy that their contemporary Lysias, whose language was held up to later generations as 'the best model of the attic dialect' (Dion. Hal. *Lys.* 2), was not an Athenian citizen, but a son of the Syracusan Cephalus, who followed Pericles' invitation to settle in Athens. Still, Lysias was born in Athens, probably about 445, and spent the first fifteen years of his life there. After the death of their father, he and his brothers settled in Thurii, where he is said to have studied rhetoric with the Syracusans Tisias and Nicias. The family returned to Athens in 412/11 after the Sicilian disaster, and it was from that time on until his death about 380 that he won his renown as a forensic speaker, and participated in the political life of Athens to the extent that it was possible for a metic to participate. With the exception of a brief stay in Megara, where he had taken refuge from the Thirty, and from where he actively supported the opponents of their regime, he seems to have remained in Athens.[97]

V. PHILOSOPHY, RHETORIC AND SCIENCE

Plato and his master Socrates are mainly responsible for our regarding Athens as the centre of philosophy in antiquity and as the focus from which it has radiated into the West for two and a half millennia. Socrates never left Athens, except on military duties, and Plato founded his Academy there, which attracted as its star pupil Aristotle of Stagira, who in due course established his own school, the Lyceum, in Athens. The number of foreigners who came to Athens to study at these institutions is prefigured by those mentioned by Phaedo, himself a native of Elis, as having been present – or expected to be present – at the death of Socrates: Simmias, Cebes and Phaedondes had come from Thebes, Euclid and Terpsion from Megara, while the absence of Aristippus of Cyrene and Cleombrotus of Ambracia is explained in that they are said to have been detained in Aegina (Pl. *Phd.* 59c). Numerous foreigners are

[97] See above, p. 309.

mentioned elsewhere in Plato's dialogues and in the writings of Xenophon as part of Socrates' circle.

But Athens cannot be regarded as the birthplace of *philosophia* in the broad sense it has in Greek as 'the disinterested pursuit of wisdom by means of the human intellect', which includes not only philosophy as we understand it but also science, scholarship and the arts of communicating with our fellow-men which are subsumed under the name of rhetoric. However, Athens did provide the fertile soil in which seeds imported from abroad could develop and be brought to fruition in the comprehensive systems of Plato and Aristotle. The 'soil' she provided consisted intellectually in tragedy, which probes the dilemmas posed by human life, and in comedy, which comments on them and tries to rise above them through laughter; politically it consisted in the development of empire, which made her a focal point of the social, economic and political life of Greece as well as of an intellectual life which, in the view of Hippias of Elis, transcended conventional social boundaries (Pl. *Prt.* 337c–d). The 'seeds' came in two strains, primarily from Asia Minor and from the Greek settlements in southern Italy and Sicily. The first consisted in the study of external nature which had flourished in Ionia ever since Thales in the early sixth century, and included also the exploration of knowable reality which preoccupied thinkers in the West; Anaxagoras of Clazomenae was the first representative of Ionian thought to come to Athens (Clem. Al. *Strom.* 1.63), and Parmenides of Elea the first to bring Western thought. The second strain was imported into Athens by Protagoras of Abdera and Gorgias of Leontini, who turned their considerable intellectual powers away from a concern with external nature and toward the exploration of human society and the problems of communication within it.

There is general agreement that Anaxagoras was born *c.* 499/8 at Clazomenae, that he died in 428/7 at the age of seventy-two in Lampsacus, and that he spent two or three decades of his life in Athens (D.L. ii.7). However, since much of the ancient evidence about his life is beset by obscurities, ambiguities and contradictions, the time of his sojourn in Athens and its length have been the subject of much controversy. Some scholars date his stay in Athens early, usually from *c.* 480 to *c.* 450, lengthening his time in Lampsacus,[98] while others prefer a later date, terminating in the 430s. The dates 456/5 to 437/6, which have recently been proposed, seem to be the least unsatisfactory, especially since they best accommodate the traditions about his relations with Pericles.[99] Although it is unlikely that he gave formal instruction other

[98] So, recently, Schofield 1980 (J 93) 33–5, and Woodbury 1981 (J 115) 295–315, with bibliography on p. 296 n. 2.

[99] Mansfeld 1979 (J 76) 53–5 with nn. 52 and 53, 1980 (J 76) 87–8.

than a few public lectures, his impact on Athens was enormous. Pericles and Euripides are most prominent among the 'pupils' tradition assigns to him. In the case of Euripides this need mean no more than that Anaxagoras' influence can be detected in numerous passages in his plays,[100] but for Pericles several ancient authors, some close to his lifetime, attest cordial relations between him and Anaxagoras, including Pericles' defence of him at his trial for impiety.[101] Further, Thucydides is said to have attended his lectures (Marcellin. 22), and Socrates was not only familiar with his published work (Pl. *Phd.* 97bc, cf. Ap. 26d) but is said to have been a friend and disciple of Archelaus, the earliest Athenian philosopher, who is himself said to have studied with Anaxagoras (D. L. II.16, cf. 23, Suda s.v. Ἀρχέλαος).

Parmenides is reported by Plato (*Prm.* 127a–c) to have visited Athens together with his disciple Zeno for the Panathenaic festival at the age of sixty-five, which will have been *c.* 450, and to have conversed with the young Socrates on that occasion. No trace of his influence can, however, be detected in Athens before Plato. Zeno, on the other hand, allegedly attracted Pericles to his lectures (Plut. *Per.* 4.5, 5.3) and had among his paying pupils Pythodorus, who was exiled in 424 for his failures when general in Sicily.[102] He refused to settle in Athens, preferring the simplicity of Elea to Athenian boastfulness (D. L. IX.28).

Democritus of Abdera, the father of atomism, and Diogenes of Apollonia are the only other 'natural philosophers' whom we have reason to believe visited Athens in the fifth century. In the case of Democritus, this can only be inferred from his own celebrated statement: 'For I came to Athens and no one knew me' (D–K 68 B 116), which, in view of his serene but shy scholarly character, more probably expresses relief at having escaped the social adulation accorded to celebrities in the big city than a complaint. As with Parmenides, there is no evidence that he left any imprint on Athenian thought or literature of the fifth century. The opposite is the case with Diogenes, a contemporary of Anaxagoras: there is no evidence that he ever visited Athens, but a famous passage in Aristophanes' *Clouds* (227–33), in which Socrates celebrates Air as encompassing the earth and keeping it suspended, and as the seat of intelligence and divinity, is so close to the thought of a surviving fragment of his work (D–K 64 B 5) and to no other similar sentiment of which we know in the fifth century that we have to assume that his theories were familiar enough in Athens to be parodied in comedy, and perhaps also to be used in tragedy (Eur. *Tro.* 884).

---

[100] For a list, see Guthrie 1965 (J 49) II.323–5; cf. also D. L. II.10; Schol. Pind. *Ol.* 1.92; Satyr. *Vit. Eur.* frs. 371–81 (Arrighetti); Schol. Eur. *Or.* 896 and *Tro.* 884.

[101] Pl. *Phd.* 269e–270a, *Alc.* 1.118c; Isocr. xv. *Antid.* 235; Diod. XII.39.2; Plut. *Per.* 4.5, 6.1–2, 16.7–9, and 32.1–2; D. L. II.12 and 13.

[102] Pl. *Alc.* 1.119a, *Prm.* 126c and 127b; cf. Thuc. III.115.2, IV.2.2 and 65.3.

Political success depended in the Athenian democracy to a large extent on effective public speaking. To influence legislation and public policy, Council and Assembly needed to be persuaded, and in the law courts, where many political issues were aired and resolved, large juries of laymen needed to be swayed. Themistocles and Pericles had been endowed with rhetorical talents by nature, and even Cleon seems to have owed his success to a native vulgarity in speech as well as in manner of delivery, which gave him a hold over the masses. The lesson which these and other prominent men had to impart, namely that effective public speaking was an important avenue to power, was not lost on ambitious young men, especially of the upper classes, and they sought to acquire by training the rhetorical skills which had come as a natural gift to others. The supply to fill this kind of demand came from abroad, and the men who provided it are known as 'sophists'. For our knowledge of who they were, what they taught, and what effect they had on fifth-century Athens we depend largely on the testimony of Plato, who is more trustworthy as a philosopher than as a historian, and whose attitude to the sophists was hostile. But by a judicious attempt to sift fact from prejudice and by bringing whatever other sources may be available to bear upon his statements, a more objective view of their achievements can be attained.[103]

The earliest sophist and the first to identify himself as such was Protagoras of Abdera, whose visit to Athens *c.* 433 is vividly recorded in the Platonic dialogue which bears his name. Obviously Protagoras would not have called himself a professional *sophistes*, if the term had had for him the same pejorative connotations which it was to assume in the fourth century, although his statement that his predecessors identified their profession differently 'because they feared its odium' (Pl. *Prt.* 316d) shows that Plato imputed to him an awareness of a pejorative meaning. The choice of this term reveals Protagoras' revolutionary intent: from its earliest occurrence on, *sophistes* describes a person endowed with some special skill or expertise which he activates so as to make a contribution to the life of his society. This explains why Protagoras omits from his list of intellectual precursors the Ionian 'natural philosophers', who were interested in the exploration of external nature for its own sake, and why he aligns himself instead with the great poets, religious leaders, physical trainers, and music teachers of the past on the one hand, and dissociates himself from the teaching of arithmetic, astronomy, geometry and literature on the other (Pl. *Prt.* 316de, 318de). Evidently, he wanted to impart his knowledge of human concerns to other human beings; he did not wish to gain scientific knowledge of the physical universe merely for his own satisfaction. For him a *sophistes* was a person who wanted to *do*

103 For such a view, see Kerferd 1981 (J 58).

something with his wisdom. This will have been the reason why he stated at the beginning of his work that 'man is the measure of all things': what is and what is not is established by the commonsense experience of human beings, not by abstruse speculations about the structure of the universe.

Protagoras' radical departure from the past consisted in his emphasis on man as the proper study of mankind. But his social thought was far from revolutionary. He proposed no scheme of social reform and no ideal state, but was content to let each state live according to laws (*nomoi*) binding for it but for no other state. No set of laws is any closer to an absolute truth than any other: laws are morally neither right nor wrong but simply valid. This, however, does not prevent some laws from being 'better' than others. Just as a healthy person has a better perception than a sick patient of what is bitter and what is not, and just as a physician can change the patient's state from worse to better by means of drugs, so Protagoras claims

that wise and good political speakers make good things rather than bad seem to be just to cities. Since whatever sorts of things seem just and honourable to a particular city are in fact just and honourable for it, as long as it so regards them, it is the wise man who makes all the things which used to be bad for them be good. On that principle, the sophist who is able to educate his students in this manner is also wise and worth a lot of money to those whom he has educated' (Pl. *Tht.* 166d–167c).

Consistent with this, Plato has Protagoras profess to teach 'sound judgement [*euboulia*] in personal affairs, to enable a person to run his household in the best way, and in the affairs of the city, to make his contribution to public affairs most effective in action and speech', and he agrees to the definition of this discipline as *politike techne*, 'political science' or 'art of citizenship' (Pl. *Prt.* 318e–319a). There is evidence that Protagoras' teaching of rhetoric was the corollary of his political principles. If we can trust Diogenes Laertius (IX.51) that Protagoras was the first to maintain that there is an argument for opposed to an argument against on every issue, 'sound judgement' will have been arrived at for Protagoras by marshalling arguments for commending or rejecting a given course of action for a given society under a given set of circumstances, since no issue can be true or false, and consequently the teaching of the *sophistes* will consist in the formulation of what kinds of arguments suit what kinds of circumstances. This somewhat pragmatic emphasis on what is commendable rather than what is true will have been interpreted by Protagoras' contemporaries and by later generations as indifference to truth and falsehood in the discussion of a given issue, and will have given him the reputation, which we find recorded in

Aristotle's *Rhetoric* (II.24, 1402a22–8), that he presented the weaker argument as stronger.

As Protagoras himself realized (Pl. *Prt.* 326c), his teaching had most to offer to the upper classes, whose sons would have to prepare themselves for the administration of their private property as well as for public affairs, and who alone were capable of paying the fee he demanded for his services (*ibid.* 349a, D. L. IX.52). This is borne out by the setting of the dialogue which Plato named after him. It takes place in the sumptuous home of Callias son of Hipponicus, one of the richest men in Athens, who is said to have spent more money than anyone else on the sophists (Pl. *Ap.* 20a); among foreign celebrities the sophists Prodicus of Ceos and Hippias of Elis are in attendance, and of the list of young Athenians present reads like a 'Who's Who' of the upper class: Pericles' sons Paralus and Xanthippus, Alcibiades, Critias, Charmides, Phaedrus, Eryximachus, Pausanias, Agathon, Adeimantus son of Cepis, and his namesake, son of Leucolophides, who was to have a chequered career as general toward the end of the Peloponnesian War (Pl. *Prt.* 314e–316a). In view of this array it is rather surprising that only Athenians are named as his pupils.[104]

Protagoras was, as far as we know, not only the first but also the only person to identify himself as a *sophistes*. But, from Plato on, the term was applied in a more or less loose way to a number of men who appeared in Athens from *c.* 430 onwards primarily as teachers of rhetoric. There is no precise list of their names, since the criteria on which names are included or excluded by different scholars are elusive. Those most widely accepted as 'sophists' are Gorgias, Prodicus, Hippias, Antiphon, Thrasymachus, Euthydemus and Dionysodorus, of whom all but Antiphon were foreigners.[105] What these men had in common was that, regardless of what other interests they showed or taught, all were primarily concerned with rhetoric and argumentation and that, like Protagoras, all charged a fee for their instruction.[106] But, unlike Protagoras, these sophists were not philosophers in the sense that they propounded a consistent doctrine of man and society; they can be regarded as Protagoras' heirs only in the sense that they developed that teaching of rhetoric which was for Protagoras no more than an offshoot, however important, of his 'art of citizenship'.

[104] Isocrates at Schol. Pl. *Rep.* 600c; Euathlus (a prosecutor of Thucydides son of Melesias, Ar. *Ach.* 703–12 with schol. on 710) at D. L. IX.54 and 56; and probably Pythodorus (who moved the appointment of the commissioners who ushered in the Four Hundred in 411, and who was archon under the Thirty, Arist. *Ath. Pol.* 29.1 and 35.1) at D. L. IX.54.

[105] This list is based on Kerferd 1981 (J 58) 42–58. Omitted from it are the Athenians Callicles and Critias, who were politicians educated by the sophists rather than sophists themselves; the authors of the *Dissoi Logoi* and the *Anonymus Iamblichi*, whose identities are not known; Socrates, who can be regarded as a sophist only with strong qualifications; and the Hippocratic writers.

[106] The fundamental study of this aspect is still Gomperz 1912 (J 45).

Gorgias of Leontini first came to Athens as an ambassador in 427 to negotiate his city's request for an alliance and ships against Syracuse (Diod. XII.53.2; cf. Thuc. IV.86.3). Not only did he impress the Assembly with his rhetorical skill, but he also displayed it in public performances and, in addition, made a lot of money by private instruction (Pl. *Hp. Ma.* 282b). Whether his long life as an itinerant teacher, which took him to Olympia, Delphi, Thessaly and many other places, brought him to Athens for further visits we do not know. Neither the fragments surviving from his writings nor the picture drawn of him by Plato suggest that his interests and his teaching were concerned with anything other than rhetoric. Whatever speculative or social thought is embedded in the fragments or in reports about his publications is put into the service of rhetoric, and even his celebrated treatise *On that which is not* betrays no serious interest in philosophy.[107] Similarly, his delving into mythology in his *Praise of Helen* and his *Defence of Palamedes* reveals little interest in a moral assessment of the situation in which these figures found themselves, but serves merely to demonstrate Gorgias' ability to marshal arguments in the support of unpopular causes and to sway his audience by the power of his speech. Questions of right and wrong were of little interest to him in his teaching, and, unlike Protagoras, he made no claim to inculcate moral excellence (*arete*) in his students (Pl. *Meno* 95c), but merely aimed to make them powerful speakers. However, he seems to have been of too good a conventional moral character to have understood that his teaching did have moral and political conse-quences.[108] That it did have such consequences, disastrous in Plato's view, is shown in his sketch of Gorgias' pupil, Callicles, who is presented as Gorgias' host (Pl. *Gorg.* 447b) and as a well-educated member of the Athenian upper class (*ibid.* 487b, 512d). Regardless of whether he was an actual historical person or an imaginative composite character invented by Plato to demonstrate what he regarded as the salient traits of the young Athenian intellectuals who were attracted to the sophists in the 420s, Callicles despises the masses as being an obstacle to the self-realization of the superior man, yet he caters to their every whim, because he recognizes that he has to persuade them through his rhetorical prowess to give him the means to get absolute power into his own hands. That Plato's fears had some substance to them is shown by the tradition that he impressed Critias and Alcibiades during his presence in Athens, and that his style left its mark on Thucydides (Philostr. *VS* 1.9.1).[109]

Isocrates is said to have been a pupil not only of Gorgias but also of

---

[107] For an opposite view, see Kerferd 1981 (J 58) 95–8.
[108] See E. R. Dodds, ed. *Plato: Gorgias* (Oxford, 1959) 6–10; Segal 1962 (J 96) 99–155, esp. 103.
[109] The statement that he also influenced Pericles is to be discarded on chronological grounds.

Prodicus (Dion. Hal. *Isoc.* 1). Like Gorgias, Prodicus came to Athens as
an ambassador of his native city, Iulis on the island of Ceos, but his visits
seem to have been more numerous than those of Gorgias. He, too, used
the opportunity to make some money by public displays of his rhetorical
talent as well as by giving private instruction to young aristocrats (Pl.
Hp. Ma. 282c). He charged his fees on a sliding scale from one to fifty
drachmae, depending on the level of instruction desired (Pl. *Crat.* 384b;
Arist. *Rhet.* III.14, 1415b12–17). There is a lively description of him on
the occasion of his first attested presence in Athens at the reception for
Protagoras in Callias' house in 433, in which Plato pokes fun at his
idiosyncrasies and at his deep, resounding voice (Pl. *Prt.* 315de); but he
was widely respected for his learning and his teaching (*ibid. Symp.* 177b,
Tht. 151b; Xen. *Mem.* II.1.21); Socrates acknowledged him as a friend
and teacher (Pl. *Meno* 96d; *Chrm.* 163d; *Hp. Ma.* 282c), and even
Aristophanes speaks of him with respect (*Clouds* 361; *Birds* 692, fr. 490),
which suggests that he was well known and frequently seen in Athens.

Prodicus' teaching of rhetoric seems to have been dominated by three
major concerns. The first of these was correct linguistic usage (*onomaton
orthotes*) (Pl. *Euthyd.* 277e, *Crat.* 384b), in which he drew distinctions
between different words of similar meaning, a skill of which we get a
demonstration in Plato's *Protagoras* (337a–341d), and whose relevance to
rhetoric is obvious.[110] The second differentiates him from Gorgias in
that he devoted much attention to moral problems, as is shown in his
allegory on *The Choice of Heracles*, which has been preserved for us by
Xenophon (*Mem.* II.1.21–34). This tract is said to have formed part of a
larger work, possibly his only published work, the *Horae* (Seasons)
(Schol. Ar. *Clouds* 361), in which he seems to have traced the origins and
development of human civilization. Protagoras had already felt constrained to deal with this subject in order to explain the need for the kind
of instruction in the social virtues which he claimed to offer. But
Prodicus seems to have cast his net considerably wider than this, though
it is not altogether clear how the book was related to his rhetorical
pursuits or how it was organized. Possibly it was an offshoot of his
linguistic researches. What we do know about it from a number of late
ancient sources suggests that it contained a rationalization of the origin
of religion, which went so far that it later earned him the reputation of
being an atheist.[111] Prodicus seems to have distinguished two phases in
the development of religion. In the first of these, ancient men venerated
as gods all those primary natural forces on which their sustenance and
well-being depended: sun and moon, rivers and springs and the like

110 See Classen 1976 (J 16), 215–47, esp. 230–7.
111 For a translation of the most important ancient sources, see Guthrie 1969 (J 49) III.238–9, to
which add now *P. Herc.* 1428, fr. 19.

(Sext. Emp. *Math.* IX.18); in the second phase the appellation 'god' was extended to great human benefactors of the past whose skills had provided mankind with shelter or taught them the preparation of foodstuffs, such as bread or wine, whose givers were now identified as Demeter and Dionysus, respectively.[112] Whether this kind of outlook deserves to be identified as 'atheism' remains a moot point. Sure enough, it denied the existence of the traditional gods as gods, who did not merit being worshipped as such by intelligent men; still, the benefactions they had bestowed on men were real and lasting: would Prodicus have objected to simple folk acknowledging their debt to them by venerating them as gods? Wherever the truth may lie, there is no doubt that Prodicus' theory contributed to a split between intellectuals and the common people: the tradition that, like Socrates, he was condemned to drink the hemlock for corrupting the young (Schol. Pl. *Rep.* 600c = Suda s.v. *Πρόδικος*) does not deserve credence, but it is no wonder that it arose. Apart from Isocrates, his only known Athenian pupil was Theramenes, who played a crucial but ambivalent role in the establishment as well as in the overthrow of oligarchical regimes in Athens in 411 and 404/3 (Schol. Ar. *Clouds* 361; Ath. V.220B).

The fact that no names of any pupils of Hippias have come down to us is probably due to the frequent demands of his native Elis made on him to serve as its ambassador, so that he may not have stayed anywhere long enough to produce pupils. That he ever came to Athens in an official capacity, as Gorgias and Prodicus did, can only be inferred from the opening of one of the two Platonic dialogues named after him (Pl. *Hp. Ma.* 281ab). But this dialogue as well as the *Hippias Minor* and Xenophon's *Memorabilia* (IV.4.5–25) attest several private visits to Athens on which he engaged in conversation with Socrates. If we can draw any inferences from his presence at the house of Callias in the *Protagoras* (314bc, 337c–338b) he will have visited the city at least as early as 433 B.C. No doubt his frequent appointments as an ambassador will have been due in large measure to his effectiveness as a speaker, and, like Gorgias and Prodicus, he earned a lot of money by lecturing in the places he visited (Pl. *Hp. Ma.* 282de, 300cd).

Of all the sophists of whom we know, Hippias was the most versatile and commanded the most encyclopaedic knowledge in practical as well as in theoretical matters. At an appearance in Olympia he boasted that everything he was wearing – from the ring on his finger to his cloak and his sandals – had been made by himself (Pl. *Hp. Mi.* 368bc). In the subjects he knew he was helped by a prodigious memory, which enabled him to repeat in proper order a list of fifty names upon having heard it once (Pl. *Hp. Ma.* 285e; Philostr. *VS* 1.11), and his teaching tried to

[112] See Henrichs 1975 (J 51) 93–123, and 1976 (J 52) 15–21.

develop the memory of his pupils (Xen. *Symp.* IV.62). No trace of any writings has been preserved of his studies in astronomy, geometry, arithmetic, grammar, literary criticism, painting, sculpture and various other subjects, which he introduced in his lectures (Pl. *Hp. Ma.* 285b–d; Philostr. *VS* 1.11), nor of the epic, tragic and dithyrambic poetry he composed (Pl. *Hp. Mi.* 368cd). But vestiges of two kinds of writing survive, which are of special interest. The content of a tract called *Names of Peoples* (D–K 86 B 2) escapes us completely; the title suggests a treatment of ethnographic and historical matters on a philological basis. Along these lines, Hippias' *List of Olympic Victors* (Plut. *Num.* 1.6), although now lost, will have been one of the most important and original contributions to historical studies. Since the Olympic Games were panhellenic celebrations which regularly recurred every fourth year, Hippias' list could provide a panhellenic frame of time-reckoning through which events in different parts of the Greek world could be synchronized and correlated in a way superior to that of Hellanicus, whose list of the priestesses of Hera at Argos was, after all, only a local chronicle. The discovery of this use of the list of Olympic victors is to be credited to Hippias, and although we have no evidence that he based any historical studies on it, it provided the groundwork for much later chronography.

The title *Troïkos* is the only surviving evidence for a second kind of writing by Hippias. Our information that it consisted of Nestor's answer to Neoptolemus' question after the fall of Troy – what pursuits will gain fame for a young man (Pl. *Hp. Ma.* 286ab, Philostr. *VS* 1.11) – indicates that it dealt with moral problems. We have no indication what the substantive content of Nestor's admonitions may have been, but we can guess that its subject will not have been very different from the moral issues discussed by Hippias and Socrates in Plato's two *Hippias* dialogues and in Xenophon's *Memorabilia* (IV.4.5–25). The former deal with moral excellence, noble pursuits, and truth and falsehood as embodied in Achilles and Odysseus respectively, while the latter constitutes a discussion of the relation between a just act (*dikaion*) and adherence to the laws (*nomimon*). That Hippias did have thoughts of his own on these subjects, banal though they may have been, is shown also in Plato's *Protagoras* (337cd), where he addresses the intellectuals assembled as 'kinsmen, relatives and fellow-citizens by nature [*physei*] but not in law [*nomoi*]' since 'like is kin to like by nature, but law, being a tyrant over men, often does violence to nature'. If we could rely on Plato's chronological data, as we cannot, this would be the earliest testimony to the *nomos–physis* antithesis, which is otherwise not attested until the 420s and of which more will have to be said later. Yet there is no reason to doubt that Plato is here paraphrasing, perhaps even quoting, views articulated by Hippias in a context which we cannot determine. This makes it difficult to extrapolate any doctrine from his words beyond saying that he gave precedence to the demands of nature (*physis*) over those of law and convention (*nomos*), that he regarded political boundaries as artificial, and perhaps that he regarded physiological kinship as less natural than intellectual ties among like-minded men.[113]

The presence in Athens of Thrasymachus of Chalcedon as a teacher of rhetoric is attested as early as 427 B.C. (Ar. *Dait.*, fr. 205 K–A). While he was celebrated in antiquity primarily for his innovative contributions to rhetorical theory and practice,[114] he is best known to us for the political views attributed to him by Plato in the first book of the *Republic* (336b–354c), namely that justice consists in obedience to the laws which have been enacted by those in power to safeguard their own interests. How closely Plato's formulation and treatment reflects the actual views of Thrasymachus is uncertain.[115] But we know from the fragment of a speech he wrote for delivery by a young Athenian that he was vitally interested not only in political principles but also in the political issues which disturbed the internal life of Athens in the wake of the disastrous end of the Sicilian Expedition (Dion. Hal. *Dem.* 3), and in which his only known pupil Cleitophon was prominently involved.[116] The setting of the *Republic*, moreover, shows, as does also the *Protagoras*, the cosmopolitan character of the Athenian society to which Thrasymachus had access. The dialogue takes place in the house of the metic Cephalus in the Piraeus, at which not only his sons Polemarchus, Lysias and Euthydemus are present, but also Plato's brothers Glaucon and Adeimantus, Charmantides and Cleitophon (Pl. *Rep.* 1.328b).

Three further foreign teachers of rhetoric should be mentioned, even though they are little more than names to us. Plato's *Euthydemus* introduces us to the two brothers Euthydemus and Dionysodorus who were natives of Chios, had joined the panhellenic colony of Thurii, but who were exiled and came to Athens and other Greek cities as itinerant teachers of rhetoric.[117] Another, Euenus of Paros, owes his fame primarily to Socrates' prominent mention of him as a popular teacher of virtue, who charges a fee for his services (Pl. *Ap.* 20bc). His distinctive mark is that he also wrote mainly elegiac poetry to help train the memory of his students in rhetoric (Pl. *Phdr.* 267a).[118]

The culture produced in fifth-century Athens is one of the momentous

---

[113] A similar sentiment may underlie his statement at Xen. *Mem.* IV.4.14 that the laws need not be obeyed since those who enact them often change them. For the mathematical achievement attributed to Hippias, see below, p. 349.

[114] The evidence is assembled in D–K 85 A 1–14.

[115] See Dahrendorf 1968 (J 18) 129–50.

[116] Pl. *Clitoph.* 406a and 410c, cf. *Rep.* I, 328b and 340a–c. For his political involvement in 411 B.C., see Arist. *Ath. Pol.* 29.3.   [117] For details, see Kerferd 1981 (J 58) 53–4.

[118] For fragments of his poetry, see *IEG* 63–7.

achievements of the human mind in that it constitutes an attempt on many fronts to comprehend man, his society and the universe in which he has been placed by rational means with the least possible recourse to supernatural explanations of the way things are. The road toward this development had been paved as early as the sixth century in Ionia, and, as we have seen, foreigners from there as well as from other parts of the Greek world made a considerable contribution to stimulating its growth in Athens. Anaxagoras, Diogenes and probably also Democritus brought the fruits of rational explorations of the physical universe, and the sophists had accompanied their teaching of rhetoric by far-reaching rational analyses and criticisms of the structure of human society and the problems besetting it. It is not surprising that this movement also provided a climate conducive to new endeavours in mathematics and science, if we confine 'science' in this context to astronomy, which is closely related to mathematics anyway, and to medicine.

The polymath Hippias of Elis is credited by Plato with proficiency in arithmetic, geometry and astronomy (Pl. *Prt.* 318e; *Hp. Mi.* 366c–368c), and it is probably the same Hippias who is credited by some with the discovery of the quadratix, which he is said to have used to solve the problem of trisecting an angle.[119] The chief impetus for mathematical and astronomical studies in fifth-century Athens seems, however, to have come from Pythagoreans or, at least, from men steeped in the mathematical doctrines which formed the nucleus of Pythagorean philosophy, of whom three are mentioned by Proclus: Oenopides and Hippocrates of Chios and Theodorus of Cyrene.[120] Oenopides, who is described as a younger contemporary of Anaxagoras, was the earliest of these and will have been active in the second half of the fifth century. His interest in mathematical methodology is indicated by the report that he worked on the problem of finding the perpendicular to a straight line with the help of rule and compasses only.[121] In astronomy he is said to have been the first to discover the obliquity of the zodiac and to have calculated the period of the 'great year', that is, the period in which all heavenly bodies return to their original relative positions (D–K 41 A 7). There is no direct evidence that he worked in Athens, but since his work on the great year is closely related to the Athenian Meton's interest in the same problem, and since he seems to have based some of his calculations on the Attic calendar of festivals, the presumption of a prolonged stay in Athens is almost inevitable.

[119] Proclus, *In primum Euclidis Elementorum librum commentarii* (Friedlein), pp. 272.3–10 and 356.6–12. For a full discussion with bibliography, see Bulmer-Thomas 1972 (J 10) 405–10.

[120] Proclus (above, n. 119) 65.21–66.8 with the discussions of Bulmer-Thomas 1974 (J 11) 179–82, 1972 (J 10) 410–18, and 1976 (J 12) 314–19.

[121] Proclus (above, n. 119) 283.7–10 and 322.5–6 with von Fritz 1937 (J 40) 2258–72, esp. 2267–71.

For his fellow-Chian contemporary Hippocrates, on the other hand, an extensive sojourn in Athens is explicitly mentioned in John Philoponus' commentary on Aristotle's *Physics* (*Comm. in Arist. Graeca* XVI.31.3–9). According to this story, Hippocrates was a merchant who, having been robbed of his cargo by pirates, went to Athens to prosecute them; as the prosecution dragged on, he decided to attend lectures on geometry, and became so proficient that he tried to find a solution to the problem of squaring the circle. Other sources confirm that he engaged in commerce (Plut. *Solon* 2), and Aristotle (*Eth. Eud.* H 14.5, 1247a17–21) has a variant version of the way in which Hippocrates lost his money. His achievements include the discovery of a way of squaring the lune (D–K 42 A 1 and 3), working on the problem of doubling the cube (*ibid.* A 4), and the publication of the earliest book on the elements of geometry (Proclus (above, n. 119) 66.7–8). In astronomy, he studied the galaxy and comets (Arist. *Mete.* 1.6, 342b30–343a20).

Most of our knowledge of the life of Theodorus of Cyrene is derived from Plato's *Theaetetus*, the dramatic date of which is shortly before Socrates' death in 399 B.C. As he is presented as being advanced in years and of about the same age as Socrates, a date around 465 is commonly assumed for his birth, and the dialogue is regarded as testimony that he visited Athens in Socrates' lifetime. This seems corroborated by the fact that Socrates mentions him as a good geometer in Xenophon (*Mem.* IV.2.10). His appearance in Plato's *Sophist* and *Politicus* may indicate that he visited Athens again later, after the death of Socrates, while the instruction in astronomy, harmony and arithmetic, which Theaetetus claims to have received from Theodorus (Pl. *Tht.* 145cd), may have been given either in Athens or Cyrene. Plato, however, is said to have gone to Cyrene to study with him (D. L. III.6, cf. II.103). We further learn from the *Theaetetus* (164e–165a) that he had started out as a pupil of Protagoras but soon left him to devote himself to geometry. His main contribution to mathematics was, however, the demonstration of the irrationality of the square root of all natural numbers from 3 to 17 (except, of course, of 4, 9 and 16) (Pl. *Tht.* 147d–148b). He is the only one of the four mathematicians we have been discussing to be included in Iamblichus' list of Pythagoreans (*VP* 267).

Although we cannot with confidence attach a name to any foreigner who came to Athens in the fifth century for the teaching or practice of medicine, there can be no doubt that treatises attributed to Hippocrates of Cos were known and that medical training given by foreigners was available. Our evidence for the former consists in Plato's mention of his works in the *Phaedrus* (270bc) and for the latter in the *Protagoras* (311bc). However, we do not know how dependent Athenian medicine was on

foreigners or by whom and when such Athenian physicians as Eryximachus and his father Acumenus had been trained. However, we cannot go
far wrong in assuming that the rational approach taken by Hippocrates'
school, its rejection of magic and of philosophical and cosmological
principles, and its emphasis on observation, environment, prophylaxis,
and on the psychological condition of the patient, will have found a
sympathetic audience among the Athenian intelligentsia.

VI. THE IMPACT ON ATHENS

All layers of Athenian society will have been beneficiaries of the stimulus
which the influx of foreigners brought to the economic life of the city.
But their impact on its cultural life, which was to prove the most
enduring and most seminal for the development of western civilization,
will have been most immediately felt by the upper classes. Painters and
sculptors, poets and prose writers had been enticed to Athens by
members of the upper classes, who gave them work, support and
protection. Cimon had brought Polygnotus; Alcibiades had Aglaophon
commemorate his victories, Agatharchus decorate his house, and had
rescued Hegemon from the clutches of the law; Zeuxis, Ion and
Herodotus moved in the highest circles of Athenian society.[122] At the
same time, the presence of foreign artists and authors had a stimulating
effect on the work of their Athenian colleagues: Polygnotus collaborated
with Micon, Alcamenes and Agoracritus worked with Phidias, and the
relation between Herodotus and Sophocles was beneficial for both.[123].
Still the most pervasive and lasting cultural imprint was left on Athens
by the sophists and the philosophers who preceded them.

Their appeal, too, was primarily to the upper classes. Anaxagoras was
closely associated with Pericles, and Pythodorus extended generous
hospitality to Parmenides and Zeno, Callias to Protagoras, Hippias and
Prodicus, and Callicles to Gorgias.[124] But the influence of these foreigners extended far beyond class and affected the political as well as the
cultural life of the city. Anaxagoras brought philosophy into a city,
which had not yet produced any philosophers of its own; by the end of
the century, public readings of his work had taken place, his books were
for sale for as little as one drachma, and familiarity with his doctrines
among the intelligentsia could be taken for granted (Pl. *Phd.* 97bc; *Ap.*
26d; *Gorg.* 465d). Some of the credit for this familiarity goes to
Euripides: so many passages in his tragedies bear the marks of Anaxagoras' doctrines that ancient biographers concluded that he had been

---

[122] See above, pp. 317–18, 318–19, 324–6, 330–1.   [123] See above, pp. 317, 321–2, 333–5.
[124] See above, p. 340 with nn. 101 and 102, and pp. 343, 344.

Anaxagoras' pupil, and some modern scholars believe that the two were at least personally acquainted with one another.[125]

On a more professional level, the earliest Athenian philosopher of whom we know, Archelaus – who is also said to have been Socrates' teacher – had studied with Anaxagoras (D. L. ii.16, Suda s.v. Ἀρχέλαος; Porph. *Histor. Philos.*, fr. xii (Nauck²)) and was influenced by his doctrines of homoeomers as the primary irreducible constituents of all things and of Mind (*Nous*) as the original cause of motion.[126]

Archelaus' historical significance, however, consists less in giving Ionian natural philosophy a home in Athens than in combining it with social theories which may also have their roots among the Greeks of Asia Minor and which reached Athens through the sophists. Late doxographers attribute to him the view that 'things are just and disgraceful not by nature (*physei*) but by conventional belief (*nomoi*)' (D. L. ii.16, Suda s.v. Ἀρχέλαος). If this is a genuine quotation, it constitutes the earliest statement we possess of the *nomos–physis* antithesis which was to become a major theme in Athenian intellectual life from the last quarter of the fifth century on. But since there are no indications that Archelaus ever related his physical theories to a social philosophy, it is more likely that his view of cultural development resembled that which Plato attributes to Protagoras, according to which the development of norms of right and wrong takes a different path in different societies. This would credit Archelaus with the belief that, unlike natural phenomena, the *nomoi* of each state are not determined by an invariable absolute standard, but by different and shifting moral notions; this would mean that the realm of *nomos* is different from, but not necessarily opposed to, the realm of *physis*. It is, then, more likely that the opposition of the two was imported by later doxographers who, more conversant with the *nomos–physis* antinomy, paraphrased Archelaus' doctrine so as to attribute a moral theory to him, couched in terms which were part of their own – but not Archelaus' – conceptual framework.[127] Archelaus is more likely to have juxtaposed rather than opposed *nomos* and *physis* to one another in a way similar to the Hippocratic treatise *On Airs, Waters and Places* (14 and 16), where they complement rather than contradict one another. Both explain qualities peculiar to different peoples as due either to their social traditions or to their natural environment, and in the case of the Macrocephali we even get an instance in which *nomos* develops into *physis*.[128] For the development of the antinomy between the two, we must therefore look elsewhere.

Although the absence of any information on the intellectual developments in cities other than Athens must make us wary, there are strong

125 Guthrie 1965 (J 49) II 323–5.   126 See Guthrie 1965 (J 49) II 339–44.
127 Heinimann 1945 (J 50) 111–14.   128 Heinimann 1945 (J 50) 26–8.

indications that the antinomy developed in Archelaus' native Athens, and that it owes its origin to the influence of the sophists. To understand it, we must remember that the range of *nomos* and *physis* is considerably wider than 'law' and 'nature' would suggest, and for that reason we shall leave them untranslated in the following discussion. *Nomos* denotes any social and political norm, ranging from 'law' and 'custom' to 'way of life', 'conventional belief,' 'religious practice', and 'proper conduct of an individual'. Its sanction is purely human and its authority is based on its acceptance by a given group of people as valid and binding for themselves; consequently, it is as mutable or immutable as purely human concerns are.[129] *Physis*, on the other hand, refers to an unchangeable 'natural' force which has made things and persons what they intrinsically are: it describes natural phenomena or the process of their development from their origin to their decay, and it is used of the innate, unschooled, native endowment of a person, his stock or his inborn character. Thus, although the *physis* of one individual may differ from that of another, *physis* can also be treated as a force to which all men, regardless of the society in which they live, are subject: for Thucydides (III.82.2) the harsh experiences to which states are and always will be subject in times of civil disorder (*stasis*) are a condition of 'human nature' (*anthropine physis*).

It is in this last sense in particular that *physis* became the opponent of *nomos* at some undeterminable point in the last third of the fifth century. There is no evidence that the antinomy between the two was imported fully developed into Athens from abroad. The indications are rather that it developed in Athens as an instrument of social and political criticism under the impact of the doctrines of the natural philosophers as popularized by the teaching of the sophists. Ever since the reforms of Cleisthenes, *nomos* as the ratification of norms accepted as valid and binding by society as a whole had been the watchword of the Athenian democracy.[130] In the latter part of the fifth century, it is still praised as the preserver of the state (Soph. *Ant.* 663–76; Eur. *Supp.* 312–13), as a guarantor of freedom (Eur. *Supp.* 438, cf. Hdt. VII.104.4–5), and as a bulwark against tyranny (Eur. *Supp.* 429–32; Ar. *Wasps* 463–7, Thuc. III.62.3); it was regarded as the basis of social as well as of legal norms (Thuc. II.37.3), as having no class distinctions in the administration of justice (Thuc. II.37.1; Eur. *Hec.* 291–2), as the guarantor of justice in state and society (Soph. *Ant.* 23–5; *OC* 913–4, 1382; Eur. *Hec.* 799–801; *Suppl.* 433–8), and as granting freedom of speech to rich and poor alike (Eur. *Supp.* 435–6). Yet by the 420s it had also been recognized that *nomos*, especially in its written form as 'statute', inhibits human freedom of action (Eur. *Hec.* 864–7), and that other values may have a higher claim to human allegiance. This recognition will have been precipitated

[129] Ostwald 1969 (D 64) 20–56.   [130] Ostwald 1969 (D 64) 137–60.

by too rigid an emphasis on the part of the democratic establishment of *nomos* as the exclusive social norm. As early as the 440s Sophocles' *Antigone* had disputed the monopoly of the *nomoi* of the state by affirming an equal validity for the unwritten *nomima* dictated by family religion; in the early 420s, Cleon's insistence that a state is stronger when it enforces inferior *nomoi* which are inviolable than when it has good laws which lack authority, and his praise of the humble citizen who, unlike the intellectual who wants to be smarter than the established *nomoi*, recognizes that he is less competent than the laws (Thuc. III.37.3–4), had forged *nomos* into an instrument to enforce a levelling conformity, indifferent to quality and excellence.

This will not have gone over well with the upper classes and especially with those of them whose wits had been sharpened by foreign philosophers and sophists. They are likely to have been familiar with the doubts raised about the absolute validity of *nomos* by thinkers such as Empedocles, who accepted the terms 'birth' and 'death' only as a matter of common parlance (*nomos*) but as opposed to his intellectual conviction that they are really no more than mixture and separation (D–K 31 B 9), or such as Democritus, whose knowledge that only atoms and the void have reality (*eteei*) made him reject the common notions (*nomos*) which accept colour, sweet and bitter as real. Under the influence of contemporary natural philosophers present in Athens, such as Anaxagoras, Democritus and Diogenes, *physis* will have entered the lists as a potential opponent of *nomos*, and through the sophists it will have become a weapon of social criticism.

The *physis* of the natural philosophers does not occupy a prominent place in the thinking of Protagoras, the earliest sophist, and he explicitly dissociates himself from the professional training in arithmetic, astronomy, geometry and literature which, he claims, is dispensed by his competitors (Pl. *Prt.* 318de). Yet popular opinion closely associated natural philosophy with sophistic teaching: in Aristophanes' *Clouds* (94–9) the propagation of physical doctrines elsewhere attributed to Meton, Hippon and Diogenes is conflated with the teaching of successful speaking for pay, and Socrates' accusers are said to have regarded him as 'a smart man [*sophos aner*] who thinks about things in mid-air, has conducted research into whatever is beneath the earth, and makes out the weaker argument to be the stronger' (Pl. *Ap.* 18b). That there was substance to this association is shown in that Prodicus was credited not only with research into correct linguistic usage but also with scientific pursuits as part of his moral and rhetorical teaching,[131] and in that

<hr>

[131] Prodicus' interest in language: Pl. *Crat.* 384b; *Euthyd.*277e; *Prt.* 337a–c, 340a; *Meno* 75e; *Lach.* 197b and d; *Chrm.* 163b–d; interest in *physis*: Ar. *Clouds* 360–1; Schol. Ar. *Birds* 692; Suda s.v. Πρόδικος; rhetorical teaching: Pl. *Ap.* 19e, *Hp. Ma.* 282c, Xen. *Mem.* II.1.21–34, Philostr. *VS* 1.12.

Hippias included discussions of geometry, astronomy, literature and rhythms in his discourse (Philostr. *VS* 1.11). Their scientific pursuits do not seem to have been an end in themselves, but were intended to give their pupils a general education on which to draw in making public speeches. None of the sophists is credited with an original doctrine concerning the physical universe, so that it is reasonable to assume that what natural science they taught was the product of others and that natural science was subordinate to their primary concern, the teaching of rhetoric.

Interestingly enough, with the exception of Hippias we hear of no foreign sophist who used *physis* as an instrument of social criticism of *nomos*, and Plato's attribution to Hippias of the statement that the bonds uniting intellectuals are closer, because based on *physis*, than the *nomos*-based bonds of kinship and society, has not only been seen to be chronologically unreliable,[132] but is also so commonplace that an earlier currency of the antithesis must be assumed. Among the sophists and their immediate disciples the antinomy is found only in the arguments of the Athenians Antiphon and Callicles (D–K 87 B 44; Pl. *Gorg.* 482e–484c) and in a way which also suggests that it was already well known in Athens before we find it first articulated.

It is, therefore, not surprising that the opposition of *physis* to *nomos* is first attested not in a philosophical or sophistic tract but in popular literature. Aristophanes' *Clouds*, produced in 423, presents Wrong as boasting that it was the first to conceive the idea of contradicting the *nomoi* and the regulations of justice (1039–40) and as encouraging its devotees to 'do as nature [*physis*] bids, skip, jump, laugh, and not be inhibited by conventional notions [*nomizе*] of what is disgraceful' (1075–8). What is more, not only is the debate between Right and Wrong modelled on the sophistic practice of presenting arguments for and arguments against a given issue in speech and debate, a practice first attested for Protagoras,[133] and explicitly made into a contest between the old and the new education (Ar. *Clouds* 937 and 961), but the entire setting of the play is a parody on sophistic teaching. Traits are attributed to Socrates which he himself categorically rejected but attributed to the sophists, foremost among them teaching for pay and speculation about the physical universe, and the product of his school is a Pheidippides who boasts: 'how pleasant it is to be familiar with the latest clever gimmicks and to be able to soar so high in thought as to look down upon the established laws [*nomoi*]' (1399–1400).[134] Clearly, Aristophanes was thoroughly familiar with the impact which the sophists had on Athens,

132 Pl. *Prt.* 337cd with pp. 347–8 above.
133 See above, pp. 342–3 with Kerferd 1981 (J 58) 84–92.
134 For a full discussion see K. J. Dover, ed. *Aristophanes: Clouds* (Oxford, 1968) xxxii–lvii.

and although he often presents the simple, unsophisticated older generation with sympathy and compassion – Dicaeopolis, Strepsiades, Demos, Philocleon – he must himself have been a member of a younger generation, which learned its use of language and argumentation from the sophists.[135]

While no foreign sophist is mentioned as Aristophanes' teacher, Euripides is said to have been a disciple not only of Anaxagoras, but also of Protagoras, Prodicus and Socrates.[136] Regardless of whether these traditions preserve a kernel of historical truth, their very existence manifests an awareness of the extent to which Euripides was open to the foreign influences which flooded Athens during his lifetime. This is especially true of his criticism of the gods of traditional religion, which is born of his concern for social justice. From its first appearance to its final attempt in the *Bacchae* to come to grips with the phenomenon of religion as such, it shows traces of contemporary thought about the gods which were believed to be the product of sophistic teaching. Plays written just before or during the Archidamian War remind us of Protagoras' agnostic despair that we can never come to know any truth about the gods (D–K 80 B 4) and of Prodicus' denial of the existence of the conventional gods: a speech in the *Philoctetes* (431 B.C.) inveighs against seers who claim to have clear knowledge of divine matters, while in reality they manipulate people by persuasion (fr. 795N²); a long extract from the *Bellerophon* (before 425) rejects the existence of the heavenly gods not on intellectual grounds, as Prodicus had done,[137] but because wicked and impious tyrants prosper and because small god-fearing states fall victim to powerful impious states (fr. 286N²). Traces of Protagoras, Archelaus or Prodicus have been seen in Hecuba's heart-rending appeal: 'for the gods are strong and the *nomos* which controls them; for by *nomos* do we believe in the gods and define the rules of right and wrong by which we live': an affirmation of divine power is almost immediately undercut by the statement that the gods are controlled by norms (*nomoi*), and this is in turn undercut by the statement that this affirmation has no sanction beyond the human conventions (*nomoi*) which require gods for establishing social norms in human society.[138]

When the questioning of the morality of the gods recedes in Euripides' later works and ontological problems come to the fore, ideas first found in the Ionian natural philosophers seem to be grafted onto thoughts derived from the sophists. Echoes of Diogenes (D–K 64 B 5), of Heraclitus, of the atomists, and of Anaxagoras' 'Mind' have been

---

[135] See further, de Carli 1971 (J 21).
[136] See Γένος Εὐριπίδου II (Arrighetti); Gell. *NA* xv.20.4, Suda s.v. Εὐριπίδης.
[137] Sext. Emp. *Math.* IX.18 with the two articles by Henrichs cited above, n. 112.
[138] Eur. *Hec.* 799–801 with Heinimann 1945 (J 50) 121–2.

detected in Hecuba's outcry in the *Trojan Women* (415 B.C.): 'You who are
the stay of the earth and have your seat on the earth, whoever you are,
hard to guess and hard to know, Zeus, whether you are nature's necessity
or mortal's mind, I invoke you.'[139] But the quest for the divine reality in
the power underlying natural phenomena also betrays a mind steeped in
sophistic thinking. Doctrines of Prodicus may be reflected in Teiresias'
speech in the *Bacchae* (274–84), which gives a rationalized version of the
blessings bestowed on man by Demeter and Dionysus.[140] But nowhere is
Euripides' indebtedness to the natural philosophers and the sophists
more in evidence than in Sisyphus' speech in the satyr play which bore
his name and which, it is now believed, formed part of the same tetralogy
as the *Trojan Women*.[141]

No name can be attached to the theory with which the fragment
opens, that men originally lived 'beastlike and disorganized' (1–2); but
the thought occurs with increasing frequency in the last quarter of the
fifth century.[142] The invention of laws (*nomoi*) to curb and discipline the
excesses of the wicked and to establish justice as a tyrant (5–8) is not
attributed to an individual lawgiver but, as in Plato's account of
Protagoras' doctrine, to enactment by mankind (Pl. *Prt.* 324a–b, 325a–b,
326c–d). The invention of religion, designed by a 'shrewd man wise in
judgement' to inhibit secret wrongdoing in action, speech, or thought
(9–11, 14–15) by instilling the fear of an immortal, powerful, all-hearing
and all-seeing divinity from whom no thought is hidden (16–24),
reminds us of Antiphon's recognition that law provides no safeguard
against secret wrongdoing (D–K 87 B 44 A 2.3–23) and of Democritus'
attribution to 'a few intelligent men' of the invention of an omniscient
and omnipotent Zeus (D–K 68 B 30), and also to his belief that the notion
of the gods was implanted in primitive man by the fear engendered by
experiencing thunder, lightning and eclipses of sun and moon (D–K 68 A
75). And finally, Prodicus' views may lurk behind Sisyphus' mention of
the benefits accruing to man from such celestial phenomena as sun and
rain (30–1, 34–6 with D–K 84 B 5). In short, there can be no doubt that
Euripides' religious views were tinged by doctrines which had been
imported into Athens by foreign philosophers and sophists.

It is less easy to find parallels to Euripides' all-pervasive social
criticisms in specific doctrines known to have been propagated by
natural philosophers and sophists. Still we know how deeply the
argumentation and language of his plays was indebted to the rhetorical

[139] Eur. *Tro.* 884–7 with Heinimann 1945 (J 50) 130–1.

[140] E. R. Dodds, ed. *Euripides: Bacchae*, 2nd edn (Oxford, 1960) 104–5.

[141] The attribution of this speech to Critias by Sext. Emp. *Math.* ix.54 used to be generally
accepted, until Dihle 1977 (J 23) 28–42 showed cogent reasons for accepting their assignment to
Euripides by Aëtius in *Dox. Graec.* 294 and 298; cf. Scodel 1980 (J 94) 122–37. The citations in the
following are based on Snell's text in *TGrF* 1.43 F 19.   [142] Heinimann 1945 (J 50) 148–9.

teaching current in Athens in his lifetime,[143] and we cannot go far wrong in attributing to the same influences also his attacks on social conventions, usually described as *nomoi* or in similar terms, in the name of values represented by *physis* or features derived from it. More often than not, *nomos* is in Euripides a rigid force of restraint and an impediment to true justice. The Cyclops is happy to be able to indulge his appetites unencumbered by the *nomoi* which complicate human life (Eur. *Cycl.* 336–46); in the *Ion* we are told not only that the observance of *nomos* depends on the circumstances and persons involved (1045–7), but there are complaints that the gods who 'write' laws for men behave themselves lawlessly, and that it is not right that *nomos* should permit unjust men to find protection at an altar (442–3, 1312–13). Elsewhere, the Greek *nomos* is criticized which attaches too high a value to athletic contests (fr. 282.13–15N²); the value of the law enjoining monogamy is doubted (fr. 402N²); the disabilities inflicted on illegitimate children exist by convention (*nomos*) or in name (*onoma*) only: nature (*physis*) recognizes no difference between legitimate and illegitimate birth (frs. 141, 168, and 377N²). Sometimes *physis* is a countervalue before which *nomos* pales (cf. fr. 920N²), at other times it is the force of circumstances in the guise of *ananke* (*Hec.* 846–9, *Or.* 486–8), or again a good character can be regarded as more reliable than the law (fr. 597N²).

No play uses *physis* more pungently as a tool of social criticism and to prove that reality belies the appearance of the underdog and the regard in which he is conventionally held than the *Electra*. *Alexandros*, produced only a few years before or after the *Electra*, expresses the sentiment that nobility conferred by birth and wealth is unreal and merely conventional (*nomoi*) in comparison with god-given nobility which consists in good sense and intelligence (fr. 52, esp. 8–10). This becomes a theme of the *Electra*: the sterling qualities of the poor farmer to whom Electra is married baffle Orestes into questioning the relation between real and apparent nobility (367–90). The criterion for detecting true nobility of character consists in the company a man keeps and the qualities he displays; what is rejected is judgement based on the prestige of his family, which is attributed to opinionated vacuity, and on mere physical prowess. Consistently with this view, Electra vaunts later in the play over the body of Aegisthus:

You used to boast that you were one whose strength lay in his money; but money is with us only for a brief moment or not at all: it is our innate character [*physis*] that remains steadfast, not our money. For character is always with us and helps us overcome adversity, but when prosperity comes with injustice and stupidity it flies out of the house after flourishing but a short time.   (939–44)

---

[143] Solmsen 1975 (J 101) is entirely devoted to a study of this phenomenon in Euripides and Thucydides.

Wealth, poverty, and family prestige are social norms opposed to *physis*; *physis* alone has permanence and a reality which status symbols and other external social trimmings lack. Intelligence is on the side of *physis*; only the stupid and empty-headed attach value to transitory externals (cf. also fr. 495.40–3).

If the *Electra* contains the most concentrated expression of the use of the *nomos–physis* antithesis for purposes of social criticism and of sophistic influence on tragedy, Thucydides is the foremost Athenian exponent of the influence of the sophists on prose literature.[144] Ancient traditions that Thucydides studied philosophy under Anaxagoras and rhetoric under Antiphon, and that he admired Gorgias and Prodicus for their style[145] are reliable only to the extent that they attest an awareness of the contemporary influences to which he was exposed, drawing inferences from his work rather than citing independent external evidence for them. For the fact that he shares with Gorgias a penchant for balanced clauses and antithesis, and with Prodicus a concern for precision in language does not necessarily mean that he consciously imitated them. That, like Anaxagoras (D–K 59 B 21a), he preferred rational to theological explanations of phenomena and looked beyond them to underlying causes does not imply that he was actually his student, and his expressed admiration for Antiphon (VIII.68.1) does not warrant the conclusion of a teacher–student relationship between them. Still, since all these analogies are based on correct observations, there can be no disputing the fact that Thucydides was open to the influence of the philosophers and sophists who came to fifth-century Athens from abroad. That influence goes considerably further and deeper than was recognized in antiquity. Indeed, Thucydides seems to have absorbed all the intellectual currents of his day so thoroughly that, even where specific similarities between him and a particular thinker can be detected, it is impossible to feel certain that it was that thinker who helped shape Thucydides' outlook; rather, he reflects the intellectual atmosphere of his time as a whole.

The heritage bequeathed by Protagoras to all subsequent sophistic teaching is more manifest in Thucydides than in any other fifth-century author. It is seen not only in his use of speeches to explore the deeper meaning of the events he narrates, but the antithetical way in which he arranges them reflects the Protagorean principle of *antilogia*, that is, the consciousness that there are arguments for and arguments against any given issue. The term *antilogia* introduces (1.31.4) the first set of paired

---

[144] For a fuller discussion of the problems touched upon in the following, see Solmsen 1975 (J 101), Finley 1942 (C 30) 36–73, and Hornblower 1987 (C 52) 110–35.

[145] Antyllus *ap.* Marcellin. 22 and 36, cf. 51; for Antiphon, see also Βίος Θουκυδίδου 2 and Caecilius in [Plut.] *X orat.* 832E.

speeches in his work, in which the Corcyreans argue for (1.32–6) and the Corinthians against (1.37–43) the conclusion of an alliance between Athens and Corcyra, exploring the implications and repercussions such an alliance would have for the Greek world at large in a way in which simple narrative cannot do it. This antithetical pairing is used to special advantage in the speeches attributed to the Corinthians (1.68–71) and the Athenian ambassadors (1.73–8) at the Congress of the Peloponnesian League which preceded the declaration of war. Taken together, they analyse as precisely and as dispassionately as that could be done the factors which, in Thucydides' view, made the war between Athens and Sparta inevitable. They include not only the temperamental differences between the restless, enterprising Athenians and the complacent and sluggish Lacedaemonians, but also a brilliant justification of the Athenian possession of empire through an astute analysis of the dynamics which drove them to create it. In some of the paired sets, such as the debate between Cleon and Diodotus on the fate of the people of Mytilene (III.37–40, 42–8) or the speeches of the Plataeans and the Thebans before the five Lacedaemonian judges (III.53–9, 61–7), the antithesis enters even the structure of the speeches themselves in that argument and counter-argument are given in the same sequence.

There are two further features in which Thucydides may be thought to resemble Protagoras. One of these is his reconstruction of the early history of Greece by means of arguments from probability (*to eikos*) and on the basis of whatever plausible indices (*tekmeria*) he can find in myth, literature, contemporary primitive customs, geography and material remains, in order to prove the magnitude of the Peloponnesian War (1.2–19), just as Protagoras had accounted for the development of the social virtues by his reconstruction of the origin of society (Pl. *Prt.* 320c–328d). The second is that his agnostic attitude in matters of religion, most explicitly articulated in the Melian Dialogue (v.105), may be regarded as an application to human conduct of convictions stated by Protagoras apparently in an epistemological context (D–K 80 B 4). Yet the differences in the use of these and similar features are more decisive than the similarities. For, while Protagoras and the sophistic teachers of rhetoric used these devices to score a point in argument, Thucydides employs them to cut through the palpable momentary situation so as to isolate what he regards as the true issues underlying it, to isolate a reality which applies not merely to the particular situation under discussion but is valid for the human condition regardless of time and place.

Thucydides' conviction that the physiological and psychological structure of man, his needs, his aspirations, and the kind of external situations with which he is faced, form the constant which gives the study of the past the perennial value which it has (1.22.4), shows that he shared with Protagoras a man-centred universe. There is no systematic exposition of this conviction, but its contours emerge from general remarks, scattered throughout the work, on man and his condition. So long as human nature (*anthropeia physis*) remains what it is, the hardships brought about by civil disorder (*stasis*) will recur (III.82.2); the desire to rule others, especially when they are weaker, is ingrained in man's nature (1.76.3; v.89, cf. 105.2; vi.61.5), so that acceptance of imperial rule is consistent with the way men are (*tou anthropeiou tropou*): prestige, fear and material benefits will see to it that, once acquired, empire is not relinquished (1.76.2–3), for when left free rein, no laws and no terror can inhibit human nature (III.45.7). Yet Thucydides also recognizes its limitations: human calculations can be fallible (III.40.1, cf. 45.3 and VIII.24.5) and cannot control external fortune (vi.78.2); the plague was beyond human nature (*anthropeia physis*) to endure, and no physician or human skill (*anthropeia techne*) could prevail against it (II.47.4, 50). Moreover, the most intelligently conceived plans of statesmen and generals are consistently foiled by factors over which human planning has no control.[146]

These insights are surely Thucydides' own. But the mind which perceived and formulated them will have been sharpened to its task by sophistic influences as well as by medical writings which, as some believe, schooled him to look behind the symptoms for true causes.[147] Furthermore, Thucydides' method of presenting these insights is frequently informed by the *nomos–physis* antithesis. The conflict between what is morally right (*to dikaion*) and the public interest (*to xympheron*) dominates both the question of the treatment to be meted out to the Mytileneans and the argument between Melians and Athenians; the *nomos–physis* polarity is brought into both discussions, and so is the role of necessity (*ananke*) in human affairs.[148] That these terms formed part of the stock-in-trade of the sophists is amply attested by the argument between Right and Wrong in Aristophanes' *Clouds* (1036–45, 1068–79). But there are telling differences. In the Mytilenean debate, Cleon supports his advocacy of the brutal deployment of imperial power by arguments from *nomos* and what is right, while Diodotus' opposition is based on arguments from *physis* and the public interest. For Cleon a city is strong only so long as its laws remain unchanged and these laws, represented by the decision taken at an earlier meeting of the Assembly, demand a harsh punishment of the wrong (*adikia*) done by the Mytileneans as being both right (*dikaia*) and in the public interest (Thuc. III.37.3, 38.1, 39.1, 3 and 6, 40.4); for Diodotus no law is adequate to inhibit the fallibility of human nature (*anthropeia physis*) or stop it once it

146 Stahl 1966 (c 96).   147 So especially, Cochrane 1929 (c 19).
148 See Ostwald 1988 (c 74).

has embarked upon its course; the issue is not whether the Mytileneans were right or wrong, but what policy serves the public interest, and terrifying *nomoi* serve the state less well than a policy of cultivating the allegiance of the common people in allied states to nip incipient revolts in the bud (III.45.3 and 5, 44.1, 2, 3, and 4, 47.5).

In the Melian Dialogue, however, the policy of ruthless exercise of imperial power is entirely predicated on a view of *physis* which looks like the application to a concrete political situation of Democritus' belief that 'ruling belongs by nature to the stronger' (D–K 68 B 267); its aim is less to preserve the empire than to extend it. Arguments from justice are excluded by the Athenians from the outset on the ground that 'what is right is decided in human reckoning when the pressure that can be exerted by the two sides is equal, but what is possible is achieved by those who have superior power and is acquiesced in by the weak' (v.89). Like Diodotus, the Athenians combine arguments from public interest with arguments from *physis* (v.91.2). However, their perspective on *physis* differs radically from that of Diodotus. For while Diodotus envisages the *physis* of the allies as the mainspring which makes their attempts at revolt inevitable, the Athenians at Melos think only of the *physis* of the imperial power, which nothing can inhibit and which harks back to the statement of the Athenian ambassadors at Sparta before the war, in which the growth of the Athenian empire is ascribed to the natural human impulse toward dominion over others (1.76.3). To the constraints of this *physis*, the Athenians assert, even the gods are subject; and when they proceed to call this a 'law' (*nomos*) they do so with tongue in cheek, obviously realizing that an inescapable fact of nature cannot be the product of human legislation (v.105.1–3). In other words, the contrast of *nomos* and *physis* which Diodotus had used to argue that human nature cannot be suppressed by legislation (III.45.7) is here revaluated to make human attempts to establish *nomoi* look futile and ridiculous when faced with the natural impulse to assert superior power.

The influence of two foreign historians on Thucydides deserves a brief word here. Hellanicus of Lesbos is criticized at 1.97.2 for his cursory and chronologically imprecise account of the fifty years which separated the end of the Persian from the outbreak of the Peloponnesian War (*pentekontaëteia*). Since Thucydides' own narrative of this period is open to the same objections, we cannot be sure what exactly he found fault with in Hellanicus' work on Attica (*Attike xyngraphe*). However, since he censures the use of archon-lists and other lists of officials for chronological purposes, preferring his own system of reckoning by summers and winters (v.20.2–3), and since we know that Hellanicus' work depended for its structure on the Athenian archon-list (see above, p. 337), this is the probable target of Thucydides' criticism. Still, criticism is not wholesale condemnation: the few instances of dating by Athenian archons and Spartan ephors (II.2.1 and v.19.1) or by the priestesses of Hera at Argos (II.2.1 and IV.133.2–3) may well have been taken from Hellanicus' chronologies.[149]

Herodotus is not mentioned by name anywhere in Thucydides. Yet he looms large in the background of the entire work. Thucydides' programmatic statements that he is more interested in historical truth than in attractive presentation (1.21.1), and that he regards the search of a clear understanding of the past as of more permanent value than the momentary delight in a story well told (1.22.4), are generally believed to be criticisms of Herodotus, from whose method Thucydides sharply differentiates his own. Nevertheless, Thucydides' narrative of the sequel of the Persian Wars begins where Herodotus had left off; he takes the Herodotean narrative for granted without criticizing it or attempting to correct it, except in a few details,[150] which suggest that he was thoroughly familiar with it.

While the imprint left by foreign intellectuals is most noticeable for us in Athenian literature, their contemporaries will have been more concerned with the effect of their teaching on Athenian politics. Plato makes Protagoras say that the most influential men, whom he identifies with the wealthiest, are best able to give their sons the maximum of education (Pl. *Prt.* 326c), and it was in the hands of these sons, trained by the sophists, that much of the fate of Athens rested during the last two decades of the fifth century. Their social background and intellectual training will have made them wish to distance themselves from the levelling conformity of the Athenian democracy, to whose establishment their own forebears had, in many cases, made significant contributions. Many of those who worked for the overthrow of the Athenian democracy in 411 and in 404, and participated in the oligarchical regimes which replaced it, had been pupils of foreign sophists, and several did not shrink from engaging in treasonous activities against their country.[151]

The influence which Anaxagoras and Zeno are alleged to have had upon Pericles has already been mentioned, as has Zeno's relation to the general Pythodorus son of Isolochus.[152] Another pupil of Zeno, Aristoteles, had served the democracy as general in 431/0 and as a *hellenotamias* ten years later, before, as a general under the Four Hundred, he became one of the die-hards who pushed for the fortification of Eetioneia in

---

[149] See Gomme 1950 (C 37) I 2–8.

[150] For example, 1.20.3 corrects Hdt. IX.53.2–3 on the existence of a 'Pitane company' in the Spartan army, and possibly Hdt. IX.57.5 on the two votes of each Spartan king; 1.126.8 corrects Hdt. v.71.2 on the 'prytaneis of the naucrari' at the time of the Cylonian revolt.

[151] See Ostwald 1986 (A 96) 346–8, 359–72, 460–6, 507–50.

[152] See above, pp. 339–40.

order to secure access to the Piraeus for the Peloponnesians; he spent part of his exile with Lysander and acted as his personal representative at the peace negotiations with Theramenes, and returned as an old man to Athens in 404 to become one of the Thirty, being instrumental in obtaining a Spartan garrison for their protection.[153] Adeimantus son of Leucolophides is described sitting as a boy at the feet of Prodicus in Plato's *Protagoras* (315e); some eighteen years later, he was denounced for participation in the profanation of the Mysteries, his considerable wealth was confiscated and sold at auction,[154] and he went into exile (Andoc. 1.16). Although he had not joined the oligarchical movement either in 411 or in 404, but had fought along with Alcibiades in the Hellespont in 407/6, had been re-elected as general to replace those deposed after Arginusae, and had been captured by the Spartans after Aegospotami, the fact that he alone was spared by Lysander put him under suspicion of having betrayed the fleet at Aegospotami (Xen. *Hell.* 1.4.21, 7.1, II.1.30; Diod. XIII.69.3; Plut. *Alc.* 36.6). Theramenes, a disciple of Prodicus, played a leading part in establishing and overthrowing the Four Hundred, in setting up the intermediate regime of the Five Thousand, in conducting the peace negotiations with Sparta in 404, and in establishing the oligarchy of the Thirty to whom he was to fall victim. His close associate in 404, Cleitophon, who had in 411 offered an amendment to the motion establishing the commission which ushered in the oligarchy (Arist. *Ath. Pol.* 29.3 and 34.3), had been a student of Thrasymachus (above, n. 116); Andron, who had been one of the Four Hundred (Harp. and Suda s.v. Ἄνδρων), but turned against them and became the chief prosecutor of Antiphon, Onomacles and Archeptolemus ([Plut.] *X orat.* 833E), is said by Plato (*Prt.* 315c) to have sat at the feet of Hippias as a young man. Pythodorus, who had prosecuted Protagoras, presumably for overcharging him for his instruction, made the motion in 411 to which Cleitophon offered his amendment, himself became one of the Four Hundred and is probably identical with the man in whose archonship the Thirty came to power (Xen. *Hell.* II.3.1, Lys. VII.9, Arist. *Ath. Pol.* 35.1 and 41.1).[155] Charmides, who served as one of the Ten in the Piraeus under the Thirty and was killed in the street-fighting which followed their overthrow (Xen. *Hell.* II.4.19) is probably identical with the person at whose house some of the profanations of the

---

[153] Pl. *Prm.* 127d; for his generalship in 431/0 see *IG* I³ 366.6; for his service as *hellenotamias*, see *ATL* List 34 with Lewis 1961 (D 49) 118–23, esp. 120–21; for his activities in 411, Xen. *Hell.* II.3.46 with Thuc. VIII.90.1 and 91.2; for his activities in 404, Xen. *Hell.* II.2.18 and 3.2 and 13

[154] *IG* I³ 422.187–92; 426.10–22, 43–51, 141–2, 185–90; 430.3, 10–12, 27–30 with Aurenche 1974 (D 4) 130–1.

[155] Arist. *Ath. Pol.* 29.1, D. L. IX.54, where the association of his name with that of Euathlus (cf. D. L. IX.56, Quint. *Inst.* III.1.10, Gell. *NA* V.10) suggests the motive for prosecution. Cf. n. 104 above.

Mysteries had taken place in 415 (Andoc. 1.16), and is shown by his nephew Plato not only as a frequent companion of Socrates, but also in the company of Protagoras.[156]

Two sophistic disciples deserve special mention because of the prominent roles they played in the downfall of Athens, Critias and Alcibiades. But apart from the fact that both are said to have been impressed by Gorgias (above, p. 344) and that both entered the house of Callias together to listen to Protagoras and participated in the discussion that followed (Pl. *Prt.* 316a, 347b), nothing is known about any foreigners whose students they may have been, except that Pericles' superannuated Thracian slave Zopyrus is said to have been a teacher of Alcibiades (Pl. *Alc.* 1, 122b, cf. Plut. *Alc.* 1–3). Yet their close association with Socrates, so close that later apologists went out of their way to clear Socrates' name from contamination with them,[157] shows that they moved in intellectual circles in which foreigners easily mingled with Athenians. It is not easy to make sense of Critias' chequered career, which was already unusual in that he first emerged into the political limelight when, well over forty years old, he was implicated in the mutilation of the Herms but was freed by the testimony of his kinsman Andocides (Andoc. 1.47 and 68). If he participated in the oligarchy of the Four Hundred ((Dem.) LVII.67), his involvement was not deep enough to force him into exile after their overthrow.[158] What we know of his acts between 411 and the ruthless role he played as leader of the Thirty suggests that he was prompted more by personal and intellectual commitments than by political considerations. His vengeful motion to have the bones of Phrynichus exhumed and cast outside the boundaries of Attica (Lycurg. *Leoc.* 113), as well as his motion for the recall of Alcibiades (Plut. *Alc.* 33.1), seem to betray a strong loyalty to Alcibiades rather than political principles. The same reason is likely to have caused Cleophon to drive him into exile after Alcibiades' fall (Arist. *Rhet.* 1.15, 1375b31–2), which he spent in Thessaly, allegedly 'fomenting democracy and arming the *penestai* against their master' (Xen. *Hell.* 11.3.36). It is difficult in the light of his later oligarchical activities in Athens to give this conduct a political interpretation.[159] It rather seems to indicate a strong puritanical streak in him which may well have outraged whatever sense of social justice his philosophical training has fostered in him. The same streak may have moved him on his return to Athens after the peace in 404/3 'to purge the city of unjust men and to turn the rest of the citizens to goodness and justice' (Lys. XII.5) by trying to remake Athens

[156] Pl. *Chrm.* 154ab, 155a; *Symp.* 222b; *Theages* 128d; *Prt.* 315a; cf. Xen. *Symp.* 1.3 and III.1–2; *Mem.* III.6.1. [157] Xen. *Mem.* 1.2.12–16 and 24–39.

[158] G. Adeleye, 'Critias: member of the Four Hundred?', *TAPA* 104 (1974) 1–9.

[159] For attempts at a political interpretation, see Wade-Gery 1958 (A 121) 271–92, esp. 280–1; Mossé 1969 (A 91A) 122 n. 3; Krentz 1982 (D 44A) 46.

in the image of an idealized Sparta.[160] The extremes to which he went in
the pursuit of this goal were, according to an ancient commentator on
Aeschines (1.39), reflected in a monument erected after his death by his
sympathizers, which showed Oligarchy setting a torch to Democracy
with the inscription: 'This is a memorial to noble men who for a short
time kept the accursed commons of Athens from its arrogance.'

A commitment to social justice was, however, not one of the
mainsprings of Alcibiades' conduct. What had he learned from the
sophists he pressed into the service of satisfying his own boundless
ambition for political power. The evidence for this is so copious that it
would be pointless to try to rehearse it exhaustively here. But it is well
illustrated by the rhetorical brilliance of two speeches which Thucydides
attributes to him, the speech in which he argues against Nicias in favour
of the Sicilian Expedition,[161] and his justification of his earlier anti-
Spartan policy, which he delivered before the Spartans after he had
defected to them.

What stands out in his speech to the Athenian Assembly is an
exploitation of the *nomos–physis* antithesis, in which he presents himself,
paradoxically enough, as the champion of *nomos*, after having based his
claim to leadership on the distinction of his ancestors (vi.16.1), which
one would expect to lead to an argument from *physis*. Instead, Alcibiades
turns to his own victories at Olympia and says of them:

this sort of thing is conventionally [*nomoi*] regarded as an honour, and at the
same time the achievement creates an impression of power. Again, it is only
natural [*physei*] that my fellow citizens envy me for the splendour I enjoy in the
city for equipping choruses and providing other public services, but this too
creates an impression of strength in the eyes of foreigners.   (16.2–3)

In other words, *nomos* is responsible for the honour which redounds to
Athens from his victories, while the carping of *physis* tends to undermine
his reputation. Moreover, he credits what his opponents consider as his
unnatural (*para physin*) youthful madness with his success in dealing with
the Peloponnesians (17.1), and in his peroration he exhorts the Athenians, in language reminiscent of Cleon's speech on the fate of the
Mytileneans, not to rescind their vote on the grounds that 'those men
live most securely whose government least deviates from the character
and the *nomoi* they have, even if they are inferior' (18.7). To have a man
argue for *nomos* whose personal conduct is characterized by *paranomia*
(Thuc. vi.15.4), and to have a man who had spared no effort to
undermine Nicias' peace treaty with Sparta argue for the Sicilian
Expedition on the grounds 'that we must defend our Sicilian allies,
inasmuch as we have sworn to do so and without objecting that they

---

[160] Krentz 1982 (D 44A) 63–8.   [161] Cf. Macleod 1983 (A 82) 68–87.

have not defended us' (18.1) is an irony which, in this context, is a clear instance of the sophistic practice of making the worse argument appear to be better.

Alcibiades' assertion of his own superiority over the common people in this speech and his regarding it rather as their good fortune that they have him to look up to (16.4–5) reveals an arrogance of the intellectual aristocrat *vis-à-vis* the masses that may well have characterized the attitude of many other sophist-trained politicians of his time. In its disarming frankness it anticipates his defence of his earlier policies at Sparta:

> We gave leadership to the people as a whole, because we thought it right to preserve the form of government under which our city had attained the peak of its greatness and freedom and which came to us as an inheritance, while as intelligent people we realized what democracy is, and I no less than anyone in that I have more reason to revile it. However, nothing new can be said about what everyone agrees to be madness, and to change it did not seem a safe course for us to take, when you, our enemy, were standing at the gates. (VI.89.3–6)

The Athenian democracy was for Alcibiades neither an article of faith nor an offence to social justice, but a condition whose reality must be included in one's political calculations.

However rampant similar sentiments may have been among the upper class and especially its younger intellectuals, they will not have been shared by the majority of Athenians, particularly by the older generation which suspected that foreign influences had been at work in shaping them and which attributed the erosion of traditional civic religion to the spread of sophistic rationalism. Some feeling against the presence of foreigners in Athens had been latent at least since the middle of the fifth century and seems to have been shared by members of all social classes. We have seen it (above, p. 307 with n. 8) in the support given to Pericles' citizenship law in 451/0, which placed encumbrances on unions between Athenians and foreigners; it is apparent in the Old Oligarch's censure of the free and easy way in which metics mingled with Athenians ([Xen.] *Ath. Pol.* 1.10); it comes to the fore again in the severity with which the Thirty proceeded against the metics (Xen. *Hell.* II.3.21–2, 41; Lys. XII.6; Diod. XIV.5.6), as well as in Archinus' opposition to Thrasybulus' bill enfranchising Lysias and other foreigners who had returned to Athens from the Piraeus ([Plut.] *X orat.* 835F–836A; cf. Arist. *Ath. Pol.* 40.2), in Phormisius' proposed restriction of citizenship to landowners (Dion. Hal. *Lys.* 32), and in Theozotides' exclusion of the children of foreigners from the support he proposed to be given to the orphans of those who had fought for the democracy against the oligarchs.[162] But from the 430s

---

[162] Lys. frs. VI.I.1 and 2 (Gernet–Bizos), with Stroud 1971 (D 94) 280–301, esp. 299–300. On this period see Strauss 1987 (D 93) 90–104.

on, the sophists in particular became the butt of what Athenian xenophobia there existed. Democratic stalwarts such as Laches and Anytus expressed their revulsion against them (Pl. *Lach.* 197d; *Meno* 91c), and even those young aristocrats who were eager to be instructed by them were wary of the odium they might incur by associating with the sophists.[163] They wanted to be smart, but they did not want to be unpopular.

The main reason for the unpopularity of foreign sophists was the conviction that the intellectual training they administered undermined the authority of religion. Greek religion demanded of its adherents no more than participation in traditional forms of worship. It was free from dogma and a concept of faith was alien to it. Dissenting beliefs held by individuals could be tolerated so long as they did not serve to discourage people from worshipping the gods by traditional prayers, sacrifice and other rites. The doctrines of the Ionian physicists as popularized by the rationalism of the sophists, however, were thought to be doing precisely that and were, therefore, regarded by many as a threat to the established religion. Actions of various kinds were taken against foreign propounders of subversive views. Anaxagoras was prosecuted for impiety for having asserted that the sun is a fiery stone, thus detracting from its divinity and from its worship,[164] and he had to leave Athens as a result. His accuser was a certain Diopeithes, a divine of sorts possessed with an evangelistic fervour, which gave him the reputation of being slightly crazy (Ar. *Birds* 988 with schol.; *Wasps* 380 with schol.). With Anaxagoras in mind, he proposed a decree, stipulating the procedure of *eisangelia* – usually invoked in cases of crimes against the state, especially those for which no written legislation existed – to be applied to 'those who do not pay the customary respect to the divine or teach doctrines about celestial phenomena' (Plut. *Per.* 32.2). Plutarch's assertion that Pericles was the real target of Diopeithes' attack (cf. also Diod. XII.39.2) is made credible by the close relation between statesman and philosopher; but it makes the proceeding testify no less to offended sensibilities on the part of the religious majority in that it shows that the association had exposed Pericles to censure on religious grounds.[165] Similarly, Pericles' foreign mistress, Aspasia, is said to have been prosecuted for impiety by the comic writer Hermippus, but was acquitted as a result of Pericles' impassioned plea.[166] Judicial proceedings were also instituted against Prodicus, if a late tradition, which may be contaminated by the fate of

[163] Ar. *Clouds* 102–25; Pl. *Prt.* 312a, *Gorg.* 485a–d and 519e–520a; *Phdr.* 257d.
[164] D. L. II.12, Joseph, *Ap.* II.265, Plut. *De Superst.* 169F with Burkert 1985 (K 16) 86, 175, 230.
[165] For a full discussion, see Derenne 1930 (J 22) 13–41. For a sceptical view of the tradition, see Dover 1976 (J 33) 25–54, esp. 27–34.
[166] Plut. *Per.* 32.1 and 5; Ath. XIII.589e; Schol. Ar. *Knights* 969.

Socrates, can be trusted: he was forced to drink the hemlock for corrupting the young (see p. 346 above).

A fate of a different kind befell Protagoras for his agnostic assertion: 'Concerning the gods I am in no position to know either that they exist, or that they do not exist, or what kind of shape they have; for many factors prevent knowing, such as the impossibility of attaining certainty and the fact that man's life is short' (D–K 80 B 4). For this belief, we are told, he was expelled from Athens and his books were burned in the Agora.[167] Evidently, the questions raised by this foreigner were too disconcerting for the common people, too prone to undermine the public worship of the gods.

The measures taken against Diagoras of Melos seem to have been motivated by more substantial reasons. He was a dithyrambic poet who is likely to have spent some time in Athens in the 420s, if he is the 'Melian' credited in Aristophanes' *Clouds* (828–30) with the doctrine that Zeus had been supplanted as king by Dinos (= 'pot'). An ancient tradition reports that Diagoras had so maligned the Mysteries that many prospective initiates did not go through with their initiation, and that the Athenians, therefore, published on a bronze stela a proclamation promising one silver talent to anyone who would kill him and two to anyone who would produce him alive in Athens.[168] A variant tradition (Diod. XIII.6.7) has the proclamation follow Diagoras' escape from Athens before being tried on a slanderous charge of impiety, and dates the proclamation in 415/14, a date which seems to be corroborated by the unmistakable parody of the proclamation against Diagoras in Aristophanes' *Birds* (1072–8), first performed in 414. Whatever public statement Diagoras may have made, it will have been especially offensive coming from a foreigner ([Lys.] VI.17–18) and that at a time when young Athenian intellectuals from the upper classes had been discovered in the illicit performance – and thus profanation – of the Mysteries.[169] This was a time when the Athenians, on the eve of their expedition against Sicily, were more nervous about disturbances in the equilibrium of the state than they had ever been before, and when the profanations of the Mysteries and the desecration of the Herms were viewed by many as a prelude to a coup designed to overthrow the democracy. However hospitable and open the Athenians had been to foreigners a decade earlier, they could not now afford to let anyone, citizen or foreigner, endanger the state by undermining its religion.

[167] D. L. IX.52, 54, and 55; cf. Cic.*Nat. D.* 1.23.63, Schol. Pl. *Rep.* 606c; Plut. *Nic.* 23.4, Philostr. *VS* 1.103. Here, too, Dover 1976 (J 33) 34–7 is sceptical.

[168] Schol. Ar. *Birds* 1073 and *Frogs* 320; Melanthius *FGrH* 326 F 3, and Craterus *FGrH* 342 F 16.

[169] See Jacoby 1959 (J 56); Woodbury 1965 (J 114) 178–211.

CHAPTER 9

THE ARCHIDAMIAN WAR

D. M. LEWIS

I. THE CAUSES OF THE WAR

It is not an unreasonable attitude to be interested in the Peloponnesian War for what Thucydides made of it and not for its own sake, and few episodes in history are so closely associated with their chronicler. This chapter cannot replace the reading of his history, and makes no attempt to provide a substitute. At best, it may be possible to give a narrative which clarifies some of his thinking and calls attention to points which he has obscured.[1]

Open warfare between Athens and the Peloponnesian League began in 431. Thucydides oscillates between two beginnings of the war, the Theban attack on Plataea in the spring (II.1–7.1) and the Spartan invasion of Attica eighty days later (I.125.2, II.12.3, 19.1). The two are apparently conjoined at VII.18.2, and at V.20.1 Thucydides seems to treat the date of the former as the date of the latter. In an important passage (VII.18.2) the Spartans acknowledge that the Thebans should not have attacked Plataea in a time of peace and that they themselves should not have taken up arms while the Athenians were offering arbitration under the terms of the Thirty Years' Peace; Athenian ambassadors had warned them (I.78.4) not to outrage the gods by whom that peace had been sworn. It was thus agreed that Sparta had formally and illegally opened the continuous war, but matters were not as simple as that;[2] as Polybius said (III.6.6), while abstaining from using this instance, one should not confuse the beginning (arche) of a war with its causes (aitiai).

The causes lay further back and would be seen differently by different people. In our other sources emphasis is laid on Athenian relations with Megara (Ar. *Ach.* 515–39, *Peace* 606–9; Andoc. III.8; Diod. XII.39.4–5; Plut. *Per.* 29.4–31.1) and Aegina (Andoc. III.6, cf. Thuc. II.27.1). Thucydides took a different line.[3] When he set out the *aitiai* (for him, 'causes of complaint') and the *diaphorai* (disputes) 'so that no one should have to

---

[1] Guidance on specific points is generally available from *HCT* or from Kagan 1969, 1974 (G 17–18). In this chapter, de Ste Croix refers to G 36, unless otherwise stated.

[2] They are for de Ste Croix 65, but see 290–2 for a more cautious statement.

[3] Cf. Dover, *HCT* v 422–3.

seek how so great a war arose' (1.23.5), he held firmly to a line of narrative which placed Athenian relations with Corinth in the foreground (1.24ff, cf.118.1). His story begins, surprisingly, with party strife in remote Epidamnus, well up the Adriatic Sea, some five years before war broke out, and it is the Corinthians who are the most active characters in Book 1, in words (more than a tenth of the book consists of Corinthian speeches) and in deeds. Thucydides certainly knew what he believed, and we cannot show that he was wrong. Aegina and Megara do get their place. As we look at the other evidence, we can see a belief that Megara was intimately associated with the outbreak of war and that its affairs were somehow disproportionate to the size of the war which they caused; since Thucydides says that the repeal of the Megarian Decree was the principal Spartan demand (1.139.1, 140.4) and reports Pericles as saying that the demand was less important in itself than as a test of Athenian resolve (1.140.4–5), he should not be accused of failing to account for this belief. What we can complain of is that he has made up his mind so resolutely about what was important that he has left us without the facts to check him; no ingenuity enables us to discover, for example, the chronological relationship of the Megarian Decree (p.376) to his main narrative.[4]

Thucydides, however, does not confine himself to Corinth. Whatever her bellicosity, it was Sparta which had to be persuaded into war and the Spartan attitude had to be accounted for. Three passages deepen the account. At 1.23.6, after the undertaking to describe the *aitiai* and *diaphorai*, they are joined, I would say, subordinated, to the sentence:

'The truest *prophasis*,[5] most inconspicuous in talk, I think, was that the growth of Athenian power provoked fear in the Spartans and forced them [*anankasai*] to make war.

At 1.88 we are told:

The Spartans voted that the Peace had been broken and that war should start, not so much because they were persuaded by their allies' arguments as because they were afraid that the Athenians might grow even more powerful, seeing that much of Greece was already under their control.

---

[4] The reference to Corinthian suspicion of Athens over Megara at 1.42.2 *could* be a reference to the Megarian Decree, but could equally well be one to Athens' reception of Megara into alliance in 460, the start of Corinthian hatred for Athens (1.103.4).

[5] Much effort has been spent on the etymology and implications of the word *prophasis*, which in the fifth century did not yet always bear the meaning of 'excuse' (and probably a false one), which it did for Polybius when he tried to sort out the terminology of the causes of wars (III.6); see Kirkwood 1952 (c 60); Pearson 1952 (c 76); Rawlings 1975 (A 103). However, the word does not stand in isolation here, but is combined with *alethestate* (truest). The other appearance of that combination in Thucydides is at VI.6.1, where it produces a total reversal of the terminology in the parallel passage, III.86.4. There is no important distortion in translating as 'the truest reason'.

At 1.118.2 it is said that the Fifty Years were years

in which the Athenians made their empire stronger and themselves reached a
high point of power, but the Spartans, though they saw them, only made small
attempts to prevent them and kept quiet most of the time, being even before this
not quick to go to war unless they were forced, and in part prevented by wars of
their own, until the power of the Athenians was clearly at its height and they
were laying hands on their alliance. Then they thought it no longer tolerable;
they thought they had to make every effort and bring down their power, if they
could, by starting this war.

We can hardly concern ourselves here with the most notorious of
Thucydidean problems. There are some[6] who think that the original
design of Book 1 did concentrate on the *aitiai* and *diaphorai*, but that, after
Sparta resumed war in 413 in a period of Corinthian weakness,
Thucydides, needing wider causes for the whole war, inserted these
three passages and the account of the Fifty Years. Others[7] see no need for
such a hypothesis and find the 'truest *prophasis*' omnipresent in the book.
Even if the growth of Athenian power is omnipresent, Spartan fear is not
(only in 1.33.3), and the inadequacy of the account of the Fifty Years and
its lack of relation to the main narrative are powerful reasons for
supposing that there has been some reworking.

On any view about the composition of Book 1, Thucydides' final
judgement was that the Spartans acted out of necessity (*ananke*); they had
no choice.[8] It may be doubted whether he thought that the Athenians
had much choice either. Given his general views on the nature of power,
particularly as expressed in the Athenian national character, he is
unlikely to have thought that they would turn back. At one crucial point
(1.49.7) they are also involved in *ananke*, and Pericles' last words before
the war are that *ananke* must be willingly accepted (1.144.3). Almost his
last words; his last words are that they must not diminish the achievements of their ancestors (1.144.4), in almost the same words as the
Corinthians had told the Spartans not to diminish the achievements of
theirs (1.71.7). Thucydides saw the war as inevitable. At Sparta he allows
Archidamus a plea for delay; at Athens the opponents of war are
dismissed in a line or so (1.139.4).

How widely had the war been thought inevitable and for how long? In
June 433 Thucydides reports the Athenians as accepting the Corcyraean
assertion that there would be war with the Peloponnesians whatever

  6 Schwartz 1929 (C 91) 92–167; Andrewes 1959 (G 4).
  7 De Romilly 1951 (C 85) 21–37; de Ste Croix 56–63.
  8 For a closer study of *ananke* in this context, see Ostwald 1988 (C 74). Since no one ever makes
any concrete proposals about how the arbitration so freely spoken of should be conducted, it
appears that the matter was only of importance in fixing responsibility for the breach of the Thirty
Years' Peace; even Archidamus (1.85.2) is only urging delay, and caution on this point.

they did (1.44.2, cf.33.3). As it happens, we can confirm this. Athenian decrees passed within the archon-year 434/3 (M–L 58 = *IG* I³ 52), at the end of the main phase of financing the building programme (see p. 125), place strict limits on future public expenditure, order the spending of certain surplus money on the dockyards and the walls, and in general put Athenian finance on a war footing. It cannot be formally proved[9] that they antedate the deepening of the crisis involved in accepting the alliance with Corcyra (below, p. 374), but they probably do. Thucydides does not explain why the Athenians held this belief. We can in part fill his gap by remembering the Peloponnesian League conference of 440 (p. 144) and observing that Pericles in 432 is made to talk of long-standing Spartan plots (1.140.2; cf. Plut. *Per.* 8.7, Pericles saying that he already saw war approaching from the Peloponnese). Thucydides names no speaker in 433, but at 1.127.3 he attests Pericles' constant opposition to the Spartans, his unwillingness to yield and his drive to war.[10]

Some aspects of the strengthening of Athenian power in the thirties have already been noted (pp. 145–6). The tribute-lists, very lacunose in this period, allow others to be seen more dimly. From 438, additional charges (*epiphorai*) are made on some states, perhaps fines for late payment, and from 434 there are voluntary accessions by states which had not been assessed, either as a state matter or with individuals paying on their behalf; these have been seen as moved by a desire to enter the Athenian economic system, but are more likely to be politically motivated.[11] There was some tendency for tributes reduced in 446 (p. 138) to move up again; a more complex pattern on the Thracian coast east of the Strymon is probably connected with the rise of the Odrysian kingdom.[12] There was doubtless some restlessness: Mytilene, despite her loyalty in 440 (p. 144), had contemplated revolt before the war (Thuc. III.2.1). Athenian fleets were on the move in 435 and 434 (*IG* I³ 464.105–7, 465.128–9), in what theatre we do not know; one may have gone as far as Naples (Timaeus *FGrH* 566 F 98). Shortly before 433 Athens abandoned her alliance with Perdiccas king of Macedon[13] to back his brother Philip and another prince.

Thucydides starts his path to war with the affairs of Epidamnus, where there was a democratic revolution shortly before 435. The new government asked the help of the mother-city Corcyra (see *CAH* III².3, 132–3). Rejected by her, they went on to her mother-city Corinth, from which

---

[9] Meiggs 1972 (E 53) 201, is too optimistic, and see Thompson 1970 (D 96) 57–8. See now Kallet-Marx 1989 (G 21), doubting the orthodox dating of the Callias Decrees.

[10] de Ste Croix 65 says that the drive is to the war which the Spartans have already declared, but hardly explains the three imperfect tenses.

[11] Against the wrong interpretation offered by *ATL* I 455–6, see Lepper 1962 (E 40) (economic), Schuller 1981 (E 80) (political). [12] *ATL* III 309–13.

[13] The date of his accession is uncertain; see Hammond *et al.*1972–88 (F 29) II 103–4.

their founder had come. Relations between Corinth and Corcyra had long been bad (cf. Plut. *Them.* 24.1), and Corinth, glad to assert her position, sent help. Corcyra resented the interference, and attacked Epidamnus. Corinth raised the stakes and proclaimed a new colony to Epidamnus; Athens was not the only city which could raise new cities among barbarian neighbours.[14] Drawing on all her reserves of good will with her friends, she raised a fleet of seventy-five ships and prepared to move on Epidamnus. (1.24–7).

Up until now, Corcyra had no formal ties with any large state. Reputedly wealthy, her distinguishing feature was her possession of the second largest fleet in Greece, a nominal 120 ships. Why she needed it, except to assert her descent from the nautical Phaeacians of the *Odyssey*, is not clear, but she may have had trouble with Adriatic pirates. Nevertheless, her first reaction was to attempt to come to terms with Corinth. In her diplomatic approaches she invoked the aid of Sparta and Sicyon, evidently not enthusiastic about supporting Corinth. Corinth refused all offers of settlement, made her expedition and met with disaster in the battle of Leucimme (435). Corcyra settled affairs at Epidamnus to her satisfaction, and for some time controlled the Ionian Sea, taking reprisals against Leucas and Elis, who had backed Corinth. (1.28–30).

Corinth started to prepare an expedition on an even larger scale. Corcyra would need help, and applied to Athens for alliance (spring 433). Her ambassadors argued on the assumption that war was coming; Corcyra occupied a strategic position on the route for fleets to Italy and Sicily, and her naval strength would be crucial for the balance of power at sea. Corinthian ambassadors made light of the possibility of war and made unconvincing reference to their past services to Athens and their rights over Corcyra, but pointed to a real danger to the Thirty Years' Peace if Athens should accept Corcyra while she was actually at war with Corinth. The Assembly lasted for two days and came to a compromise: the alliance would not be a full *symmachia*, by which Athens would undertake to have the same friends and enemies as Corcyra, but would take the new, perhaps unprecedented, form of an *epimachia*, by which the partners only bound themselves to assist each other in the event of an actual attack on Corcyraean or Athenian territory. The Athenian position thus defined gave her a plausible position in relation to her treaty obligations and would be sufficient to encourage Corcyraean resistance. It fell a long way short of warning Corinth off, and Thucydides gives Athens no such motive; the first stage in the war which the Athenians agreed to be inevitable would be the use of Corcyra to weaken the naval strength of Corinth and her associates. (1.31–44).

The Athenian squadron which now went to Corcyra (M–L 61 = *IG* 1³

14 For a numismatic reflection, see Kraay 1976 (C 190) 84.

364) had clear instructions which followed from the treaty; force was only to be used against the Corinthians if they attempted to land on Corcyra or any of her dependencies. Only ten ships went, which was no deterrent, and the Corinthians were not deterred. They had raised their fleet to a strength of 150, against which the Corcyraeans put out 110. Off the islands of Sybota the fleets met (August 433). By Athenian standards it was an uncouth, old-fashioned affair, with no pure naval technique, fought like a land-battle with masses of troops on deck and the ships often stationary. Thucydides first notes the reluctance of the Athenian generals to become involved, but, eventually, as the Corinthians got on top, 'no distinction was now made, and matters came to that point of necessity that the Corinthians and Athenians laid hands on one another' (1.49.7). The Athenian generals had exceeded their instructions; it may well be thought that they had not been easy to execute. (1.45–9).

The Corinthians were about to push their advantage home when twenty more Athenian ships appeared, sent on the correct assumption that the first squadron might be inadequate to save Corcyra. The Corinthian commanders decided that further success was unlikely. After a brief negotiation, in which the Corinthians complained of the Athenian breach of the Thirty Years' Peace and the Athenians returned to the position that they had no instructions except to protect Corcyraean territory, which would not be such a breach, the Corinthians withdrew without much further incident. Athens had saved Corcyra, at some cost to the neatness of her diplomatic manoeuvres to maintain the Peace. That the route to the west seemed more important than Thucydides lets us see in detail emerges from the renewal, within the archon-year 433/2, of the treaties with Leontini and Rhegium, at their request (M–L 63, 64 = IG i³ 53, 54; cf. SEG XXVI.12). (1.50–5).

Some Corinthian reaction was clearly likely. One obvious Athenian weak point was Potidaea, a substantial city on the isthmus of Pallene, in the front line as far as Athenian relations with Perdiccas of Macedon were concerned (p. 373) and retaining strong links with her mother-city Corinth; she had perhaps already caused trouble to Athens (p. 138). Athens requested her to dismiss her Corinthian magistrates and pull down a wall. The Potidaeans spent the winter negotiating with Athens and, simultaneously, with Perdiccas' connivance, put out feelers to Corinth and Sparta, securing a pledge from the highest circles at Sparta[15] to invade Attica if the Athenians proceeded against them. Perdiccas also encouraged their neighbours in Chalcidice to revolt from Athens. The Athenians evidently found it hard to believe that there would be a revolt (the malcontents bought time by paying their normal tribute at the Dionysia of 432). However, when an Athenian squadron of thirty ships

[15] But see Andrewes, HCT IV 135, holding that the Spartan Assembly is referred to here.

arrived to enforce the demands on Potidaea, it found not only Potidaea, but her neighbours, representing over $7\frac{1}{2}$ per cent of the tribute of the empire, in revolt. With only a thousand hoplites on hand, its commanders moved on to their other task, the support of the rebels against Perdiccas. (1.56–9).

Fearing for Potidaea, the Corinthians collected a force of 2,000 troops, Corinthian volunteers and paid troops from the Peloponnese, and sent it north under Aristeas, son of Adeimantos the commander of 480 (Hdt. VIII.5.1 etc.).[16] Athens responded with another forty ships and 2,000 hoplites. These began by joining the first force in the siege of Pydna, evidently on the assumption that the main enemy was Perdiccas,[17] but patched up an agreement with him (which he broke almost immediately) and moved on Potidaea by land. A battle north of the isthmus broke the communications between Potidaea and her neighbours, and yet another squadron from Athens completed the siege works to the south of the city. This point of repose marks the second stage in Thucydides' chain of grievances (1.66). The Corinthians complained of Athenian actions against their colony and that Peloponnesians were under siege; the Athenians that the Peloponnesians had promoted the revolt of a subject city and were fighting openly on its behalf. (1.60–6).

There had as yet been no sign of Spartan willingness to implement the pledge to Potidaea, and the Corinthians demanded action and an official decision that the Athenians had broken the Peace. The Spartans called for all complainants to speak before their Assembly. At this point, Thucydides introduces two subsidiary matters. Aegina was sending secret complaints that her autonomy, guaranteed by the Peace, was being infringed; we have no real idea what this was about.[18] The Megarians had some substantial complaints, notably that they were barred from the harbours in the Athenian empire and 'the Attic Agora' ($\tau\hat{\eta}s$ $'A\tau\tau\iota\kappa\hat{\eta}s$ $\dot{a}\gamma o\rho\hat{a}s$) against the terms of the Peace. (1.67).

We have already noted that we have no clue to the chronology of the Megarian affair. We are later told (1.139.1–2) that the ban on the Megarians 'using' the harbours and the Agora was expressed in an Athenian decree and that the Athenians' reason for it was that the Megarians had been cultivating undelimited sacred land and receiving runaway slaves. It has been argued[19] that there is no more to the decree

---

[16] This was certainly an official Corinthian action. See, against Gomme, *HCT* 1 224–5, de Ste Croix 82–5.

[17] As late as the second prytany of the conciliar year 432/1, a payment is still made 'for Macedonia', with no mention of Potidaea (*IG* 1³ 365.5). But see Chronological Notes, pp. 502–3.

[18] It is universally assumed that Aegina made a very short payment of tribute in 432, and thought possible that Athens had retaliated, but we cannot exclude the possibility that her tribute had been reduced since the last evidence for it in 440; it is now certain (Kraay 1976 (C 190) 47) that she had been allowed to continue her coinage.   [19] de Ste Croix *passim*.

than this, that the Megarians had rendered themselves accursed by their cultivation of sacred land and were therefore being banned from the Athenian Agora in its most literal sense, that area in the centre of Athens from which homicides and other undesirables were certainly banned.[20] If this were so, it would be difficult to understand why the two references we have so far considered give priority to the harbours in the empire; a third (1.144.2), more rhetorically phrased, has *agora* before 'harbours', but omits the definite article for *agora*. Two passages support the view that some kind of trade ban was involved. The first is Aristophanes *Ach.* 535, which says that the Megarians were slowly starving as a result of the decree; no amount of argument[21] to show that this cannot have been true overthrows the implication for the decree's intentions. The second has had rather less attention.[22] At Thucydides 1.120.2, the Corinthians, stirring the Peloponnesians to war, are made to say:

Those of us who have already had dealings with the Athenians do not need teaching that one should be on one's guard against them, but those who live more inland and not on their path should know that, if they do not defend those on the coast, they will find it harder to bring down their produce in its season and get back again what the sea gives to the mainland.

It is hard to interpret this except as saying that some allies are already under economic threat of some kind. There is no parallel for the phrase ἡ Ἀττικὴ ἀγορά, but nothing against the belief that *agora* means something like 'market' in an abstract sense here.[23]

The only motives for the Athenian decree in ancient sources outside Thucydides are personal motives of Pericles, whether specifically as a favour to his mistress Aspasia or as a general attempt to divert attention from political moves against him and his friends (e.g. Diod. XII.38–9; Plut. *Per.*30–2).[24] Modern suggestions have taken various forms. Little support can be found nowadays for any general theory of commercial rivalry taken to extremes;[25] there would be more to be said for a view that Athens was trying to block materials for Peloponnesian naval development.[26] Another possible view[27] is that pressure on Megara is in effect not so much a cause of the war but a first blow in it, designed to force

[20] de Ste Croix, Appendix LXIII.   [21] de Ste Croix 241–4.

[22] But see Legon 1973 (G 23, on which see Meiggs 1982 (L 99) 492–3), and Legon 1981 (F 45) 217–21.

[23] The position of de Ste Croix has been criticized by Gauthier 1975 (G 14); Sealey 1975 (G 37) 103–5; Legon 1981 (F 45) 210–27, and defended by MacDonald 1983 (G 28). See also the references collected by Legon 1981 (F 45) 214 n.51 and MacDonald 1983 (G 28) 385 n.1.

[24] Most of this arises from the belief that Ar. *Ach.*515–39, *Peace* 605–24 were to be taken seriously.

[25] The view, most closely connected with Cornford 1907 (C 24), is well criticized by de Ste Croix 214–20.   [26] Legon 1981 (F 45) 219–22.

[27] Wade-Gery 1970 (C 105) 1069; Sealey 1975 (G 37) 105.

Megara back into the empire; we shall need to return to this later, in the context of Periclean strategy.

The debate at the Spartan Assembly is covered by Thucydides in four speeches. He saw no reason to repeat the complaints of Sparta's allies which he had already described, and the Corinthian speech, improbably, confines itself to a general survey of the growth of Athenian power and wrongdoing as opposed to Spartan slowness. The sting is in the tail, a threat to seek help elsewhere, presumably at Argos, if Sparta does not do her duty. A speech by an Athenian embassy, mysteriously present on other business, then follows, abstaining from detailed reply on the allied complaints, surveying Athens' past services to Greece, justifying her empire and her conduct of it, and warning Sparta against precipitate breach of the Thirty Years' Peace. It would be easier to believe in the historicity of this embassy and this speech if the 'other business' had been identified, and the thought that Thucydides' purposes are wider than those of simple reporting is hard to repress.[28] The difficulties are only increased by the speech of king Archidamus which follows (the other Spartan king, Pausanias, was a minor). It is not unlikely that he urged caution, more thorough preparation and exploration of the Athenian offers of arbitration, but his well-considered analysis of the strength of Athens' strategic position, amply justified by later events, is not fully in accord with his conduct of the campaign of 431 or with the thoughts Thucydides attributes to him during it. That a decisive, short speech was made by the ephor Sthenelaidas, urging Sparta to do her duty to her allies without delay, is entirely credible. The Spartans agreed by a large majority that the Athenians had broken the Peace, and it was decided to hold a League congress to take a formal vote for war. A mission went to consult Delphi, and Apollo promised his support. (1.67–88, 118.3).

At the League congress, the stress is again on Corinth. She has been lobbying for support among the allies, and there is yet another Corinthian speech, not only arguing for war, but making practical suggestions as to how it should be conducted.[29] There was again a majority for war and preparations for it began, though not to the total exclusion of diplomacy. (1.119–26.1).

A first embassy to Athens appears to have confined itself to propaganda points. The Spartans demanded the expulsion of those subject to the Cylonian curse (*CAH* III².3, 368–70), in the hope of embarrassing

---

[28] So Schwartz 1929 (C 91) 105–6 (cf. Schwartz 1926 (C 90) 79–80), hotly scorned by Gomme 1937 (A 49) 158. It must be admitted that, if we dismiss the factual statement about the embassy's departure at 1.87.5, there are few rational grounds on which we can accept anything Thucydides says. On the speech, see also Raubitschek 1973 (C 81).

[29] In this speech there are no obvious allusions to Archidamus' doubts about the way to fight the war; the cross-references are all with the corresponding section of Pericles' speech at 1.140–4, which provides the pair to it, despite the disunity of place and time.

Pericles, thus identifying him as the main advocate of war at Athens (Thucydides agrees). The Athenians riposted by a similar demand directed against the murderers of Pausanias (p. 101); it is not clear who these were, but the demand gave Thucydides an occasion for finishing the stories of Pausanias and Themistocles from where Herodotus had left them (see p. 6). (1.126.2–139).

In a second phase, perhaps involving more than one embassy, there was a more serious attempt at negotiation. Potidaea and Aegina were raised, but the greatest emphasis was placed on the Megarian Decree. The Athenians refused to repeal it or even suspend its operation.[30] A last embassy, more intransigent, simply announced that the Spartans wanted peace and that, if the Athenians made their allies autonomous, there would be peace. An assembly debate followed, apparently on the basis that the previous proposals were still on the table. Thucydides wastes no time on those who argued that the Megarian Decree should not stand in the way of peace but be repealed, but concentrates on Pericles' case for war and his demonstration of how it should be fought. His case for war is no more than an assertion of Spartan unreliability. Any concessions would be met with further Spartan demands, and Athens must stand firm. He proposed that the specific Spartan demands be met with simple rudeness; the Megarian Decree would be repealed if the Spartans renounced their occasional practice of banning foreigners from their territory;[31] the allies would be allowed autonomy if they had been autonomous in 446 and if the Spartans gave up interfering in the affairs of their own allies; the Athenians maintained their offer to go to arbitration under the terms of the Peace, but national honour dictated that they would not yield any point otherwise. The Spartan embassy treated this as a rejection, and there were no more embassies. (1.139–46).

Athens had stood firm on the Megarian Decree; the reference to the possibility of autonomy for allies who had been autonomous in 446 could conceivably have had some meaning for Aegina and possibly Potidaea, had it not been accompanied by the remark about Sparta's allies. On the other hand, the Spartans had not gone beyond a hint that Potidaea and the rest might be negotiable, if the Athenians abandoned the Megarian Decree; if an explicit offer was made, for example, to see to the withdrawal of troops from Potidaea, we do not know about it. It is hard to believe that there was any effective wish for peace on either side. Thucydides sees the truest cause in Spartan fear of the growth of Athenian power. Nothing was offered to remove that, and Thucydides

---

[30] The anecdote (Plut. *Per.* 30.1), in which the Spartan Polyalces suggests turning the decree's face to the wall, is apparently authentic. See Lewis 1977 (A 76) 49 n.157 on Ar. *Ach.*537. de Ste Croix 322 agrees that the Spartans were negotiating seriously at this point.

[31] Cf. II.39.1, but there is no evidence that the practice had been frequent or troublesome.

in any case says it was inconspicuous. There is no need to be surprised at that. Athens would not go to war saying that the Spartans were afraid of them; it was more comfortable to say that the Spartans were plotting against them. Sparta would not go to war saying that she was afraid of the Athenians; it was more comfortable to rest on her duty to her allies.

II. WAR

Thucydides determines our view of the narrative shape of the war even more firmly than of the preliminaries. It is not only presumptuous, but also overwhelmingly difficult, to quarrel with or modify his analysis. Sometimes he provides facts which suggest another view, but we may reasonably be concerned that we do not have all the facts. The cases of the invasions of the Megarid and of tribute-collecting expeditions have already been discussed (above, p. 5), and have shown the likelihood that the narrative is not as all-embracing as it may appear. Since we have epigraphical evidence (*IG* I³ 75; 424/3?) of a treaty with Halieis which he does not mention, we cannot safely deny the historicity of a Euboean expedition in 424 reported by Philochorus (*FGrH* 328 F 130). In a slightly different way, we do not learn until late 429, when it becomes relevant to the narrative, that there was a fort and a squadron of three ships on the north coast of Salamis blockading Megara (II.93.4); it is reasonable to assume that it had been there since the beginning of the war, possibly even earlier. Problems of more substance are raised by Thucydides' unwillingness to concern himself with what did not happen. He tells us (II.56.4) that there was an expectation that Pericles' expedition of 430 would capture Epidaurus, but our curiosity about what would have been done with it, if it had been taken, is left unsatisfied, even though it is hard to find an answer which fits Periclean strategy as Thucydides describes it. There are scholars who have suspected that Thucydides has played down or omitted facts or intentions which endangered his strategic analysis or his dramatic picture.[32]

1. Athenian strategy and its problems

Thucydides gives a clear picture of Periclean strategy, makes it purely personal to him, and endorses it wholeheartedly, particularly in II.65, written after the end of the whole war. After Pericles' death, he makes no very clear attempt to characterize alternative Athenian strategies, beyond general indications that he thought that there was a greater tendency to irrelevant operations (II.65.7), nor does he expound with any clarity how strategic questions were determined at Athens and what

[32] See, e.g., Hunter 1973 (C 33)

the role of the board of *strategoi* was. We have some epigraphical evidence (M–L 69 = *IG*i³ 71.46–8) that the board was expected to engage in financial planning, but are ill-informed about how much it could do without reference to the Assembly. At one extreme, our evidence suggests that naval expeditions had to be authorized by the Assembly. This would raise problems about security (cf. iv.42.3), but there might have been some attempt to cloak specific operations under generalities (cf. vi.8.2, where Syracuse is not even mentioned). On the other hand, it is unlikely that local operations needed such authorization, and in 424 there is an extensive mobilization for the attack on Megara which can hardly have waited for the Assembly (iv.68.5; cf. iv.90.1). There are various indications of the *strategoi* engaging in diplomatic and secret work preparatory to operations (ii.79.2, iv.54.3, 66.3, 76.2), and occasionally we may suspect that they had plans which they had not divulged to the Assembly at all.[33] It seems safe to suppose that most operations were originated on their board, which is not to say that the Assembly would accept them unaltered; there are at least two operations (ii.85.5, iv.2.4) which look very much like proposals made directly to the Assembly by individuals. Ideas about expeditions are often attributed by Thucydides to individual *strategoi* (iii.51.2, iv.66.3, 89), but suggestions that the annual election was fought on strategic issues[34] are implausible (see above, p. 86), though the known views of an individual could have been relevant.

No considerations about colleagues and relatively few about the Assembly are allowed for in Thucydides' picture of how Pericles intended to conduct the war.[35] That picture is consistent (1.141.2–144.1, ii.13.2, 65.7). What is portrayed is a defensive strategy: evacuation of Attica without any attempt to meet Peloponnesian invasion by land; careful maintenance of the fleet, since control of the sea was essential for maintaining alternative food supplies and control of the allies; control of the allies was itself essential to maintaining Athens' financial resources, already at a level to which Peloponnesian public finance could not hope to aspire; avoidance of irrelevant operations, particularly the acquisition of additional territory during the war. Offensive operations are referred to only as means of retaliation: the ravaging of Attica would be met by raids on the Peloponnese, more damaging since the Peloponnesians had no alternative food resources; the establishment of a fort in Attica could be met by a parallel sea-based operation. The impression left is that Pericles' aim was to make the Peloponnesians recognize that they could not break Athens' position and had no alternative but to come to terms

[33] Consider iii 91 with Andrewes, *HCT* iv 156 n.1.
[34] An unargued postulate of Beloch 1884 (D 5) 19–92. See also Whibley 1889 (D 107) 121–31; West 1924 (D 106). [35] On this picture see, e.g., Cawkwell 1975 (G 12); Holladay 1978 (G 16).

on something like the existing balance of power. But this aim is never explicitly stated. It can only be said that it seems to represent Thucydides' view of a satisfactory outcome of the war; he clearly thinks that the failure to accept the Spartan offer of the status quo in 425 was a mistake.[36]

The picture requires some scrutiny and expansion. The policy of evacuation, though implicit in the original decision to build the Long Walls (p. 113), was revolutionary; centuries of tradition, in which a state whose fields were invaded by a hoplite force was expected to meet it with its own hoplites, were rejected. It should be noted that Thucydides' narrative shows that the land was not simply abandoned; an active use of cavalry (II.19.2, 22.2, III.1.2, cf. VII.27.5) limited the operations of at least the enemy's light-armed foragers.[37] He has little to say about the border forts,[38] though they must have been intended to serve a purpose: the fort at Oenoe caused Archidamus trouble in 431 (II.18–19.1), though its only attested achievement is in 411 (VIII.98.2); another at Panactum plays no visible part until the Boeotians capture it in 422 (V.3.5), but this hardly proves that it did nothing.

The emphasis on maintaining the fleet fits into an important strand of Thucydides' narrative. Before the war, the Corinthians are made to say that naval skill can be acquired (1.121.3–4), a proposition doubted by Pericles (1.142.6–9), who lays stress on the length of time needed to acquire it (cf. [Xen.] *Ath. Pol.* 1.19–20 on the wide spread of naval expertise at Athens). As against the old-fashioned land-battle by sea fought at Sybota (p. 375) we are eventually presented with Phormio's two victories at Naupactus in 429, where sheer manoeuvrability presents Athenian naval ability at its finest flowering. In between those two battles, Thucydides reports (II.85.1–2):

The Spartans sent advisers to Cnemus and the fleet, telling him to make a better sea-battle and not be kept off the sea by a few ships. For, especially since it was the first time they had tried a sea-battle, they found the result most surprising and did not think that their fleet was so inferior, but that there had been some cowardice, not comparing the long experience of the Athenians with their own shortness of practice. It was in anger then that they sent the advisers.

By sea, at any rate, the Peloponnesian War is not a story of the development of new techniques, except for the Corinthian and Spartan moves of 413 to counter Athenian skills (pp. 458–9). It is a story of how the Athenians lost those skills.

Pericles' emphasis on the need to keep the allies in hand requires much more extended comment. As we have seen, Athens had a substantial revolt on her hands when the war started. Not all the Chalcidic cities

---

[36] Note the various nuances at IV.21.2, 22.3, 41.4, 65.4, V 14.2.
[37] Busolt 1893–1904 (A 12) III 930; Hanson 1983 (A 58) 77–8, 105–6; Ober 1985 (G 31).
[38] On which see Ober 1985 (G 32).

were easily accessible to Athenian sea-power, and even Potidaea, which was, provided a very substantial and expensive distraction (II.13.3, 70.2, III.17) until its surrender in winter 430/29. The prevention and subjugation of revolts was a key point in Athenian policy. We have come a long way since Athens indicated her willingness to lead a league for mutual protection against the Persians, and Thucydides' picture is not equivocal. He always uses the language of subjection, even slavery, for the allies, and even Athenians (Pericles, II.63.2; Cleon, III.37.2) are made to speak of the empire as a tyranny. At the start of the war, Thucydides (II.8.4–5) asserts that most people favoured the Spartans, especially since they were proclaiming that they were liberating Greece, and that there was great excitement against the Athenians, amongst those who wished to be freed from their rule and those who were afraid that they might be ruled themselves.

It has been argued[39] that this is a misleading picture, that the essential feature of the period was a class struggle between the upper and the lower classes, and that Thucydides tended to see things through the eyes of his own class. On this view, only the upper classes in the empire were really hostile to Athens; the lower classes valued Athenian rule as a protection against their own oligarchs.[40] For a formal claim that the fifth-century empire had been systematically favourable to the lower classes and to democracy, we have to wait for Isocrates' *Panegyricus* of 380 (IV.105–6; cf. Arist. *Pol.* 1307b22–4), but one Athenian speaker in Thucydides claims (III.47.2) that the *demos* in all the cities favours Athens and either does not join the oligarchs in revolt or, if forced to revolt, remains hostile to the revolt and an asset for Athens. The specific case he is arguing is that of Mytilene (p. 403) and his account of the *demos'* attitude to that revolt is not quite the same as that of Thucydides' narrative.[41] In other cases, the argument against Thucydides depends very largely on Thucydides' own narrative. When the sponsors of revolt are identifiable, they tend to be oligarchs, and there is a great deal more resistance in the cities to revolt and attack from the enemy than one would expect from Thucydides' general attitude.

There is of course plenty of civil strife (*stasis*) in Thucydides. Casual reference to the *demos*, the *dunatoi* (the powerful) and the *oligoi* (the few) starts as soon as the main narrative (1.24.5) and never stops. The main formal analysis (III.82–3) is attached to the troubles on Corcyra in 427, taken as an early case of troubles which affected practically the whole

---

[39] De Ste Croix 1954/5 (E 75).

[40] The sentiments attributed to Phrynichus at VIII.48.6 are rather different. What he appears to be saying is that the Athenian *demos* had moderated the rapacity of the Athenian upper classes towards the cities and their upper classes.

[41] III.47.3 against III.27–8; see Bradeen 1960 (E 12) 263–5; Westlake 1976 (E 93); but contrast de Ste Croix 1981 (A 109) 603–4.

Greek world, as 'the leaders of the *demos* (οἱ τῶν δήμων προστάται) tried to bring in the Athenians, the *oligoi* the Spartans'. In the narrative there are occasional hints of underlying economic motives (murder of creditors, III.81.4, redistribution of land, VIII.21), but there is nothing of this in the analysis, which concentrates on the deformation of political language, values and conduct among what seem to be fairly small groups; Thucydides does not say that *stasis* was between the *oligoi* and the *demos* as a whole. The impression of small groups is sometimes sustained by the narrative. The leaders of the *demos* who form a plot to hand Megara over to Athens in 424 are evidently a very small group, and one particular group at Samos which first makes a 'democratic' revolution (VIII.21) and then turns itself into an oligarchic group (VIII.73.2) is said to number three hundred.[42]

An alternative model is perhaps possible. Even at Athens, it is distinctly difficult to find anything approaching class struggle before 404, and, even at Athens, democratic leaders tend to have wealth or birth or both. There are not all that many cities in the empire where conditions were as favourable to a potential split between the landed and the landless. It seems possible to suppose that in many cities the effective political class was very restricted in number and that the majority of the citizen body was not politically concerned. If so, it may be the case that the essential feature of the situation was not the class struggle, but the polarization of power between Athens and Sparta, and that all internal rivalries in the political class were shaped by the bipolarity of power in such a way that those who counted on Athenian support would express themselves as democrats, those who wanted Spartan help as oligarchs. The easiest way of taking the controversial line (Ar. *Ach.* 642) in which Aristophanes claims to have shown 'what democracy meant for the people of the allied cities' (tr. Sommerstein) is that some scepticism might be possible about the nature of what were claimed to be democracies.

We have already seen (pp. 131–2) that many Athenian imperial measures were taken for the preservation of individuals favourable to Athens. These will have become more and more identified with the ruling power as the empire continued. As it came to an end, some were executed for 'atticism' (VIII.38.3; cf. *Hell. Oxy.* 17.1). If Plato wrote (*Ep.* VII, 322b) that 'the Athenians preserved their empire for seventy years by having friends in each of the cities', there is a corollary to that; the friends in the cities were preserved by the Athenian empire. We cannot rule out the possibility that, in cases where allied cities resist 'liberation' by the Spartans, the reins of power are in the hands of men with much to lose (cf. Xen. *Hell.* 1.6.13). Effectively, it is not obvious that Thucydides is

[42] But the *demos* of III.27.2–3 is not a small group.

wrong in assuming that the normal collective will of a city was to independence and that it will have moved in that direction whenever it was or seemed to be the case that Athenian power was insufficient to stop it (IV.108.3–6, VIII.2.2, 24.5).[43] But, except in such conditions and where cities were exposed to pressure from their hinterland, the Athenians felt that the general strength of their position and the loyalty of their local supporters was enough to stop revolts; few allied cities were garrisoned.

Allied loyalty is linked, by way of the tribute, to finance, and here Thucydides' picture is curiously incomplete. The emphasis on Athenian reserves of capital as against the likely improvisations of the Peloponnesians, pervasive in Pericles' first speech (1.141.3–5, 142.1, 143.1), is given impressive detail at II.13.3–5. Imperial income was 600 talents a year,[44] coined reserves 6,000 talents,[45] even without the possibility of drawing on temple treasures and the gold plates on Phidias' chryselephantine statue of Athena. Greek city states normally adjusted their annual income to their annual expenditure, and, until Lycurgus' Periclean revival of 336–324, we have little reason to believe that such an accumulation of reserves was aimed at anywhere. The figures are impressive, but even II.13.3 notes that Potidaea was proving costly. Two later references (II.70.2, III.19; III.17 seems to be an unattached draft on the same theme) show the development of Athenian financial anxieties. Thucydides then drops the subject, never drawing the consequences for his admiration of Pericles' foresight, failing even to mention the great assessment of 425 (p. 420); it does not reappear until VI.12.1.[46] Epigraphic evidence (M–L p.217) substantiates Thucydides' picture of heavy drains on the reserve in the early years of the war; close to 4,000 talents were spent, apart from annual income, in the three financial years 432–429.[47] Thereafter, the drain was limited, not perhaps without some strains on the temper of the Athenian rich and the patience of the allies.

[43] de Romilly 1966 (E 72).

[44] Calculation on the tribute quota-list for spring 432 shows receipts in actual tribute of only about 390 talents, but at least allowance for revenue from overseas estates is reasonable; see *ATL* III 333–6, Gomme, *HCT* II 17–19. Xen. *Anab.* VII.1.27 gives total Athenian revenue at the start of the war as 1,000 talents. This is hardly a documentary text, but the figure of 400 talents which it implies for internal income is consistent with other evidence.

[45] The manuscript text says that the reserves at their highest point had been 9,700 talents, but that expenditure on the building programme and Potidaea had brought them down. It is extremely difficult to calculate any way by which this figure could have been reached (Kolbe 1929 (D 43) is still the best attempt), and the authors of *ATL* prefer an alternative text, by which the balance had been steady for some time at 6,000 talents and was temporarily down to 5,700; see *ATL* III 118–31, 338; Gomme 1953/4 (G 15) and *HCT* II 26–33; Meritt 1954 (C 71); Wade-Gery and Meritt 1957 (D 103). It used to be held that Thucydides was capable of having simply added total expenditure to the reserve in 431 and assuming that the result had all once existed at one time (Beloch 1912–27 (A 2) II².2, 338–42; Meyer 1899 (A 87) 119), and perhaps the idea is due for revival (cf. Accame 1935 (C 111) 491 and 1952 (C 114) 244–5).

[46] Thereafter VII.28.4, VIII 1.2 (falsified by 15.1) and much else.

[47] Some of this expenditure falls before the report at II.13.3.

Avoidance of irrelevant operations, particularly the acquisition of additional territory during the war, is a Periclean aim which raises more complex problems. There were indeed formal extensions of Athenian power even in 431, notably the bringing of Cephallenia into alliance (II.30; cf. also II.26.2, 32). Thucydides certainly omits the acquisition of Dorian Thera, outside the empire in 431 (II.9.4), in it not later than 426 (M–L 68.21 = IG I^3 68.22), and a strong, but not quite certain, case can be made for attributing this to Pericles' lifetime.[48] Whatever Pericles meant, Thucydides clearly read it as a warning against ventures in Sicily and perhaps Boeotia. We shall have to consider some possible indications that, inside those limits, Pericles may have had more offensive ideas than Thucydides allows.

A certain amount of Athenian strategy, both before and after Pericles' death, was of course determined simply by the need to react to revolts in the empire or to Peloponnesian movements. The new elements after Pericles' death can be roughly characterized as methods designed to make things more unpleasant for the enemy rather than simply waiting for him to tire. The most successful was the attempt to bring greater pressure to bear on Sparta's own position by the fortification of Pylos in 425 and the capture of Cythera in 424. The first resulted incidentally in the capture of 120 Spartiate prisoners, the second, to judge by Thucydides' description of Spartan morale during a week of ravaging of Laconia itself (IV.55–6), came near to winning the war in a way which would go far beyond any Periclean or Thucydidean notions of simple survival. What we do not hear of along this line is any considered attempt to promote Messenian and helot revolt;[49] the reasons remain obscure. The most explicit reason relevant to the war against the Peloponnese given for the Sicilian Expedition of 427–424 was the desire to cut off corn supplies for the Peloponnese at their source, that is, an attempt to extend the ravaging of Peloponnesian fields, but it is reasonably clear that irrelevant ambition played its part.

Other attempts to change the situation had deeper historical roots. However effective the Periclean defensive strategy might be, it still involved tolerating Peloponnesian invasions of Attica virtually every year, and left Boeotian activity, with or without Peloponnesian cooperation, possible. The contrast with the 450s was marked. In that period Athens had controlled Boeotia, the Argive alliance had provided a hoplite counterpoise to Sparta in the Peloponnese, and above all Athenian control of the Megarid had made Peloponnesian moves north of the Isthmus virtually impossible, a fact not irrelevant to control of Boeotia. During the Archidamian War, Argos' thirty years' peace with Sparta of 451/0 (p. 120) eliminated her from the scene almost entirely.

[48] See p. 409 n.110.   [49] Lewis 1977 (A 76) 28.

But Alcibiades (p. 435) was not the first to see the possible advantage of an Argive policy; there is clear evidence (Ar. *Knights* 465–9) that Cleon was negotiating in Argos in winter 425/4.[50]

Athenian ideas about Boeotia were more immediate, but the position is more complex. It seems safe to say that Pericles had seen no possibility of doing anything useful and had regarded even Plataea as expendable, though Thucydides does not make the dishonourable point explicit. In the first years of the war Thebes used the threat of Athenian activity to bring many smaller states under her direct control; at least six such virtually ceased to exist (*Hell. Oxy.* 17.3) even before the fall of Plataea in 427. Theban predominance in Boeotia was now assured and she is credited with designs on Thespiae, at least, before 423 (IV.133.1). It might well be thought that there was scope for Athenian diplomacy here, and by 424 the Athenian generals Hippocrates and Demosthenes were apparently convinced that there might be widespread support for a movement which was for democracy and (by implication) against Thebes (IV.76). Demosthenes had had an attack on Boeotia in mind in 426 (III.95), and the idea developed in 424 into an elaborate and disastrous plan ended at the battle of Delium. The explicit point made to the Athenian force before that battle was that success would bring the end of Boeotian cavalry support for Peloponnesian invasions of Attica (IV.95.2), but the campaign's ambitions for power in Boeotia were surely more far-reaching than this military problem.

It was Megara which remained the key point. It was essential for communications between the Peloponnese and Boeotia (IV.72.1) (and points further north), and the events of 446 (p. 134) had shown the difference that its possession made to the security of Attica. Good evidence shows the importance attached to it in Athens. On the one occasion when Thucydides gives us a clear statement about Athenian peace-terms, in 425, Cleon asks for the return of Nisaea, Pegae, Achaea and Troezen (IV.21.3). That demand was couched with reference to the terms of the Thirty Years' Peace (p. 137), and was disingenuous. It had been the case when that Peace was made that Megara had revolted and her two ports remained under Athenian control, but that was an unstable situation which had to be resolved; if Cleon is asking for Nisaea and Pegae as part of a permanent settlement, that is a demand for Megara as a whole. In 424 Hippocrates and Demosthenes had a plan for recapturing Megara, battered by seven years of Athenian invasion and internal strife, and succeeded in capturing Nisaea. Thucydides suggests (IV.73.4) that this was a sufficient gain and that the generals would not have been justified in taking risks to capture Megara itself. At that moment this may have been true, since the possession of the Spartiate prisoners would in

---

[50] For the dubious relevance of Pericles' Epidaurus campaign in 430 see. p. 398.

itself inhibit Peloponnesian invasion of Attica, but the impression
persists that Thucydides was not all that interested in Megara and may
not be a reliable guide. It remains a possibility that Pericles himself had
seen the acquisition of Megara as a desirable war aim and that the
Megarian Decree, the invasions of the Megarid and the blockade of
Nisaea had all been designed to produce the softening up of Megara
which nearly bore fruit in 424.[51]

It is easy to underestimate the effect of blockade, still easier to
underestimate what might have been hoped from it, and it is true that the
sea-keeping abilities of the Greek trireme could not match the effectiveness of more modern blockade. As we have seen, Pericles in Thucydides
speaks of sea-borne raids more in terms of retaliation than as offensive
measures in themselves. But a contemporary ([Xen.] *Ath.Pol.* 2.13)
noted, among the advantages of sea-power, that 'by every mainland
there is a protruding cape or an offshore island or a strait where those
who rule the sea can lie offshore and damage those who live on the
mainland'. This is an exaggeration, and some parts of the Peloponnesian
coast are less open than is suggested. Nevertheless, from Salamis and
Aegina a good deal of the Saronic Gulf could be covered, though there
was always room for improvement (III.51). Pericles' attack on Epidaurus
in 430 fits into this context (see p. 398), and posts at Methana (IV.45) and
Halieis (*IG* I³ 75, 424/3?, not in Thucydides) later tightened the Athenian
grip on the east coast of the Peloponnese. From autumn 430 an Athenian
squadron at Naupactus had the task of stopping Corinthian trade in the
Crisaean Gulf. Excavation is beginning to provide evidence of the
effects of blockade. At Corinth a wholesale fish merchant, accustomed to
import salt fish in quantity from both the eastern and western Mediterranean, seems to have closed down pretty abruptly in the 420s.[52]

2. Peloponnesian strategy and its problems

Let us turn to the Peloponnesian side.[53] As we have seen, there are
speeches in Book I purporting to show that some of them realized that
the war would not be easy. Archidamus' analysis of the strengths of the
Athenian position (1.80–1[54]) is hardly different from that of Pericles and
warns that they should not assume that a quick victory can be assured by
ravaging Attica; the war may be bequeathed to their children, and a

---

[51] See n. 27 and add Wick 1979 (G 43).
[52] Williams 1978–80 (F 72), summarized by Salmon 1984 (F 61) 128. Note also the evidence for
silver shortage at Corinth, Kraay *ap.* Salmon *op. cit.*172. But see MacDonald 1982 (G 27). It might be
suggested that, if the blockade from the east and south had not been fairly complete, the
Peloponnese would have caught the plague, which it did not (II 54.5).
[53] Brunt 1965 (G 10) is fundamental; see also Cawkwell 1975 (G 12); Kelly 1982 (G 22).
[54] For reservations about this speech see p. 378.

prolonged build-up of allies, both Greek and barbarian, in the hope of securing ships and money will be necessary. The Corinthians also (1.121–2.1) have little to say about the effects of ravaging Attica, but are much more optimistic about raising money and building naval strength, throwing in the possibility of promoting revolts in the empire and building a fort in Attica as well. We have no reason to doubt that these thoughts could have occurred in 432, but they do not seem to be near the centre of Greek expectations. Thucydides is clear that the Spartans believed that direct invasion of Attica would produce a quick end to the war (IV.85.2, V.14.3) and that this belief was widely shared: 'at the beginning of the war some thought the Athenians would last a year, some two years, no one more than three years if the Peloponnesians invaded Attica' (VII.28.3). Despite the sentiments attributed to him in Book I, when Archidamus invades Attica in 431, he is presented as hopeful that the Athenians will come out to fight for Attica or even give in before it is ravaged (II.11.6–8, 12.1, 18.5, 20[55]).

The Athenians did not come out to fight and the effect of ravaging Attica was limited. During the Archidamian War there were five invasions, only hampered by Athenian cavalry who kept the light-armed away from the city itself (the Peloponnesians were short of cavalry and largely dependent on Boeotian help in this arm); the hoplite force made no attempt to test the strength of the Long Walls. The longest invasion, in 430, lasted forty days (II.57), the shortest, in 425, fifteen (IV.6). The latter was particularly ineffective, since it had come too early and the corn was still green. The invasions of 430 and 427 were said to be particularly damaging (III.26.3), but the total effect was not great. The land was used when the Peloponnesians went home (VII.27.4); 'it had suffered very little in the earlier invasions' (Hell. Oxy. 17.5).[56] The results did not repay the very substantial forces which were taken to Attica. Figures are scarce (Plut. Per. 33.5 gives 60,000 for 431; Androtion FGrH 324 F 39 is corrupt), but the normal force was a two-thirds levy of the Peloponnesian League (II.10.2, 47.2, III.15). The Spartans were risking disillusion, not only for themselves, but for their allies (III.15.2). Strains were imposed on Athens, but they were hard to see from outside.

The alternative ideas attributed to the Corinthians and to Archidamus were not totally neglected. The Corinthians had already built up their fleet considerably for the war against Corcyra, and the Spartans themselves had the nucleus of a fleet, though we know little about it; six other states in the alliance (II.9.3) could be counted on for naval contributions. There were some grandiose ideas about. Supporters in Sicily and Italy were asked for two hundred ships, with a view to building up a total fleet

---

[55] de Ste Croix 207.

[56] But both these passages are contrasting the situation after the fortification of Decelea in 413.

of five hundred.[57] The problem of finance was here overpowering. We have virtually no evidence about Peloponnesian war finance,[58] and, although the Corinthians may have suggested (1.121.3) borrowing money from Olympia and Delphi to hire rowers, nothing seems to have been done. The inferiority of Peloponnesian naval forces in the Archidamian War was recognized on both sides. They are repeatedly ineffectual or hesitant (e.g. III.33.1, 79.3) and, after Athens gained sixty ships by sharp practice at the armistice of 425 (p. 416), naval activity comes to an end.

Hopes of western help came to nothing in the Archidamian War, though the hopes seem to have been matched, at least in 433, by local fears of Syracuse and acceptance by Athens that the position of Corcyra on the sea-route to and from the west might be helpful (p. 375). Nor, despite Archidamus' allusion to barbarian help, was anything to be obtained from Persia. Though one embassy in 430 failed to get through (II.67), others evidently did (IV.50). The Athenians in winter 425/4 captured a Persian envoy going to Sparta with a message complaining of the incoherence of Spartan requests. This is hardly surprising. If Sparta was fighting as the champion of Greek freedom, she had little to offer the King, whose main relevant wish will have been to recover the Greeks of Asia.[59]

It has been thought a problem that in 432 the Corinthians contemplate a fort in Attica (1.122.1) and that Pericles discusses its difficulties and the possibility of retaliation (1.142.2–4), though in the narrative there is no question of such fortification before the Spartans threaten it in 421 (V.17.2). The probable answer is[60] that any permanent base in Attica would have needed active and effective cooperation from Boeotia and that no confidence was felt in Boeotian abilities before their success at Delium in 424. In contrast, the Spartans in 426 did embark on an imaginative and substantial venture, the foundation of Heraclea Trachinia just north of Thermopylae (III.92–3; Diod. XII.59.3–5), hoping to create a naval base which would threaten Euboea and to control the route to the north. This had no important consequences; the locals were hostile and Spartan commanders inefficient (cf. V.51–2.1).

Mention of the route to the north suggests that ideas were beginning to develop on how to implement the Corinthian suggestion of promoting revolt in the Athenian empire. The development had been slow. When Mytilene revolted in 428, a fleet was manned, but only to help Mytilene. When it failed to arrive in time, its commander rejected local suggestions that it be used to start revolt in Ionia and hastened home

---

[57] II.7.2 must be emended on the basis of Diod. XII.42.1; Brunt 1965 (G 10) 261 is in error here.
[58] M–L 67 may not be relevant to it; see Jeffery 1988 (F 36), but a new fragment complicates the matter.   [59] Brunt 1965 (G 10) 262; Lewis 1977 (A 76) 63–6.
[60] Brunt 1965 (G 10) 267–70.

(III.31); such a plan was evidently far beyond his instructions and ideas. The initiation of a proper policy had to wait until Brasidas' spectacular successes in the Thraceward region in 424. Here the Athenian empire was not protected by sea, but vulnerable to a long and enterprising march by land, a possibility discounted in Athens ([Xen.] *Ath. Pol.* 2.5). Brasidas' operations, however, were conducted under the handicap that influential circles in Sparta were sceptical, jealous and preoccupied with putting an end to the war.

One of the purposes served by the Corinthian speech at 1.68–71 is to illustrate the themes of Athenian enterprise and Spartan sloth, and Thucydides was not impressed with the Spartan ability to conduct war (1.118.2, IV.55.2 and, above all, VIII.96.5, where the Spartans are contrasted not only with the Athenians, but with the Syracusans, 'Athens' most efficient opponents'; cf. VII.55.2). A system designed to produce obedience and conformity only rarely produced enterprise,[61] and other reasons constrained Spartan policy. Tensions inside the ruling class were endemic and even institutionalized.[62] Spartan manpower was a comparatively small part of the resources of the Peloponnesian League, and her ability to keep her allies in hand depended on her military prestige and success. Above all, the Spartan system depended on her ability to control her large subject population. When that control seemed under threat, as it did in 425 and after, no other consideration took priority.[63]

3. General considerations

The more open society of Athens encouraged more enterprise, but had its own disadvantages. Thucydides draws attention to the instability of purpose of large groups (e.g. Athens, II.65.4; Syracuse, VI.63.2), and much of his final case for Pericles (II.65.7–10) is devoted to his ability to control the Assembly, both in its optimistic and in its pessimistic moods. Pericles would have stopped some of the more obvious mistakes, principally the great Sicilian expedition; we may guess that Thucydides also thought he would have taken some of the opportunities for peace, particularly in 425. The Assembly could be held to be particularly attracted to what seemed bright and plausible ideas (III.38.5, VI.9.3) and seems to have been incapable of turning down any offer of alliance, however unprofitable.[64] The conditions of decision-making made it hard to arrive at rational decisions based on reliable information. Some forms of information should have been ascertainable. There should have been a

[61] Finley 1975 (A 39) 161–77; Lewis 1977 (A 76) 29; Hodkinson 1983 (F 30).
[62] Lewis 1977 (A 76) 34–49. [63] Lewis 1977 (A 76) 27–9, 144.
[64] VI.13.2 seems a fair statement about Athens, in any period.

rough idea of what the enemy was capable of doing, even though Thucydides could not fix the size of a Spartan army (v.68.2); it was not like the campaign of 480 when all ideas about Persian strength must have been total guesswork. Even in the Sicilian Expedition of 415, it should have been possible to gauge the size of the problem, though little attempt was made.[65] For other kinds of intelligence the problem was much harder. On matters like the state of opinion in Megara, Boeotia or Sicily, the Assembly was dependent on individual speakers, with little ground for judging their reliability.

National characters and institutions played their part in the way in which war policies were formed. We should not expect this or any other war to be conducted in any severely rational way, and it would be mistaken to think of fifth-century Greece as particularly rational.[66] It is clear enough from Thucydides (II.21.3, 54.2–4, v.26.3–4) and Aristophanes' *Knights*, as well as much other evidence, that oracles, official and unofficial, were on constant offer during the war, and that omens and signs were of major importance.[67] Thucydides allows them some weight when they affected actions and attitudes (I.118.3, II.8.2–4, III.104.1, VI.27.3, VII.50.4), despite his own personal scepticism.[68] He himself is more impressed with the importance of the accidental.[69] Speakers in Thucydides are well aware that things do not go according to plan (I.78.1–2, 122.1, IV.18.3–5, 62.3–4, VII.61.3; but Pericles, I.140.1, II.64.1, thinks that most things are predictable). Nor is Thucydides unaware of the fog of battle; the participants in his war do not always know what is happening to them and around them.[70]

In the more formal fighting of the war, some traditions of older Greek warfare (cf. *CAH* III².3, 340) survived. The possibility of a set-piece battle to decide a single point of dispute (cf. *ibid.* 356) was now regarded even by Spartans as 'nonsense' (v.41.2–3), but individual actions were still regularly brought to an end by the defeated side sending a herald to ask for a truce to bury the dead[71] and the victors setting up a trophy.[72] But the amount of Greek land which was ravaged and the disturbance to the general population was greatly increased by Athenian amphibious warfare and the growing use of fixed bases for raiding. In general, it seems, war became more 'total'; one would guess that the whole number of casualties, even neglecting the Athenian plague, was far larger than

[65] VI.1.1. But Nicias (VI.20) may have been doing more than the official observers (VI.6.3, 8.1–2).

[66] For some general points about Athens, see Dodds 1951 (J 26) 188–95, but curse-tablets are earlier than he suggests.   [67] Much useful materal is collected by Powell 1979 (K 75).

[68] For Thucydides' attitude to oracles, see Dover 1988 (A 27) 65–73.

[69] For discussion of Thucydides' use of *tyche* and related words, see Edmunds 1975 (C 29) 174–204.

[70] I.51.1–2, II 3.1, 4.2, 81.7, 94.1, III.22.5, 24.3, 110.1, 112.3, IV.68.2, 96.3, 96.5, 115.3, 130.5.

[71] Lateiner 1977 (A 74); Pritchett 1971–85 (A 101) IV 246–9.

[72] Pritchett 1971–85 (A 101) II 246–75.

that of those who died in battle. Internal strife was perhaps most bitter and damaging, but a sequence of captured cities were treated with a severity enhanced by the length of their resistance or a feeling on the victors' part that they had behaved badly. Greek theory (Xen. *Cyr.* VII.5.72, cf. *Mem.* IV.2.15; *Dissoi Logoi* 90 F3.5 D–K) had perhaps always recognized the absolute discretion of the captor of a city; in this war, execution of part or whole of the male population and enslavement of the rest became acceptable options.[73] Other forms of brutality are to be noted. From the beginning of the war the Spartans executed all those they caught at sea, even neutrals (II.67.4), and the Athenians used this as justification for some executions of individuals who fell into their hands. There was more disposition to hold on to prisoners taken in regular action, who could be used for ransom or bargaining; not all of them were kept in the most comfortable conditions.[74] The voice of humanity was never stilled, and, even towards the end of the war, Callicratidas, for example (p. 491), proclaimed himself against the enslavement of Greeks (Xen. *Hell.* 1.6.14–15[75]), but, in general, the realities were harsh.

4. 431 B.C.

The first action of spring 431 was at Plataea, only twelve miles from Thebes across the Asopus, but long allied to Athens (*CAH* IV² 298). By arrangement with a pro-Theban group there, two boeotarchs led 300 or so Thebans (400 in Hdt. VII.233.2) to seize Plataea before the war got under way. No guard had yet been set (it was also in some sense a sacred month, III.56.2), the Plataeans had done nothing to evacuate their fields, and the force easily secured its entry early in the night. Despite the plea of the pro-Thebans for more drastic action, its first move was a simple proclaimed invitation to join the Boeotian League. The initial reaction was acquiescence, but it soon became clear that the Theban force was not very large and that the pro-Athenian feelings of the people had a chance. Regrouping in the night, the Plataeans, supported by their women and slaves, attacked in heavy rain and the half-light before dawn and forced those 180 Thebans whom they did not kill into surrender. The main Theban army, delayed by the rain, was held off by a threat to kill the prisoners and withdrew. The Plataeans then killed them anyway, which, according to the Thebans, they had sworn not to do; an Athenian request to leave them for further consideration came too late. The Athenians seized all Boeotians in Attica, provided Plataea with corn and reinforce-

---

[73] de Ste Croix 1954/5 (E 75) 14–16; Kiechle 1958 (A 72). The fifth-century precedent for the enslavement of a population cited by the former, the Argives at Mycenae (p. 109), is dubious, since Diod. XI.65.5 is contradicted by Paus. VII.25.6.

[74] On the treatment of prisoners in this war, see Panagopoulos 1978 (G 33).

[75] In the event, he sold an Athenian garrison.

ments and evacuated the non-combatants. The war had got off to a
bloody start. The dangers of *stasis* in a city had been illustrated; oaths
may have been violated; Thebes had lost close to 15 per cent of her first-
line troops in a day. (II.1–6).

The main event then got under way. The Peloponnesian force
gathered at the Isthmus under king Archidamus. One last messenger was
sent to Athens. Repulsed without a hearing, he said as he crossed the
border: 'This day will begin great evils for the Greeks.' Meanwhile,
Pericles' plans were being implemented. Flocks and farm animals were
sent to Euboea and other islands; women, children and household
equipment were brought from the country into the city. Vacant areas,
temples and shrines were occupied by temporary establishments, and
these eventually spread down to the area of the Long Walls and to the
Piraeus. Athens' population was still largely rural, and there was a good
deal of dissatisfaction. Time was, however, provided by the slow
progress of Archidamus, who made an unsuccessful attempt to reduce
the fortress of Oenoe before finally moving into Attica by Eleusis and
establishing himself at Acharnae, eight miles from Athens. His expectation, Thucydides thought, despite the prognostications attributed to
him in Book 1, was that the Athenians would come out and fight in the
orthodox way. Some certainly wanted to: besides the Acharnians
themselves, we can point to one Cleon, making his first appearance, who
was associated with the view (Hermippus F47 K–A ap. Plut. *Per*.33.8).
By means which are not clear[76] Pericles avoided summoning any meeting
which might revoke the previous plan, and relied on the Athenian
cavalry (for which reinforcements had come from Thessaly, cf. *IG* I³ 55)
to curb the ravaging, in which it was generally successful, except on one
occasion when a promising engagement against Boeotian cavalry ran
into some hoplite opposition. The central plain was unaffected in this
year, and Archidamus eventually moved across northern Attica to
Oropus and out into Boeotia, after a very restrained campaign (cf. Hdt.
IX.73.3). (II.10–23).

Meanwhile, an Athenian squadron of a hundred ships had been
circumnavigating the Peloponnese. It may have started with raiding on
the south coast of the Saronic Gulf.[77] It was at some point joined by fifty
ships from Corcyra. An attack on Messenian Methone was beaten off by a
Spartan officer named Brasidas, 'the first person in the war to be praised
in Sparta'. In Elis, the possibilities of amphibious warfare were demonstrated. Two days' ravaging was done before the main Elean army
arrived and, despite a storm which forced the fleet to sea, part of the
landing party briefly held the port of Pheia before it was re-embarked.

---

[76] See Hansen and Christensen 1983 (D 36).
[77] Diod. XII.43.1, Steph. Byz. s. v. Ἀκτή point to a possible lacuna in our text of Thucydides.

The main objectives, however, seem to have been at the mouth of the Corinthian Gulf. The Corinthian port of Sollium was taken and presented to friendly Acarnanians. The tyrant of Astacus was expelled and the town taken into alliance. Most importantly, the island of Cephallenia with its four cities came over without a fight; Thucydides (II.7.3) had already named it along with Corcyra, the Acarnanians and Zacynthos, all already in alliance, as an object of an embassy to make sure of firm friendship, which would enable Athens to make war on the Peloponnese from all round. That these gains touched the apprehensions or pride of the Corinthians is made clear by their attempt to reverse them later in the year at a time classified by Thucydides as winter. The tyrant of Astacus was restored, but there was no success in Acarnania and a positive reverse at Cranium in Cephallenia; oaths seem to have been broken again here. (II.23.2, 25, 30, 33).

Smaller Athenian expeditions gave attention to narrow waters. The Euboean channel was vulnerable to Locrian pirates; thirty ships took hostages from one threatening town, won a small victory over a Locrian force and set up a base on the offshore island of Atalante (II.26, 32). More dramatically, a chapter of history was brought to a temporary end with the expulsion of the once proud Aeginetans from Aegina and their replacement with an Athenian colony. It was felt that the Aeginetans bore some responsibility for the outbreak of war and they lived far too near the Peloponnese for safety (II.27); a base on Aegina would usefully supplement the force on the north coast of Salamis (p. 380).

In the north a splendid diplomatic coup brought alliance with the Odrysian kingdom and, through the king's chief minister, Nymphodorus of Abdera, a negotiated rapprochement with Perdiccas. Though the siege of Potidaea dragged on throughout the year, it seemed possible that the Chalcidian revolt might be brought to an end. (II.29).

Even after the Peloponnesians had gone home, it will not have been a comfortable year at Athens. To the inevitable batch of oracles, some even predicting that the war would last twenty-seven years (V.26.4), others no doubt more optimistic,[78] was added the alarm of a solar eclipse on 4 August; Pericles demonstrated the advantage of the sophistic movement by giving the people a lesson in astronomy (Cic. Rep 1.16.25; Plut. Per. 35.2, wrongly dated). The end of Aeginetan independence will have brought some satisfaction, and those who had remained at home throughout the summer were eventually rewarded with a grand outing (II.31). All the first-line citizen hoplites in Attica, to the number of 10,000 together with 3,000 or so metics, apparently replacing the force at

---

[78] I remember, as a small boy in 1939, being obscurely comforted by the information that the first German president had had five letters in his name and lasted five years and that Hindenburg had had ten years in office; that gave Hitler only to 1940.

Potidaea, and a large number more lightly armed were taken by Pericles
to ravage the Megarid and joined by the fleet returning from Cephallenia; Thucydides remembered it as the largest of all Athenian expeditions,
when the city was still in its prime and had not yet fallen sick, and
reinforces his picture of Athens before the plague with his account of the
Funeral Speech delivered by Pericles over the dead of the war's first year.
The Athenian society depicted in the speech is inevitably an idealization
which the Athenians did not achieve in practice, and there are aspects of
the patriotism recommended in it which carry less conviction now than
they did to the Edwardians, but Thucydides' attempt to reproduce
Pericles' aspirations for Athens is a literary and political achievement
which puts subject and author on a very high human plane. (II.34–46).

f. 430 B.C.

One sentence on the Peloponnesian invasion of 430 gets that campaigning season under way before the description of the plague
which changed Athenian history. In view of what seems to be the well-
established ability of diseases to change their character, it is unprofitable
to attempt to put a label on the disease which struck Athens with such
violence.[79] The calamity was so awesome that, were it not for Thucydides and literary echoes of Thucydides, we should hardly have known
that it occurred; classical Athenian literature is nearly silent about it.[80]
For four years or more, no Athenian can have been free from fear of it; in
430 and 429, and again in 426, it was active (III.87.1–3 supplements the
main narrative in II.47–54). What is meant by 'active' emerges from
II.58.3; Hagnon lost 1,050 hoplites out of 4,000 from the plague in forty
days. Camp conditions constitute a special case, but the figures that
Thucydides was able to extract from the official lists of hoplites and
cavalry (4,400 dead hoplites, 300 cavalry) suggest that the death-rate
over the whole period was of this order and justify his view that nothing
affected Athenian strength so much. Various explanations were offered
from the factual (the Peloponnesians had poisoned the wells) to the
theological (Apollo was fulfilling his promise (p. 378) to the Peloponnesians). The effect on the Athenian social and economic structure must
have been considerable.[81] On a more general level, Thucydides attributes to the plague a general breakdown of moral standards; if there was

---

[79] Poole and Holladay 1979 and 1984 (D 72 and 73).

[80] Pl. *Symp.* 201d is a rare exception.

[81] I do not accept the view of Fine 1951 (L 35) 167–208, that Athenian patterns of land-tenure
were totally altered, but Thucydides' picture of rapid changes of individual fortune probably has
something to it.

such a tendency, it is hard to see how the effect of the plague could be distinguished from other factors.[82]

This was the longest of the Peloponnesian invasions of Attica. In forty days Archidamus' force went through the central plain, moved down the south coast to the silver mines of Laurium and then turned north up the east coast, ravaging 'all the land'; no opposition is reported. Pericles maintained the policy of the previous year and was confident enough about Athenian acceptance of it to take the main fleet to sea himself (II.56). The Athenian component was again a hundred ships, but, since no operations on the west coast of the Peloponnese were contemplated, the reinforcement of fifty ships came from Chios and Lesbos this year, not from Corcyra. However, the forces carried were substantially strengthened, no doubt as a result of the experience in Elis. The 431 squadron had made do with its thousand marines as land-forces,[83] but in this year the hoplite force was raised to four thousand, and three hundred cavalry were taken as well, on transports converted from old triremes; the objects of this expedition would not be able to face it in the field. In size, as Thucydides notes later (VI.31.2), it was similar to the force which went to Sicily in 415, though it would not be away for so long and needed far less in the way of supply.

While Pericles was in command of this force, he made three uses of it. The first move was against Epidaurus. The force was so large that the Epidaurians made no attempt to face it in the field. Their land was ravaged and there was an unsuccessful attempt to take the city; Thucydides makes no comment on the motive (cf. p. 380). Other Peloponnesian cities further south, Troezen, Hermione and Halieis, were then subjected to simple ravaging. Finally, Pericles crossed the twenty miles or so across the Argolic Gulf to the Laconian coast and sacked the perioecic city of Prasiae (modern Leonidhion), virtually isolated by land from Laconia proper; this doubtless gave the Athenians some satisfaction.[84] The expedition then went back to Athens, and was immediately taken by Pericles' colleagues, Hagnon and Cleopompus, up to Chalcidice; the intention was clearly to finish off the siege of Potidaea and the whole revolt, but the outbreak of plague on the expedition (p. 396) wrecked the plan. (II.56,58).

It would seem certain that Potidaea was part of the original plan for the year and that Pericles, in his preliminary use of the force on the Peloponnesian coast, was therefore working to some kind of time limit.

[82] Given the generality of II.53, one would have expected to find echoes of its language and thought elsewhere in the history; they are curiously absent.

[83] Gomme's view (HCT II 80) that Thucydides never counts the marines is unacceptable.

[84] Cf. Ar. Peace 242–3 and Cartledge 1979 (F 14) 238.

The question is whether anything more elaborate than ravaging enemy fields was in his mind. We notice no attempt to anticipate the later posts at Methana and Halieis, but, since capture of Epidaurus is talked of, he surely intended to do something with it; it was no Prasiae to be sacked and abandoned. Thucydides' observations on its strategic importance come at v.53: in a situation when Argos and Athens were already in alliance, it would improve communications between them, and it would keep Corinth quiet. It is not necessary, in the context of 430, to suppose that Pericles was already thinking to the renewal of the Argive alliance (but see p. 387). To complete the chain of Athenian posts across the Saronic Gulf and Corinth's eastern approaches, already in 431 extended to Aegina, was ample motive to seize Epidaurus; Pericles' intentions should not be restricted by over-tight definition of his injunction against extending the empire.

If Pericles had taken Epidaurus, the situation which faced him on his return might have been different. According to Thucydides, the second Peloponnesian invasion and the plague turned the Athenians against the war and Pericles. Ambassadors went to Sparta and returned without success; we have no idea what they offered or what was asked of them. Pericles' position was not strengthened, and formal attacks on him began. Thucydides gives him a defence, and says that it stopped the moves to peace, but not proceedings which resulted in a fine and deposition.[85] How long it was before he was re-elected is unclear. (II.59–65.4). Thucydides ascribes no further specific actions to him and does not record his death in autumn 429 (II.65.6) in its place.

The Peloponnesians did not confine themselves to land operations this year. They managed to put a hundred ships to sea in an unsuccessful attempt to detach Zacynthos from the Athenian alliance (II.66), and the Ambraciots, in a more local operation, made an attempt on Amphilochian Argos (II.68); the schemes would be combined next year. Further evidence came to Athens that there was long-range thinking among the enemy when the Odrysian king handed over a Peloponnesian embassy, which was attempting to win him over on the way to its primary objective, a mission to Persia. The temper of the Athenian Assembly showed itself when the ambassadors were put to death without trial (II.67; cf. p. 393). That at least Pissuthnes, satrap of Sardis, saw that there was profit for Persia to be made out of the war had been made clear by the fall of Colophon to a Persian-backed faction (III.34.1).

---

[85] Plut. *Per.* 35.4–5 provides a variety of proposers and fines, none of them from an *Atthis*; there is a temptation to use the apparently more respectable detail of 32.3–5, but the procedure there described is clearly incomplete and Plutarch dates it to 432. The same chapter contains material about the decree of Diopeithes against impiety, said to be directed against Anaxagoras, and a prosecution of Aspasia. Despite Adcock, *CAH* v¹ 577–80 and Gomme, *HCT* II 184–9, I see no particular attraction in putting them here; for the dates of Anaxagoras see p. 339.

Later in the year the Athenians decided to blockade the Corinthian Gulf with a fleet of twenty ships under Phormio. There was a minor disaster in far-off Lycia when a tribute-collecting expedition (see p. 5), trying to check possible action from Peloponnesian privateers on the trade-route from southern Asia Minor and Phoenicia, ran into trouble and lost its general. Some compensation came when Potidaea at last surrendered. Its garrison and inhabitants were allowed to go free, and Athenian public opinion thought the terms too generous, early evidence that even success might not protect generals from criticism. A thousand Athenians took over the town (Thuc. II.70.4; Diod. XII.46.7; M–L 66 with commentary), but the Chalcidian revolt was far from over. (II.69–70).

6. 429 B.C.

In 429 the main Peloponnesian army was turned on to settling with Plataea, no doubt under pressure from Thebes (III.68.4). The name of Plataea meant much for Spartan sentiment, and Archidamus made some attempt at a settlement on the basis of a Plataean return to neutrality; the attempt broke down when the Athenians promised they would not abandon the Plataeans. Prolonged siege operations got nowhere, and Archidamus eventually decided to starve the city out by circumvallation; 400 Plataean citizens, 80 Athenians and 110 women were cut off from the outside world. (II.71–8).

Meanwhile, the Athenians attempted to follow up the capture of Potidaea by finishing the Chalcidic revolt. Only two thousand hoplites could be spared this year, and the attempt failed at Spartolus with 430 killed in an interesting battle, the first of which we have any detail in which hoplites were mauled by light-armed peltasts, equipped with the small Thracian shield, and by cavalry. (II.79).

If the Peloponnesian attack on Plataea did not show much strategic imagination, their other main plan for the year certainly did. The initiative seems to have come from Ambracia, still smarting from the pre-war defeat (p. 145). This year their aim was not only Amphilochian Argos, but the whole of Acarnania. Supported by their mother-city Corinth, they sold the Spartans the proposition that, with adequate support by land and sea, it would be possible to clear Acarnania, Zacynthos and Cephallenia; Athenian circumnavigation of the Peloponnese would become impossible (cf. II.80.1 *fin.* with 7.3); Corcyra would be isolated;[86] even Naupactus might fall. To their local Greek allies they added impressive forces from a wide variety of barbarians; the thousand Peloponnesian infantry they had asked for arrived under the Spartan

[86] This obvious point can surely be added.

admiral Cnemus, but the fleet was delayed. The Acarnanians, expecting
attack from all sides, failed to concentrate, but one engagement ended
the land campaign. The allied force decided to begin with Stratus. Their
thousand Chaones rushed on ahead into an ambush and were routed; the
remaining barbarians took to flight, and the Stratian slingers harassed
the Greek forces from a distance. This was not the kind of fighting
Cnemus was used to, and he withdrew; the expedition then broke up.
(11.80–2).

In 430 Cnemus had been able to concentrate his hundred ships against
Zacynthos without difficulty, but in this year the naval threat to the
Acarnanian coast did not develop. The local ships were waiting at
Leucas for the main squadron from Corinth and Sicyon, and this now
had to pass Phormio's force at Naupactus. The Corinthian commanders
did not think this much of an obstacle since they had forty-seven ships
against Phormio's twenty, and were not prepared for battle. Phormio
nevertheless attacked. Some thought had evidently been given to the
possibility and to methods of dealing with superior Athenian manoeuvrability. The fleet formed itself into a circle, inside which were placed the
small supply ships and a reserve of five good triremes; there would be no
line for the Athenians to break. Phormio made no attempt to break in,
but formed column of line and sailed round and round the circle, forcing
it to become tighter and tighter. When the dawn wind he had been
anticipating got up, the circle was reduced to a cursing mess of colliding
ships; at this point he attacked, sinking several ships and capturing
twelve as the remainder fled to the coast of Achaea. They then retired to
Cyllene in Elis, where they were joined by Cnemus and the ships from
Leucas, and started piecing themselves together under the goad of
Brasidas and two other Spartan 'advisers', who arrived with an incredulous and angry message (p. 382). Phormio reported his victory to Athens
and asked for reinforcements. The Assembly voted him twenty ships,
but gave them a small and unimportant job to do in Crete as well.[87]
(11.83–5).

Phormio therefore only had his original twenty ships to face the
Peloponnesian force, now enlarged to fifty-seven.[88] The preliminary
manoeuvres and Peloponnesian practising took place west of the
narrows at Rhium, which would make sense if the Peloponnesian
objective was still Acarnania, and gave the Athenians more room for
deploying their superior skill. But the first Peloponnesian objective was
now the destruction of Phormio, and he was drawn into the narrows by
the show of a threat against Naupactus. He lost nine ships immediately

---

[87] See p. 381. The dying Pericles might have improved the Assembly's geography, had he been
well.

[88] Most editors prefer the seventy-seven provided by the other family of manuscripts, but this
seems unduly large, in terms both of what could have been mobilized and of the course of the battle.

and the rest made for the security of Naupactus, with the enemy in hot and incoherent pursuit. However, the last and slowest Athenian ship had a cool-headed commander. Sailing round an anchored merchant-ship, he rammed his leading pursuer full amidships. This was sufficient to bewilder the enemy and reinvigorate his colleagues. Six Peloponnesian ships were taken, and the initial Athenian losses were recovered, except for one ship which remained to make a Peloponnesian trophy for the first phase of the battle. The Peloponnesians did not remain to await the Athenian reinforcements; the Leucadians went home and the rest withdrew to Corinth. Even overwhelming numbers had not conquered Athenian naval skills. The lesson of the importance of the sea was driven home when Phormio mounted an operation to tighten the grip of Athens' friends on Acarnania; only Oeniadae on its delta remained inviolate, protected by the autumn rising of the Achelous.[89] (II.86–92, 102–3).

Cnemus and Brasidas were not yet beaten, and accepted a Megarian plan. There were forty ships at Nisaea, the Megarian port on the Saronic Gulf. Crews were marched from the defeated fleet across the Isthmus to man these for a raid on the Piraeus, where the Athenians had as yet seen no need for any precautions. Thucydides thought this a well-conceived plan and contemptuously reports the talk of a wind, which led it to being abandoned in favour of a raid on Salamis. As far as this went, it was successful. The three ships based at the north end of the island (p. 380) were captured and a good deal of other damage was done before the arrival of large Athenian forces and worries about the state of the ships, not fully seaworthy after long inactivity, forced withdrawal. But, compared to the chance which had been missed, this did not amount to much, and the Athenians rapidly took measures against any renewal of the idea. (II.93–4).

The last event of 429 promised more than it achieved. The hopes cherished since 431 (p. 395) that Sitalces the Odrysian might deploy his power on the Athenian side, pressed by an Athenian as senior as Hagnon, at last materialized, despite the fact that scepticism at Athens kept away the Athenian support he had been promised. He moved in enormous force, but with more zeal in trying to impose his will on Perdiccas than in finishing the Chalcidic revolt for the Athenians; neither of his aims came to much. (II.95–101).

7. 428 B.C.

Initially, it looked as if 428 was to revert to the pattern of 430. With Plataea still under siege, Archidamus invaded Attica again, with limited results (III.1), and the Athenians had been contemplating a naval

[89] And by a substantial wall-circuit, still well preserved (see Lawrence 1979 (I 96) 475).

expedition to the Peloponnese, omitted in 429, doubtless because of the plague, and of only forty Athenian ships.[90] In the situation after the plague, Athenian resources were limited and the first rumours which reached Athens from Tenedos, Methymna and loyal Mytileneans (cf. Arist. *Pol.* 1304a) that Mytilene was synoecizing the three smaller cities of the island with a view to revolt were only met with a warning embassy. When this was rejected, action was clearly necessary. The fleet designed for the Peloponnese was diverted to Mytilene with instructions to catch the Mytileneans outside the walls at a festival if it could and to demand the demolition of their fortifications and the cession of their fleet; the ten ships already at Athens were seized and their crews jailed. The news of the fleet's coming reached Mytilene on the third day, and it was forced to show its hand prematurely, before preparations were complete and corn and archers ordered from the Black Sea had come in. After a small naval engagement, the Mytileneans asked the Athenian fleet, itself not confi-dent that it had enough force for the job, for an armistice, nominally to send an embassy to Athens, in reality to gain time to ask for Spartan help. After the return of the embassy from Athens, they declared the armistice at an end but did nothing very decisive. It may have seemed a good idea to wait for what Sparta would provide, but the effect was that even those Athenian allies who had been hesitant up till now (the Chians?) came in. The Athenians could now block both of Mytilene's harbours, though they controlled no land outside their own camps. (III.2–6).

The Mytilenean embassy to Sparta was diverted to Olympia, where it was a year of the Games and a meeting of the Peloponnesian League could be conveniently held. They asked for direct help and a second invasion of Attica; Athens was exhausted by the plague and financially, and would not be able to fight in more than one place. They were accepted into alliance, and it was agreed to repeat the invasion immedi-ately and support it with ships brought across the Isthmus. An invasion as late as this, during the Peloponnesians' own harvest, was slow to get under way, and the Athenian response to the news was to put a hundred ships to sea off the Isthmus, making up the crews from the ranks of the hoplites, and even landing in places; at the same time news came in that Phormio's son, Asopius, on his way to a new campaign in Acarnania, was active on the Laconian coast. Athens was evidently very far from finished, whatever the Mytileneans said. Sparta started preparing a relief squadron to Lesbos of forty ships under the new admiral Alcidas. (III.7–16).

---

[90] Ten ships had arrived from Mytilene (III.3.4) and presumably there were to be Chians as well, as in 430. It should be noticed that Thucydides has nothing whatever to say about Chios in the context of the revolt of Mytilene, despite their identical situations (III.10.5). This is an exhibition of Chian prudence (VIII.24.4–5, Quinn 1981 (E 64) 40–1), but could the Athenians take it for granted?

Meanwhile, the Mytileneans used their superiority by land to strengthen their position on the island, though an attempt on Methymna failed. The Athenians recognized their lack of land forces, and sent out a thousand hoplites under Paches; they were now able to invest Mytilene by land as well as by sea. Despite the demonstration off the Isthmus strains were showing. A property tax was introduced for the first time in the war.[91] (III.18–19). There were further reverses. Asopius failed to take Oeniadae and was killed in an attack on Leucas (III.7); Lysicles, perhaps the new patron of Aspasia, in command of a tribute-collecting expedition, got himself killed in Caria. (III.19). That over two hundred of the Plataea garrison extricated themselves in an adventurous escape was no great comfort; the Plataeans were given Athenian citizenship (Dem. LIX.104–6) instead of the help that they had been promised. (III.20–4).

8. 427 B.C.

Mytilene had a depressing winter, as the corn started to run out, but an incipient wish for surrender was checked by the arrival of the Spartan Salaethus, announcing the imminent arrival of Alcidas' squadron and an impending invasion of Attica. The latter happened, under the command of Cleomenes, regent for Pausanias, the Agiad king who was still a minor,[92] and was thought particularly effective; Alcidas moved slowly, and when he finally reached the coast of Asia, the rumours which had reached him as he crossed the Aegean were confirmed; Mytilene had fallen seven days before. (III.25–9).

Salaethus' assurances of the coming of Alcidas had worn thin, even for himself. It seemed to him that the best chance of breaking the siege was to increase hoplite strength; on his advice, hoplite weapons were distributed to the lower classes. When this was done, the new hoplites demanded a fairer distribution of corn; if they did not get it, they would surrender the city. It does not follow from what Thucydides says here (III.27–8) that they had been pro-Athenian all along, though this was later asserted in Athens (III.47.1–3). Perhaps there was no corn for the upper classes to distribute; in any case, they took the view that the city would have to surrender anyway and that they might as well get what credit there was to be got by surrendering themselves.[93] The final terms would be whatever an embassy could secure from the Athenian Assembly; meanwhile Paches would neither kill nor imprison nor

[91] It raised 200 talents. Whether there was also an extraordinary reassessment of tribute, as maintained by *ATL* III 70, remains uncertain. See Mattingly 1961 (E 44) 166–8, 1961 (E 46) 155–60, 1966 (E 48) 179–83, 1970 (C 143) 133–42; Meiggs 1972 (E 53) 531–7; Bradeen and McGregor 1973 (C 121) 20–3; Piérart 1984 (E 62) 172–6.

[92] Archidamus died this year, but we cannot fix the date.

[93] For the varied interpretations of this episode see p. 383 n. 41.

enslave anyone.[94] Those most deeply implicated fled to altars, but were persuaded that no wrong would be done to them and were put in safe custody on Tenedos; it is not clear whether they were being protected from the Athenian force or from their own people.

Alcidas accepted his failure. His instruction had been to relieve Mytilene, and he was deaf to suggestions that a surprise attack there might retrieve it or that, by the seizure of some city on the coast of Asia Minor, he could promote revolt in Ionia and threaten Athenian revenues; all he wanted to do was go home. He had picked up some prisoners on the voyage, and could think of nothing better to do than execute them; a mission from the Samian exile settlement of Anaea (p. 144) did at least convince him that this was no way to free Greece and would drive potential allies back into the arms of Athens, but no real development followed. When he realized that he had been seen by Athenian despatch vessels, he made straight for the Peloponnese. Paches had been alarmed by the news of his presence, thinking that, even if he did not stay in Ionia, he might do some damage to the unwalled Ionian cities[95] and set off in pursuit; he failed to catch him and was somewhat relieved, since, if a blockade had been called for, his forces would have been over-stretched. Having been drawn as far south as Patmos, he took the opportunity of rectifying the situation at Notium, which had deteriorated since the loss of Colophon in 430; Athens reinforced his settlement with a new colony. He then returned to Lesbos, mopped up the two cities still in revolt, and despatched to Athens Salaethus, who had been hiding in Mytilene, and the principal rebels, including the Mytileneans he had consigned to Tenedos; they added up to slightly more than a thousand (III.50.1[96]). (III.29–35).

The Athenian Assembly had been capable of merciless decisions during Pericles' lifetime (p. 398), though perhaps while he was in eclipse, and it had been very frightened over Mytilene; Salaethus was executed, for no very obvious reason, and the debate turned to the fate of the Mytilenean prisoners. (III.36).

In retrospect, after the war (II.65.10), Thucydides thought of the politicians after Pericles as competing with others on a similar level for primacy, and therefore inclined to give the *demos* what it wanted. This charge does not seem to be made out against the first man of whom we get a clear picture. In 427, we are told (III.36.6), Cleon was the most violent of the citizens and far the most persuasive to the people; the

[94] An atrocity story (*Anth. Pal.* VII.614) survived for nine centuries according to which he had raped two women whose husbands he had executed, and he certainly seems to have committed suicide while on trial at Athens (Plut. *Nic.* 6.1).

[95] Wade-Gery 1958 (A 121) 219–20 for lack of walls in Ionia, but see Meiggs 1972 (E 53) 149–51; Brunt 1966 (E 13) 92 n.54.

[96] The figure has been doubted, but we have to allow for Eresus, Antissa and Pyrrha as well.

overlapping second introduction at IV.21.3 omits the violence and introduces the word 'demagogue' (leader of the people). Later writing made much play with the word 'demagogue'. It is not invariably used pejoratively, and could be applied to figures who were not normally thought of as extreme democrats, but by and large the implications are hostile. There was certainly a function for something of the kind in democratic Athens, and Thucydides is capable of using the second element of the word, though not the word itself, in connexion with Pericles (1.127.3, 11.65.8). To be generally the most persuasive politician is not to hold an office and does not imply an unbroken run of successful persuasion, but it is entirely plausible that the Assembly would become accustomed to listen regularly to someone who sounded as if he knew what he was talking about, even if he was no Pericles.[97] Cleon did not belong to an old family, though his father seems to have been of liturgic status as early as 459, and there is no evidence for landholding; besides alleged political receipts, his only attested source of income is a workshop of slave-tanners, which gave comedy a good subject.[98] It has been held[99] that Cleon's apparent newness has nothing to do with a lack of ancestors or land, but rather in his professed willingness to put the interests of the city as a whole above the traditional ties of friendship, but along these lines there is nothing which can be inferred of Cleon which could not be said of Pericles, and some of the attitudes to Cleon surely arise from snobbery and dislike of his style.[100] Our main sources on Cleon, Thucydides and Aristophanes, both heartily disliked him, which makes it harder to see his qualities; he surely had some, and it may be possible to deduce from Aristophanes, whose portrait has elements absent from Thucydides, not only violence and a considerable parade of oracles, but also a genuine interest in finance and administration.[101]

In what earlier debates his violence had manifested itself we can only guess. On this occasion, he carried a motion for the execution, not only of those Lesbians sent by Paches, but of all adult male Mytileneans and for the enslavement of the women and children; for an autonomous ally to revolt was particularly inexcusable and it must have been a deep-laid plan which had brought Peloponnesian ships to Ionia. A trireme went off to Paches to give him these orders. The next day, some revulsion could be detected; it was a cruel and portentous decision to destroy a whole city and not the guilty only. It proved surprisingly easy to call a second Assembly for reconsideration, and, after a close-fought debate, the decree was repealed; contrary to what the reader of 11.65.10 might

[97] For discussions of demagogy, see Finley 1962 = 1974 (D 26); Andrewes 1962 (C 5) 82–4; Connor 1971 (D 16) 109–10.

[98] For facts about Cleon and his family connexions, see Davies 1971 (L 27) 318–20; Bourriot 1982 (D 9).   [99] Connor 1971 (D 16) *passim*.   [100] Lewis 1975 (D 52).

[101] Woodhead 1960 (D 109); Andrewes 1962 (C 5) 79–85.

have expected. Cleon set himself against the clear tide of public opinion.[102] A second trireme, starting a day and a night after the first, made enormous efforts and arrived just as Paches had read the first despatch. But his first selection of guilty parties was executed *en bloc* at Athens, and Mytilene paid the usual penalty for revolt, loss of her fleet and fortifications. Moreover, she lost her extensive colonial possessions on the mainland, which became direct tribute-paying members of the empire.[103] (III.36–50).

Thucydides brings another major actor on the Athenian stage in 427. Nicias is just as much a new man as Cleon,[104] more so, in fact, since we know nothing of his father but his name and deme, but he is enormously more wealthy than Cleon and the source of his wealth less obtrusive; almost certainly the fortune had been made in the silver-mines since the 480s.[105] A combination of evidence (Ar. *Birds* 363; Phrynichus F 22 Edm.; cf. Pl. *Lach*.181e–182d) suggests a reputation for technical military interests; perhaps this expertise should be thought of as not dissimilar from Cleon's financial interests. He was well into his forties this year, when we first find him in the generalship (there is no support for Plutarch's assertion (*Nic.* 2.2) that he had often been a colleague of Pericles), and it may have taken him time to establish himself by a calculated programme of conspicuous liturgic expenditure. But what we find him doing shows both strategic thinking about the need to conduct the blockade of Megara from closer in (not only goods but excursions by privateers and a repetition of the raid in 429 are in question) and a fairly technical approach to doing it.[106] (III.51).

While this was going on, the abandoned garrison of Plataea, now reduced to 225 or so, at last gave in. After the semblance of a trial they were executed, even the Athenians, against whom no charge could be brought; the women were sold into slavery. The city was briefly granted to Megarian exiles and then destroyed, disappearing from the map until after the King's Peace of 386, a time when Sparta was less concerned with

---

[102] It is clear enough that horror and pity played a large part in the change of mind; Thucydides has chosen two speeches, one by Cleon, one by an unknown Diodotus, which treat them as irrelevant and only argue about what is expedient for Athens. For discussions of Thucydides' debate, see Andrewes 1962 (C 5) 71–9; Macleod 1983 (A 82) 88–102.

[103] For these 'Aktaiai Poleis', long settled by Mytilene, see *CAH* II³.2, 781–2; J. M. Cook 1973 (F 19) *passim*, especially 197, 383. Thucydides also reports a complex arrangement by which all Lesbos, except Methymna, was broken up into three thousand lots. Three hundred of these would go to the gods, the rest to Athenian cleruchs, though the Lesbians continued to work the land, paying 200 drachmae a year for each lot. What the details of this arrangement were, whether Athenian cleruchs actually went to Lesbos (or stayed if they did), and how long the arrangement lasted, constitute a nexus of unsolved questions. See Gomme, *HCT* II 328–31; Jones 1957 (D 40) 175–6; Brunt 1966 (E 13) 81–4; Meiggs 1972 (E 53) 261–2; Quinn 1981 (E 64) 36–7 with n. 63.

[104] No ancient writer makes the point, but Plutarch could find nothing when he wrote his life and neither inscriptions nor ostraca have helped.   [105] See Davies 1971 (L 27) 403–7.

[106] For the details see Gomme, *HCT* II 333–6; Beattie 1960 (G 8) 20–43; Legon 1981 (F 45) 29–32.

Theban interests. This was not a matter of much consequence for the war, and the seventeen chapters it occupies in Thucydides are partly there to make the contrast between Mytilene, which had narrowly escaped destruction, and Plataea, which had not.[107] All this happened in the ninety-third year of Plataea's alliance with Athens; the reader is left wondering whether this is only intended as a date. (III.52–68).

At this point, Thucydides has perhaps become less interested in the course of the war than in its violent consequences, and the next episode is even nastier. No Corcyrean activity whatever has been reported since 431; it emerges that there has been *stasis* there. The Corinthians had released, ostensibly on enormous bail, 250 Corcyraeans, many of them notables, who had been taken prisoner at Sybota (1.55.1); they had been persuaded to detach Corcyra from the Athenian alliance. After various moves and counter-moves, starting in the courts and ending with the assassination in the council-chamber of Peithias, the leading pro-Athenian, and members of his party, they persuaded the Assembly that they had been in danger of enslavement to Athens and should declare their neutrality. The whole plot was carefully watched at Corinth and Sparta. Alcidas, on his return from Ionia, was given Brasidas' assistance and sent to support the plot, in conjunction with the naval allies of the north west. The new regime courteously informed Athens of the change in the situation. Its envoys were not well received, and Athens sent sixty ships under Eurymedon to Corcyra, since its nearest available commander, Nicostratus at Naupactus, had only twelve ships. (III.69–72.1, 80.2).

Civil war now broke out, determined to some extent by the likely timing of great-power intervention. The oligarchs started it, with only one Corinthian trireme present. An initial success gave them the Agora and one of the harbours, but the *demos* kept control of the acropolis, other high ground and the other harbour. Eight hundred mercenaries from the mainland strengthened the oligarchs, but the *demos* secured a good deal of support from the servile population of the countryside, and, although the centre of the city was in flames, it had already gained the upper hand when Nicostratus arrived from Naupactus with five hundred of its Messenian inhabitants. He made an attempt to arrange a settlement. Only ten men, no longer present, would be regarded as guilty; the rest should live in harmony, but convert the alliance with Athens to the full offensive and defensive form (cf. p. 374). The democratic leaders were not fully satisfied. Nicostratus might return to Naupactus, as he wished, but he should leave them five triremes as a precaution, which they would replace with five of their own, to which they nominated political opponents. These refused to go, which the democratic leaders took as

[107] See Macleod 1983 (A 82) 103–22, on the debate.

evidence of their insincerity, and Nicostratus had to intervene to protect them and others of their party. (III.72.2–75).

At this point, Alcidas and Brasidas arrived with fifty-three ships. The Corcyraeans endeavoured to put sixty ships to sea, but these put out in no kind of order and thirteen were lost; that the losses were no worse was to the credit of Nicostratus, fighting a neat defensive engagement against the bulk of the Peloponnesians. Although Brasidas wanted to renew the direct attack the next day, Alcidas overruled him and did nothing except ravage the countryside for a morning. At night fire-signals announced the impending arrival of Eurymedon and his fleet from Athens; Alcidas did not even consider waiting and made for home, hauling his ships over the isthmus which joined Leucas to the mainland to avoid a possible collision with Eurymedon. Even before Eurymedon arrived, the demo-cratic leaders had begun their purge. No altar or shrine was inviolate, pretence of legal process was rare, and many preferred suicide to an inevitable end. Once killing had started, it went far beyond political motives (cf. p. 384). Unlike Nicostratus, Eurymedon made no attempt to intervene, and his fleet remained for seven days while the slaughter continued. If his instructions had been to make Corcyra safe for Athens, he had hardly succeeded even in that. Five hundred Corcyraeans escaped the massacre and, first from the mainland, then from a base on the island itself, made a great deal of Corcyraean land unworkable and produced famine in the city. (III.76–85).

One of Corcyra's original attractions to Athens (p. 374) had been its position on the route to Italy and Sicily. In the autumn, long-cherished Athenian plans at last got under way. The occasion was the ambition of Syracuse to foreclose on the Chalcidian area of north-eastern Sicily (p. 165). With the support of all Dorian Sicily, except Camarina, who took the other side, she moved against Leontini, supported by her Chalcidian neighbours and Rhegium across the Straits of Messina, and brought it under siege. Athens was tied by treaty to Leontini and Rhegium at least (pp. 143, 375), and Leontini sent the greatest of living orators, Gorgias, to make her case (Diod. XII.53, entirely credible, despite Thucydides' silence). Athens sent twenty ships under Laches and Charoiades to defend her Ionian relatives; the real reasons, according to Thucydides, were to cut Peloponnesian corn-supplies from Sicily at their source and to test the possibility of gaining control of Sicily. Having said this, he more or less abandons all attempt to explain the course of operations in this theatre, giving no clue as to why the first venture of the expedition he describes should be, with help from Rhegium, against the unimpor-tant Syracusan allies on the Aeolian islands. This is virtually the only occasion in the Archidamian War where we have a historical text to fill in the gaps. A papyrus (*FGrH* 577 F 2 = *PSI* XII 1283), perhaps of Philistus, shows the Athenian fleet had been divided into two sections, with Charoiades off Camarina, where he got killed, and Laches off Messene, before they reunited for the attack on the Aeolian islands; it would appear that their original attention to the main theatre of war was greater than Thucydides lets us see, though it is entirely plausible that some later operations were influenced by the views and wishes of Rhegium.[108] (III.86, 88).

In winter, the plague struck again, and there was a portentous series of earthquakes and consequent tidal waves (III.87). The earthquakes had this much advantage for Athens; the first invasion of Attica to be headed by Archidamus' son Agis was called off at the Isthmus, apparently on the assumption that the divine warnings were against an invasion (III.89.1). More is going on in Sparta than Thucydides lets us see at this point. At some time in the second half of 427 or early in 426 (we have no means of relating it to the death of Archidamus), steady pressure from Delphi and an unknown amount of support in Sparta had produced the revocation of the banishment (p. 137) of king Plistoanax, who returned from exile to the accompaniment of the same dances and sacrifices as those which were believed to have been performed at the inauguration of the Spartan kingship (v.16.3). Not everybody at Sparta was happy, however, and it would be a long time before Plistoanax was again allowed to command an army in the field.

9. 426 B.C.

Besides Sicily, where nothing very coherent is reported, the Athenians chose two theatres of operation for 426.[109] Generals new to us, Demosthenes and Procles, took thirty ships to collaborate with the Acarnanians along the lines envisaged for Asopius in 428 (p. 403). Nicias went with sixty ships and two thousand hoplites to try to force the Dorian island of Melos into the empire.[110] He got nowhere within the time he had available before keeping an appointment to meet the main Athenian army from the city in the territory of Tanagra. This is the first Athenian invasion of Boeotia of which we hear in the war (but cf. *Hell.*

---

[108] See also Ampolo 1987 (G 1), redating *IG* I³ 291 to this period. The consequence is to show that much of the costs of the expedition were borne locally.

[109] Though, taken together, they could be held to anticipate some of the features of the plan for 424 (p. 425), Thucydides makes no suggestion that they were connected; he was probably already close enough to the highest strategic thinking for his silence to be taken seriously.

[110] Thucydides offers no explanation except the unwillingness of Melos to join. There are attractions in the view (Piérart 1984 (E 62)) that it was the expedition of Alcidas in 427 which attracted Athenian attention to the need to strengthen control in the southern Cyclades. The problem is Thera, mentioned by Thucydides in 431 as neutral along with Melos, but never again. It certainly had come under Athenian control by 426/5 (M–L 68 = *IG* I³ 68.21–5); how long before depends on the readings and dating of *ATL* List 27 = *IG* I³ 283; see n. 91.

Oxy. 17.3), and the only easy explanation for the change of mind is to think of it as a belated reprisal for Plataea. There was a small, but satisfying, victory over Tanagraean and Theban troops, and Nicias went on to ravage the coasts of Locris, where nothing has been reported since 431, except perhaps from Atalante (see p. 395 and III.89.3). (III.91).

The original plan for the force commanded by Demosthenes and Procles was to renew the attack on Leucas; all Athenian allies in the area could agree on that, and the Acarnanians were particularly keen. However, the Messenians of Naupactus suggested that it would be more useful to attack the Aetolian tribes, whom they saw as a threat to them. In a wild speculation, Demosthenes dreamed of creating a powerful block of allies, which would link up with Ozolian Locris and Phocis and open a new route into Boeotia. The Acarnanians and Corcyraeans disliked the idea and went home. Much depended on the willingness of the Ozolian Locrians to provide javelin men, but Demosthenes did not wait for them; he proceeded, on Messenian advice, on a course of attacking Aetolian villages. Unaware of the proper rules of Greek warfare, the Aetolians took to the hills and made periodic javelin-attacks. When the Athenians ran out of archers, there was nothing to protect them and the force dissolved, losing 120 of the 300 Athenian hoplites and the general Procles; the allies also had heavy losses. Demosthenes retired to Naupactus, and sent his fleet home, remaining at Naupactus himself, 'fearing the Athenians because of his actions'. (III.94–8).

The Aetolians had been aroused and given confidence. A mission to Sparta and Corinth[111] pointed out the possibilities for an attack on Naupactus. The Spartans were convinced and, though it was somewhat late in the year, sent 3,000 allied hoplites, 500 from the newly founded colony of Heraclea Trachinia (p. 390), under the command of Eurylochus. Assembling his force at Delphi, Eurylochus shook the nominal allegiance to Athens of the Ozolian Locrians and met the Aetolians in the territory of Naupactus. He moved into the area outside the walls and took the outlying village of Molycreum; Naupactus itself was in danger, since it was doubtful whether there was enough force there to hold its wall-circuit. However, Demosthenes had had ample warning to send to the Acarnanians. Despite their disagreement with him over the Aetolian campaign, they saw that Naupactus could not be allowed to fall and shipped in a thousand hoplites; the city was now secure. (III.100–2.5).

Unlike Alcidas at Mytilene, Eurylochus, having failed in the task for which he had been sent, was flexible enough to consider other objectives. The Ambraciots convinced him that there was enough force available to clear Athenian influence out of Amphilochia and Acarnania; in a mirror-

---

[111] This is the probable time, within a year or so, of the Spartan treaty with Aetolia: *SEG* xxvi 461, cf. xxviii 408; earlier dates should not be considered. See Jeffery 1988 (F 36).

image of Demosthenes' conduct earlier in the year, he switched fronts. Though the season was far advanced, the Ambraciots sent three thousand hoplites to seize the hill town of Olpae, three miles or so north of Amphilochian Argos. The Acarnanians could not concentrate against them, since they had to watch for the approach of Eurylochus. It was now their turn to send for help, to Demosthenes at Naupactus and to a new Athenian squadron of twenty ships, evidently despatched at the initial news of Eurylochus' campaign. Every scrap of force in the region now concentrated on the south-east corner of the Gulf of Ambracia. Eurylochus joined the Ambraciots at Olpae; the Acarnanians concentrated at Argos, and were joined by the Athenian squadron and by Demosthenes from Naupactus, with two hundred Messenian archers and sixty Athenian archers. Demosthenes took over the command and marched out to Olpae. When, after five days, battle was joined, Eurylochus' larger force overlapped Demosthenes' right. But, as it curled round, an ambush of four hundred Acarnanians, planted by Demosthenes for the purpose, took Eurylochus in his rear. He was killed and the Peloponnesian line rolled up; the Ambraciots, who had been successful on their flank, were involved in the disaster and had heavy losses; only Eurylochus' Mantinean troops retreated to Olpae in any semblance of order. (III.102.5–7, 105–8).

The only Spartiate left, Menedaeus, found the situation uncomfortable. Olpae was already besieged by land and the Athenians blocked the sea. During the truce for the burial of the dead, he sought terms for an unhampered withdrawal; Demosthenes and the Acarnanians would only grant this to him and his Peloponnesians, but he nevertheless accepted. Without telling the Ambraciots, the Peloponnesians began to leave, pretending at first to be foraging and then moving faster; the Ambraciots attempted to join them, and lost another two hundred men. Demosthenes and the Acarnanians could reasonably hope that no one in those parts would trust a Spartan or a Peloponnesian for some considerable time. (III.109–11).

The reinforcements from Ambracia knew nothing of these events, and were ambushed on their way, losing in their turn more than a thousand men. No Greek city in the war, Thucydides comments, suffered so great a disaster in so short a time, and he will not give the casualty figures, since they will sound incredible. Ambracia was not quite wiped out, and put small numbers of ships to sea later in the war, but it needed a Corinthian garrison for its protection. The Acarnanians were evidently content to see its ambitions merely curbed, and gave easy terms. (III.112–14). Freed from worries about Ambracia, they captured Anactorium in 425 (IV.49) and in 424 Oeniadae at last joined the Athenian alliance (IV.77.2).

It is hard to see that this theatre of war had ultimately repaid the effort Athens had put into it, and much of the campaigning of this year gives the impression of simple action and reaction, but even that portion of the spoils which survived the journey home left no doubt that this was a substantial victory, the first clear victory over enemies for three years.[112] Demosthenes' career had seemed broken and was now restored, with some justification; he had certainly learnt a good deal about campaigning in rough country fairly rapidly.

The plague had been bad this year, and this no doubt contributed to Athenian willingness to accept an oracle which urged the purification of Delos, one of the homes of Apollo, god of plague.[113] Pisistratus had purified Delos in his time (*CAH* III².3, 403), but evidently not thoroughly enough; during the winter all discoverable graves were dug up and removed to Rheneia (cf. 1.8.1), and birth and death on Delos were henceforth forbidden. In the following spring, the old festival of the Delia was renewed on a much grander scale; perhaps the god would now be satisfied, and the solidarity of those members of the empire who looked to Delos as a cult-centre might be increased. (III.104). Further thought suggested that the god was not satisfied, and in 422 the Delians themselves were expelled as impure (v.1); this was going too far, Apollo said (v.32.1).

10. 425 B.C.

Another festival in the month before the Delia is accidentally important for us and our picture of Athens. At the Lenaea of 425, the winning comedy was the *Acharnians* of Aristophanes, the earliest of his eleven surviving plays, nine of which fall within the Peloponnesian War. Henceforth, we have closely datable evidence about some of the topics and personalities which were thought funny and newsworthy at Athens. Care, however, is needed about the presuppositions which we bring to that evidence, and we should not assume too rashly that any single analogy, whether it be comedy in any of its later forms or journalism or political cartooning, will entirely explain the methods and aims of Old Comedy. That there will have been a basic tendency to attack the prominent is obvious enough (cf. [Xen.] *Ath. Pol.* 2.18), but the seriousness of the poet's aims is harder to estimate. The *Acharnians* itself happens to be the hardest play to evaluate. Almost the only proposition about which confidence can be felt is that the Acharnian charcoal-

---

[112] For various victory dedications by Athenians and Messenians, see M–L 74 with comm. and *SEG* XIX 392.

[113] For Athenian care for Apollo-cults in this period, cf *IG* I³ 130, 131, 137, 138; the dates are all uncertain, but this is a remarkable proliferation.

burners are still (cf. p. 394) identified with extreme bellicosity, and scholars are still deeply divided as to whether the success of the farmer hero Dicaeopolis in making a separate peace for himself without the rest of the city should be read as a fantasy of successful selfishness or as a commendation of a real negotiated peace and an end to the war;[114] we can therefore hardly be certain what the play tells us about the current atmosphere at Athens.

Sicily is only mentioned in the play as a place where expensive and useless ambassadors go (line 606), and it may be doubted whether the average Athenian was clearer about what had been going on in that theatre in 426 than we are. Thucydides' details are sparse and his order suspect, to judge from the coverage of the year in the papyrus history (p. 408). Messene was certainly won over, and there was a good deal of collaboration from the native Sicels, resentful of Syracuse,[115] but we can hardly tell what reasoning lay behind the widely scattered operations, ranging as far west as Himera. Periodic visits to Italian Locri were presumably needed to encourage her neighbour Rhegium, where there was *stasis*. One effect was to provoke naval rearmament at Syracuse, and a new Chalcidian embassy convinced the Athenians that a larger fleet was necessary; it perhaps also asked for a new commander. During the winter Laches was relieved by Pythodorus,[116] as a precursor of a fleet of forty ships planned for the spring. Even before that fleet could leave, the situation worsened. Syracusan and Locrian ships recovered Messene, while a Locrian invasion held Rhegium inactive; it might even be possible to capture Rhegium before the Athenians arrived in force. (III.90, 99, 115–16, IV.1).

The normal spring invasion of Attica, under Agis, had arrived before the fleet set out, under Eurymedon and Sophocles.[117] They had acquired additional tasks. The Peloponnesians had at last heard the pleas of the Corcyraean oligarchs in their fort (p. 408) and sent sixty ships to help them against the hungry democrats in the city; Eurymedon was the expert on Corcyra, and no one would doubt that forty Athenian ships could deal with sixty from the Peloponnese. A further afterthought, perhaps produced in the Assembly (p. 381), gave Demosthenes, at present out of office, but presumably already elected for the forthcoming archon-year, some right to use the ships round the Peloponnese, if he wished. (IV.2).

He did in fact have a clear plan in mind; a year's service with the Messenians of Naupactus had suggested the possibility of establishing

---

[114] For the former see Forrest 1963 (J 37); Dover 1972 (J 32) 84–8. For the latter de Ste Croix 355–71; MacDowell 1983 (J 73).   [115] Confirmed by *IG* I³ 291 (see p. 409 n.108).

[116] It is no longer much believed that the mock prosecution of Laches by Cleon in the *Wasps* (of 422) necessarily reflects a real trial; see MacDowell's edition (1971), 164–5, 251.

[117] Not the poet, though he was general at least once in this period.

some of them in a raiding post in their own land, specifically, on the promontory of Pylos, at the north end of the present Navarino Bay. Eurymedon and Sophocles were unenthusiastic. The Peloponnesian fleet was well ahead of them, and the loss of Corcyra was certainly a greater danger than the loss of an opportunity. However, *by chance*, a storm forced the fleet into Pylos. Even here, no one would listen to Demosthenes' strategic arguments and nothing was done, until *an urge overcame* the idle expedition to fortify the place. Once the idea took hold, six days' work, with every kind of improvisation, greatly improved the naturally strong position. Eurymedon and Sophocles, now apparently partly converted to the idea, left five ships with Demosthenes and hurried on to Corcyra and Sicily.[118] (IV.3–5).

Though news had come to Sparta that this was going on, it was a time of festival and the danger was held to be neither great nor urgent. Agis and those on the expedition in Attica took a very different view and rushed for home, after a mere fifteen days of ravaging; they had in any case come too early, in a wet spring, and were hungry and uncomfortable. The Spartiates among them made straight for Pylos, summoning help from all over the Peloponnese and recalling the fleet from Corcyra; this once again (cf. p. 408) came over the isthmus of Leucas, avoiding the Athenian ships, which had reached Zacynthos. It was there that despatch ships from Demosthenes found them, to report the concentration of Peloponnesian forces and the threat to the new fort. Since the danger to Corcyra was now deferred, Eurymedon and Sophocles could reasonably think that their immediate business was with the Peloponnesian fleet, whatever their original views about the fort. (IV.6–8.4).

In order to guard against their arrival and reduce the fort without interruption, the Spartans endeavoured to block the entrances to the bay and put a hoplite force on to the island of Sphacteria, which lies across it (Fig. 38).[119] Demosthenes strengthened his position and armed his force as best he could, with help from the contingents of two vessels which arrived from Naupactus, clearly by arrangement. He correctly foresaw the part of the shore where the Spartans would try to land, and held that. The forty-three Peloponnesian ships were too many for the purpose, and attacked in relays. Brasidas was particularly vocal and active, uncharac-

---

[118] My italics mark what seem to me to be certainly loaded phrases in Thucydides (and there may be more), and indicate some doubt as to whether Thucydides has represented their previous attitude entirely correctly. That Thucydides was indicating that success at Pylos and Sphacteria was due to chance was argued by Cornford 1907 (C 24) 82–109 in an exaggerated form. Gomme's reaction (*HCT* III 488–9) goes too far; see e.g., Edmunds 1975 (C 29) 178–9, 197.

[119] Thucydides had evidently never visited the area. He habitually refers to the bay as a harbour, and greatly underestimates the length of Sphacteria and the width of the south channel. That he does not mention the lagoon on the eastern side of the Pylos promontory, separated from the bay by a sandbar, is a matter of geographical change rather than error. See in general Pritchett 1965–85 (A 100) I 6–29; Wilson 1979 (G 44); Strassler 1988 (G 38).

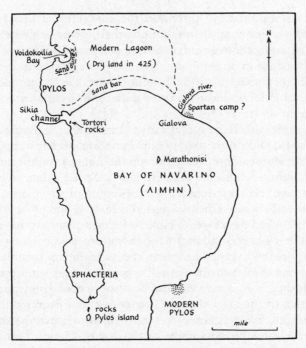

Fig. 38. Plan of Pylos–Sphacteria. (After Wilson 1979 (G 44) 143 map
8.)

teristically losing his shield, though not until after fainting from many
wounds. More than a day was spent in the fruitless attack and the
Spartans were already considering constructing siege-engines when the
Athenians arrived from Zacynthos. After a day to consider the situation,
they drew up for battle. When the Peloponnesians did not come out, they
went in, meeting virtually no opposition by sea; much of the engagement
was fought over ships already beached. At the end of the battle, Athenian
ships were sailing round Sphacteria on permanent watch. Four hundred
and twenty Lacedaemonians, of whom perhaps two-fifths were Spartiates, and notable ones (v.15.1), with their helots, were stranded on the
island. (IV.8.5–14).

The whole further course of the war was thus changed. We cannot
here consider in detail the decline of Spartiate manpower in the fifth
century,[120] but it is amply clear that the fate of the Spartiates on
Sphacteria was a matter of the gravest concern at Sparta. A high-ranking
commission, sent to the spot, concluded that the island could not be
relieved and that its garrison would be starved out or overwhelmed; it
forthwith concluded a local armistice, on the most unfavourable terms.

[120] See p. 108 n.42.

It would be legitimate to provision the garrison and the Athenians would make no move against it, but no other restrictions would be put on their freedom of movement; a Spartan embassy would go to Athens, on an Athenian ship, to negotiate a general peace, and Spartan sincerity would be guaranteed by their handing over, for the period of the armistice, the Peloponnesian fleet on the spot and all triremes in Laconia, sixty ships in all. (IV.15–16).

We may infer that there was already a disposition at Sparta to believe that the war could not be won;[121] the invasions of Attica had had no visible effect and sea-borne operations in the Aegean and the north west had been uniformly unsuccessful. All talk of Sparta's duty to her allies was forgotten, and there seems to have been no pretence of consulting them. The embassy to Athens expected an easy hearing (the Athenians had after all asked for peace in 430), and seems simply to have offered peace on the status quo and future collaboration; Thucydides gives it no further arguments except a lesson on the mutability of fortune and the desirability for the Athenians of making sure of success while they had it. Some influence from later events can be suspected, and the remainder of his narrative of the Archidamian War is cast in a form to justify the Spartan advice. It is not, however, totally surprising that the Athenians should have attempted to improve the terms. Cleon demanded the handover of the force on Sphacteria, as a guarantee of Spartan willingness to implement specific terms, particularly the return of Megara to Athenian control (see p. 387), but pressed too hard. The Spartan ambassadors were prepared to negotiate, but only in private session, and Cleon chose to treat this as a sign of insincerity; the Assembly had a right to hear. There was, however, a substantial body of opinion[122] which thought the terms good enough, and one vote had to be taken three times before they were rejected (Philochorus *FGrH* 328 F 128). (IV.17–22).

The Spartan embassy went home, and the armistice came to an end. The Spartans asked for their fleet back, but the Athenians discovered some breaches of the armistice to justify its retention; Peloponnesian naval activity was thus ended for the rest of the Archidamian War. Twenty more ships joined the blockade to bring the total up to seventy and surround the island by night; by day two ships, on opposite courses, went round and round it. Their situation was by no means comfortable: food supplies were short; there was only one spring at Pylos; there was little room for so large a force to eat, and none to beach the ships. The

---

[121] Cf. III.52.2 for an indication that the possibility of a negotiated peace had been contemplated in 427, and Ar. *Ach.* 652–3 suggests that feelers had been put out for a peace of which one term would be the restoration of Aeginetan independence.

[122] That Nicias spoke for peace is asserted by Plutarch (*Nic.* 7.2); it is not clear that he had evidence for it. On the episode see also Gomme 1962 (A 51) 104–7.

Peloponnesian army sat watching, making attacks on Pylos and waiting for some opportunity to turn up; but it had remarkable success in keeping Sphacteria provisioned, offering large rewards to anyone who could beat the blockade in small boats or as a swimmer towing skins of poppy-seed mixed with honey and crushed linseed. Over a month passed, and nothing changed. Demosthenes was considering a landing and did not like it. If the fleet's rowers were excluded, he had only seven or eight hundred fighting men and had to hold Pylos as well. The island was covered with dense scrub and he remembered his Aetolian experience. (IV.23, 26).

At Athens the mood changed; perhaps it had been too readily assumed that Sphacteria could be taken. It was already late July, and the weather would not hold indefinitely. They were having enough difficulty in provisioning the fleet in summer and, if the blockade could not be maintained, the garrison might come out in the way that its food was going in. Cleon felt the tide of opinion moving against him, as the Assembly met to discuss the situation. There are few passages of Thucydides which are as redolent of bias and dislike as the account of this Assembly, and it is by no means easy to determine how much correction is needed. The facts, after all, will turn out to be that Cleon turns from demagogue to commander and wins a great victory, and this could be said in court in the fourth century (Dem. XL.25); Thucydides would have us believe that he was trapped by his own braggadocio into a command which he did not want and somehow succeeded. His first move was to reject a suggestion that he himself go to inspect the situation. The answer, he said, must be an assault on the island and it could not be all that difficult; if the generals were real men, they would have made it already, as he would have done if he were in their place. This was aimed at Nicias, spokesman for the board, and Nicias accepted the challenge; as far as they were concerned, he could take whatever force he wanted and try. It cannot be totally excluded that Cleon really wanted this, but, if Thucydides is right that he did not, the most likely reading of the situation is that, whatever military experience he may have had, it had simply never occurred to him that he could aspire to the *strategia*, reserved so far for men of birth and wealth (Eupolis F 384 K–A; [Xen.]*Ath. Pol.* 1.3); he could not believe that Nicias was serious. Nicias pressed the point, and the Assembly took it up, shouting for Cleon to take the command. Eventually, he gave in. Even if he had not planned for this, he knew enough about what those more expert were saying to ask for the Lemnian and Imbrian cleruchs and some peltasts from Aenus who were in Athens and for the provision of four hundred archers. With these and the present force at Pylos, he would destroy the Sphacteria garrison or bring it back alive within twenty days. For that last bit of boasting he should not be excused; no operation of war is that certain. (IV.27–8).

He knew something of Demosthenes' mind, and had him associated in the command. He arrived to find the troops on the spot more than ready for the assault, as an escape from their present discomforts, and the operation had been made easier by an accidental fire which had cleared the scrub. After offering the Spartans on the mainland one more chance to surrender the garrison as a preliminary to a general peace and taking a further day for preparation, the Athenians landed eight hundred hoplites just before dawn, both from the sea and from the bay. They achieved complete surprise. As the sun came up, the rest of the force followed, not only trained troops, eight hundred archers and a similar number of peltasts, but seven or eight thousand rowers, who, except for the odd special skill, will have mostly just thrown stones. Demosthenes' aim was to fill the island with small groups, who would take any scrap of high ground; wherever the Spartans were, there would be someone in their rear or flank. (IV.29–32).

The only tactic available to the Spartan commander Epitadas, with the troops he had, was to try to close the Athenian hoplites and beat them, but this was impossible. The missiles of the light troops limited his freedom of movement and, on the rough ground, he could do nothing to catch them. Slowly the attacking force, accustomed to think of Spartans as invincible, realized that they were not, and gained confidence. The shouting became louder and louder and, in a cloud of dust and missiles, with a growing number of dead and wounded, the Spartans withdrew to the high ground at the north of the island, where they held out for most of the rest of the day, tired, thirsty and hot. Eventually, the Messenians found a way round and came out on the same level; a new Thermopylae was in the making. (IV.33–6).

This would not suit Cleon and Demosthenes, who wanted live Spartans to take back to Athens. They called off the fighting and offered quarter, which the greater part of the enemy was disposed to accept. Epitadas was dead and his second-in-command left for dead; their successor asked to consult the Spartans across the bay. The final, hardly creditable, word from there was that the survivors should use their own discretion, provided they did nothing disgraceful (*aischron*); they then surrendered. In all, 128 hoplites had died; 292 were taken to Athens, about 120 of them Spartiates.[123] Cleon was back within twenty days, his promise fulfilled. That Spartans had surrendered rather than die fighting was a great blow to Spartan prestige. Their own morale was not improved when Pylos came into use as Demosthenes intended. A Messenian garrison there started raiding territory hitherto inviolate, and

---

[123] For a shield taken on this occasion see Fig.39.

Fig. 39. Bronze shield captured from the Spartans by the
Athenians at Pylos and dedicated in the Stoa Poikile at Athens.
(After *Hesperia* 6 (1937) 346, fig. 11.)

helots began to desert to it. A succession of Spartan embassies went to
Athens to negotiate for the return of Pylos and the prisoners, without
success; the Athenians 'wanted more' and sent them away. Maddeningly,
Thucydides gives no details; he is too intent on demonstrating an
Athenian lack of moderation, which will have a price to pay. (IV.37–41).

Nicias and the regular board of generals had not ceased to plan, and
soon had a success of their own to show. A very large force, by post-
plague standards, eighty ships, two thousand Athenian hoplites and two
hundred cavalry, reinforced, for the first time that we hear of, by allied
land-forces, from Miletus, Andros and Carystus, landed on the coast of
the Corinthiad. The Corinthians had warning (cf. p. 381) of the
expedition, but, not knowing precisely where it would land, had to split
their forces. In a hard-fought engagement the Athenian cavalry was
decisive; over two hundred Corinthians were killed for the loss of fifty
Athenians. Some damage was done in Corinthian territory, but the most
permanent result, which had perhaps been the main objective, was the
establishment of another fortified raiding-post, on the isthmus of
Methana. From here Troezen, Halieis and Epidaurus were all vulnerable
to raids; life for Sparta's allies was becoming increasingly uncomfortable. (IV.42–5). Troezen had made terms for an armistice before spring
423 (IV.118.4), and Halieis came further over to Athens than that to
judge by *IG* I³ 75 (424/3?).[124]

[124] For the satisfaction felt about this expedition at Athens, see the happy chorus of Aristophanes'
Knights (595–610) of the next spring; for some elucidation of the topography, see Stroud 1971 (G 40).

At some time close to this[125] we have to fit in an event ignored by Thucydides (though known to Plutarch, *Arist.*24.5), a major reassessment of tribute (ATL I and II A9 = M–L 69 = IG i³ 71). As we have seen (p. 385), Thucydides abandons the theme of the financial strains on Athens after 428, and there is indeed reason to say that the drain on Athens' treasury was more or less stanched for a year or two after that (M–L p. 217), though we cannot fix with any precision how far allied tribute was being pushed up and how often the property-tax on wealthy citizens was resorted to.[126] Borrowing from Athena took a mild upward turn in 426/5 (M–L *ibid.*), and it is a fair, though by no means certain, inference from the language of the assessment-decree of 425 that there had been no reassessment of tribute at the Great Panathenaea of 426, as would have been normal, and that the omission was controversial. In late summer 425 there was a reassessment. The decree of Thudippus, which proposed it, is couched in exceptionally violent language, not so much against the allies, about whom the worst which is said is that no tribute shall be reduced, except in cases of manifest incapacity to pay, as against any Athenian who impedes in any way the rapid passing of the assessment through the complex procedures proposed. There is some reason[127] to suppose that Thudippus was Cleon's son-in-law and to see in the decree the hand of Cleon, closely associated with finance in the *Knights* of the next spring, forcing through a long-cherished plan in the afterglow of his victory. The list of tributes which resulted can be substantially reconstructed. It is certain that the grand total was between 1,460 and 1,500 talents, and some of the individual assessments are enormously higher than in the thirties.[128] How much realism there was about the lists is more questionable. We get the impression that any state that had ever been in the alliance or to which Athens had laid claim was included, and should not assume, for example, that the appearance of Melos, with a tribute of 15 talents, proves anything about its relationship to the empire. That the old subjects of Mytilene (p. 406) appear is reasonable, but could Athens really expect to collect from over forty states in the Black Sea? Nevertheless, there are some very large tributes from states firmly in Athenian control, and it is more than surprising that this assessment does not appear as a factor when Thucydides has to discuss allied attitudes to Athens in the next year. The tradition known to Plutarch asserted that the cause of the assessment was not so much the length and expense of the war as excessive public expenditure on distributions to the *demos* and construction of statues and temples. We

---

[125] See Chronological Notes, p. 503.

[126] Ar. *Knights* 923–6 suggests it is a familiar institution in 424.

[127] But see Bourriot 1982 (D 9) 411–18.

[128] For a more detailed discussion, see Meiggs 1972 (E 53) 324–32.

can make some guesses as to projects which might be meant by that, but one very obvious measure is the increase in jury-pay. We cannot fix precisely when it was increased from 2 to 3 obols a day, but the 3 obols are prominent in the *Knights* of the next spring, which certainly associates Cleon with the jurors. Whatever the rich might think and say about it, 3 obols does not seem an extravagant sum, as far as we can tell, and it is entirely plausible that war conditions had driven up the cost of living.

In a second, slightly later, decree, Thudippus proposed that all cities assessed should also bring a cow and a suit of armour to the Panathenaea[129] and take part in the Panathenaic procession like Athenian colonists. Both parts of the proposal have the same implication; Athens is to be recognized as the mother-city. Doubtless some allies were not flattered, but, if we remember the reorganization of the Delia in the spring, we can detect a systematic attempt to soften the picture of the tyrant-city.

Elements in our picture of Athens, quite independent of Thucydides, are not very attractive. Thucydides makes Cleon say in 427 that Athenian life is unsuspicious and not used to plots (III.37.2), but Thudippus' decree (ll.36–8) regards the slothfulness of officials as sabotage. This lends credibility to the frequency of accusations of plotting in the *Knights*, accusations which seem increasingly to have been linked with alleged oligarchic or tyrannical sympathies.[130] The temper of the mother-city was unreliable, and in late winter 425/4 Chios, the main surviving autonomous ally, whose loyalty had apparently been unshaken even during the Lesbian revolt, was ordered to pull down a new wall and give further sureties of good behaviour (IV.51).

Another event of the winter throws light on the protracted theme of the return of Persia to Greek affairs. It is clear enough that embassies had been going to Artaxerxes from both Athens and Sparta since the start of the war (Thuc. II.7.1, 67; Ar. *Ach.* 61–125, 646–51), but an Athenian squadron at the mouth of the Strymon now picked up a Persian, Artaphernes, on his way to Sparta. On him they found letters from the King, complaining of the unclarity of Spartan requirements and suggesting that an embassy with a clear mandate sent back with Artaphernes might be more efficient. The Athenians thought that there might be some profit in using Artaphernes themselves, but an embassy sent with him had got no further than Ephesus when it heard of Artaxerxes' death and turned back (IV.50). The Persian empire was then plunged into a succession crisis of considerable dimensions, and disappeared as a

[129] Whether there was anything new about this besides the compulsion is very controversial; see Meritt and Wade-Gery 1962 (C 152) 69–71.

[130] For the continuance of the theme, see Ar. *Wasps* 478–507, with which cf. Thuc. VI. 60.1 (referring to 415), and Eupolis F 193 K–A, closely comparable with American cartoons of the McCarthy era.

diplomatic factor for some time.[131] Nevertheless, at some stage, Athens did make a treaty with Darius II, the successful claimant (Andoc. III.29[132]).

One side-effect of the Pylos campaign had been to defer the planned enlargement of the Sicilian venture. When Eurymedon and Sophocles were at last free, they had to carry out their mission in Corcyra. They secured the surrender of the oligarchic fort, promising that the fate of its occupants would be an Athenian matter, but their efforts to protect their prisoners were at best half-hearted. Thucydides strongly implies that they let them be butchered (it is one of the nastier stories in the history), because it would be too much of a nuisance, and would bring themselves no credit, to send them back to Athens. The fleet which was waiting for them in Sicily had a difficult summer in 425 stopping defection from the alliance. It saved its vital base at Rhegium with a small victory over the new Syracusan fleet and contrived to hold its Chalcidian friends together against the expansion of their former ally Messene, but Dorian Camarina was reported wavering. The effect of the eventual arrival of Eurymedon and Sophocles seems to have been adverse. So large a squadron provided grounds for Syracuse to arouse suspicion of Athenian ambitions, and at the Conference of Gela in summer 424 the Syracusan Hermocrates argued successfully for a policy of Sicily for the Sicilians and a general peace on the status quo. The Athenian fleet then went home. Its generals were charged with having been bribed to withdraw when they could have conquered Sicily; Pythodorus and Sophocles were exiled and Eurymedon fined. Thucydides marks a turning point in his narrative with further emphasis on Athenian overweening self-confidence, which made no distinction between possible and impossible ventures. (IV.24–5, 46–8, 58–65).

II. 424 B.C.

However, before he reached that point in his narrative, he had events to record in which Athens built more than adequately on the success of Cleon and Demosthenes. The first change from the past was negative, and Thucydides does not mention it. There was no invasion of Attica in

---

[131] For a discussion of this episode see Lewis 1977 (A 76) 2–3, 69–80. But it is wrong on one substantial point, antedating the earliest Babylonian evidence for recognition of Darius II by five to six months; see Stolper 1983 (B 14).

[132] The supporting evidence is M–L 70 = IG i³ 227. A new fragment of this (SEG XXXII 10; Walbank 1983 (c 173), cf.1982 (c 172)) now makes it certain that this text honours Heracleides of Clazomenae, who has been useful to Athenian ambassadors in relation to spondai with the basileus. This is surely the Heracleides who later became an Athenian general and politician and was nicknamed ὁ βασιλεύς. The date of these spondai remains uncertain; see the discussion in Lewis 1977 (A 76) 76–7, but Stolper 1983 (B 14) shows that dating the treaty to the year 424/3 (as argued by Wade-Gery 1958 (A 121) 207–11) gives a very tight timetable.

424; the Athenians had given notice (IV.41.1) that they would execute their prisoners if there were. The situation was in general transformed, and the mood of confidence is confirmed by the *Knights*; Aristophanes' references to peace are perfunctory this year.[133] The military operations of the year are certainly all distinguished by a new spirit of enterprise. The first can be put down to the new realization that Spartans were not invincible and was made possible by the elimination of the Peloponnesian fleet. The importance to Sparta of Cythera, the island off the open southern shore of Laconia, had long been recognized (cf. Hdt. VII.235). After preliminary soundings of some of its perioecic inhabitants, Nicias descended on it with sixty ships and a large force of hoplites (including Milesians again), and won it over with little effort. Some malcontents were deported, a tribute was imposed, and an Athenian base was established. (IV.53–4).

The coast of Laconia was now open to the fleet, and for seven days it did more or less as it pleased, unhindered by the small Spartan forces dispersed around the countryside, perhaps more to deter possible helot revolt than to face landing-parties. One such force did fight, and lost men and weapons; the Athenians set up a trophy over Lacedaemonians in Laconia. Thucydides, who, we happen to know for once, was 300 miles away, was given a gruesome picture of Spartan morale in this period. If it was true (and we can name at least one Spartan who was resilient enough to be planning a counter-stroke), Athens came very near winning the war that week. But the attempt was not pressed. The fleet sailed back towards Athens, made a raid on Epidaurus Limera, still in Laconia, and then burnt Thyrea, in the Cynurian borderland between Laconia and Argos. Here the Spartans had settled the dispossessed Aeginetans, but, on the approach of the fleet, their Spartan garrison deserted them, for fear of being caught in a siege. Those Aeginetans who were not killed on the spot were transported to Athens and killed there, on the orders of the Assembly, still pursuing the oldest of Athenian feuds. (IV.55–7).

Meanwhile, the long sustained pressure on Megara was at last bearing fruit. The democrats in Megara, strained by the combined effects of the regular Athenian invasions and raids from their own exile party in Pegae, had at first thought, not of returning to the democratic yoke of Athens which they had shaken off in 446, but of offering the exiles terms for return. However, a reassessment of the situation by the leaders (*prostatai*) of the *demos* suggested to them that democracy might not survive a restoration of national unity and that their own best chance of personal survival lay in handing the city over to Athens. They arranged with

[133] Comic and other evidence suggests that Cleon had remained on the generals' board and was playing on his triumph, but, though Thucydides himself was general this year, he makes no suggestion that Cleon was behind any of the operations during it.

Demosthenes and Hippocrates, Pericles' nephew,[134] that the Athenians should first seize the Long Walls which linked the city to Nisaea (p. 112), where there was a Peloponnesian garrison, and then move on the city. The conspirators successfully got the Athenian advance-force into the Long Walls, but failed in their further attempt to open the gates of the city itself. By this time 4,000 Athenian hoplites and 600 cavalry had arrived, having marched from Eleusis through the night. The generals, realizing that something had gone wrong with the plan for the city, turned the army's attention to walling off Nisaea, where the bewildered Peloponnesian garrison had long decided that Megara itself had revolted. After watching two days of busy building, it had had enough. The Peloponnesian allies would pay ransom for their liberty, and the Athenians might do as they pleased with any Spartan present; the Spartans could learn that loyalty between allies was a two-way process. The Athenians took over Nisaea and began to reorganize against Megara. (IV.66–9).

So far the Athenians had done well out of refusing peace in 425; from now on it was downhill practically all the way. Thucydides marks the transition by springing a surprise. It happened that at this time Brasidas was in the area of Sicyon and Corinth, preparing an expedition to Thrace, of which we have been given no warning. Hearing of the capture of the Megarian Long Walls, he put together 4,000 or so hoplites (about two-thirds from Corinth), sent to the Boeotians, who needed no telling about the importance of preserving Megara, and marched for Megara, hoping to save Nisaea. He was too late for that, and could not persuade the Megarians to join in an attempt to recover it. They were paralysed by the mutual suspicion of their factions, who could agree on nothing except the desirability of awaiting events. The Boeotians arrived, and their cavalry came into play. The Athenian light-armed were sent running to the sea, and there was a formal cavalry battle, without clear outcome. Brasidas then challenged a hoplite battle. He had a very mixed force, but probably outnumbered the Athenians by about seven to five. His real advantage was that he would win even if the Athenians refused battle, for then Megara would fall into his lap. And the Athenians did refuse battle; the generals reckoned that they had got most of what they had come for (see p. 387) and that Megara was not worth the risk of damage to the best of their hoplites; they withdrew. Brasidas was now admitted to Megara, and then went back to preparing his Thracian expedition. The Megarians most deeply implicated in the plot with Athens fled; the remainder brought back the exiles from Pegae. After a

---

[134] He had been *strategos* already in 426/5 (M–L 72 = *IG* i³ 369.3), but this is his first appearance in Thucydides.

purge of another hundred suspected pro-Athenians, Megara became an extreme oligarchy.[135] (IV.70-4).

Part of the reason for not pressing the attack on Megara was that Hippocrates and Demosthenes[136] had even more far-reaching plans in mind, which might convert Boeotia to democracy and bring it over to the Athenian side; they were already in touch with various Boeotian exiles and sympathetic elements there. On the return from Megara, Demosthenes went straight off to the Corinthian Gulf, where, with the Acarnanians, he at last won over Oeniadae. The idea was that, with the western allies, he would seize Siphae in the territory of Thespiae; at the same time, with the aid of Orchomenians, long hostile to Thebes, and neighbouring Phocians, the revolt of Chaeronea would be procured. While these moves distracted Boeotian attention, Hippocrates would march out with the main Athenian army and fortify the shrine of Apollo at Delium in the territory of Tanagra. With increased pressure from both ends of Boeotia, widespread democratic and anti-Theban movements could be expected. (IV.76-7).

The scheme depended on careful timing and secrecy, and secured neither. Demosthenes arrived too early at Siphae, and nevertheless found the whole Boeotian army present to secure Siphae and Chaeronea; a Phocian had betrayed the plan. That put a stop to possible Boeotian plotters. When Hippocrates marched out to Delium, he had the two days he needed to fortify it, but, while he was withdrawing, he was forced into a battle by the Boeotian army, which had had time to concentrate again at Tanagra. The Athenian right wing successfully outflanked and curled round the Boeotian left, killing a great many Thespians[137] and some of their own men, before being scattered by a Boeotian cavalry force which appeared from behind a hill. The Athenian left was already being pushed back by the Theban right; this had a depth of twenty-five men to the normal Athenian eight and pushed correspondingly harder. As night fell, the whole army broke into flight. Delium held out for seventeen days, before being stormed with the use of a primitive, but terrifying, flame-thrower. The Boeotians, who had up to that point stood on the impiety of the Athenians in occupying the shrine, at last released the Athenian dead, nearly a thousand hoplites, including Hippocrates, and many others; Boeotian losses were under five hundred, very few of

[135] At this point IV.75 reminds us, in effect, of the variety of Athens' commitments. One naval detachment cleans Mytilenean exiles out of Antandrus, where they had been threatening the whole Troad (IV.52); another, under Lamachus, collecting tribute in the Black Sea, loses ten ships in a flood and has a 150-mile march back to Calchedon.

[136] The clear implication of IV.77.1 is that Thucydides thought of Hippocrates as the senior partner, surprisingly to us.

[137] Perhaps as many as three hundred; see Clairmont 1983 (K 17) 232-4 on IG VII 1888, unknown to Gomme; IG VII 585 (Clairmont, ibid. 230-1), from Tanagra, with sixty-one citizens and two Eretrian dead, may also refer to this battle.

whom can have been Thebans. The victory, unlike Coronea (p. 133), had been over the whole Athenian army and did wonders for Theban self-esteem, so badly dented in the Persian Wars.[138] (IV.89–101).

All this was bad enough, but there was worse elsewhere. We must now return to Brasidas. The initiative for his march to the north had come from the north, from the Chalcidians in revolt from Athens who thought that the tide of Athenian success would soon turn in their direction and from Perdiccas, who suspected Athenian feelings towards him[139] and was having trouble with the Lyncestian king Arrhabaeus; he offered half the pay for any force sent.[140] A northern expedition offered Sparta some prospect of diverting Athenian pressure on the Peloponnese, and it would also be convenient to get some of the more active helots out of the country. Freedom was offered to those who were prepared to serve abroad, and Brasidas was given seven hundred of them;[141] another thousand hoplites were hired in the Peloponnese. Brasidas, who so far had had no independent command of any consequence, jumped at the idea; events would show that he was capable of improving it beyond anything dreamed of or thought desirable in Sparta. (IV.74.1, 79–80).

No one at Athens had believed the enemy capable of a long march by land. Provisioning such a march would be difficult, and there would be hostile or suspicious country to cross. But Brasidas had sympathetic Thessalians to guide him, and, by speed (he did well over 32 km on the first day, with a stop for a conference) and bluff, he got through from Heraclea to territory under Perdiccas' control in four days. Perdiccas' first task for him was to deal with Arrhabaeus, and he was not pleased when Brasidas preferred to negotiate with Arrhabaeus rather than fight him; if he was paying half the piper he wanted to call the whole programme. (IV.78, 82–3).

With the Chalcidians Brasidas moved on Acanthus, at the base of the Athos prong of Chalcidice, reaching there just before the grape harvest. There was a pro-Chalcidian party there prepared to receive him, but the *demos* was reluctant. Only concern for their fruit made them allow him in, alone, to address them. Thucydides gives him a full speech on this occasion.[142] He revived Sparta's claim to be fighting the war for Greek

---

[138] To round the troubles of the campaign, Demosthenes, landing at Sicyon to do something with the force intended for Siphae, was caught by the Sicyonian army and lost more men.

[139] Rightly; see Hermippus F 63.8 K–A and M–L 65 = *IG* I³ 61.46–51; the previous decree on the same stone (430/29?) takes a very patronizing line with him.

[140] Presumably the Chalcidians would pay the other half, but we are never told.

[141] It was said that the first two thousand to volunteer mysteriously disappeared. The relation of this recruitment to the new hoplite force of ex-helots, the *neodamodeis*, which dates to about this time (see p. 434), is not clear.

[142] This is the only Thucydidean speech which is demonstrably not free composition, in that it contains one remark (IV.85.5) which Thucydides later refers to (IV.108.5) as part of Brasidas' propaganda; it happens, as Thucydides says, to be a lie.

liberty and invited them to join in that crusade. He denied any intention of interfering in internal affairs or of imitating Athenian imperialism, and made light of Athenian ability to retaliate. He seemed both honest and attractive, and they were very worried about their grapes. A secret ballot decided on revolt, provided that he reaffirmed the pledge he had brought from home that all allies he acquired would have autonomy. He was then allowed to bring his army into the city; the small neighbouring state of Stagira, also an Andrian colony, joined the revolt. (IV.84–8).

After this bloodless victory, Brasidas and the Chalcidians went for the greatest prize. Amphipolis (p. 145) had a very small Athenian element in its population, and there were supporters both of Perdiccas and the Chalcidians; those Argilians who had been absorbed in it were particularly unreliable. There was an Athenian garrison, commanded by a general, Eucles,[143] but no warning reached him before Brasidas marched through a snowy night to force the bridge over the Strymon at dawn and appear outside the city; many were caught in the country. Eucles got a message off to Thucydides, in command of seven ships at Thasos, half a day's sail away. This is Thucydides' only command that we know of. He lets us see that he was a name to conjure with in the area. Brasidas was told that he owned gold mines there and had great influence in Thrace (see p. 1) and was convinced by this that speed was essential. He offered generous terms to all the population, whether they wanted to stay or go. The Athenians thought it would be safer to go, and no one else had much to lose. Eucles' authority collapsed and the city surrendered. Thucydides arrived in time to save the port of Eïon; elsewhere defection began to spread. The news of Delium was now known, and everything that Brasidas said about Athenian powerlessness was believed. All reports of the man himself were favourable, and revolt became fashionable. (IV.102–8.6).

At Athens confidence had been turned to terror in a few months. Amphipolis had been a source of pride, precious metals and ship-timber, and its strategic position was vital. Brasidas' original march had shown them that their allies as far as the Strymon could be reached by the Spartans, but now that control of the Strymon crossing had been lost, anything was possible. Allied opinion was reported unstable, and such garrison forces were sent out as was possible in winter.[144] Brasidas was certainly thinking on a large scale. He sent to Sparta for more troops and began to build triremes on the Strymon. While waiting for his reinforcements, he continued his winter campaign. On Athos he brought over several small cities, but ran into resistance at two for the first time. They

[143] It is not clear whether this was a regular arrangement or was occasioned by the news of Brasidas' appearance in the theatre; IV.82 is very vague about Athenian counter-measures.

[144] Somewhere we have to fit in the mysterious expedition to Euboea (p. 380) of Philochorus 328 F 130. The defeat at Delium will certainly have had some effect on opinion there; cf. the two Eretrians who may have died on the Boeotian side at Delium (n. 137).

were no great prize, and a more attractive opportunity presented itself at Torone on Sithonia, the middle prong. Treachery let him into the city, but there was tough resistance from an Athenian garrison and its local supporters, who held a fort by the sea for a day or so before an unnecessary panic sent them too running to their ships. Brasidas at last rested for what remained of the winter, that is, he strengthened the places which he held and plotted to take more. (IV.108.1, 7; 109–16).

12. 423 B.C.

His ambitious plans found no welcome at Sparta. The 'first men' there were jealous of him, and had their minds, not on greater enterprises, but on getting back the prisoners and settling the war, while he was still successful; to let him go further might even prejudice that aim.[145] We do not know who made the first approaches,[146] but an armistice was agreed, to run for a year while peace terms were discussed. The Athenians thought that, even if a general settlement could not be reached, they would at least be stopping Brasidas until they themselves were better organized to deal with him; the Spartans thought that, once the Athenians had got a taste of peace, they would be more willing to give back the men and negotiate a long-term settlement. (IV.117–19).

The armistice was not in time to stop Brasidas. His winter plotting had been in Pallene, the western prong, where there had been receptive ears, despite the presence of the Athenians at Potidaea; there they blocked the isthmus, making the peninsula, strategically, into an island vulnerable to Athenian sea-power. Here Scione revolted, so close in time to the armistice that it was arguable which event came first, and greeted Brasidas with unprecedented enthusiasm. When news of the armistice reached him, he argued about the dates and refused to give up his prize. The Athenians were furious, refused arbitration, provided for by the armistice and offered by the Spartans, and accepted Cleon's proposal to sack Scione and execute its population. Their anger was still further increased when Scione's neighbour Mende also revolted and Brasidas found reasons to accept her, sending the two cities what troops he could spare and a Spartan commander. He himself had to pay some long-

---

[145] The task of conflating IV.108.7 and 117.2 is made harder by the difficulty of settling the sense of the latter passage.

[146] We have: (a) a document setting out the detailed terms, drawn up from the Spartan point of view, and approved by a meeting of the Peloponnesian League; (b) an Athenian decree, moved by Laches, accepting the terms; (c) a note, with a Spartan date, but evidently reporting oath-taking at Athens. The oaths were sworn by the Athenian generals, Nicias, Nicostratus and Autocles, three Spartan ambassadors, and representatives from Corinth, Sicyon, Megara and Epidaurus; Sparta's allies outside the Peloponnese are not covered (for a discussion of whether they were members of the Peloponnesian League, see de Ste Croix 335–8, who concludes that they were, but recalcitrant on this occasion).

deferred attention to his paymaster Perdiccas and assist another expedition against Arrhabaeus. It was a difficult campaign and he had one eye
over his shoulder on the situation at Mende; Perdiccas began to regret
his switch from Athens to Sparta. (IV.120–8).

By the time Brasidas extricated himself from this campaign, Mende
had already fallen to the Athenian punitive expedition, under Nicias and
Nicostratus. With adequate naval power and Potidaea as a base, they
could press both cities. The democratic party in Mende rapidly had
second thoughts about the revolt and themselves turned on their new
allies. In the confusion the Athenians burst in and made a sensible
settlement; Mende's defection would be forgotten and they could deal
themselves with those responsible for the revolt.[147] Scione proved a
tougher nut to crack, and all that was done there this summer before the
army went home was to tighten the siege. It is, however, possible that
Perdiccas' changed attitude was helping to ease the general situation in
Thrace.[148] (IV.129–31).

The armistice had not been a great success, though it seems to have
held in the other theatres of war.[149] Sparta did make an attempt to
reinforce Brasidas, but Perdiccas used his influence in Thessaly to block
the route; only a few Spartiates got through to provide Brasidas with
some much needed officers (IV.132). If there were further negotiations,
we hear nothing of them, and the armistice was allowed to lapse.[150]

13. 422 B.C.

The Thraceward area remained the main theatre of war. Besides a
diplomatic initiative in Magna Graecia, which we discuss in the next
chapter (p. 447), the only known event elsewhere of consequence was the
loss to the Boeotians by treachery of the border fort of Panactum. Cleon
took over the Thracian command,[151] and sailed north with thirty ships;
of Athenian troops he had 1,200 hoplites and 300 cavalry, but there was
also an unspecified number of allies. The siege of Scione was no urgent

[147] Note the difficulty the generals had in restraining their troops from butchering the
population; it is not often that we get an insight into the ordinary Athenian's attitude to revolting
allies.
[148] The elaborate Athenian treaty with Perdiccas and Arrhabaeus, IG I³ 89, has often been placed
in this year, though it has also been placed around 435. It seems best to put it towards the end of
Perdiccas' reign. On the other hand, the undated treaty, IG I³ 76, by which Athens recovered some
control in Bottiaea, should belong hereabouts.
[149] There was an extreme case of return to local priorities in the Peloponnese where, in winter
423/2 (IV.134), Mantinea and Tegea, both allies of Sparta, fought a drawn battle in the interests of
their common tendency to expand into western Arcadia (p. 104).
[150] Hostilities, however, seem to have been suspended for some months beyond the original year;
there are difficulties about V.1.
[151] For a discussion of Thucydides' account of Cleon's last campaign, see Gomme 1962 (A 51)
112–21.

matter, and he took troops from the blockading force there. Whether or not it was part of his original plan, he moved across to Torone, learning that Brasidas was not there, and took it neatly and economically with an amphibious attack from two sides. The women and children were enslaved, the men, both the citizens and their allies, sent to Athens. (v.2–3).

He moved on to the mouth of the Strymon. Athens still held Eïon as a convenient base (he had Thucydides to thank for that); from there he recaptured Galepsus to the east, but not Stagira to the west. As for Amphipolis itself, he clearly reckoned that he would need more and different troops for that. He sent to Perdiccas for help and tried to hire troops in Thrace; meanwhile he waited in Eïon. Brasidas had followed him round and watched his movements closely; he too hired Thracians on a large scale. In terms of Greek forces, the armies were fairly evenly matched in number, though Cleon's force was perhaps of better quality. Cleon made a reconnaissance in force against Amphipolis, apparently still not intending battle, but his movements were clumsy and inexperienced,[152] and a sudden attack from the city caught him unprepared. He died in the battle,[153] and his force was overwhelmingly defeated, losing about six hundred Athenian dead. On the other side there were only seven dead, but one of them was Brasidas himself, who had, unknown to the Athenians, been mortally wounded; the Amphipolitans gave him a splendid funeral and heroic honours, treating him as the colony's new founder.[154] (v.6–11).

More reinforcements had been on their way to Brasidas from home, but they turned back on the news of his death, rightly judging that the mood for peace would now prove irresistible. As Thucydides judged the situation, the predominant Spartan view had been for peace ever since Sphacteria. They were disillusioned with the failure of their invasions, they wanted their prisoners back, and the raiding from Pylos and Cythera raised the ever-present prospect of a new Helot Revolt.[155] A further threat was now impending; the thirty years' peace with Argos (p. 120) was running out, and it looked as if renewing it would be far from easy; the dangers of an Athenian–Argive alliance or any allied defection to Argos were, it seemed, enormous. It was Athens, therefore, which had to be convinced of the merits of peace, and at Athens Delium and Amphipolis had wrought a great change since 425; there had been

[152] See Anderson 1965 (G 2).

[153] It is doubtful whether anyone ever managed to distinguish the facts of his death from what they wanted to believe; Thucydides does his worst, but see Diod. XIII.74.2.

[154] For what may well be the grave, see *Archaeological Reports for 1984–85*, 47. The real founder, Hagnon, was still alive and well in Athens.

[155] We are not dependent on Thucydides' judgement, since the alliance with Athens of 421 contained a specific clause (v.23.3) by which Athens would help if the helots did revolt.

something to be said for the warning that the Spartan ambassadors had given them then. Elaborate calculations have been made to determine how close Athens was to financial exhaustion, but the two most recent attempts[156] both treat the 1,000 talents reserve fund of II.24.1 as if it had disappeared, which it had not. At the worst, a quarter of the reserve of spring 431 remained intact. More relevantly to resources and morale, assessment of front-line strength by land would have shown very heavy losses, to judge by the increasing use of allied land-power and the smallness of the Athenian force Cleon took to Amphipolis. (v.13–14).

It is hard to believe that any serious war-party survived at Athens or Sparta, and the simultaneous deaths of Cleon and Brasidas were universally treated as symbolic (cf. with Thuc. v.16.1, Ar. *Peace* 261–86). Thucydides abandons attempts at impersonality here, when it might have been particularly in point, to contrast the dead men with the Athenian Nicias, eager to save his fellow-citizens from toils and to preserve his own reputation for success (Mende had evidently outweighed Scione), and the Spartan king Plistoanax, shaky in his position and eager for a diplomatic success. They were particularly concerned to see the negotiations succeed, but we hear little of the detail,[157] which took the whole winter. Apparently, the Athenians were thought to be sticking on some points towards the end, and the Spartans applied the pressure of proclaiming an expedition to establish a fort in Attica. But the Spartans had trouble with their own allies and the final terms were unacceptable to Boeotia, Corinth, Elis and Megara, who all declined to vote for them, as well as to the Chalcidians, so that it can reasonably be said that Sparta was determined on peace, whatever her allies thought. (v.15–17).

The framework selected was that each side should return its gains in the war (III.52.2 shows that this had been long in Spartan minds as a possible formula). The most obvious exceptions were Plataea and Nisaea. The Thebans claimed that Plataea had surrendered and not been taken by force, so the Athenians made the same claim about Nisaea. That Potidaea and Aegina, both intimately associated with the causes of the war, were now Athenian settlements was tacitly forgotten, and there was a similar silence about the changes in the region of Acarnania. Sparta also in effect gave up all pretence of interest in the north. Amphipolis would be returned, and the Athenians could do as they pleased with any city in their control, including Scione, which was not; later in the summer it did fall, and Cleon's savage proposal (p. 428) was carried out (v.32.1, without comment). As for the main Chalcidian states in revolt, an

---

[156] *ALT* III 341–5, Gomme, *HCT* III 687–9.
[157] Laches was also involved as an Athenian negotiator (v.43.2); see also Andrewes and Lewis 1957 (G 7).

extraordinary formula declared them neutral and autonomous, provided they paid the tribute 'as assessed by Aristides'; if they did this, Athens was not to take up arms against them; if she persuaded them to return to her alliance, Sparta would have no objection. Panactum would also be returned. None of this cost Sparta anything. In return, Athens would give back Pylos and Cythera to Sparta and satisfy Sparta's allies in the eastern Argolid by evacuating Methana and the Opuntian Locrians by evacuating Atalante. There would be a general exchange of prisoners; it was clear enough who would principally benefit by that. After ten years of war, Sparta had abandoned, not only all attempt to destroy the Athenian empire, but also some cherished interests of major allies, bargaining the liberation of Greece for the security of her own system. Athens had won the war. (v.18–19).

CHAPTER 10

THE PEACE OF NICIAS AND THE SICILIAN EXPEDITION

A. ANDREWES

I. THE FAILURE OF THE PEACE

Athens had won the war, but it quickly proved to be a hollow victory. Sparta had abandoned her project of liberating the subjects of Athens and her own alliance was in some disarray, but she was very far from being crushed; and though the terms of the Peace of Nicias were decidedly favourable to Athens the latter was in no position to enforce them. There follows a period of confused negotiation and inconclusive conferences, on which Thucydides has not succeeded in imposing that degree of order which he seems in general to aim at.[1]

The difficulty of implementing the Peace made itself felt at once. The lot obliged Sparta to act first, and she released the prisoners she held; but when Clearidas claimed that he could not hand over an unwilling Amphipolis, the home government allowed him instead merely to withdraw his troops. Roughly at the same time a meeting of her allies at Sparta reiterated the refusal of several of them to accept the Peace.[2] To counter this and for security from Argos (below), the Spartans negotiated a defensive alliance with Athens, which procured them the return of the Pylos prisoners, but nothing more, and the main effect was to foster suspicion that Sparta and Athens were conspiring against the rest of Greece. Corinthian envoys on their way home from Sparta called on the Argives to come to the rescue of the Peloponnese by setting up a defensive alliance of their own.

Argos had done well out of her neutrality in the Archidamian War (v.28.2; cf. Ar. *Peace* 475–7), and the prospect of leadership in a new alliance appealed to a people conscious of their heroic past. Further, their thirty years' peace with Sparta would shortly run out; the exact date is

---

[1] The narrative of this chapter is necessarily based on Thuc. v–vII; references not otherwise specified are to these books. For comment and bibliography down to 1970 see *HCT* IV. That v.21–83 are less coherent than the record of the Archidamian and Sicilian Wars is not simply a subjective judgement: see *HCT* v 375–8, and cf. 364–7 on IV.102–v.13. It must be remembered that Thucydides was in exile after 424.

[2] See *HCT* IV 21–2; Gomme (*HCT* III 690–2) and others take this not as a separate meeting but as a continuation of the main peace conference. Thucydides' confused account (v.21–27.1) may perhaps be a conflation of two versions written at different times (*HCT* v 428–31).

not clear (above, p. 120), but it is during winter 422/1 that Thucydides notes this (v.14.4). The weakness of Argos lay in her internal divisions: democratic sympathy with Athens in the end proved stronger than the preference of some among the upper class for oligarchy and friendship with Dorian Sparta, but not before much damage had been done. The first applicant for membership of the new alliance was Mantinea, afraid that Sparta would dismantle her minor empire in west Arcadia: later in this summer a Spartan expedition in fact took Parrasia from her control. Mantinean democracy, possibly of quite recent origin,[3] was a further bond with Argos. Next came Elis, also a democracy, in dispute with Sparta over Lepreum in Triphylia, a former dependency of Elis which Sparta had recently declared autonomous; a little later the Spartans settled there the helots who had served with Brasidas in Thrace, and the *neodamodeis*, a recently created class of helots liberated for hoplite service (above, p. 426 n. 141), first mentioned here (v.34.1). Then the Corinthians formally joined, and the cities of Chalcidice, the latter let down by Sparta in the Peace, while Corinth had not only lost Sollium and Anactorium but must also have suffered more from the war than states better sheltered from Athenian naval power. But an attempt to bring Tegea in failed; her robust loyalty to Sparta on this occasion may owe something to habitual opposition to Mantinea. The Corinthians, though discouraged, then approached the Boeotians, but they too had done well out of the war and their victory at Delium had raised their morale; they distrusted Argive democracy and were content with their existing truce with Athens. The other state that had rejected the Peace, Megara, which had not recovered its port of Nisaea, waited to see what would happen (v.28–34).

Thucydides sums this stage up by saying that the summer (of 421) was quiet, with free intercourse between Sparta and Athens, but their mutual suspicions grew. Athens had not got Amphipolis back, and Sparta did nothing to implement her verbal assurances that she would compel her reluctant allies to accept the Peace and recover for Athens the prisoners held by Boeotia and the frontier fort of Panactum captured in 422. They claimed they had done all they could and asked for Pylos, which was naturally refused, though in the end the Messenian garrison was withdrawn and settled in Cephallenia. It was hardly to be expected that Sparta should send her army out to coerce Corinth or Boeotia, and with her prestige at its present low ebb (cf. v.28.3) she had no other way to impose her will, as was demonstrated when she sent an embassy to Corinth during the summer (v.30). The Spartans were not accustomed to being frustrated in this way, and it is not surprising that some of the

[3] So Bölte 1930 (F 10) 1319–21, but others have dated it much earlier; see pp. 102–4.

ephors who took office in the autumn were, as Thucydides notes, hostile to the Peace (v.35).

In the winter two of these ephors, Cleobulus and Xenares, proposed to the Corinthian and Boeotian envoys after another inconclusive conference that Boeotia should join the Argive alliance, and the alliance then be swung round to the Spartan side. It is hard to see how this curious plot could ever have succeeded, but it attracted the boeotarchs; however, the second part of the plan had to be kept secret and could not be explained to the Boeotian councils,[4] which rejected the idea of joining in with Corinth, now in revolt against Sparta. One ingredient of the plot had been for Sparta to obtain Panactum and restore it to Athens in exchange for Pylos, and the Spartans continued to press for this, but the price the Boeotians demanded was a separate alliance with Sparta parallel to that which the Spartans now had with Athens. That would clearly contravene the undertakings Sparta had given to Athens and safeguard Boeotia against being forced to accept the Peace, and it was not till the end of the winter that the Spartans made up their minds to it. The Argives, imagining that Sparta, Athens and Boeotia were ganging up together, took fright at the prospect of their total isolation and began peace negotiations with Sparta. In fact the Spartan envoys sent to take over Panactum found that its fortifications had been completely razed. That affront greatly strengthened the position of the Athenian opponents of the Peace, and Alcibiades sent a message to Argos urging that an embassy should be sent, jointly with Elis and Mantinea, to propose an alliance with Athens. The Argives at once broke off the negotiations begun in Sparta. (v.36–44).

This is Thucydides' first mention of Alcibiades. Born around 452, he would have been thought young in any other city, as Thucydides notes, but at Athens his birth and wealth allowed him an early start; he had already tried to renew his family's Spartan proxeny, renounced by his grandfather, through services to the Sphacteria prisoners; but in the peace negotiations the Spartans preferred to deal with Nicias and Laches, and Alcibiades resented this. Here as later Thucydides gives full weight to his personal motives, but he allows that he genuinely believed the Argive alliance to be the better policy for Athens. The Argive embassy duly arrived, followed by a hasty embassy from Sparta. Alcibiades is said to have tricked the latter into denying before the Assembly what they had asserted to the Council, that they had come with full powers to negotiate, upon which he denounced their perfidy. The story has the authority of Thucydides, but it contains serious difficulties;[5] the exiled

---

[4] For the political machinery of the Boeotian League see *CAH* vi² ch.9.
[5] Hatzfeld 1951 (D 37) 89f; *HCT* IV 51–3.

historian may perhaps have accepted too readily a touched-up version of a manoeuvre by which Alcibiades discredited the embassy. Nicias, stressing Athens' gains under his treaty, obtained the despatch of another embassy to Sparta, but its demands, which inevitably included renunciation of the alliance with Boeotia, were as inevitably rejected, and nothing was obtained but the renewal of Sparta's oaths to the Peace. Athens at once concluded a defensive alliance with Argos, Elis and Mantinea (the 'Quadruple Alliance').[6] (v.43–7).

So the situation became that much clearer. At Athens the war-weariness which had recommended the Peace was yielding to anger and frustration, and the city was ready for any hostile action short of war. Sparta, humiliated by the Peace itself and by her general loss of influence, felt much the same; no more was heard of the Athenian alliance, which lost all significance if the Peace itself were in danger. The Argive alliance was developing into an outright anti-Spartan coalition, and Corinth at once withdrew; what she had proposed was an alliance to be directed against the combination of Athens and Sparta, and, if that no longer held, her interest brought her over to the Spartan side. The Boeotians would support Sparta if it came to a showdown, but meanwhile felt free for independent action, as they shortly showed. (v.48).

The threat to the cohesion of the Peloponnesian League thus became much less immediate. The fabric might be loosened by Sparta's neglect of the proclaimed interests of her allies, as Thucydides' Corinthians complain in 432 (1.68), or by her insistence that they maintained suitable constitutions, as Pericles charged (1.144.2, cf. 1.19); but from outside Argos was never strong enough or sufficiently united to challenge Sparta effectively, and from inside the League it looks as if Corinth's attitude was of decisive importance, as also the capacity of her oligarchic leaders to control the city's foreign policy. In 432 Corinth took the lead in a movement that could theoretically have developed into widespread secession, but that ended when Sparta yielded to the threat (p. 378 above). In 421/0 Corinth again took the lead and this time matters were taken further, with a new league actually created under Argive auspices and then joined by Corinth, originally with the object of protecting specifically the Peloponnese; but as relations between Sparta and Athens worsened the new league lost its usefulness to Corinth, whose leaders had no difficulty in executing a complete reversal of policy. By 395, when Corinth had already for some years refused to support Spartan campaigns, she was ready to join an overtly anti-Spartan coalition which even included her old enemy Athens; but this change of policy did affect her internal balance (see *CAH* vi[2], ch.4). The main lines of the pattern are clear enough.

[6] On the relation between *IG* i[3] 83 and Thuc. v.47 see *HCT* iv 54–62, v 457.

The Olympic festival of 420 demonstrated the general uneasiness. The Eleans excluded Sparta on the charge of having sent troops into Lepreum during the Olympic truce and failing to pay the substantial fine then imposed. Sparta denied the charge, and for fear she might intervene troops were summoned from Elis' allies; fear was increased when the wealthy Spartan Lichas, who had entered a chariot under the name of the Boeotian League, was prevented from crowning his victorious charioteer, but no disturbance followed. In the winter the colonists of Heraclea Trachinia were defeated by their neighbours and their commander was killed; in spring 419 the Boeotians took the place over, dismissing the new commander on the ground that he was incompetent and the Athenians might seize Heraclea. The Spartans were displeased, but the Boeotians fought as their allies in 418 and Heraclea was back in Spartan hands by 412 (Thuc. VIII.3.1). (V.49–52.1).

In the same spring Alcibiades, now a general, led an allied force with a small Athenian contingent 'through the Peloponnese' to Patrae, which he persuaded to build walls down to the sea; the march was a striking gesture, if not much more. Thereafter operations centred on a quarrel between Argos and Epidaurus, formally over the non-payment of dues owed to Apollo Pythaeus, a cult over which Argos presided;[7] control of Epidaurus would open a much quicker route between Athens and Argos, and would be a blow to Corinth. The summer of 419 saw only desultory operations, but in the winter the Spartans got 300 men into Epidaurus by sea. The Argives complained that Athens had not prevented this, and demanded that in return they should install the Messenian garrison in Pylos again; this they did, and they inscribed on the stela of the Peace a note that the Spartans had not kept their oaths. The proposal was made by Alcibiades, whose policy now clearly predominated. (V.52.2–56).

II. MANTINEA AND THE AFTERMATH

By 418 the Spartans had decided that some larger initiative was needed to restore their authority, but it was not till the middle of summer that their army set out for Argos under king Agis. The Argives tried to stop them at Methydrium when only their Arcadian allies had joined them, but Agis dodged round them by night and reached Phlius, where a formidable allied force had assembled. The Argives made ready to meet him on the regular road down from Nemea, but Agis divided his force and with the Spartans and a few allies reached the Argive plain by a steep mountain route further west. The Argives, hurrying back, believed they had trapped him between their own army and the city; the Spartans were

---

[7] Barrett 1954 (J 3); *HCT* IV 71–2.

equally confident, expecting the Boeotians and others to take the Argives in the rear when they arrived by the Nemea road, and it looks as if Thucydides thought this expectation the better founded. But before battle was joined two Argive leaders, one a general, approached Agis with a proposal for a truce, to be followed by negotiations for peace. Agis, who evidently favoured such negotiations, accepted a four-month truce and led his army away. The Argive general barely escaped stoning and had his property confiscated, but the truce was not repudiated. Agis, who had consulted none of his allies and only one Spartan officer, was followed by his army, obedient but complaining; and Thucydides at this point remarks that it was the finest army yet seen in Greece, capable of defeating a force twice as strong as that of the Argive coalition. At Sparta, resentment increased over the lost opportunity for a great victory, and a little later Agis with difficulty beat off proposals to raze his house and inflict an enormous fine, but he had to accept a board of ten advisers.[8] (v.57–60, 63).

Meanwhile Athenian hoplites and cavalry had arrived in Argos, and after some argument about the validity of the truce they set off for Orchomenus, which capitulated quickly. The other allies then planned to attack Tegea, but the Eleans insisted on Lepreum as the next objective, and when this was rejected they took their 3,000 men home. The threat to Tegea brought the Spartan army out again in a hurry, this time joined only by some Arcadians; the remoter allies were summoned but could not arrive in time. Agis advanced into Mantinean territory and encamped near the Heracleum, on the east side of the plain not far from the city;[9] the enemy took up a strong position on Mt Alesium close by. Agis then began an unpromising uphill attack on them, but suddenly called it off and went back into Tegeatis, where he diverted on to Mantinean land water over which the cities quarrelled because of the damage it did.[10] The allied troops, indignant that their generals had let Agis go unhindered, came down to camp on level ground, which may have been the effect Agis aimed to produce. (v.60–2, 63–5).

Next day he marched back towards the Heracleum, and encountered the allied army a short distance away. Thucydides speaks in strong terms of the alarm this caused the Spartans,[11] but in fact there was time for Agis

---

[8] In Thucydides they offer no military advice, and a probable emendation of v.63.4 (see *HCT* IV 90–1) restricts their function to consultation about the withdrawal of the army from enemy territory: that is, the objection was not to Agis' generalship but to his policy towards Argos.

[9] Pritchett 1965–85 (A 100) II ch.5.

[10] There have clearly been large changes in the hydrography of this area, and modern attempts to elucidate this manoeuvre have not proved successful: see *HCT* v 457–8, correcting IV 97–8 in the light of Pritchett's study (n.9 above).

[11] This is the one serious difficulty in Thucydides' otherwise clear account; it is hard to see how Agis can have failed to know at least the rough location of the enemy: see *HCT* IV 100–1 and v 458–60. An uncertain factor is the wood mentioned by Pausanias (VIII.11.1) but not by Thucydides, or by Xenophon or Polybius in their accounts of the battles of 362 and 207 B.C.

to draw his army up and for a last-minute attempt to alter its formation. Each army had edged to the right, as Greek armies were apt to do because of the right-hand man's fear of having his right, unshielded, side exposed, and the Spartans and Tegeates on Agis' right outflanked the Athenians on the allied left, while the Mantineans on the allied right projected beyond Agis' left to an extent that he judged dangerous. He therefore ordered the units on his left, the Scirites, Brasidas' soldiers and the *neodamodeis*, to move to the left to face the Mantineans, thus leaving a gap between them and the Spartan units next in line, while two other Spartan units from the right wing were to pass behind the line and come in to fill the gap. This order was given just as the armies were on the point of engaging; the two polemarchs from the right wing failed to carry it out, for which they were later exiled, and the gap remained. (v.66–72.1).

As a result the Mantineans put Agis' left to flight, and they and the thousand Argive picked troops next to them moved into the gap and pushed back the Spartans they encountered. But in the centre the main body of the Spartans defeated the main body of the Argives and part of the Athenian contingent, while on their right the Spartans and Tegeates enveloped the rest of the Athenians. The latter were thus in grave trouble till Agis turned to rescue his left wing, at which they could retire under less pressure, having lost the generals Laches and Nicostratus and 200 men; the Argives lost 700. The allied right could not resist Agis' main force and fled; the Mantineans lost 200, but the Argive picked troops mostly got away. Spartan losses were thought to be about 300. (v.72.3–74).

The Spartans set up a trophy and went home to celebrate the Carnea.[12] The main result of the battle was to restore their prestige, severely damaged by the surrender on Sphacteria, the betrayal of their allies in the Peace and their general irresolution; Mantinea showed that it was premature to think of a Spartan collapse, and after these years of vacillation their policy took an alarmingly positive turn. The Argive alliance had learnt that it had not the force to dominate the Peloponnese, but it too was not yet broken. An attempt at the circumvallation of Epidaurus issued only in the construction of an Athenian fort, and operations then ceased for the winter. (v.75).

The full effect of the defeat on Argos had yet to be shown. At the beginning of this winter the Spartans marched out again as far as Tegea and sent to Argos proposals for a settlement, and after much argument these were accepted. Evidently the balance of Argive politics had altered in favour of those who had negotiated the truce in the summer; Ephorus (Diod. xii.80.2–3, cf.75.7) assigned a large part in this to the corps of specially trained Argive troops mentioned above, and Aristotle's state-

---

[12] The Carnean month is equated by Plut. *Nic.* 28.2 with the Attic Metageitnion, August/ September. It was thus still high summer when the battle was fought.

ment (*Pol.*1304a25–7) that at Argos the upper class gained credit at Mantinea and tried to overthrow the democracy probably refers to this occasion, and is not entirely incompatible with Thucydides' version. Soon afterwards this preliminary accord was developed into a full alliance, in a remarkable document (v.79; see *HCT* IV 134–45) which in form set up a league based on the cities of the Peloponnese under the joint leadership of Sparta and Argos, an arrangement which Sparta could not have tolerated even on paper unless she were assured of her control of Argive policy. Athens was told to evacuate her forts in the Peloponnese; an embassy was sent to the cities of Chalcidice, last heard of in 421 when they joined an Argive alliance with very different aims; and Perdiccas was seduced from his current friendship with Athens. The latter, seeing no promising alternative, sent Demosthenes to evacuate the fort at Epidaurus. The Mantineans submitted to Sparta and gave up what remained of their Arcadian holdings. The Spartans installed a tighter oligarchy at Sicyon; and finally, about March 417, Spartan and Argive troops overthrew the democracy at Argos and set up an oligarchy. (v.76–81).

With the last step the new allies had gone too far. In the spring the Argive *demos* began to recover its nerve and to plot against the oligarchs; by midsummer they were ready, and chose the moment when the Spartans were occupied with the festival of the Gymnopaedia. The revolt succeeded after a fight inside the city. Thucydides notes, before the end of his summer of 417, that the Argives thought of renewing their alliance with Athens. That is perhaps the time when they made the first approaches; surviving fragments of the decree (*IG* I³ 86) show that it was passed in the same prytany in which the first payments were made for the expedition against Melos, i.e. well into the spring of 416. Thucydides gives no hint of this delay or of any reason for it. Meanwhile the Argives had begun to build Long Walls from their city to the sea, some five miles away, with the help of craftsmen from Athens. (v.82).

III. ATHENIAN POLICY AND POLITICS

Many historians have blamed Athens for not supporting her Peloponnesian allies with larger forces in 418, attributing this to indecision between the policies of Nicias and Alcibiades. Much has been made of a victory for the 'peace party' in the elections to the generalship in 418,[13] but Athenian elections were not of a kind to give clear-cut or lasting victory to one policy group, and the record does not suggest that Nicias had recovered much influence since 420. Thucydides' estimate of the strength of the force assembled by Sparta for the first campaign of 418

[13] E.g. Beloch 1912–27 (A 2) II.1, 348; Busolt 1893–1904 (A 12) III.ii, 1237.

should give us pause, and it is hard to feel confident that a larger Athenian contingent would have given victory over the smaller but still formidable force deployed at Mantinea.[14] In the dubious boast which Thucydides (VI.16.6) ascribes to Alcibiades in 415, that he had brought together the most powerful elements in the Peloponnese to put the Spartans to the test of a single battle at Mantinea, he is made to claim that this was done 'without great danger or expense to Athens'; and he might well have made such a claim.

Argument about Athens' recovery from the financial strain of the Archidamian War has centred on the level at which tribute was now levied on the empire. The thesis that there was a substantial lowering at the conclusion of peace has now been abandoned, largely as a result of closer study and redating of the quota-lists;[15] it seems that tributes were reduced for some but not all of the island states, while elsewhere the rates set in 425 were broadly maintained, a policy not likely to have been controversial at Athens. Andocides (III.9) says that as a result of the Peace over 1,200 talents came in annually from the tribute; this, like Thucydides' 600 for 431 (see p. 385), cannot be true of the tribute alone but may not be far out for Athens' imperial revenues as a whole. This would allow some replenishment of the reserve, but Andocides' further assertion that 7,000 talents were carried up to the Acropolis can be no indication of the amount actually saved, though it may reflect aspiration expressed in a decree. The accounts for 418/17 do not suggest acute shortage – it was the Sicilian Expedition that dissipated whatever had been accumulated – but when Alcibiades in 420 first propounded his policy of actively supporting the Peloponnesians opposed to Sparta, it may have seemed prudent to assure the Assembly that it did not involve large expenditure.

Defeat in battle and the loss of Argos brought this policy to an abrupt halt, and some effort was made to implement the alternative favoured by Nicias, re-establishing Athens' position in the north. Thucydides records preparations for an expedition to be led by Nicias, which was then abandoned, mainly because of Perdiccas' attitude; his statement that the Athenians then 'blockaded' (κατέκλῃσαν) Macedon is not easy to interpret, but it implies further Athenian activity in the north, and the accounts for 418/17 (M–L 77.4–10) include payment for at least one (earlier) expedition to Thrace. The counter-revolution in Argos opened other prospects. The despatch of craftsmen (above) involved no danger,

---

[14] Thucydides (v.68.2, 71.3) says that the Spartan army was the larger. On the implication that his figures for the Spartans' own contingent must be corrected, see HCT IV 110–17; *contra*, Cawkwell 1983 (F 16) 385–90.

[15] West 1925 (C 175); ATL III 347ff; Meritt and McGregor 1967 (C 151) 85f; M–L pp.226–7; Meiggs 1972 (E 53) 340–3. The main change is the dating of ATL list 33 to 418/17 rather than 422/1; for a new fragment of this list see Meritt 1972 (C 150A) 418–20, IG I³ 287.

though in the winter of 417/16 a Spartan army came and demolished the new walls; they then took the Argive village of Hysiae and killed all the free men captured there, an atrocity which drew no comment from Thucydides and has drawn little since. But the proposal to renew the alliance was more hazardous: when Sparta next attacked Argos Athens would be committed to military help, and even if she avoided another set battle it would be hard to avoid some clash like that which took place in summer 414 and caused the resumption of full-scale war. This was a prospect that might daunt others besides Nicias, and it accounts for the delay in making the new treaty. (v.83).

In all probability this is the context of the last ostracism, in which supporters of Nicias and Alcibiades unexpectedly combined to turn the vote against Hyperbolus, the man who had proposed holding an ostracism. Theopompus is cited (*FGrH* 115 F 96) as saying that he was ostracized for six years, and sense has been made of this by taking it as the interval between an ostracism in 417 and Hyperbolus' death in 411. But there are some grounds for thinking that Hyperbolus was still in Athens later than spring 417, and a slight emendation of the scholiast who quotes Theopompus makes the six years the period of Hyperbolus' dominance as a demagogue, from the death of Cleon in 422 to the ostracism.[16] According to Plutarch's main sources the contest was mainly between Nicias and Alcibiades, the old and the men of peace against the young warmongers, and if this is right[17] an ostracism in spring 416 makes sense: in winter 418/17 there could be no thought of reviving Alcibiades' Peloponnesian policy, whereas by winter 417/16 the issue was alive again and decision was needed, whether to renew the Argive alliance and on what terms.

By the collusion of Nicias and Alcibiades this issue was evaded, so that both were available as generals when a graver decision was made in 415; and this was the end also of ostracism as a means of choosing between two policies which had nearly equal and dangerously heated support. Decision about the alliance evidently went in Alcibiades' favour. The new treaty names Spartan aggression as the *casus foederis*, and even makes explicit provision for the possibility that Sparta may want to make peace; though the details are lost, it looks as if Athens' military commitment was much more specific than in the treaty of 420; most striking of all, a specific sum of money[18] is to be committed from the tribute. The

---

[16] Raubitschek 1955 (D 74); Connor 1968 (C 21) 160 n.36. For Hyperbolus' presence in Athens in summer 417, see Woodhead 1949 (C 180) and McGregor 1965 (D 56) 31–2, 43–6 on *IG* I³ 85.

[17] Plutarch, *Nic.* 11.10 ascribes to Theophrastus the view that Alcibiades' main opponent was not Nicias but Phaeax, and four ostraca with the latter's name survive; but we know of no issue that needed to be settled between them.

[18] The number of talents is lost; *IG* I³ 86.11 restores 'not less than forty'. The treaty is discussed in *HCT* v 261–3.

Spartans invaded the Argolid in winter 416/15 and threatened to in summer 414, and it is astonishing that outright war with Athens was avoided till 413: Thucydides comments on the fact that Sparta did not treat an Athenian raid from Pylos in summer 416, which took much booty, as releasing them from the Peace of Nicias.

It thus looks as if Alcibiades could safely have risked a straight contest with Nicias in the ostracism and the compact against Hyperbolus not only left important issues unresolved but had a damaging effect on the rest of Alcibiades' career. Hyperbolus, the 'lamp-seller', is to us a somewhat colourless figure:[19] contemporary comic poets paid him attention enough, but he carried no measure to compare with Cleon's raising of jury-pay and he did not live in Athenian memory as a great champion of the people. He was perhaps unlucky in coming to the fore under the shadow of Cleon's defeat at Amphipolis, and for the next few years the limelight was first on Nicias and the negotiation of his Peace, then on Alcibiades and his efforts to wreck it. Hyperbolus had no recorded part in all this. It is likely enough that he opposed the Peace, but if that aligned him with Alcibiades the combination can never have been easy; and the trick now played on Hyperbolus ended any hope that Alcibiades could become an accepted leader of the whole people in the style of Pericles. In 415 when Androcles, then the dominant radical leader, was whipping up feeling over the profanation of the Mysteries, Thucydides comments (VI.28.2) that Alcibiades' enemies regarded him as an obstacle to their domination that had to be removed.

It has never been easy to sum him up. His brilliance dazzled contemporaries, but the mass of detail that was accumulated about his life and character is mostly gossip-column material, no great help towards serious assessment. Historians today must rely on their interpretation of the events in which he took part, and on the judgements of his more responsible contemporaries. Thucydides' verdict must carry great weight, that personal motives predominated throughout,[20] though twice, in writing of 420 (V.43.2) and 411 (VIII.47.1), he allows that Alcibiades genuinely believed in the policies he advocated; the two speeches given to him in Book VI, in Athens and at Sparta, are in their different ways damaging; another passage, VI.15.3–4, which appears to present a revised view influenced by the military successes of 411–408, still harps on the distrust which he aroused and the consequent refusal to give him an unfettered command. Plato's more intimate portrait does not seriously conflict with Thucydides; the accounts by Xenophon and

[19] For what is known of his career see Connor 1971 (D 16) 81–2. He is there placed in the category of 'new politicians' in the style of Cleon, and the meagre data do not conflict with this, but they do not do much to clarify the concept.

[20] On the competitive character of Athenian politics at this time see Davies 1978 (A 23) 139.

others of his reception at Athens in 407 (p. 488 below), and Aristophanes' brief comment in the *Frogs* on public opinion in 405, estimate his
intentions very variously but all testify to the uneasiness of his relations
with his city. His collusion with Nicias in spring 416 did him permanent
harm.

IV. MELOS

In the same spring of 416 Alcibiades sailed to Argos and took measures
against some three hundred men still suspected of pro-Spartan sympathies; and an expedition was sent under Cleomedes and Tisias against
Melos. When the Melians refused to submit, their city was walled off and
a garrison was left to maintain the siege, which dragged on, with some
minor Athenian reverses, till a further force was sent in the following
winter, and Melos surrendered. The adult males were killed, the women
and children sold into slavery. A casual allusion to 'Melian hunger' in
Aristophanes' *Birds* (186) shows that this did not weigh on the Athenians' conscience in spring 414, but later it headed the list of atrocities to
be charged against the Athenian empire. The more complex controversy
that now surrounds it is in large part due to Thucydides' treatment of it.
His sketch of the background is meagre: Melos was a colony of Sparta,
neutral at the outbreak of war, an open enemy since Athens ravaged her
land, i.e. since Nicias' attack of 426 (p. 409). From this Thucydides jumps
directly to the expedition of 416, so that we are left with the fact of a state
of war, but no indication why an attack should have been made in this
particular year, or how the matter was presented to the allies who were
summoned to take part.[21] (v.84).

When the armament reached Melos the Athenian generals sent
envoys, who were not permitted to address the people but only the
authorities and 'the few'. The negotiations were embodied by Thucydides not in a pair of antithetic speeches but in the unique form of a
dialogue. The form makes for more vivid presentation, but the basic
purpose of the author remains a matter for argument. The Dialogue is
formally not about the morality of the eventual execution, but about the
Melian response to the Athenians' first demand, that Melos should
submit. By the time it was written the execution had taken place and was
known to the author, so that when we read what the Melians are made to
say about their impending fate we inevitably think of that as death.
Again, the Athenian expedition to Sicily had surely sailed and most
probably come to its disastrous end before the Dialogue was finished,
and critics have been very ready to see a connexion in Thucydides' mind
between that and the massacre of the Melians. That is possible, even

---

[21] See Andrewes 1960 (c 4) 1–2; *HCT* iv 156–8.

likely, but he has given no explicit indication of the kind of connexion he envisaged.[22] We have also to take account of the fact that he chose not to give us a debate in Athens about the execution,[23] and in the first instance we must keep the two questions apart, about the assault on the Melians' independence and about their execution.

Forcible incorporation in the League was nothing new, whatever we may think of its justification in a particular case; there is no reason to suppose that Thera, also neutral in 431, suffered acutely from having been compelled to join soon afterwards.[24] There is that much basis for the Athenians' claim that their demands on Melos were 'moderate', though the arguments they are given here are highly theoretical and disagreeably bleak; when they maintain that Athens' imperial position could be seriously harmed by leaving Melos alone, few modern readers will want to concede that. Thucydides, with his strong feeling for the power and glory of Athens, may have seen this differently and regarded the Melians' heroics as foolish and unrealistic; and the fact that they had been offered a relatively painless alternative might affect his view of the massacre. There is not much to show what he would have thought about that: he had at least noted the Athenians' revulsion against their first decision to execute the whole adult population of Mytilene (III.36.4), and he deplored the slaughter at Mycalessus in 413 (below, p. 458; though that is not strictly parallel), but he had no word of direct condemnation for the judicial murder of the Plataeans, and the cases of Hysiae and Scione pass without comment. His record of the Melian execution is equally bare. (v.116.4.).

It was not impossible, though it may have been difficult, for him to obtain much genuine information about what was said on this occasion; many of the topics raised are ones that would naturally come up, for instance the chances of Spartan intervention (104–5). As in less controversial speeches, it is to be assumed that he would omit matter that did not seem significant for the theoretical issues in which he was primarily interested,[25] and sharpen the expression of what he did think important. But when the Athenians at the start demand that argument should be based on what the parties really think, and follow that with the assertion that both know that justice is not applicable between states of very unequal power (89), we have moved a long way from the normal language of Greek diplomacy as it is exhibited in later published speeches. The peculiar tone of the Dialogue furnishes a main argument to those critics who regard Thucydides' speeches as his free compo-

---

[22] The passage in the Dialogue with the strongest claim to be treated as looking forward to the Sicilian venture is the disquisition on hope at v.103.1. On the danger of treating the juxtaposition of Melos and Sicily as if it had been created by Thucydides, see Dover 1973 (C 27) 41.

[23] The fact that there would be some overlap with the Mytilene debate in Book III can hardly by itself have determined Thucydides' choice.   [24] See above, p. 409 n. 110.   [25] Cf. HCT v 397–8.

sition, and those who take the opposite view may still suspect that he has here more than in other instances shaped the argument to his own purposes; and to the extent that we accept this view we must ask what his purpose here was. It has been supposed by many[26] that he meant to illustrate the moral decline of Athens under the stress of war, but comparison with the line taken by the Athenians in 1.73–8 does not suggest that Thucydides envisaged a linear development from 432 to 416. The fact that Melos stands out so prominently in judgements about the Athenian empire is certainly in large part due to the attention that Thucydides' Dialogue has focused on it, but the feeling he displays elsewhere about that empire makes it questionable if he intended to produce the revulsion which most readers of the Dialogue feel. The alternative is to suppose that his mind was actually and not only formally on the original question of the coercion of Melos, and that the theoretical issue underlying the Dialogue is the question what consideration, if any, should limit the exercise of imperial power. That would not be a defence of Athens, but nor is it a vindication of Melos. This interpretation leaves Thucydides curiously insensitive to the effect his Dialogue might have,[27] but that may be right.

To return to the event itself, we are told no more about the reasons for the execution than we were told about the reasons for the original attack. Thucydides names no proposer for the decree, as he named Cleon in the case of Scione, and that tells against Plutarch's assertion that Alcibiades was the author. Mass executions came more easily now, and that can be counted a debasing effect of war, though not of the kind noted in Thucydides' famous excursus; the main cause here may simply be exasperation at the trouble and expense of reducing an island which should have known better than to offer hopeless resistance. If it was also intended to impress on others the futility of opposing Athens, the effect was entirely nullified by the Sicilian disaster.

V. SICILY: THE FIRST PHASE

In the same winter ambassadors from Segesta sought the help of their ally Athens[28] against their neighbour Selinus, assisted by Syracuse. Issues familiar from the 420s[29] were rehearsed again, and envoys were sent from Athens to investigate. In the spring they returned with 60 talents of silver and the report that more was available. Thucydides only summarizes the decision to send sixty ships under Alcibiades, Nicias and Lamachus, to help Segesta against Selinus, to restore Leontini, and what

---

[26] E.g. J. H. Finley 1942 (C 30) 208–12.
[27] Not only on modern readers; cf. Dion.Hal., *Thuc.* 37–41.
[28] For this alliance see above, p. 53.   [29] See above, p. 408.

else they thought best. Fragments of the decree (M–L 78 = IG i³ 93) show that the Assembly had first to vote whether to appoint a single general or three, and the objective is stated less precisely; Syracuse is not named, but presumably the debate went into more detail and would justify Thucydides' assumption that the real intention was to subjugate all Sicily. (vi.6).

Discussion in the form of speeches is reserved for a second Assembly, held four days later to deliberate about preparations. Nicias reopens the issue of sending an expedition at all, stressing the difficulties and the opening it might give to Athens' enemies nearer home; better to reconquer the Thraceward area, which would be easier to hold thereafter; and without naming Alcibiades he castigates the rashness and ambition of the proponents of the expedition. Alcibiades' reply is arrogant and forceful, with echoes of the more expansionist phrases attributed to Pericles in earlier books, and complete assurance that Sicilian disunity guaranteed success. Nicias, realizing that his first plea had failed, then tries to deter enthusiasm by calling for much enlarged forces, at least 100 triremes, 5,000 hoplites, archers and slingers and the rest in proportion. The Assembly, more eager than ever, gave the generals full powers to decide the scale of the armament. The debate was not secret, and there is no reason to doubt that Thucydides has the main course of it correctly, and the substance of the arguments. (vi.8–26).

Athens' interest in the west was not new. It had been clear to Thucydides, still in Athens, that the expedition of 427 was to explore the possibility of gaining control over all Sicily (iii.86.4), and the generals who assented to the Peace of Gela had been punished for not pursuing that objective more resolutely (iv.65.3). The record of that desultory[30] war, with its changes of side and internal dissension in the cities, would support Alcibiades' thesis of the rootlessness of the Siceliots and their incapacity for resolute corporate action; and since 424 another upheaval had put Messene for a time under the control of Syracuse's ally Locri (v.5.1). The *demos* of Leontini had been expelled and the upper class absorbed into Syracuse; this led to the mission of Phaeax to the West in 422, who encouraged the Leontine remnant on the spot and hoped to help them further by building a coalition against Syracuse. This got nowhere, but in 415 Leontine envoys came with those from Segesta, and their plea carried weight.

Leontini being a colony of Chalcis, they could appeal as Ionians oppressed by their Dorian neighbour, but hostility to Syracuse was not simply based on that traditional antithesis.[31] Phaeax had been well received at two Dorian cities: Camarina which was allied to the

[30] But see above, pp. 408–9, for the possibility that Thucydides' presentation is misleading.
[31] On that see Alty 1982 (A 1).

Chalcidian cities in 427 but in 424 initiated the process which led to the Peace of Gela; Acragas which had disputed the leadership of Sicily till her defeat by Syracuse in 446/5, when she retired into a surprisingly complete and sustained neutrality, which Phaeax did not in practice interrupt. Rebuffed at Gela, he concluded that the other cities would not join, and went home. Resentment against Syracuse, in spite of the phrases given to Hermocrates at VI.78.2–3, did not help Athens in 415, when only Naxus voluntarily joined her; the mere size of the force is probably a factor here, arousing suspicion about Athens' intentions.[32] In Italy fear of Locri had kept Rhegium steady in her old alliance with Athens during the earlier war, but in 415, though she alone of the Italiot cities allowed the fleet provisions, Rhegium refused the Athenians entry into the city, and declared that she would do whatever the other cities jointly decided; that looks like prevarication, for there is no other sign of concerted Italiot action, nor any likelihood of it.

Equally there was no rush to support Syracuse; the strength of the Athenian force may be a factor here too, and the poor performance of the Syracusan infantry at their first serious encounter with the Athenians will have discouraged their friends. Only minimal assistance was given at that stage, and after Nicias' victory late in 415 there might be more inclination to support Athens. The change comes with the arrival of Gylippus (p. 455), who at once got over a thousand men sent by Himera, which so far had taken no part except to refuse entry to the Athenian fleet when it passed. Subsequent recruiting journeys produced more reinforcements, till at VII.33.2 it can be said that almost all Sicily except for Acragas had joined Syracuse against the Athenians. They were not disposed to unite spontaneously, but vigorous diplomacy could unite them.

Thucydides uses the strong term ἔρως for the feeling at Athens about the expedition, and specifies the hope of the people for an inexhaustible source of public pay, to which he adds the same note of disapproval with which he had ended his account of Athens' reaction to the Peace of 424 (VI.24.3–4). In his first introduction (VI.1.1) he stressed the ignorance of the people about the size of Sicily and its population, and no answer is recorded anywhere to Nicias' question, how to hold Sicily if it were conquered; the instability which Alcibiades counted as an advantage for Athens would add to the difficulty of holding down any city that had once submitted. Nicias was also right to maintain (VI.20.2) that Athens could not in this case offer liberation or a possibly attractive change of regime (as it had been thought in 424 that the Boeotians might welcome democracy, IV.76.2). Naturally enough no one at this stage contemplated the possibility that the fleet might lose command of the sea and find its

[32] For an apparently similar reaction in 425/4 see above, p. 422.

retreat cut off. Later (II.65.11) Thucydides modified his judgement to the extent of saying that the Sicilian venture was 'not so much[33] an error in their estimate of the enemy they were to attack', but he still reckons the expedition as the worst of the mistakes committed after Pericles' death. We can hardly see this decision of the Assembly as other than disastrous. It may be conceded that the expedition could have returned safely with some result achieved, and we may even agree with what Thucydides appears to be saying,[34] that the worst could have been avoided if Alcibiades had not been recalled, but it was still an appalling gamble to send so many ships and men so far away while the tense situation in Greece was unresolved.

While preparations were under way, almost all the numerous busts of Hermes which stood in the streets of Athens were mutilated in a single night.[35] This was seen not only as a bad omen but as evidence of widespread conspiracy against the state, and the alarm was very great. Invitation to informers produced no firm evidence about the mutilation, but charges were made about sacrilegious parodies of the Mysteries, and here it was easy for his enemies to incriminate Alcibiades. Thucydides' brief account is supplemented, with a wealth of detail, from Andocides' speech 'On the Mysteries', delivered in his own defence fifteen years later: a suspect witness, from his character as well as his involvement, but since this was a case which many of the jurors would remember, the public details can mostly be trusted, as that the first information on the Mysteries was produced to an Assembly held for the generals when the fleet was on the point of sailing. Alcibiades begged for an immediate trial, but his enemies, afraid of an acquittal, procured a decision that the sailing should not be delayed, and so the expedition left with one of its commanders under the threat of recall for trial on a charge of the utmost gravity. (VI.27–9).

Denunciations followed, and many were arrested while others fled abroad. The most substantial information came relatively late, from one Dioclides (Andoc. 1.37ff) who said he had got up early for a journey to Sunium, and by the light of a full moon had seen some 300 men in the streets; later, realizing that these were the perpetrators, he named 42, including Andocides, and further arrests and flights followed. In the hope of halting the inquisition Andocides was persuaded by a fellow prisoner to confess to the mutilation. Thucydides (VI.60.2) was not sure whether the confession was true or false, and says that the clear truth was not discovered then or later; and he indicates no motive for the outrage.

---

[33] The Greek phrase οὐ τοσοῦτον does not cancel but subordinates the proposition it precedes. See Westlake 1958 (c 109).   [34] See, most recently, HCT v 423–8.

[35] On what follows see MacDowell's edition (1962) of Andocides On the Mysteries, and HCT IV 264–88.

Andocides' statement (1.61, cf.67) that Euphiletus proposed the plan to his 'club' (*hetaireia*) while they were drinking hardly helps; it was the scale of the sacrilege and the degree of organization implied that made the people suspect what Thucydides (VI.60.1) calls 'an oligarchic and tyrannical conspiracy', however improbable the mutilation may seem to us as a political act. Alcibiades could not have wished for such a bad omen for his expedition, but the ordinary man readily saw danger in upper-class behaviour that flouted law or convention, and that made the connexion in the public mind between the parody of the Mysteries and the mutilation, and so implicated Alcibiades. His danger remained, but the people accepted Andocides' confession about the mutilation. Dioclides then owned that his information was false, so most of those he had denounced were freed and this phase of the turmoil ended.

The chronology of the investigation and that of the departure of the fleet are closely connected, one main question being whether the Hermae were mutilated at a full or a new moon. Plutarch and Diodorus have stories (not identical) of an informer who claimed to have identified suspects by the light of the moon and was discredited because the night in question was a new moon, and it has always been tempting to identify this informer as Dioclides, who did claim a full moon; but Andocides, who was out to refute Dioclides, mentions this moon without comment (1.38). Probably therefore full, and taking other factors into account[36] it is likely that the mutilation took place about 25 May 415 and that the fleet sailed early in June.

So it set out, with prayers and elaborate ceremony, the largest and most magnificently equipped fleet ever despatched from a Greek harbour. At Corcyra they joined up with their allies and held a review of the whole force: 134 triremes, 5,100 hoplites, some archers and other light-armed troops; 100 ships and over 2,000 of the hoplites were Athenian, the rest from the allies. Supply ships, and freelance operators out for profit, more than doubled the number of vessels. The expedition then made its crossing, divided into three to avoid overcrowding Italian harbours, but its reception along the south coast was discouraging; only Taras and Locri actually refused water and anchorage, but no city would offer provisions till the whole fleet was reunited at Rhegium, and the Rhegines declared for neutrality (p. 448). There they waited for the return of three ships sent ahead to Segesta, which then brought the depressing report that no more money was available from Segesta in spite of earlier professions. (VI.30–32.2, 42–6).

At the ensuing conference Nicias proposed that they should sail to Selinus and try to settle the quarrel with Segesta, then return home, demonstrating Athenian power to the cities they passed. Alcibiades was

[36] See *HCT* IV 274–6.

for negotiation with the other cities and with the Sicels before attacking Syracuse and Selinus; he laid particular stress on the convenience of Messene as a base. Lamachus wanted an immediate attack on Syracuse, where surprise might bring a victory which would overawe the other cities, whereas Athenian delay would give them time to recover confidence. A later comment (VII.42.3) shows that Thucydides, like most later historians, thought Lamachus was right. In the event he added his vote to that of Alcibiades, but the diplomatic plan miscarried too. Messene offered food but refused admittance, a serious setback for Alcibiades, and the adherence of Naxus was little compensation. Catana at first refused, but while the generals were addressing the Assembly some of their troops got inside the town, and the Catanaeans in alarm agreed to an alliance, giving the Athenians the base they required. It was also reported that Camarina might join Athens, but that too came to nothing, and on return to Catana the fleet found the state galley *Salaminia*, waiting for Alcibiades and others charged with parody of the Mysteries. Andocides' confession had not stilled that panic, and their alarms even led to the Athenians sleeping one night in the Theseum under arms. A formal charge was preferred by Cimon's son Thessalus, and the *Salaminia* was despatched; the men charged followed as far as Thurii, but there they went ashore and were lost. Later Alcibiades made his way to the Peloponnese, while at Athens he and others were condemned to death in absence. (VI.47–53.1, 60–1).

The other two generals then set off with the whole fleet towards the west on an exploratory mission. Rebuffed at Himera, the only Greek city on the north coast, they went on to capture the small Sican town of Hyccara and enslaved the inhabitants; from there they turned back, the infantry by land through Sicel territory, making an unsuccessful attack on Hybla Geleatis on their way, while the fleet brought back the Sican captives who were sold for 120 talents. Nicias meanwhile collected 30 from Segesta; we are not told what he thought of the situation in western Sicily, but the sequel shows that he as well as Lamachus was now persuaded of the need for direct action against Syracuse. The Syracusans, regaining confidence, began to think of an attack on the Athenian camp at Catana, and the Athenians adroitly encouraged them through an agent; and so the entire Syracusan army was lured out to the north at the beginning of winter while the Athenians set out by night and landed in the Great Harbour of Syracuse not far from the Olympieum. Next day the Syracusans returned and offered battle, which the Athenians refused; but on the next day, when the Syracusans were less on the alert, Nicias attacked, and after a long struggle the Syracusans were put to flight. Then, after burying their dead, the Athenians sailed back to Catana to await the spring. (VI.62–71).

Thucydides gives their reasons: it was winter, and they needed cavalry and money. He makes no comment at this point, but later (VII.42.3) he criticized the withdrawal, and subsequent historians have judged the decision severely. Winter would not have been an obstacle if they had not delayed their attack on Syracuse for so long. The Syracusan cavalry, which had already prevented the Athenians from following up their victory, was a real danger which the archers and slingers of the Athenians failed to counter. The force assembled on the Athenian side next spring performed better, but later on the Syracusan cavalry again dominated. Money, Thucydides says, was not only to be sought from Athens but collected in the West.[37]

At Syracuse Hermocrates called for tighter discipline, and got the board of fifteen generals replaced by one of three, including himself. Embassies were sent to Corinth and Sparta, and a new wall was built northwards from the city to make it harder for the Athenians, if they again defeated Syracuse in the field, to wall the city off.[38] The Athenians had a further setback when the fleet went on from Catana to Messene in the hope that it might be betrayed; but Alcibiades before he left had given the plot away to the Messenian friends of Syracuse. The fleet retired to Naxus, and while it was there the Syracusans came out in force and burnt their camp at Catana. Later the Athenians made another attempt to win Camarina over, which had sent token help to Syracuse but might prove more persuadable after Nicias' victory. Thucydides gives us another debate: Hermocrates appeals to Dorian sentiment, as he could not do in the context of 424, and this time openly faces the fact that some other cities might be glad to see Syracuse humbled; the Athenian Euphemus, not otherwise known, made the most of the danger of Syracusan domination, and argued that Athenian policy called not for the enslavement of Sicily but for the establishment of free allies against their enemies. The Camarineans were not impressed and declared that, since they had alliances with both sides, they would stay out of the conflict. (VI.72–88.2).

The Syracusan plea for Spartan help was supported by Corinth, but the authorities were reluctant. Thucydides ascribes decisive effect to the intervention at this point of Alcibiades, who had been invited to Sparta under safe conduct. Handicapped by the distrust always felt for a man

[37] A fragmentary inscription at Athens (*IG* I³ 291) lists money contributions from Naxus, Catana, the Sicels and Rhegium, some of them substantial. Meritt 1957 (C 153) 200, followed by *HCT* IV 316, referred this to 415, in which case it must be seen as an effect of Nicias' first victory, and reinforces Lamachus' argument (above) on what might have been gained by a swift stroke against Syracuse at the start. But Ampolo 1987 (G 1), mainly because of Rhegium's unwelcoming attitude when the Athenians first arrived (above), revives the view of some earlier scholars that the contributions were made in the war of 427–424, and this may well be right. In that case we have no guide to what may have been collected in winter 415/14.

[38] For the position of this wall see *HCT* IV 472.

changing sides, he is made to develop unusual arguments about the nature of patriotic obligation; whether or not he spoke in such terms, Thucydides thereby distances him further from the thinking of ordinary men. He gave an alarming account of Athens' plans, after the subjugation of Sicily, to turn the resources of the West[39] against the Peloponnese; made the fruitful suggestion that a Spartan officer should be sent to command operations in Sicily; and recommended the seizure of Decelea as a measure of which the Athenians had always been afraid. The Spartans, though hesitant as always, were encouraged by this expert advice. The long interval, over a year, before they moved against Decelea, has led some to suppose that Alcibiades' advice was really tendered at a later date,[40] and others to deny that it had the effect Thucydides claims,[41] but this is to underrate the scruples Sparta still felt about breaking the Peace of Nicias. There was no delay in the appointment to the Sicilian command of Gylippus, son of that Cleandridas who after his exile in 446 had made a career for himself in the West (VI.104.2). He had the Corinthians send two ships to Messenian Asine while they made others ready. (VI.88.3–93.3).

VI. SICILY: GYLIPPUS AND THE TURN OF THE TIDE

In spring 414 the Athenians began with minor raids, before the arrival from Athens of 250 horsemen, for whom horses were to be found in Sicily, 30 horse-archers and 300 talents of silver. Syracusan preparations were concentrated on Epipolae, the high ground that slopes up to the west from the city, where they meant to station a body of 600 picked troops. The Athenians outwitted them again, landing their entire force north of Syracuse and pressing on to capture the heights before the six hundred could reach them from the meadow by the river Anapus where a review was being held. The Syracusans refused battle next day, so the Athenians fortified a post called Labdalum somewhere on the north edge of the plateau as a store for their siege materials. Next they established another base some way to the south, referred to as 'the circle', from which they began to build their circumvallation to the north at a speed which alarmed the Syracusans. (VI.94, 96–8).

Cavalry harassment failed in face of the cavalry the Athenians now had, from Segesta and the Sicels as well as their own. Hermocrates and his colleagues decided against another full-scale battle, and instead began to build a counter-wall across the line the Athenians would have to take

---

[39] At VI.90.2 the subjugation of Carthage is part of these plans (cf.15.2). In this same winter the generals in Sicily sent a trireme to Carthage proposing friendship (88.6). At 34.2 Hermocrates is credited with a proposal to ask for Carthaginian help for Syracuse in 415.

[40] Wilamowitz 1925 (C 110).   [41] Bloedow 1973 (D 7) 19–20.

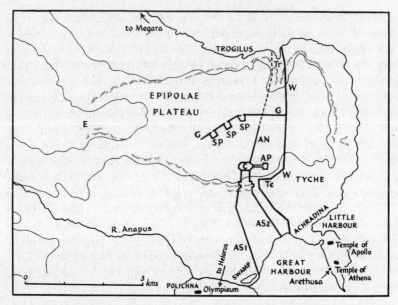

Fig. 40. Plan of Syracuse. (After Gomme *et al.* 1945–81 (C 37) IV (1970) map 2 opp. 469.)

when they brought their wall down to the level ground south of Epipolae. The Athenians did not interfere till after the work was complete, when they took it by a sudden attack, mainly the work of three hundred picked men. The next day the Athenians started to build southwards from their circle towards the harbour, and the Syracusans again tried to block them, with a palisade and ditch through the marshes to the south of the first counter-wall. The Athenian infantry then came down from Epipolae and rapidly took the stockade, and this led on to a more general battle in which the Syracusan right wing was driven back into the city while the left fled along the Anapus. The Athenian three hundred made a dash for the bridge, but the Syracusans rallied and repulsed them and went on to attack the Athenian right wing. Lamachus, coming from further left to help, crossed a ditch with only a few men and was there cut off and killed. Meanwhile the Syracusans in the city sent a detachment up on to Epipolae to attack the Athenian circle, which they hoped to find undefended; but Nicias, who had been left behind sick, ordered his attendants to set fire to the timber stacked by the circle, and this held the attackers off till the Athenians from below came to the rescue. At the same time the Athenian fleet, till now stationed at Thapsus between Megara and Syracuse, sailed into the Great Harbour. (VI.99–102).

The Syracusans were now convinced that they could not prevent the

Athenians building further, and the double wall from Epipolae to the sea was quickly brought near completion. Supplies came in to the Athenians from many parts of Italy, and three penteconters from Etruria. The discouraged Syracusans, in a common Greek reaction to ill-success, deposed their generals and elected three others in their place, and some inconclusive approaches were made to Nicias. Meanwhile Gylippus and the ships from Corinth had reached Leucas, where they were told that Syracuse was now completely walled off. To secure what he could in Italy Gylippus set off with Pythen of Corinth in four ships to Taras, and tried unsuccessfully to win over Thurii, whose troops his father had once commanded. Then, after being blown out to sea by a storm, he returned to Taras to repair his ships. Nicias had not thought this small force worth attention. (VI. 103–4).

Events in Greece foreshadowed other trouble for Athens. Desultory warfare continued between Sparta and Argos, and in summer 414 thirty Athenian ships, which had come to their ally's help, were induced to join the Argives in landings on Laconian territory. The Athenians had refused other such invitations, but now their ravaging of Epidaurus Limera and Prasiae was an unequivocal breach of the letter of the Peace of Nicias. That satisfied the Spartan conscience, hitherto troubled by the thought that in refusing the offer of arbitration in 432 they had broken the Thirty Years' Peace (see p. 370), and the way was open for the occupation of Decelea in the following spring. (VI. 105).

Gylippus and Pythen went on to Locri, where they learnt that the Athenians walls were after all not yet completed. Nicias had by now sent off four ships to intercept them, but Gylippus had already left for Himera, which agreed to join him and furnished hoplite arms for 700 men of his crews. Help was also sent by Selinus, Gela and some of the Sicels; the Sicels were more ready to join since the recent death of Archonides the powerful ruler of Herbita, a firm friend of Athens (cf. p. 164). So with a force of some 3,000 men they set off for Syracuse. The Corinthians from Leucas were now on their way, and one ship under the Corinthian Gongylus made exceptional speed and reached Syracuse shortly before Gylippus' arrival. When they learnt that he was close, the Syracusans' courage abruptly revived; they abandoned a meeting which was to have discussed negotiations and went out in full force to meet him. The Athenians made no move to prevent the junction on Epipolae; soon after, when the armies were drawn up for battle but Syracusan disarray had caused Gylippus to retire to more open ground, Nicias still did not attack. (VII. 1–3.3)

Epipolae was now the centre of action. Of the Athenian walls north of the circle, part were finished, part had been begun, and for most of the rest the stone was in place for building. First Gylippus, keeping his main force opposite the enemy fortifications, sent a detachment to capture the fort at Labdalum, out of sight of the Athenians. Then the Syracusans began a third counter-wall, out from the city to the north of the circle. The Athenians had finished the short stretch of their walls by the harbour that was still to do, and brought their army up on to Epipolae, and some minor action followed. But Nicias now decided to fortify Plemmyrium, the cape which bounds the Great Harbour to the south, so as to keep a better watch on the Syracusan fleet in the Little Harbour and reduce the distance they would have to cover to meet any enemy naval movement. Three forts were built and gear was stored there; but the area was short of water, and parties sent out for water or firewood were harassed by the Syracusan cavalry, a third of which was now stationed near the Olympieum. Thucydides dates from this point the serious deterioration of the Athenian naval force. (VII.3.4–4.6).

Gylippus went on with the counter-wall, with the forces of both sides drawn up before their walls. When he decided to attack, his first attempt was made in too narrow a space for the cavalry to operate and he was defeated. Admitting his mistake, on the next day he drew up his hoplites further outside the fortifications; the Athenians were compelled to fight, since the new wall had almost passed the line of their own, and in the less confined space the Syracusan cavalry routed the Athenian left wing and the rest were driven back to their walls, the first defeat the Athenians had suffered at Syracuse. The next night the counter-wall passed the critical point. Twelve Corinthian and other ships now arrived, after evading the twenty that Nicias had sent to intercept them, and their crews joined in the wall building while Gylippus set out to collect military and naval forces elsewhere in Sicily. The Syracusans began training for a sea fight. (VII.5–7).

In face of this Nicias sent home a letter, whose substance must be roughly as Thucydides gives it, though expressed in his individual style. After outlining the situation, he explains that his ships are waterlogged after long service, since the need to keep watch on the enemy prevented drying them out, and the crews were reduced by desertion and demoralized by their living conditions; the Athenians know that a crew cannot be kept at full efficiency for long and they must not be surprised that he is afraid for the fleet as well as for the land force. Either the expedition must be recalled, or another of no less strength sent out; and he asks to be replaced in command because of his kidney trouble. There is no knowing how far the despairing tone of the letter is due to Thucydides' presentation, but it fits his picture of Nicias and he has already noted in the narrative how Nicias lost heart at the first arrival of Gylippus (VII.4.4). Athenian actions at this stage show none of the energy displayed down to the capture of the Syracusan palisade across the marshes, and it is tempting to ascribe the change to the loss of Lamachus on that occasion; but this may be unfair to Nicias. Thucydides assigns no individual responsibility for the stratagems that got the Athenian force to Syracuse in 415 or in 414, or for the decision to retire to Catana in the winter; but he does ascribe to Nicias the victory late in 415, and Nicias' resource and competence show through in the account of the last disastrous retreat. Athenian confidence in him was undimmed, based on the record to which Thucydides alludes in v.16.1, and two comedies of spring 414 refer in passing to his skill.[42] But it was fear of taking on fresh risks that impelled him to press for peace in 422, and the same attitude appears in the debates at Athens in 415. It seems that he could not bring himself at short notice to take the steps that might have prevented Gylippus from entering Syracuse, or defeated him on Epipolae before the Syracusans had fully recovered confidence; and it is hard to believe that the circumvallation could not have been completed in time. (VII.8, 10–15).

The Athenians inevitably rejected the alternative of recalling the expedition. They would not even release Nicias, but appointed two officers on the spot to assist him, Menander and Euthydemus, while they prepared a fresh force under Demosthenes, a commander of great vigour but not consistent success, and Eurymedon who had experience in Sicily. Eurymedon set out at once, around the time of the winter solstice, with ten ships and 120 talents, and twenty ships were sent round the Peloponnese to block reinforcements that the Corinthians were getting ready. The Corinthians also manned twenty-five ships with a view to battle in the Gulf; and the Spartans, released from their scruples by the Athenian raid in the summer (p. 455), spent the winter preparing for the occupation of Decelea. In the spring the allied army set out under Agis and set about the fortification, dividing the labour between the cities. (VII.16–19.2).

A force of 600 helots and *neodamodeis* and 300 Boeotians set out from Taenarum to sail direct to Sicily, and the Corinthians sent off 500 and the Sicyonians 200, while the twenty-five Corinthian ships held off the Athenian squadron at Naupactus. In Sicily Gylippus returned with what troops he had been able to collect, and he and Hermocrates encouraged the Syracusans to challenge the Athenians by sea. They began with a combined operation, in which Gylippus led the infantry round by night for a dawn attack on Plemmyrium, while forty-five ships from the Little Harbour were to force their way into the Great Harbour and join the thirty-five there. There was a long struggle at the entrance against the thirty-five ships sent out by the Athenians, but Gylippus' surprise attack on the forts was at once successful. In the Great Harbour the Syracusans

---

[42] Aristophanes' *Birds* (363); Phrynichus' *Monotropos* (fr.22).

at first did well, but then fell into disorder and lost eleven ships to three Athenian. But the action suggested that the Athenians were not in principle invincible at sea; large quantities of stores and materials had been captured at Plemmyrium; the Athenians were now confined to a much narrower space on the shore, and provisions could no longer be brought in from outside without a fight. (VII.19.3–5, 21–4).

At home Demosthenes was ready to sail, with sixty Athenian and five Chian ships, to be supplemented with what he could collect on the way. Charicles and some Argives were landed opposite Cythera to establish a fort there, as a refuge for helots and a base for raids. Meanwhile 1,300 Thracian peltasts had arrived at Athens too late to sail with Demosthenes, and they were sent home as too expensive to use against Decelea; and Thucydides (VII.27–8) takes this occasion to describe, in part by anticipation, the effects of the occupation of Decelea.[43] Pressure on the countryside was now continuous; more than 20,000 slaves deserted; provisions from Euboea had now to be brought round by sea instead of overland through Oropus; the troops were worn out keeping watch from the walls. The cost of all this, added to the costs of the Sicilian Expedition and coupled with the loss of much internal revenue, led to the institution of a 5 per cent tax on seaborne trade in place of the allied tribute, probably in autumn 413. It was hoped that this would increase income: there is no direct evidence of the working of the new system, but collection would present problems and it is not surprising that tribute was reimposed in the summer of 410.[44] Dieitrephes, who was to escort the Thracians home, had orders to raid enemy coasts in passing, and the savage massacre perpetrated at the small Boeotian town of Mycalessus moved Thucydides to comment that it was 'as lamentable as anything suffered in the war'. (VII.20, 26–30).

The second expedition eventually assembled at Corcyra, after Demosthenes had recruited troops in the north west and Eurymedon had returned from Syracuse with the news of the loss of Plemmyrium; and Conon from Naupactus had obtained the detachment of ten ships to help him against the Peloponnesian squadron in the Corinthian Gulf. After Demosthenes' departure the latter got ready for battle and stationed themselves in the crescent-shaped bay of Erineus, to the east of the narrows, with their infantry in support on shore. Thirty-three Athenian ships, now under Diphilus, attacked them there, and three Corinthian ships were sunk while seven Athenian were badly damaged; the Corinthians had strengthened the projecting anchor-blocks[45] in their

---

[43] On these difficult chapters see *HCT* IV 400–9.

[44] Meritt 1936 (C 148) 386–9; *ATL* III 91–2; Meiggs 1972 (E 53) 438–9. Mattingly 1967 (C 142) 13–14 dissents.

[45] A beam was laid across the bow, whose projecting ends (*epotides*) are the feature here concerned. See Morrison and Williams 1968 (A 91) 198, 281–2, with fig. 9 on p.282.

bows so as to carry away the outriggers of their opponents, an innovation that was to be developed further at Syracuse. Demosthenes meanwhile crossed to Iapygia, and was well received at Metapontum; and at Thurii found that the anti-Athenian faction had been expelled and the city was ready to join him. (VII.31, 34–5).

In Sicily envoys sent by Syracuse to the western cities had collected hoplites, who had to go through the interior because Acragas refused them passage; and Nicias persuaded the Sicels to ambush them, some 800 being killed, though 1,500 got through. This, though offset by the arrival of contingents from Camarina and Gela, induced a pause in Syracusan operations, but when they heard of Demosthenes' approach they renewed their efforts to finish Nicias off first. They shortened the bows of their ships and supported the anchor-blocks with heavy struts reaching six cubits back, an improvement on the Corinthians' device. The Athenians, relying on speed and skill, had long and light bows; they avoided head-on ramming and rowed through the enemy's line or round it to attack from the rear and break the ships' oars, but their sophisticated tactics needed sea-room which inside the harbour was not available. Gylippus began by leading out his troops from the city and the Olympieum to distract attention from the sudden naval attack which followed; but the Athenians managed to get out seventy-five ships against eighty Syracusan and the battle proved indecisive. After a day's interval the assault was renewed early in the morning, but at midday the Syracusans withdrew and the Athenians assumed they had broken off for the day; but this was a stratagem of the Corinthian Ariston, by which food had been brought down to the shore for the crews to take a quick meal before resuming attack on the unfed Athenians. The latter got to sea in some disorder, and after some skirmishing decided their best plan was a quick attack. The modified prows of the enemy ships now took their toll, as did the Syracusan javelin-men on board, and the Athenians were routed with the loss of seven ships and damage to many more. The Syracusans, having in effect cut the Athenians off from the sea, hoped they could now overcome the land force. (VII.32–3, 36–41).

While they were preparing, Demosthenes and Eurymedon sailed in. Their force now comprised seventy-three ships, about 5,000 hoplites and ample light troops. Demosthenes urged that they should strike at once, without giving the enemy time to recover from their immediate consternation. The Athenians now controlled the plain of the Anapus again, but a first assault on Gylippus' counter-wall was beaten off and Demosthenes' siege-engines burnt. The alternative was to take it in the rear, and this involved an ascent in force which could not go undetected by day, so a night attack was mounted, to be led by Demosthenes and two colleagues while Nicias stayed by the Athenian fortifications. The ascent at Euryelos was unobserved and the fort there taken; and the Athenians pressed on to defeat the Syracusan élite six hundred and even began to pull the wall down. But as they advanced they lost coherence, and first the Boeotians threw them back and then a general rout began. Thucydides stresses the confusion in this, the only large night-battle of the war: the bright moonlight was not enough to distinguish friend from foe, the Athenian password became known. Apart from the casualties of the battle, many were lost and more threw down their arms in the narrow and abrupt descent from Euryelos. Syracusan hopes rose again, and Gylippus set out once more to collect fresh troops. (VII.42–6).

VII. SICILY: THE FINAL DISASTER

The Athenians, apart from this wreck of their hopes, suffered from the unhealthy position of their camp in the marshes. Demosthenes was urgent that they should sail home at once, or at least withdraw to Thapsus or Catana where conditions would be easier, and Eurymedon agreed. Nicias maintained that Syracuse was near collapse under the financial strain of war (Thucydides adds, as a statement of fact, that there was a faction in the city that still wished to negotiate); most of all, the Athenians at home would not accept the necessity of retreat and charges of bribery would be made. Then Gylippus came back with fresh Sicilian troops, and Peloponnesians who had set off in the spring but been blown off course to Libya, where Cyrene helped them on their way to Selinus. Nicias at last gave up his resistance, and secret orders had been given for withdrawal when an eclipse of the moon (27 August) caused a panic revulsion among the troops, and Nicias declared that he would not even deliberate further till the 'thrice nine days' prescribed by the seers had elapsed. (VII.47–50).

All this was quickly known to the Syracusans and highly encouraging, so after some days of practice they sailed out with seventy-six ships against eighty-six Athenian. On the Athenian right Eurymedon extended his line too far in an attempt to outflank the enemy and was cut off from the Athenian centre, and he and the ships with him were caught in a corner of the harbour and destroyed. The Syracusans then drove the main fleet back to land; some ships beached outside the Athenian stockade were attacked by Gylippus, but their Etruscan guards resisted and the Athenians saved these ships. But eighteen had been lost, and the superiority which the arrival of Demosthenes had given had now slipped away again. After a failure with a fireship the Syracusans, who could now move freely about the harbour, blocked the entrance, little more than a kilometre wide, with triremes broadside on and other boats at anchor. The Athenians, with no other hope of importing provisions, had to try

to force the entrance.[46] They therefore abandoned Epipolae and brought
the whole force down to the shore, and set afloat every ship they could to
a total of 110 and crowded on to them all the men they could. Weight was
no matter, for this was no contest of skill but a floating land-battle.
Nicias drew up the infantry to cover as large a section of the shore as he
could, while the other generals made straight for the harbour mouth and
defeated the ships stationed there. But the Syracusans, with roughly the
same number as the seventy-six ships of the last battle, had placed
themselves in a circle round the harbour, and now attacked the
Athenians from all sides before they could demolish the barrier. A long
confused struggle followed, which Thucydides does not try to disentangle in detail; instead he describes types of encounter that took place,
and the feelings of the troops who looked on and the participants. In the
end the Athenians were forced back to the shore. (VII.51–71).

They were too dispirited even to make the usual request for the return
of their dead for burial. Demosthenes noted that they still had more
seaworthy ships than the enemy – the Athenians had lost about sixty, the
Syracusans less than fifty – and proposed that they should make another
attempt to break out at dawn; Nicias agreed, but the crews refused to
embark. The Syracusans were out of action for an opposite reason.
Hermocrates suggested that they should go out at once to block the land
roads away from the city, but the authorities refused on the ground that
the troops were too far gone in celebration of their victory and of a
festival of Heracles; so instead he sent a message, as from Nicias'
Syracusan friends, to tell the Athenian generals that their route was
already blocked. The Athenians took another day to recover and
organize their retreat, and the Syracusan infantry did then set out to
block the way, while the navy sailed in unhindered to tow away the
surviving Athenian ships. (VII.72–4).

On the following day some 40,000 men took their lamentable
departure, leaving behind not only their dead but the sick and wounded
whom they could not carry. They marched in two divisions, Nicias
leading and Demosthenes behind, in a 'square' with the hoplites outside
and the light-armed and baggage within, and they crossed the Anapus,
driving off the guard there. They then turned west in the direction of the
modern village of Floridia; Thucydides' topographical indications are
not precise,[47] but the speech he gives to Nicias holds out hope of a safe
refuge among the Sicels, presumably somewhere near Acrae. On this day
they covered some 6–7 km, on the next half that distance, bringing them
to fertile and inhabited ground where they might find food and water,
but the Syracusans blocked the head of the valley before them,

[46] Before the final battle, Thucydides gives a catalogue, analysed in *HCT* IV 432–40, of the forces
involved.   [47] See *HCT* IV 455–7.

dominated by a hill named Acraeum Lepas. Two days were spent trying
to force this passage, after which they retired to more open country,
defeating an attempt to block the valley in their rear. The next day saw a
short advance, presumably to find a way round the obstacle, but at night
the generals decided to change direction and make for the sea. (VII.75–9).

Leaving many fires to deceive the enemy, they reached the shore by
dawn, Nicias in good order and well ahead; the plan was to strike inland
up the river Cacyparis (Cassibile), but their guides then sent them on to
the next river, Erineus (Cava Mammaledi, now dry). In the morning the
Syracusans hurried to catch them up. Demosthenes' contingent, less well
ordered and already labouring, was surrounded and harassed all the rest
of the day; a call to the islanders to desert found little response, but in the
end Demosthenes surrendered on the assurance, not later honoured, that
no one should be killed by violence or starvation. Only 6,000 gave up
their arms; if Thucydides' earlier figure was correct, the casualties of the
retreat must have been very great. When Demosthenes was halted Nicias
was already some 7–9 km ahead and he went on to cross the Erineus.
Next day, after being allowed to verify the fact of Demosthenes'
surrender, he offered to pay the Syracusans all their costs of war if they
would let his men go; that was refused, and the Athenians spent another
hungry night. At dawn they set off again, but at the river Assinarus
(Fiumara di Noto?) discipline collapsed, from thirst and their anxiety to
cross. The carnage in the river-bed was appalling, till Nicias personally
surrendered to Gylippus, who then ordered his troops to take prisoners;
but many became their captors' private booty, and in the confusion only
a thousand ended as state captives. Many, however, escaped to scatter
over the island, with Catana as an eventual refuge. (VII.80–5).

The prisoners were shut up in the great quarries still visible to the east
of the theatre in Syracuse, and Nicias and Demosthenes were executed,
against the wishes of Gylippus. The prisoners suffered greatly, from
stifling heat in the day and cold in the autumn nights, crowded together
and uncared for, on the most meagre rations. After seventy days some
were sold, but the Athenians and the western Greeks who had joined
them were kept on starvation rations for eight months in all; Thucydides
does not say how many survived[48] or what then happened to them.
(VII.86–7).

So the ambitious and costly venture came to its desolate end. Much
must be laid to the charge of the leaders: the withdrawal at the end of 415,
Nicias' inactivity at the time of Gylippus' arrival, his refusal to sail away
when that was still possible; the collapse of the reinforced fleet in the last

---

[48] The 100 minae given by Epicerdes of Cyrene (Dem. xx. 41–2; *IG* i³ 125) saved some from death
by hunger, but we are not told how they got out of the quarries.

battles may be put down to the poor condition of the original ships and crews, and failure of morale after the ill success of Demosthenes' one bold stroke. Thucydides' comment at VIII.96.5 (cf. VII.55.2) that the Syracusans, the closest in character to the Athenians, also fought best against them, overlooks the despair which at one time overtook them, but the spirit they showed when Gylippus had reinvigorated them justifies him.

CHAPTER 11

THE SPARTAN RESURGENCE

A. ANDREWES

I. WAR IN IONIA AND PERSIAN INTERVENTION

The news from Sicily was hard to accept at Athens, but when it was confirmed the people's anger fell on the orators and seers who had backed the expedition. They appointed a board of ten elderly men to deliberate on policy and prevent rash decision; but these are not seen to play much part in the next eighteen months and the division of responsibility between them and the democratic Council, which continued to meet, is far from clear; the oligarchic ring of their title, *probouloi* (Ar. *Pol.* 1299b31, 1323a7), may not be significant.[1] Short of ships, money and men, the Athenians feared immediate assault from Syracuse and revolt among their allies; preparations were resolutely undertaken and expenses were curtailed. Greece at large expected the fall of Athens imminently. The Spartans laid down a ship-building programme for themselves and their allies, and they too thought Syracuse would soon intervene, but no western ships appeared till late in 412 (VIII.26.1).[2] Agis in winter 413/12 went north to collect money and hostages round the Malian Gulf, which implies that Sparta had regained control of Heraclea Trachinia (cf. p. 437 above). He was also the recipient, at Decelea, of the earliest overtures from Athenian allies, first Euboea and then Lesbos. (VIII.1–3, 5.1–2).

At Sparta envoys from Chios and Erythrae were supported by one from Tissaphernes, satrap of Sardis. He had got the satrapy after helping to suppress the revolt of the former satrap Pissuthnes (Ctesias 53), at an uncertain date. Thucydides, silent about Persia since the death of Artaxerxes (IV.50.3), has said nothing of all this, but it is clearly implied in Book VIII (19.2, 28.2, 54.3) that in 412 Athens was committed to support of Amorges, the bastard son of Pissuthnes who continued or

---

[1] 'The first step . . . on the road to constitutional change', according to Hignett 1952 (D 38) 269, and the revolutionaries of 411 did make some use of them; but in Aristophanes' plays earlier that year they are merely mocked (*Lys.* 387–613; *Thesm.* 808–9).

[2] References of this type are to Thucydides, who remains the primary source till autumn 411. On the special problems of Book VIII see *HCT* v 1–4 and p. 469 below.

renewed the revolt in Caria. This substantiates Andocides' allegation (III.29) that Athens had broken her treaty with Darius II: the mere recklessness of this act assigns it to a time when Athenian confidence was high; the general at Ephesus who received a payment in spring 414 (M–L 77.78–9) could well have been there to assist Amorges, and that gives a suitable date. In winter 413/12 Darius had recently demanded from Tissaphernes, and from Pharnabazus satrap of Dascyleum, the tributes of the Greek cities of Asia which Athens had so far prevented them from collecting; and Tissaphernes was ordered to bring Amorges in, dead or alive. (VIII.5.4–5).

Tissaphernes promised pay for a fleet, while envoys from Pharnabazus brought 25 talents of silver to Sparta; the target they proposed, the Hellespont, offered better hopes of quick victory, but the Chians had sixty ships immediately available and Alcibiades was urgent in their favour, so Chios and Erythrae were taken into alliance. The Spartans moved no faster than usual, and it was not till June that a meeting at Corinth ordered that all the ships there should be hauled over the Isthmus into the Saronic Gulf, to go first to Chios, then to Lesbos, then to the Hellespont; in the event twenty-one were brought over, and still the Corinthians would not start till after the Isthmia. The Chians were by now suspect at Athens, so a contribution to the Athenian fleet was demanded, and seven ships were sent. When the Peloponnesian fleet at last set out, the Athenians chased it into Piraeus (Peiraios),[3] a deserted harbour near the border between Corinth and Epidaurus. The original plan had included the despatch of ten ships from Laconia, but after an earthquake the admiral Melanchridas was deposed and the squadron was reduced to five. The check to the main fleet's move discouraged the home authorities still further, but Alcibiades insisted that the ships should be sent before the Chians heard of the setback, and to the ephor Endius, with whom he had a family connexion, he urged the political advantage he might gain by getting in ahead of Agis. So after all the five ships sailed under Chalcideus, Alcibiades with them. The Chian oligarchs were ready, and the revolt from Athens had begun. Soon after, with another twenty Chian ships, Chalcideus reached Miletus, where Alcibiades' influence with the leading men helped to obtain the revolt of this important city, which now served as the main Peloponnesian base. (VIII.6–12, 14, 16–17).

The Athenians reacted swiftly, lifting the ban on the use of the thousand talents held in reserve since the outbreak of the war, and sending out by instalments twenty ships which from the small island of

[3] Since K. O. Müller this has usually been emended to Spiraeum, but see Bölte 1929 (F 9) and *HCT* v 24–5.

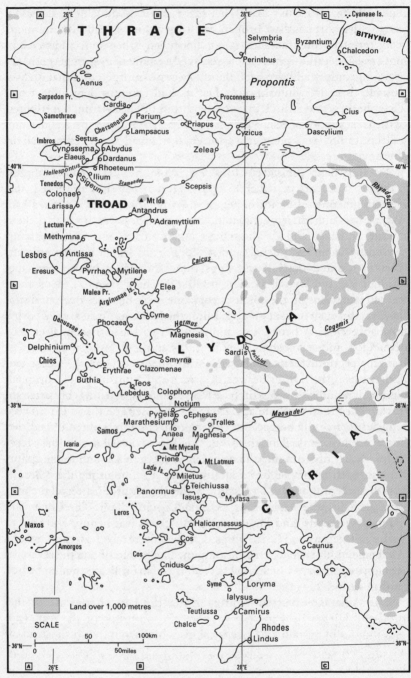

4 Western Asia Minor and the Hellespont

Lade nearby effectively besieged Chalcideus in Miletus. The stage was
thus set for some twelve months of disjointed warfare,[4] the Peloponnesians trying to extend the revolt, the Athenians to contain it. Thucydides
puts in here (VIII.16) the 'first treaty' between Sparta and Persia, a brief
working agreement which left much unsettled. Next (VIII.21) is a
popular uprising in Samos against a non-democratic regime whose
character is not wholly clear;[5] whether it was of recent installation or not,
Athens had confidence enough in it to use Samos as her base at the start
of this campaign, but equally the uprising had the goodwill of the
Athenians present. Thucydides appears not to know the decree *IG* I³ 96,[6]
not exactly dated but clearly belonging in this context, which refers to
Samians who had invited the Peloponnesians in; but he tells us that
Athens granted autonomy to Samos as being now secure. Meanwhile the
Peloponnesians had broken out of Piraeus, and four ships under the new
Spartan admiral Astyochus reached Chios, then joined thirteen Chians in
Lesbos, which had already achieved the revolt of Methymna and
Mytilene. The counter-attack was rapid and effective: twenty-five ships
under Leon and Diomedon recovered Mytilene without a blow and the
revolt elsewhere in Lesbos was soon quelled. A small Peloponnesian
land force which had set off towards the Hellespont turned back, having
probably brought over Cyme and Phocaea which soon after appear on
the Peloponnesian side. An Athenian landing at Panormus south of
Miletus brought Chalcideus and a small force to the spot, and he was
killed. Leon and Diomedon turned their attention to Chios and made
several landings, and after three defeats the Chians no longer resisted the
ravaging of their rich land. (VIII.15, 18–24).

These were only beginnings. At the end of summer a major Athenian
force reached Samos under Phrynichus and two colleagues, forty-eight
ships with 1,000 Athenian hoplites, 1,500 Argives and 1,000 islanders.
Crossing to the mainland they defeated the Milesians and their allies and
were proceeding to wall the city off when they heard, the same evening,
that the Spartan Therimenes was at hand with fifty-five ships, twenty of
them Syracusan under Hermocrates; and these sailed into the Gulf of
Iasus to Teichiussa. The Athenian generals were ready to fight them, but
Phrynichus dissuaded them, arguing that Athens' only remaining
armament must not be exposed to such risk; they should retire to Samos,
collect all the ships there, and then see what could be done. Thucydides
warmly praises Phrynichus for this, presumably with Pericles' prudence

---

[4] The incoherence of the subject matter has been made responsible for obvious incoherences in
Thuc. VIII, but the trouble goes deeper than that: see *HCT* v 369–75 and p. 469 below.

[5] Will 1969 (E 94) and others (see p. 144 n. 107) suppose that oligarchy was continuous from 439
to 412; those who assume that democracy was restored in 439, as Barron 1966 (C 181) 100, have to
suppose a brief return of oligarchy shortly before this rising. See also *HCT* v 44–7.

[6] See Lewis 1954 (C 138) 29–31.

in mind, but his judgement may be questioned. The Peloponnesians, who did not yet feel the confidence the Syracusans had acquired, steadily refused battle at this stage even when they had some superiority in numbers; but they held the initiative and could choose where to start the next revolt against Athens, as at Rhodes in winter 412/11 or when Dercylidas marched by land to the Hellespont in the next spring, and inevitably the Athenian rescue arrived too late. The Athenians' need therefore was to bring the Peloponnesians to battle and the problem was to achieve this. In the present case Therimenes would have had no option; the result might have been the disaster that Phrynichus feared, but given the numbers of the two fleets and their current standards of performance the chances of an Athenian victory were surely high, and victory at this stage, with most of the empire intact, would have done much more for Athens than the victory at Cyzicus eighteen months later. As it was, the Argives went home in anger, having lost 300 men in the land battle, and the Peloponnesians took Iasus, capturing Amorges and rich booty; his mercenaries, mostly Peloponnesians, were sent with Pedaritus to Chios. (VIII.25–8).

Early in winter 412/11 another substantial Athenian reinforcement arrived, thirty-five ships under Strombichides and two others, and the whole fleet was now brought together at Samos. Thirty ships and some hoplites were sent to Chios under Strombichides; those left at Samos were inferior in numbers to the Peloponnesians in Miletus, but the latter did not contest their control of these waters. Astyochus now set out from Chios, but after an attempt on Clazomenae his ships were scattered by a storm and got back to Chios with difficulty. Pedaritus had reached Erythrae and was ferried across to Chios, but a quarrel then arose between him and Astyochus, to whose command he was not subordinated. A further twelve ships, including ten from Thurii under Dorieus, arrived at Cnidus but half of them were soon taken by the Athenians. Astyochus then arrived at Miletus to find the fleet well supplied, from the Persian subsidy and the booty of Iasus, but the treaty with Tissaphernes was thought unsatisfactory and was re-negotiated (p. 470). (VIII.30–6).

At the battle of Miletus Alcibiades fought against the Athenians, and after it he rode to Teichiussa to summon Therimenes to the rescue of Miletus. After this[7] he fell under grave suspicion from the Peloponnesians, and Thucydides says that Astyochus received an order from Sparta to kill him; the enmity of king Agis is mentioned, but not the story found in later sources that Alcibiades had seduced his wife. This was drastic

---

[7] Lewis 1977 (A 76) 96 n.2 takes the battle here mentioned to be the small battle at Panormus (above; Thuc. VIII.24.1); but in this context (45.1) 'the' battle at Miletus must be the major battle, which was literally fought there.

action against a man who had just rendered important service and the fact of the order has been doubted;[8] but Alcibiades did disengage himself from the Peloponnesians and attach himself to the court of Tissaphernes, where he intrigued against them, representing to the satrap that the Spartans, the declared liberators of Greece, were dangerous allies and that the best policy for Persia was to keep a balance between the combatants. The satrap's weapon was his money, and at this point (45.2) Thucydides says that Alcibiades persuaded him to halve the sailors' pay from a drachma to 3 obols a day and to pay it irregularly. (VIII.26.5, 45).

It is questionable how this should be related to an earlier statement (29) that at the beginning of the winter, after the capture of Iasus, Tissaphernes paid a month's subsidy at the drachma rate, but then proposed to reduce it to 3 obols; resistance led by Hermocrates produced a compromise by which he paid slightly more. From this point Thucydides carries on a consecutive narrative (30–44), mainly concerned with the Peloponnesians, till their move to Rhodes (p. 471); he then goes back in time to the breach between Alcibiades and the Peloponnesians (45.1), starting a fresh narrative sequence which overlaps extensively with that of the preceding chapters. The dislocation greatly exceeds any to be found elsewhere in his work, and the lack of correlation between the two sequences is most eccentric. This is one of the main bases for the theory that the eighth book is unfinished not only in that it breaks off so abruptly, but that Thucydides had not yet integrated the various reports he received into a unitary narrative like that of earlier books, though down to the end of the text we have he had rendered them into his own individual style.[9] Much remains in doubt: many commentators[10] have concluded that the reduction of pay at 45.2 is simply another version of the reduction at 29; the alternative is to take 45.2 as a separate and later transaction, and while both hypotheses have their difficulties, the latter gives an easier chronology.

Tissaphernes, who was so far paying the subsidy out of his own resources, also saved money when Alcibiades as his mouthpiece resisted appeals for financial help from Chios and other Greek cities. The King might later pay the subsidy himself, and the Phoenician fleet of which much is heard for the next year was certainly the King's, from outside Tissaphernes' satrapy. We first hear of the plan to bring this fleet into play very much in passing, in the account of Alcibiades' intrigues, but it does not occur in the other sequence and we are never told when the

[8] See *HCT* v 95 and Lewis *loc. cit.*

[9] This is not the only base, and the theory has taken many forms. Already in antiquity it was realized that the character of Book VIII required some special explanation: cf. Marcellin. *Vita* 43–4.

[10] Holzapfel 1893 (C 50) 436–7, followed by many; *contra*, Steup (C 17) *ad loc.*

project was formed or when it was communicated to the Peloponnesians. Trouble over payment of the subsidy continued and worsened
while the fleet stayed in Tissaphernes' area.

The new treaty between Sparta and Persia[11] was a little more formal
than its predecessor. There are straightforward clauses about joint
conduct of the war; the Spartans are expressly forbidden to exact tribute
from the Greek cities, but the King is committed to paying 'such forces
as he has sent for', though no rate is specified. A later clause possibly
refers to separate agreements between the cities and the King;[12] though
there is no hint of this elsewhere, such agreements might explain the fact
that the cities do not seem to resent being handed over to the Persians.
Meanwhile the Athenians had fortified a strong point at Delphinium in
Chios, some 15 km north of the city with a useful harbour.[13] There was
some internal dissension in Chios, which Pedaritus dealt with harshly.
He also appealed to Astyochus for help, and when that was denied he
wrote to Sparta to denounce him. His standing in Sparta seems to have
been high, and the next Peloponnesian squadron to arrive brought a
commission of eleven Spartiates to advise Astyochus, and to depose him
if they saw fit. In fact they left him in command, so presumably they
acquitted him, though Thucydides continues to report disaffection in the
fleet. (VIII.37–39.2).

The new squadron, twenty-seven ships under Antisthenes, had been
prepared with the help of Pharnabazus' agents and carried with it
Clearchus, to command whatever ships reached the Hellespont. Setting
out around the winter solstice, near Melos they met with ten Athenian
ships; they took three, but for fear that the others would report their
presence they then made a large detour to the south and eventually
arrived at Caunus in Caria, and sent word to Miletus. Astyochus set off at
once, and arrived at Cnidus by night. An Athenian patrol of twenty ships
under Charminus was somewhere to the south watching for the ships at
Caunus, and the Cnidians urged Astyochus to sail straight on and catch
them unawares. In the course of a stormy night his fleet was scattered,
but when the encounter took place in the morning Charminus was put to
flight and lost six ships, escaping with the rest to Halicarnassus. The
combined Peloponnesian fleet concentrated at Cnidus; the Athenians
from Samos came as far as Syme and Loryma, but neither side risked an
attack. (VIII.39–43.1).

There followed a conference with Tissaphernes at Cnidus, at which
the leading Spartan Lichas objected to both the treaties that had been

---

[11] Thucydides (37) puts this after the arrival of Astyochus, but later refers to it as the treaty of
Therimenes; the latter had perhaps done the preliminary negotiation.

[12] This depends on an interpretation of the difficult wording of 37.5 which is far from agreed. See
HCT v ad loc.

[13] Full description and an account of the excavation in Boardman 1956 (G 9).

made, because they allotted to the King all the territory he or his predecessors had held. Taken literally this would have restored Persian rule in Greece as far south as Boeotia; it is unlikely that anything like that was seriously meant and it should have been easy to confine the King's claim to Asia, as in the third treaty a few months later, but Tissaphernes withdrew in perhaps simulated anger. The Peloponnesians received an opportune invitation to Rhodes, where they landed at Camirus and persuaded the whole island to revolt, contributing 32 talents to their upkeep. The Athenians, too late to stop them, based themselves on Chalce to the north and on Cos; the Peloponnesians beached their ships and remained for eighty days. The chronology of this is disputable: reckoning forward from the time of Antisthenes' departure from the Peloponnese these eighty days could not end before early April. (VIII.43.2–44).

II. THE BEGINNINGS OF THE ATHENIAN REVOLUTION

Before all this, plots were hatching in the Athenian camp. Alcibiades tried not only to reduce Persian help to the Peloponnesians, but to get support given to Athens, which would facilitate his return there. Thucydides, though doubtful about Tissaphernes' mind, seems to have believed that Alcibiades had some real influence with him, but the sequel shows that it was not enough to switch him to the Athenian side. Conversations were begun, probably in November, between Alcibiades and powerful men in the fleet at Samos, on the basis that the constitution of Athens should be changed to reassure the King. Wealthy men among the conspirators resented the increasing financial burdens of the war and wished to get control of the state into their own hands, not yet with a view to ending the war but in the hope of attracting Persian money. Alcibiades' proposals were put to the men of the fleet, who disliked the prospect of oligarchy but did not mutiny. (VIII.47–8.3).

But there was opposition from Phrynichus, who argued that Alcibiades was not interested in oligarchy as such (Thucydides agreed), only in securing his return to Athens, and that the King had no good ground for preferring Athens to Sparta. In a unique passage Thucydides presents him as opposing a plan to set up oligarchies in the allied cities; this would not increase their loyalty to Athens, for it was the upper classes at Athens who had most oppressed them, and all they wanted was their freedom. This argument found no favour, and Pisander, once a demagogue much mocked in comedy, was sent from Samos to present Alcibiades' case at Athens. But if Alcibiades were back in favour Phrynichus would be at risk, which he attempted to evade by writing to Astyochus to expose the intrigues of Alcibiades. When this odd manoeuvre backfired, he adroitly extricated himself, and the end result of the complicated affair was rather to diminish the credit of Alcibiades at Samos and to enhance his own. All this took place before Astyochus left Miletus for Cnidus, which means that the despatch of Pisander to Athens occurred not later than the latter part of December. Alcibiades kept up his efforts to bring Tissaphernes over to the support of Athens, and the quarrel with Lichas (p. 471) gave him a lever not available at any other time. (VIII.48.4–52).

Pisander can hardly have arrived in Athens later than the beginning of January 411, and Thucydides gives the impression that he put his plans for reform to the Assembly at once and left Athens when the same Assembly authorized him to negotiate with Tissaphernes. This cannot be quite right, for the meeting with Tissaphernes took place at the very end of Thucydides' winter; probably Pisander in fact spent some time after his arrival consulting with sympathizers in Athens before he made his plans public. Aristophanes in *Lysistrata* 490–1,[14] staged near the beginning of February, presents him as still up to his old tricks, trying to make money out of the war, and there is no hint of constitutional change; this suggests that something was known of a plan to get money from the Persians, but that the meeting described by Thucydides had not yet taken place. When it did, Pisander stressed enemy strength and Athenian weakness and argued that their only hope was to procure Persian help through Alcibiades. According to Thucydides' informant this silenced all opposition. That may be over-dramatized – it would be surprising if no democrat answered that Athens' position had rather improved lately – but he got his way and was appointed with ten colleagues to go and negotiate; the people disliked the proposal for oligarchy but let it stand provisionally in the belief that they could later reverse it. Pisander also obtained the deposition of Phrynichus on the ground that his decision not to fight at Miletus had caused the loss of Iasus and Amorges. (VIII.53–54.3).

Before he left he took in hand the upper-class clubs (*hetaireiai*) which, apart from their social aspect, furthered their members' interests in lawsuits and elections but had never yet joined forces for any larger purpose. This they were now urged to do, and the terrorist campaign unleashed in the summer was their work. But Aristophanes' *Thesmophoriazusae*, produced in mid-April when the programme of reform had been made public, indicates that terror had not broken out by then. There are indeed hints of impending trouble (esp.352–71), but the chorus takes a conventional democratic line, denouncing the breaking of oaths and the overthrow of law and attributing corrupt motives to the proposers of reform; and later (808–9) there is a gibe at the councillors of 413/12 who

---

[14] The evidence of Aristophanes' two plays of 411 is analysed in *HCT* v 184–93.

had surrendered powers to the *probouloi*. The clubs did not then set to work quite so soon as Thucydides' narrative suggests, but at some point after the Dionysia the murders began, and the victims included the current democratic leader, Androcles, who had had a large part in the exiling of Alcibiades (above, p. 443), and no one sought the culprits. Thucydides gives a vivid picture of the general mistrust: some unexpected figures proved to be oligarchs, no man could trust his neighbour, and in their ignorance they overestimated the strength of the conspiracy. (VIII.54.4, 65–6).

Meanwhile the war went on. Leon and Diomedon, sent out to replace Phrynichus and another deposed general, made raids on Rhodes; Pedaritus was killed in an attack on the beached ships of the Athenians, and the Chians starved. Near the end of winter the Athenian conference with Tissaphernes took place, at which Pisander and his colleagues first agreed to surrender all Ionia, then the offshore islands, but at the third session they baulked at the demand that the King should be allowed to build and sail as many ships as he wished along his Aegean coast.[15] Thucydides is equivocal on the extent to which Alcibiades was responsible for the breakdown, but the King could hardly in fact have asked less for transferring support to his long-standing enemy. But the Athenians were sure that Alcibiades had deliberately wrecked a negotiation that he could have brought to a successful conclusion, so the legend of his influence over Tissaphernes survived to serve him later. (VIII.55–6).

Tissaphernes set off at once to Caunus and negotiated a third treaty with the Peloponnesians, and paid their subsidy. The King's territorial claim was now restricted to Asia, but no doubt was left about his total control there; there is no mention of the Greek cities, and it later appears that they are included in the King's territory; the ships already present are to be paid 'on the terms agreed' (not stated) until the King's ships arrive; then the Peloponnesians must provide for themselves, or if they prefer to be paid by Tissaphernes they must repay him after the war. The treaty has a formal heading with dates in Spartan and Persian terms, and the statement that it was made in the plain of the Maeander. Since the negotiations had taken place at Caunus, there was evidently a gap before ratification, in which the terms could have been referred to Sparta; it later appears that Lichas did not object to them. It is clear that the King is taking a hand, and it looks as if he had now determined to fight the war with his own fleet and to depend as little as possible on Sparta; Thucydides' anxious exploration of the possible motives of Tissaphernes may be out of place, but the operations of the King's fleet had

---

[15] His right to that might seem self-evident, and the simplest explanation of the Athenian attitude is that Persian ships had been formally excluded from the Aegean by the Peace of Callias (above, p. 122), and it seemed intolerable that they should be allowed to return.

been put in his charge and his control of the subsidy was still an important factor. (VIII.57–8).

The Peloponnesian fleet returned to Miletus intending to relieve Chios, but at the same time the Athenians came back to Samos to block them. Before this Leon, appointed to succeed Pedaritus, had reached Chios from Miletus with twelve ships, and the Chians in desperation came out to fight at sea, successfully to the extent that they had not been defeated when the battle was broken off in the evening. Dercylidas with a small force got to the Hellespont by land, and Abydus and then Lampsacus came over to him and Pharnabazus. That was a danger the Athenians could not neglect, so Strombichides hurriedly left Chios with twenty-four ships, recovered Lampsacus easily but failed at Abydus, and then crossed the strait to establish Sestus as the Athenian base in this area. This took the pressure off Chios, and Astyochus went there to bring back the ships that had gone with Leon. With his force thus concentrated he came out to offer battle to the Athenians, but they refused because of their internal dissensions. (VIII.60.2–63.2).

After the conference with Tissaphernes, Pisander and the rest came to Samos and apparently spent some time there, among other things preparing an oligarchic coup among the Samians. Though they had broken with Alcibiades and lost their hope of Persian money, the conspirators had gone too far to retreat, though they still intended to continue the war with Sparta. Half of the envoys who had come with Pisander were sent to set up oligarchies elsewhere in the empire, and Dieitrephes, designated to a command in the Thraceward area, on his way dissolved the democracy at Thasos; and in less than two months Thasos went over to the Peloponnesians, vindicating Phrynichus' expectation (p. 471). Pisander himself with the other envoys was to set up other oligarchies on his way to Athens, which he reached at the end of May or the beginning of June. (VIII.63.3–65.1).

III. THE FOUR HUNDRED

For the central events of the revolution we have two conflicting sources. Thucydides, the contemporary, was an exile dependent on information brought to him from Athens, and as in earlier parts of this book his information may not always yet be complete; but his critical intelligence was not in abeyance and he had the very great advantage of knowing many of the actors personally. The *Athenaion Politeia*, whether or not it is the direct work of Aristotle, was written nearly a century later when more varied sources were available. It is partly based on documents, which many scholars greeted with enthusiasm when *Ath. Pol.* reappeared in 1891, but they have been very variously assessed both then and later. The mainly narrative sequence, 29 and 32.2–3, not too distant from Thucydides' version but tending to exculpate the reformers, may well be based on the *Atthis* of Androtion,[16] whose father Andron belonged to the Four Hundred, but to the moderate group which in the end followed Theramenes. For the two constitutions described in 30 and 31 see below.

Before the return of Pisander the oligarchs had published a programme, including the abolition of public pay and the restriction of political rights to a body of not more than five thousand; but this, according to Thucydides, was a sham to cover the intentions of the group which in the event seized power. After Pisander's arrival a commission was set up to bring forward constitutional proposals on a fixed day: according to *Ath. Pol.* 29.2, whose source appears to quote the decree, twenty men were added to the existing ten *probouloi*. When the day came, the Assembly was summoned to Colonus a short way outside the city walls; it is not clear why.[17] The commissioners recommended only the lifting of constitutional safeguards, especially the *graphe paranomon* by which a proposal could be indicted as illegal.[18] Thucydides notes the fact that the commissioners produced no substantive proposal, but he offers no explanation; here, as in the comment noted above, he seems implicitly to deny the existence of a body of more moderate reformers opposed to the extremists, and this for him cuts out what would seem the obvious answer, that the commissioners were unable to agree. (VIII.65.3–67.2).

At this point our two main sources diverge radically. Thucydides (VIII.67.3) goes straight to what he saw as the heart of the matter, the installation of a Council of Four Hundred to be appointed on the spot by an easily manipulable procedure of indirect election; he adds that the Four Hundred were to summon the Five Thousand when they thought fit, so the decree, proposed by Pisander, provided for the creation of a body of Five Thousand; till then the Four Hundred were given absolute power. *Ath. Pol.* 29.5–30.1 ascribes the new constitution to the commissioners; five thousand is the minimum number, not the maximum as in Thucydides, for the new franchise, and the list of them is to be drawn up by a hundred cataloguers. Thus far this is roughly reconcilable with Thucydides, and Lysias xx, delivered little more than a year later in defence of one Polystratus, confirms that the Assembly had formally voted to hand power over to Five Thousand, and that cataloguers were appointed. But then, instead of the immediate creation of a new Council, *Ath. Pol.* gives us a leisurely process of reform, the appointment by the

16 This would be the obvious up-to-date source when *Ath. Pol.* was written. On the evidence of *Ath. Pol.* see Rhodes 1981 (c 83), *HCT* v 212–51; on the date of its composition see Rhodes 51–8.
17 The distance is so short that little weight can be given to the explanation sometimes given, that only armed men would venture to Colonus. The location must have some special significance which eludes us. 18 See Hignett 1952 (D 38) 360, 373.

Five Thousand of their own constitutional commission, two constitutions brought out by them (30.2–6 'for the future', 31 'for the present'), and the adoption of these by an Assembly, with the unlikely implication that the Four Hundred were established only after all this, by the not very clear provisions of 31.1.

Somewhere in this there must be a considerable element of fiction. Thucydides gives us revolution by a sudden coup, and even in exile he can hardly have got the character of the event to that extent wrong; and he was sure that no Five Thousand came into being before the fall of the Four Hundred. A persistent theory[19] holds that the process apparently spread out over a period in *Ath. Pol.* was in fact rushed through at the Colonus meeting, the details having been worked out beforehand; but this 'reconciles' *Ath. Pol.* and Thucydides by charging both with error. Almost as persistent is the view that the constitution 'for the future' is the one established after the fall of the Four Hundred,[20] but some of its provisions are so impractical that it is hard to imagine them actually being enacted, let alone put into effect. A simpler answer is more plausible, that the constitutions are fiction perpetrated by the Four Hundred themselves, published soon after their coup[21] as the work of a Five Thousand who did not exist.[22] But other solutions will continue to be argued.

At this point Thucydides names and describes the leaders of the revolution, introducing two new figures. Antiphon, the earliest in the canon of the ten Attic orators, had taken no part in public politics but helped his friends in the law courts; here he is said to be 'the man who put the whole affair together' and had given most thought to it; he was presumably responsible for the radical turn the revolution now took. In spite of the praise here given to his abilities, the sequel shows that Thucydides had no sympathy with his politics. Theramenes, more succinctly praised, is more equivocal. His father Hagnon, a colleague of Pericles and founder of Amphipolis, is found in old age among the *probouloi* of 413, but he is not on record as playing an active part. This is the first mention of Theramenes, though presumably not the beginning of his career; his subsequent changes of side, much criticized by contemporaries, are perhaps best explained by supposing a genuine belief in some sort of moderate oligarchy, not the kind of regime Athens could ever tolerate for long. (VIII.68).

The archon Callias and some other officers were not deposed, and the

---

[19] For bibliography on these and other theories see Rhodes 1981 (C 83) 385ff, HCT v 254–6.

[20] Ferguson 1926 (D 23) and in *CAH* v¹ 338–40; *contra*, Hignett 1952 (D 38) 376–8; de Ste Croix 1956 (D 83) 14–20.   [21] Meyer 1899 (A 87) 433–5; Hignett 1952 (D 38) 360, 373.

[22] At the time of the counter-revolution, according to Thuc. VIII.92.11, the Four Hundred did not want the Five Thousand brought into being, but they did not want it known that they did not exist, so uncertainty persisted.

Four Hundred may have intended to let the old Council finish out its time, but if so they changed their minds and dissolved it with armed support, paying the councillors for the remaining month of their year. Their next action was to send to Decelea and propose negotiations to Agis, a radical change of policy since the start of the conspiracy at Samos. Agis, thinking that a city in the throes of revolution would be in no state to resist, sent for extra troops and soon afterwards came down from Decelea in force; but the defence had by no means collapsed, and after his withdrawal the overtures of the Four Hundred were better received. (VIII.69–71).

Envoys were also sent off to the fleet at Samos. There the oligarchic plot set up by Pisander had achieved the murder of the ostracised Hyperbolus, but when 300 conspirators (see p. 384 above) tried to overthrow the democracy they were resisted with support from the Athenian sailors. Of the generals present, Charminus was an oligarch, Leon and Diomedon democrats, and the crisis threw up two new leaders, Thrasybulus son of Lycus now a trierarch, and Thrasyllus serving as a hoplite. The crew of the state galley *Paralus* took an active part, and after the triumph of the democrats they were sent to Athens to announce this, with Chaereas from the main fleet. The Four Hundred imprisoned two or three of them, but Chaereas got back to Samos and reported, according to Thucydides falsely, brutal oppression and threats against the sailors' families. Thrasybulus and Thrasyllus calmed the sailors down, and oaths were sworn to maintain democracy and carry on the war, and they elected new generals. The envoys of the Four Hundred, learning this, waited at Delos. (VIII.72–7).

Astyochus, faced with near mutiny against the inactivity, sailed out along the south coast of Mycale while Milesian troops advanced by land. The Athenians withdrew to Samos, inferior in numbers and expecting the return of Strombichides from the Hellespont; next day he arrived, and now the Athenians offered battle and the Peloponnesians refused. Shortly after, Clearchus was sent off with forty ships; these were scattered by a storm and Clearchus returned to Miletus, but ten got through and procured the revolt of Byzantium, which compelled the Athenians to detach a squadron to counter them. Unrest in the Peloponnesian fleet continued, and worsened when Thrasybulus persuaded the Athenian fleet to invite Alcibiades to join them. He was then elected to the generalship, and at once went back to confer with Tissaphernes, increasing the Peloponnesians' suspicion that the latter was dealing dishonestly with them. In a minor riot Astyochus had to flee to an altar; the Milesians were encouraged to take over a fort built in the city by Tissaphernes; Lichas objected, arguing that the Milesians must put up with Tissaphernes' actions while the war lasted. Mindarus now arrived to take over the command from Astyochus, who set off home accompanied by envoys from Tissaphernes and the Milesians sent to complain of one another, and by Hermocrates. Evidently each party thought it had a legitimate grievance, but it is not clear what the position of the Greek cities of Asia was supposed to be under the latest treaty.[23] Nor do we know certainly what the Spartan Assembly made of all this, though Xenophon (*Hell.* 1.1.31) gives an incidental glimpse in a note on Hermocrates: he denounced Tissaphernes at Sparta, with support from Astyochus,[24] and was thought to have the right of it. Further, the sequel suggests that Mindarus came with authority from Sparta to break with Tissaphernes if he got no satisfaction from him. Meanwhile an internal upheaval in Syracuse sent Hermocrates into exile and three new generals to Miletus in his place.[25] (VIII.78–85).

Tissaphernes now left for Aspendus, a little way up the river Eurymedon, where the King's fleet of 147 Phoenician ships had arrived. Thucydides was sure of that much, but uncertain why they came no further, and he saw this almost entirely as a problem about Tissaphernes' motives. Frustratingly his text breaks off in mid-sentence (VIII.109), as Tissaphernes a little later set out for the Hellespont to explain matters to the Peloponnesians; Xenophon (*Hell.* 1.1.9) is no help here, but Diodorus (XIII.46.6) makes him say that he had sent the ships away on learning that the kings of Arabia and Egypt were plotting against Phoenicia, and it seems that there was a revolt in Egypt in 411[26] which could be the factual basis for Diodorus' not very accurate statement. Tissaphernes' continuing failure to pay the subsidy regularly or in full may be due to a desire to loosen his ties with Sparta, as the terms of the third treaty suggest; but this so exasperated the Spartans that before the end of summer Mindarus accepted an invitation from Pharnabazus and a sudden movement took his entire fleet north to the Hellespont, so that when the Phoenician ships were withdrawn Tissaphernes was left with no fleet at all. For the next three years Pharnabazus' satrapy was the main seat of the war. (VIII.87, 99).

Alcibiades had consolidated his position at Samos, where his supposed influence with Tissaphernes still served him as an asset, and when the envoys of the Four Hundred in the end arrived he was able to restrain the anger of the sailors and prevent a decision to sail at once against the Piraeus, which Thucydides recognized as a signal service to Athens, the first that Alcibiades had done her. He also formulated the reply to the envoys, that he had no objection to the rule of the Five Thousand, but

[23] Lichas' objection to the Milesians (above) does not settle the issue; see Lewis 1977 (A 76) 110–14.

[24] This perhaps implies a more favourable view of Astyochus than we find in Thuc. VIII.

[25] Xenophon (*Hell.* 1.1.27–31) places this in summer 410; for argument against this see *HCT* v 281–5.   [26] Lewis 1958 (G 24); see *CAH* IV² 284.

the Four Hundred must go and the old Council of Five Hundred be restored; measures of economy were in order but the war must be carried on. The crew of the *Paralus* reappeared: the Four Hundred had unwisely entrusted to them the transport of three ambassadors to Sparta, but instead they delivered them to the Argives and brought an Argive embassy to Samos with offers of help; these were gratefully acknowledged, but at this stage operations on land were not contemplated. (VIII.86).

IV. THE FIVE THOUSAND REPLACE THE FOUR HUNDRED

Alcibiades' reply, when reported at Athens, proved to be a turning point in the fortunes of the oligarchy. There was already some disillusion among the rank and file, and a group of the leaders headed by Theramenes and Aristocrates was calling for a regime more widely based. The extremists in alarm sent off the last of several embassies to Sparta, led by Phrynichus and Antiphon, to obtain any tolerable agreement they could get, and they pressed on with the construction of a wall at Eëtionea, the short promontory which encloses the Piraeus harbour on the west; the purpose was probably to defend the 'few men' they had stationed at the harbour entrance against attack from the increasingly disaffected city.[27] The embassy brought back no satisfactory answer from Sparta; the Spartans presumably thought it would be more profitable to wait on events than to grant terms to a Four Hundred no longer in firm control. At the same time a fleet of forty-two ships was known to be at Las in Laconia, preparing to answer an appeal from Euboea; Theramenes asserted that their real destination was the Piraeus and that the Eëtionea wall was meant to secure their entry. (VIII.89–91).

The crisis came to a head with the murder of Phrynichus on his return from Sparta. The murderer escaped, but an accomplice revealed that he knew of meetings at the house of the commander of the frontier guards (*peripoloi*).[28] The Four Hundred took no action on this, a further sign that their grip was failing. The ships from Las, commanded by Agesandridas, reached Epidaurus and overran Aegina, reinforcing Theramenes' suspicions. Finally hoplites building the Eëtionea wall rebelled and arrested Alexicles, a general of the oligarchy. The Four Hundred threatened Theramenes, who offered to go and rescue Alexicles; confusion and alarm in the city and Piraeus was stilled, partly by the mediation of Thucydides of Pharsalus; Theramenes, faced by the hoplites, agreed that

[27] Our text of Thuc. VIII.90.4 has the new wall being built along the inner side of the promontory at the harbour edge, but it is hard to see how that would help, and emendation is necessary; see *HCT* v 303–8.

[28] This is Thucydides' version (VIII.90.2); on its discrepancy with other versions see *HCT* v 309–11.

the wall should be demolished, and it was. The hoplites did not call for immediate return to democracy but for the establishment of the Five Thousand; no one was yet certain if they existed or who might turn out to be one of them. (VIII.92).

Next day the hoplites released Alexicles and marched up to the city. Feeling now ran less high, and it was agreed to hold an Assembly 'about concord' in the temple of Dionysus on a fixed day; but on that day the fleet of Agesandridas was sighted, coming from Megara past Salamis. There was an immediate rush to the Piraeus to man what ships there were, but Agesandridas went on to round Sunium and eventually to Oropus, captured by the Boeotians in the previous winter. The Athenians followed under Thymochares to Eretria, but with the ships already there they had only thirty-six against forty-two and by a trick of the Eretrians the crews had scattered to buy provisions at the moment when Agesandridas attacked from Oropus. In a brief battle outside the harbour the Athenians lost twenty-two ships, and the whole of Euboea revolted except for Oreus, held by Athenian cleruchs. The Piraeus was wide open to attack, and Thucydides comments on the advantage to Athens of an unadventurous opponent who did not seize the opportunity. But this was the heaviest blow yet, for the occupation of Decelea had made Athens more than ever dependent on Euboea. (VIII.93–5).

They hastened to put their affairs in order; the Four Hundred were formally deposed and power given to the Five Thousand, defined as those who could provide arms, which even after the losses in Sicily would mean more than a literal five thousand. No detail is known of the constitution now established, not even for the Council whose vote is recorded in the one decree that survives ([Plut.] *X Orat.* 833D); but, though the contrary has been argued,[29] those outside the 'Five Thousand' were certainly not given the vote. Thucydides' emphatic praise for this regime (VIII.97.2) should not be referred to its constitutional merits, for he shows little interest in such things elsewhere, concentrating rather on the quality of political leadership; what mattered to him here was the conduct of affairs, and his praise is confined to the early months of the regime, the dividing line probably at the point when Cleophon procured the rejection of the Spartan offer after Cyzicus.[30] The extremist leaders, Pisander and others, escaped to Decelea, but Antiphon surprisingly stayed in Athens, where perhaps it was not at once clear what the attitude of the new regime would be, since many of its leaders had been members of the Four Hundred. In the event he and two others were charged with treason, the last embassy to Sparta, and he was executed; the decree was

[29] de Ste Croix 1956 (D 83); *contra*, Rhodes 1972 (D 76).
[30] On this difficult passage see *HCT* v *ad loc.*

proposed by Andron father of Androtion (p. 475), and the main accuser was Theramenes.[31] (VIII.96–8).

V. THE HELLESPONT CAMPAIGNS AND THE RETURN OF ALCIBIADES

It was at about the same time that Mindarus set off for the north with seventy-three ships (p. 478). Detained by storms at Icarus, he got through to Chios, but Thrasyllus with fifty-five ships had gone to join Thrasybulus, who with five was dealing with trouble in the west of Lesbos; but Mindarus boldly pushed on between Lesbos and the mainland, avoiding the Athenians, and reached the Hellespont. Most of the Athenian ships at Sestus escaped into the open sea, and the whole fleet concentrated at Elaeus, at the tip of the Chersonese; and after five days of preparation seventy-six ships re-entered the Hellespont, clinging to the European shore. Part had rounded the headland of Cynossema when eighty-six Peloponnesian ships attacked from the opposite shore, at first successfully. Then as so often with Greek fleets after an initial success, their order relaxed; the Athenians rallied and routed them, but the narrowness of the straits enabled them to save most of their ships. Their losses were not disastrous, twenty-one against fifteen Athenian, but Athenian superiority at sea had been reasserted, and when the news reached Athens it restored morale badly damaged by the Euboean defeat. The Athenians also regained Cyzicus, sailed on into the Propontis, and captured a small squadron coming from Byzantium; the Peloponnesians sent for their recently victorious fleet from Euboea, but that was largely wiped out by a storm off Athos. (VIII.99–107).

Alcibiades returned from Aspendus in the autumn, claiming to have prevented the intervention of the Phoenician fleet. Thucydides (VIII.108) adds two more snippets, the expulsion of Persian garrisons from Antandrus and Cnidus, and brings Tissaphernes as far as Ephesus on his journey to the Hellespont before he breaks off, the summer of 411 not quite completed. His magisterial account, which tells us nothing of his informants and rarely mentions a variant, now gives place to two divergent versions, which might in principle be a more healthy situation, if both were fully preserved. In a world which judged historians by their style, Xenophon's charm ensured his survival: capable of vivid reporting where his interest was engaged, oddly incurious when it was not, wilfully silent on matters which he found distasteful, he had none of Thucydides' restless determination to search out the facts and analyse

---

[31] See, besides [Plut.] *loc. cit.* (above), the Geneva papyrus with part of a text of Antiphon's speech in his own defence, reprinted in the Teubner *Antiphon* (Thalheim 1914) and discussed in *HCT* v 198–200.

what lay beneath them. The only other continuous account is the lazy and unintelligent epitome of Ephorus by the Sicilian Diodorus written in the time of Augustus, which regularly differs in detail and in substance from Xenophon's. The universal history of Ephorus of Cyme,[32] written in the middle of the fourth century, became a standard work in antiquity but was not very highly regarded; and in modern times Xenophon the contemporary was generally preferred until the publication in 1908 of fragments of the *Hellenica Oxyrhynchia* revealed that the ultimate source of Diodorus' narrative for 396 was an unknown near-contemporary historian whom Ephorus evidently preferred to Xenophon. Smaller fragments found since, concerned with the Ionian War, confirm the guess that he was a continuator of Thucydides. The author (hereafter 'P')[33] was a solid historian, stylistically unambitious, well informed about what was going on among both Athenians and Spartans, and indeed elsewhere. Like Thucydides he used a system of numbered years, and within a year he made frequent transitions from one scene of action to another. He had none of Thucydides' urge to generalize – for P, politics dissolve into a series of manoeuvres by individuals, and the Corinthian War has no *alethestate prophasis* – but in matters of fact the papyrus fragments allow some convincing corrections of Xenophon, and it would certainly make a great difference to our picture of this period if we had P entire. As it is we get only glimpses, mostly where Diodorus' epitome is fuller than usual; all too often we can see that Ephorus' version was different from Xenophon's, but not precisely how it differed.[34]

Shortly after the battle of Cynossema, Dorieus the Thurian, whom Mindarus had detached to deal with trouble in Rhodes, reached the Hellespont, was seen by Athenian lookouts, and driven ashore either near Rhoeteum or at Dardanus. Our two sources differ widely: the main problem with Xenophon, how Mindarus could see what was going on from Ilium, may be soluble;[35] Diodorus' statement (XIII.45.2) that the Athenians brought out their entire fleet against Dorieus can hardly be right, but he is always capable of introducing his own muddle into an otherwise sensible account (see e.g. p. 490 below on Notium). The main battle was long and hard fought till Alcibiades appeared with twenty ships, on which the Peloponnesians fled to the shore, where Pharnabazus helped them to save most of their ships. Then all but forty of the Athenians left the Hellespont to collect money; Thrasyllus went home with the good news and a request for more ships and men; from Athens

---

[32] *FGrH* 70; above, p. 7.   [33] Above, p. 8.
[34] Hereafter X = Xen. *Hell.*, D = Diod. XIII.
[35] See Tuplin 1986 (c 101) 54–5. This case does not exemplify what was said at the end of the previous paragraph: Diodorus is full enough, but no clear outline emerges.

Theramenes set out with thirty ships, failed to prevent the building of a causeway over the Euripus, and eventually went on to assist Archelaus of Macedon in his siege of Pydna. Tissaphernes arrived at the Hellespont, but Xenophon says nothing of his dealings with the Peloponnesians (see p. 478 above), only that he had orders from the King to make war on the Athenians, so he seized Alcibiades and imprisoned him in Sardis, but after a month he made his escape and rode to the coast. (X 1.1.2–10; D 45–7, 49.1).

As the winter ended, Mindarus gathered all his forces, in the first place for an attack on Cyzicus, and the Athenians at Sestus in alarm sailed round to Cardia on the north coast of the Chersonese. In Xenophon's highly dramatic account of the following operations everything depends on the whirlwind leadership of Alcibiades; but there are some loose ends, and in two crucial places the development rests on improbable chances. Diodorus' summary (49–51) is more extensive than usual and this time allows us to see a more coherent version.[36] The generals at Cardia, not named, sent for Thrasybulus from Thrace and Theramenes who had now joined him; and for Alcibiades, engaged in unspecified activity at Lesbos. The fleet moved to Elaeus, then passed Abydus by night, to conceal not the fact of its passage but its increased numbers, and so to Proconnesus, the large island north west of Cyzicus, where again precautions were taken to avoid the reinforcement being reported to Mindarus. Next day under cover of a rainstorm they approached Cyzicus in three divisions; Alcibiades went ahead with a force sufficient to lure the whole enemy fleet out of harbour, while Thrasybulus and Theramenes were concealed behind the promontory south of Artace, from which they emerged to cut off Mindarus' retreat and force him to land where Pharnabazus' mercenaries were. A long and involved fight ensued, and in the end Mindarus was killed and his troops routed. The Syracusans burnt their ships, but the Athenians carried off the rest. (X 1.1.11–18; D 49–51).

This brilliant victory for the time being changed the face of the war. Apart from the need to find a more reliable paymaster, Mindarus' move to the north had carried with it a substantial shift in strategy; instead of the slower but perhaps safer method of avoiding battle and picking off Athenian allies one at a time, there was now the possibility of ending the war more quickly by cutting off Athens' corn supply. That involved a greater risk of getting caught up in a full-scale battle, though of course it was not inevitable that Mindarus should fall into this particular trap. But the corn route from the Black Sea was now free, and a post was established at Chrysopolis at the entrance to the Bosporus to collect dues from shipping; but of the Hellespontine cities only Perinthus now

[36] See Andrewes 1982 (G 6) 19–25.

came over, and further advance in this area had to wait till 408. (X 1.1.21–2).

The recovery of confidence at home spelt the end of the regime of the Five Thousand. Support was already crumbling when the Spartans after Cyzicus made an offer of peace, which was opposed by Cleophon (D 52–3), the 'lyre-maker', a demagogue whose first appearance in literature is in Aristophanes' *Thesmophoriazusae*, but he is already named on an ostracon which cannot be later than 416; as the son of a general of the Archidamian War[37] Cleophon probably belonged to the Five Thousand, but the pressure from his unprivileged supporters will have been the decisive factor for rejection. The restoration of the democratic Council appears to have taken place before the end of the archon-year 411/10; this restoration is treated as an epoch in the decree of Demophantus (Andoc. 1.96–8), which imposed on all Athenians an oath to kill anyone attempting to overthrow the democracy, but the archon and other officers finished out their term. The popular mood remained suspicious: Andocides (1.75–6) gives a curious list of categories of people whose civic rights were partly suspended, and the speaker of Lysias 25, not a wholly satisfactory witness, complains of a wave of malicious prosecutions.

The revolution of the Four Hundred never had more than a precarious basis. The provisional acceptance of Pisander's first proposals at Athens rested on the hope of Persian money, which was proved vain even before the actual coup, and the approaches of the oligarchs to Sparta would be generally seen as mere treason; Alcibiades' message and the action of the hoplites at Eëtionea opened up a fatal split among the oligarchs themselves. Thucydides (VIII.89.3) hints at other internal divisions, noting that an oligarchy newly set up by revolution was especially vulnerable because individual members expected too much from it for themselves. The Five Thousand was no narrow oligarchy, if it meant 'those who could provide arms' (Thuc. VIII.97.1), and government was again open, but the hoplites as such had no political *esprit de corps* and offered no resistance to the restoration of democracy. Some no doubt had anti-democratic leanings, such as those who on the day after the confrontation at Eëtionea were ready to do a deal with the Four Hundred, and it is significant that in Andocides' list (above) we find that soldiers who had remained in the city in the time of the Four Hundred were forbidden to speak in the Assembly or serve on the Council, though they retained their other rights; but others, probably the bulk of them, were ordinary democrats with no special enthusiasm for the political role that had been assigned to them.

One important legacy survived, a commission set up to revise the laws

37 Vanderpool 1952 (D 99) and 1968 (D 100) 120.

of Athens. Conspicuous examples of its activity are the republication of Draco's law of murder (*IG* i³ 104), inscribed in 409/8, and the laws regulating the work of the Council (*IG* i³ 105) of similar date. The task was still not completed at the end of the war, but after the fall of the Thirty it was resumed and finished. A more immediate and unwelcome legacy was an empty treasury; the accounts for 410/9 (M–L 84; *IG* i³ 375) record only expenditure from current income. They now put into effect a reform adumbrated in *Ath. Pol.* 30.2 (the 'constitution for the future'), by which the number of the *hellenotamiai* was doubled to twenty and these took over the duties of the old *kolakretai*, who now disappear. The reintroduction of the tribute probably improved the situation: a fragmentary decree (*IG* i³ 99) contemplates repayment of the state's debt to Athena, and work was actually restarted on the Erechtheum in 409/8 (*IG* i³ 474). The second prytany of 410/9 shows the first payment for the *diobelia* introduced by Cleophon, probably a payment of 2 obols to poorer citizens whose sufferings will have been greatly increased by the occupation of Decelea and the loss of Euboea.

Still in summer 410 Agis led a foraging raid close up to the walls of Athens, but retired when Thrasyllus drew up the available troops by the Lyceum. The Athenians were now encouraged to vote Thrasyllus the forces for which he had come home after Cynossema, and in spring 409 he sailed with 1,000 hoplites, 100 horsemen and thirty ships,[38] with 5,000 of his sailors armed as peltasts. After a minor victory at Pygela he went to Notium and recovered Colophon, then collected rich booty in Lydia before turning to his main objective, Ephesus. Meanwhile Tissaphernes had assembled a large force, and men from the Syracusan fleet helped with the defence, and when Thrasyllus landed at two points near the city he was driven back with the loss of 400 men.[39] The capture of four ships out of a Syracusan squadron of twenty-five that was heading north for the Hellespont hardly compensated for the defeat. When Thrasyllus sailed to Sestus to join Alcibiades and they moved to Lampsacus for the winter, there was friction between the two forces, which Xenophon attributes to the scorn of the victors of Cyzicus for Thrasyllus' defeated men; but there may also have been a political issue. Of the leaders in the Hellespont, Theramenes was one of the founders of the Five Thousand and Alcibiades had at one point in 411 endorsed them, while Thrasybulus, the enemy of the later oligarchy of the Thirty, may at this stage have shared their views. There was, if not actual hostility, a certain distance between the democracy in Athens and the Hellespontine force, which

---

[38] So D 64.1; X 1.1.34 says fifty were voted, in the previous winter.

[39] The most recently published fragments of P (Koenen 1976 (c 62); see now McKechnie and Kern 1988 (c 69)) come from a detailed account of this engagement; the very tattered papyrus shows no serious divergence from the briefer versions of X and D, which roughly agree.

made its own plans and ran its own finances;[40] and in sending Thrasyllus to Ionia rather than to the Hellespont the democrats at home may have hoped for a success there that would balance the glamour of Cyzicus. A victory won jointly over Pharnabazus near Abydus healed the breach. (X 1.1.33–2; D 64.1–4).

In the same winter[41] the Messenian garrison of Pylos surrendered to the Spartans who were besieging them; a relief force of thirty ships under Anytus had been prevented by storms from rounding Cape Malea, and at his subsequent trial Anytus, later notorious as the accuser of Socrates, was alleged to have secured his acquittal by bribery (*Ath. Pol.* 27.5), a large undertaking given the size of Athenian juries. The colonists of Heraclea Trachinia lost 700 men and their Spartan commander in battle against their neighbours the Oeteans. The Megarians recaptured their port of Nisaea from the Athenians, who then sent out 1,000 hoplites and 400 cavalry, and in a battle near the border they defeated a larger army of Megarians and a Spartan detachment; this is probably the 'battle at Megara' in which Plato's brothers, Adeimantus and Glaucon, distinguished themselves (*Rep.* 368a). A small fragment of P describes the end of the battle, and adds that the Athenians were angry with their generals for the risk they had taken but overjoyed at having overcome a Spartan force.[42]

In spring 408 the attack on the Hellespontine cities was resumed, beginning with Calchedon. After Alcibiades had forced the Bithynians to hand over the cattle which the Calchedonians had entrusted to them, the city was walled off from sea to sea. The Spartan harmost Hippocrates came out and fought a hard battle with Thrasyllus' hoplites, but when Alcibiades and the cavalry arrived he was killed and his men fled back into the city; Pharnabazus, outside the circumvallation, failed to break through[43] and could only return to his camp. Alcibiades then left to collect money, and the other generals came to terms with Pharnabazus: he was to pay them 20 talents on behalf of Calchedon and convey an Athenian embassy to the King. Calchedon was to pay its regular tribute to Athens, with arrears, and the Athenians were not to attack it again till the embassy returned. Pharnabazus insisted that Alcibiades too must swear, and on his return from Selymbria they exchanged oaths and the mission of the embassy was put in hand. (X 1.3.2–12; D 66.1–4).

Selymbria had given money in 410 but had not rejoined the alliance. In 408 Xenophon (1.3.10) says only that it was taken, Diodorus (66.4) adds that this was by treachery; only Plutarch (*Alc.* 30.3–10) gives a detailed

---

[40] See Andrewes 1953 (G 3) 2–5.   [41] See Chronological Notes, pp. 503–5.

[42] This fragment confirms the account of D 65.1–2; X omitted the battle altogether.

[43] Tuplin 1986 (C 101) 44 discusses the topographical problem of X 1.3.2.

story.[44] The conspirators within, afraid they had been betrayed, gave their signal too soon, but Alcibiades pressed on and was admitted with only a small force; in great danger, he had it proclaimed that the Selymbrians were not to oppose the Athenians, and during the confusion this caused the rest of the Athenian force arrived. Alcibiades prevented his Thracian troops from sacking the city, and treated it well. This last we can confirm from the decree (M–L 87) proposed at Athens by Alcibiades in 407 to ratify the settlement: hostages to be returned and no more taken, autonomy guaranteed, Athenian and allied claims for property lost during the war abandoned except for land and houses. This was no time for ferocious punishment; there were others to be enticed back on to the Athenian side.

Next Byzantium was walled off, where the Spartan Clearchus had Megarian and Boeotian troops as well as a few of his own. The siege made slow progress till Clearchus left to get money from Pharnabazus and to collect ships, and in his absence discontent, due mainly to his distribution of the available food to the soldiers and not to the population in general, led a group of Byzantines to offer to betray the city to Alcibiades. To facilitate his entry, fleet and army pretended to withdraw from the siege, but in the night the fleet returned to make a noisy attack on the harbour, distracting attention while Alcibiades' troops were let in by a landward gate. After a struggle the Megarians and Boeotians surrendered and were sent to Athens, while Byzantium rejoined the empire, again on mild terms. Pharnabazus and the Athenian envoys heard the news at Gordium in Phrygia, where they had stopped for the winter. (X 1.3.14–4.1; D 66.4–67).

The victorious campaign, which left only Abydus in Peloponnesian hands, opened up the possibility of a return to Athens, welcome not only to Alcibiades but to many of his men who had been several years abroad. Leaving a detachment in the Hellespont, the rest sailed to Samos; from there Thrasybulus returned with thirty ships to finish off the siege of Thasos, Thrasyllus and the main body set out for Athens, and Alcibiades took twenty ships to Caria, where he collected 100 talents. Even then he did not make straight for Athens, but stopped at Paros, then went to Gytheum to check a report that a Spartan fleet was being prepared there; then, hearing that he had been appointed general, he at last went home, arriving on the day of the Plynteria (at the beginning of June 407), a day of ill omen when no Athenian would embark on serious business. He still hesitated till he saw on the quayside Euryptolemus and other relatives and friends, then he landed to a rapturous reception, defended his record

[44] Suspicion has been roused by the similarity of this to some elements in Diodorus' account of the recapture of Byzantium; see Hatzfeld 1951 (D 37) 288 n.1.

in speeches to Council and Assembly, and was given complete charge of the conduct of the war, no one daring to resist this proposal.[45] Thrasybulus had also been appointed general, in absence, as had Conon, who was available at home.[46] Alcibiades' exile was rescinded, the stela of his condemnation was thrown into the sea, the Eleusinian authorities were ordered to lift the curses that had been pronounced against him, and his property was restored. To crown all, he escorted by land the annual procession to Eleusis, which had gone by sea since the occupation of Decelea. Agis did not intervene. (X 1.4.8–20; D 68–69.3).

Xenophon's sketch of the feeling in Athens (1.4.13–17) contains a long and disingenuous vindication of Alcibiades' past, with only a single sentence for opponents who thought him responsible for all the city's troubles. Diodorus (68.4) says that the upper classes thought they had found a man capable of openly and stoutly resisting the *demos*, while the poor expected him to turn the city upside down and relieve their poverty; this might be a coarse summary, at third hand, of an analysis by P of the contradictory expectations that he aroused, the contradiction masked for the moment by enthusiasm for his leadership in war. Plutarch (*Alc.* 34.7–35.1) claims that the lower classes passionately longed for him to set up as tyrant, brushing the constitution aside and putting the sycophants to flight. He adds that it is uncertain what view Alcibiades took on this; but we may perhaps assume that he would be content with having, for the moment, attained by general consent the commanding position which Thucydides ascribes to Pericles at the end of his life, and hoping to consolidate that by further victories. Strategically we can only presume that he relied on his understanding with Pharnabazus for his holiday at home and thought that operations in Ionia could wait till the return of the Athenian ambassadors from the King. Thrasybulus meanwhile had reduced Thasos[47] and Abdera, and his force was now free to campaign in the east.

At some point in the last decade of the fifth century comes an episode not recorded in any extant ancient source, the violent destruction of the temple of Zeus at Nemea. Excavation[48] has revealed an extensive burnt layer, with enough iron spear-points and bronze arrowheads to indicate

[45] Xenophon (1.4.20) says he was ἀναρρηθεὶς ἁπάντων ἡγεμὼν αὐτοκράτωρ, which may or may not mean formal appointment as στρατηγὸς αὐτοκράτωρ, the title which Diodorus (69.3) and Plutarch (*Alc.* 33.2) give him.

[46] Conon was last heard of intervening in a fresh outbreak of civil strife at Corcyra (D 48). This chapter interrupts the account of Theramenes' voyage at the end of 411 (above, p. 483), and Conon's action should also be dated to 411, not to 410/9 where Diodorus puts the operations of both commanders. It looks then as if Conon had been in Naupactus in 411 and so escaped involvement in the revolution. Gomme on Thuc. IV.48.5 is too sceptical.

[47] *IG* II² 8827–8 are the tombstones of two men described as Thasian hostages who died in Attica, presumably taken by Thrasybulus on this occasion.

[48] See Miller's annual reports (1 115), especially 46 (1977) 9ff, 21f; for the date 49 (1980) 179.

that the fire was not accidental but the result of a deliberate attack. That warns us of our ignorance, even for a period so relatively well documented as the late fifth century.

VI. LYSANDER AND THE COLLAPSE OF ATHENS

In the spring of 407 the Athenian envoys on their way up-country met a Spartan embassy on its way down, under one Boeotius, claiming to have obtained all that they could wish from the King, together with Cyrus the King's younger son coming as satrap of Lydia, Great Phrygia and Cappadocia, and commander of all Persian forces in the west. He was to give firm support to Sparta, and 30 minas a month per ship – but to any number the Spartans wished, a change from the grudging offers made in 411. Xenophon says nothing of any further concession, but the form of later negotiations suggests that the doubtful status of the Greek cities (above, p. 478) was now regulated: they were to be autonomous while they paid tribute to Persia. (X 1.4.1–4; D 70.3).

Sparta had been slow to recover from Cyzicus. Ships were built at Antandrus with Pharnabazus' help, and Clearchus had hoped to collect more. Of the admiral for 408,[49] Cratesippidas, we know only that he had helped a faction on Chios to expel 600 of their opponents, who settled at Atarneus on the mainland (D 65.3–4).[50] In summer 408 (Androtion, FGrH 324 F 44, the first entry for this archon-year) a Spartan embassy came to Athens and negotiated an exchange of prisoners; if they also made soundings about a compromise peace, these were rejected. Early in 407 the new admiral, Lysander, came to Rhodes, where the three old cities had just coalesced into a single state, and with the ships he found there and those he had brought with him, seventy in all, he settled at Ephesus to await Cyrus' arrival in Sardis. (X 1.5.1; D 70.1–2, 75.1).

Nothing is known of his earlier career, but he was to show himself not only an able general but a ruthless politician determined to build up a personal following in the cities accessible to him. His diplomatic skill was shown at his first meeting with the youthful Cyrus,[51] who promised to continue support beyond the 500 talents he had brought, then in the end was persuaded to increase the daily wage from 3 obols to 4. Athenian envoys tried to counter this with the help of Tissaphernes,[52] who would

---

[49] Sealey 1976 (F 63) may well be right to argue that the nauarchy had only recently been limited to an annual tenure, starting in the spring; as a corollary it was not iterable.

[50] It is often supposed that these were democrats who had somehow regained power, but a split among the oligarchs is at least as likely. The mention of Pedaritus (P fr.2; Theopompus FGrH 115 F 8) may suggest that these two had supported rival groups.

[51] Plutarch (Artox. 2.4) says he was born after Darius' accession; if so, he could not now be more than sixteen.

[52] For the puzzling fragmentary decree in honour of Euagoras (IG i³ 113), which appears to mention Tissaphernes and regard the King as an ally of Athens, see Lewis 1977 (A 76) 129–31.

have liked to reinstate his policy of balancing the two Greek powers, but they were rebuffed; their own envoys to the King were meanwhile detained by Pharnabazus on Cyrus' orders. Lysander beached his ships, now ninety, at Ephesus to repair and dry them out, but took no military action for the rest of the summer. (X 1.5.2–10; D 70.3).

Before the end of August Alcibiades set out from Athens with 1,500 hoplites, 150 horsemen and a hundred ships. He failed to take Andros,[53] across the route from the Hellespont to Athens, and left Conon there while he went on to Samos and carried out raids from there. Later he moved to Notium, closer to the enemy at Ephesus, and early in spring 406 he went to join Thrasybulus at Phocaea, leaving the main fleet in charge of his helmsman Antiochus with strict instructions not to engage in battle. Xenophon gives only a blurred account of what followed, but P fr.4 gives us some opportunity of correcting and completing Diodorus' alternative version.[54] The opening moves are not clear, but probably P said that Lysander had been in the habit of sending out a group of three or four ships for some purpose, and Antiochus decided to pick them off. So he took ten of his best ships, and left most of them in ambush while he went ahead to entice the enemy detachment out of harbour. But Lysander was too quick for him: his three ships sank Antiochus, and he then brought his full fleet out to chase the ships in ambush. The Athenians in Notium, seeing their danger, manned their ships as fast as they could, but in the disorder they lost twenty-two ships outside the harbour. If Antiochus had planned only a limited operation and not a general battle, he mismanaged his ambush and failed to realize how this might embroil the main fleet. Alcibiades hurried back and challenged Lysander afresh, but he was content with what he had achieved. (X 1.5.11–15; D 71).

This was not an overwhelming defeat, but disastrous for Alcibiades. Even before it he had failed to give an effective start to his Ionian campaign, and feeling against him rose in the fleet; Thrasybulus of Collytus, a man with a long democratic career ahead of him, went home to lead a chorus of complaint. Plutarch (*Alc.* 35.2–4) was surely right, that the extravagant hopes formed in the previous summer were a decisive element in his downfall; the distrust of Alcibiades' intentions which Thucydides had noted was fully reactivated. The board of generals that now took over is virtually identical with the board for 406/5; probably the battle took place near the time of their election and they were instructed to assume command prematurely. Alcibiades himself withdrew to the castles in Thrace which he had secured during his time in the Hellespont. Conon brought his twenty ships from Andros, and

---

[53] There is no record of the defection of Andros, but it could have followed on the revolt of Euboea.   [54] See Andrewes 1982 (G 6) 15–19.

improved the quality of the fleet at Samos by reducing its numbers from a hundred to seventy, keeping the better of the rowers available.[55] Diodorus (72.3–73.2) has a complicated story of a night approach by Agis to the walls and confrontations on the following days: he has this after Notium and before Alcibiades' deposition, which suggests early 406,[56] but he has the whole sequence under 408/7 and inserts after Notium a condensed account of Thrasybulus' operations of 410 in the north. (X 1.5.16–20; D 74.1–2).

Spring 406 also brought a successor to Lysander, Callicratidas, who according to our sources disdained waiting on barbarians for money and would have preferred to reconcile Sparta and Athens. Lysander greatly resented his recall – we know too little of the internal politics of Sparta, but if it is true (above, p. 489 n.49) that the rule against iteration had only recently been instituted his attitude is more intelligible – and returned to Cyrus the remainder of the money he had been given; Cyrus refused Callicratidas an interview, Lysander's partisans put every obstacle in his way, and they complained of the folly of the Spartans in sending an inexperienced commander to succeed one who knew his business. However, he succeeded in imposing his authority at Miletus and collected some money and 140 ships, with which he set off for Lesbos. On the way a quick attack secured the surrender of Delphinium, the Athenian base on Chios, and he took Teus before proceeding to Methymna; this had an Athenian garrison and a record of supporting Athens, but his assault succeeded, the Methymnaeans were given their freedom, and he went on to Mytilene. Conon had followed, arriving in time to hear of the loss of Methymna, and he encamped on one of the Hecatonnesia, just south of the Gulf of Adramyttium; here it was easy for Callicratidas to cut off his retreat to Samos. Conon's fleet was in good heart, but he could not face Callicratidas who now had 170 ships, so he made a dash for Mytilene, but in the fight which was forced on him outside the harbour he lost thirty ships. Callicratidas forced an entry into the larger northern harbour, and Conon was besieged in the smaller harbour and the city, with far too many mouths to feed. (X 1.6.1–19; D 76–79.7).

The problem of getting word to Athens was solved by sending two fast ships out one midday, of which the one that made for the open sea was caught, but the other reached the Hellespont. At Athens 110 ships were somehow found; citizens of all classes embarked, and metics, and slaves who were given 'Plataean' citizenship (Ar. Frogs 694; Hellanicus

---

[55] Plutarch (Lys. 4.6–7) has a rhetorical passage slightly earlier, just before Notium, about the sailors deserting the Athenian fleet for the higher pay they could get on the other side.

[56] It would thus be possible, but only just, for Soph. OC 92–3 to refer to this episode (there are Boeotian cavalry in D 72.4.8). Beloch 1912–27 (A 2) II².1, 418 n.2 was probably right to reject the view that this is a duplicate of Agis' attack in 410.

FGrH 323a F 25); and the golden Nikae and other dedications were coined into money (*Frogs* 720; Hell. F 26; Philochorus, *FGrH* 328 F 141).[57] At Samos another 30 ships had been collected and the Samians provided 10, making a total of 150. Meanwhile Cyrus had relented and sent Callicratidas money; and Diomedon, coming to Conon's help, got into the channel between the island part of the city and the land, but then lost ten of his twelve ships to a sudden enemy sortie. The new Athenian fleet sailed north to the Arginusae islands, close to the Asiatic shore opposite the south-east cape of Lesbos; Callicratidas left 50 ships with Eteonicus to keep up the siege of Mytilene, and came to meet the Athenians with 120. (X 1.6.18–26; D 97.1–3).

Xenophon sets out the order of battle. Since the Spartans now had the better sailors, the Athenians posted on each wing two squadrons of fifteen ships, with a second line of two similar squadrons to cover the gaps and prevent the enemy from sailing through the front line;[58] in the centre the Samians and others formed a single line. On the other side Callicratidas held the right wing, the Boeotians under Thrasondas the left. It is not easy to see how the battle developed: Xenophon only says it went on for a long time, at first in formation and then with the ships more scattered; Diodorus' more extensive version is mostly portents and padding and this time gives no effective illumination; and there are some errors.[59] They agree that the turning-point was Callicratidas' death, when first the Peloponnesian right wing and then the left was routed, and they fled to Chios and Phocaea. News was got to Eteonicus, who prevented panic by pretending the message was of victory, and so got his ships off to Chios while he retired with the infantry to Methymna. (X 1.6.28–33, 36–8; D 97.4–99, 100.5).

The Spartans had lost over seventy ships, the Athenians twenty-five, but of these many were still afloat with survivors clinging to them, and the failure to rescue these proved fatal to the victorious generals. It is common ground that a rising storm prevented them from either picking up the survivors or going ahead to raise the siege of Mytilene, and that the generals' first despatch to Athens said no more than this; but Xenophon's determination to see the generals as innocent victims has produced a jerky and in places illogical account of the reaction at Athens, to which Diodorus (or at least XIII.101) is probably a better guide.[60] In

[57] Hellanicus attributes both measures to the archon-year 407/6, in which case they must belong to the very end of the year, around the beginning of July 406; and the battle to 406/5, probably in August.   [58] See Morrison and Coates 1986 (A 90) 88–91.

[59] D 98.3 puts the younger Pericles on the right wing, but the narrative at 99.4 implies that he was on the left, where Xenophon puts him. The narrative at 97.1 can hardly be right, that only 60 ships were got ready at Athens and 80 had been assembled at Samos; and the 140 ships given to Callicratidas at 97.3 might be another error.

[60] See Andrewes 1974 (D 2). But Diodorus speaks throughout of the recovery of corpses, not of living men: surprisingly reaffirmed at xv.35.1.

spite of elation at the victory, feeling rose about the casualties; Theramenes and Thrasybulus had come home before the rest, and the generals
supposed they were responsible for the agitation; so they sent a second
letter, asserting that these two had been assigned the duty of recovering
the men.[61] That turned the people's anger against them, but their defence
was accepted and the generals were deposed except for Conon who was
left in charge; the eight surviving were summoned home for trial, of
whom six obeyed. The flight of the other two is intelligible in view of
known public feeling and the record of Athens in treatment of her
generals, but it must have done harm to the cause of those who did go
home. (X 1.6.34–5, 7.1–2; D 100.1–4, 101.1–5).

At the first meeting they seemed to be favourably received, but
decision was put off to a further Assembly, and in the interval came the
Apaturia, the family festival celebrated in October, when the appearance
of many men in mourning inflamed feeling afresh. In the Assembly the
Council put forward the motion of one Callixenus,[62] that since accusation and defence had been heard at the previous meeting they should
proceed to an immediate vote, with death as the penalty on conviction.
An attempt to have this motion declared illegal was howled down, and
when some of the *prytaneis* declined to put it to the vote they too were
intimidated, except for Socrates. The alternative motion of Euryptolemus, for separate trials according to the 'decree of Cannonus',[63] at first
prevailed, but after an objection and a second vote it was lost, and the six
were condemned to death: among them Thrasyllus, Aristocrates and
Diomedon, all experienced commanders, and Pericles' homonymous
son. (X 1.7.2–34; D 101.6–7).

The victims belonged to the board that took office at Alcibiades'
downfall, whereas Theramenes and Thrasybulus had been his associates;
but political feeling enters into this depressing affair only to the extent
that it may have sharpened the generals' original suspicion of their
former opponents. The democracy's execution of loyal democrats, after
victory at such a critical moment, can only be called hysteria, attributable
to the long strain of a war that was now going badly. Revulsion was
rapid, and fatal to Callixenus, though stories differ about his fate;
Theramenes, according to his enemy Lysias (XIII.10), was elected general
next spring but rejected on his *dokimasia* as no friend of the people.

[61] Xenophon has this in his main narrative (1.6.35) and when he returns to the subject at 7.17,
29ff; but at II.3.35 Theramenes in his last speech is allowed to say that he did not start the quarrel but
had been attacked first by the generals.

[62] Otherwise unknown; Xenophon makes him an agent of Theramenes and charges the latter
with procuring bogus mourners for the Apaturia. Diodorus has nothing of this, but does not treat
Theramenes as merely innocent (101.7); no one suggests that Thrasybulus played an active part.

[63] Known only from this occasion (X 1.7.20), an intimidating but legal process for use against
those who had harmed the state.

Cleophon is not recorded as taking any part in this affair, but *Ath. Pol.* 34.1 makes him responsible for the rejection of a Spartan peace offer at this point; this has justifiably been regarded as a misplaced version of the similar offer and rejection in 410. (X 1.7.35, D 103.2).

In the winter the Greek cities and Cyrus sent embassies to Sparta demanding the restoration of Lysander to his command, and the Spartans got round the rule against a second term by sending him nominally as second-in-command (*epistoleus*) to Aracus. On arrival at Ephesus he sent for Eteonicus, who had spent an unhappy winter on Chios, and set about creating a larger fleet; Cyrus pointed out that all the money he had from the King and much more had been spent, but still gave to Lysander. The Athenians had returned to Samos, and manned 173 ships; Adeimantus and Philocles had come to share the command with Conon. Cyrus was now summoned to his father's sickbed, and he sent for Lysander to Sardis, telling him not to fight unless he had many more ships than the Athenians, and detailing to him the tributes from the cities which were at his disposal.[64] At this point Diodorus and Plutarch put in a notorious example of Lysander's perfidy, his conduct during an oligarchic coup in Miletus, and after an excursion to Caria[65] they send him off on a brief visit to Attica and Agis, from which he returned before the Athenians could catch him. (X 11.1.1–7, 10–15; D 100.7–8, 104).

But through most of the summer there was no serious activity, for when Lysander finally went north it was, according to Xenophon (11.1.17) 'for the sailing out of the ships', that is, the ships bringing the corn from the Black Sea, and that should be late August or early September; we also know that the final battle was fought in the archon-year 405/4. He went first to Abydus, then to capture the rich city of Lampsacus; the Athenians followed with three new generals, Menander, Tydeus and Cephisodotus, and 180 ships to Elaeus and Sestus, then to Aegospotami, a bare beach opposite Lampsacus where the Hellespont is still very narrow, some distance from the nearest supply base at Sestus. For four successive mornings they offered battle, and Lysander kept his ships ready but did not come out; and he could observe how the crews scattered for rest or food when they got back to their beach. Alcibiades, coming from his Thracian base, warned the Athenians of their danger and urged them to move to a safer position, but they would have none of him. Aristophanes' *Frogs*, with its unusually serious and overtly political parabasis calling for the recall of good men from exile, asks at the end of the play (1422–32) what should be done about Alcibiades, whom the city 'longs for and hates and wishes to have'; evidently his recall had been mooted, if only informally, and mistrust persisted. The generals at

---

[64] For Cyrus' right to this revenue see Lewis 1977 (A 76) 119.

[65] This, though not the rest, also comes in Xenophon's version, but with different details.

Aegospotami could also fear the consequences to themselves if Alcibiades took a hand. (X 11.1.17–26; D 105).

On the fifth day Lysander struck. The dispersal of the Athenians was signalled from mid-channel, his fleet raced across the strait, and the Athenians had no time to man their ships.[66] Conon with eight or nine ships escaped to Cyprus, the *Paralus* to Athens, but the rest fell into Lysander's hands, and some 3,000 prisoners including the generals Adeimantus and Philocles. The last was executed, along with the Athenians among the captives, in reprisal for atrocities which Athens was charged with committing or threatening against prisoners she took; only Adeimantus was spared. Lysander then cleared the rest of the Hellespont, and Lesbos, sending all Athenians home to swell the number that would need feeding. The army of the Peloponnesian League marched to Attica under Pausanias, Agis came down from Decelea, and Lysander came to Aegina, then moored outside the Piraeus with 150 ships and waited. (X 11.1.27–2.2, 2.5–9; D 106.1–8, 107.1–2).

The Athenians blocked the harbour and manned the walls, and in conscious imitation of the amnesty of 480 they restored citizen rights to all who had been deprived of them (Andoc. 1.77–9); and they gave Athenian citizenship to the Samians (M–L 99). When food ran short they sent to Agis offering to become allies of Sparta, retaining their walls and the Piraeus; he referred them to Sparta, and at the frontier they were told to go home and think again. Archestratus was imprisoned for advocating acceptance of a Spartan proposal that ten stades of the walls should be pulled down, and a decree forbade further discussion of terms like these. In the end Theramenes offered to go to Lysander to find out whether Sparta wished to enslave the city; and he stayed away for three months, detained (he said) by Lysander. By the time he came back, saying that Lysander had told him to apply to the ephors at Sparta, Athens was no longer in a state to resist; and Cleophon, the main obstacle to surrender, had been disposed of.[67] Theramenes was appointed as the head of an embassy of ten,[68] and when they stated at the frontier that they had full powers they were allowed to proceed. Many Spartan allies, headed by Corinth and Thebes, opposed a treaty and urged that Athens should be destroyed, but Sparta refused to enslave a city which had rendered such service to Greece in her hour of danger; we may fairly

---

[66] So Xenophon. Diodorus (106.1) has Philocles, whose turn it was to command, set out ahead with thirty ships, telling the rest to get ready to follow, but we are not told what his plan was. The rest of the fleet was not manned when Lysander attacked, so the surprise and disaster were as complete as in the other account: cf. Ehrhardt 1970 (G 13).

[67] Xen. 1.7.35 and Lys. XIII.12 differ about his fate.

[68] Lys. XII.68–9 makes much of the fact that Theramenes refused to state in advance the terms he was prepared to accept for Athens. The 'Theramenes papyrus' (Merkelbach and Youtie 1968 (c 72); Henrichs 1968 (c 47)) restates the charge very nearly in Lysias' exact words, then gives Theramenes a spirited and sophisticated reply (see Andrewes 1970 (c 6)).

suppose that they were also concerned about the ways in which a vacuum in Attica might be filled. The eventual terms included dismantling the Long Walls and the Piraeus, the surrender of all but twelve ships, the return of exiles and the standard commitment of the Peloponnesian League, to have the same friends and enemies as the Spartans and to follow wherever they led by land or sea. The only fear of the crowd that anxiously awaited Theramenes' return was that he might have failed to obtain a treaty, and this was accepted with minimum resistance. Then Lysander sailed into the Piraeus and the demolition of the walls began to the sound of flutes. Xenophon comments that they 'thought this day was the beginning of freedom for the Greeks'; whatever view he may have taken at the time, in the end the admirers of Sparta were to be adequately disillusioned about the freedom she sponsored. (X 11.2.6–23; D 107.3–4).

VII. EPILOGUE

The story may end, as it began, with Thucydides. He was sure that Athens could have 'got the better' of the Peloponnesians if they had stuck to the rules laid down by Pericles, and his most uncompromising statement of the defensive nature of Pericles' strategy comes in the same late-written chapter (11.65) in which he acclaims Pericles' foresight. That is by no means a simple judgement. Pericles' insight had told him that it would be quite easy to stand up to the Peloponnesians taken by themselves, but it is recognized that the odds were radically changed when first the Sicilians joined in, then revolts among the allies multiplied, and lastly Cyrus gave Sparta support without reservation. Thucydides still insists on the Athenians' successful resistance to these increased pressures and claims that they only succumbed because of their internal dissensions.

He has already (11 65.11) noted the baleful effect of quarrels at home on the fate of the expedition to Sicily, and there his mind seems to be on the exile of Alcibiades (p. 449 above). Here (65.12) it is hardly possible to pinpoint a specific outbreak between the arrival of Cyrus and the final defeat at Aegospotami; revulsion after the Arginusae trial may have deprived Athens of the services of Theramenes as a general, but that could not be seen as a decisive factor; more important, there is no doubt of the general feeling of suspicion and unease that followed the overthrow of the Four Hundred (p. 480 above), replacing the resolute mood in which Athens had faced the Sicilian disaster (Thuc. VIII.1). We should also take into account Thucydides' judgement on the Five Thousand (VIII.97.2), where in my belief the basis for ascribing to them a μετρία ξύγκρασις (moderate mixture) between the Many and the Few is that this regime was able to employ men of very different political colours, both Thrasyllus and Theramenes; the parabasis of Aristophanes' *Frogs* expresses a similar point of view. But another late-written passage brings us back to Alcibiades: VI.15.4 where Thucydides boldly says outright that Athens was wrecked because her citizens could not overcome their distrust of Alcibiades and give him the command. His performance between his recall by the fleet in 411 and his return to Athens in 407 gives something of a base for this judgement, but it does not follow that he could have coped equally well with the combination of Cyrus and Lysander, or that he had grown to be safe from the effects of his flamboyant character. It would be more comfortable if Thucydides had settled for saying in general that the current atmosphere of distrust was inimical to good planning. But he may have been among those who thought that the final disaster could have been avoided if the generals at Aegospotami had been willing to listen to Alcibiades.

If Pericles had intended no more than to demonstrate to the Spartans that they could not defeat Athens, it must be supposed that he would have pressed for acceptance of the Spartan peace offer in 425, which Thucydides himself evidently favoured (p. 382 above). It remains difficult to understand how that great statesman came to think that it was worth exposing the land of Attica to some years of Spartan ravaging for so slight a result, or how he could have supposed that a settlement reached in this context could have lasted; the affront to Sparta's allies would have been more deeply felt in 425, when Athens' triumph had not yet been checked, than it was in 421. But Thucydides thought that the defensive strategy made sense, and so have enough modern critics.

In practice it proved impossible to end the war except by the victory of one side. For a time during the Archidamian War, more especially after Pylos and before Delium, Athens had a chance of outright victory (p. 386 above), which was not exploited. After the Sicilian disaster, and Athens' reckless antagonization of the King of Persia, that chance virtually disappeared, and the prospects for a compromise peace, though one might have been negotiated in 410, were no higher than before. In Thucydides' view the fault lay with the successors of Pericles, whose competition for dominance led them to propose vote-catching measures; hence mistakes which were fatal to the city. It has never been entirely easy to know how to take this, except for his prime example, the expedition to Sicily, which he claims the people saw as opening up large funds for public pay, and which certainly displayed dissension among Athens' leaders. Other mistakes were of course made, but few of them fit Thucydides' analysis, and that analysis is surely incomplete: alongside the positive mistakes the missed opportunities deserved a mention.

Thucydides' thesis is conditioned by his concentration on the defensive; a significant indication is his judgement, which was surely wrong, on Phrynichus' performance at Miletus in 412 (p. 468 above).

The length of the war increased its destructive power. The material damage, worst for Attica, was repaired sooner than might have been expected, and in a relatively short period Athens re-emerged as a major power in Greece; but impressive as the fourth-century achievements of the city and its individual citizens were, the momentum of the fifth century was not quite recovered. Spartan leadership held no promise for the future of Greece, and her rule proved harsher than the 'tyranny' of Athens; any hope that Thebes might improve on this died with Epaminondas. Inevitably one wonders what would have followed from an Athenian victory in the war, but this is scarcely profitable; to maintain an enlarged empire or achieve the unity of Greece, a radical change of attitude would be needed at Athens, and the end product might be widely different from the Greece that we know and admire.

CHRONOLOGICAL NOTES

D. M. LEWIS

(Note 13 by A. Andrewes)

(1) The dating of Leotychidas' operations in Thessaly is tied up with an insoluble problem. Diodorus' chronological source seems to have had correct reign lengths for the fifth-century Eurypontid kings, which Diodorus reports under archon-dates which are wrong by seven years. He reports Leotychidas' death in 476/5 after a reign of 22 years (XI.48.2), though 491 is the year which best fits Herodotus' account of his accession (VI.65–72; *CAH* IV² 498–9), and then gives Archidamus 42 years from 476/5 to 434/3 (Diod. XII.35.4), and Agis 27 years from 434/3 to 407/6 (XII.35.4). However, Archidamus almost certainly died in 427 (see p. 403) and Agis in 400 (Andrewes 1971 (F 3) 216 n. 18). Many have been tempted to believe that the slip has been caused by confusion between the exile of Leotychidas in 476 and his death in 469, but this will hardly account for confusion about Archidamus and Agis. The error is perhaps more mechanical, caused by a confusion between Phaidon, Athenian archon in 476/5, and the archon of 469/8, really called Apsephion, who appears in Diodorus' MSS as Phaion or Phaidon. The first solution will give us a date for Leotychidas' exile and thus for his Thessalian expedition. The second will not; at least, it certainly will not if Leotychidas' regnal years include his years of exile, as they certainly did for Plistoanax (Diod. XIII.75.1), though not for the king Pausanias (XIII.75.1, XIV.89.1). Beloch (1912–1927 (A 2) I.2, 186–7) deferred Leotychidas' exile to 469 to justify the reign length, but it is not clear how he could have reconciled his birth date of 545 for him (*ibid.*, 182; perhaps a little high), with Herodotus' statement (VI.72.1) that he did not grow old in Sparta. For the whole question and a solution in which there was no Eurypontid king between 476 and 469, see Connor 1985 (L 25) 99–102.

(2) Further points favour a long stay by Pausanias at Byzantium. A long stay, extending into the period of Themistocles' residence at Argos, is implied by the Letters of Themistocles, a second-century A.D. fictitious collection which has some good material (Doenges 1981 (C 26)), and at least one story of Pausanias' behaviour at Byzantium (Plut. *Cim.* 6.4–7) falls into this period and implies a longish time-sequence.[1]

---

[1] Notice the journey to the oracle at Pontic Heraclea, but there is a variant for this (Paus. III.17.8–9). Both versions attach the story to Pausanias' behaviour in 478, but this is proved wrong by Plutarch's making it the occasion for an expulsion of Pausanias from Byzantium by Cimon.

(3) That a boy boxer was proclaimed as a Tirynthian at Olympia in 468 (*P. Oxy.*
222 = *FGrH* 405 F 1, line 42) does not in itself prove that the move to Halieis had
not yet taken place; Paus. II.17.5 may, however, imply that Argos had already
recovered the Heraeum at the time of the capture of Tiryns and that this
happened after the fall of Mycenae. No other text links the Argos–Tiryns
sequence with any ally or enemy, unless we include the dateless episode (Hdt.
VII.137.2) in which a Spartan captured Halieis, and this is likely to be too late to
be relevant. Some have placed the Argive capture of Tiryns before that of
Mycenae; for Forrest 1960 (F 24) 230–2, the campaigns overlap in 465.

(4) There is unanimity in the ancient sources that the Helot Revolt lasted ten
years, and this seems to be true both of direct references and of dates which seem
to be calculated on that assumption. Thucydides, the primary source, describes
its beginning in connexion with the revolt of Thasos. That revolt is connected
with the colony at Drabescus which he seems to have dated to 465/4 (see p. 13).
He places the end of the Revolt in the tenth year (1.103.1–4), a statement which
should be taken seriously, although the passage interrupts a sequence of events
which belong to 461 or 460. An unnecessary belief in the strict order of
Thucydides' account has frequently led in modern times (e.g. Gomme, *HCT* I
410–11; *ATL* III 162–8; Klaffenbach 1950 (B 6); Lewis 1953/4 (B 8)) to the
emendation of the numeral, even though the emendation would in its turn
involve assuming a remarkably early intrusion by Athens into the Corinthian
Gulf (1.103.4). No ancient author seems to have taken the course of emendation,
but there is evidence for a different use of the ten years, one which calculated
them back from the point at which Thucydides appears to put the end and which
therefore started the Revolt in 469/8 or thereabouts. Diodorus (XI.63) starts it in
that year (and finishes it in 456/5, XI.84.8, though giving the length as ten years
at XI.64.4). More importantly, since it is not clear how much Diodorus has been
using his chronological source, at least one *Atthis* seems to have done so; Schol.
Ar. *Lys.* 1144, where the archon-year and the time-lapse after Plataea guarantee
each other, placed an Athenian expedition to help Sparta against the Messenians
in 468/7. This school of thought has had its modern successors (Scharf 1954/5 (B
12); Hammond 1955 (B 5) 371–81. A variant: Sealey 1957 (B 13); Badian 1988 (B
1) 304–10), but this is not a likely interpretation of Thucydides, and the dating
offers no hope of even approximating the one obviously independent dating,
that to the fourth year of Archidamus' reign in Plut. *Cim.* 16.4.[2] Certainty would
be foolish, but a start in winter 465/4 and an end some time in 456/5 does least
violence to Thucydides and offers a plausible sequence of events.

(5) Events at Athens (pp. 69–70) suggest that the return of Cimon's expedition
from Ithome and the alliances with Argos and Thessaly belong to the archon-
year 462/1. The most valuable evidence is the casualty list M–L 33: 'These men
of the Erechtheid tribe died in the war, in Cyprus, in Egypt, in Phoenicia, in
Halieis, in Aegina, at Megara.' The most natural interpretation (but see

---

[2] The dating by the 79th Olympiad and the Athenian archon of 464/3 in Paus. IV.24.5 obviously
rests on calculation.

Gomme, *HCT* I 311) is that the first year of the Egyptian expedition was the same as the first year of fighting in mainland Greece. The Egyptian expedition lasted six years and ended in a summer (Thuc. 1.109.4–110.1; Megabyxus can hardly have diverted the Nile in flood). The only method of fixing its end is to make the assumption that the disaster occasioned the transfer of the allied treasury from Delos to Athens, completed by spring 453 (*IG* I³ 259.3). But, if the Egyptian expedition ended in 454, we still cannot tell whether its six years are, on Thucydides' normal practice, six summers and six winters, in which case it started in 460 (as argued by Gomme, *HCT* I 410), or six campaigning seasons, in which case it started in 459 (as argued by Kolbe 1937 (C 63) 266–7; see also p. 13). The former view seems incompatible with the evidence (Diod. XI.78.4) that the siege of Aegina, begun in the first year of the war (M–L 33 and Thuc. 1.105.2) and completed after the battles of Tanagra and Oenophyta (Thuc. 1.108.5), lasted only nine months. The main text proceeds from the conclusion that 459 was the first war-year and that Tanagra and Oenophyta belong to 458.³

(6) Thucydides follows the surrender of Aegina, without any indication of time interval, with Tolmides' circumnavigation of the Peloponnese. The *Atthis* date for that was the archon-year 456/5 (Schol. Aeschin. II.75).⁴ The date has been disregarded by many, for various reasons. Thucydides' order should not be regarded as a reason, as it is, e.g., by *ATL* III 168–72. The imperfect tenses at the beginning of 1.109 should warn us that this chapter on the Egyptian expedition begins with resumptive matter; it appears that what led Thucydides to go back to the Egyptian expedition at this point was the arrival of Megabyxus' large force, generally and rightly dated to 456. I am reluctant to reject the *Atthis* date for Tolmides. The consequence, given the views expressed in note (5), is that Thucydides gives us nothing for 457.

(7) Similarly, it is not unlikely that Thucydides' account of the Egyptian expedition also overlaps at its end with material which he defers to 1.111. Time-indications in that chapter make it likely that all its events belong to one campaigning season; we cannot tell whether it is that of 455 or 454.

(8) That the date of Cimon's Cyprus expedition is 451 was argued by Meiggs 1972 (E 53) 124–6, strongly influenced by the apparent evidence of the papyrus commentary on Demosthenes (p. 126 n. 26) that financial measures implying the

³ Diodorus' evidence about the length of the siege of Aegina seems straightforward but is generally disregarded; Busolt 1893–1904 (A 12) III 322 n. 3 quotes a long list of authorities who found it incompatible with Thucydides' chronology. It is not incompatible, as shown by Gomme, *HCT* I 412 n. 2 (with different years from mine), and Gomme's own reason for rejecting it is simply that he thinks that Thuc. 1.108.3 guarantees that the Long Walls were completed before the surrender of Aegina. I incline to think that the last clause of 1.108.3 is a response to 1.107.4 and that it is by no means certain what part of the whole sequence is referred to by μετὰ ταῦτα in 108.4. Hammond 1955 (B 5) 404 n. 1 would have been able to accommodate the nine months (again with different years), had he not been committed to taking seriously Diodorus' dating of Tanagra to the archon-year 458/7 and Oenophyta to 457/6.

⁴ On general principles, we should not regard the fact that Diodorus (XI.84) dates it to the same year as supporting evidence, since there is no clear reason to think that he is using his chronological source.

conclusion of peace with Persia were taken at Athens before the end of the archon-year 450/49. Diodorus (XII.3–4) spreads the campaign over two of his years, 450/49 and 449/8, and treatments before Meiggs (e.g. Gomme, *HCT* I 396 (tentatively) and *ATL* III 178, 298–9 (with a tight and elaborate timetable)) preferred 450. The problems are complex, and involve a number of questions. Did Cimon return early from ostracism? What is the precise meaning of Thuc. 1.112.1? Did the Spartans break the truce referred to there in invading Attica in 446? The nearest thing we have to useful evidence is the appearance of some Carian names at the end of *ATL* List 4, say, in early summer 450; these were connected with Cimon's expedition by Nesselhauf 1933 (E 57) 25–6, and their position in the list perhaps suits 450 better. Nothing in Thucydides excludes Diodorus' view that the campaign extended over two years, and that may be something Ephorus knew, not a matter of calculation.

(9) The Coronea campaign has normally been dated late in 447. *ATL* III 178, accepting the MS reading in Philochorus *FGrH* 328 F 34, and arguing that Thucydides' language implied that the Euboean revolt followed soon after the evacuation of Boeotia, preferred spring 446. If the casualty-list M–L 48 belongs to 447, as would seem to follow from the quota-list chronology followed here, and if the casualty-list discussed on p. 133 n. 60 refers to Coronea (Bradeen 1964 (C 119) 21–9 and 1969 (C 120) 154), Coronea does belong to the campaigning season of 446.

(10) On the chronology of the Samian revolt see Fornara 1979 (E 26) which I only partially accept. I assume here that all three payments recorded on M–L 55 are for Samos, the first, 128 talents, in 441/0, the second, 368 talents, in 440/39, but before the Panathenaea, the third, 908 talents, in 440/39 after the Panathenaea. Fornara may be right to give the first payment to the fleet which set up the democracy; I think it unlikely that this was in 442/1, as he thinks. It is not clear from what point the nine months of Plut. *Per.* 28.7 are reckoned.

(11) Thucydides (II.2.1) has an elaborate chronological statement relating the Theban attack on Plataea to the Thirty Years' Peace, the priestess of Hera at Argos, the Spartan ephor, the Athenian archon and the battle of Potidaea. It has proved distressingly difficult to accept all his statements as transmitted in the manuscripts, though Thomson 1968 (G 41) has managed it. The essential difficulty is that if, as is stated in the MSS, the attack on Plataea was in the sixth month after the battle of Potidaea, what can Thucydides mean in implying at 1.125.1 that the Spartan invasion of Attica came the best part of a year (precise interpretation varies) after the declaration of war by the congress of the Peloponnesian League? Gomme (*HCT* I 222–4, 421–5) claimed to be arguing not only from this, but also from Thucydides' narrative of the Potidaea affair, in dating the revolt of Potidaea to April 432, the battle of Potidaea to June and the two meetings at Sparta to July and August; this not only requires emending Thucydides' interval between the battle of Potidaea and the attack on Plataea, but seems to run up against the inscription cited on p. 376 n. 17. The bibliography is large; de Ste Croix 1972 (G 36) 317–28 is a useful introduction.

We have lost a vital clue, since Thucydides has omitted all reference to the Olympic Games of 432.

(12) The tribute-assessment decree of 425 (M–L 69) contains at line 34 a reference to an expedition which is away while the decree is going through the Council and the Assembly. It was maintained by Wade-Gery and Meritt 1936 (G 42) that the expedition was Cleon's expedition against Sphacteria. There are difficulties in detail about this, quite apart from the more general question about whether this is a plausible moment to place the initiation of such a far-reaching and optimistic operation. It may be better to put the decree later in the sequence of events and think it influenced by the glow of victory; the expedition referred to will then be Nicias' expedition to the Corinthiad; so M–L pp. 194–6.

(13) Between the battles of Cyzicus early in 410 and Arginusae in summer 406 Xenophon has noted the opening of a new year or campaigning season in only three passages, *Hell.* 1.2.1, 3.1, 4.2, leaving one year-change unmarked and no direct indication where it should come. Somewhere in these four years we have to locate a gap in military activity of roughly a year. Busolt (1893–1904 (A 12) III.ii 1529 n. 1), followed by E. Meyer and others, put the gap at the end of the doubtful period: Thrasyllus sailed out to Ionia in summer 410, the Athenian campaign in the Hellespont follows in 409, Alcibiades went home to Athens in 408, the battle of Notium belongs to spring 407 (the 'early' chronology). Beloch (1912–27 (A 2) II.ii, 243–54) argued that the gap is at the beginning, so that the events listed above must all come down a year; this 'late' chronology was adopted by W. S. Ferguson (*CAH* v¹ 463–5, and 1932 (D 24) 38–45) and Lotze 1964 (G 26). Uniquely, Robertson 1980 (G 35) follows the 'early' chronology as far as the Hellespont campaign, then stretches *Hell.* 1.4.8–9 to cover almost the whole year 408; thereafter he follows the 'late' chronology for Alcibiades' visit to Athens and the battle of Notium.

The 'early' scheme has certain advantages. Diodorus XIII.64.7 says that the Athenian occupation of Pylos lasted 15 years to the Spartan recapture, and if this took place in winter 410/9 the figure is correct, whereas on the 'late' scheme it should be 16. Again, the Athenian ambassadors to the King who set off with Pharnabazus in the winter after the Hellespont campaign were detained on Cyrus' order, and according to Xenophon (1.4.7) three years elapsed before they were released and got back to the Athenian camp; the 'early' scheme will just allow this, but if their detention did not start till the beginning of 407 there would be no camp to return to after three full years. But if Notium was fought in spring 407 and Arginusae in about August 406, this is an impossible point at which to insert a full year of military inactivity, with both Cyrus and Lysander on the scene. Worse still, the board of Athenian generals appointed soon after Notium is the same board that commanded at Arginusae; it is not conceivable that it was re-elected entire for a second year. It is surprising that the 'early' chronology found so much favour in the generation of Busolt and Meyer.

The intermediate solution proposed by Robertson has the attraction that it allows us to keep the 15 years of the occupation of Pylos and the three years of the Athenian envoys' detention while giving us reasonable dates for Notium and Arginusae. The trouble is to believe the central proposition. Xen. 1.4.8 clearly represents Alcibiades as being in a hurry; Robertson makes much of the difficulty of raising so large a sum as 100 talents from Caria in quick time, but to spend an entire year squeezing these small communities would not be a sensible policy. Again, Cyrus on this theory had already come far enough west to be seen by the Athenian envoys (Xen. 1.4.4) by the beginning of spring 408, but he does not reach Sardis till well into the summer of 407; it is not enough to say that things moved slowly in the Persian empire.

At the beginning the 'late' chronology has the advantage of giving the Syracusans time to rebuild their fleet. After Cyzicus Pharnabazus provided money and timber at Antandrus (Xen. 1.1.25–6), and when Thrasyllus reached Ephesus, roughly in the middle of June, the Syracusans were there with twenty ships, plus five more recently arrived from home; if this was in 410 the rebuilding had been done with astonishing speed, if in 409, there is no problem. Busolt and Beloch, with their various followers, accept from Xenophon that Hermocrates was deposed after Cyzicus and that the new generals took over the fleet at Miletus (1.1.31), whereas here (above, p. 478) the alternative view has been followed, that the deposition and the take-over are wrongly dated by Xenophon and really belong to the summer of 411 (Thuc. VIII.85.3, see HCT ad loc.).

As regards the shipbuilding this makes little difference, but Beloch built further on what follows, 1.1.32–6. 'At this time' an event occurred which led, it is not clear how much later, to the exile of Pasippidas from Sparta, and Cratesippidas was sent out to the ships which Pasippidas had collected from the allies. Critics have argued about the meaning of 'at this time'; Cratesippidas was the immediate predecessor of Lysander (Hell. 1.5.1), who took over in 407, but he might have been sent out before his formal term of office began. Next (1.1.33), 'about this time' Thrasyllus led out Athenian troops to the Lyceum (we must now be back in 410) against a demonstration by Agis, who withdrew to Decelea. From there he could see the many ships bringing grain to the Piraeus, and realized that it was no good merely blocking the Athenians' access to their land; so he decided to send Clearchus son of Ramphias to Byzantium, and did so.

Clearchus however had already reached the Hellespont in summer 411 (Thuc. VIII.80.3), and we have not been told that he had gone home in the interval; Xenophon shows no sign of knowing of his earlier arrival, and it is a natural guess that he has simply misdated the despatch of Clearchus by a year (so Robertson, 283 n. 4). But this is a more doubtful case than that of the deposition of Hermocrates: the circumstances of the despatch of Clearchus are quite different this time, and the details about his arrival, and Xenophon has not here involved himself in contradictions like those found in the Hermocrates narrative. It may then be that Clearchus had come back to Greece and was at Agis' disposal. If so, we should note that the 'many' ships suggest the regular autumn sailing, necessarily after the victory at Cyzicus had cleared the way, and this means that Thrasyllus was still in Athens in autumn 410.

The standard argument against the 'late' chronology has always been that it leaves the Athenian generals in the Hellespont totally inactive for a full year after Cyzicus, especially surprising for so energetic a leader as Alcibiades. In 1953 (G

3) 2–5 I argued that at this time the democratic leaders in Athens were not ready to collaborate with the Hellespontine generals, and that this accounts for the fact that the necessary reinforcements requested by the latter were not sent in 410 (p. 482 above). This was accepted by Lotze, but not by Robertson (285 n. 13), who found it untypical for the democracy or for Alcibiades. The 15 years for Pylos (above) have then to be taken as an error, perhaps Diodorus' own. The detention of the ambassadors was imposed by Cyrus to prevent the Athenians learning what was going on at the time (Xen. *Hell.* 1.4.5–6), and to extend this for three years never made much sense; I have no specific remedy to propose.

CHRONOLOGICAL TABLE

Persia, Egypt, etc.	Greece and the Aegean: Political History
	490 Battle of Marathon
485 Death of Darius. Accession of Xerxes	
c. 484 Persia recovers Egypt	
480 Xerxes' invasion of Greece	480 Battles of Artemisium, Thermopylae, Salamis
479 Revolt of Ionia. Persia loses Sestus and Hellespont	479 Battles of Plataea and Mycale, capture of Sestus (winter)
478 Persia loses Byzantium and the Bosphorus	478 (− 6?)
Greek cities in Cyprus liberated from Persia	Leotychidas in Thessaly
	478 (winter)
	Recall of Pausanias; formation of Delian League
	476–5 Cimon's campaign in Thrace; capture of Eïon and Scyros
	475–69 Subjugation of Carystus
	Revolt and suppression of Naxos
	c.? 473–0
	Battle of Tegea
	c.? 473–69
	Battle of Dipaieis
	c. 471 Ostracism of Themistocles
c. 470 Persia recovers Cyprus	471–0 Synoecism of Elis
469–6 Battle of the Eurymedon	469–6 Battle of the Eurymedon
	c. 466 Death of Pausanias; flight of Themistocles

S. Italy, Sicily and Carthage	Greek Literature, Philosophy, Art
	c. 499/8 Birth of Anaxagoras
	497/6 Birth of Sophocles
	490–480 Latest pediments of the temple of
	Aphaea at Aegina
	Athenian Treasury at Delphi
485 Gelon becomes tyrant of Gela and later of Syracuse	485 Comedy added to City Dionysia
480 Sicilian victory at Himera	*c.* 480 Birth of Euripides
478 Death of Gelon: Hiero succeeds at Syracuse	
478–7 Polyzalos in Italy, then ruler of Gela Syracuse and Acragas at war	
476 Foundation of Aitna Resettlement of Himera Olympic victories of Hiero and Theron Death of Anaxilas of Rhegium–Messana; Micythos regent there	476 Bronze Tyrant-slayers of Critius and Nesiotes dedicated Pindar, *Olympian* I–III, *Pythian* II, *Nemean* I; Bacchylides V Aeschylus' first visit to Sicily; *Aetnaeae* performed at Aetna
475 Eruption of Etna	
474 Battle of Cyme Hieron's Pythian victory	474–3 Pindar, *Pythian* III
472 Death of Theron; Thrasydaeus succeeds at Acragas	472 Aeschylus, *Persae*
472–1 War between Syracuse and Acragas Expulsion of Thrasydaeus; end of Emmenid tyranny at Acragas, Gela and Himera	
471 and after. Mercenaries' war in territories of Gela and Acragas Battle of Crastus	
470 Hiero's Pythian victory	*c.* 470 Birth of Socrates
	c. 470–460 Polygnotus (painter) *flor.* Stoa Poikile at Athens
	470–69 Pindar, *Pythian* I, *Olympian* XII, *Isthmian* II; Bacchylides IV
468 Hiero's Olympic victory	468 First production by Sophocles Death of Simonides
	468–7 Pindar, *Olympian* VI; Bacchylides III
467–6 Death of Hiero; Thrasybulus succeeds at Syracuse Micythos retires; Anaxilas' sons succeed at Rhegium–Messana	467 Aeschylus, *Seven against Thebes*
466 Revolution at Syracuse; Thrasybulus retires to Locri	

Persia, Egypt, etc.	Greece and the Aegean: Political History
465 (August) Xerxes murdered Artaxerxes I becomes king	465 Attempt to found colony at Ennea Hodoi Revolt of Thasos
	465–4 Helot Revolt
	? Argos captures Mycenae
	463 Surrender of Thasos
c. 462 Revolt in Egypt under Inaros	462 Spartan appeal for Athenian help
	? Ephialtes' reform of the Areopagus Cimon dismissed by Spartans from Messenia Alliance of Athens with Megara, Argos and Thessaly
	461 Ostracism of Cimon; Ephialtes assassinated
459? Athenian fleet in Cyprus turns to Egypt and sails up the Nile	459? Athenian expedition to Cyprus and Egypt Athenian defeat at Halieis Battles of Cecryphaleia and in Megarid Athenian Long Walls begun
	458? Spartan expedition to Doris Battles of Tanagra and Oenophyta Surrender of Aegina
	457 Archonship opened to *zeugitae*
	? Introduction of payment for jurors
456 Persian army under Megabyxus reaches Egypt	456 Surrender of Messenians on Ithome Expedition of Tolmides round Peloponnese
	455–4 Thessalian expedition Pericles in Corinthian Gulf
454 Athenian expedition to Egypt ends in disaster	454 Treasury of Delian League moved to Athens Unrest in Ionia
	451 Five Years' Truce between Athens and Sparta Thirty Years' Peace between Argos and Sparta Pericles' citizenship law Return of Cimon to Athens
c. 450 Rebellion of Megabyxus in Syria	450? Cimon's expedition to Cyprus and death
450? Cimon's expedition to Cyprus Unrest in Egypt continues	449? Peace of Callias
449? Peace of Callias	448–7 Irregularities of tribute-payment
	448 Spartan invasion of Attica
	? Pericles in Chersonese
	446 Athenian defeat at Coronea and loss of Boeotia Revolt of Euboea Spartan invasion of Attica
445–4 Psammetichus' gift of corn to Athens	446–5 Thirty Years' Peace
	443? Ostracism of Thucydides son of Melesias

S. Italy, Sicily and Carthage	Greek Literature, Philosophy, Art
466–1 Civil war at Syracuse. Revolution in subject-cities and 'Common Resolution' to end civil war	
463 'Democracy' and Festival of Liberty at Syracuse	463 Aeschylus, *Supplices*
461 Restoration of Catana, Naxus and Camarina First appearance of Ducetius Expulsion of Anaxilas' sons and republican restoration at Rhegium and Messana	*c.* 460 Birth of Hippocrates
459–8 Rise of Sicel movement; foundation of Menainon and conquest of Morgantina by Ducetius	458 Aeschylus, *Oresteia*
458–7? Athenian treaty with Segesta	
	c. 456 Anaxagoras comes to Athens Temple of Zeus at Olympia complete with its sculpture *c.* 460–440 Myron *flor.* 456 Death of Aeschylus
454–3 Tyndarides' attempt at tyranny; petalism introduced at Syracuse War between Segesta and (?) Lilybaeum	455 First production by Euripides *c.* 455 Birth of Thucydides
453–2 Foundation of Palice; consolidation of Sicel *synteleia* Syracusan expeditions against Etruscans	
451–0 Siege of Motyum; Ducetius defeats Syracusans and Acragantines	*c.* 450 Beginning of building of Hephaesteum
450–49 Ducetius defeated at Nomae and exiled to Corinth	*c.* 450–430 Phidias, Polyclitus *flor.* 447 Beginning of building of Parthenon *c.* 446 Birth of Aristophanes
446 Ducetius returns to Sicily; foundation of Kale Akte Acragas defeated by Syracuse	Latest extant ode of Pindar (*Pythian* VIII) *c.* 445 Birth of Lysias
444–3 Foundation of Thurii	
c. 443 Athenian treaties with Leontini and Rhegium Athenian fleet at Naples	*c.* 442 Work on metopes and frieze of Parthenon begins 442 Comedy added to Lenaea

Persia, Egypt, etc.	Greece and the Aegean: Political History

440 Pissuthnes in touch with Samian revolt	441–0 (winter)
	    Revolt of Samos
	439 (spring)
	    Surrender of Samos
	    c. 438 Phormio in Acarnania

	c. 437 Pericles' Pontic expedition 437–6 Foundation of Amphipolis

	435 Quarrel between Corinth and Corcyra about Epidamnus
	    Battle of Leucimme
	433 Athenian alliance with Corcyra
	    Decrees of Callias
	    Battle of Sybota
	432 Revolt of Potidaea
	  ? Megarian Decree
	    Conference at Sparta
	431 Theban attack on Plataea
	    War begins
	    Peloponnesian invasion of Attica
	    Athenian fleet round Peloponnese

430 Pissuthnes intervenes at Colophon	430 Peloponnesian invasion of Attica
	    Plague breaks out at Athens
	    Pericles' Peloponnesian expedition
	    Pericles deposed and fined
	    Phormio sent to Naupactus
	    Fall of Potidaea
	429 Siege of Plataea begins
	    Death of Pericles
	    Defeat of Cnemus and successes of Phormio
	428 Peloponnesian invasion of Attica
	    Revolt of Mytilene
	    Property-tax at Athens
	427 Peloponnesian invasion of Attica
	    Fall of Mytilene
	    Fall of Plataea
	    Stasis at Corcyra
	    Athenian expedition to Sicily
	426 Demosthenes in north west
	    Nicias at Melos
	425 Peloponnesian invasion of Attica
	    Fortification of Pylos
	    Athenians refuse Spartan peace-offer
	    Re-assessment of tribute
	    Athenian capture of Sphacteria

424–3 (winter) Death of Artaxerxes I	424 Athenians capture Nisaea
	    Athenians capture Cythera and raid Laconia
	    Battle of Delium
	    Brasidas reaches north, captures Acanthus, Amphipolis, Torone

S. Italy, Sicily and Carthage	Greek Literature, Philosophy, Art
440 Death of Ducetius; Syracuse annexes Sicel area	
	438 Euripides, *Alcestis* Partial completion of Parthenon; the Athena of Phidias dedicated
	438–2 Work on pediments of the Parthenon
	437 Work begun on the Propylaea
	c. 436 Death of Empedocles Prosecution of Anaxagoras
	c. 435 Phidias at Olympia (cult statue of Zeus)
433–2 Renewal of Athenian treaties with Rhegium and Leontini	c. 433 Protagoras in Athens
	431 Euripides, *Medea*
	c. 430 Attic Classical grave-relief series begins
	428 Euripides, *Hippolytus*
427 Embassy of Gorgias of Leontini to Athens	427 Aristophanes, *Daitales* Gorgias in Athens Birth of Plato
427–4 Athenian forces in Sicily	
	426 Aristophanes, *Babylonians*
	425 Aristophanes, *Acharnians*
424 Conference of Gela	424 Aristophanes, *Knights* Exile of Thucydides

Persia, Egypt, etc.	Greece and the Aegean: Political History
423 (February?) Ochus becomes King as Darius II ? Renewal of peace between Persia and Athens	423 (April) Armistice for one year between Athens and Sparta 422 Cleon recaptures Torone Battle of Amphipolis; death of Cleon and Brasidas Negotiations for peace 421 Peace of Nicias (April) Fifty years' alliance between Athens and Sparta Destruction of Scione 420 Alliance between Sparta and Boeotia Four-Power alliance 419 Nicias and Alcibiades generals Alcibiades operates in Peloponnese 418 Spartan victory at Mantinea 418–17 Fifty years' alliance between Sparta and Argos Oligarchy established at Argos 417 Oligarchy overthrown at Argos; alliance with Athens renewed
c. 416? Pissuthnes revolts. Tissaphernes satrap in Sardis Athenian support of Amorges	416 (spring) Ostracism of Hyperbolus? Athenians attack and subjugate Melos 415 Segesta appeals to Athens against Selinus Mutilation of the Hermae Athenian fleet sails for Sicily Recall and flight of Alcibiades 414 Argive invasion of Thyrea Spartans ravage Argive country Athenian landings in Laconia
413 (autumn) Darius asks Tissaphernes and Pharnabazus for action	413 Spartans renew the war and seize Decelea 5 per cent duty substituted for tribute
412–11 Treaties between Sparta and Persia	412 Revolt of Athenian subject-allies Treaties between Sparta and Persia
411 Trouble in Egypt?	411 Revolution of the Four Hundred Government of the Five Thousand Army and fleet at Samos faithful to democracy; Alcibiades in command Athenian victories at Cynossema and Abydus 410 Athenian victory at Cyzicus Full democracy restored at Athens Athenians refuse Spartan peace offers
408 Trouble in Media 408–7 Mission of Spartan Boeotius; Cyrus sent to west	408 Athenians regain Byzantium Founding of the city of Rhodes 407 Alcibiades returns to Athens Lysander takes over Spartan fleet 406 Athenian defeat at Notium; withdrawal of Alcibiades Athenian victory at Arginusae Trial of the generals
405–4 (winter) Death of Darius II; Arsaces becomes King as Artaxerxes II 401 Revolt of Cyrus; battle of Cunaxa 401–0 Amyrtaeus king of Egypt	405 Battle of Aegospotami 405–4 Siege of Athens 404 Peace between Sparta and Athens; destruction of Long Walls

S. Italy, Sicily and Carthage	Greek Literature, Philosophy, Art
	423 Aristophanes, *Clouds*
422 Athenian envoys in S. Italy and Sicily	422 Aristophanes, *Wasps*
	421 Aristophanes, *Peace*
	c. 420 Polyclitus' Hera at Argos
	c. 420–400 Zeuxis, Parrhasius (painters) *flor.*
	420–410 Temple of Athena Nike balustrade
415 Athenian expedition arrives in Sicily	415 Euripides, *Troades*
414 Siege of Syracuse	414 Aristophanes, *Birds*
Death of Lamachus	
Arrival of Gylippus	
414–13 Eurymedon sails to Sicily	
413 Second Athenian expedition reaches Sicily	
Athenian disaster in Sicily	
	412 Euripides, *Helen* and *Andromeda*
	411 Aristophanes, *Lysistrata* and *Thesmophoriazusae*
409 Hannibal's expedition to Sicily; destruction of Selinus and Himera	409–406 Completion of the Erechtheum
	409 Sophocles, *Philoctetes*
	408 Euripides, *Orestes*
406 Second Carthaginian expedition to Sicily; fall of Acragas	406 Death of Euripides in Macedon; death of Sophocles
405 Rise of Dionysius	405 Aristophanes, *Frogs*
Peace between Syracuse and Carthage	
	401 Production of Sophocles, *Oedipus Coloneus*

BIBLIOGRAPHY

Abbreviations

AAA	*Athens Annals of Archaeology*
Abh. Sächs. Ak. Wiss. zu Leipzig	
	Abhandlungen der sächsischen Akademie der Wissenschaften zu Leipzig
AfP	*Archiv für Papyrusforschung*
AHR	*American Historical Review*
AIIN	*Annali: Istituto Italiano di Numismatica*
AJA	*American Journal of Archaeology*
AJAH	*American Journal of Ancient History*
AJP	*American Journal of Philology*
AMI	*Archäologische Mitteilungen aus Iran*
Annales E.S.C.	
	Annales, Economies, Sociétés, Civilisations
Ann. Fac. di Lett. di Perugia	
	Annali della facoltà di lettere di Perugia
Ant. Class.	*Antiquité classique*
Arch. Anz.	*Archäologischer Anzeiger*
Arch. Delt.	*'Αρχαιολογικὸν Δελτίον*
ASAA	*Annuario della scuola archeologia di Atene*
ASNP	*Annali della Scuola Normale Superiore di Pisa, Classe di Lettere e Filosofia*
ASS	*Archivio storico siciliano*
ASSO	*Archivio storico per la Sicilia orientale*
Ath. Mitt.	*Athenische Mitteilungen. Mitteilungen des deutschen archäologischen Instituts, Athenische Abteilung*
ATL	B. D. Meritt, *et al. The Athenian Tribute Lists* I–IV. Cambridge, Mass. – Princeton, 1939–53
BAR	British Archaeological Reports
BCH	*Bulletin de correspondance hellénique*
Bibl. Ec. fr. Ath. et Rome	
	Bibliothèque des Ecoles françaises d'Athènes et de Rome
BICS	*Bulletin of the Institute of Classical Studies of the University of London*
Boll. d'Arte	*Bollettino d'Arte*
Boll. Ist. Naz. Dramma Ant.	
	Bollettino del Istituto nazionale dello studio della dramma antica

BSA	*Annual of the British School at Athens*
CA	*Classical Antiquity* (formerly *California Studies in Classical Antiquity*)
CAH	*The Cambridge Ancient History*
CEG	P. A. Hansen, *Carmina Epigraphica Graeca*. Berlin, 1983–9
CID	*Corpus des Inscriptions de Delphes*
CJ	*Classical Journal*
Class. et Med.	*Classica et Mediaevalia*
Cl. Phil.	*Classical Philology*
Cl. Rh.	*Clara Rhodos*
CQ	*Classical Quarterly*
CR	*Classical Review*
CRAI	*Comptes-rendus de l' Académie des inscriptions et belles lettres*
Cron. di Arch.	*Cronache di Archeologia*
CSCA	*California Studies in Classical Antiquity*
CW	*Classical Weekly*
DGE	*Dialectorum Graecarum Exempla Epigraphica*
DHA	*Dialogues d'histoire ancienne*
Ditt. *Syll.*	W. Dittenberger (ed.) *Sylloge Inscriptionum Graecarum*. 3rd edn. Leipzig, 1915–21
D–K	H. Diels and W. Kranz, *Die Fragmente der Vorsokratiker*. 6th edn. Berlin, 1951–4
Dox. Graec.	Diels, *Doxographi Graeci*. Berlin, 1879
EMC/CV	*Echos du Monde Classique/Classical Views*
FGrH	F. Jacoby, *Die Fragmente der griechischen Historiker*. Berlin and Leiden, 1923–58
FHG	C. Müller, *Fragmenta Historicorum Graecorum*. Paris, 1841–70
G&R	*Greece and Rome*
GGM	C. Müller, *Geographi Graeci Minores* i–iii. Paris, 1855–82
GRBS	*Greek, Roman and Byzantine Studies*
HCT	A. W. Gomme, A. Andrewes and K. J. Dover, *A Historical Commentary on Thucydides* i–v. Oxford, 1945–81
Hesp.	*Hesperia*
Hill, *Sources*[2]	G. F. Hill, rev. R. Meiggs and A. Andrewes, *Sources for Greek History between the Persian and Peloponnesian Wars*. Oxford, 1951
HN	B. V. Head, *Historia Numorum*. Oxford, 1911
HSCP	*Harvard Studies in Classical Philology*
HThR	*Harvard Theological Review*
IEG	M. L. West (ed.) *Iambi et Elegi Graeci ante Alexandrum cantati* ii. Oxford, 1972

IEK   *Die Inschriften von Erythrai und Klazomenai* (C 130)
IG   *Inscriptiones Graecae*. Berlin, 1873–
I. J. Naut. Arch.
               International Journal of Nautical Archaeology
Ist Mitt.   *Istanbuler Mitteilungen. Mitteilungen des deutschen archäologischen Instituts, Abteilung Istanbul*

JHS   *Journal of Hellenic Studies*
JNG   *Jahrbuch für Numismatik und Geldgeschichte*
JÖAI   *Jahreshefte des Österreichischen archäologischen Instituts, Wien*
JRS   *Journal of Roman Studies*

K–A   R. Kassel and C. Austin, *Poetae Comici Graeci*. Berlin and New York, 1983–

LCM   *Liverpool Classical Monthly*
LIMC   *Lexicon Iconographicum Mythologiae Classicae*. Zurich–Munich, 1981–
LSAM   F. Sokolowski, *Lois sacrées de l'Asia Mineure*. Paris, 1955
LSCG   F. Sokolowski, *Lois sacrées des cités grecques*. Paris, 1969
LSS   F. Sokolowski, *Lois sacrées des cités grecques, Supplément*. Paris, 1962

MBNG   *Mitteilungen der Bayerischen Numismatischen Gesellschaft*
MEFRA   *Mélanges de l'Ecole française de Rome, Antiquité*
Mem. Torino   *Memorie dell' Accademia delle Scienze di Torino*
Milet   A. Rehm (ed.) *Das Delphinion in Milet*. Berlin, 1914
M–L   R. Meiggs and D. M. Lewis, *Greek Historical Inscriptions*. Oxford, 1969
Mus. Helv.   *Museum Helveticum*

NNM   Numismatic Notes and Monographs
Not. Scav.   *Notizie degli scavi di antichità*
Num. Chron.   *Numismatic Chronicle*

OCD   *Oxford Classical Dictionary*
OIP   Oriental Institute Publications

PA   J. Kirchner, *Prosopographia Attica*. Berlin, 1901–3
PCPhS   *Proceedings of the Cambridge Philological Society*
PMG   D. L. Page, *Poetae Melici Graeci*. Oxford, 1962
PP   *Parola del Passato*
Proc. Amer. Philos. Soc.
               Proceedings of the American Philosophical Society
Proc. Br. Acad.
               Proceedings of the British Academy

Proc. Royal Irish Academy
    Proceedings of the Royal Irish Academy
PSI   Papiri della società italiana
P–W   Pauly–Wissowa–Kroll–Mittelhaus, *Real-Encyclopädie der klassischen Altertumswissenschaft*. Stuttgart, 1893–

RBP*h*   *Revue belge de philologie*
REA   *Revue des études anciennes*
REG   *Revue des études grecques*
REH   *Revue des études historiques*
Rend. Linc. *Rendiconti della Accademia nazionale dei Lincei*
Rev. Phil.   *Revue de philologie, de littérature et d'histoire anciennes*
RGVV   *Religionsgeschichtliche Versuche und Vorarbeiten*
Rh. Mus.   *Rheinisches Museum*
RIDA   *Revue internationale des droits de l'antiquité*
Riv. di Filol. *Rivista di filologia e d'istruzione classica*
Röm. Mitt. *Römische Mitteilungen. Mitteilungen des deutschen archäologischen Instituts, Römische Abteilung*
RSA   *Rivista di storia antica*

SBAk. Berlin Sitzungsberichte der Akademie der Wissenschaften zu Berlin
SB Heidelberg
    Sitzungsberichte der Heidelberger Akademie der Wissenschaften
SBAk. Wien Sitzungsberichte der Österreichischen Akademie der Wissenschaften
SEG   *Supplementum Epigraphicum Graecum*. Leiden, 1923–
SGDI   H. Collitz and F. Bechtel, *Sammlung der Griechischen Dialekt-Inschriften* I–IV. Göttingen, 1885–1910
SIG   W. Dittenberger (ed.) *Sylloge Inscriptionum Graecarum*. 3rd edn, Leipzig, 1915–24
SO   *Symbolae Osloenses*

TAPA   *Transactions and Proceedings of the American Philological Association*
TAPS   Transactions of the American Philosophical Society
TGrF   B. Snell and S. Radt (eds.) *Tragicorum Graecorum Fragmenta*. Göttingen, 1971–
Tod, GHI M. N. Tod, *Greek Historical Inscriptions*. Oxford, 1946–8

VDI   *Vestnik Drevnei Istorii*

Wien. Stud. *Wiener Studien*

YCS   *Yale Classical Studies*

ZfN   *Zeitschrift für Numismatik*
ZPE   *Zeitschrift für Papyrologie und Epigraphik*

A. GENERAL

1. Alty, J. 'Dorians and Ionians', *JHS* 102 (1982) 1–14
2. Beloch, K. J. *Griechische Geschichte*. 2nd edn. 4 vols. in 8. Strassburg–Berlin/Leipzig, 1912–27
3. Bengtson, H. *Die Verträge der griechisch-römischen Welt von 700 bis 338 v. Chr.* (Die Staatsverträge des Altertums II). Munich–Berlin, 1962. (2nd edn 1975)
4. Bengtson, H. *Griechische Geschichte*. 5th edn. Munich, 1977
5. Berve, H. *Die Tyrannis bei den Griechen.* I–II. Munich, 1967
6. Boardman, J. *The Greeks Overseas.* 2nd edn. London, 1980
7. Boardman, J., Griffin, J. and Murray, O. (eds.) *The Oxford History of the Classical World.* Oxford, 1986
8. Bonner, R. J. and Smith, G. *The Administration of Justice from Homer to Aristotle* I–II. Chicago, 1930–8
9. Bradeen, D. W. and McGregor, M. F. (eds.) Φόρος: *Tribute to Benjamin Dean Meritt.* Locust Valley, 1974
10. Brunt, P. A. 'The Hellenic league against Persia', *Historia* 2 (1953–4) 135–63
11. Burn, A. R. *Persia and the Greeks.* London, 1962. (2nd edn with a Postscript by D. M. Lewis. London, 1984)
12. Busolt, G. *Griechische Geschichte bis zur Schlacht bei Chaeroneia.* I², II², III. i, III. ii (to 404). Gotha, 1893–1904
13. Cameron, A. and Kuhrt, A. (eds.) *Images of Women in Antiquity.* London–Canberra, 1983
14. Cameron, G. G. *Persepolis Treasury Tablets* (OIP 65). Chicago, 1948
15. Carpenter, R. *Beyond the Pillars of Hercules. The Classical World seen through the Eyes of its Discoverers.* New York, 1966
16. Carradice, I. A. (ed.) *Coinage and Administration in the Athenian and Persian Empires* (BAR International Series 343). Oxford, 1987
17. Cartledge, P. and Harvey, F. D. (eds.) *Crux. Essays presented to G. E. M. de Ste Croix on his 75th birthday.* Exeter, 1985
18. Cary, M. and Warmington, E. H. *The Ancient Explorers.* 2nd edn. Harmondsworth, 1963
19. Casson, L. *The Ancient Mariners. Seafarers and Sea Fighters of the Mediterranean in Ancient Times.* London, 1959
20. Casson, L. *Ships and Seamanship in the Ancient World.* Princeton, 1971
21. Cowley, A. E. *Aramaic Papyri of the Fifth Century B.C.* Oxford, 1923
22. Daux, G. 'Remarques sur la composition du conseil amphictionique', *BCH* 81 (1957) 95–120
23. Davies, J. K. *Democracy and Classical Greece.* Hassocks, 1978
24. Diller, H. 'Die Hellenen–Barbaren–Antithese im Zeitalter der Perserkriege', in *Grecs et barbares* (Entretiens ... Fondation Hardt 8), 37–82. Vandoeuvres–Geneva, 1962
25. Dodds, E. R. *The Ancient Concept of Progress and Other Essays on Greek Literature and Belief.* Oxford, 1973

26. Dover, K. J. *Greek and the Greeks: Collected Papers* I: *Language, Poetry, Drama.* Oxford, 1987

27. Dover, K. J. *The Greeks and their Legacy: Collected Papers* II: *Prose Literature, History, Society, Transmission, Influence.* Oxford, 1988

28. Dow, S. 'Greek numerals', *AJA* 56 (1952) 21–3

29. Dunbabin, T. J. *The Western Greeks*, Oxford, 1948

30. Duncan-Jones, R. P. 'Metic numbers in Periclean Athens', *Chiron* 10 (1980) 101–9

31. Eadie, J. W. and Ober, J. (eds.) *The Craft of the Ancient Historian: Essays in Honor of Chester G. Starr.* Canham, MD, 1985

32. Ehrenberg, V. *Polis und Imperium.* Zurich–Stuttgart, 1965

33. Ehrenberg, V. L. *The Greek State.* 2nd edn. London, 1969

34. [Ehrenberg] *Studies in Ancient Societies and Institutions presented to Victor Ehrenberg on his 75th Birthday.* Oxford, 1966

35. Evans, J. A. S. 'The Settlement of Artaphernes', *Cl. Phil.* 71 (1976) 344–8

36. Finley, M. I. *The World of Odysseus.* 3rd edn. Harmondsworth, 1962

37. Finley, M. I. 'The problem of the unity of Greek law', in *Atti del 1° Congresso internazionale della società italiana di storia del diritto*, 129–42. Florence, 1966

38. Finley, M. I. *Democracy, Ancient and Modern* (M. W. Gross Lectures). New York, 1973

39. Finley, M. I. *The Use and Abuse of History.* London, 1975

40. Finley, M. I. 'The ancient city from Fustel de Coulanges to Max Weber and beyond', *Comparative Studies in Society and History* 19 (1977) 305–27 (= L 41, 3–23)

41. Finley, M. I. 'Classical Greece', in *Second International Conference of Economic History* I: *Trade and Politics in the Ancient World*, 11–35. Paris, 1965

42. Finley, M. I. *Ancient Slavery and Modern Ideology.* London, 1980

43. Freeman, K. *Greek City-States.* London, 1959

44. Garlan, Y. 'Etudes d'histoire militaire et diplomatique', *BCH* 89 (1965) 332–48

45. Gernet, L. *Anthropologie de la Grèce antique.* Paris, 1968

46. Gillis, D. *Collaboration with the Persians* (*Historia* Einzelschr. 34). Wiesbaden, 1979

47. Glotz, G. with Cohen, R. *Histoire grecque* II. Paris, 1938

48. Gomme, A. W. *The Population of Athens in the Fifth and Fourth Centuries B.C.* (Glasgow University Publications 28). Oxford, 1933

49. Gomme, A. W. *Essays in Greek History and Literature.* Oxford, 1937

50. Gomme, A. W. 'The population of Athens again', *JHS* 79 (1959) 61–8

51. Gomme, A. W. *More Essays in Greek History and Literature.* Oxford, 1962

52. Graham, A. J. *Colony and Mother City in Ancient Greece.* Manchester, 1964

53. Gschnitzer, F. *Abhängige Orte im griechischen Altertum* (Zetemata 17). Munich, 1958

54. Hammond, N. G. L. *Studies in Greek History.* Oxford, 1973

55. Hansen, M. H. 'The number of Athenian hoplites in 431 BC', *SO* 56

(1981) 19–32

56. Hansen, M. H. *Demography and Democracy: the Number of Athenian Citizens in the Fourth Century B.C.* Herning, 1986
57. Hansen, M. H. 'The origin of the term *demokratia*', *LCM* 11 (1986) 35–6
58. Hanson, V. D. *Warfare and Agriculture in Classical Greece* (Biblioteca di studi antichi 40). Pisa, 1983
59. Harrison, A. R. W. *The Law of Athens* I–II. Oxford, 1968–71
60. Hasebroek, J. *Staat und Handel im alten Griechenland. Untersuchungen zur antiken Wirtschaftsgeschichte.* Tübingen, 1928
61. Hasebroek, J. *Griechische Wirtschafts- und Gesellschaftsgeschichte bis zur Perserzeit.* Tübingen, 1931
62. Hasebroek, J. *Trade and Politics in Ancient Greece* (transl. of A 60 by L. M. Fraser and D. C. MacGregor). London, 1933
63. Hill, G. F., rev. Meiggs, R. and Andrewes, A. *Sources for Greek History between the Persian and Peloponnesian Wars.* Oxford, 1951
64. Hornblower, S. *Mausolus.* Oxford, 1982
65. Hornblower, S. *The Greek World 479–323 B.C.* London–New York, 1983. (Reprinted with corrections 1985)
66. Humphreys, S. C. *Anthropology and the Greeks.* London–Henley–Boston, 1978
67. Humphreys, S. C. *The Family, Women and Death: Comparative Studies.* London–Boston–Melbourne–Henley, 1983
68. Huss, W. *Geschichte der Karthager* (Handbuch der Altertumswissenschaft, Abt. 3, Teil 8). Munich, 1985
69. Jeffery, L. H. *Archaic Greece.* London, 1976
70. Jüthner, J. *Hellenen und Barbaren. Aus Geschichte des Nationalbewusstseins.* Leipzig, 1923
71. Karavites, P. ''Ελευθερία and αὐτονομία in fifth-century interstate relations', *RIDA* ser. 3, 29 (1982) 145–62
72. Kiechle, F. 'Zur Humanität in der Kriegführung der griechischen Staaten', *Historia* 7 (1958) 129–56
73. Kirsten, E. *Die griechische Polis als historisch-geographisches Problem des Mittelmeeresraumes.* Bonn, 1956
74. Lateiner, D. 'Heralds and corpses in Thucydides', *CW* 71 (1977–8) 97–106
75. Latte, K. *Kleine Schriften zu Religion, Recht, Literatur und Sprache der Griechen und Römer*, eds. O. Gigon, W. Buchwald and W. Kunkel. Munich, 1968
76. Lewis, D. M. *Sparta and Persia* (Cincinnati Classical Lectures 1). Leiden, 1977
77. Lewis, D. M. 'Democratic institutions and their diffusion', in Πρακτικὰ τοῦ Η΄ διεθνοῦς συνεδρίου Ἑλληνικῆς καὶ Λατινικῆς Ἐπιγραφικῆς, τόμος Α΄, 55–61. Athens, 1984
77A. Lewis, D. M. 'Public property in the city', in A 93A, 243–62
78. Lipsius, J. H. *Das Attische Recht und Rechtsverfahren.* I, II. i, II. ii, III. Leipzig, 1905–15
79. Lloyd, C. 'Greek urbanity and the polis', in Marchese, R. R. (ed.) *Aspects*

of Graeco-Roman Urbanism. Essays on the Classical City. (BAR International Series 188), 11–41. Oxford, 1983 [1984]

80.   McDonald, W. A. *The Political Meeting Places of the Greeks.* Baltimore, 1943

81.   MacDowell, D. M. *The Law in Classical Athens.* London, 1978

82.   Macleod, C. W. *Collected Essays.* Oxford, 1983

83.   [Manni]. *Φιλίας χάριν. Miscellanea in onore di Eugenio Manni.* Rome, 1979

84.   Marrou, H. I. *Histoire de l'éducation dans l'antiquité.* 3rd edn. Paris, 1956

85.   Martin, R. *L'urbanisme dans la Grèce antique.* Paris, 1956. 2nd edn. 1974

86.   Meiggs, R. 'A note on the population of Attica', *CR* n.s. 14 (1964) 2–3

87.   Meyer, E. *Forschungen zur alten Geschichte* II. Halle, 1899

88.   Momigliano, A. *Alien Wisdom. The Limits of Hellenization.* Cambridge, 1975

89.   Momigliano, A. *Quinto contributo alla storia degli studi classici e del mondo antico* I–II. (Edizioni di storia e letteratura). Rome, 1975

90.   Morrison, J. S. and Coates, J. F. *The Athenian Trireme.* Cambridge, 1986

91.   Morrison, J. S. and Williams, R. T. *Greek Oared Ships, 900–322 B.C.* Cambridge, 1968

91A.   Mossé, C. *La tyrannie dans la Grèce antique.* Paris, 1969

92.   Mossé, C. 'Citoyens actifs et citoyens passifs dans les cités grecques', *REA* 81 (1979) 241–9

93.   Murray, O. *"Ο 'ΑΡΧΑΙΟΣ ΔΑΣΜΟΣ", Historia* 15 (1966) 142–56

93A.   Murray, O. and Price, S. *The Greek City: From Homer to Alexander.* Oxford, 1990

94.   Ormerod, H. A. *Piracy in the Ancient World: an Essay on Mediterranean History.* Liverpool, 1924

95.   Ostwald, M. *Autonomia: its Genesis and Early History* (American Classical Studies II) [U.S.A.], 1982

96.   Ostwald, M. *From Popular Sovereignty to the Sovereignty of Law.* Berkeley–Los Angeles, 1986

97.   Peacock, D. P. S. *Pottery in the Roman World: an Ethnoarchaeological Approach.* London–New York, 1982

98.   Pistorius, T. *Hegemoniestreben und Autonomiesicherung in der griechischen Vertragspolitik klassischer und hellenistischer Zeit.* Frankfurt, 1985

99.   Pomeroy, S. B. *Goddesses, Whores, Wives and Slaves: Women in Classical Antiquity.* London, 1976

99A.   Powell, A. *Athens and Sparta. Constructing Greek Social and Political History from 478 B.C.* London–New York, 1988

100.   Pritchett, W. K. *Studies in Ancient Greek Topography* I–V (University of California Publications in Classical Studies 1, 4, 22, 28, 31). Berkeley–Los Angeles, 1965–85

101.   Pritchett, W. K. *The Greek State at War* I–IV. (The first volume was originally published as *Ancient Greek Military Practices.*) Berkeley–Los Angeles, 1971–85

102.   Raubitschek, A. E. 'The Covenant of Plataea', *TAPA* 91 (1960) 178–83

103.   Rawlings, H. R. *A Semantic Study of 'Prophasis' to 400 B.C.* (*Hermes* Einzelschr. 33). Wiesbaden, 1975

104. Rawson, E. *The Spartan Tradition in European Thought*. Oxford, 1969
105. Rhodes, P. J. 'Ephebi, bouleutae and the population of Athens', *ZPE* 38 (1980) 191–201
106. Roberts, J. W. *City of Sokrates. An Introduction to Classical Athens*. London, 1984
107. Roy, J. 'The mercenaries of Cyrus', *Historia* 16 (1967) 287–323
108. de Ste Croix, G. E. M. 'Political pay outside Athens', *CQ* n.s. 25 (1975) 48–52
109. de Ste Croix, G. E. M. *The Class Struggle in the Ancient Greek World*. London, 1981
110. Schwabl, H. 'Das Bild der fremden Welt bei den frühen Griechen', in *Grecs et Barbares* (Entretiens... Fondation Hardt 8), 1–36. Vandoeuvres–Geneva, 1962
111. Sealey, B. R. I. *Essays in Greek Politics*. New York (1967)
112. Snodgrass, A. M. *Archaic Greece: the Age of Experiment*. London–Melbourne–Toronto, 1980
113. Starr, C. G. *The Economic and Social Growth of Early Greece*. New York, 1977
114. Thomas, R. *Oral Tradition and Written Record in Classical Athens*. Cambridge, 1989
115. Toynbee, A. J. *Some Problems of Greek History*. Oxford, 1969
116. Ucko, P. J., Tringham, R. and Dimbleby, G. W. (eds.) *Man, Settlement, and Urbanism*. London, 1972
117. Vernant, J.-P. 'Remarques sur la lutte de classe dans la Grèce ancienne', *Eirene* 4 (1965) 5–19 (= A 118, 11–29; Eng. transl. A 119, 1–18)
118. Vernant, J.-P. *Mythe et société en Grèce ancienne*. Paris, 1974
119. Vernant, J.-P. *Myth and Society in ancient Greece* (transl. of A 118 by J. Lloyd). Hassocks, 1980
120. Veyne, P. *Le pain et le cirque: sociologie historique d'un pluralisme politique*. Paris, 1976
121. Wade-Gery, H. T. *Essays in Greek History*. Oxford, 1958
122. Welskopf, E. C. (ed.) *Hellenische Poleis, Krise–Wandlung–Wirkung*. Berlin, 1974
123. Westlake, H. D. *Essays on the Greek Historians and Greek History*. Manchester, 1969
124. Whittaker, C. R. 'The Western Phoenicians: colonization and assimilation', *PCPhS* n.s. 20 (1974) 58–79
125. Wilamowitz-Moellendorff, U. von. *Aristoteles und Athen* I–II. Berlin, 1893
126. Will, E. *Le monde grec et l'orient*. I. *Le Ve siècle (510–403)*. Paris, 1972
127. Wolff, H. J. *'Normenkontrolle' und Gesetzesbegriff in der attischen Demokratie*. SB Heidelberg 1970, no. 2

B. CHRONOLOGY
(See also F 71; G 29, 30, 35, 41)

1. Badian, E. 'Towards a chronology of the Pentekontaetia down to the renewal of the Peace of Callias', *EMC/CV* n.s. 7 (1988) 289–320

2. Bayer, E. and Heideking, J. *Die Chronologie des Perikleischen Zeitalters* (Erträge der Forschung 36). Darmstadt, 1975
3. den Boer, W. 'Political propaganda in Greek chronology', *Historia* 5 (1956) 163–77
4. Deane, P. *Thucydides' Dates 465–431 B.C.* Don Mills, Ontario, 1972
5. Hammond, N. G. L. 'Studies in Greek chronology of the sixth and fifth centuries B.C.', *Historia* 4 (1955) 371–411
6. Klaffenbach, G. 'Das Jahr der Kapitulation von Ithome und der Ansiedlung der Messenier in Naupaktos', *Historia* 1 (1950) 231–5
7. Lenardon, R. J. 'The chronology of Themistokles' ostracism and exile', *Historia* 8 (1959) 23–48
8. Lewis, D. M. 'Ithome again', *Historia* 2 (1953/4) 412–18
9. Milton, M. P. 'The date of Thucydides' synchronism of the siege of Naxos with Themistokles' flight', *Historia* 28 (1979) 257–75
10. Parker, R. A. and Dubberstein, W. H. *Babylonian Chronology, 626 B.C. – A.D. 75* (Brown University Studies 19). Providence, 1956
11. Samuel, A. E. *Greek and Roman Chronology: Calendars and Years in Classical Antiquity* (Handbuch der Altertumswissenschaft Abt. 1, Teil 7). Munich, 1972
12. Scharf, J. 'Noch einmal Ithome', *Historia* 3 (1954/5) 153–62
13. Sealey, R. 'The Great Earthquake in Lacedaemon', *Historia* 6 (1957) 368–71
14. Stolper, M. W. 'The death of Artaxerxes I', *AMI* 16 (1983) 223–36
15. Stolper, M. W. 'Some ghost facts from Achaemenid Babylonian texts', *JHS* 108 (1988) 196–8
16. Unz, R. K. 'The chronology of the Pentakontaetia', *CQ* n.s. 36 (1986) 68–85
17. van der Waerden, B. L. and Pritchett, W. K. 'Thucydidean time-reckoning and Euctemon's seasonal calendar', *BCH* 85 (1961) 17–52

C. SOURCES

I. HISTORIOGRAPHY

1. Aly, F. and Sbordone, F. 'Zum neuen Strabon Text', *PP* 5 (1950) 228–63
2. Ameling, W. 'Plutarch, Perikles 12–14', *Historia* 24 (1985) 47–63
3. Anderson, J. K. *Xenophon*. London. 1974
4. Andrewes, A. 'The Melian Dialogue and Perikles' last speech', *PCPhS* 186 (1960) 1–10
5. Andrewes, A. 'The Mytilene Debate: Thucydides 3.36–49', *Phoenix* 16 (1962) 64–85
6. Andrewes, A. 'Lysias and the Theramenes Papyrus', *ZPE* 6 (1970) 35–8
7. Andrewes, A. 'Diodoros and Ephoros: one source of misunderstanding', in A 31, 189–97
8. Baladié, R. *Strabon. Tome V (Livre VIII)* (Budé). Paris, 1978
9. Barber, G. L. *The Historian Ephorus*. Cambridge, 1935
10. Bartoletti, L. *Hellenica Oxyrhynchia* (Teubner). Leipzig, 1959
11. Bloch, H. 'Studies in the historical literature of the fourth century B.C. I:

The *Hellenica of Oxyrhynchus* and its authorship', *HSCP* Suppl. 1, 303–41. (Cambridge, MA, 1940)

12. Breitenbach, H. R. *Historiographische Anschauungsformen Xenophons.* Freiburg, 1950

13. Breitenbach, H. R. 'Xenophon', P–W IXA2 (1967) 1569–1928

14. Bruce, I. A. F. *An Historical Commentary on the 'Hellenica Oxyrhynchia',* Cambridge, 1967

15. Casevitz, M. *Diodore de Sicile, Bibliothèque Historique,* XII (Budé). Paris, 1972

16. Cawkwell, G. L. *Xenophon: History of My Times.* Harmondsworth, 1979

17. Classen, J. and Steup, J. *Thukydides.* Various dates and editions, reprinted Berlin, 1963

18. Cobet, J. *Herodots Exkurse und die Frage der Einheit seines Werkes* (*Historia* Einzelschr. 17). Wiesbaden, 1971

18A. Cobet, J. Review of C 29A in *Gnomon* 46 (1974) 737–46

19. Cochrane, C. N. *Thucydides and the Science of History.* London, 1929

20. Connor, W. R. 'History without heroes: Theopompus' treatment of Philip of Macedon', *GRBS* 8 (1967) 133–54

21. Connor, W. R. *Theopompus and Fifth-Century Athens.* Washington, 1968

22. Connor, W. R. *Thucydides.* Princeton, 1984

23. Connor, W. R. 'Narrative discourse in Thucydides', in *The Greek Historians: Literature and History,* 1–17. Stanford, 1985

24. Cornford, F. M. *Thucydides Mythistoricus.* London, 1907

25. Delebecque, E. *Essai sur la vie de Xénophon.* Paris, 1957

26. Doenges, N. J. *The Letters of Themistocles.* New York, 1981

27. Dover, K. J. *Thucydides* (*G&R,* New Surveys in the Classics 7). Oxford, 1973

28. Drews, R. D. 'Diodorus and his sources', *AJP* 83 (1962) 383–92

29. Edmunds, L. *Chance and Intelligence in Thucydides.* Cambridge, MA, 1975

29A. Fehling, D. *Die Quellenangaben bei Herodot.* Berlin–New York, 1971 (transl. into English as *Herodotus and his 'Sources'* by J. G. Howie. Leeds, 1989)

30. Finley, J. H. *Thucydides.* Cambridge, MA, 1942

31. Finley, J. H. *Three Essays on Thucydides.* Cambridge, MA, 1967

32. Fornara, C. W. *Herodotus: an Interpretative Essay.* Oxford, 1971

32A. Fornara, C. W. 'Evidence for the date of Herodotus' publication', *JHS* 91 (1971) 25–34

32B. Fornara, C. W. 'Herodotus' knowledge of the Archidamian War', *Hermes* 109 (1981) 149–56

33. von Fritz, K. 'The historian Theopompus', *AHR* 46 (1941) 765–87

34. von Fritz, K. 'Die griechische ἐλευθερία bei Herodot', *Wien. Stud.* 78 (1965) 5–31

35. Frost, F. J. 'Some documents in Plutarch's Lives', *Class. et Med.* 22 (1961) 182–94

36. Frost, F. J. *Plutarch's Themistocles. A Historical Commentary.* Princeton, 1980

37. Gomme, A. W., Andrewes, A. and Dover, K. J. *A Historical Commentary on Thucydides* I–V. Oxford, 1945–81

38. Griffith, G. T. 'The Greek historians', in Platnauer, M. (ed.) *Fifty Years of Classical Scholarship*, 150–92. Oxford, 1954. (Revised with Addenda as *Fifty Years (and Twelve) of Classical Scholarship*. Oxford, 1968)

39. Grundy, G. B. *Thucydides and the History of his Age*. London, 1911. (2nd edn with an additional volume. Oxford, 1948)

40. Habicht, C. 'Falsche Urkunden zur Geschichte Athens im Zeitalter der Perserkriege', *Hermes* 89 (1961) 1–35

41. Hamilton, J. R. *Plutarch: Alexander. A Commentary*. Oxford, 1969

42. Hampl, F. 'Herodot. Ein kritischer Forschungsbericht nach historischen Gesichtspunkten', *Grazer Beiträge* 4 (1975) 97–136

43. Harding, P. E. 'Androtion's view of Solon's *Seisachtheia*', *Phoenix* 28 (1974) 282–9

44. Harding, P. 'Atthis and Politeia', *Historia* 26 (1977) 148–60

45. Harvey, F. D. 'The political sympathies of Herodotus', *Historia* 15 (1966) 254–5

46. Hatzfeld, J. 'Notes sur la composition des Helléniques', *Rev. Phil.* ser. 3, 4 (1930) 115–27, 209–26

47. Henrichs, A. 'Zur Interpretation des Michigan-Papyrus über Theramenes', *ZPE* 3 (1968) 101–8

48. Herter, H. (ed.) *Thukydides* (Wege der Forschung 98). Darmstadt, 1968

49. Holzapfel, L. *Untersuchungen über die Darstellung der griechischen Geschichte von 489 bis 413 vor Chr. bei Ephoros, Theopomp u.a. Autoren*. Leipzig, 1879

50. Holzapfel, L. 'Doppelte Relationen im VIII. Buche des Thukydides', *Hermes* 28 (1893) 435–64

51. Hornblower, J. *Hieronymus of Cardia*. Oxford, 1981

52. Hornblower, S. *Thucydides*, London, 1987

53. Hunter, V. *Thucydides, the Artful Reporter*, Toronto, 1973

54. Jacoby, F. 'Hellanikos', P–W 8 (1913) 104–53 (=C 59, 262–87)

55. Jacoby, F. 'Herodotos', P–W Suppl. 2 (1913) 205–520 (=C 59, 7–164)

56. Jacoby, F. 'Some remarks on Ion of Chios', *CQ* 41 (1947) 1–17 (=C 58, 144–68)

57. Jacoby, F. *Atthis: the Local Chronicles of Ancient Athens*. Oxford, 1949

58. Jacoby, F. *Abhandlungen zur griechischen Geschichtschreibung*. Leiden, 1956

59. Jacoby, F. *Griechische Historiker*. Stuttgart, 1956

60. Kirkwood, G. M. 'Thucydides' words for "cause"', *AJP* 73 (1952) 37–61

61. Kleinknecht, H. 'Herodot und Athen', *Hermes* 75 (1940) 241–64

62. Koenen, L. 'Fieldwork of the International Photographic Archive in Cairo. 2. A new fragment of the Oxyrhynchite Historian', *Studia Papyrologica* 15 (1976) 55–76

63. Kolbe, W. 'Diodors Wert für die Geschichte der Pentekontaetie', *Hermes* 72 (1937) 241–69

64. Lane Fox, R. 'Theopompus of Chios and the Greek world, 411–322 B.C.', in F 7, 105–20

65. Laqueur, R. 'Diodorea', *Hermes* 86 (1958) 257–90

66. Lewis, D. M. 'A Loeb *Constitution of the Athenians*', *CR* n.s. 19 (1969) 45–7

67. Lotze, D. 'War Xenophon selbst der Interpolator seiner Hellenika I–II?',

Philologus 118 (1974) 215–17

68. Luschnat, O. 'Thukydides der Historiker', P–W Suppl. 12 (1971) 1085–354, 14 (1974) 759–86

69. McKechnie, P. R. and Kern, S. J. *Hellenica Oxyrhynchia*. Warminster, 1988

70. Maclaren, M. Jr. 'On the composition of Xenophon's Hellenica', *AJP* 55 (1934) 121–39, 249–62

71. Meritt, B. D. 'Indirect tradition in Thucydides', *Hesp.* 23 (1954) 185–231

72. Merkelbach, R. and Youtie, H. C. 'Ein Michigan-Papyrus über Theramenes', *ZPE* 2 (1968) 161–9

73. Montgomery, H. *Gedanke und Tat: zur Erzählungstechnik bei Herodot, Thukydides, Xenophon und Arrian*. Lund, 1965

74. Ostwald, M. *ANAΓKH in Thucydides*. Atlanta, 1988

75. Pearson, L. *The Local Historians of Attica* (American Philological Association Monograph 11). Philadelphia, 1942

76. Pearson, L. '*Prophasis* and *Aitia*', *TAPA* 83 (1952) 205–23

77. Pearson, L. 'The pseudo-history of Messenia and its authors', *Historia* 11 (1962) 397–426

78. Pelling, C. B. R. 'Plutarch's adaptation of his source-material', *JHS* 100 (1980) 127–40

78A. Pomeroy, S. B. *Xenophon: Oeconomicus: a Social and Historical Commentary*. London, 1990

79. Pouilloux, J. and Salviat, F. 'Lichas, lacédémonien, archonte à Thasos, et le livre VIII de Thucydide', *CRAI* (1983) 376–403

80. Raubitschek, A. E. 'Die sogenannten Interpolationen in den ersten beiden Büchern von Xenophons' Griechischer Geschichte', in *Akten des VI. Internationalen Kongresses für Griechische und Lateinische Epigraphik München 1972*, 315–25. Munich, 1973

81. Raubitschek, A. E. 'The speech of the Athenians at Sparta', in C 95, 32–48

82. Rhodes, P. J. 'Thucydides on Pausanias and Themistocles', *Historia* 19 (1970) 387–400

83. Rhodes, P. J. *A Commentary on the Aristotelian 'Athenaion Politeia'*. Oxford, 1981

84. Rhodes, P. J. *Thucydides, History II*. Warminster, 1988

85. de Romilly, J. *Thucydide et l'impérialisme athénienne*. 2nd edn. Paris, 1951. (Eng. transl. by P. Thody, *Thucydides and Athenian Imperialism*. Oxford, 1963)

86. Russell, D. A. F. M. 'Plutarch's Life of Coriolanus', *JRS* 53 (1963) 21–8

87. Schachermeyr, F. *Stesimbrotus und seine Schrift über die Staatsmänner* (SBAk. Wien, Phil.-Hist. Kl. 247.5).Vienna, 1965

88. Schwartz, E. 'Diodoros', P–W V. 1 (1903) 663–701 (= C 92, 35–97)

89. Schwartz, E. 'Ephoros', P–W VI. 1 (1907) 1–16 (= C 92, 3–26)

90. Schwartz, E. Review of F. Taeger, *Thukydides*, in *Gnomon* 2 (1926) 65–82

91. Schwartz, E. *Das Geschichtswerk des Thukydides*. 2nd edn. Bonn, 1929

92. Schwartz, E. *Griechische Geschichtsschreiber*. Leipzig, 1957

93. Sordi, M. 'I caratteri dell'opera storiografica di Senofonte nelle

Elleniche', *Athenaeum* n.s. 28 (1950) 1–53, 29 (1951) 273–348

94. Stadter, P. A. *Plutarch's Historical Methods: an Analysis of the 'Mulierum Virtutes'*. Cambridge, MA, 1965
95. Stadter, P. A. (ed.) *The Speeches in Thucydides*. Chapel Hill, 1973
95A. Stadter, P. A. *A Commentary on Plutarch's 'Pericles'*. Chapel Hill–London, 1989
96. Stahl, H.-P. *Thukydides: die Stellung des Menschen im geschichtlichen Prozess* (Zetemata 40). Munich, 1966
97. Strasburger, H. 'Herodot und das perikleische Athen', *Historia* 4 (1955) 1–25 (= Marg, W. (ed.) *Herodot*, 574–608. Munich, 1962)
98. Strasburger, H. 'Thukydides und die politische Selbstdarstellung der Athener', *Hermes* 86 (1958) 17–40 (= C 48, 498–530)
99. Theander, C. *Plutarch und die Geschichte* (Bull. soc. des lettres de Lund 1950–1951, 1). Lund, 1951
100. Thompson, W. E. 'Andocides and Hellanicus', *TAPA* 98 (1967) 483–90
101. Tuplin, C. J. 'Military engagements in Xenophon's Hellenica', in Moxon I., Smart, J. D. and Woodman, A. J. (eds.) *Past Perspectives: Studies in Greek and Roman Historical Writing*, 37–66. Cambridge, 1986
102. Verdin, H. 'Hérodote historien? Quelques interprétations récentes', *Ant. Class.* 44 (1975) 668–85
103. Volquardsen, C. A. *Untersuchungen über die Quellen der griechischen und sicilischen Geschichten bei Diodor, Buch XI bis XVI*. Kiel, 1868
104. Wade-Gery, H. T. 'Two notes on Theopompos, *Philippica*, x', *AJP* 59 (1938) 129–34 (= A 121, 233–8)
105. Wade-Gery, H. T. 'Thucydides', in *OCD*, 1067–9. 2nd edn. Oxford, 1970
106. Walker, P. K. 'The purpose and method of "The Pentekontaetia" in Thucydides, Book I', *CQ* n.s. 7 (1957) 27–38
107. Waters, K. H. 'Herodotos and politics', *G&R* n.s. 19 (1972) 136–50
108. Westlake, H. D. 'Thucydides on Pausanias and Themistocles – a written source', *CQ* n.s. 27 (1977) 95–110
109. Westlake, H. D. 'Thucydides 2.65.11', *CQ* n.s. 8 (1958) 102–10 (= A 123, 161–73)
110. Wilamowitz, U. von. 'Lesefrüchte CXCV', *Hermes* 60 (1925) 297–300

II. INSCRIPTIONS

111. Accame, S. 'Il decreto di Callia nella storia della finanza ateniese', *Riv. di Filol.* 63 (1935) 468–96
112. Accame, S. 'Un nuovo decreto di Lindo del v sec. a.C.', *Cl. Rh.* 9 (1938) 211–29
113. Accame, S. Review of B. D. Meritt, *Documents on Athenian Tribute*, in *Riv. di Filol.* 66 (1938) 409–16
114. Accame, S. 'Note storiche su epigrafi attiche del v secolo', *Riv. di Filol.* 80 (1952) 111–36, 223–45
115. Baumbach, L. *Studies in Mycenaean Inscriptions and Dialect 1953–1964*

(Incunabula Graeca 20). Rome, 1968

116. Bingen, J. 'Le décret SEG x 64 (Le Pirée, 413/2?)', *RBPh* 37 (1959) 31–44

117. Blinkenberg, C. *Lindos: Fouilles et recherches, 1902–1914*, II: *Inscriptions*, i–ii. Copenhagen, 1941

118. Bousquet, J. 'Inscriptions de Delphes', *BCH* 109 (1985) 221–53

119. Bradeen, D. W. 'Athenian casualty lists', *Hesp.* 33 (1964) 16–62

120. Bradeen, D. W. 'The Athenian casualty lists', *CQ* n.s. 19 (1969) 145–59

121. Bradeen, D. W. and McGregor, M. F. *Studies in Fifth-Century Attic Epigraphy.* Norman, 1973

122. Bravo, B. 'Une lettre sur plomb de Berezan: colonisation et modes de contact dans le Pont', *DHA* 1 (1974) 111–87

123. Bridges, A. P. 'The Athenian treaty with Samos, ML 56', *JHS* 100 (1980) 185–8

124. Camp, J. McK., II. 'Greek inscriptions', *Hesp.* 43 (1974) 314–24

125. Capps, E. 'Greek inscriptions. A new fragment of the list of victors at the City Dionysia', *Hesp.* 12 (1943) 1–11

126. Clairmont, C. 'New light on some public Athenian documents of the 5th and 4th century', *ZPE* 36 (1979) 123–6

127. Crosby, M. 'The leases of the Laureion mines', *Hesp.* 19 (1950) 189–312

128. Crosby, M. 'More fragments of mining leases from the Athenian Agora', *Hesp.* 26 (1957) 1–12

129. Dunst, G. 'Archaische Inschriften und Dokumente der Pentekontaetie aus Samos', *Ath. Mitt.* 87 (1972) 99–163

129A. Dunst, G. 'Der Opferkalender des attischen Demos Thorikos', *ZPE* 25 (1977) 243–64

130. Engelmann, H. and Merkelbach, R. *Die Inschriften von Erythrai und Klazomenai*, 1. Bonn, 1972

131. Etienne, R. and Piérart, M. 'Un décret du Koinon des Hellènes à Platées en l'honneur de Glaucon, fils d'Etéoclès d'Athènes'. *BCH* 99 (1975) 51–75

132. Guarducci, M. 'Nuove note di epigrafia siceliota arcaica', *ASAA* n.s. 21–2 (1959–60) 249–87

133. Hansen, P. A. *Carmina Epigraphica Graeca*, I–II. Berlin, 1983–9

134. Henry, A. S. 'The dating of fifth-century Attic inscriptions', *CSCA* 11 (1978) 75–108

135. Jeffery, L. H. 'Comments on some archaic Greek inscriptions', *JHS* 69 (1949) 25–38

136. Jeffery, L. H. 'Further comments on archaic Greek inscriptions', *BSA* 50 (1955) 67–84

137. Jeffery, L. H. *The Local Scripts of Archaic Greece.* Oxford, 1961. 2nd edn ed. A. W. Johnston. Oxford, 1989

138. Lewis, D. M. 'Notes on Attic inscriptions', *BSA* 49 (1954) 17–50

139. Lewis, D. M. 'The treaties with Leontini and Rhegion', *ZPE* 22 (1976) 223–5

140. McGregor, M. F. 'The ninth prescript of the Attic Quota-Lists', *Phoenix* 16 (1962) 267–75

141. McGregor, M. F. 'Athens and Hestiaia', *Hesp.* Suppl. 19 (1982) 101–11

142. Mattingly, H. B. 'Two notes on Athenian financial documents', *BSA* 62 (1967) 13–17

143. Mattingly, H. B. '"Epigraphically the Twenties are too late"', *BSA* 65 (1970) 129–49

144. Mattingly, H. B. 'The Athenian decree for Miletos (*IG* i² 22 + = *ATL* II.D 11): a postscript', *Historia* (1981) 113–17

145. Meiggs, R. 'The dating of fifth-century Attic inscriptions', *JHS* 86 (1966) 86–97

146. Meritt, B. D. *The Athenian Calendar in the Fifth Century*. Cambridge, MA, 1928

147. Meritt, B. D. *Athenian Financial Documents of the Fifth Century*. Ann Arbor, 1932

148. Meritt, B. D. 'Greek Inscriptions', *Hesp.* 5 (1936) 355–430

149. Meritt, B. D. *The Athenian Year*. Berkeley–Los Angeles, 1961

150. Meritt, B. D. 'The tribute quota list of 454/3 B.C.', *Hesp.* 41 (1972) 403–17

150A. Meritt, B. D. 'Two new fragments of the tribute lists', *Hesp.* 41 (1972) 418–21

151. Meritt, B. D. and McGregor, M. F. 'The Athenian quota-list of 421/0 B.C.', *Phoenix* 21 (1967) 85–91

152. Meritt, B. D. and Wade-Gery, H. T. 'The dating of documents to the mid-fifth century', *JHS* 82 (1962) 67–74, 83 (1963) 100–17

153. Meritt, B. D., Woodhead, A. G. and Stamires, G. A. 'Greek inscriptions', *Hesp.* 26 (1957) 198–270

154. Moretti, L. *Iscrizioni agonistiche greche*. Rome, 1953

155. Pečírka, J. *The Formula for the Grant of Enktesis in Attic Inscriptions* (Acta Universitatis Carolinae Philosophica et Historica, Monographia 15). 1966

156. Pritchett, W. K. 'The Attic Stelai, Part II', *Hesp.* 25 (1956) 178–317

157. Pritchett, W. K. 'Calendars of Athens again', *BCH* 81 (1957) 269–301

158. Pritchett, W. K. 'The height of the *Lapis Primus*', *Historia* 13 (1964) 129–34

159. Pritchett, W. K. 'The top of the *Lapis Primus*', *GRBS* 7 (1966) 123–9

160. Pritchett, W. K. 'The location of the *Lapis Primus*', *GRBS* 8 (1967) 113–19

161. Raubitschek, A. E. 'Athens and Halikyai', *TAPA* 75 (1944) 10–14

162. Raubitschek, A. E. *Dedications from the Athenian Akropolis*. Cambridge, MA, 1949

163. Raubitschek, A. E. 'Die Inschrift als geschichtliches Denkmal', *Gymnasium* 72 (1965) 511–22

164. Sokolowski, F. *Lois sacrées de l'Asia Mineure*. Paris, 1955

165. Sokolowski, F. *Lois sacrées des cités grecques: Supplément*. Paris, 1962

166. Sokolowski, F. *Lois sacrées des cités grecques*. Paris, 1969

167. Stroud, R. S. 'An Athenian law on silver coinage', *Hesp.* 43 (1974) 157–88

168. Stroud, R. S. 'The gravestone of Socrates' friend, Lysis', *Hesp.* 53 (1984) 355–60

169. Tracy, S. V. 'Hands in fifth-century B.C. Attic inscriptions', in *Studies*

Presented to Sterling Dow on his Eightieth Birthday, 277–82. Durham, N.C., 1984

170. Walbank, M. B. 'Criteria for the dating of fifth-century Attic inscriptions', in A 9, 161–9

171. Walbank, M. B. *Athenian Proxenies of the Fifth Century B.C.* Toronto–Sarasota, 1978

172. Walbank, M. B. 'A correction to *IG* ii² 65', *ZPE* 48 (1982) 261–3

173. Walbank, M. B. 'Herakleides of Klazomenai: a new join at the Epigraphical Museum', *ZPE* 51 (1983) 183–4

174. Walbank, M. B. 'Leases of sacred properties in Attica', I–II, *Hesp.* 52 (1983) 100–35 and 177–99

175. West, A. B. 'Aristidean tribute in the assessment of 421 B.C.', *AJA* 29 (1925) 135–51

176. Wick, T. E. 'A note on the date of the Athenian–Egestan alliance', *JHS* 95 (1975) 186–90

177. Wick, T. E. 'The date of the Athenian–Egestan alliance', *Cl. Phil.* 76 (1981) 118–21

178. Wilhelm, A . 'Der älteste griechische Brief', *JÖAI* 7 (1904) 94–105 (= *id.*, *Abhandlungen und Beiträge zur griechischen Inschriftenkunde* I, 186–97. Leipzig, 1984)

179. Wilhelm, A. 'Attische Urkunden, xxxi. *IG* i² 70, 16, 166', *SBAk. Wien, Phil.-Hist. Kl.* 217. 5 (1939) 52–72 (= *id. Akademieschriften zur griechischen Inschriftenkunde* I, 572–92. Leipzig, 1974)

180. Woodhead, A. G. '*IG* i² 95 and the ostracism of Hyperbolus', *Hesp.* 18 (1949) 78–83

III. COINAGE
(See also H (VI) for Sicily)

181. Barron, J. P. *The Silver Coins of Samos.* London, 1966

182. Caltabiano, M. 'Documenti numismatici e storia del Koinon arcade dalle origini al sec. v a.C', *Helikon* 9–10 (1969/70) 423–59

183. Cook, R. M. 'Speculations on the origins of coinage', *Historia* 7 (1958) 257–62

184. Fowler, B. H. 'Thucydides 1.107–8 and the Tanagran Federal Issues', *Phoenix* 11 (1957) 164–70

185. Grierson, P. *The Origins of Money* (Creighton Lecture in History, 1970). London, 1977

186. Herrmann, F. 'Die thessalische Münzunion im 5. Jahrhundert', *ZfN* 33 (1922) 33–43

187. Herrmann, F. 'Die Silbermünzen von Larissa in Thessalien', *ZfN* 35 (1924–5) 1–69

188. Kraay, C. M. 'Hoards, small change, and the origin of coinage', *JHS* 84 (1964) 76–91

189. Kraay, C. M. *Greek Coins and History.* London, 1969

190. Kraay, C. M. *Archaic and Classical Greek Coins.* London, 1976

191. Kraay, C. M. 'The Asyut Hoard: some comments on chronology', *Num. Chron.* (1977) 188–98

192. Kraay, C. M. and Hirmer, M. *Greek Coins*. London, 1966
193. Lacroix, L. *Monnaies et colonisation dans l'occident grec*. Brussels, 1965
194. Martin, T. R. *Sovereignty and Coinage in Classical Greece*. Princeton, 1985
195. Price, M. J. 'Early Greek bronze coinage', in Kraay, C. M. and Jenkins, G. K. (eds.) *Essays in Greek Coinage presented to Stanley Robinson*, 90–104. Oxford, 1968
196. Price, M. J. and Waggoner, N. *Archaic Greek Coinage; the Asyut Hoard*. London, 1975
197. Starr, C. G. *Athenian Coinage 480–449 B.C.* Oxford, 1970
198. Vickers, M. 'Early Greek coinage: a reassessment', *Num. Chron.* (1985) 1–44
199. Williams, R. T. *The Confederate Coinage of the Arcadians in the Fifth Century B.C.* (NNM 155). New York, 1965

D. ATHENS: INTERNAL AFFAIRS

1. Andrewes, A. 'Philochoros on phratries', *JHS* 81 (1961) 1–15
2. Andrewes, A. 'The Arginusae trial', *Phoenix* 28 (1974) 112–22
3. Andrewes, A. 'The opposition to Perikles', *JHS* 98 (1978) 1–8
4. Aurenche, O. *Les groupes d'Alcibiade, de Léogoras et de Teucros. Remarques sur la vie politique athénienne en 415 avant J. C.* Paris, 1974
5. Beloch, K. J. *Die attische Politik seit Perikles*. Leipzig, 1884
6. Bicknell, P. J. *Studies in Athenian Politics and Genealogy (Historia Einzelschr. 19)*. Wiesbaden, 1972
7. Bloedow, E. *Alcibiades Re-examined (Historia Einzelschr. 21)*. Wiesbaden, 1973
8. Boegehold, A. L. 'The establishment of a central archive at Athens', *AJA* 76 (1972) 23–30
9. Bourriot, F. 'La famille et le milieu social de Cléon', *Historia* 31 (1982) 404–35
10. Calhoun, G. M. *Athenian Clubs in Politics and Litigation* (Bulletin of the University of Texas 262). Austin, 1913
11. Carawan, E. M. '*Eisangelia* and *Euthyna*: the trials of Miltiades, Themistocles and Cimon', *GRBS* 28 (1987) 167–208
12. Cavaignac, E. 'Eschyle et Thémistocle', *Rev. Phil.* ser. 2, 45 (1921) 102–6
13. Cavaignac, E. 'Miltiade et Thucydide', *Rev. Phil.* ser. 3, 3 (1929) 281–5
14. Cawkwell, G. L. 'νομοφυλακία and the Areopagus', *JHS* 108 (1988) 1–12
14A. Chandler, L. 'The north-western frontier of Attica', *JHS* 46 (1926) 1–21
15. Cole, J. R. 'Cimon's dismissal, Ephialtes' revolution and the Peloponnesian Wars', *GRBS* 15 (1974) 369–85
16. Connor, W. R. *The New Politicians of Fifth-Century Athens*. Princeton, 1971
17. Davies, J. K. 'Demosthenes on liturgies: a note', *JHS* 87 (1967) 33–40
18. Davies, J. K. *Wealth and the Power of Wealth in Classical Athens*. New York, 1981
19. Derenne, E. *Les procès d'impiété intentés aux philosophes à Athènes*. Liège, 1930
20. Develin, R. *Athenian Officials 684–321 B.C.* Cambridge, 1989

21.   Dover, K. J. 'δέκατος αὐτός', *JHS* 80 (1960) 61–77 (= A 27, 159–80)

22.   Dow, S. 'The Athenian Calendar of Sacrifices: the chronology of Nikomakhos' second term', *Historia* 9 (1960) 270–93

23.   Ferguson, W. S. 'The constitution of Theramenes', *Cl. Phil.* 21 (1926) 72–5

24.   Ferguson, W. S. *The Treasurers of Athena*. Cambridge, MA, 1932

25.   Ferguson, W. S. 'The Attic Orgeones', *HThR* 37 (1944) 96–104

26.   Finley, M. I. 'The Athenian demagogues', *Past and Present* 21 (1962) 3–24 (= *id.* (ed.) *Studies in Ancient Society*, 1–25. London, 1974)

27.   Flacelière, R. 'Sur quelques points obscurs de la vie de Thémistocle', *REA* 55 (1953) 5–28

28.   Fornara, C. W. 'The hoplite achievement at Psyttaleia', *JHS* 86 (1966) 51–4

29.   Fornara, C. W. *The Athenian Board of Generals from 501 to 404* (*Historia* Einzelschr. 16). Wiesbaden, 1971

30.   Hansen, M. H. *'Eisangelia': the Sovereignty of the People's Court in Athens in the Fourth Century B.C. and the Impeachment of Generals and Politicians* (Odense University Classical Studies 6). Odense, 1975

30A. Hansen, M. H. *'Apagoge', 'Endeixis' and 'Ephegesis' against 'Kakourgoi', 'Atimoi' and 'Pheugontes'* (Odense University Classical Studies 8). Odense, 1976

31.   Hansen, M. H. 'How did the Athenian *Ecclesia* vote?', *GRBS* 18 (1977) 123–37. (Reprinted with addenda in D 34, 103–21)

32.   Hansen, M. H. 'Misthos for magistrates in classical Athens', *SO* 54 (1979) 5–22

33.   Hansen, M. H. 'Eisangelia in Athens: a reply', *JHS* 100 (1980) 89–95

34.   Hansen, M. H. *The Athenian Ecclesia: a Collection of Articles 1976–83*. Copenhagen, 1983

35.   Hansen, M. H. 'The Athenian Board of Generals', in *Studies in Ancient History and Numismatics presented to Rudi Thomsen*, 69–70. Aarhus, 1988

36.   Hansen, M. H. and Christensen, J. 'What is *syllogos* at Thucydides 2.22.1?', *Class. et Med.* 34 (1983) 15–29

37.   Hatzfeld, J. *Alcibiade*. Paris, 1951

38.   Hignett, C. *A History of the Athenian Constitution to the End of the Fifth Century B.C.* Oxford, 1952 (Reprinted with corrections 1958)

39.   Humphreys, S. C. 'Public and private interests in classical Athens', *CJ* 73 (1977–8) 97–104 (= A 67, 22–32)

40.   Jones, A. H. M. *Athenian Democracy*. Oxford, 1957

41.   Jordan, B. *The Athenian Navy in the Classical Period. A Study of Athenian Naval Administration and Military Organization in the Fifth and Fourth Centuries B.C.* (University of California Publications: Classical Studies 13). Berkeley–Los Angeles–London, 1975

42.   Koerner, R. 'Die Entwicklung der attischen Demokratie nach dem Peloponnesischen Krieg in Verfassung, Verwaltung und Recht', in A 122, I 132–46

43.   Kolbe, W. 'Studien über das Kalliasdekret: Bausteine zu einer Geschichte des Schatzes der Athena', SBAk. Berlin 1929, 273–89 = *id.*,

Thukydides im Lichte der Urkunden, 50–91. Stuttgart, 1930

44. Krentz, P. 'Foreigners against the Thirty: *IG* II² 10 again', *Phoenix* 34 (1980) 298–306

44A. Krentz, P. *The Thirty at Athens*. Ithaca–London, 1982

45. Kron, U. 'Demos, Pnyx und Nymphenhügel', *Ath. Mitt.* 94 (1979) 49–75

46. Leake, W. M. *The Topography of Athens and the Demi of Attica*. London, 1841

47. Lenardon, R. J. *The Saga of Themistocles*. London, 1978

48. Lévy, E. *Athènes devant la défaite de 404: histoire d'une crise idéologique*. (Bibl. Éc. fr. Ath. et Rome 225). Paris, 1976

49. Lewis, D. M. 'Double representation in the *strategia*', *JHS* 81 (1961) 118–23

50. Lewis, D. M. 'Cleisthenes and Attica', *Historia* 12 (1963) 22–40

51. Lewis, D. M. 'After the profanation of the Mysteries', in A 34, 177–91

52. Lewis, D. M. 'Athenian politics', review of D 16, *CR* n.s. 25 (1975) 87–90

53. Lewis, D. M. Review of V. Gabrielsen, *Remuneration of State Officials in Fourth-Century B.C. Athens*, *JHS* 102 (1982) 269

54. Loraux, N. *L'invention d'Athènes, histoire de l'oraison funèbre dans la 'cité classique'*. Paris, 1981. (English transl. by A. Sheridan, *The Invention of Athens*. Cambridge, MA, 1986)

55. MacDowell, D. M. *The Athenian Homicide Law in the Age of the Orators*. Manchester, 1963

56. McGregor, M. F. 'The genius of Alkibiades', *Phoenix* 19 (1965) 27–46

57. Martin, J. 'Von Kleisthenes zu Ephialtes: Zur Entstehung der athenischen Demokratie', *Chiron* 4 (1974) 5–42

58. Meiggs, R. 'The political implications of the Parthenon', in I 121, 36–45

59. Mikalson, J. D. *The Sacred and Civil Calendar of the Athenian Year*. Princeton, 1975

60. Mossé, C. *La fin de la démocratie athénienne*. Paris, 1962

61. Ober, J. *Mass and Elite in Democratic Athens. Rhetoric, Ideology and the Power of the People*. Princeton, 1989

62. Oliver, J. H. *The Athenian Expounders of the Sacred and Ancestral Law*. Baltimore, 1950

63. Osborne, M. J. *Naturalization in Athens* (Verhandelingen van de Koninklijke Academie voor Wetenschapen, Letteren en Schone Kunsten van België). 43, no. 98, Brussels, 1981; 44, no. 101, Brussels, 1982; 45, no. 109, Brussels, 1983

64. Ostwald, M. *Nomos and the Beginnings of the Athenian Democracy*. Oxford, 1969

65. Patterson, C. *Pericles' Citizenship Law of 451–450 B.C.* New York, 1981

66. Pecorella Longo, C. *'Eterie' e gruppi politici nell'Atene del IV sec. a. C.* Florence, 1971

67. Piérart, M. 'À propos de l'élection des stratèges athéniens', *BCH* 98 (1974) 125–46

68. Plassart, A. 'Les archers d'Athènes', *REG* 26 (1913) 151–213

69. Podlecki, A. J. 'The political significance of the Athenian

"Tyrannicide"-cult', *Historia* 15 (1966) 129–41

70. Podlecki, A. J. 'Cimon, Skyros and "Theseus' bones"', *JHS* 91 (1971) 141–3

71. Podlecki, A. J. *The Life of Themistocles: a Critical Survey of the Literary and Archaeological Evidence.* Montreal, 1975

72. Poole, J. C. F. and Holladay, A. J. 'Thucydides and the Plague of Athens', *CQ* n.s. 29 (1979) 282–300

73. Poole, J. C. F. and Holladay, A. J. 'Thucydides and the Plague: a further footnote', *CQ* n.s. 34 (1984) 483–5

74. Raubitschek, A. E. 'Theopompos on Hyperbolos', *Phoenix* 9 (1955) 122–6

75. Rhodes, P. J. *The Athenian Boule.* Oxford, 1972. (Reprinted with additions and corrections 1985)

76. Rhodes, P. J. 'The Five Thousand in the Athenian revolutions of 411 B.C.', *JHS* 92 (1972) 115–27

77. Rhodes, P. J. 'εἰσαγγελία in Athens', *JHS* 99 (1979) 103–14

78. Rhodes, P. J. 'Athenian democracy after 403 B.C.', *CJ* 75 (1979/80) 305–23

79. Rhodes, P. J. 'Notes on voting in Athens', *GRBS* 22 (1981) 125–32

80. Rudhardt, J. 'La définition du délit d'impiété d'après la législation attique', *Mus. Helv.* 17 (1960) 87–105

81. Ruschenbusch, E. 'Ephialtes', *Historia* 15 (1966) 369–76

82. Ruschenbusch, E. *Athenische Innenpolitik im 5. Jahrhundert v. Chr.* Bamberg, 1979

83. de Ste Croix, G. E. M. 'The Constitution of the Five Thousand', *Historia* 5 (1956) 1–23

84. Sartori, F. *Le eterie nella vita politica ateniese del VI e V secolo a. C.* Rome, 1957

85. Schachermeyr, F. *Religionspolitik und Religiosität bei Perikles (SBAk. Wien Phil.-Hist. Kl.* 258, 3). Vienna, 1968

86. Seager, R. 'Lysias against the corn-dealers', *Historia* 15 (1966) 172–84

87. Sealey, B. R. I. 'Ephialtes', *Cl. Phil.* 59 (1964) 11–22 (= A 111, 42–58)

88. Sealey, B. R. I. 'Ephialtes, *eisangelia* and the council', in Shrimpton, G. S. and McCargar, D. J. (eds.) *Classical Contributions: Studies in Honour of Malcolm Francis McGregor,* 125–34. Locust Valley, 1981

89. Sinclair, R. K. *Democracy and Participation in Athens.* Cambridge, 1988

90. Solders, S. *Die ausserstädtischen Kulte und die Einigung Attikas,* Lund, 1931

91. Stevenson, G. H. 'The financial administration of Pericles', *JHS* 44 (1924) 1–9

92. Stockton, D. 'The death of Ephialtes', *CQ* n.s. 32 (1982) 227–8

93. Strauss, B. S. *Athens after the Peloponnesian War: Class, Faction, and Policy 403–386 B.C.* London–Sydney, 1987

94. Stroud, R. S. 'Theozotides and the Athenian orphans', *Hesp.* 40 (1971) 280–301

95. Thompson, H. A. 'Athens faces adversity', *Hesp.* 50 (1981) 343–55

96. Thompson, W. E. 'Notes on the Treasurers of Athena', *Hesp.* 39 (1970) 54–63

97. Toepffer, J. *Attische Genealogie.* Berlin, 1889

98.   Tolbert Roberts, J. *Accountability in Athenian Government* (Wisconsin Studies in Classics). Madison–London, 1982

98A.   Traill, J. S. *Demos and Trittys*. Toronto, 1986

99.   Vanderpool, E. 'Kleophon', *Hesp.* 21 (1952) 114–15

100.   Vanderpool, E. 'New ostraka from the Athenian Agora', *Hesp.* 37 (1968) 117–20

101.   Wade-Gery, H. T. 'Studies in the structure of Attic society, II. The laws of Kleisthenes', *CQ* 27 (1933) 17–29 (= A 121, 135–54)

102.   Wade-Gery, H. T. 'Themistokles' archonship', *BSA* 37 (1936/7) 263–70 (= A 121, 171–9)

103.   Wade-Gery, H. T. and Meritt, B. D. 'Athenian resources in 449 and 431 B.C.', *Hesp.* 26 (1957) 163–97

104.   Wallace, R. W. 'Ephialtes and the Areopagos', *GRBS* 15 (1974) 259–69

105.   Wallace, R. W. *The Areopagos Council, to 307 B.C.* Baltimore, 1989

106.   West, A. B. 'Pericles' political heirs'. *Cl. Phil.* 19 (1924) 124–46, 201–28

107.   Whibley, L. *Political Parties in Athens during the Peloponnesian War*. Cambridge, 1889

108.   Whitehead, D. *The Demes of Attica 508/7 – ca. 250 B.C. A Political and Social Study*. Princeton, 1986

109.   Woodhead, A. G. 'Thucydides' portrait of Cleon', *Mnemosyne* ser. 4, 13 (1960) 289–317. (German transl. in C 48, 557–93)

E. THE ATHENIAN EMPIRE

1.   Andrewes, A. 'Could there have been a battle at Oinoe?', in Levick, B. M. (ed.) *The Ancient Historian and his Materials: Essays in Honour of C. E. Stevens on his Seventieth Birthday*, 9–16. Farnborough, 1973

2.   Asheri, D. 'The site of Brea', *AJP* 90 (1969) 337–40

3.   Badian, E. 'The Peace of Callias', *JHS* 107 (1987) 1–39

4.   Balcer, J. M. *The Athenian Regulations for Chalkis: Studies in Athenian Imperial Law* (Historia Einzelschr. 33). Wiesbaden, 1978

5.   Barns, J. 'Cimon and the first Athenian expedition to Cyprus', *Historia* 2 (1953–4) 163–76

6.   Barron, J. P. 'Milesian politics and Athenian propaganda c. 460–440 B.C.', *JHS* 82 (1962) 1–6

7.   Barron, J. P. 'Religious propaganda of the Delian League', *JHS* 84 (1964) 35–48

8.   Barron, J. P. 'The fifth-century *horoi* of Aigina', *JHS* 103 (1983) 1–12

9.   Barron, J. P. 'Chios in the Athenian Empire', in F 7, 89–108

10.   Blackman, D. J. 'The Athenian navy and allied naval contributions in the Pentecontaetia', *GRBS* 10 (1969) 179–216

11.   Bosworth, A. B. 'The Congress Decree: another hypothesis', *Historia* 20 (1971) 600–16

12.   Bradeen, D. W. 'The popularity of the Athenian Empire', *Historia* 9 (1960) 257–69

13.   Brunt, P. A. 'Athenian settlements abroad in the fifth century B.C.', in A 34, 71–92

14.   Cawkwell, G. L. 'The foundation of the Second Athenian Confederacy', *CQ* n.s. 23 (1973) 47–60

15.   Chambers, M. H. 'Four hundred sixty talents', *Cl. Phil.* 53 (1958) 26–32

16.   Culham, P. 'The Delian League: bicameral or unicameral', *AJAH* 3 (1978) 27–31

17.   Earp, A. J. 'Athens and Miletos ca. 450 B.C.'. *Phoenix* 8 (1954) 142–7

18.   Eddy, S. K. 'Four hundred sixty talents once more', *Cl. Phil.* 63 (1968) 184–95

19.   Eddy, S. K. 'Some irregular amounts of Athenian tribute', *AJP* 94 (1973) 47–70

20.   Ehrenberg, V. 'The foundation of Thurii', *AJP* 69 (1948) 149–70 (= A 32, 298–315)

21.   Ehrenberg, V. 'Thucydides on Athenian colonisation', *Cl. Phil.* 47 (1952) 143–9 (= A 32, 245–53)

22.   Erxleben, E. 'Das Münzgesetz des delisch-attischen Seebundes', *AfP* 19 (1969) 91–139, 20 (1970) 66–132, 21 (1971) 145–62

23.   Erxleben, E. 'Die Kleruchien auf Euböa und Lesbos und die Methoden der attischen Herrschaft im 5. Jh.', *Klio* 57 (1975) 83–100

24.   Fehr, B. 'Zur religionspolitischen Funktion der Athena Parthenos im Rahmen des delisch-attischen Seebundes', *Hephaistos* 1 (1979) 71–91, 2 (1980) 113–25, 3 (1981) 55–93

25.   Finley, M. I. 'The Athenian Empire: a balance sheet', in Garnsey, P. D. A. and Whittaker, C. R. (eds.) *Imperialism in the Ancient World*, 103–26. Cambridge, 1978 (= L 41, 41–61)

26.   Fornara, C. W. 'On the chronology of the Samian War', *JHS* 99 (1979) 7–19

27.   Francis, E. D. and Vickers, M. 'Argive Oenoe', *Ant. Class.* 54 (1985) 105–15

28.   French, A. 'The tribute of the allies', *Historia* 21 (1972) 1–20

29.   French, A. 'Athenian ambitions and the Delian Alliance', *Phoenix* 33 (1979) 134–41

30.   Gauthier, P. 'A propos des clérouquies athéniennes du Ve siècle', in L 40, 163–78

31.   Gehrke, H.-J. 'Zur Geschichte Milets in der Mitte des 5. Jahrhunderts v. Chr.', *Historia* 29 (1980) 17–31

32.   Giovannini, A. and Gottlieb, G. *Thukydides und die Anfänge der athenischen Arche*. SB Heidelberg, 1980, no. 7

33.   Hammond, N. G. L. 'The origins and nature of the Athenian alliance of 478/7 B.C.', *JHS* 87 (1967) 41–61 (= A 54, 311–45)

34.   Herrmann, P. 'Zu den Beziehungen zwischen Athen und Milet im 5. Jahrhundert', *Klio* 52 (1970) 163–73

35.   Highby, L. I. *The Erythrae Decree: Contributions to the Early History of the Delian League and the Peloponnesian Confederacy* (*Klio* Beiheft 36). Leipzig, 1936

36.   Holladay, A. J. 'The détente of Kallias?', *Historia* 35 (1986) 503–7

37.   Jackson, A. H. 'The original purpose of the Delian League', *Historia* 18 (1969) 12–16

38. Jones, A. H. M. 'Two synods of the Delian and Peloponnesian Leagues', *PCPhS* n.s. 2 (1952–3) 43–6

39. Larsen, J. A. O. 'The constitution and original purpose of the Delian League', *HSCP* 51 (1940) 175–213

40. Lepper, F. A. 'Some rubrics in the Athenian quota-lists', *JHS* 82 (1962) 25–55

41. Lewis, D. M. 'The origins of the First Peloponnesian War', in Shrimpton, G. S. and McCargar, D. J. (eds.) *Classical Contributions: Studies in Honour of Malcolm Francis McGregor*, 71–8. Locust Valley, 1981

42. Lewis, D. M. 'The Athenian Coinage Decree', in A 16, 53–63

43. Libourel, J. M. 'The Athenian disaster in Egypt', *AJP* 92 (1971) 605–15

44. Mattingly, H. B. 'The Athenian Coinage Decree', *Historia* 10 (1961) 148–88

45. Mattingly, H. B. 'Athens and Euboea', *JHS* 81 (1961) 124–32

46. Mattingly, H. B. 'The Methone Decrees', *CQ* n.s. 11 (1961) 154–65

47. Mattingly, H. B. 'The growth of Athenian imperialism', *Historia* 12 (1963) 257–73

48. Mattingly, H. B. 'Athenian imperialism and the foundation of Brea', *CQ* n.s. 16 (1966) 172–92

49. Mattingly, H. B. 'Periclean imperialism', in A 34, 193–233

50. Mattingly, H. B. 'The Athenian Coinage Decree and the assertion of empire', in A 16, 65–71

51. Meiggs, R. 'The growth of Athenian imperialism', *JHS* 63 (1943) 21–34

51A. Meiggs, R. 'A note on Athenian imperialism', *CR* 63 (1949) 9–12

52. Meiggs, R. 'The crisis of Athenian imperialism', *HSCP* 67 (1963) 1–36

53. Meiggs, R. *The Athenian Empire*. Oxford, 1972

54. Meister, K. *Die Ungeschichtlichkeit des Kalliasfriedens und deren historische Folgen* (Palingenesia XVIII). Wiesbaden, 1982

55. Meritt, B. D., Wade-Gery, H. T. and McGregor, M. F. *The Athenian Tribute-Lists* I–IV. Cambridge, MA, and Princeton, 1939–53

56. Meyer, H. D. 'Vorgeschichte und Gründung des delisch-attischen Seebundes', *Historia* 12 (1963) 405–46

57. Nesselhauf, H. *Untersuchungen zur Geschichte der delisch-attischen Symmachie* (*Klio* Beiheft 30). Leipzig, 1933

58. Oliver, J. H. 'The Peace of Callias and the Pontic expedition of Pericles', *Historia* 6 (1957) 254–5

59. Piérart, M. 'Les *ΕΠΙΜΗΝΙΟΙ* de Milet', *Ant. Class.* 38 (1969) 365–88

60. Piérart, M. 'Milet dans la première liste de tributs', *ZPE* 15 (1974) 163–7

61. Piérart, M. 'Athènes et Milet', *Mus. Helv.* 40 (1983) 1–18, 42 (1985) 276–99

62. Piérart, M. 'Deux notes sur la politique d'Athènes en mer Égée', *BCH* 108 (1984) 161–76

63. Pritchett, W. K. 'The transfer of the Delian Treasury', *Historia* 18 (1969) 17–21

64. Quinn, T. J. *Athens and Samos, Lesbos and Chios, 478–404 B.C.* Manchester, 1981

65. Raaflaub, K. 'Beute, Vergeltung, Freiheit? Zur Zielsetzung des delisch-

attischen Seebundes', *Chiron* 9 (1979) 1–22

66. Rawlings, H. R. III. 'Thucydides on the purpose of the Delian League', *Phoenix* 31 (1977) 1–8

67. Reece, D. W. 'The Battle of Tanagra', *JHS* 70 (1950) 75–6

68. Rhodes, P. J. *The Athenian Empire*. (*G&R* New Surveys in the Classics 17). Oxford, 1985

69. Robertson, N. D. 'The true nature of the "Delian League", 478–461 B.C.', *AJAH* 5 (1980) 64–96, 110–33

70. Robertson, N. D. 'Government and society at Miletus, 525–442 B.C.', *Phoenix* 41 (1987) 356–98

71. Robinson, E. S. G. 'The Athenian Currency Decree and the coinages of the allies', *Hesp.* Suppl. 8 (1949) 324–40

72. de Romilly, J. 'Thucydides and the cities of the Athenian Empire', *BICS* 13 (1966) 1–12

73. Ruschenbusch, E. 'Das Machtpotential der Bündner im ersten attischen Seebund', *ZPE* 53 (1983) 144–8

74. Ruschenbusch, E. 'Tribut und Bürgerzahl im ersten attischen Seebund', *ZPE* 53 (1983) 125–43

75. de Ste Croix, G. E. M. 'The character of the Athenian Empire', *Historia* 3 (1954/5) 1–41

76. de Ste Croix, G. E. M. 'Notes on jurisdiction in the Athenian Empire', *CQ* n.s. 11 (1961) 94–112, 268–80

77. Salmon, P. *La politique égyptienne d'Athènes: vf et vf siècles*. Brussels, 1965

78. Schuller, W. *Die Herrschaft der Athener im ersten attischen Seebund*. Berlin, 1974

79. Schuller, W. 'Die Einführung der Demokratie auf Samos im 5. Jahrhundert v. Chr.', *Klio* 63 (1981) 281–8

80. Schuller, W. 'Über die ἰδιῶται-rubric in den attischen Tributlisten', *ZPE* 42 (1981) 141–51

81. Seager, R. 'The Congress Decree: some doubts and a hypothesis', *Historia* 18 (1969) 129–41

82. Sealey, B. R. I. 'The origin of the Delian League', in A 34, 233–55

83. Smart, J. D. 'Athens and Egesta', *JHS* 92 (1972) 128–46

84. Smart, J. D. 'Kimon's capture of Eion', *JHS* 87 (1967) 136–8

85. Thompson, W. E. 'The Peace of Callias in the fourth century', *Historia* 30 (1981) 164–77

86. Unz, R. K. 'The surplus of the Athenian *phoros*', *GRBS* 26 (1985) 21–42

87. Wade-Gery, H. T. 'The question of tribute in 449/8 B.C.', *Hesp.* 14 (1945) 212–29

88. Walsh, J. 'The authenticity and the dates of the Peace of Callias and the Congress Decree', *Chiron* 11 (1981) 31–63

89. Walters, K. R. 'Diodorus 11.82–4 and the second battle of Tanagra', *AJAH* 3 (1978) 188–91

90. Welwei, K.-W. '"Demos" and "Plethos" in athenischen Volksbeschlüssen um 450 v. Chr.', *Historia* 35 (1986) 177–91

91. West, A. B. 'The tribute lists and the non-tributary members of the Delian League', *AHR* 35 (1929/30) 267–75

92. Westlake, H. D. 'Thucydides and the Athenian disaster in Egypt', *Cl. Phil.* 45 (1950) 209–16 (= A 123, 61–73)
93. Westlake, H. D. 'The commons at Mytilene', *Historia* 25 (1976) 429–40
94. Will, E. 'Notes sur les régimes politiques de Samos', *REA* 71 (1969) 305–19
95. Woodhead, A. G. 'The institution of the *Hellenotamiae*', *JHS* 79 (1959) 149–52
96. Woodhead, A. G. 'West's panel of ship payers', in A 9, 170–8

F. THE GREEK STATES

1. Adshead, K. *The Politics of the Archaic Peloponnese*. Aldershot, 1986
1A. Anderson, J. K. 'A topographical and historical study of Achaea', *BSA* 49 (1954) 72–92
2. Andrewes, A. 'Sparta and Arcadia in the early fifth century', *Phoenix* 6 (1952) 1–5
3. Andrewes, A. 'Two notes on Lysander', *Phoenix* 25 (1971) 206–26
4. Andrewes, A. 'Argive Perioikoi', in Craik, E. M. (ed.) *'Owls to Athens': Essays on Classical Culture presented to Sir Kenneth Dover*, 171–8. Oxford, 1990
5. Bérard, V. 'Tégée et la Tégéatide', *BCH* 16 (1892) 528–49
6. Blamire, A. 'Pausanias and Persia', *GRBS* 11 (1970) 295–305
7. Boardman, J. and Vaphopoulou-Richardson, C. E. (eds.) *Chios. A Conference at the Homereion in Chios 1984*. Oxford, 1986
8. Bölte, F. 'Kleonai', P–W 11 (1922) 721–8
9. Bölte, F. 'Speiraion' P–W IIIA (1929) 1592–9
10. Bölte, F. 'Mantinea', P–W XIV (1930), 1290–344
11. Buck, R. J. *A History of Boeotia*. Edmonton, 1979
12. Callmer, C. *Studien zur Geschichte Arkadiens*. Lund, 1943
13. Cartledge, P. 'A new 5th-century Spartan treaty', *LCM* 1 (1976) 87–92
14. Cartledge, P. *Sparta and Lakonia*. London–Boston–Henley, 1979
15. Cartledge, P. A. 'A new lease of life for Lichas Son of Arkesilas?', *LCM* 9 (1984) 98–102
16. Cawkwell, G. L. 'The decline of Sparta', *CQ* n.s. 33 (1983) 385–400
17. Chamoux, F. *Cyrène sous la monarchie des Battiades*. (Bibl. Éc. fr. Ath. et Rome 177). Paris, 1953
18. Cook, J. M. 'The problem of Classical Ionia', *PCPhS* n.s. 7 (1961) 9–18
19. Cook, J. M. *The Troad*. Oxford, 1973
20. Demand, N. H. *Thebes in the Fifth Century: Heracles Resurgent*. London–Boston–Melbourne–Henley, 1982
21. Edgerton, H. and Scoufopoulos, N. C. 'Sonar search at Gythion harbor', *AAA* 5 (1972) 202–6
22. Effenterre, H. van. 'La fondation de Paestum', *PP* fasc. 192 (1980) 161–75
23. Fornara, C. W. 'Some aspects of the career of Pausanias of Sparta', *Historia* 15 (1966) 257–71
24. Forrest, W. G. 'Themistokles and Argos', *CQ* n.s. 10 (1960) 221–41

25. Forrest, W. G. 'Legislation in Sparta', *Phoenix* 21 (1967) 11–19
26. Franke, P. R. 'Phethaloi–Phetaloi–Petthaloi–Thessaloi. Zur Geschichte Thessaliens im 5. Jahrhundert v.Chr.', *Arch. Anz.* (1970) 85–93
27. Graham, A. J. Review of F 53 in *CQ* n.s. 28 (1978) 105–6
28. Guhl, E. *Ephesiaca*. Berlin, 1843
29. Hammond, N. G. L., Griffith, G. T. and Walbank, F. W. *A History of Macedonia* I–III. Oxford, 1972–88
30. Hodkinson, S. 'Social order and the conflict of values in classical Sparta', *Chiron* 13 (1983) 239–81
31. Hodkinson, S. 'Land tenure and inheritance in classical Sparta', *CQ* n.s. 36 (1986) 378–406
32. Holladay, A. J. 'Sparta's role in the First Peloponnesian War', *JHS* 97 (1977) 54–63
33. Holladay, A. J. 'Sparta and the First Peloponnesian War', *JHS* 105 (1985) 161–2
34. Hönle, A. *Olympia in der Politik der griechischen Staatenwelt* (Diss. Tübingen, 1968)
35. Huxley, G. L. *Early Sparta*. London, 1962
36. Jeffery, L. H. 'The development of Lakonian lettering: a reconsideration', *BSA* 83 (1988) 179–81
37. Jones, A. H. M. *Sparta*. Oxford, 1966
38. Kahrstedt, U, 'Synoikismos', P–W IVA 2 (1932) 1435–45
39. Kahrstedt, U. *Beiträge zur Geschichte der thrakischen Chersones* (Deutsche Beiträge zur Altertumswissenschaft 6). Baden-Baden, 1954
40. Kuhn, E, *Ueber die Entstehung der Staedte der Alten. Komenverfassung und Synoikismos*. Leipzig, 1878
41. Lang, M. L. 'Scapegoat Pausanias', *CJ* 63 (1967/8) 79–85
42. Larsen, J. A. O. 'The constitution of the Peloponnesian League I', *Cl. Phil.* 28 (1933) 257–76
42A. Larsen, J. A. O. 'Orchomenus and the formation of the Boeotian Confederacy', *Cl. Phil.* 55 (1960) 9–18
43. Larsen, J. A. O. 'A new interpretation of the Thessalian Confederacy', *Cl. Phil.* 55 (1960) 229–48
44. Lazenby, J. F. 'Pausanias, son of Kleombrotos', *Hermes* 103 (1975) 235–51
45. Legon, R. P. *Megara: the Political History of a Greeek City-State to 336 B.C.* Ithaca–London, 1981
46. Lippold, A. 'Pausanias von Sparta und die Perser', *Rh. Mus.* 108 (1965) 322–6
47. Lotze, D. 'Selbstbewusstsein und Machtpolitik: Bemerkungen zur machtpolitischen Interpretation spartanischen Verhaltens in den Jahren 479–477 v. Chr.', *Klio* 52 (1970) 255–75
48. Lotze, D. 'Zur Verfassung von Argos nach der Schlacht bei Sepeia', *Chiron* 1 (1971) 95–109
49. Maier, F. G. 'Factoids in ancient history: the case of fifth-century Cyprus', *JHS* 105 (1985) 32–9
50. Mastrokostas, E. Ἀρχαιότητες καὶ μνημεῖα Αἰτωλίας καὶ Ἀκαρνανίας,

Arch. Delt. 19B (1964) 294–300

51.   Mitchell, B. M. 'Cyrene and Persia', *JHS* 86 (1966) 99–113
52.   Moggi, M. 'Συνοικίζειν in Tucidide', *ASNP* ser. 3, 5 (1975) 915–24
53.   Moggi, M. *I sinecismi interstatali greci*, I: *Dalle origini al 338 a.c.* Pisa. 1976
54.   Morrison, J. S. 'Meno of Pharsalus, Polycrates and Ismenias', *CQ* 36 (1942) 57–78
55.   Ollier, F. *Le mirage spartiate. Etude sur l'idéalisation de Sparte dans l'antiquité grecque de l'origine jusqu'aux Cyniques* I. Paris, 1933
56.   O'Neil, J. L. 'The exile of Themistokles and democracy in the Peloponnese', *CQ* n.s. 31 (1981) 335–46
57.   Peek, W. *Ein neuer spartanischer Staatsvertrag. (Abh. Sächs. Ak. Wiss. zu Leipzig* 65.3). 1974
58.   Pouilloux, J. *Recherches sur l'histoire et les cultes de Thasos* I (Etudes thasiennes 3). Paris, 1954
59.   Pouilloux, J. and Salviat, F. 'Les archontes de Thasos', Πρακτικὰ τοῦ Η' διεθνοῦς συνεδρίου Ἑλληνικῆς καὶ Λατινικῆς Ἐπιγραφικῆς, *Proceedings of the Eighth Epigraphic Congress 1982* I 233–58. Athens, 1984
60.   Roux, G. *L'Amphictionie, Delphes et le Temple d'Apollon au IVe siècle.* Lyons, 1979
61.   Salmon, J. B. *Wealthy Corinth.* Oxford, 1984
62.   Salviat, F. 'Les colonnes initiales du catalogue des théores . . .', *Thasiaca (BCH* Supp. 5), 107–27. Paris, 1979
63.   Sealey, R. 'Die spartanische Nauarchie', *Klio* 58 (1976) 335–58
64.   Shipley, G. J. *A History of Samos, 800–188 B.C.* Oxford, 1987
65.   Siewert, P. *Der Eid von Plataiai* (Vestigia 16). Munich, 1972
66.   Sordi, M. 'La posizione di Delfi e dell'Anfizionia nel decennio tra Tanagra e Coronea', *Riv. di Filol.* n.s. 36 (1958) 48–65
67.   Swoboda, H. 'Elis', P–W 5 (1905) 2368–432
68.   Tigerstedt, E. N. *The Legend of Sparta in Classical Antiquity* I. Stockholm–Göteborg–Uppsala, 1965
69.   Vinogradov, Yu. G. 'Sinopa i Olbiya v V v. do n. e. Problema politicheskogo ustroistva', *VDI* 1981, 2, 65–90
69A. Wallace, P. W. *Strabo's Description of Boiotia* (Bibliothek der klassischen Altertumswissenschaften NF 2. Reihe, 65). Heidelberg, 1979
70.   Wallace, W. P. 'Kleomenes, Marathon, the Helots, and Arkadia', *JHS* 74 (1954) 32–5
71.   White, M. E. 'Some Agiad dates: Pausanias and his sons', *JHS* 84 (1964) 140–52
72.   Williams, C. K. Corinth excavation reports in *Hesp.* 47 (1978) 1–39, 48 (1979) 105–44, 49 (1980) 107–34
73.   Zeilhofer, G. *Sparta, Delphoi und die Amphiktyonen im 5. Jahrhundert vor Christus.* Diss. Erlangen, 1959

G. THE PELOPONNESIAN WAR

1.   Ampolo, C. 'I contributi alla prima spedizione ateniese in Sicilia', *PP* 42 (1987) 5–11

2. Anderson, J. K. 'Cleon's orders at Amphipolis', *JHS* 85 (1965) 1–4
3. Andrewes, A. 'The generals in the Hellespont', *JHS* 73 (1953) 2–9
4. Andrewes, A. 'Thucydides on the causes of the War', *CQ* n.s. 9 (1959) 223–39
5. Andrewes, A. 'Thucydides and the Persians', *Historia* 10 (1961) 1–18
6. Andrewes, A. 'Notion and Kyzikos: the sources compared', *JHS* 102 (1982) 15–25
7. Andrewes, A. and Lewis, D. M. 'Note on the Peace of Nikias', *JHS* 77 (1957) 177–80
8. Beattie, A. J. 'Nisaea and Minoa', *Rh. Mus.* 103 (1960) 20–43
9. Boardman, J. 'Delphinion in Chios', *BSA* 51 (1956) 41–54
10. Brunt, P. A. 'Spartan policy and strategy in the Archidamian War', *Phoenix* 19 (1965) 255–80
11. Cavaignac, E. 'Les Dékarchies de Lysandre', *REH* 90 (1924) 285–316
12. Cawkwell, G. L. 'Thucydides' judgement of Periclean strategy', *YCS* 24 (1975) 53–70
13. Ehrhardt, C. 'Xenophon and Diodorus on Aegospotami', *Phoenix* 24 (1970) 225–8
14. Gauthier, P. 'Les ports de l'Empire et l'*Agora* Athénienne: à propos du "Décret Mégarien"', *Historia* 24 (1975) 498–503
15. Gomme, A. W. 'Thucydides ii 13, 3', *Historia* 2 (1953/4) 1–21
16. Holladay, A. J. 'Athenian strategy in the Archidamian war', *Historia* 27 (1978) 399–427
17. Kagan, D. *The Outbreak of the Peloponnesian War*. Ithaca, 1969
18. Kagan, D. *The Archidamian War*. Ithaca, 1974
19. Kagan, D. *The Peace of Nicias and the Sicilian Expedition*. Ithaca, 1981
20. Kagan, D. *The Fall of the Athenian Empire*. Ithaca, 1987
21. Kallet-Marx, L. 'The Kallias Decree, Thucydides, and the outbreak of the Peloponnesian War', *CQ* n.s. 39 (1989) 94–113
22. Kelly, T. 'Thucydides and Spartan strategy in the Archidamian War', *AHR* 87 (1982) 25–54
23. Legon, R. P. 'The Megarian Decree and the balance of Greek naval power', *Cl. Phil.* 68 (1973) 161–71
24. Lewis, D. M. 'The Phoenician fleet in 411', *Historia* 7 (1958) 392–7
25. Littman, R. J. 'The strategy of the Battle of Cyzicus', *TAPA* 99 (1968) 265–72
26. Lotze, D. *Lysander und der peloponnesische Krieg* (*Abh. Sächs. Ak. Wiss. zu Leipzig*, Phil.-Hist. Kl. 57.1). 1964
27. MacDonald, B. R. 'The import of Attic pottery to Corinth and the question of trade during the Peloponnesian War', *JHS* 102 (1982) 113–23
28. MacDonald, B. R. 'The Megarian Decree', *Historia* 32 (1983) 385–410
29. Meritt, B. D. 'The end of winter in Thucydides', *Hesp.* 33 (1964) 228–30
30. Meritt, B. D. 'The chronology of the Peloponnesian War', *Proceedings of the American Philosophical Society* 115 (1971) 97–124 (cf. 122 (1978) 287–93)
31. Ober, J. 'Thucydides, Pericles and the strategy of defense', in A 31, 171–88

32. Ober, J. *Fortress Attica: Defense of the Athenian Land Frontier 404–322 B.C.* Leiden, 1985

33. Panagopoulos, A. *Captives and Hostages in the Peloponnesian War*. Athens, 1978

34. Rhodes, P. J. 'Thucydides on the causes of the Peloponnesian War', *Hermes* 115 (1987) 154–65

35. Robertson, N. 'The sequence of events in the Aegean in 408 and 407 B.C.', *Historia* 29 (1980) 282–301

36. de Ste Croix, G. E. M. *The Origins of the Peloponnesian War*. London, 1972

37. Sealey, R. 'The causes of the Peloponnesian War', *Cl. Phil.* 70 (1975) 89–109

38. Strassler, R. B. 'The harbor at Pylos, 425 B.C.', *JHS* 108 (1988) 198–203

39. Strauss, B. S. 'Aegospotami reexamined', *AJP* 104 (1983) 24–35

40. Stroud, R. S. 'Thucydides and the Battle of Solygeia', *CSCA* 4 (1971) 227–47

41. Thompson, W. E. 'The chronology of 432/1', *Hermes* 96 (1968) 216–32

42. Wade-Gery, H. T. and Meritt, B. D. 'Pylos and the assessment of tribute', *AJP* 57 (1936) 252–60

43. Wick, T. E. 'Megara, Athens and the West in the Archidamian War: a study in Thucydides', *Historia* 28 (1979) 1–14

44. Wilson, J. B. *Pylos 425 B.C.: a Historical and Topographical Study of Thucydides' Account of the Campaign*. Warminster, 1979

H. SICILY

I. GENERAL

1. Arrighetti, G. 'Civiltà letteraria della Sicilia antica fino al V sec. a. C.', in H 6, II.1 129–53

2. Bidez, J. *Empédocle d'Agrigente*. Paris, 1969

3. Burelli, L., Culasso Castaldi, E. and Vanotti, G. *I tragici greci e l'Occidente* (Introduction by L. Braccesi). Bologna, 1979

4. Calder, W. M., III *The Inscription from Temple G at Selinus* (Greek, Roman and Byzantine Monographs 4). Duke University, 1963

5. De Waele, J. A. 'La popolazione di Acragas antica', in A 83, 747–60

6. Gabba, E. and Vallet, G. (eds.) *La Sicilia antica*. 2 vols. Naples, 1980

7. Gallavotti, G. *Empedocle*. Verona, 1975

8. La Genière, J. de. 'Ségeste et l'hellénisme', *MEFRA* 90 (1978) 33–49

9. Hackforth, R. Chapter VI, 'Sicily', in *CAH* VI¹ (1927) 145–64

10. Maddoli, G. 'Il VI e V secolo', in H 6, II.1 1–102

11. Manni, E. *Geografia fisica e politica della Sicilia antica*. Rome, 1981

12. Panagitou, S. 'Empedocles on his own divinity', *Mnemosyne* 36 (1983) 276–85

13. Treu, M. 'Sizilische Mythologie bei Simonides', *KOKALOS* 14–15 (1968–9) 428–38

14. Van Compernolle, R. 'Ségeste et l'hellénisme', *Phoibos* 5 (1950–1) 183–228

15. Voza, G. 'Cultura artistica fino al V secolo a. C.', in H 6, II.1 103–28

II. HIERO AND THERON

16. Battaglia, R. 'Eschilo e il teatro greco di Gela', *ASSO* ser. 4, 10 (1957) 168–72
17. Bury, J. B. 'The constitutional position of Gelon and Hiero', *CR* 13 (1899) 98–9
18. Cataudella, Q. 'Eschilo in Sicilia', *Dioniso* 37 (1963) 5–24
19. Daux, G. 'Chronique des fouilles 1959', *BCH* 84 (1960) 721
20. De Waele, J. A. *Acragas graeca. Die historische Topographie des griechischen Akragas auf Sizilien*, I: *Historischer Teil*. Rome, 1971
21. Gentili, B. 'I tripodi di Delfi e il carme III di Bacchilide', *PP* 8 (1953) 199–208
22. Guardi, T. 'L'attività teatrale nella Siracusa di Gerone I', *Dioniso* 51 (1980) 25–47
23. Guarducci, M. 'Arcadi in Sicilia', *PP* 8 (1953) 209–11
24. La Rosa, V. 'Le *Etnee* di Eschilo e l'identificazione di Xouthia', *ASSO* 70 (1974) 151–64
25. Lavagnini, B. 'I Persiani d'Eschilo al teatro di Siracusa', *Boll. Ist. Naz. Dramma Ant.* (1930) 36–44
26. Piccirilli, L. 'La controversia fra Ierone I e Polizelo', *ASNP* ser. 3, 11 (1971) 69–79
27. Podlecki, A. A. 'Simonides in Sicily', *PP* 34 (1979) 5–16
28. Stanford, W. B. 'Traces of Sicilian influences in Aeschylus', *Proc. Royal Irish Acad.* 44 C (1937–8) 225–59
29. Vallet, G. 'Note sur la "maison" des Deinomenides', in A 83, 2141–56
30. Wilamowitz-Moellendorff, U. von. 'Hiero und Pindar', SBAk. Berlin (1901) 1273–1318 (= *id. Kleine Schriften* VI (1972) 234–85)

III. FALL OF TYRANNIES, CONSTITUTIONAL HISTORY

31. Asheri, D. 'Rimpatrio di esuli e ridistribuzione di terre nelle città siciliote, ca. 466–461 a.C.', in A 83, 145–58
32. Barrett, W. S. 'Pindar's twelfth *Pythian* and the fall of the Deinomenidai', *JHS* 93 (1973) 23–35
33. Bonacasa, N. 'Il problema urbanistico di Himera', *Quaderno Imerese*, 1–16. Rome, 1972
34. Consolo Langher, S. 'Problemi di storia costituzionale siceliota', *Helikon* 9–10 (1969–70) 107–43
35. Consolo Langher, S. N. 'Naxos di Sicilia. Profilo storico', in A 83, II 537–62
36. Coppola, G. 'Una pagina del περὶ Σικελίας di Filisto in un papiro fiorentino', *Riv. di Filol.* 58 (1930) 449–66
37. De Sanctis, G. 'Una nuova pagina di storia siciliana', *Riv. di Filol.* 33 (1905) 66–73 (= *id.*, *Scritti minori* I, 113–20. Rome, 1966)
38. Hüttl, W. *Verfassungsgeschichte von Syrakus*. Prague, 1929

39. La Genière, J. de. 'Réflexions sur Sélinonte et l'Ouest sicilien', *CRAI* 1977, 251–64

40. La Genière, J. de. 'Nuove ricerche sulla topografia di Selinunte', *Rend. Linc.* ser. 8, 36 (1981) 211–17

41. La Genière, J. de. 'Sélinonte. Recherches sur la topographie urbaine (1975–1981)', *ASNP* ser. 3, 12 (1982) 469–79

42. Manganaro, G. 'La caduta dei Dinomenidi e il *politikon nomisma* in Sicilia nella prima metà del V sec. a.C.', *AIIN* 21–2 (1974–5) 9–39

43. Meier-Welcker, H. *Himera und die Geschicke des griechischen Sizilien.* Boppard am Rhein, 1980

44. Pais, E. 'Il papiro di Oxyrhynchos nr. 665 relativo alla storia antica della Sicilia', *Rend. Linc.* ser. 5, 17 (1908) 329–43

45. Rizza, G. 'Scoperta di una città antica sulle rive del Simeto: Etna-Inessa?', *PP* 14 (1959) 465–74

46. Vallet, G. *Rhégion et Zankle. Histoire, commerce et civilisation des cités chalcidiennes du détroit de Messine.* Paris, 1958

47. Wentker, H. *Sizilien und Athen. Die Begegnung der attischen Macht mit den Westgriechen.* Heidelberg, 1956

IV. SICEL MOVEMENT

48. Adamasteanu, D. 'L'ellenizzazione della Sicilia e il momento di Ducezio', *KOKALOS* 8 (1962) 167–98

49. Bello, L. 'Ricerche sui Palici', *KOKALOS* 6 (1960) 71–97

50. Boehringer, C. 'Die barbarisierten Münzen von Akragas, Gela, Leontinoi und Syrakus im 5. Jahrhundert v.Chr.', *AIIN*, Suppl. 20 (1975) 157–90

51. Childs, W. A. P. 'Morgantina, past and future', *AJA* 83 (1979) 377–9

52. Croon, J. H. 'Ducetius, dux Siculorum', *Tijdschrift v. Geschiedenis* 65 (1952) 301–17

53. Croon, J. H. 'The Palici – an autochthonous cult in ancient Sicily', *Mnemosyne* IV, 5 (1952) 116–29

54. Erim, K. 'Morgantina', *AJA* 62 (1958) 79–90

55. Maddoli, G. 'Ducezio e la fondazione di Calatte', *Ann. Fac. di Lett. di Perugia* 15 (1977–8), n.s. 1 (Studi Classici)

56. Manni, E. '"Indigeni" e colonizzatori nella Sicilia pre-romana', in *Assimilation et résistance à la culture gréco-romaine dans le monde ancien. Travaux du VIᵉ Congrès Internationale d'Études Classiques* (Madrid, 2–6 septembre 1976), 181–211. Bucarest–Paris, 1976

57. Manni, E. 'Quattro note filologico-topografiche', *ASS* ser. 4, 2 (1976) 5–17

58. Meister, K. Review of H 67, in *Gnomon* 47 (1975) 772–7

59. Messina, A. 'Menai-Menainon ed Eryke-Palike', *Cron. di Arch.* 6 (1967) 87–91

60. *Morgantina Studies.* I: M. Bell, *The Terracottas.* Princeton, 1981; II: T. V. Buttrey, *The Coins.* Princeton, 1989

61. Mussinano, L. 'Montagna di Marzo: relazione preliminare', *Chron. di Arch.* 5 (1966) 55–66

62. Mussinano, L. 'Iscrizioni da Montagna di Marzo', *KOKALOS* 16 (1970) 166–83

63. Orlandini, P. *Vassallaggi* I (*Not. Scav.*, Suppl. 25). 1971

64. Pais, E. 'Piacus', in *Ancient Italy*, 123–9. Chicago, 1908

65. Piraino, M. T. 'Morgantina e Murgentia nella topografia dell'antica Sicilia orientale', *KOKALOS* 5 (1959) 174–89

66. *Preliminary Reports I–XI* on 'Excavations at Serra Orlando' or 'at Morgantina (Serra Orlando)', by R. Stillwell and/or E. Sjöqvist, and by H. L. Allen, *AJA* 61 (1957) – 68 (1964); 71 (1967); 74 (1970); 78 (1974)

67. Rizzo, F. P. *La repubblica di Siracusa nel momento di Ducezio*. Palermo, 1970

68. Rizzo, F. P. 'Contrasto greco-siculo o crisi di rapporti fra Sicelioti nel periodo 466–451 a.C.?', *KOKALOS* 16 (1970) 139–43

69. Sjöqvist, E. 'Perchè Morgantina?', *RAL* 15 (1960) 291–300

70. Sjöqvist, E. 'I Greci a Morgantina', *KOKALOS* 8 (1962) 52–68

71. Sjöqvist, E. *Sicily and the Greeks. Studies in the Interrelationship between the Indigenous Population and the Greek Colonists.* Ann Arbor, 1973

V. SYRACUSE AND TYRRHENIAN AFFAIRS

72. Colonna, G. 'La Sicilia e il Tirreno nel V e IV secolo', *KOKALOS* 26–7 (1980–1) 157–91

73. De Sensi Sestito, G. 'I Dinomenidi nel basso e medio Tirreno tra Imera e Cuma', *MEFRA* XIII c 2 (1981)

74. De Waele, J. A. 'Intorno ad una iscrizione della Malophoros', *KOKALOS* 9 (1963) 195–204

75. Giuffrida Ientile, M. *La pirateria tirrenica. Momenti e fortuna* (Suppl. to *KOKALOS* 6). Rome, 1983

76. Merante, V. 'La Sicilia e Cartagine dal V secolo alla conquista romana', *KOKALOS* 18–19 (1972–3) 77–103

77. Torelli, M. 'Beziehungen zwischen Griechen und Etruskern im 5. und 4. Jahrhundert v.u.Z.', in A 122, II 823–40

VI. COINAGE

78. Bernabò Brea, L. In *AIIN* Suppl. 20 (1975) 45–9 (on Piacus)

79. Boehringer, C. 'Hierons Aitna und das Hieroneion', *JNG* 19 (1968) 67–98

80. Boehringer, E. *Die Münzen von Syrakus.* Berlin–Leipzig, 1929

81. Cahn, H. A. *Die Münzen der sizilischen Stadt Naxos.* Basel, 1944

82. Consolo Langher, S. *Contributo alla storia della antica moneta bronzea in Sicilia.* Milan, 1964

83. Gabrici, E. *La monetazione del bronzo nella Sicilia antica.* Palermo, 1927

84. Gutmann, P. and Schwabacher, W. 'Die Tetradrachmenprägung und Didrachmenprägung von Himera (472–409 v.Chr.)', *MBNG* 47 (1929) 101–44

85. Hill, G. F. *Coins of Ancient Sicily.* London, 1903

86. Jenkins, G. K. 'The coinage of Enna, Galaria, Piakos, Imachara, Kephaloidion and Longano', *AIIN* Suppl. 20 (1975) 77–103
87. Jenkins, G. K. *The Coinage of Gela*. Berlin, 1970
88. Jenkins, G. K. 'Himera: the coins of Akragantine type', *AIIN* Suppl. 15–16 (1971) 21–36
89. Jenkins, G. K. *Coins of Greek Sicily*. 2nd edn. London, 1976
90. Kraay, C. M. 'The demareteion reconsidered. A reply', *Num. Chron.* (1972) 13–24
91. Mazzarino, S. 'Documentazione numismatica e storia Syrakousana del V secolo a.C.', in *Anthemon, Scritti di Archeologia e di Antichità Classica in onore di Carlo Anti*, 41–65. Florence, 1955
92. Schwabacher, W. 'Die Tetradrachmenprägung von Selinunt', *MBNG* 43 (1925) 1–89
93. Westermark, U. and Jenkins, K. *The Coinage of Kamarina*. London, 1980
94. Williams, R. T. 'The damareteion reconsidered', *Num. Chron.* (1972) 1–11

I. ART AND ARCHITECTURE

1. Amandry, P. 'Thémistocle à Mélitè', in *Charisterion for A. K. Orlandos IV*, 265–79. Athens, 1967
1A. Amyx, D. A. 'The Attic Stelai, Part III', *Hesp.* 27 (1958) 163–310
2. Anti, A. *Teatri greci arcaici*. Padua, 1947
3. Anti, A. and Polacco, L. *Nuove ricerche sui teatri greci arcaici*. Padua, 1969
4. Arias, P. E., Hirmer, M. and Shefton, B. B. *A History of Greek Vase Painting*. London–New York, 1962
5. Ashmole, B. and Yalouris, N. *Olympia, the Sculptures of the Temple of Zeus*. London, 1967
6. Ashmole, B. *Architect and Sculptor in Classical Greece*. London–New York, 1972
7. Athens. *The Athenian Agora; a Guide to the Excavation and Museum*. 3rd edn. Athens, 1976
8. Aupert, P. *Fouilles de Delphes*, II: *Topographie et Architecture. Le stade*. Paris, 1979
9. Barron, J. P. 'New light on old walls: the murals of the Theseion', *JHS* 92 (1972) 20–45
10. Bell, M. 'Stylobate and roof in the Olympieion at Akragas', *AJA* 84 (1980) 359–72
11. Berger, E. (ed.) *Parthenon-Kongress Basel*. Mainz, 1984. (With very full bibliography on the building)
12. Bergquist, B. *The Archaic Greek Temenos*. Lund, 1967
13. Berve, H. and Gruben, G. *Greek Temples, Theatres, and Shrines*. New York, 1962; London, 1963
14. Beschi, L. 'Il monumento di Telemachos, fondatore dell'Asklepieion ateniese', *ASAA* n.s. 29–30 (1967–8) 381–436
15. Bieber, M. *History of the Greek and Roman Theater*. 2nd edn. Princeton, 1961
16. Boardman, J. *Athenian Black Figure Vases*. London, 1974

17.   Boardman, J. *Athenian Red Figure Vases: the Archaic Period.* London, 1975
18.   Boardman, J. 'The Parthenon frieze – another view', in *Festschrift für Frank Brommer*, 39–49. Mainz, 1977
18A.   Boardman, J. *Greek Sculpture: the Archaic Period.* London, 1978
19.   Boardman, J. 'Herakles, Theseus and Amazons', in Kurtz, D. C. and Sparkes, B. A. (eds.) *The Eye of Greece: Studies in the Art of Athens*, 1–28. Cambridge, 1982
20.   Boardman, J. *Greek Sculpture: the Classical Period.* London, 1985
21.   Boardman, J. *Athenian Red Figure Vases: the Classical Period.* London, 1989
22.   Boardman, J. and Finn, D. *The Parthenon and its Sculpture.* London, 1985
23.   Boersma, J. S. *Athenian Building Policy from 561/0 to 405/4 B.C.* Groningen, 1970
24.   Boulter, C. (ed.) *Greek Art, Archaic into Classical* (Cincinnati Symposium 1982). Leiden, 1985
25.   Brommer, F. *Die Skulpturen der Parthenon-Giebel.* Mainz, 1963
26.   Brommer, F. *Die Metopen des Parthenon.* Mainz, 1967
27.   Brommer, F. *Der Parthenonfries, Katalog und Untersuchung.* Mainz, 1977
28.   Brommer, F. *Hephaistos.* Mainz, 1978
29.   Brommer, F. *The Sculptures of the Parthenon.* London, 1979
30.   Broneer, O., *Isthmia*, I. *Temple of Poseidon.* Princeton, 1971
31.   Broneer, O. *Isthmia, II: Topography and Architecture.* Princeton, 1973
32.   Bruneau, P. and Ducat, J. *Guide de Délos.* Paris, 1965
33.   Brunnsåker, S. *The Tyrant-Slayers of Kritios and Nesiotes.* Stockholm, 1971
34.   Bruno, V. *Form and Color in Greek Painting.* New York, 1977
35.   Bundgaard, J. A. *Mnesikles, a Greek Architect at Work* (on Propylaea). Copenhagen, 1957
36.   Bundgaard, J. A. *Parthenon.* Copenhagen, 1976
37.   Burford, A. 'Temple building at Segesta', *CQ* n.s. 11 (1961) 87–93
38.   Burford, A. M. 'The builders of the Parthenon', in I 121, 23–35
39.   Burford, A. 'The economics of Greek temple building', *PCPhS* n.s. 11 (1965) 21–34
40.   Burford, A. *Greek Temple Builders at Epidauros.* Liverpool, 1969
41.   Burns, R. A. 'Hippodamus and the planned city', *Historia* 25 (1976) 414–28
42.   Carpenter, R. *The Architects of the Parthenon.* Harmondsworth, 1970
43.   Castagnoli, F. *Ippodamo di Mileto e la Pianta Ortogonale.* Rome, 1956. (Engl. transl. by V. Caliandro, *Orthogonal Town Planning in Antiquity.* Cambridge, MA and London, 1971)
44.   Chamoux, F. *Fouilles de Delphes*, IV, 5. *L'Aurige.* Paris, 1955
45.   *La cité des images.* Lausanne–Paris, 1984. (Eng. transl. by C. Bérard *et al. A City of Images.* Princeton, 1989)
46.   Clarke, M. L. 'The architects of Greece and Rome', *Architectural Review* 1963, 9–22
47.   Cook, R. M. *Greek Painted Pottery.* 2nd edn. London, 1972
48.   Coulton, J. J. 'Towards understanding Doric design: the stylobate and

intercolumnations', *BSA* 69 (1974) 61–86

49. Coulton, J. J. 'Towards understanding Greek Temple design: general considerations', *BSA* 70 (1975) 59–99
50. Coulton, J. J. *The Architectural Development of the Greek Stoa.* Oxford, 1976
51. Coulton, J. J. *Greek Architects at Work, Problems of Structure and Design.* London, 1977
52. Coulton, J. J. 'Doric capitals: a proportional analysis', *BSA* 74 (1979) 81–153
53. Courby, M. F. *Fouilles de Delphes*, II.1: *La terrasse du temple.* Paris, 1927
54. Courby, F. *Exploration archéologique de Délos*, XII: *Les temples d'Apollon.* Paris, 1931
55. Delorme, J. *Gymnasion.* Paris, 1960
56. Despinis, G. I. Συμβολὴ στὴ μελέτη τοῦ ἔργου τοῦ Ἀγορακρίτου. Athens, 1971
57. De Waele, J. A. 'Der Entwurf der dorischen Tempel von Akragas', *Arch. Anz.* (1980) 180–241
58. De Waele, J. A. 'Der Entwurf der dorischen Tempel von Paestum', *Arch. Anz.* (1980) 367–400
59. Dinsmoor, W. B. *Observations on the Hephaisteion* (*Hesp.* Supp. 5). Princeton, 1941
60. Dinsmoor, W. B. *The Architecture of Ancient Greece.* 3rd edn. London–New York, 1950
61. Dinsmoor, W. B. Jr. *The Propylaia to the Athenian Akropolis*, I: *The Predecessors*, Princeton, 1980
62. Drerup, H. 'Parthenon und Vorparthenon; zum Stand der Kontroverse', *Antike Kunst* 24 (1981) 21–37
63. *Due Bronze da Riace. Rinvenimento, Restauro, Analisi ed Ipotesi di Interpretazione* (*Boll. d'Arte*, Serie Speciale, 3). Rome, 1985
64. Francis, E. D. and Vickers, M. 'The Oenoe painting in the Stoa Poikile and Herodotus', *BSA* 80 (1985) 99–103
65. Frickenhaus, A. 'Lenäenvasen', *72. Programm zum Winckelmannsfeste.* Berlin, 1912
66. Fuchs, W. *Die Skulptur der Griechen*, 3rd edn. Munich, 1983
66A. Gardiner E. N. 'Panathenaic amphorae', *JHS* 32 (1912) 179–93, esp. 184–7
67. Gardiner, E. N. *Olympia. Its History and Remains.* Oxford, 1925
68. Gauer, W. *Weihgeschenke aus den Perserkriegen* (*Ist. Mitt.* 2). Tübingen, 1968
69. von Gerkan, A. *Griechische Städteanlagen: Untersuchungen zur Entwicklung des Städtebaues im Altertum.* Berlin–Leipzig, 1924
70. Graef, B. and Langlotz, E. *Die antiken Vasen der Akropolis zu Athen* II. Berlin, 1933
71. Graham, J. W. 'Origins and interrelations of the Greek house and the Roman house', *Phoenix* 20 (1966) 3–31
71A. Graham, J. W. 'Houses of Classical Athens', *Phoenix* 28 (1974) 45–54
72. Gruben, G. *Die Tempel der Griechen.* Munich, 1966

73. Hammond, N. G. L. 'Dramatic production to the death of Aeschylus', *GRBS* 13 (1972) 387–450

73A. Harrison, E. B. *The Athenian Agora*, II. *Archaic and Archaistic Sculpture.* Princeton, 1965

74. Harrison, E. B. 'Alkamenes' sculptures for the Hephaisteion', *AJA* 81 (1977) 137–78, 265–87, 411–26

75. Hill, B. H. *The Temple of Zeus at Nemea.* Princeton, 1966

76. Hill, I. T. *The Ancient City of Athens.* London, 1953

77. Hoepfner, W. and Schwandner, E.-L. *Haus und Stadt im klassischen Griechenland* (Wohnen in der klassischen Polis 1). Munich, 1986

78. Hopper, R. J. *The Acropolis.* London, 1971

79. Immerwahr, H. R. 'Book-rolls on Attic vases', in Henderson, C. Jr (ed.) *Classical, Medieval and Renaissance Studies in Honor of Berthold Louis Ullman* I, 17–48. Rome, 1964

80. Jannoray, J. *Fouilles de Delphes*, II: *Topographie et Architecture. Le gymnase.* Paris, 1953

81. Jeffery, L. H. 'The Battle of Oinoe in the Stoa Poikile: a problem in Greek art and history', *BSA* 60 (1965) 41–57

82. Jones, J. E. 'Town and country houses in Attica in classical times', in *Miscellanea Graeca*, I: *Thorikos and Laurion in Archaic and Classical Times.* Ghent, 1975

83. Jones, J. E., Graham, A. J. and Sackett, L. H. 'An Attic country house below the Cave of Pan at Vari', *BSA* 68 (1973) 355–452

84. Jones, J. E., Sackett, L. H. and Graham, A. J. 'The Dema House in Attica', *BSA* 57 (1962) 75–114

85. Judeich, W. *Topographie von Athen.* 2nd edn. (Handbuch der Altertumswissenschaft, Abt 3, Teil 2, bd 2). Munich, 1931

86. Kalligas, P. ''Εργασίαι . . . 'Ιεροῦ Διονύσου 'Ελευθερέως', *Arch. Delt.* 18 (1963) BI, 12–18

87. Keaney, J. J. 'Heliodorus F 1 and Philochorus F 41', *Historia* 17 (1968) 507–9

88. *Kerameikos, Ergebnisse der Ausgrabungen* I–XI. Deutsches Archäologisches Institut, Berlin, 1939–80

89. Knell, H. 'Vier attische Tempel klassischer Zeit', *Arch. Anz.* (1973) 94–113

89A. Knell, H. 'Die Gruppe von Prokne und Itys', *Antike Plastik* 17 (1978) 9–19

90. Knell, H. *Perikleische Baukunst.* Darmstadt, 1979

91. Knigge, U. *Der Kerameikos von Athen. Führung durch Ausgrabungen und Geschichte.* Athens, 1988

92. Kolb, F. *Agora und Theater, Volks- und Festversammlung* (DAI, Archäologische Forschungen 9). Berlin, 1981

93. Kolb, F. *Die Stadt im Altertum.* Munich, 1984

94. Lawrence, A. W. 'Archimedes and the design of Euryalus fort', *JHS* 66 (1946) 99–107

95. Lawrence, A. W. *Greek Architecture* (Pelican History of Art). 3rd edn. Harmondsworth, 1973

96. Lawrence, A. W. *Greek Aims in Fortification*. Oxford, 1979
97. Lippold, G. 'Polygnotos (1)', P–W 42. Halbb. (1952) 1630–9
98. Lorenz, T. *Polyklet*. Wiesbaden, 1972
99. McCredie, J. R. 'Hippodamos of Miletos', in Mitten, D. G., Pedley, J. G. and Scott, J. A. (eds.) *Studies presented to George M. A. Hanfmann*, 95–100. Cambridge, MA, 1971
100. McDonald, W. A. *Political Meeting-Places of the Greeks*. Baltimore, 1943
101. Maier, F. G. *Griechische Mauerbauinschriften*. Heidelberg. 1959–61
102. Mallwitz, A. *Olympia und seine Bauten*. Munich, 1972
103. Mallwitz, A. x. *Bericht über die Ausgrabungen in Olympia*. Berlin, 1981
104. Mallwitz, A. and Herrmann, H.-V. *Die Funde aus Olympia*. Athens, 1980
105. Martin, R. *Recherches sur l'agora grecque, Etudes d'histoire et d'architecture urbaines* (Bibl. Éc. fr. Ath. et Rome 174). Paris, 1951
106. Martin, R. *Manuel d'Architecture Grecque*, I: *Matériaux et Techniques*. Paris, 1965
107. Martin, R. *L'Urbanisme dans la Grèce Antique*. 2nd edn. Paris, 1974
108. Mattingly, H. B. 'The Athenian Nike temple reconsidered', *AJA* 86 (1982) 381–5
109. Meritt, L. S. 'The Stoa Poikile', *Hesp.* 39 (1970) 233–64
110. Metzger, H. *Recherches sur l'Imagérie Athénienne*. Paris, 1965
111. Miles, M. M. 'The date of the temple on the Ilissos River', *Hesp.* 49 (1980) 309–25
112. Miles, M. M. 'The Theseum architect', *AJA* 85 (1981) 207
113. Miller, S. G. *The Prytaneion*. Los Angeles, 1978
114. Miller, S. G. Review of 18, *AJA* 85 (1981) 504–6
115. Miller, S. G. and Miller, S. G. 'Excavations at Nemea' (1973–4 and following years), *Hesp.* 44 (1975) 143–72, 45 (1976) 174–202, 46 (1977) 1–26, 47 (1978) 58–88, 48 (1979) 73–103, 49 (1980) 178–205, 50 (1981) 45–67, 51 (1982) 19–40, 52 (1983) 70–95, 53 (1984) 171–92
116. Mussche, H. *Thorikos, a Guide*. Brussels, 1974
117. Mussche, H. and others. *Thorikos, Preliminary Reports* 1963–
118. Oikonomides, A. N. *The Two Agoras in Ancient Athens*. Chicago, 1962
119. Orlandos, A. K. Τὰ ὑλικὰ δομῆς τῶν ἀρχαίων Ἑλλήνων. 2 vols. Athens, 1955–8. (French transl. by V. Hadjimichali, *Les matériaux de construction et la technique architectural des anciens grecs* I–II. Paris, 1966–8)
120. Overbeck, J. *Die antiken Schriftquellen zur Geschichte der bildenden Künste bei den Griechen*. Leipzig, 1868
121. *Parthenos and Parthenon*. (*G&R* Suppl. to 10). Oxford, 1963
122. Paton, J. M., Stevens, G. P., Caskey, L. D. and Fowler, H. N. *The Erechtheum*. Cambridge, MA 1927
123. Pétracos, B. 'La base de la Némésis d'Agoracrite', *BCH* 105 (1981) 227–53
124. Pickard-Cambridge, A. W. *The Theatre of Dionysos in Athens*. Oxford, 1946
125. Picon, C. A. 'The Ilissos Temple reconsidered', *AJA* 82 (1978) 47–81
126. Plommer, W. H. *Ancient and Classical Architecture*. London, 1957. 3rd impr. 1963

127.   Pollitt, J. J. *Art and Experience in Classical Greece*. Cambridge, 1972
128.   Pollitt, J. J. *The Ancient View of Greek Art*. London–New Haven, 1974
129.   *Princeton Encyclopedia of Classical Sites*, ed. R. Stillwell, W. L. MacDonald and M. H. McAllister. Princeton, 1976
130.   Richter, G. M. A. *The Archaic Gravestones of Attica* (with an epigraphical appendix by M. Guarducci). London, 1961
131.   Richter, G. M. A. *The Portraits of the Greeks*. London, 1965
132.   Richter, G. M. A. *The Sculpture and Sculptors of the Greeks*. London–New Haven, 1970
133.   Richter, G. M. A. *The Portraits of the Greeks*. Condensed edition by R. R. R. Smith. Oxford, 1984
134.   Rider, B. C. *Ancient Greek Houses*. Cambridge, 1916
135.   Ridgway, B. S. *The Severe Style in Greek Sculpture*. Princeton, 1970
136.   Ridgway, B. S. *Fifth Century Styles in Greek Sculpture*. Princeton, 1981
137.   Ridgway, B. S. *Roman Copies of Greek Sculpture*. Ann Arbor, 1984
138.   Robertson, D. S. *Greek and Roman Architecture*. 2nd edn. Cambridge, 1959
139.   Robertson, [C.] M. *Greek Painting*. Geneva, 1959; New York, 1979
140.   Robertson, C. M. *A History of Greek Art* I–II. Cambridge, 1975
141.   Robinson, D. M., Graham, J. W. *et al. Excavations at Olynthus*. Baltimore, 1929–1946, especially vols. VIII, X and XII (on houses)
142.   Rolley, C. *Greek Bronzes*. London–Stevenage, 1986 (= *Les Bronzes Grecs*. Fribourg, 1983)
143.   Romano, D. G. 'An early stadium at Nemea', *Hesp.* 46 (1977) 27–31
144.   Romano, D. G. 'The stadia of the Peloponnesos'. Diss. Pennsylvania, 1981
145.   Rumpf, A. 'Parrhasius', *AJA* 55 (1951) 1–12
146.   Schauenberg, K. Εὐρυμέδον εἰμι, *Ath. Mitt.* 90 (1975) 97–121
147.   Schefold, K. *The Art of Classical Greece*. New York, 1966
148.   Schläger, H. 'Beobachtung am Tempel von Segesta', *Röm. Mitt.* 75 (1968) 168–9
149.   Scranton, R. L. *Greek Walls*. Cambridge, MA, 1941
150.   Scranton, R. L. 'Greek architectural inscriptions', *Harvard Library Bulletin* 14 (1960) 149–82
151.   Shear, T. L. Jr. 'The demolished temple at Eleusis', *Hesp.* Suppl. 20 (1982) 128–40
152.   Shoe, L. T. *Profiles of Greek Mouldings*. Cambridge, MA, 1936
153.   Shoe, L. T. *Profiles of Western Greek Mouldings*, Rome, 1952
154.   Simon, E., Hirmer, M. and A. *Die griechischen Vasen*. Munich, 1976
155.   Sourvinou-Inwood, C. 'Theseus lifting the rock and a cup near the Pithos Painter', *JHS* 91 (1971) 93–109
156.   Sparkes, B. A. 'Illustrating Aristophanes', *JHS* 95 (1975) 122–35
157.   Stanier, R. S. 'The cost of the Parthenon', *JHS* 73 (1953) 68–76
158.   von Steuben, H. *Der Kanon des Polyklet*. Tübingen, 1973
159.   Stuart, J. and Revett, N. *The Antiquities of Athens* I. London, 1762
160.   Stuart Jones, H. *Select Passages from Ancient Writers Illustrative of the History of Greek Sculpture*. London, 1895

161. Stupperich, R. *Staatsbegräbnis und Privatgrabmal im klassischen Athen*. Diss. Münster, 1977
162. Taplin, O. *The Stagecraft of Aeschylus*. Oxford, 1977
163. Thompson, H. A. 'Activities in the Athenian Agora: 1957', *Hesp.* 27 (1958) 145–60
164. Thompson, H. A. 'Activity in the Athenian Agora: 1966–1967', *Hesp.* 37 (1968) 36–72
165. Thompson, H. A. 'Athens faces adversity', *Hesp.* 50 (1981) 343–55
166. Thompson, H. A. and Wycherley, R. E. *The Athenian Agora*, XIV, *The Agora of Athens, the History, Shape and Uses of an Ancient City Center*. Princeton, 1972
167. Threpsiades, J. and Vanderpool, E. *'ΠΡΟΣ ΤΟΙΣ ΕΡΜΑΙΣ'*, *Arch. Delt.* 18 (1963) A 99–114
168. Threpsiades, J. and Vanderpool, E. 'Themistocles' sanctuary of Artemis Aristoboule', *Arch. Delt.* 19 (1965) A 26–36
169. Tomlinson, R. A. *Greek Sanctuaries*. London, 1976
170. Travlos, J. *Πολεοδομικὴ Ἐξέλιξις τῶν Ἀθηνῶν*. Athens, 1960
171. Travlos, J. *Pictorial Dictionary of Ancient Athens*. London–New York, 1971
172. Vanderpool, E. 'The date of the pre-Persian city-wall of Athens', in A 9, 156–60
173. Vos, M. F. *Scythian Archers in Archaic Attic Vase-Painting*. Groningen, 1963
174. Wachsmuth, G. *Die Stadt Athen im Altertum* I–II. Leipzig, 1874, 1890
175. Walker, S. 'Women and housing in classical Greece: the archaeological evidence', in A 13, 81–91
176. Ward-Perkins, J. B. *Cities of Ancient Greece and Italy: Planning in Classical Antiquity*. New York, 1974
177. Webster, T. B. L. *Potter and Patron in Classical Athens*. London, 1972
177A. Willers, D. *Zu den Anfängen der archaistischen Plastik in Griechenland*. (*Ath. Mitt.* Beiheft 4), 33–47. 1975
178. Williams, D. 'Women on Athenian vases: problems of interpretation', in A 13, 92–106
179. Winter, F. E. *Greek Fortifications*. London, 1971
180. Winter, F. E. 'Tradition and innovation in Doric design, I: Western Greek temples', *AJA* 80 (1976) 139–45
181. Winter, F. E. 'Tradition and innovation in Doric design, II: Archaic and Classical Doric east of the Adriatic', *AJA* 82 (1978) 151–61
182. Wycherley, R. E. *The Athenian Agora*, III: *Literary and Epigraphical Testimonia*. Princeton, 1957
183. Wycherley, R. E. 'Neleion', *BSA* 55 (1960) 60–6
184. Wycherley, R. E. *How the Greeks Built Cities*. 2nd edn. London, 1962; New York, 1976
185. Wycherley, R. E. 'Hippodamus and Rhodes', *Historia* 13 (1964) 135–9
186. Wycherley, R. E. '*Archaia agora*', *Phoenix* 20 (1966) 285–93
187. Wycherley, R. E. *The Stones of Athens*. Princeton, 1978

J. LITERATURE AND PHILOSOPHY

1. Backhaus, W. 'Der Hellenen–Barbaren–Gegensatz und die Hippokratische Schrift Περὶ ἀέρων ὑδάτων τόπων', *Historia* 25 (1976) 170–84

2. Bacon, H. H. *Barbarians in Greek Tragedy*. New Haven, 1961

3. Barrett, W. S. 'Bacchylides, Asine, and Apollo Pythaieus', *Hermes* 82 (1954) 421–44

4. Barrett, W. S. 'The Oligaithidai and their victories', in Dawe, R. D., Diggle, J. and Easterling, P. E. (eds.) *Dionysiaca*, 1–20. Cambridge, 1978

5. Bowie, E. L. 'Early Greek elegy, symposium, and public festival', *JHS* 106 (1986) 13–35

6. Bowra, C. M. 'Xenophanes and the Olympian games', in *Problems in Greek Poetry*, 15–37. Oxford, 1953

7. Bowra, C. M. 'Euripides' epinician for Alcibiades', *Historia* 9 (1960) 68–79 (= *id. On Greek Margins*, 134–48. Oxford, 1970)

8. Bowra, C. M. *Greek Lyric Poetry*. 2nd edn. Oxford, 1961

9. Bowra, C. M. *Pindar*. Oxford, 1964

10. Bulmer-Thomas, I. 'Hippias of Elis', 'Hippocrates of Chios', *Dictionary of Scientific Biography* VI, 405–10, 410–18. New York, 1972

11. Bulmer-Thomas, I. 'Oenopides of Chios', *Dictionary of Scientific Biography* X, 179–82. New York, 1974

12. Bulmer-Thomas, I. 'Theodorus of Cyrene', *Dictionary of Scientific Biography* XIII, 314–19. New York, 1976

13. Burkert, W. 'Iranisches bei Anaximandros', *Rh. Mus.* 106 (1963) 97–134

14. Burnett, A. P. *Catastrophe Survived. Euripides' Plays of Mixed Reversal*. Oxford, 1971

15. Burnett, A. P. *The Art of Bacchylides*. Cambridge, MA, 1985

16. Classen, C. J. 'The study of language amongst Socrates' contemporaries', *Sophistik* (Wege der Forschung CLXXXVII, ed. C. J. Classen), 215–47. Darmstadt, 1976

17. Conacher, D. J. *Euripides: Myth, Theme and Structure*. Toronto, 1967

18. Dahrendorf, R. 'In praise of Thrasymachus', *Essays in the Theory of Society*. Stanford, 1968

19. Dale, A. M. 'The metrical units of Greek lyric verse I–III', in *Collected Papers*. Cambridge, 1969

20. Davison, J. A. *From Archilochus to Pindar: Papers on the Literature of the Archaic Period*. London, 1968

21. de Carli, E. *Aristofane e la sofistica* (Pubblicazioni della Facoltà di Lettere e Filosofia dell'Università di Milano LVII). Florence, 1971

22. Derenne, E. *Les procès d'impiété intentés aux philosophes à Athènes au Ve et IVe siècles avant J.-C.* (Bibliothèque de la Faculté de Philosophie et Lettres de l'Université de Liège, fasc. 45). Liège–Paris, 1930

23. Dihle, A. 'Das Satyrspiel "Sisyphos"', *Hermes* 105 (1977) 28–42

24. Diller, H. 'Sophokles: die Tragödien', in J 95, 51–104

25. Diller, H., Lesky, A. and Schadewaldt, W. *Gottheit und Mensch in der Tragödie des Sophokles*. Darmstadt, 1963

26. Dodds, E. R. *The Greeks and the Irrational*. Berkeley–Los Angeles, 1951
27. Dodds, E. R. 'Notes on the Oresteia', *CQ* n.s. 3 (1953) 11–21
28. Dodds, E. R. 'Morals and politics in the "Oresteia"', *PCPhS* n.s. 6 (1960) 19–31 (= J 29, 45–63)
29. Dodds, E. R. *The Ancient Concept of Progress*. Oxford, 1973
30. Dover, K. J. 'The political aspect of Aeschylus's *Eumenides*', *JHS* 77 (1957) 230–7 (= A 26, 161–75)
31. Dover, K. J. *Lysias and the Corpus Lysiacum*. Berkeley–Los Angeles, 1968
32. Dover, K. J. *Aristophanic Comedy*. London, 1972
33. Dover, K. J. 'The freedom of the intellectual in Greek society', *Talanta* 7 (1976) 24–54 (= A 27, 135–58)
34. Dover, K. J. 'Ion of Chios: his place in the history of Greek literature', in F 7, 27–37 (= A 27, 1–12)
35. Elliott, R. T. *The Acharnians of Aristophanes*. Oxford, 1914
36. Färber, H. *Die Lyrik in der Kunsttheorie der Antike*. Munich, 1936
37. Forrest, W. G. 'Aristophanes' *Acharnians*', *Phoenix* 17 (1963) 1–12
38. Forssman, B. *Untersuchungen zur Sprache Pindars*. Wiesbaden, 1966
39. Fränkel, H. *Early Greek Poetry and Philosophy*, transl. by M. Hadas and J. Willis. Oxford, 1975
40. von Fritz, K. 'Oinopides', P–W 34. Halbb. (1973) 2258–72
41. Gaspar, C. *Essai de chronologie Pindarique*. Brussels, 1900
42. Gellie, G. H. *Sophocles. A Reading*. Melbourne, 1972
43. Gelzer, T. 'Aristophanes der Komiker', P–W Suppl. 12 (1970) 1391–570
44. Gelzer, T. 'Aristophanes', in J 95, 258–306
45. Gomperz, H. *Sophistik und Rhetorik*. Leipzig–Berlin, 1912
46. Görgemanns, H. 'Aischylos: die Tragödien', in J 95, 13–50
47. Griffith, M. *The Authenticity of 'Prometheus Bound'*. Cambridge, 1977
48. Grube, G. M. A. *The Drama of Euripides*. London, 1941
49. Guthrie, W. K. C. *A History of Greek Philosophy* II–III. Cambridge, 1965–9
50. Heinimann, F. *Nomos und Physis: Herkunft und Bedeutung einer Antithese im griechischen Denken des 5. Jahrhunderts* (Schweizerische Beiträge zur Altertumswissenschaft 1). Basel, 1945
51. Henrichs, A. 'Two doxographical notes: Democritus and Prodicus on religion', *HSCP* 79 (1975) 983–123
52. Henrichs, A. 'The atheism of Prodicus', *Cronache Erculanese* 6 (1976) 15–21
53. Hermann, G. 'Commentatio de metris Pindari', in Heyne, C. G., *Pindari Carmina et Fragmenta* III. Oxford, 1809
54. Huxley, G. *Pindar's Vision of the Past*. Belfast, 1975
55. Irigoin, J. *Histoire du texte de Pindare*. Paris, 1952
56. Jacoby, F. 'Diagoras ὁ "Αθεος', *Abh. Berlin. Kl. f. Sprachen, Literatur und Kunst*. Berlin, 1959
57. Kennedy, G. A. *The Art of Persuasion in Greece*. London, 1963
58. Kerferd, G. B. *The Sophistic Movement*. Cambridge, 1981
59. Kitto, H. D. F. *Sophocles, Dramatist and Philosopher*. Oxford, 1958
60. Kolb, F. 'Polis und Theater', in J 95, 504–43

61.   Lattimore, R. 'Aeschylus on the defeat of Xerxes', in *Classical Studies in Honor of W. A. Oldfather*, 82–93. Urbana, 1943

62.   Lefkowitz, M. R. '*ΤΩ ΚΑΙ ΕΓΩ*: the first person in Pindar', *HSCP* 67 (1963) 177–253

63.   Lefkowitz, M. R. *The Lives of the Greek Poets*. London, 1981

64.   Lesky, A. 'Die Datierung der Hiketiden und der Tragiker Mesatos', *Hermes* 82 (1954) 1–13

65.   Lesky, A. *A History of Greek Literature*, transl. by J. Willis and C. de Heer. London, 1966

66.   Lesky, A. *Die tragische Dichtung der Hellenen*. 3rd edn. Göttingen, 1972

67.   Lesky, A. *Greek Tragic Poetry*, transl. by M.Dillon. New Haven–London, 1983

68.   Linforth, I. M. 'Religion and drama in "Oedipus at Colonus"', *University of California Publications in Classical Philology* 14 (1951) 75–191

69.   Lloyd-Jones, H. 'Zeus in Aeschylus', *JHS* 76 (1956) 55–67

70.   Lloyd-Jones, H. *The Justice of Zeus*. Berkeley–Los Angeles–London, 1971. (2nd edn 1983)

71.   Lloyd-Jones, P. H. J. 'Modern interpretation of Pindar: the Second Pythian and Seventh Nemean Odes', *JHS* 93 (1973) 109–37

72.   Lloyd-Jones, H. 'Pindar', *Proc. Brit. Acad.* 68 (1982) 139–63

73.   MacDowell, D. 'The nature of Aristophanes' *Akharnians*', *G&R* n.s. 30 (1983) 143–62

74.   Macleod, C. W. 'Politics and the *Oresteia*', *JHS* 102 (1982) 124–44 (= A 82, 20–40)

75.   Maehler, H. *Die Lieder des Bakchylides. Erster Teil: Die Siegeslieder* I–II. Leiden, 1982

76.   Mansfeld, J. 'The chronology of Anaxagoras' Athenian period and the date of his trial', *Mnemosyne* ser. 4, 32 (1979) 39–69; 33 (1980) 17–95

77.   Marcovich, M. 'Xenophanes on drinking parties and Olympic games', *Illinois Classical Studies* 3 (1978) 1–26

78.   Matthiessen, J. 'Euripides: die Tragödien', in J 95, 105–54

79.   von der Mühll, P. 'Der Anlass zur zweiten Pythie Pindars', *Mus. Helv.* 15 (1958) 215–21

80.   Mullen, W. *Choreia: Pindar and Dance*. Princeton, 1982

81.   Nisetich, F. J. *Pindar's Victory Songs*. Baltimore–London, 1980

82.   Page, D. L. *Further Greek Epigrams*. Cambridge, 1981

83.   Paquet, L. *Les cyniques grecs*. Ottawa, 1975

84.   Pickard-Cambridge, A. W. *Dithyramb, Tragedy, and Comedy*. 2nd edn rev. by T. B. L. Webster. Oxford, 1962

85.   Pickard-Cambridge, A. W. *The Dramatic Festivals of Athens*. 2nd edn rev. by J. Gould and D. M. Lewis. Oxford, 1968. (Reprinted with addenda, 1988)

86.   *Pindare* (Fondation Hardt Entretiens sur l'antiquité classique XXXI). Geneva, 1985

87.   Podlecki, A. J. *The Political Background of Aeschylean Tragedy*. Ann Arbor, 1966

88. Rich, A. N. M. 'The Cynic concept of αὐτάρκεια', *Mnemosyne* ser. 4, 9 (1956) 23–9
89. Rivier, A. *Essai sur le tragique d'Euripide*. 2nd edn. Paris, 1975
90. Rosenmeyer, T. *The Art of Aeschylus*. Berkeley–Los Angeles, 1982
91. Schadewaldt, W. *Der Aufbau des Pindarischen Epinikions*. Halle, 1928
92. Schmid, W. and Stählin, O. *Geschichte der griechischen Literatur* (= *Handbuch der Altertumswissenschaft*, 7 Abt.) I, 2–5. Munich, 1934–48
93. Schofield, M. *An Essay on Anaxagoras*. Cambridge, 1980
94. Scodel, R. *The Trojan Trilogy of Euripides* (Hypomnemata 60). Göttingen, 1980
95. Seeck, G. A. (ed.) *Das griechische Drama*. Darmstadt, 1979
96. Segal, C. P. 'Gorgias and the psychology of the logos', *HSCP* 66 (1962) 99–155
97. Seidensticker, B. 'Das Satyrspiel', in J 95, 204–57
98. Severyns, A. *Bacchylide: essai biographique*. Liège, 1933
99. Solmsen, F. 'The Erinys in Aeschylus' *Septem*', *TAPA* 68 (1937) 197–211
100. Solmsen, F. 'Strata of Greek religion in Aeschylus', *HThR* 40 (1947) 211–26
101. Solmsen, F. *Intellectual Experiments of the Greek Enlightenment*. Princeton, 1975
102. Spira, A. *Untersuchungen zum Deus ex machina bei Sophokles und Euripides*. Kallmünz/Opf., 1960
103. Sutton, D. *The Greek Satyr Play*. Meisenheim am Glan, 1980
104. Thummer, E. *Pindar: die Isthmischen Gedichte* I–II. Heidelberg, 1969
105. Vickers, B. *Towards Greek Tragedy*. London, 1973
106. Walton, F. R. 'A problem in the Ichneutae of Sophocles'. *HSCP* 46 (1935) 167–89
107. West, M. L. 'The Prometheus trilogy', *JHS* 99 (1979) 130–48
108. West, M. L. 'Ion of Chios', *BICS* 32 (1985) 71–8
109. von Wilamowitz-Moellendorff, U. *Timotheos: die Perser*. Leipzig, 1903
110. von Wilamowitz-Moellendorff, U. *Pindaros*. Berlin, 1922
111. Winnington-Ingram, R. P. *Euripides and Dionysus. An Interpretation of the Bacchae*. Cambridge, 1948
112. Winnington-Ingram, R. P. 'Zeus in the *Persae*', *JHS* 93 (1973) 210–19
113. Winnington-Ingram, R. P. *Sophocles. An Interpretation*. Cambridge, 1980
114. Woodbury, L. 'The date and atheism of Diagoras of Melos', *Phoenix* 19 (1965) 178–211
115. Woodbury, L. 'Anaxagoras and Athens', *Phoenix* 35 (1981) 295–315

K. RELIGION AND FESTIVALS

1. Amandry, P. 'Sur les concours argiens', in *Études Argiennes* (*BCH* Suppl. VI), 211–53. 1980
2. *Athletics in Ancient Greece. Ancient Olympia and the Olympic Games*. Athens. 1976 (published under the supervision of N. Yalouris)

3.   Bengtson, H. *Die Olympischen Spiele in der Antike.* 2nd edn. Zürich–Stuttgart, 1972

4.   Bianchi, U. *La religione greca,* in Tacchi Venturi, P. (ed.) *Storia della religione,* 81–394. 6th edn. Turin, 1971

5.   Bilínski, B. *Agoni ginnici: componenti artistiche ed intellettuali nell'antica agonistica greca* (Academia Polacca delle Scienze, Biblioteca e Centro di Studi a Roma, Conferenze 75). Wrocław, 1979

6.   Bouché-Leclercq, A. *Histoire de la divination dans l'antiquité* i–iv. Paris, 1879–82

7.   Brelich, A. *Guerre, agoni e culti nella Grecia arcaica* (Antiquitas 1.7). Bonn, 1961

8.   Broneer, O. 'The Isthmian victory crown', *AJA* 66 (1962) 259–63

9.   Brumfield, A. C. *The Attic Festivals of Demeter and their Relation to the Agricultural Year.* New York, 1981

10. Burkert, W. 'Kekropidensage und Arrhephoria', *Hermes* 94 (1966) 1–25

11. Burkert, W. 'Buzyge und Palladion', *Zeitschrift für Religions- und Geistesgeschichte* 22 (1970) 356–68

12. Burkert, W. *Homo Necans, Interpretationen altgriechischer Opferriten und Mythen.* Berlin, 1972. (Eng. transl. K 15)

13. Burkert, W. *Griechische Religion der archaischen und klassischen Epoche.* Stuttgart–Berlin–Cologne–Mainz, 1977. (Eng. transl. K 16)

14. Burkert, W. *Structure and History in Greek Mythology and Ritual.* Berkeley–Los Angeles, 1979

15. Burkert, W. *Homo necans.* (Eng. transl. of K 12 by P. Bing). Berkeley–Los Angeles, 1983

16. Burkert, W. *Greek Religion: Archaic and Classical.* (transl. of K 13 by J. Raffan). Oxford, 1985

17. Clairmont, C. *Patrios Nomos: Public Burial in Athens during the Fifth and Fourth Centuries B.C.* (BAR International Series 161) Oxford, 1983

18. Classen, C. J. 'The Libyan god Ammon in Greece before 331 B.C.', *Historia* 8 (1959) 349–55

19. Clinton, K. *The Sacred Officials of the Eleusinian Mysteries* (TAPS 64, 3). Philadelphia, 1974

20. Crahay, R. *La littérature oraculaire chez Hérodote.* Paris, 1956

21. Davison, J. A. 'Notes on the Panathenaea', *JHS* 78 (1958) 23–42 (= J 20, 28–66)

22. Davison, J. A. 'Addenda to "Notes on the Panathenaea"', *JHS* 82 (1962) 141–2 (= J 20, 66–9)

23. Deubner, L. *Attische Feste.* Berlin, 1932

24. Drees, L. *Olympia, Gods, Artists and Athletes* (transl. by G. Onn). London, 1968

25. Ebert, J. *Griechische Epigramme auf Sieger an gymnischen und hippischen Agonen* (Abh. Sächs. Ak. Wiss. Phil.-Hist. Kl. 63.2). Berlin, 1972

26. Fahr. W. Θεοὺς νομίζειν. *Zum Problem der Anfänge des Atheismus bei den Griechen* (Spudasmata 26). Hildesheim–New York, 1969

27. Farnell, L. R. *The Cults of the Greek States* i–v. Oxford, 1896–1909

28. Feaver, D. D. 'Historical development in the priesthoods of Athens',

YCS 15 (1957) 121–58

29. Finley, M. I. and Pleket, H. W. *The Olympic Games: the First Thousand Years*. London, 1976
30. Fontenrose, J. 'The hero as athlete', *CSCA* 1 (1968) 73–104
31. Fontenrose, J. *The Delphic Oracle, its Responses and Operations*. Berkeley–Los Angeles, 1978
32. Foucart, P. *Les mystères d'Eleusis*. Paris, 1914
33. Gardiner, E. N. *Greek Athletic Sports and Festivals*. London, 1910
34. Gardiner, E. N. *Athletics of the Ancient World*. Oxford, 1930
35. Graf, F. *Eleusis und die orphische Dichtung Athens in vorhellenistischer Zeit*. Berlin, 1974
36. Harris, H. A. *Greek Athletes and Athletics*. London, 1964
37. Harris, H. A. *Sport in Greece and Rome*. London, 1972
38. Harrison, E. Review of κ 39, in *AJA* 61 (1957) 268–9
39. Herington, C. J. *Athena Parthenos and Athena Polias*. Manchester, 1955
40. Herrmann, H.-V. *Olympia. Heiligtum und Wettkampfstätte*. Munich, 1972
41. Herter, H. 'Phallos', P–W 38. Halbb. (1938) 1681–748
42. Humphreys, S. C. 'Family tombs and tomb cult in ancient Athens: tradition or traditionalism?' *JHS* 100 (1980) 96–126 (= A 67, 79–130)
43. Jacoby, F. '*Patrios Nomos:* state burial in Athens and the public cemetery in the Kerameikos', *JHS* 64 (1944) 37–66 (= C 58, 260–315)
44. Jordan, B. *Servants of the Gods* (Hypomnemata 55). Göttingen, 1979
45. Jüthner, J. and Brein, F. *Die athletischen Leibesübungen der Griechen* (SBAk. Wien 249.1–2). Vienna, 1965–8
46. Kadletz, E. 'The race and procession of the Athenian oscophoroi', *GRBS* 21 (1980) 363–71
47. Kahil, L. 'Autour de l' Artémis Attique', *Antike Kunst* 8 (1965) 20–33
48. Kahil, L. 'L'Artémis de Brauron: rites et mystères', *Antike Kunst* 20 (1977) 86–98
49. Kearns, E. 'Change and continuity in religious structures after Cleisthenes', in A 17, 189–207
50. Kett, P. *Prosopographie der historischen griechischen Manteis bis auf die Zeit Alexanders des Grossen*. Diss. Erlangen, 1966
51. Klee, T. *Zur Geschichte der gymnischen Agone an griechischen Festen*. Leipzig, 1918
52. Kramer, K. *Studien zur griechischen Agonistik nach den Epinikien Pindars*. Diss. Cologne, 1970
53. Kron, U. *Die zehn attischen Phylenheroen* (*Ath. Mitt.* Beiheft 5). Berlin, 1976
54. Kurtz, D. C. and Boardman, J. *Greek Burial Customs*. London, 1971
55. Kutsch, F. *Attische Heilgötter und Heilheroen* (*RGVV* 12.3). Giessen, 1913
56. Kyle, D. G. *Athletics in Ancient Athens*. Leiden, 1987
57. Lewis, D. M. 'Athena's robe', *Studia Classica Israelitica* 5 (1979–80) 28–9
58. Linders, T. *Studies in the Treasure Records of Artemis Brauronia found in Athens*. Stockholm, 1972
59. McGregor, M. F. 'Cleisthenes of Sicyon and the panhellenic games', *TAPA* 72 (1941) 266–87

60. Meuli, K. 'Griechische Opferbräuche', in *Phyllobolia, Festschrift Peter Von der Mühll*, 185–288. Basel, 1946 (= *id.*, *Gesammelte Schriften* II, 907–1021. Basel, 1975)

61. Mikalson, J. D. 'Religion in the Attic demes', *AJP* 98 (1977) 424–35

62. Miller, S. G. 'The date of the first Pythiad', *CSCA* 11 (1978) 127–58

63. Mommsen, A. *Feste der Stadt Athen im Altertum*. Leipzig, 1898

64. Moretti, L. *Olympionikai. I vincitori negli antichi agoni Olimpici*. Rome, 1957

65. Moretti, L. 'Supplemento al catalogo degli Olympionikai', *Klio* 52 (1970) 295–303

66. Mylonas, G. E. *Eleusis and the Eleusinian Mysteries*. Princeton, 1962

67. Nilsson, M. P. *Cults, Myths, Oracles and Politics in Ancient Greece*. Lund, 1951

68. Nilsson, M. P. 'Bendis in Athen', *Opuscula Selecta* III (Skrifter utgivna av Svenska Institutet i Athen 8°, II:3), 55–80. Lund, 1960

69. Nilsson, M. P. *Geschichte der griechischen Religion*, I: *Die Religion Griechenlands bis auf die griechische Weltherrschaft*. 3rd edn. Munich, 1967

70. Nock, A. D. 'Religious attitudes of the ancient Greeks', *Proc. Amer. Philos. Soc.* 85 (1942) 472–82 (= *id.*, *Essays on Religion and the Ancient World*, 534–50. Cambridge, MA, 1972)

71. Parke, H. W. *Festivals of the Athenians*. London, 1977

72. Parke, H. W. and Wormell, D. E. W. *The Delphic Oracle*. Oxford, 1956

73. Parker, R. 'Greek states and Greek oracles', in A 17, 298–326

74. Patrucco, R. *Lo sport nella Grecia antiqua*. Florence, 1972

75. Powell, C. A. 'Religion and the Sicilian Expedition', *Historia* 28 (1979) 15–31

76. Robinson, R. S. *Sources for the History of Greek Athletics*. Cincinnati, 1955

77. Rose, H. J. 'The religion of a Greek household', *Euphrosyne* 1 (1957) 95–116

78. Rotroff, S. I. 'An anonymous hero in the Athenian Agora', *Hesp.* 47 (1978) 196–209

79. Rougemont, G. 'La hiéroménie des Pythia et les trêves sacrées d'Éleusis, de Delphes et d'Olympie', *BCH* 97 (1973) 75–106

80. Roux, G. *Delphes. Son oracle et ses dieux*. Paris, 1976

81. Rudhardt, J. *Notions fondamentales de la pensée religieuse et actes constitutifs du culte dans la grèce classique*. Geneva, 1958

82. Rumpf, A. 'Attische Feste – attische Vasen', *Bonner Jahrbücher* 161 (1961) 208–14

83. Schlaifer, R. 'Notes on Athenian public cults', *HSCP* 51 (1940) 233–60

84. Simon, E. *Die Götter der Griechen*. 2nd edn. Munich, 1980

85. Simon, E. *Festivals of Attica. An Archaeological Commentary*. Madison, 1983

86. Sourvinou-Inwood, C. 'Persephone and Aphrodite at Locri: a model for personality definitions in Greek religion', *JHS* 98 (1978) 101–21

87. Trumpf, J. 'Fluchtafel und Rachepuppe', *Ath. Mitt.* 73 (1958) 94–102

88. Van Hoorn, G. *Choes and Anthesteria*. Leiden, 1951

89. Wachsmuth, D. 'Aspekte des antiken mediterranen Hauskults', *Numen* 27 (1980) 34–75

90. Weiler, I. *Der Sport bei den Völkern der alten Welt.* Darmstadt, 1981
91. Young, D. C. *The Olympic Myth of Greek Amateur Athletics.* Chicago, 1984

L. SOCIETY AND ECONOMY

1. Andreyev, V. N. 'Some aspects of agrarian conditions in Attica in the fifth to third centuries B.C.', *Eirene* 12 (1974) 5–46
2. Asheri, D. *Distribuzioni di terre nell'antica Grecia.* (Mem. Torino, ser. 4, 10). Turin, 1966
3. Austin, M. M. and Vidal-Naquet, P. *Économies et sociétés en grèce ancienne.* Paris, 1972
4. Austin, M. M. and Vidal-Naquet, P. *Economic and Social History of Ancient Greece: an Introduction.* London, 1977
5. Behrend, D. *Attische Pachturkunden: ein Beitrag zur Beschreibung der μίσθωσις nach den griechischen Inschriften* (Vestigia XII). Munich, 1970
6. Biscardi, A. 'Sul regime della comproprietà in diritto Attico', in *Studi in onore di Ugo Enrico Paoli,* 105–43. Florence, 1956
7. Blackman, D. J. 'Ancient harbours in the Mediterranean', *International Journal of Nautical Archaeology* 11 (1982) 79–104 and 185–211
8. Böckh, A. *Die Staatshaushaltung der Athener.* 2nd edn. Berlin, 1840
9. Böckh, A., ed. M. Fränkel, *Die Staatshaushaltung der Athener* I–II. 3rd edn. Berlin, 1886
10. Bogaert, R. *Les origines antiques de la banque de dépôt. Une mise au point accompagnée d'une esquisse des opérations de banque en Mésopotamie.* Preface by F. M. Heichelheim. Leiden, 1966
11. Bogaert, R. *Banques et banquiers dans les cités grecques.* Leiden, 1968
12. Bourriot, F. *Recherches sur la nature du génos. Étude d'histoire sociale athénienne: periodes archaique et classique.* Paris, 1976
13. Bravo, B. 'Remarques sur les assises sociales, les formes d'organisation et la terminologie du commerce maritime grec à l'époque archaïque', *DHA* 3 (1977) 1–59
14. Bravo, B. 'Sulân. Représailles et justice privée contre des étrangers dans les cités grecques', *ASNP* ser. 3, 10 (1980) 675–987
15. Bravo, B. 'Le commerce des céréales chez les Grecs de l'époque archaïque', in L 56, 17–29
16. Brelich, A. *Paides e Parthenoi.* Rome, 1969
17. Brockmeyer, N. *Antike Sklaverei* (Erträge der Forschung CXVI). Darmstadt, 1979
18. Burford, A. M. *Craftsmen in Greek and Roman Society.* London, 1972
19. Burford Cooper, A. 'The family farm in Greece', *CJ* 73 (1977–8) 162–75
20. Carter, L. B. *The Quiet Athenian.* Oxford, 1986
21. Cartledge, P. '"Trade and politics" revisited: Archaic Greece', in L 55, 1–15
22. Cassola, F. 'Sull'alienabilità del suolo nel mondo greco', *Labeo* 11 (1965) 206–19
23. *Colloque 1971. Actes du Colloque 1971 sur l'esclavage* (Annales Littéraires de

l'Université de Besançon CXL). Paris, 1973

24.   *Colloque 1975. Actes du Colloque sur l'esclavage, Nieborów 2–6* XII *1975*, ed. I.
Biezuńska-Malowist and J. Kolendo (Prace Instytutu Historycznego
Uniwersytetu Warszawskiego X). Warsaw, 1979

25.   Connor, W. R. 'The razing of the house in Greek society', *TAPA* 115
(1985) 79–102

26.   Davies, J. K. 'Demosthenes on liturgies: a note', *JHS* 87 (1967) 33–40

27.   Davies, J. K. *Athenian Propertied Families.* Oxford, 1971

28.   Davies, J. K. Review of L 3, in *Phoenix* 29 (1975) 93–102

29.   Davies, J. K. 'Athenian citizenship: the descent group and the
alternatives', *CJ* 73 (1977–8) 105–21

30.   Davies, J. K. *Wealth and the Power of Wealth in Classical Athens.* New
York, 1981

31.   Donlan, W. *The Aristocratic Ideal in Ancient Greece. Attitudes of Superiority
from Homer to the End of the Fifth Century B.C.* Lawrence, KS, 1980

32.   Dover, K. J. *Greek Homosexuality.* London, 1978

33.   Duncan-Jones, R. P. 'Metic numbers in Periclean Athens', *Chiron* 10
(1980) 101–9

34.   Ehrenberg, V. *The People of Aristophanes.* 2nd edn. Oxford, 1951

35.   Fine, J. V. A. *Horoi: Studies in Mortgage, Real Security and Land Tenure in
Ancient Athens (Hesp.* Suppl. IX) [Princeton], 1951

36.   Finley, M. I. *Studies in Land and Credit in Ancient Athens: 500–200 B.C.* New
Brunswick, 1952

37.   Finley, M. I. 'Land, debt, and the man of property in classical Athens',
Political Science Quarterly 68 (1953) 249–68 (= L 41, 62–76)

38.   Finley, M. I. (ed.) *Slavery in Classical Antiquity.* Cambridge, 1960

39.   Finley, M. I. *The Ancient Economy.* London–Berkeley–Los Angeles, 1973

40.   Finley, M. I. (ed.) *Problèmes de la terre en Grèce ancienne.* Paris–The Hague,
1973

41.   Finley, M. I. *Economy and Society of Ancient Greece*, ed. with an
introduction by R. P. Saller and B. D. Shaw. London, 1981

42.   Finley, M. I. 'Problems of slave society: some reflections on the debate',
Opus 1 (1982) 201–11

43.   Fisher, N. R. E. *Social Values in Classical Athens.* London–Toronto, 1976

44.   Forbes, H. A. 'Strategies and soils: technology, production and
environment in the peninsula of Methana, Greece'. Ph.D. thesis,
University of Pennsylvania, 1982

45.   Foxhall, L. 'Household, gender, and property in classical Athens', *CQ*
n.s. 39 (1989) 22–44

46.   Foxhall, L. and Forbes, H. A. 'Sitometreia: the role of grain as a staple
food in classical antiquity', *Chiron* 12 (1982) 41–90

47.   Frederiksen, M. W. 'Theory, evidence and the ancient economy'.
Review of L 39 in *JRS* 65 (1975) 164–71

48.   French, A. *The Growth of the Athenian Economy.* London, 1964

49.   Fuks, A. 'Social revolution in Greece in the Hellenistic Age', *PP* 21
(1966) 437–48 (= *id., Social Conflict in Ancient Greece*, 40–51. Jerusalem
and Leiden, 1984)

50. Garlan, Y. *Slavery in Ancient Greece*, rev. edn, transl. by J. Lloyd. Ithaca–London, 1988

51. Garland, R. *The Piraeus from the Fifth to the First Century B.C.* London, 1987

52. Garnsey, P. D. A. (ed.) *Non-slave Labour in the Greco-Roman World* (*PCPhS* Suppl. 6). Cambridge, 1980

53. Garnsey, P. D. A. 'Grain for Athens', in A 17, 62–75

54. Garnsey, P. D. A. *Famine and Food Supply in the Graeco Roman World. Responses to Risks and Crisis.* Cambridge, 1988

55. Garnsey, P. D. A., Hopkins, M. K. and Whittaker, C. R. (eds.) *Trade in the Ancient Economy.* London, 1983

56. Garnsey, P. D. A. and Whittaker, C. R. (eds.) *Trade and Famine in Classical Antiquity.* (*PCPhS* Suppl. 8). Cambridge, 1983

57. Gauthier, P. *Symbola: les étrangers et la justice dans les cités grecques* (Annales de l'est 42). Nancy, 1972

58. Gernet, L. 'Comment caractériser l'économie de la Grèce antique?' *Annales d'histoire économique et sociale* (1933) 561–6

59. Giroux, H. 'Trois images de l'éducation grecque', in Caron, J.-B., Fortin, M. and Maloney, G. (eds.) *Mélanges d'études anciennes offerts à Maurice Lebel.* Quebec, 1980

60. Golden, M. 'Slavery and homosexuality at Athens', *Phoenix* 38 (1984) 308–24

61. Gould, J. P. 'Law, custom, and myth: aspects of the social position of women in classical Athens', *JHS* 100 (1980) 38–59

62. Grierson, P. 'Commerce in the Dark Ages: a critique of the evidence', *Trans. Royal Hist. Soc.* ser. 5, 9 (1959) 123–40

63. Gschnitzer, F. *Griechische Sozialgeschichte von der mykenischen bis zum Ausgang der klassischen Zeit.* Wiesbaden, 1981

64. Halstead, P. 'Traditional and ancient rural economy in Mediterranean Europe: plus ça change?' *JHS* 107 (1987) 77–87

65. Harvey, F. D. 'Literacy in the Athenian democracy', *REG* 79 (1966) 585–635

66. Harvey, F. D. 'The maritime loan in Eupolis' "Marikas" (*P. Oxy.* 2741)', *ZPE* 23 (1976) 231–3

67. Hind, J. G. F. 'Pyrene and the date of the "Massaliot Sailing Manual"', *RSA* 2 (1972) 39–52

68. Hodkinson, S. J. 'Animal husbandry in the Greek polis', in L 142, 35–74

69. Hopper, R. J. 'The Attic silver mines in the fourth century B.C.', *BSA* 48 (1953) 200–54

70. Hopper, R. J. 'The Laurion mines: a reconsideration', *BSA* 63 (1968) 293–326

71. Humphreys, S. C. 'Economy and society in classical Athens', *ASNP* ser. 2, 39 (1970) 1–26 (= A 66, 136–58)

72. Humphreys, S. C. 'Town and country in ancient Greece', in A 116, 763–8 (= A 66, 130–5)

73. Humphreys, S. C. 'The Nothoi of Kynosarges', *JHS* 94 (1974) 88–95

74. Humphreys, S. C. 'Oikos e polis', *RSI* 91 (1979) 545–63. Eng. transl. as

'Oikos and polis' in A 67, 1–23

75.   Humphreys, S. C. 'Law as discourse', History and Anthropology 1 (1985) 241–64

76.   Humphreys, S. C. 'Social relations on stage: witnesses in classical Athens', History and Anthropology 1 (1985) 313–69

77.   Humphreys, S. C. 'Kinship patterns in the Athenian courts', GRBS 27 (1986) 57–91

78.   Isager, S. 'The marriage pattern in classical Athens: men and women in Isaios', Class. et Med. 33 (1981) 81–96

79.   Ito, S. 'The enrolment of Athenian phratries', Legal History Review 31 (1981) 35–60 (in Japanese, Eng. summary pp. 7–8)

79A.   Ito, S. 'Phrateres as Athenian citizens', Journal of Classical Studies 30 (1983) 1–18 (in Japanese, Eng. summary pp. 149–50)

79B.   Ito, S. 'An interpretation of the so-called Demotionid Inscription', Journal of History 71 (1988) 677–713 (in Japanese, Eng. summary p. 828)

80.   Jameson, M. H. 'Agriculture and slavery in classical Athens', CJ 73 (1977–8) 122–41

81.   Jameson, M. H. 'Famine in the Greek world', in L 56, 6–16

82.   Jeanmaire, H. Couroi et Courètes. Lille, 1939

83.   Johnston, A. W. 'The rehabilitation of Sostratos', PP 27 (1972) 416–23

84.   Johnston, A. W. 'Trademarks on Greek vases', G&R n.s. 21 (1974) 138–52

85.   Johnston, A. W. Trademarks on Greek Vases. Warminster, 1979

86.   Just, R. 'Freedom, slavery, and the female psyche', in A 17, 169–88

87.   Just, R. Women in Athenian Law and Life. London, 1990

88.   Kent, J. K. 'The temple estates of Delos, Rheneia, and Mykonos', Hesp. 17 (1948) 243–338

89.   Knorringa, H. Emporos. Data on Trade and Trader in Greek Literature from Homer to Aristotle. Amsterdam, 1926

90.   Lacey, W. K. The Family in Classical Greece. London, 1968

91.   Lane Fox, R. J. 'Aspects of inheritance in the Greek world', in A 17, 208–32

92.   Latte, K. 'Phratrie', P–W xx, 1 (1941) 746–58 (= A 75, 423–34)

93.   Lauffer, S. Die Bergwerkssklaven von Laureion. 2nd edn. Wiesbaden, 1979

93A.   Lévy, E. 'Métèques et droit de résidence', L'étranger dans le monde grec: actes du colloque organisé par l'Institut d'Etudes Anciennes, 47–67. Nancy, 1987

94.   Lewis, D. M. 'The Athenian Rationes Centesimarum', in L 40, 187–212

95.   Lotze, D. Μεταξὺ ἐλευθέρων καὶ δούλων. Studien zur Rechtstellung unfreier Bevölkerungen in Griechenland bis zum 4. Jahrhundert v. Chr. Berlin, 1959

96.   Lotze, D. 'Zwischen Politen und Metöken: Passivbürger im klassischen Athen?' Klio 63 (1981) 159–78

97.   MacDowell, D. M. 'Bastards as Athenian citizens', CQ n.s. 26 (1976) 88–91

98.   MacDowell, D. M. 'The oikos in Athenian Law', CQ n.s. 39 (1989) 10–21

99.   Meiggs, R. Trees and Timber in the Ancient Mediterranean World. Oxford, 1982

100. Mele, A. *Il commercio greco arcaico. Prexis ed Emporie* (Cahiers du Centre Jean Bérard IV). Naples, 1979

101. Michell, H. *The Economics of Ancient Greece.* Cambridge, 1940. 2nd edn 1957

101A. Millett, P. 'Patronage and its avoidance in classical Athens', in Wallace-Hadrill, A. (ed.), *Patronage in Ancient Society*, 15–47. London, 1989

102. Momigliano, A. D. 'Sull'amministrazione delle miniere del Laurio', *Athenaeum* 10 (1932) 247–58 (= A 89, 531–43)

103. Musti, D. *L'economia in Grecia.* Rome–Bari, 1981

104. Noonan, T. S. 'The grain trade of the Northern Black Sea in antiquity', *AJP* 94 (1973) 231–42

105. Oertel, F. Anhang, in L 116, 511–85

106. Osborne, R. G. *Demos: the Discovery of Classical Attika.* Cambridge, 1985

107. Osborne, R. G. 'Law in action in classical Athens', *JHS* 105 (1985) 40–58

108. Osborne, R. G. *Classical Landscape with Figures: the Ancient Greek City and its Countryside.* London, 1987

109. Osborne, R. G. 'Social and economic implications of the leasing of land and property in classical and Hellenistic Greece', *Chiron* 18 (1988) 279–323

110. Owens, E. J. 'The koprologoi at Athens in the fifth and fourth centuries B.C.', *CQ* n.s. 33 (1983) 44–50

111. Panagos, C. T. *Le Pirée, Etude économique et historique depuis les temps les plus anciens jusqu'à la fin de l'empire romain.* French transl. by P. Gerardat. Athens, 1968

112. Parry, J. J. 'The harbours of ancient Greece, with special reference to those of the Aegean in the classical period', I–II. M. Phil. thesis, University of Liverpool, 1987

113. Patterson, C. *Pericles' Citizenship Law of 451–50.* New York, 1981

114. Pearson, H. W. 'The secular debate on economic primitivism', in L 117, 3–11

115. Pečírka, J. 'Homestead farms in classical and Hellenistic Hellas', in L 40, 113–47

115A. Pesando, F. *Oikos e Ktisis. La casa greca in età classica.* Perugia, 1987

116. von Pöhlmann, R. *Geschichte der sozialen Frage und des Sozialismus in der antiken Welt.* 3rd edn. Munich, 1925

117. Polanyi, K., Arensberg, C. M. and Pearson, H. W. (eds.) *Trade and Market in the Early Empires.* Glencoe, IL, 1957

118. Randall, R. H., Jr. 'The Erechtheum workmen', *AJA* 57 (1953) 199–210

119. Reed, C. M. 'Maritime traders in the Greek world of the Archaic and Classical periods'. D. Phil. thesis, University of Oxford, 1981

120. Rhodes, P. J. 'Bastards as Athenian citizens', *CQ* n.s. 28 (1978) 88–92

121. Ste Croix, G. E. M. de 'Some observations on the property rights of Athenian women', *CQ* n.s. 20 (1970) 273–8

122. Ste Croix, G. E. M. de 'Ancient Greek and Roman maritime loans', in Edey, H. and Yamey, B. S. (eds.) *Debts, Credits, Finance and Profits. Essays in Honour of W. T. Baxter*, 41–59. London, 1974

123. Sallares, R. *The Ecology of the Ancient Greek World.* London, 1991

124. Salviat, F. and Vatin, C. 'Le cadastre de Larissa', *BCH* 98 (1974) 247–62
125. Sartre, M. 'Aspects économiques et aspects réligieux de la frontière dans les cités grecques', *Ktéma* 4 (1979) 213–24
126. Schaps, D. M. 'Women in Greek inheritance law', *CQ* n.s. 25 (1975) 53–7
127. Schaps, D. M. 'The woman least mentioned', *CQ* n.s. 27 (1977) 323–30
128. Schaps, D. M. *Economic Rights of Women in Ancient Greece*. Edinburgh, 1979
129. Snodgrass, A. M. 'Heavy freight in archaic Greece', in L 55, 16–26
130. Sundwall, J. *Epigraphische Beiträge zur sozial-politischen Geschichte Athens im Zeitalter des Demosthenes. Klio* Beiheft 4 (1906)
131. Thomson, W. E. 'An interpretation of the "Demotionid" decrees', *SO* 62 (1968) 51–68
132. Thompson, W. E. 'Athenian marriage patterns: remarriage', *CSCA* 5 (1972) 211–25
133. Thompson, W. E. 'The Athenian entrepreneur', *Ant. Class.* 51 (1982) 53–85
134. Tod, M. N. 'The economic background of the fifth century', *CAH* v¹ (1927) 1–32
135. Van Effenterre, H. 'Reflexions sur la fiscalité dans les cités grecques archaïques' in Van Effenterre (ed.) *Points de vue sur la fiscalité*, 19–30. Paris, 1979
136. Van Effenterre, H. 'Le statut comparé des travailleurs étrangers en Chypre, Crète et autres lieux à la fin de l'archaïsme', in *Acts of the International Archaeological Symposium, 'The Relations between Cyprus and Crete c 2000–500 B.C.'*, 279–93. Nicosia, 1979
137. Vélissaropoulos, J. *Les nauclères grecs*. Geneva–Paris, 1980
138. Wade-Gery, H. T. 'Studies in the structure of Attic society, I: Demotionidai', *CQ* 25 (1931) 129–43 (= A 121, 116–34)
139. Walters, K. R. 'Pericles' citizenship law', *CA* 2 = *CSCA* 14 (1983) 314–36
140. Webster, T. B. L. *Athenian Culture and Society*. London, 1973
141. Whitehead, D. *The Ideology of the Athenian Metic (PCPhS* Suppl. 4). Cambridge, 1977
142. Whittaker, C. R. (ed.) *Pastoral Economies in Classical Antiquity (PCPhS* Suppl. 14). Cambridge, 1988
143. Wiedemann, T. *Greek and Roman Slavery*. London–Canberra, 1981
144. Will, E. 'Trois quarts de siècle de recherches sur l'économie grecque antique', *Annales E.S.C.* 9 (1954) 7–22
145. Wolff, H. J. 'Marriage law and family organisation in ancient Athens', *Traditio* 2 (1944) 43–95
146. Wood, E. M. 'Agricultural slavery in classical Athens', *AJAH* 8 (1983) [1986] 1–47
147. Wood, E. M. *Peasant-citizen and Slave: the Foundations of Athenian Democracy*. London, 1988

INDEX

References in italics are to maps (by map number) and illustrations (by page number).

Arrangement of material within entries is predominantly chronological, though some material of a topical nature is alphabetically ordered.

Footnotes are referred to only where the subject is not mentioned in the corresponding page of text.

Attica (*cont.*)

394, (forts) 381, 382, 389, 390; Spartan occupation of Decelea 453, 455, 457, 458, 464, 485, 488; Agis raids 485; rebuilding after Peloponnesian War 498

cult of Hyakinthides 280; houses 200, *201*; landholding patterns 19, 288, 295; mining area 292, 303, (industrial premises) 202, 291, (ownership) 296, 406, (Peloponnesian raid) 430, (workforce) 297, 298n42, 301; public building projects 81, 498, 315; quarries 296; settlement patterns 288, 292; temples 315; *see also individual places*

Autocles (Athenian general) 428n146

Avienus; *Ora maritima* 26

Bacchylides (poet) 31; on after-life 243; dithyramb 327; on envy 234; epinician odes 223, 238, 240, 242; myth and history in 228; poetic style 240, 242; and Sicily 147n, 150, 153, 226, 238

banking 24, 287–8, 303

barbarians, Greek identification of 16, 36, 125, 152

barter 21

Basile, Athenian shrine of 192

basileus (Athenian archon) 87, 245–6, 250, 254–5

Bassae, temple of Apollo at 191, *192*, *193*, 316n; Corinthian order 188; frieze 179, 180

bath-houses 198

Battiad monarchy of Cyrene 27

Bendis, cult of 262, 263, 298n42, 313

Berezan letter of Anaxagores 22n28

Bisaltae (Thracian tribe) *1 Cb*, 127, 129n41

Bithynians 486

Black Sea: corn supplies 26, 146, 301; Pericles' expedition 145–6; tribute collecting expedition (424) 425n135

blood-guilt 17

Boeae *2 Cd*, 117n80

Boeotia *1 Cc*, *2 Bb–Cb*; settlement after Persian Wars 96; hoplite democracies 96–7; Athenian interest in (450s) 111; in First Peloponnesian War 114, 115, 116, 117; troops in Athenian expedition to Thessaly 119; disaffection from Athens 133, 137; federal constitution, and Theban hegemony 133; settlers at foundation of Thurii 142–3; in Archidamian War 386–7, 390, 392, 394, 409–10, 424, 448, (battle of Delium) 390, 425–6, (loss of Panactum) 382, 429; refuses terms of Peace of Nicias 431, 433, 434; rejects Argive alliance 434; Spartan alliance 435, 436, 437, 438, (and Sicilian campaign) 457, 460, (and campaign in Hellespont and

north) 487, 492

coinage 96, 116, 133; constitutions 92–3, 94; vase-painting 180

Boeotius (Spartan envoy) 489

Bolkon (Syracusan general) 163

book trade 268, 351

booty: and Athenian economy 304; Cimon and 63–4, 325

Boreas, cult of 261

Bottiaea 429n148

bouleuteria, see under Athens; Olympia

Boulis (a Spartan) 332

Bouselos, division of estate of 291

Boutadai (Attic deme) 298

boxing 228, 229, 235

Brasidas (Spartan general): repulses Athenians at Methone 394; and Cnemus' expedition 400; raid on Salamis 401; and Corcyrean civil war 407, 408; at battle for Sphacteria 414–15; protects Megara against Athens 424; expedition to Thrace 391, 424, 426–30; death 430, 431

Brauron *2 Dc*; pottery *257*; stoa 218; *see also under* Artemis

Brauronia (festival) 257

Brae, decree establishing 129, 312

bronze: coinage 24, 170; working in Athens 202

Brygos (potter) 320

building: craftsmen, mobility of 187; materials 185–6, 199, 200, 208, 214, (transport of) 185, 187, 206; tools 185; *see also* architecture

Buphonia (religious ceremony) 245, 247, 251

Buthia *1 Ec*, 57

Buzygai (Athenian *genos*) 259

Byzantium *4 Ca*; Cimon in 325; alliance with Athena 30, 36; Pausanias in 12, 35, 43, 46, 97, 100, 108, 499; possible Athenian campaign (447) 128, 129, 132; and Samian revolt 145; revolt 477; Alcibiades regains 487

Cacyrium, Sicily 155

Calamis (sculptor) 163n17, 209

Calchedon *4 Ca*, 486

calendar: of Attic festivals 249–56, 349; Council of Five Hundred uses solar year 12; months 16, 245, 249–50; regional variations 16; of sacrifices 248; Solon's codification 246

Calliades (archon, 480/79) 12

Callias (archon, 412/11) 476

Callias (II), son of Hipponicus, negotiates Thirty Years' Peace 136; *see also* Peace of Callias

Callias III, son of Hipponicus 343; and sophists 351; town houses 296n36

Callicles, and sophists 343n105, 344, 351, 355

foreign contacts and 306–12; innovations, Athenian 302–5; market 287, 302–3; plague and 396; public, Athenian 302, 303–5; *see also* self-sufficiency

Edonians 145

education: breakdown of traditional 244; formal schools 32; memory training 346–7, 348; sophists 198, 311, 341, 344, 345, 354; use of palaestra to meet pupils 198

Eëtionea 309, 363–4, 479–80, 484

egalitarianism 33, 272, 300

Egesta *see* Segesta

Egypt: Delian League expeditions 13, 39, 50–3, 54, 61, 111, 112, 117, 120, 501; Psammetichus' gifts of corn to Athens 54, 77, 299; revolt (411) 478
    Athenian trade 50, 301, 312; religion 17, 18

Eïon *1 Cb*; Cimon captures from Persians 41, 42, 45–6, 47, 99, 210; Athenians receive tribute payments at 129; Thucydides prevents Brasidas taking 427, 430

eisangelia (impeachment) 71–2, 73, 82, 368

eisphora (property tax) 84, 403, 420

Elaeus *1 Eb, 4 Ba*, 128, 494

Elba 166

election to office 85, 89, 294, 475; *see also* lot

Eleusinian Mysteries 264–5; agricultural connexions 252, 264, 265; and belief in after-life 264–5; Aristophanes parodies 248; *basileus* in charge of 246; city sanctuary 219, 248, 264, 314; Eumolpids and 263; festival of Asclepius integrated with 262; first-fruit offerings by allies 261, 264, 312–13; Lesser Mysteries 265; and panhellenism 312–13; procession 264, 265, 488; profanation (415) 309, 364–5, 443, 449–50, (Alcibiades and) 267, 449, 450, 451, 488; prominence 246

Eleusis *2 Cb*; Demeter's gift of grain to 252, 264; stone for Erechtheum 220; Telesterion 64n6, 196, 264, 265, 316; *see also* Eleusinian Mysteries

Eleutherae *2 Cb*, 133, 255

Elis *1 Bd, 2 Aa*; synoecism 28, 103, 230; subjugates smaller local communities 104; in Persian Wars 104, 230; political obscurity after Persian Wars 105n31, 109; rebuilds temple of Zeus at Olympia 105n31; supports Corinth over Epidamnus 374; Athenian raids (431) 394; refuses terms of Peace of Nicias 431, 433; alliance with Argos, Athens and Mantinea 230–1, 434, 438
    gymnasia 103; and Olympic Games 105n31, 229, 230, 231

elite, Athenian: democratic leaders 84–7; foreign influences on 351; new men 32;

openness 305; social attitudes 288; sophists and 363–7; urbanization 296; *see also* aristocracy

Elpinice (Cimon's sister) 68, 69, 146; and Polygnotus 181, 317–18

Elymians, Sicily 147, 191

Emmenid dynasty of Acragas 147, 149–50, 151, 153, 154–5, 238

Empedocles 159, 168, 169–70, 354

emporia 22, 23, 25

endeixis (judicial procedure) 28n

Endius (Spartan ephor) 465

engineering: cranes 185; drainage 159, 202; irrigation 301

Ennea Hodoi, Thrace *see* Nine Ways

Entella, Sicily *3 Bb*, 147

entrepreneurship 288

Epaminondas (Theban general) 498

ephebes and Eleusinian Mysteries 264

Ephesus *1 Ed, 4 Bc*; Themistocles in 65, 66; Athenian general at (414) 465; Thrasyllus at 485, 504; Lysander at 489, 490; possible use of ostracism 93n106; temples of Artemis 185, 261

Ephialtes 69–70; sails beyond Chelidonian islands, after Eurymedon 46, 50, 70; and Delian League 49–54, 61, 112; anti-Spartan policy 49, 63, 68, 73, 74, 112, 114; possible Spartan reaction to political success of 49, 69, 110, 114; murdered 63, 75, 309
    reforms 11, 79, 87, 91, (of Areopagus) 62, 65, 67–77, 89, 275, (enhance value of citizenship) 299, (increasing use of inscriptions after) 41, 80

ephor lists, Spartan 363

Ephorus of Cyme 7, 10, 46, 66, 121, 482

epic poetry 268, 325–6

Epicerdes of Cyrene 462n48

Epicharmus (comic poet) 153, 155n4, 167

Epidamnus *1 Ab*, 371, 373–4

Epidaurus *1 Cd, 2 Cc*; in Persian Wars 106; alliance with Corinth 110; in First Peloponnesian War 112; supports revolt of Megara 134; in Archidamian War 387n50, 388, 397–8, 419, 428n146; quarrel with Argos 437; Athenian fort 439, 440; cult of Asclepius 261–2, 313

Epidaurus Limera *2 Cd*, 423, 455

epigamia (intermarriage rights) 159

epimachia (alliances) 374

Epipolae, Syracuse 453, *454*, 455–6

Epirus 27, 65

Epitadas (Spartan general) 418

Epiteles (Athenian general) 128

eranos, eranoi (gift exchange, interest-free loans) 21, 288, 303

Eratosthenes, Lysias' prosecution of 309

juries, Athenian (*cont.*)
  participation in public life 305; payment 62,
  63, 75, 76, 81, 84, 420–1; size 76, 77, 82; and
  social norms 289; use of rhetoric to
  persuade 341; *see also heliaia*
justice: *apagoge* 28n; cases involving Mysteries
  264; Delian League; serious cases
  transferred to Athens 131–2, 310–11;
  endeixis 28n; *graphe* 28n; metics represented
  by *prostates* 307; pollution and 278; religious
  background 258–9
Justin, Epitome of Pompeius Trogus 9n28, 46

kakodaimonistai (club) 295
Kalamaia (festival) 252
Kale Akte, Sicily *3 Ca*, 164
Kallynteria (festival) 250
kalos kagathos 32
karban/karbanos (non-Greek) 16
Kerameis (Attic deme) 298
Kerykes (Athenian *genos*) 300; and cult of
  Asclepius 314; and Eleusinian Mysteries
  264, 314; Herodotus and 331; priesthood
  251
kinship, social groups based on 294
Kleophrades Painter 176
kleros (landholding) 19, 20, 290
Kokalos (legendary king of Sicily) 151n3
kolakretai (Athenian treasury officials) 81, 126,
  485
Kollytos (Attic deme) 298
Kronia (festival) 251
Kydathenaion (Attic deme) 298
Kynosarges, gymnasium of Heracles 256–7

Labdalum, near Syracuse 453, 456
labour: *oikos* context of most human 289; use
  of all available in farming 301; *see also*
  workforce
Laches (Athenian general): expedition to
  Sicily 408–9, 413; and armistice (424)
  428n146; in peace negotiations (422–1) 435;
  death at Mantinea 439; on sophists 368
Lachon of Ceos (Bacchylides' patron) 238
Laconia *2 Bc*; helots 19n13; Helot Revolt 109;
  in First Peloponnesian War 117, 118;
  Athens raids (424) 423
Lade 467
Lamachus (Athenian general): and Pericles'
  Pontic expedition 146; tribute collecting
  expedition (424) 425n135; Sicilian
  Expedition 446, 451; death 454, 457
Lampon (seer) 142, 263–4
Lampsacus *1 Eb, 4 Ba*; Anaxagoras in 339;
  coinage 131; revolt 474; in Ionian War 485,
  494
landownership 19, 20; Attica 288, 295;

Corcyrean problems 384; fragmentation of
  holdings 20, 290–1; overseas property
  ownership 295; plague and Athenian
  396n81; by temples 19, 29
land use 298, 301
language: foreign influence 298, 337–8;
  Greeks united by common 15–16; literary
  15, 168, 239–40, 337–8; Prodicus on 345; in
  Sicily 165; *see also* dialects
Laos 141
Larissa, Aleuadae of 99, 119n87
Las, Laconia *2 Bd*, 479
Lasus of Hermione 326
Laurium *2 Cc; see also* Attica (mining area)
law: on adoption 291; Assembly enacts
  Athenian 77; citizenship, Pericles' 83,
  299–300, 307–8, 367; and customs, as
  uniting Greeks 17; inscription of 248; on
  murder 25, 485; Protagoras and 142, 342;
  rapid change in 5th cent. 289–90;
  recodification of Athenian from 411/10
  289–90, 484–5; Spartan freedom under 332;
  and state intervention 299–300; Thurian
  code 142; written texts, early 90; *see also*:
  Draco; judiciary; juries; justice; Solon
Lebedus *4 Bb*, 56
lectures 329–30, 340, 346
leitourgiai see liturgies
Lemnos *1 Dc*; Delian League tribute 128; and
  Samian revolt 143; cleruchs 128, 417;
  Athenian trade 301
Lenaea (Athenian festival) 250, 252–3;
  Athenian audience 270; comedy 253, 268–9,
  284, 412; common to Ionians and
  Athenians 245; metics as *choregoi* 272, 300;
  vases 249, 253
Leocrates (Athenian general) 85, 112
Leocritus of Samos 51n58
Leon (Athenian admiral), 467, 473, 474, 477
Leontini, Sicily *3 Db*; under Syracuse 147;
  populations of Naxus and Catana resettled
  in 150, 151; autonomous republic
  established 157; Catanaeans return home
  157; Naxians return home 158; period of
  prosperity 158; renewal of Athenian treaty
  (433/2) 143n100, 375; war with Syracuse
  408, 447–8; Gorgias' embassy to Athens
  311, 344, 408; Athenian support 446, 447–8;
  coinage 157; culture 170
Leontiscus (Olympian victor) 159
Leophron (son of Anaxilas of Rhegium) 153
Leotychidas, king of Sparta: punishes
  medizers of northern Greece 35, 96, 97, 99,
  499; exile 96, 99, 101
Lepreum, Triphylia *2 Aa*; under Elis 104;
  Spartan–Elean dispute over 230, 434, 437,
  438

221–2, 246, 317n41

Posidonia 141

potagogides (women-spies) 153

Potidaea *1 Cb*; Thirty Years' Peace and 137; and problems in Delian League 129, 138; Corinth provides magistrates 138; revolt 375–6, 379, 383, 385, 395, 397, 502; surrender 399; silence of Peace of Nicias on 431

pottery: amphorae, 'Panathenaic' 306n3; Attic painted; late Archaic trade 22, 306; Corinthian late Archaic painted 22; evidence on sail-propelled ship 26n45; fine, aristocrats and 32; *krateriskos* from Brauron *257*; trademarks on Corinthian and Attic painted pottery 22; vase inscribed with name Eurymedon 47n44; *see also* vase-painting

poverty in Athens 21, 84, 87

praktores (exacters of taxes) 80

Prasiae *2 Bc*, 397, 455

Pratinas of Phlius (dramatist) 282, 324

Praxiergidae (Athenian *genos*) 70n27, 263, 300

Praxiteles of Mantinea 150n1, 158n8

pre-Socratic philosophers 177, 246

prestige 29; *see also* display

Priene *1 Ed*, *4 Bc*, 143

priestesses *see* arrhephoroi *and under* Hera

priesthoods 250, 270; family connexions 246, 251, 256, 259, 266, 292

prison, Athenian *212*, 213, *214*

prisoners, treatment of 393; Athenian Sicilian Expedition 462; Boeotia retains Athenian 434; Corcyra 408, 422; Hysiae 442, 445; Melos 444, 445, 446; Mycalessus 458; Mytilene 404–6; Peace of Nicias on 432; Plataean 406; Pylos; return to Sparta 433; release on bail during Great Dionysia 269; Selymbria 487

probouleusis 78

probouloi, ten 464, 473, 475, 476

Procles 409, 410

Proconnesus 483

Prodicus of Ceos (sophist) 344–6; Adeimantus son of Leucolophides and 364; and Euripides 356, 357; on origins and development of human civilization 345; in Plato's *Protagoras* 343; possible charge of impiety 346, 368–9; on religion 345–6, 356; and sciences 354; as sophist and teacher of rhetoric 311, 343; and Theramenes 364; Thucydides influenced by 359; visit to Athens 311, 351

Proerosia (festival) 252

property: landlord-owned 295–6; no call for redistribution in 5th cent. Athens 94; tax 84, 403, 420

property-classes, Athenian 29, 62, 75–6, 233, 304

prophasis 371

prophecy 278–9

Prosopitis, Egypt 51

prostates (legal representative for metics) 307

Protagoras of Abdera (sophist) 177, 339, 341–3; arguments for and against (*antilogia*) 342–3, 355, 359–60; Callias and 351; and Critias and Alcibiades 365; and Euripides 356; expelled from Athens for impiety 247, 369; as leader of sophistic movement 246–7; and *nomos–physis* antithesis 354; on origins and development of human civilization 345, 360; Pericles and 178, 181; *Prometheus Bound* shows influence 276; and Pythodorus 364; religion 356; social thought 342; Thucydides assimilates ideas 359–61; and Thurii 142, 316

proxeny 132, 435

prytaneion: Athens 74–5n41, 79–80, 200, 206, 211, *212*; Olympia 193, *194*

prytaneis 78, 79, 211

Psammetichus, of Egypt 54, 77, 299

Pseudo-Xenophon *see Athenian Constitution* (Pseudo–Xenophon)

public, intellectual and social life 27–33

public service *see* liturgies; offices of state

Pydna: Thermistocles in 65, 66; siege of 376, 483

Pygela *4 Bc*; battle of 485

Pylos *2 Ad*; Athenian fortification and siege of Sphacteria 386, 413–14, *415*, 416–19, 435; Messenian garrison 118, 418–19; raids on Sparta from 430; Peace of Nicias on 432; return to Sparta of prisoners from 433; Messenians withdrawn to Cephallenia 434; Messenians reinstalled 437; raid on Sparta from 443; Spartan recapture 486, 503, 505

Pythagoras of Rhegium (sculptor) 170

Pythagoras (philosopher) 170, 234, 236

Pythagoreanism 31–2, 177; Petron of Himera 170; and Polyclitus' *Canon* 182; and sciences 349, 350

Pythen of Corinth 455

Pythian Games: Amphicytonic control 231; cult of Apollo and 224; foundation 227; Hiero's victory 238; horse-races 231, 238; Megacles' victory 306; music 231; order and development 231; origins and organization 224; Pindar and 226, 327; race in armour 231

Pythion (Megarian guide to Pericles' army), gravestone 134

Pythodorus son of Isolochus (Athenian general): command in Sicily 340, 413; exiled 422; and philosophers 343n104, 351, 363, 364